THE ROUTLEDGE
COMPANION TO CULT CINEMA

The Routledge Companion to Cult Cinema offers an overview of the field of cult cinema – films at the margin of popular culture and art that have received exceptional cultural visibility and status mostly because they break rules, offend, and challenge understandings of achievement (some are so bad they're good, others so good they remain inaccessible).

Cult cinema is no longer only comprised of the midnight movie or the extreme genre film. Its range has widened and the issues it broaches have become battlegrounds in cultural debates that typify the first quarter of the twenty-first century. Sections are introduced with the major theoretical frameworks, philosophical inspirations, and methodologies for studying cult films, with individual chapters excavating the most salient criticism of how the field impacts cultural discourse at large. Case studies include the worst films ever; exploitation films; genre cinema; multiple media formats cult cinema is expressed through; issues of cultural, national, and gender representations; elements of the production culture of cult cinema; and, throughout, aspects of the aesthetics of cult cinema – its genre, style, look, impact, and ability to yank viewers out of their comfort zones.

The Routledge Companion to Cult Cinema goes beyond the traditional scope of Anglophone and North American cinema by including case studies of East and South Asia, continental Europe, the Middle East, and Latin America, making it an innovative and important resource for researchers and students alike.

Ernest Mathijs is Professor of Film Studies at the University of British Columbia, Vancouver, Canada. He teaches and writes on cult cinema. With Jamie Sexton he has written *Cult Cinema* (2011). He is the co-author of *100 Cult Films* and the author of *The Cinema of David Cronenberg*.

Jamie Sexton is Senior Lecturer in Film and Television Studies at Northumbria University, UK. He is author of *Cultographies: Stranger Than Paradise* (2018) and co-author with Ernest Mathijs of *Cult Cinema* (2011). He is currently writing a monograph on American independent cinema and indie music cultures.

THE ROUTLEDGE COMPANION TO CULT CINEMA

Edited by Ernest Mathijs and Jamie Sexton

Routledge
Taylor & Francis Group

LONDON AND NEW YORK

First published 2020
by Routledge
2 Park Square, Milton Park, Abingdon, Oxon OX14 4RN

and by Routledge
52 Vanderbilt Avenue, New York, NY 10017

Routledge is an imprint of the Taylor & Francis Group, an informa business

British Library Cataloguing-in-Publication Data
A catalogue record for this book is available from the British Library

Library of Congress Cataloging-in-Publication Data
Names: Sexton, Jamie, editor. | Mathijs, Ernest, editor.
Title: The Routledge companion to cult cinema /
edited by Ernest Mathijs and Jamie Sexton.
Description: London; New York: Routledge, 2020. |
Includes bibliographical references and index. |
Identifiers: LCCN 2019023603 (print) | LCCN 2019023604 (ebook) |
ISBN 9781138950276 (hardback) | ISBN 9781315668819 (ebook)
Subjects: LCSH: Cult films–History and criticism.
Classification: LCC PN1995.9.C84 R68 2020 (print) |
LCC PN1995.9.C84 (ebook) | DDC 791.43/653–dc23
LC record available at https://lccn.loc.gov/2019023603
LC ebook record available at https://lccn.loc.gov/2019023604

ISBN: 978-1-138-95027-6 (hbk)
ISBN: 978-1-315-66881-9 (ebk)

Typeset in Bembo
by Newgen Publishing UK

MIX
Paper from
responsible sources
FSC FSC™ C013985
www.fsc.org

Printed in the United Kingdom
by Henry Ling Limited

CONTENTS

List of images   x
List of contributors   xiii
Acknowledgements   xx

Introduction: The cult cinema studies experience   1

PART I
Genres and cycles   7
  Genres, cycles, and modes   7

1 'Naughty,' 'nasty', 'culty': Exploitation film   11
   Ernest Mathijs

2 Underground film and cult cinema   24
   Glyn Davis

3 Cult-art cinema: Defining cult-art ambivalence   33
   David Andrews

4 "It happens by accident": Failed intentions, incompetence, and
   sincerity in badfilm   40
   Becky Bartlett

5 Cult horror cinema   50
   Steffen Hantke

6 Cult science fiction cinema   59
   Mark Bould

7 Cult comedy cinema and the cultic, comic mode   69
   Seth Soulstein

8 The Italian *giallo*   76
   Alexia Kannas

PART II
Global and local cult cinema   85
   Global and local cult cinema   85

9 Latsploitation   89
   Dolores Tierney

10 Iranian cult cinema   98
   Babak Tabarraee

11 Rebels without a cause: The Bombay cult film   105
   Vibhushan Subba

12 East Asian cult cinema   111
   Robyn Citizen

13 Anime is (not) cult: Gainax and the limits of cult cinema   121
   Rayna Denison

14 Blaxploitation filmmaking   131
   Harry M. Benshoff

PART III
Critical concepts   139
   Critical concepts   139

15 Cult cinema and gender   143
   Brenda Austin-Smith

16 Cult cinema and nostalgia   152
   Renee Middlemost

17 Oc/cult film and video   161
   Anna Powell

18 Transgression in cult cinema   170
   Thomas Joseph Watson

19 Access all areas? Anglo-American film censorship and cult cinema
     in the digital era   180
     Emma Pett

20 Cult cinema and camp   190
     Julia Mendenhall

PART IV
Exhibition, distribution   199
     Cult film distribution and exhibition   199

21 Midnight movies   203
     Carter Moulton

22 Drive-in and grindhouse theatres   215
     David Church

23 Blood cults: Historicising the North American "shot on video"
     horror movie   223
     Johnny Walker

24 Cult cinema in the digital age   233
     Iain Robert Smith

25 Cult cinema and film festivals   244
     Russ Hunter

PART V
Fandom   253
     Cult fandom   253

26 Conventions and cosplay   257
     Lynn Zubernis

27 Grown woman shit: A case for *Magic Mike XXL* as cult text   266
     Amanda Ann Klein

28 The cut between us: Digital remix and the expression of self   275
     Jenna Ng

29 The professionalised fandom of careers in cult: "Passionate work"
     within academia and industry   285
     Matt Hills

Contents

PART VI
Music and sound   295
    Sound and music in cult film   295

30 Cult musicals   297
    Ethan de Seife

31 Cult soundtracks (music)   307
    James Wierzbicki

32 Sounding out cult cinema: The 'bad', the 'weird' and the 'old'   315
    Nessa Johnston

PART VII
Aesthetics and intermediality   325
    Cult film aesthetics   325

33 Inside an actor's scrapbook: Heath Ledger's aesthetic practice
    of *unbalancing*   329
    Jörg Sternagel

34 Special effects and the cult film: Cult film production and analogue
    nostalgia on the digital effects pipeline   338
    Leon Gurevitch

35 Production play: Sets, props, and costumes in cult films   349
    Tamao Nakahara

36 Cult film and adaptation   358
    I. Q. Hunter

37 Cult film – cult television   366
    Stacey Abbott

PART VIII
Auteurs   379
    Cult auteurs   379

38 "It's a strange world": David Lynch   383
    Jeffrey Andrew Weinstock

Contents

39 "You guys always bring me the very best violence": Making the
case for Joss Whedon's *The Avengers* and *Serenity* as mainstream cult   392
Erin Giannini

40 Anti-auteur: The films of Roberta Findlay   402
Alexandra Heller-Nicholas

41 Anna Biller   411
Jennifer O'Meara

42 Alejandro Jodorowsky and *El Topo*   422
Antonio Lázaro-Reboll

PART IX
Actors   431
   Cult cinema acting   431

43 Judy Garland   435
Steven Cohan

44 From the other side of the wind: Dennis Hopper   443
Adrian Martin

45 Barbara Steele   451
Nia Edwards-Behi

46 Bruce Lee: Cult (film) icon   460
Paul Bowman

47 All he needs is love: The cult of Klaus Kinski   468
Ian Cooper

48 Crispin Glover   478
Sarah Thomas

Index   488

IMAGES

Early discussions of exploitation film in *Film Comment*. Used with permission from *Film Comment* magazine and Film at Lincoln Center. © 1963   11

1.1   Lawrence Woolsey (John Goodman) as an exploitation showman in Joe Dante's *Matinee* (Dante, USA, 1993). Universal Pictures/Renfield Productions   13

4.1   *Birdemic: Shock and Terror's* objectively bad aesthetics (Nguyen, USA, 2010). Expedition Films/Moviehead Pictures   45

4.2   One of several attempts to replicate failure in *Birdemic 2: The Resurrection* (Nguyen, USA, 2013). Got A Fish Productions/Moviehead Pictures   46

5.1   "That's disgusting": Horrality in *The Fly* (Cronenberg, USA, 1986). SLM Production Groups/Brooksfilms   54

5.2   Transgressiveness in the mainstream: *Gremlins* (Dante, USA, 1984). Warner Bros/Amblin Entertainment   56

8.1   Inspector Tellini looks at a tarantula in *The Black Belly of the Tarantula* (Cavara, Italy/France, 1971). Da Ma Produzione   79

8.2   Stylized murder in *Tenebre* (Argento, Italy, 1982). Sigma Cinematografica Roma   83

12.1   Sho'nuff in the modified costumes of imperial Japanese iconography and Leroy in the iconic yellow jumpsuit of Bruce Lee from the film he was making before his death, *Game of Death*. Still from *The Last Dragon* (Schultz, USA, 1985). Delphi III Productions/Motown Productions   113

12.2   Hijikata as Jōgorō Komoda using the butoh movements that he pioneered in service of the film's thematic freakery. Still from *Horrors of Malformed Men* (Ishii, Japan, 1969). Toei Company   117

12.3   This image of a black track and field athlete hangs on Tetsuo's wall. Still from *Tetsuo: The Iron Man* (Tsukamoto, Japan, 1989). Japan Home Video/K2 Spirit/Kaiyu Theater/SEN   118

23.1 Advertising for Wizard Video's range of "violent videocassettes" and UEI's
first print ad for *Blood Cult*. Images courtesy of the Popular Film and
Television Collection. Ads from *Fangoria* magazine (issue 49, 1985)   227

30.1 Esther Williams and a bevy of bathing beauties in *Neptune's Daughter* (Buzzell,
USA, 1949). Metro-Goldwyn-Mayer. Image courtesy of George Eastman House   300

30.2 Grover Dale and George Chakiris lead a colorful dance through Rochefort's
town square in Jacques Demy's *Les Demoiselles de Rochefort* (Demy, France, 1967).
Parc Film/Madeleine Films   303

30.3 Soon-to-be-undead glam-rock star Beef (Gerrit Graham) mesmerizes his
admirers in Brian De Palma's *Phantom of the Paradise* (De Palma, USA, 1974).
Harbor Productions   304

33.1 Still from *Too Young to Die: Heath Ledger* (*Heath Ledger: Liebling der Götter*,
Freyer, GER, 2012), Broadview TV   331

33.2 Still from *Too Young to Die: Heath Ledger* (*Heath Ledger: Liebling der Götter*,
Freyer, GER, 2012), Broadview TV   331

33.3 Still from *The Dark Knight* (Nolan, USA, 2008). Warner Bros   334

37.1 Agent Cooper investigates the disappearance of Agent Desmond. Still from
Twin Peaks (ABC, USA, 1990–1991)   372

37.2 Veronica Mars walking in the rain at the end of series three. Still from *Veronica
Mars* (UPN, USA, 2004–2006)   375

38.1 Laura/Carrie screaming in *Twin Peaks* and *Twin Peaks: The Return*. Stills from
Twin Peaks (ABC, USA 1990–1991) and *Twin Peaks: The Return* (Showtime,
USA, 2017)   384

38.2 Rebekah Del Rio performing in *Mulholland Drive* and *Twin Peaks: The
Return*. Stills from *Mulholland Dr.* (Lynch, USA, 2001) and *Twin Peaks:
The Return* (Showtime, USA, 2017)   387

40.1 *Blood Sisters* (Findlay, USA, 1987). Reeltime Distribution Corporation   403

40.2 *Snuff* (Michael and Roberta Findlay, USA, 1976). August Films/Selected
Pictures   407

40.3 *Tenement* (Roberta Findlay, 1985)   409

41.1 Elaine (Samantha Robinson) lying on top of the pentagram rug that
Biller hand-pulled for *The Love Witch* (Biller, USA, 2016). Image shot by
M. David Mullen, courtesy of Anna Biller Productions   413

41.2 Anna Biller as Barbi in *Viva* (Biller, USA, 2007), with the character's costume
and pose highlighting overlaps between her stylized space and body. Image
shot by Steve Dietl, courtesy of Anna Biller Productions   414

41.3 Poster promoting *The Love Witch* 'High Tea Party' in Los Angeles, March
2018. Reprinted with permission from Anna Biller. Poster credit: Demonic
Pinfestation, with photography by Richard Foreman   417

41.4 Elaine/Samantha Robinson in *The Love Witch* (Biller, USA, 2016), as captured
using a kaleidoscope lens and colour gels. Image shot by M. David Mullen,
courtesy of Anna Biller Productions   420

43.1 Judy Garland sings "Over the Rainbow". *The Wizard of Oz* (Fleming, USA,
1939). Metro-Goldwyn-Mayer   436

43.2   Judy Garland sings "The Man that Got Away" on *The Judy Garland Show*
(CBS, 1963–64)   437

43.3   Judy Garland and Fred Astaire perform "A Couple of Swells" in *Easter Parade*
(Walters, USA, 1948). Metro-Goldwyn-Mayer   439

47.1   Klaus Kinski as the title character in *Aguirre, the Wrath of God* (Herzog,
W. Germany/Peru/Mexico, 1972). Werner Herzog Filmproduktion/Hessischer
Rundfunk   472

47.2   Klaus Kinski as the crazed landlord in *Crawlspace* (Schmoeller, USA/Italy,
1986). Empire Pictures   474

48.1   Crispin Glover's dancing moves from *Friday the 13th: The Final Chapter*
(Zito, USA, 1984). Paramount Pictures/Georgetown Productions/Sean
S. Cunningham Films   481

48.2   Crispin Glover in *Willard* (Morgan, USA, 2003). New Line Cinema/Hard
Eight Pictures   484

CONTRIBUTORS

Stacey Abbott is a reader in Film and Television Studies at the University of Roehampton. She is the editor of *The Cult TV Book* (2010) and has written on a wide range of cult television series, including *Buffy the Vampire Slayer, Angel, Torchwood, Fringe, Alias* and *Hannibal*. She is the author of *Celluloid Vampires* (2007), *Angel: TV Milestone* (2009), *Undead Apocalypse* (2016), and co-editor, with Lorna Jowett, of *TV Horror: Investigating the Dark Side of the Small Screen* (2013). She is currently co-editing, with Lorna Jowett, *Global TV Horror* (forthcoming) and writing the BFI Classic on Kathryn Bigelow's *Near Dark*.

David Andrews is a scholar who has published four books on film, literature, and pornography. His articles have appeared in many forums, including *Cinema Journal, The Journal of Film and Video, The Journal of Popular Culture, Jump Cut*, and *The Velvet Light Trap*. The University of Texas Press published his most recent book, *Theorizing Art Cinemas*. He teaches writing and literature at Loyola University Chicago.

Brenda Austin-Smith is Professor and Head of English, Theatre, Film & Media at the University of Manitoba, where she teaches courses in Cult Film, Film and Realism, and Cinephilia. She researches and writes on adaptation, melodrama, spectatorship, performance, and emotional responses to film. Among her publications are essays on Gene Hackman, Hitchcock and Henry James, Lars von Trier, Canadian women directors, animal performance, and symbolism in American literature.

Becky Bartlett is a lecturer in Film and Television at the University of Glasgow, where her teaching has included courses on cult film and television, and religion in film and television. She is currently working on her monograph, *American Badfilm 1950–1970: Analysing Incompetence and Intention* (2020), and has contributed articles to *Continuum: Journal of Media & Cultural Studies* and the edited collection, *New Heart and New Spirit: The Bible Onscreen Since 2004* (2019). Her research interests include cult cinema, bad movies, religion and film, and Hollywood gorilla men.

Harry M. Benshoff is the author of *Monsters in the Closet: Homosexuality and the Horror Film* (1997), *Dark Shadows* (2011), and *Film and Television Analysis: An Introduction to Theories, Methods,* *and Approaches* (2015). He is the editor of *A Companion to the Horror Film* (2014). With Sean Griffin, he co-authored *America on Film: Representing Race, Class, Gender, and Sexuality at the Movies* (2009 [2004]), *Queer Images: A History of Gay and Lesbian Film in America* (2006), and co-edited *Queer Cinema: The Film Reader* (2004). His numerous other essays and book chapters cover topics such as blaxploitation horror films, Hollywood LSD films, *The Talented Mr. Ripley* (1999), *Brokeback Mountain* (2005), *Milk* (2008), and *Twilight* (2008).

Mark Bould is Reader in Film and Literature at UWE, Bristol. The recipient of the IAFA Distinguished Scholarship Award (2019) and the SFRA Pilgrim Lifetime Achievement Award for Critical Contributions to the Study of Science Fiction and Fantasy (2016), he is a founding editor of the journal *Science Fiction Film and Television* and the monograph series *Studies in Global Science Fiction*. His most recent books are *The Anthropocene Unconscious* (2020), *M. John Harrison: Critical Essays* (2019), *Solaris* (2014), *SF Now* (2014) and *Africa SF* (2013).

Paul Bowman is professor of cultural studies at Cardiff University, UK. He is author of numerous monographs, including Theorizing Bruce Lee (2010), Beyond Bruce Lee (2013), Martial Arts Studies (2015), Mythologies of Martial Arts (2017) and in 2019 the open-access monograph Deconstructing Martial Arts, which is available free online from Cardiff University Press. He is co-editor of the journal Martial Arts Studies and director of The Martial Arts Studies Research Network.

David Church is a lecturer in Cinema Studies in the Department of Comparative Cultural Studies at Northern Arizona University, where he specializes in genre studies, taste cultures, and histories of film circulation. He is the author of *Grindhouse Nostalgia: Memory, Home Video, and Exploitation Film Fandom* (2015), *Disposable Passions: Vintage Pornography and the Material Legacies of Adult Cinema* (2016), and *Mortal Kombat: Games of Death* (2020).

Robyn Citizen, PhD, is a film curator, independent scholar and Texan based in Toronto. Her eclectic film background includes lecturing in the Departments of Asian Studies and Theatre and Film at the University of British Columbia from 2012 to 2017, chapters on transnational science-fiction films and *Get Out* (2017), and film festival programming. She is currently the International Programmer for the TIFF 2019 Short Cuts section.

Steven Cohan is Dean's Distinguished Professor Emeritus at Syracuse University. His books include *Masked Men: Masculinity and the Movies in the Fifties, Hollywood Musicals: The Film Reader, Incongruous Entertainment: Camp, Cultural Value, and the MGM Musical,* and *The Sound of Musicals.*

Ian Cooper is an author and screenwriter whose books include *Devil's Advocates: Witchfinder General* (2011), *Cultographies: Bring Me the Head of Alfredo Garcia* (2012), and *Frightmares* (2016). He is currently working on a book about Hitchcock's *Frenzy*.

Glyn Davis is Reader in Screen Studies at the University of Edinburgh. His publications include *Warhol in Ten Takes* (2013, co-edited with Gary Needham) and *Film Studies: A Global Introduction* (Routledge 2015, co-authored with Kay Dickinson, Lisa Patti, and Amy Villarejo). Glyn's writing has appeared in *Aniki, Cinema Journal, GLQ, MIRAJ,* and *Screen.* From 2016 to 2019, he was the Project Leader of 'Cruising the 1970s', a pan-European queer history project funded by HERA and the European Commission (www.crusev.ed.ac.uk).

Rayna Denison is a senior lecturer in Film, Television and Media Studies at the University of East Anglia, where she teaches and does research on contemporary Japanese animation and film. Rayna is the author of *Anime: A Critical Introduction* (2015), and the editor of *Princess Mononoke: Understanding Studio Ghibli's Monster Princess* (2018). She is also the co-editor of the Eisner Award-nominated *Superheroes on World Screens* (2015), and you can find her academic articles in *Cinema Journal, Japan Forum, Velvet Light Trap,* and the *International Journal of Cultural Studies.*

Nia Edwards-Behi is an independent film scholar and critic based in Aberystwyth, UK, specialising in horror and related genres. Nia is also co-director of Abertoir, Wales' International Horror Festival, a member of the European Fantastic Film Festivals Federation.

Erin Giannini is an independent scholar with a PhD in television studies from University of East Anglia. Her recent work has focused on portrayals of and industrial contexts around corporate culture on television, including a monograph on corporatism in the works of Joss Whedon. She has also published and presented work on religion, socioeconomics, production culture, and technology in series such as Supernatural, Dollhouse, iZombie, and Angel.

Leon Gurevitch is Associate Professor in the School of Design at Victoria University of Wellington, New Zealand, where he publishes academic writing, usable software, data visualisation, and media design work focused on the interface between science, technology, humanities, and design.

Steffen Hantke has edited *Horror,* a special topic issue of *Paradoxica* (2002), *Horror: Creating and Marketing Fear* (2004), *Caligari's Heirs: The German Cinema of Fear after 1945* (2007), *American Horror Film: The Genre at the Turn of the Millennium* (2010), and, with Agnieszka Soltysik-Monnet, *War Gothic in Literature and Culture* (2016). He is also author of *Conspiracy and Paranoia in Contemporary American Literature* (1994) and *Monsters in the Machine: Science Fiction Film and the Militarization of America after World War II* (2016).

Alexandra Heller-Nicholas is a film critic and author from Melbourne, Australia. She has published seven books with an emphasis on gender politics in cult and horror film and has co-edited collections on the films of Hélène Cattet and Bruno Forzani, Elaine May, Peter Strickland, and *Alice in Wonderland,* the latter coinciding with an exhibition at the Australian Centre for the Moving Image. Alexandra is a consultant for museums, filmmakers, and film festivals, and is a regular contributor to home entertainment releases from Arrow Video and Eureka Entertainment.

Matt Hills is Professor of Media and Film at the University of Huddersfield. He is the author of six monographs, including *Fan Cultures* (2002) and *The Pleasures of Horror* (2005), as well as being the editor of *New Dimensions of Doctor Who* (2013) and co-editor of *Transatlantic Television Drama* (2019). He has published more than a hundred book chapters/journal articles on fandom and cult media, including chapters in the *Wiley-Blackwell Companion to the Horror Film* (2017), the *Routledge Companion to Media Fandom* (2018) and the *Wiley-Blackwell Companion to Media Fandom and Fan Studies.* He is currently working on a follow-up to *Fan Cultures* for Routledge, entitled *Fan Studies.*

I.Q. Hunter is Professor of Film Studies at De Montfort University, Leicester, and the author of *British Trash Cinema* (2013), *Cult Film as a Guide to Life: Fandom, Adaptation, and Identity* (2016), editor of *British Science Fiction Cinema* (1999), and co-editor of eleven books, including *The Routledge Companion to British Cinema History* (2016), *Science Fiction Across Media: Adaptation/Novelization* (2013), *British Comedy Cinema* (2012), *Retrovisions: Reinventing the Past in Film and Fiction* (2001), and *Pulping Fictions: Consuming Culture Across the Literature/Film Divide* (1996).

Russ Hunter is a senior lecturer in Film and Television in the Department of Arts at Northumbria University. His research focuses on genre film festivals, Italian genre cinema, and European horror cinema. He has published on a variety of aspects of Italian and European genre cinema and is the co-editor (with Stefano Baschiera) of *Italian Horror Cinema* (2016). He has published in numerous film encyclopaedias and reference guides and works closely with a number of European genre film festivals.

Nessa Johnston is a lecturer in Media, Film and Television at Edge Hill University, UK. Her research focuses on sound in low-budget, American independent, experimental, alternative and cult films, and has been published in *Music, Sound and the Moving Image*, *The Soundtrack*, *The New Soundtrack*, *The Velvet Light Trap*, and *Continuum*. She currently has a monograph in progress on *The Commitments* for the Routledge Cinema and Youth Cultures series.

Alexia Kannas is Lecturer in the School of Media and Communication at RMIT University (Melbourne, Australia) where she teaches courses in Cinema Studies. Her research interests include cult and alternative cinemas, the cinematic modernism and sound in film and television. She is the author of *Deep Red* (Columbia University Press/Wallflower, 2017) and *GIALLO!: Genre, Modernity and Detection in Italian Horror Cinema* (2020).

Amanda Ann Klein is Associate Professor of Film Studies in the English Department at East Carolina University. She is the author of *American Film Cycles: Reframing Genres, Screening Social Problems, & Defining Subcultures* (2011), and co-editor of *Multiplicities: Cycles, Sequels, Remakes and Reboots in Film & Television* (2016). Her manuscript, *Identity Killed the Video Star: Class, Gender, and Whiteness in MTV Reality Programming* (1992–2018), is under contract with Duke University Press. Her scholarship has appeared in *Quarterly Review of Film and Video*, *Jump Cut*, *Film Criticism*, *Flow*, *Antenna*, *Salon*, *The Atlantic*, *The Chronicle of Higher Education*, *Inside Higher Ed*, and *The New Yorker*.

Antonio Lázaro-Reboll is Senior Lecturer in Hispanic Studies at the University of Kent, where he teaches in the areas of Spanish film and cultural studies. He is the author of *Spanish Horror Film* (2012) and co-editor with Ian Olney of *The Films of Jess Franco* (2018). His essays on the cross-cultural dialogue between Spanish horror and international traditions of the horror genre have been published in journals such as *New Review of Film and Television Studies* and *Film Studies*, and in edited volumes such as *A Companion to Spanish Cinema* (2012), *Spanish Erotic Cinema* (2017) and *Tracing the Borders of Spanish Horror Cinema and Television* (2017). He is currently completing a new monograph, *Spanish Comics Cultures, 1965–1975*, for Berghahn Books.

Adrian Martin is Adjunct Associate Professor of Film and Screen Studies at Monash University (Australia) and a teacher at the EQZE Film School (Spain). An internationally published film critic, he is the author of eight books, most recently *Mysteries of Cinema: Reflections on Film Theory, History and Culture 1982–2016* (2018).

Ernest Mathijs is Professor of Film Studies, University of British Columbia. He is the author of books on *Ginger Snaps* and David Cronenberg, and the co-author and co-editor of several books on *The Lord of the Rings*, European horror, and cult film. With Jamie Sexton he wrote *Cult Cinema*, and with Xavier Mendik *The Cult Film Reader* and *100 Cult Films*. He is currently researching a book on Delphine Seyrig.

Julia Mendenhall is an independent scholar who holds a PhD in English from Temple University in Philadelphia. For her dissertation, she conducted research in Toronto, Canada, on Canadian lesbian films, with a U.S. State Department Fulbright Scholarship. She is the author of the book on Patricia Rozema's film, *I've Heard the Mermaids Singing*, published by Vancouver's Arsenal Pulp Press in December 2014. She is also currently a screenwriter writing an adaptation of the groundbreaking British lesbian novel, *The Well of Loneliness,* by Radclyffe Hall.

Renee Middlemost is a lecturer in Communication and Media at the University of Wollongong, Australia. Her research focuses on fan/audience participatory practices and how these intersect with celebrity and popular culture. Her recent work has been published in *Celebrity Studies; M/C Journal,* the *Australasian Journal of Popular Culture.* She is the co-founder of FSN Australasia, and a co-editor of *Participations.*

Carter Moulton is a PhD student in Screen Cultures at Northwestern University. He received his Master's degree from the University of Wisconsin-Milwaukee, where he researched movie audiences, cinemagoing, silent cinema, and emerging technologies in film production, distribution, and exhibition.

Tamao Nakahara received her PhD from the University of California – Berkeley under the tutelage of Linda Williams and Eric Schaefer. Her publications include "Barred Nuns: Italian Nunsploitation Films," *Alternative Europe: Eurotrash and Exploitation Cinema Since 1945,* "Making up Monsters: Set and Costume Design in Horror Films," *Horror Zone,* and "The Melodrama of Masculinity: Teenage Boy and Incest Narratives in Italian Sex Comedies," *Popular Italian Cinema.*

Jenna Ng is Anniversary Lecturer in Film and Interactive Media at the University of York. She is the editor of *Understanding Machinima: essays on filmmaking in virtual worlds* (2013) and is currently working on a monograph titled *Undoing the Screen: Space, Spectacle, Surface.* She has published widely on digital visual culture, with research interests also in computational culture, digital humanities, cinephilia, and interactive storytelling.

Jennifer O'Meara is an assistant professor in Film Studies at Trinity College Dublin, where she specializes in digital theory and practice. Her monograph, *Engaging Dialogue: Cinematic Verbalism in American Independent Cinema,* was published by Edinburgh University Press in 2018. She has published on a diverse range of film and media topics in venues such as *The Velvet Light Trap, Cinema Journal, Celebrity Studies,* and *The New Soundtrack.* She is currently completing a monograph on women's voices in contemporary media.

Emma Pett is Lecturer in Film Studies at the University of East Anglia, UK. After completing an AHRC-funded PhD in collaboration with the British Board of Film Classification (BBFC), she was Research Associate on the AHRC-funded *Teenage Kicks* project (Bristol) and the AHRC-funded *Cultural Memory and British Cinema-Going in the 1960s* project (UCL). She has published on cult cinema in numerous journals, including *New Review of Film and Television Studies*, the *Journal of British Cinema and Television and Transnational Cinemas,* and is author of the forthcoming book *Experiencing Cinema: Immersive Media, Participatory Culture and the Experience Economy.*

Anna Powell retired from her post as Reader in English and Film at Manchester Metropolitan University to become an Honorary Research Fellow. She is the author of *Deleuze and Horror Film, Deleuze, Altered States and Film*, and co-author of *Teaching the Gothic*. She continues to publish articles and chapters on Deleuze and Gothic film and literature, its affects and effects. Among her recent research topics are Jan Svankmajer's Poe films, Gothic children in *The Shining* and H.P. Lovecraft. Anna is a member of the *Deleuze Studies* and *Dark Arts* editorial boards and founder of *A/V*, the online journal for Deleuze-related studies. As well as working as a visiting lecturer and running public study groups, she enjoys creative writing.

Ethan de Seife is the author of *Tashlinesque: The Hollywood Comedies of Frank Tashlin* and *This Is Spinal Tap* in the "Cultographies" series. He is currently an independent scholar in the Bay Area.

Jamie Sexton is Senior Lecturer in Film and Television Studies at Northumbria University, UK. He is author of *Cultographies: Stranger Than Paradise* (2018) and co-author with Ernest Mathijs of *Cult Cinema* (2012). He is currently writing a monograph on American independent cinema and indie music cultures for Edinburgh University Press.

Iain Robert Smith is Lecturer in Film Studies at King's College London. He is author of The *Hollywood Meme: Transnational Adaptations in World Cinema* (2016) and co-editor of the collections *Transnational Film Remakes* (with Constantine Verevis, 2017) and *Media Across Borders* (with Andrea Esser and Miguel Bernal-Merino, 2016). He is an AHRC/BBC New Generation Thinker.

Seth Soulstein is a PhD candidate in the Department of Performing and Media Arts at Cornell University, and a lecturer in Film Studies and in Theatre Studies at Ithaca College. Recent publications include "Concrete Irrationality: Surrealist Spectators and the Cult of Harry Langdon" in *Scope*, and "Classroom Clowning: Teaching (with) Humor in the Media Classroom" in the *Journal for Cinema and Media Studies.*

Jörg Sternagel is interim Associate Professor in Media Theory at the Department of Art and Design at the University of Applied Sciences Europe, Campus Berlin. Since 2016, he has been a Postdoc Researcher at the Institute for Critical Theory at the Zurich University of the Arts. His work focuses on theories of alterity and the performative, imagery and mediality, and philosophy of existence. His latest publications include the monograph *Pathos des Leibes. Phänomenologie ästhetischer Praxis* (2016) and the co-edited collection *Gegenstände unserer Kindheit: Denkerinnen und Denker über ihr liebstes Objekt* (2019).

Vibhushan Subba is a doctoral research scholar in the School of Arts & Aesthetics, Jawaharlal Nehru University in New Delhi, working on new screen cultures, trash aesthetics, and the modes of production and distribution of low budget and cult cinema.

Babak Tabarraee is a PhD candidate in the department of Middle Eastern Studies at the University of Texas at Austin. His writings in English have appeared in *Iranian Studies, Journal of Islamic and Muslim Studies, The Soundtrack*, and *Cinephile*. His publications in Farsi include three authored books of fiction, twenty-two book-format translations, and several essays, short stories, and screenplays. He is currently working on his dissertation on Iranian cult cinema.

Sarah Thomas is a lecturer in the Department of Communication and Media, University of Liverpool. She is author of *Peter Lorre – Face Maker: Constructing Stardom in Hollywood and Europe* (2012) and *James Mason* for the BFI Film Stars series (2018), and co-editor with Kate Egan of *Cult Film Stardom: Offbeat Attractions and Process of Cultification* (2012).

Dolores Tierney is Senior Lecturer in Film at the University of Sussex. She has published widely on Latin American and Latinx Media in various anthologies and journals including *Screen*, *Quarterly Review of Film and Video*, *Studies in Spanish and Latin American Cinema*, and *Porn Studies*. She is the author of *Emilio Fernandez* (2007) and *New Transnationalisms in Contemporary Latin American Cinema* (2018), and co-editor of *Latsploitation, Exploitation Cinema and Latin America* (2009) and *The Transnational Fantasies of Guillermo del Toro* (2014).

Johnny Walker is Senior Lecturer in Media at Northumbria University. His books include, as author, *Contemporary British Horror Cinema: Industry, Genre and Society* (2015) and, as co-editor, *Grindhouse: Cultural Exchange on 42nd Street, and Beyond* (2016). He is founding series co-editor of the Global Exploitation Cinemas book series.

Thomas Joseph Watson is an associate lecturer in Media at Northumbria University, Newcastle upon Tyne. His research interests focus on critical understandings of violence in contemporary cinema, music and transgressive subcultures. He is co-editor of *Snuff: Real Death and Screen Media* (2016) and has published work concerning pornography, horror cinema, crime documentary, and experimental video art.

Jeffrey Andrew Weinstock is Professor of English at Central Michigan University and an associate editor for *The Journal of the Fantastic in the Arts*. He is the author or editor of twenty-two books, the most recent of which are *The Monster Theory Reader*, *Critical Approaches to Welcome to Night Vale: Podcasting Between Weather and the Void*, *The Cambridge Companion to the American Gothic*, and *The Age of Lovecraft*. Visit him at JeffreyAndrewWeinstock.com.

James Wierzbicki teaches musicology at the University of Sydney; along with exploring questions of modernity and the postmodern, his research focuses on twentieth-century music in general and film music in particular.

Lynn Zubernis PhD is a clinical psychologist and professor at West Chester University. She has written and edited seven books on psychology and on the positive impact of fandom and popular culture in people's lives, including *Family Don't End With Blood*, written with the actors from the cult hit television show Supernatural about how the show has changed their lives and fans' lives. Dr. Zubernis chairs the Stardom and Fandom area of Southwest Popular Culture Association and is on the editorial board of the Journal of Fandom Studies. She writes for Frolic and MovieTVTechGeeks, blogs at fangasmthebook.com and can be found on social media as @FangasmSPN.

ACKNOWLEDGMENTS

We would like to thank all of the contributors for their patience in seeing the *Routledge Companion to Cult Cinema* through to completion, for their timely responses to queries and for the quality of their chapters. Collaborative scholarship can only exist in a spirit of generosity, and every chapter in this book is testament to that.

Thanks also to Natalie Foster for inviting us to edit this Companion and to our editorial assistants on the project: firstly, Sheni Kruger, and, secondly, Jennifer Vennall. A big thanks in particular to Jennifer for calmly answering a large number of queries and for playing such a crucial role in getting this large collection to completion.

Chapter 1 contains sections that first appeared as 'Exploitation Film' in *Oxford Bibliographies Online* (www.oxfordbibliographies.com, 2011). We thank Oxford University Press and Dana Linken and Krin Gabbard for their generous permission to use these arguments in this context. Part of Chapter 3 is based on 'Losing the Asterisk: A Theory of Cult-Art Cinema', which was originally published as Chapter 5 of *Theorizing Art Cinemas: Foreign, Cult, Avant-Garde, and Beyond* (University of Texas Press, 2013). A version of Chapter 28 appeared in *Humanities and the Digital* (edited by David Theo Goldberg and Patrik Svensson, Cambridge, MA: MIT Press, 2015). We thank the editors and publishers for their generosity in sharing this scholarship with a new readership.

Finally, we would like to thank colleagues in Film and Television Studies and Media Studies, especially at Northumbria University and the University of British Columbia, and Kate Egan and Xavier Mendik in particular for their continual support and advice.

INTRODUCTION
The cult cinema studies experience

Jamie Sexton and Ernest Mathijs

The cover of this book explains its subject. Pam Grier is determinedly pointing a gun at the reader. Is it in desperation; or with dedication? Determination, desperation and dedication are words often used to describe the public presence of cult cinema. They also command this book. Ours is an attempt to further the examination of an area in the study of culture at large that has persistently been side-lined yet whose traces are more than ever before prevalent across cultures – and evidenced by their consumptions, celebrations, and the anxieties that surround them. True to the word's heritage in the study of spiritual followings of dedication, and equally true to the word's adoption in studies of feasts, carnival, festivities, and cultural expressions of 'shaking it up', cult cinema is an experiential test tube for culture, where diverse formations and collections of people experiment with what can work, what doesn't, and what shouldn't to give meaning to the world through off-centre multitudes of cultural practices and considerations. Scholars such as Roland Barthes (1957), Mary Douglas (1966), René Girard (1972), Dick Hebdige (1979), Umberto Eco (1991) and Barbara Ehrenreich (2006) have, in their examinations of rituals, taboos, and trangressive expressions in photography, writing, fashion, religion, rock music, and cultural celebrations and commemorations put cultural 'maladjust-ment' front and centre. This book does, too.

It is not just Pam Grier's image. If subject of books on cult film can insist on having trans-performative Divine in a red dress on the cover, pointing a gun, or exploitation actress turned journalist Christina Lindberg with an eye-patch (the shotgun hidden from view), or spiritual filmmaker annex guru Alejandro Jodorowsky on a throne, surrounded by goats, or a bowling Viking woman, or frightening trance-stares of Jack Nance (*Eraserhead*) and Martin Sheen (*Apocalypse Now*)[1], an overload of cultural signs and indexes is presented that, at best, sums up what cult cinema is and what we should know about it, and, more likely, guides a reader's interest into understanding what cult cinema stands for and what kind of experience it entails. Culture under arrest; or culture liberated? Above all, it is culture as experience, wide-eyed, lived, and peering for meaning.

A short history of cult film (studies)

Let us track back a little. While the word 'cult' itself had been used within film culture as far back as the 1920s, it is generally assumed that the concept of the 'cult film' is a category that gained currency in the 1970s. During its initial phase cult cinema indicated the reception of films by a largely countercultural audience. As the intellectual interest in cinema increased in the 1960s, particularly amongst college students, the production and screening of films diversified: cheap, underground movies were made and new clubs and societies emerged to screen such films alongside international and repertory content; campus screenings flourished; and screenings at late hours, particularly midnight, became more common. Out of this context, the phenomenon of 'midnight movies' became notable in the 1970s, constituting an alternative to the more mainstream cinematic programme.

In the 1970s and early 1980s, when the first academic pieces on cult film were published, the concept of cult film or cult cinema was far from straightforward. It was, unusually at the time, a category that denoted types of audiences and ways of watching more than the aesthetic dimensions of the films themselves. Broadly, it referred to films which appealed to countercultural audiences, particularly films that had long runs on the midnight circuit. These could be revivals of older Hollywood films, screenings of exploitation films that would have played outside of mainstream theatres (e.g. grindhouses and drive-ins), international art-house films, or low-budget, independent films that were targeted towards the countercultural audience and launched on the midnight circuit (such as *El Topo* [1970] or *Pink Flamingos* [1972]). Yet analyses and discussions of cult cinema would also take into account factors such as its perceived anti-mainstream nature, as well as the typical filmic ingredients that commonly featured in popular midnight films.

Even though cult cinema tended to refer to reception processes more than the qualities of the films themselves, attempts have nevertheless been made to define typical properties of the cult film, though the sheer variety of films that have been considered cult have hindered any straightforward textual definitions of a 'typical cult film'. Features of films that have been considered important cult factors include: strange and weird aesthetics; transgressive content; heightened intertextual self-awareness. Many of these elements distance films from the norms of filmmaking and from the mainstream on the whole, though it is arguable that intertextual self-awareness has now itself become a typical mainstream component of filmmaking, thus drawing attention to how changing social contexts can impact upon what is considered mainstream. While these aesthetic factors are important, they certainly don't fully demarcate a cult from a non-cult text: it may be that the existence of such features may heighten the possibility of a film becoming cultified, but this is far from certain. Broader generic elements and subcultural appeal also have been considered important and can combine with more specific features. For example, in generic terms, science fiction and horror have often been associated with cult followings, though once again not all examples of these genres have become cult films. While these factors may feed into how a film is received, ultimately processes of reception can override such textual qualities in designating whether a film is cult: these include, for example, a particularly notable, devoted following and an appeal to specific niches and subcultures.

Society, culture and technology

The complexities of cult cinema are evident in the variable processes that feed into the idea of a cult film, as well as additional dimensions that have been considered important to cult status since the 1970s, including social, cultural, and technological factors. They are further heightened by regional differences relating to cult film, as studies of the phenomenon have now grown beyond looking at cult film reception in the United States. As such, it might be more convenient in the contemporary era to be aware that cult cinema is not a single phenomenon, and that it is more appropriate to think of different types of cult *cinemas*.

This collection is an attempt to do justice to the various concepts, genres, figures, contexts and cultures that have been commonly associated with cult cinema. As there are so many different aspects to consider, collecting together a range of scholars with diverse expertise is needed to do justice to the complexity of the subject. Even still, we had to be selective in terms of inclusions and exclusions, and there are various filmmaking modes, filmmakers or concepts that could have been included but which are not. We have, though, attempted to provide extensive coverage through including a number of sections which provide separate routes into a multidimensional study of cult cinema.

This collection aims to cover notable concepts, figures and processes that have informed cult film research since its beginnings to the current day, which includes coverage of longstanding issues and analyses of newer cult formations. The latter includes work on how new technological and cultural factors intertwine to reshape ideas of cultism, as well as fresh new perspectives on the notion of cult cinema. As mentioned, research on cult cinema has been dominated by a US-perspective, with other Anglo-speaking territories also being privileged to a lesser extent. This is understandable considering the phenomenon is rooted in developments in US post-war culture, but it is also the case that the idea of cult cinema today informs film cultures internationally, though not always to the same degree. This collection therefore includes a number of chapters on cult cinema in non-Western regions, from the more well-known (East Asian cult cinema) to the lesser acknowledged (Iranian cult cinema). In addition to regional limitations, both cult cinema as a phenomenon and elements of its study have been critiqued for being gendered as primarily male: that is, cult tastes – and those who have traditionally had the cultural capital to inform such tastes – have been seen as largely reflecting male preferences and prejudices of presentation and representation. Looks matter and being seen matters more. As such, gender politics inform a number of chapters: both cult film and gender, and fandom and gender, are engaged with in this collection, while the auteur section makes a point to present female figures despite the prevalence of male directors frequenting this category. The underlying point here is one that cult cinema is good at making: calling, shouting, and demanding attention for that what hegemonic culture (capitalist, patriarchal, Orientalist, …) tries to shuffle under the rug. Or, put differently, these figures were always there and now the means have been taken to call them to the front.

Overall, we have striven to provide a broad collection of chapters that range from overviews of key topics and figures, to fresh research on established topics, to less cared for areas of cult cinema. *The Routledge Companion to Cult Cinema* will be of use to students reasonably new to studying this area, as well as existing cult researchers who want to discover more about different aspects of cult cinema. One final aspect to note is that this collection is focused on *cult cinema* even though the study of other cult media – including television, for example – has also been growing in recent times. We wanted to focus mainly on cult cinema in order to adequately address the magnitude of the subject. Nevertheless, cult cinema is not a subject that can be fully demarcated from other areas, and it overlaps with other media on many occasions. As such, we have included some work on the intermedial relations between other cult cinema and other cult media (in the chapters looking at cult film and television, and cult film and literature), while other connections between media – most notably in the section on cult film and music – are addressed within various chapters. As such, this book is acknowledging the status quo of research but also, urgently, pushing for the recognition of new areas of attention – recalibrating the aim of cult cinema studies.

The cult cinema experience

Given the fugitive nature of cult cinema, efforts to study it are bound to attract criticism. Much like the unsettled status of cult films themselves, the critical and scholarly study of cult cinema is somewhat of a battlefield. Even if one looks at the ways in which the arena has been set, with pressing points such as gender, identity, heritage, region, popularity (marginal or hidden within the mainstream), or sensitivity (moral, political, policy, or otherwise) very much dominating new initiatives of research, there remains a tone of contestation when cult cinema is approached. Part of that comes from areas of the study that maintain that what is marginal in culture cannot remain so and should either be brought into 'conventional' studies, through methods commonly used and taught in psychology, sociology, or art criticism. As we have pointed out earlier (Mathijs and Sexton 2011: 13–25), cult cinema is an experience, and the reception of that experience, and equally the production and distribution contexts of that experience (such as advertising buzzwords), not to mention the philosophies, intentions and limitations involved, will always already create a field of contestation – something to be disagreed upon. There seems no way around that but to accept that contestation as a core characteristic of the field. When Jonathan Rosenbaum, a figure crucially important in outlining midnight movies as an exemplar of cult cinema, writes that 'if old terms continue to be used, but with new meanings, it becomes the responsibility of those who continue to use the term to explain what the new meanings are' in *Cineaste* (Rosenbaum 2008), it is a recognition of the fluidity and volatility of the films' diversity and the demands it poses for its students. That's settled then, cult cinema is unsettled.

There is a larger contestation at stake. Cult cinema studies questions how we come to find meaning in experiences that often resist containment. If one considers the examples of films used by Robin Wood (2018) and Robert B. Ray (2001) in their efforts to ask for attention for methods of research 'outside the box' (by proxy, by heart, by stance, for instance), one can detect that the study of cult cinema is also a study of cultural taste. Is it telling that their lamentations occurred side-by-side in a journal called *Film Criticism*, in a 1993 issue dedicated to a book called *Making Meaning*? Wood fought hard for the inclusion of the horror genre as a 'serious subject'. Ray railed against the virtual exclusion of figures such as Louis August Le Prince from the historiography of early cinema and used surrealism as a method of inquiry. Wood and Ray's examples make clear that ownership over taste is at stake here.

Pierre Bourdieu (1986) has called attention to how tastes are cemented through social forces built on robust routines and practices of 'normalcy' in the construction of aesthetic judgment, and it can be inferred from his later work that he disagreed with that. Jerome Stolnitz made a similar claim, advocating for passionate disinterestedness from the perspective of literary criticism (Stolnitz, 1960; also see Mathijs and Sexton 2011: 13–25), as did Susan Sontag (1966) in her call 'against interpretation', for popular culture (including camp). For film criticism, Noel Carroll has made several similar efforts, calling for textual readings of the films of *King Kong* (1933), Kenneth Anger, Werner Herzog and 1970s horror (De Palma, for instance) based on strategies of exception (Carroll 1998) – concentrating on what gave these films a *different* taste. After masterful analyses of the strategies we use for interpreting films, David Bordwell (1989) avoided the judgement of taste; it was left untouched in his otherwise powerful and ambitious book inspiringly called *Making Meaning*. Janet Staiger (1992, 2000) shifted the focus of discussions about taste and taste-making to the margins by considering the receptions of *A Star Is Born* (the 1954 Judy Garland version), American underground cinema, *The Texas Chainsaw Massacre* (1974), and the representations of gender in *Silence of the Lambs* (1991), and in doing so uncovered mechanisms for the construction of taste that are oppositional and 'perverse' (her words) all the while pushing the centre of cultural meaning making to acknowledge the liminal existences of some of its subjects. Pierre Bourdieu called his studies of taste a revisiting of Kantian ideals and practices of taste in the second half of the twentieth century. Miriam Hansen (2012), in her re-reading of Walter Benjamin, Siegfried Kracauer, and Theodor Adorno, similarly argues that their target was an understanding of taste in the face of modernity. Likewise,

Sianne Ngai (2003, 2012) has taken on a re-examination of Kantian aesthetics and forwarded affective categories of taste hitherto unexcavated such as 'ugly feelings', 'cute', and 'zany', all of which apply to what J.P. Telotte called, in his collection on cult film (Telotte 1991), the cult film experience.

Looking for the cult film experience, then, as both a core compass, and a contested term, equals a study of taste, approached sideways. And that entails sensitivity for the modes of expression that are not usually used in academic studies of taste (and that even theories of affect have difficulty identifying – Linda Williams 1991 and Joan Hawkins 2000 are strong efforts). It is important that the study of cult cinema does not abandon its respect for and use of solid tactics of investigation: if one wants to make claims about a film's public status one better does the groundwork of carefully studying the films, and the elements these films consist of (nut and bolts, props and excesses), collecting data, interviewing producers and patrons, and collecting collections of memories, documents from archives, poster and lobby displays, notices of platform existence – in other words, evidence. Next to that, cult cinema studies also needs to acknowledge that the language through which its subject is studied needs to reflect, respect, and pay tribute to the kinds of languages that the films themselves court: that is why words such as 'wild' and 'weird', 'mad' and 'mystical' appear so often. They should be operationalized instead of avoided. In sum, this book hopes to contribute to debates that see cult cinema, and discussions about taste and film culture as living, breeding organisms, to paraphrase *Freaks*.

Note

1 The references are, respectively, Mathijs and Mendik (2011), Mathijs and Mendik (eds) (2008), Mathijs and Sexton (2011), Rosenbaum and Hoberman (1983), and French and French (1999).

References

Barthes, Roland. 1957. *Mythologies*. London: Verso Books.
Bordwell, David. 1989. *Making Meaning: Inference and Rhetoric in the Interpretation of Cinema*. Cambridge, MA: Harvard University Press.
Bourdieu, Pierre. 1979 [1986]. *Distinction: Social Critique of the Judgement of Taste*. London: Routledge.
Carroll, Noel. 1998. *Interpreting the Moving Image*. Cambridge: Cambridge University Press.
Douglas, Mary. 1966. *Purity and Danger*. London: Routledge.
Ehrenreich, Barbara. 2006. *Dancing in the Streets: A History of Collective Joy*. New York: Metropolitan Books/Holt.
Eco, Umberto. 1991. *Travels in Hyperreality*. London: Picador.
French, Karl and Philip French. 1999. *Cult Movies*. London: Billboard Books.
Girard, René. 1972. *The Violence and the Sacred*. Baltimore, MD: Johns Hopkins University Press.
Hansen, Miriam. 2012. *The Cinema Experience: Siegfried Kracauer, Walter Benjamin, and Theodor W. Adorno*. Berkeley: University of California Press.
Hawkins, Joan. 2000. *Cutting Edge: Art-Horror and the Horrific Avant-Garde*. Minneapolis: University of Minnesota Press.
Hebdige, Dick. 1979. *Subculture: The Meaning of Style*. London: Routledge.
Mathijs, Ernest and Xavier Mendik (eds). 2008. *The Cult Film Reader*. Toronto: McGraw-Hill.
Mathijs, Ernest and Xavier Mendik. 2011. *100 Cult Films*. London: Palgrave Macmillan.
Mathijs, Ernest, and Jamie Sexton. 2011. *Cult Cinema: An Introduction*. Malden, MA: Wiley-Blackwell.
Ngai, Sianne. 2003. *Ugly Feelings*. Cambridge, MA: Harvard University Press.
Ngai, Sianne. 2012. *Our Aesthetic Categories*. Cambridge, MA: Harvard University Press.
Ray, Robert B. 2001. *How a Film Theory Got Lost and Other Mysteries in Cultural Studies*. Bloomington: Indiana University Press.
Rosenbaum, Jonathan and J. Hoberman, 1983. *Midnight Movies*. New York: Da Capo Press.

Rosenbaum, Jonathan. 2008. 'Cult Film: A Critical Symposium', *Cineaste*. 34:1 www.cineaste.com/ winter2008/cult-film-a-critical-symposium (accessed 7 May 2019).

Sontag, Susan. 1966. *Against Interpretation and Other Essays*. New York: Farrar, Straus and Giroux.

Staiger, Janet. 1992. *Interpreting Films*. Princeton: Princeton University Press.

Staiger, Janet. 2000. *Perverse Spectators: Practices of Film Reception*. New York: New York University Press.

Stolnitz, Jerome. 1960. *Aesthetics and the Philosophy of Art Criticism*. Boston, MA: Riverside Press.

Telotte, J.P. (ed.). 1991. *The Cult Film Experience*. Austin: University of Texas Press.

Williams, Linda. 1991. *Film Bodies: Genre, Gender and Excess*. Berkeley: University of California Press.

Wood, Robin. 2018. *Robin Wood on the Horror Film (edited by Barry Keith Grant, preface by Richard Lippe)*. Detroit, MI: Wayne State University Press.

PART I

Genres and cycles

Genres, cycles, and modes

As noted in the introduction to this collection, cult cinema (or cult film) is not easy to define in a straightforward manner, partly because cult film can be considered a kind of meta-genre, a category that encompasses a number of other film types. Discussing the ways that cult cannot be considered a genre in the traditional sense, Telotte has argued – drawing on Cawelti – that unlike many genres, it has no clear 'supertext', a term Cawelti uses to describe 'an abstract of the most significant characteristics or family resemblances among many particular texts' (Cawelti quoted in Telotte 1991: 6). The lack of any clear cult film supertext is related to how cult cinema indicates both reception contexts and audience responses as much as it does textual characteristics but also to the multiplicity of film modes, genres and subgenres that the category incorporates. This section contains chapters on a number of film categories that prominently feature within cult discussions and lists.

The first chapter in this section by Ernest Mathijs focuses on exploitation filmmaking. Exploitation is more of a mode than a genre, a specific type of production which has historically been demarcated from the mainstream of the film industry and which spans different genres. In particular, the exploitation film emerged in the 1920s as a mode of practice differentiated from Hollywood filmmaking: these films were low budget, tending to deal with topics considered taboo within Hollywood, and often screened in low end cinemas (particularly in grindhouse theatres). The term 'exploitation' related to the ways in which these films often exploited their sensational elements in an appeal to potential customers. (Schaefer 1999: 3–4). It is partly because of the exploitation film's marginal position within the broader film industry that it became attractive to cultists. By the 1970s, many exploitation films were being screened on the midnight circuit and gained cult reputations; since this point, the cult reputation of exploitation films has intensified, with a number of exploitation films from a broad historical range being issued on home video.

Glyn Davis explores underground film, another broad mode of filmmaking that also significantly influenced cult cinema, though not quite as markedly as exploitation film. Like exploitation films, underground film – which emerged around the late 1950s – was also often challenging in terms of presenting taboo imagery. It was, though, more artisanal and specialist than exploitation filmmaking, more linked to the world of the artist and often personal in

7

nature, as opposed to the small-scale industrial nature of most exploitation films, which were geared towards making financial profit. Yet, as Davis explains, many aspects of underground filmmaking overlap with cult cinema, including the importance of midnight screenings, transgressive aesthetics, gender politics, and stardom.

David Andrews explores a very different, and more recently coined, mode of cinema: 'artcult'. In contrast to exploitation filmmaking, this is a form of cinema which blends elements of art cinema and cult film. As a combination of modes which are themselves difficult to define in any straightforward manner, it is no surprise that 'art-cult' is itself a somewhat slippery concept. Nevertheless, it is a concept that has gained traction. Andrews contends that, while these forms of filmmaking are often opposed – in that art cinema has mostly been linked to high art status and cultural legitimacy, whilst many forms of cult film have challenged such ideas of legitimacy – there are also overlaps between them, including how they are often distinguished from the mainstream. The cult-art film, Andrews argues, is often a type of film that falls between legitimate and illegitimate modes of cinema.

Andrews refers in passing to the 'badfilm', which is a cultist category explored in this section by Rebecca Bartlett, who outlines some of the knotty philosophical issues around intention and the ways in which badfilm is embraced in ostensibly contradictory ways. Whilst exploitation and underground cinema are modal categories which pre-dated the emergence of cult cinema, and art-cult is a mode that combines a pre-existing mode *with* cult, badfilm is arguably a category of filmmaking which specifically emerges out of cultism, and is influenced by cultist audience reading strategies such as ironic readings.

The next two chapters cover horror and science fiction filmmaking, which are arguably the two most represented genres within cult film discourse. Both of these genres are linked to cult cinema, largely through their historical background as lowbrow genres (linking again to Andrews' notion of illegitimate films) and because they have both been associated with dedicated fan followings. Horror has also been linked to cult via its transgressive aesthetics, which has led to many horror films being subject to controversy and censorship, heightening for some cultists their dangerous aura. Both of these genres have, however, undergone shifting reputations and arguably have moved further into legitimate cultural positions. Yet within these genres there can be arguments amongst fans over which examples are more 'authentic' and worthwhile; as Hantke notes in his chapter, horror films which are considered mainstream are less likely to gain cult status than more marginal examples. Within science fiction this also can be the case, though there are a number of larger budgeted science fiction films that have arguably attained the status of cult classics, such as *Star Wars* (Lucas, 1977), while many contemporary mainstream science fiction films are subject to intensely dedicated fan followings. More relevant factors feeding into the cult status of science fiction films, as Bould outlines in his chapter, are gaps and fissures in certain films, which encourage fans to actively speculate about the films and the worlds they portray; such speculation is particularly encouraged in the 'puzzle film' (and while these are not confined to the science fiction genre, they are many sf puzzle films).

Comedy can exist as a mode or a genre, but while it is a particularly well-known and loved genre, Seth Soulstein highlights how it has been little discussed in cult cinema literature. This is quite surprising considering the number of comedic films that appear in cult film lists and discourse. Soulstein explores – via a detour into high and low distinctions and the Surrealists' fascination with slapstick – reasons as to why comedy has been overlooked in many studies of cult cinema, and links this partly to the ways that the comedic mode can inform other genres that might not be studied primarily as comedy. As he argues, many films which might be assigned to different generic categories nevertheless feature comedic 'kinks'.

The final chapter in this section concerns a cycle, or subgenre, in the form of the Italian giallo film. The giallo film refers to particular mode of violent crime cinema, often dating from the late 1960s to the early 1980s, which was often noted for its stylistic bravura. Alexia Kannas looks at the features of this cycle and explores its gradual cult following, which was spurred by the rise of home video throughout the 1980s and which has become even more subject to cult followings internationally. Through this process – and particularly by becoming embroiled within controversies about extreme material being released on video – it also became considered a subset of the horror film, and as such its fandoms increasingly overlapped with that of horror more broadly.

References

Schaefer, Eric. 1999. *"Bold! Daring! Shocking! True!" A History of Exploitation Films, 1919–1959*. Durham, NC: Duke University Press.

Telotte, J.P. 1991. 'Beyond All Reason: The Nature of Cult'. In Telotte, J.P. (ed.), *The Cult Film Experience: Beyond All Reason*. Austin: University of Texas Press, 5–17.

1

'NAUGHTY,' 'NASTY,' 'CULTY'

Exploitation film

Ernest Mathijs

THE
TRUTH

THE WHOLE
TRUTH

AND NOTHING BUT
THE TRUTH

ABOUT EXPLOITATION FILMS
with barry mahon

Mr. Mahon is a producer and director of exploitation films, including CUBAN REBEL GIRL, WHITE SLAVERY, GIRLS, INC., ROCKET ATTACK, U. S. A., MORALS SQUAD, JUKE BOX RACKET, VICTIMS OF SIN, NUTTY NUDES, NUDE CAMERA, NUDE LAS VEGAS, SHE SHOULD HAVE STAYED IN BED, ONE THOUSAND SHAPES OF A FEMALE, NUDES ON TIGER BEEF, and NUDES, INC.

Early discussions of exploitation film in *Film Comment*. Used with permission from *Film Comment* magazine and Film at Lincoln Center. © 1963

Introduction: From *Film Comment* to *Matinee*

In 1963, the magazine *Film Comment*, then one year old, devoted an article to exploitation film.[1] The short essay by Frank Ferrer was an eccentric account of a film circuit shunned by the mainstream media that was nonetheless a popular albeit offbeat part of the film industry. Equally a manual-of-sorts and a warning for investors, the essay is valuable because it is one of the earliest attempts to define exploitation film while it was at a crossroads – in between classical 'moral danger' film and modern risqué film, and because it highlights core industry practices. 'It is obvious that everyone exploits one another,' Ferrer writes, yet 'everyone [makes] a contribution, artistically or technically.' 'The distributor' he quickly adds, 'is a parasite. […] the man who ultimately realizes the biggest profit from the suckers who patronize this kind of film trash' (33).

In 1964, *Film Comment* returned to the topic, this time with an interview entitled 'The Truth, the Whole Truth, and Nothing but the Truth About Exploitation Films,' with director, producer and distributor Barry Mahon, of *Morals Squad* (1960), *The Love Cult* (1965) and *Nudes on Tiger Reef* (1965). Mahon refuted most of what Ferrer had claimed. Exploitation films, he said, were not an attempt at aesthetics but instead an industry necessity – a technique of salesmanship, not a craft. As a 'sexual attraction type of film' they center around the manufacturing of professional yet mediocre content with 'advertising generally overselling what you see when you get inside.' He did agree exploitation films were cheap, had a high return on investment, and that they sought out titillating subjects in order to provoke the 'hangover of religious and moral feelings' (4). Mahon identified Hershell Gordon Lewis's *Blood Feast* (1963), together with Roger Corman's and American International Pictures' Edgar Allan Poe stories, as the pinnacle of exploitation film because it added 'sadism as an offbeat form of sexuality' to the exploitation mix. Mahon thus referred to a typical motive in exploitation film: that of the sensual but monstrous woman and her ever-changing body. The move from 'naughty' to 'nasty,' and the tension between the two, would be one that typified exploitation film since – and has brought forward a lot of criticism. *Film Comment* would return to exploitation film again at several points in subsequent decades, not least when it started championing, via critic Robin Wood, horror films such as *Night of the Living Dead* (Romero, 1968) and *The Texas Chainsaw Massacre* (Hooper, 1974). It is perhaps symptomatic that the magazine that first highlighted exploitation film would grow to become one of the most esteemed in the world: an unofficial totem for global cinema taste and its critics. Like *Film Comment*, exploitation film too has grown, and it now occupies a more central spot in debates about film at large.

In 1993, Joe Dante – a filmmaker who had grown up as a fan of exploitation films and had become a film reviewer (for *Castle of Frankenstein*), one of Roger Corman's apprentices (including editing trailers to help sell films), and a successful director (*Piranha* 1978, *The Howling* 1981, *Gremlins* 1984) – directed *Matinee*, a film in which Lawrence Woolsey (John Goodman), a huckster showman and producer of B-movies, attempts to exploit the anxieties surrounding the Cuban missile crisis to sell a horror film about an Ant-Man, called *Mant*. Featuring numerous winks and nudges to exploitation films from the 1950s and 1960s, Dante's film, with its nostalgia for B-movies and genre cinema, 'matineed' exploitation film, mainstreamed it while keeping intact its cult appeal. *Matinee* showcased Mahon and Ferrer's assertions that exploitation films were primarily a product of showmen and producers, but it also paid attention to the skills of those who directed them and starred in them. In doing so, *Matinee* reflected a change in how exploitation films had been regarded since the 1970s, when Dante himself, together with John Sayles, Jonathan Demme and Stephanie Rothman (and Jean Rollin and Jess Franco in Europe) had emerged as intrepid filmmakers active in the exploitation category. *Matinee*, and Joe Dante, gave exploitation film the recognition Mahon and Ferrer had aimed at: it acknowledged and

Figure 1.1 Lawrence Woolsey (John Goodman) as an exploitation showman in Joe Dante's *Matinee* (Dante, USA, 1993). Universal Pictures/Renfield Productions

celebrated its achievements and it highlighted the films' competence (both naughty and nasty), as well as its salesmanship (both opportunistic and culturally sensitive), as professional components of a matured industry. In doing so, *Matinee* also helped put forward the understanding that the accreditation of exploitation films' success lay with its cult appeal – with the eagerness and curiosity of audiences, always ready for a new thrill, *even if* they were oversold on a promise that 'what you see when you get inside' was going to be 'something weird' (to use the name of a company specialized in distributing exploitation films). *Matinee* came at a time when repeat home viewing of films was fast becoming a staple component of enjoying them, and that repetition cemented the fandom for exploitation films (true to form, Dante has offered numerous audio commentary tracks for exploitation films released on home viewing formats, from *The Wasp Woman* [1959] to *Candy Stripe Nurses* [1974] and beyond).

Film Comment and *Matinee*, when taken in combination, are beacons for the cult trajectory of exploitation film, from a curiosity that was in need of commentary in order to 'place' it to an over-the-top self-reflection on an afternoon binge rush.

How to study this subject?

The nomenclature of cult cinema and exploitation film is often used in tandem, and there are historical and theoretical reasons to do so. For the purposes of this chapter, exploitation cinema will be regarded as a set of prime, defining elements of cult cinema. In that sense, it means that the characteristics that make up cult cinema will be highlighted in discussing exploitation cinema as a 'type' of cult cinema. That said, this chapter recognizes that exploitation film can be discussed outside the perspective of cult cinema, although, I argue, it would be near impossible to shake that perspective altogether (see Mathijs and Sexton, 2011, for an extensive overview). Whatever the angle, complete inclusiveness covering both the term 'exploitation' and 'cult' is impossible to obtain. Some sources outright refuse to handle the term and they frequently resist calling films exploitation by preferring more mobile and reception-dependent terms such as 'sleaze' or 'trash,' 'grindhouse,' or 'cinéma bis' (in French). The term 'cult' figures prominently in these corners too. To further complicate matters, within the use of exploitation film numerous small and sub-genres operate, many of which are highly formulaic, and labeled as such. 'Naughty' films and 'nasty' cinema have been mentioned already. From 'head film' to 'mockbuster', exploitation terminology further crosses over with genre terms in use in other areas of film study.

Most authoritatively defined by Eric Schaefer (1999), exploitation film is a type of cinema, often cheaply produced, that tries to create a fast profit by referring to, or exploiting, contemporary cultural anxieties. In 1963, Ferrer described it like this: 'The film industry defines an exploitation film in this manner: a low budget film that deals with sex, rape, murder, corruption, drug addiction, perversion, and any other distorted emotion' (1963: 31). For Schaefer, examples include films about drug use, nudity and striptease, sexual deviance, rebellious youths or gangs, violence in society, xenophobia, and fear of terrorism or alien invasions. Ostensibly, exploitation films claim to warn for the consequences of these problems, but in most cases their style, narrative, and inferences celebrate (or 'exploit') the problem as much as critiquing it. The low costs of production allow for quick turnarounds, enabling the exploitation film to address issues of high topicality. It also gives the films a ragged and rickety look that often fits the marginality of their topics.

Overall, the history of exploitation film is divided into a 'classical' period, that runs roughly until the 1960s, and a 'modern' period. The classical period is characterized by production routines that mimic those of Hollywood – with the key figure that of the showman/producer – and by provocative marketing and advertising, renegade distribution, and scattershot reception patterns. The modern period is distinguished by a higher degree of explicit material in the films, and a larger sense of self-awareness in its presentation to viewers, meaning that exploitation films knowingly place themselves in an existing tradition, commenting on the very notion of 'exploitation' and catering to audiences who know what they will be accessing. This self-awareness has led scholars to observe that the viewing tactics audiences employ for exploitation films simultaneously celebrate and ridicule the films, thus upsetting distinctions between highbrow and lowbrow culture. In the modern period the key figure is that of the auteur-director. The classical period of exploitation film is largely studied through a historical lens, whereas the modern period has led to extensive theorization of viewing practices. This focus on viewing practices is partly the result of the increased visibility of exploitation fandom, and of the wide variety of forms of exhibition (such as drive-ins, video, festivals, cable television, DVD, online platforms) through which modern exploitation film can be consumed. Because of this focus on viewing practices it can sometimes be argued that exploitation film is now no longer a type of film but a kind of film viewing.

Because of the low reputation of the exploitation film, scholarship has long remained scarce. Since the 1990s, however, there has been a steady increase in attention, much of it propelled by fan-scholarship from outside the academic world. Today, there is a balance between academic writings and fan-scholarship. John McCarty (1995), Jack Hunter (2002) and Harvey Fenton (2003) represent the fan-scholar perspective, and offer detailed histories and discussions of films academics often shy away from. Deborah Cartmell et al. (1997), Xavier Mendik and Graeme Harper (2000) and Mark Jancovich et al. (2003) have been important in pushing exploitation cinema onto the academy's agenda (not without obstruction). These works employ the term 'cult,' but the majority of the essays in these volumes discuss exploitation films in one form or another. Jeffrey Sconce's work (2007) is significant for the way in which it interrogates the very foundation of 'trash.' As a phenomenon on the periphery of the cinematic mainstream, exploitation film resists easy categorization and definition, and as a result its scholarly study often finds itself on the defensive, arguing for even a reason to be considered a legitimate object of research.

The very struggle for a definition has led to a situation whereby overviews of exploitation film have had to devote a lot of energy discussing meta-definitions (definitions of definitions) and try to connect the study of exploitation to that of other areas of film studies deemed more legitimate and functionalist, such as gender studies, censorship, or pedagogy (see the authoritative work of Cook, 1985). Alternatively, this separation from the mainstream of film studies has led to overly celebratory overviews from – predominantly – fan-scholars. Their importance and influence on the study of exploitation film cannot be underestimated. If nothing else, their efforts have given research into exploitation film a grassroots base, a constituency of readers and commentators with whom academics find themselves in continued debate. Some of this debate centers around the necessity (or refusal of it) for theorizing exploitation film, and it is for this reason that most overviews of the field are theory-light. Another common interest of overviews of exploitation film is a historical framework – a desire to help write the history of the subject. Because of the historical tendency to present North American exploitation film as the exemplar, or even the model, for the genre, sources that present a wide overview of that region have are generally considered 'general overviews' (see Schaefer 1999 for arguably the most commanding study of this kind).

Mostly, overviews of exploitation film tend to be 'guides': eclectic collections of reviews and commentary. Largely this is due to the fact that there have been little or no institutional initiatives to catalogue exploitation films, a result of their marginal and contested position in culture as lowbrow, 'dangerous' or 'sleazy.' Since the 1980s, however, some efforts have been made to construct encyclopedia of exploitation film. Often, these efforts have been user-generated: video technology allowed viewers to start collecting and sharing films and out of this grew the first encyclopedic catalogues, compiled by fan-scholars. Among the most notable early examples are Michael Weldon (1996) and Tim Lucas (1990), all of which started in the early 1980s as serial publications. Landis and Clifford (2002) are rooted in another user-based experience, that of New York's grindhouse theatres (the 42nd Street that both Ferrer and Mahon mention). Increasingly, websites and online catalogues and collections are taking over the function of the print encyclopedia. As a testament to the commercial origin of much exploitation film cataloguing, several of these sites are set up as online stores. Such connotations do much to help make the study of exploitation film more respectable.

Reception and fan studies are important, too, because they have acted in unison when studying exploitation film (in other areas their differences may be big enough to separate them, but not here). The philosophical backbone of reception and fan studies is phenomenology, and this has had repercussions for how exploitation film is identified: a film is an exploitation film when it is seen, or shows itself, as such. When fans talk of a film as an exploitation film, when the 'exploitation' tag is a factor of significance in a film's negotiation of its public status, and when 'exploitation' is a salient marker in a film's reception trajectory (its marketing, distribution, long-term sedimentation into culture), it is an exploitation film. This philosophy has influenced most profoundly studies of the modern period of exploitation film. Since the 1990s, reception and fan studies of exploitation film have been increasingly influential, as is evidenced by the book series Global Exploitation Cinemas (Fisher and Walker 2016).

Finally, historically, American exploitation film has dominated the scholarship in this field, for the simple reason that for many scholars it is largely a phenomenon of the American marketplace. (Clark 1995 is an excellent indication of how vast a research terrain American exploitation film is.) With regard to the classical era, studies of films from the United States cover the vast majority of the research to the point where overviews of the classical period can with reason pose for global overviews (see Schaefer 1999). Here are included studies of the classical era that concentrate on two of the pressure moments: the early 1930s and the mid- to late 1950s (Doherty 1999, 2002). Doherty (1984) offers a good analysis of American exploitation film at a crossroads in 1968. With regard to the modern era, American exploitation film takes up less of a majority in the field, and much of the scholarship is fragmented across studies of particular auteurs and regions. Overviews of American exploitation film in the modern era also tend to specify particular contexts of reception, such as the drive-in theatre or the underground scene (Mendik and Schneider 2002), although there is a vast overlap between these categories and they are used as mobile parameters rather than fixed templates. These considerations do have great pedagogical mileage as is shown by Sconce (2003), who offers a self-reflective consideration of the pedagogical challenges of teaching classical American exploitation film through the case study of Dwain Esper's *Maniac* (1934). It is worth noting that several chapters in this Companion make efforts to balance the overly U.S.-heavy emphasis that remains dominant in the study of exploitation film.

Where to look?

As previously mentioned, exploitation film is often presented as a predominantly American phenomenon. At the same time, its connection with (mostly) European arthouse and risqué cinema is frequently emphasized. Ferrer and Mahon acknowledge the influence of, for instance, Swedish and Danish films with more daring female presentations, and Dante mentions French and Italian subversive cinema in similar terms (Klein 2000). These mentions are 'cover mentions': they stand in for attitudes towards cinema, for approaches to filmmaking, and for conditions and opportunities of film consumption that do not intend to be representative of a nation, region, culture, or continent. Yet, at the same time, these regional markers have come to define how the origins of exploitation film have been studied.

There are three main reasons to study exploitation film through the perspective of national or regional cinema and to treat it as a kind of cinema specific to a country or continent. The first reason is that many exploitation films are small in scale. They are produced cheaply and distributed to a circuit limited in exposure. It is likely that, for a while at least, exploitation films might not make it out of the region in which they were first produced and screened. That said, there is a significant difference between classical exploitation film, which most definitely saw its visibility restricted to mostly regional exhibition (especially in the case of American exploitation film), and the modern period, which benefited from the development of portable exhibition platforms such as VHS and DVD, and of an accelerated circuit of distribution that, in many cases, obliterates the distinction between national and international releases. The second reason to use a national cinema perspective for exploitation film is that the desire of exploitation filmmakers to insert sensationalist topical themes into their films meant that the films latched onto local and regional sensitivities and controversies. Put bluntly, a Mexican exploitation film might have more meaning if one considers it in the context of the cultural sensitivities of Mexico. The third reason is that in several high-profile cases specific generic templates seem to develop in tandem with (or because of) unique production contexts typical to a nation's or continent's film culture and economy.

Since the modern period, there is no limit on exploitation films from all corners of the world. Italosploitation, Britsploitation and Eurotrash, for example, have attracted firm scholarship, and in more recent years Latsploitation and Asian exploitation film (often known as Asia Extreme in reference to a once dominant DVD imprint) have received a lot of attention too. There is a curious distinction between regional exploitation film's narrowly defined site-specificity and its over-generalizations informed by an Orientalist lens. Take exploitation film from the United Kingdom, Britsploitation, which has developed as a quite unique type of film, because it 'traveled quite badly' (as Upton 2001 observes). Unconcerned with aesthetics and realism from other regions and not bothered by marketplace anxieties that dominate American exploitation, it is also often seen as more muted in its imagery because of the historically tight censorship regulations. Among the unique characteristics are a fascination with vulgar comedy and science-fiction (and their combination), and an exclusive brand of horror (of which Hammer horror is the most visible exponent). Much of the terminology of Britsploitation references the emotive mobility of the spectator's position through a self-mocking deprecation (see Hunt 1998; Sheridan 2001). If pushed, one can consider this hyper-focus a form of navel-gazing. In contrast, discussions of exploitation film under a nation's or continent's banner can also contain gross generalizations on the different cultures it captures. 'Asia Extreme' and 'Eurotrash' therefore often offer a taste judgment on the aesthetics used in exploitation film from those regions. The term 'Asia Extreme' was introduced in the 1990s as a colloquial term (and also as the tag of a distribution label to denote a wave of films from Asia that caused furor on the North American and European markets). As such, there is an inference of Orientalism to its use by viewers and critics. Since then, the term has been used increasingly by scholars looking to identify a commonality in the receptions of Asian films as exploitation. Gradually, the term has enveloped most of Asian exploitation film, bringing under its umbrella the monster movie (usually arranged around Godzilla), the martial arts film (where Bruce Lee remains the centripetal figure), and anime (with tentaclesploitation and cyberpunk as pivotal sub-genres). Historically, the regions of Japan and Hong Kong have received the most attention; South Korea, Thailand, Turkey, and Indonesia started to receive attention as well (also see the chapters by Vibhushan Subba, Rayna Denison and Robyn Citizen in this volume).

European exploitation film is often nicknamed Eurotrash. Perhaps a rationale for the radical and dismissive tone of this label lies in the contrast it provides with the kind of film with which Europe is traditionally associated: state-subsidized art and auteur cinema. Even to this day, the dichotomy influences debate on European exploitation. This is acutely the case in writings on contemporary French film, as Sue Harris's 2011 study of the 1970s' most successful exploitation franchise, *Emmanuelle*, testifies, and on German film scholarship (see Hantke 2007). Most scholarship on Eurotrash covers the modern period (Mathijs and Mendik 2004 emphasize central Europe). Unlike American exploitation, the focus in Eurotrash scholarship is less on routines and practices of production and distribution (European producers remain acutely under-researched), and more on the social positioning of film as lowbrow, the textual aesthetics of realism, and on auteurist oeuvres. As an articulation of Eurotrash, Italosploitation has received quite a lot of attention, primarily because of its prolific presence in academic scholarship (especially with regard to directors active in the Spaghetti Western and Giallo sub-genres, such as Sergio Leone, Sergio Corbucci, Dario Argento and Mario Bava – see the chapter on Giallo in this volume). As these examples demonstrate, hybridity is typical for Italosploitation. The most notable items of Italosploitation are the peplum (especially the Maciste and Hercules films), nunsploitation film (sexploitation in the context of the religious orders of the Catholic Church; see Nakahara 2004), poliziottesschi (crime films with rogue cops), and cannibal and zombie films, but there are many more. Sensual aesthetics, exoticism, religious overtones, crime, mystery, and surrealism are combined in ways that have made exploitation films from Italy very successful in overseas markets. The majority of these cycles come from the 1970s (and Italy's 'years of lead' of political turmoil), though some run deep into the 1980s and 1990s (Smith 1997 offers an exhaustive guide). Mendik (2010) discusses the unique figure of Joe D'Amato, active in nearly all of these cycles, and hard-core pornography on top of it.

Compared to this, research on the exploitation film of Latin America is fairly new. Before the twenty-first century, most if not all discussion was centered around a few key figures, especially Alejandro Jodorowsky (Chilean, but mostly active in Mexico), José Mojica Marins (aka Coffin Joe, from Brazil), and Luis Buñuel (his Mexican films). Jodorowsky and Buñuel were usually discussed as 'international' directors, laying claim to 'arthouse' labels. More recently, that 'art' tag has gradually been removed from some discussions (for an example concerning Jodorowsky, who remains the seminal figure of Latsploitation, see Santos 2017). In addition, and perhaps more importantly, the twenty-first century has seen a new direction in Latsploitation studies: conceptualizations of region and nation have become more important as they have become increasingly influenced by a postcolonial theoretical perspective. This perspective is most prominently advocated by Dolores Tierney (2004, also see her chapter in this book). It has enabled the re-assessment of exploitation film in most countries of Latin America (as evidenced in Syder and Tierney 2005, and Ruétalo and Tierney 2009). Overall, the dominant region in Latsploitation has been Mexico – or Mexploitation. Mexploitaton distinguishes itself through its emphasis on generic markers (wrestling and stunt narratives, franchise horror characters such as vampires or werewolves). To this day, Mexico dominates scholarly attention for Latsploitation.

Next to that, Andes-sploitation (the Andes mountain range), Canuxploitation (Canada), Ozploitation (Australia), Nordic exploitation (propelled by the popularity of Scandinavian noir thrillers), and Turkish exploitation have received some scholarly consideration. Attention for African exploitation remains rare, with Nollywood's exploitation films (from Nigeria) and Ugandan exploitation film (called Wakaliwood; see Brown 2017) as exceptions. Historically, however, American exploitation film has dominated the research in this field, for the simple reason that for many scholars it remains largely a phenomenon of the American marketplace, if not in terms of production then at least in terms of the size of consumption and the amount of money circulating. This is especially the case with studies of the classical era that concentrate on two of the pressure moments: the early 1930s, and the mid- to late 1950s. Thomas Doherty (1999), for instance, offers excellent studies of the brief period in between the introduction of sound and the installation of Hollywood's strict self-censorship (the Hays code), in which Hollywood and exploitation were almost synonymous. Doherty's case studies include *Freaks* (Browning, 1932), the first two Tarzan films, and *King Kong* (Cooper and Schoedsack, 1933). Doherty (1984, 2002) also offers a good analysis of American exploitation film at a crossroads in 1968. Overviews of American exploitation film in the modern era tend to specify particular contexts of reception, such as the drive-in theatre or the underground scene.

Who to look for?

The challenge with exploitation film auteurs is that there is often hardly any cohesion in their career. Several filmmakers whose careers are not at all associated with exploitation film, have had exploitation trajectories. The 'apprenticeship narrative' that was mentioned in relation to Joe Dante also applies to David Cronenberg, Wes Craven, Francis Coppola, Jonathan Demme, Peter Jackson, and many filmmakers considered superb artists of cinema. At the same time, there is a lack of theoretical perspective – it is almost as if theory fails when faced with the forthrightness, brashness, and industriousness of many exploitation auteurs. This chapter's range is too small to do justice to many of the most exciting auteurs in exploitation cinema. Dario Argento, Roger Corman, Jess Franco, John Waters, William Castle, Russ Meyer, Lucio Fulci, Hershell Gordon Lewis, Radley Metzger, Paul Verhoeven, and Ed Wood Jr. have received considerable academic scrutiny (Mathijs 2011). But if a haphazard list of 'exploitation auteurs worthy of separate study' can consist of José Benazeraf, Tinto Brass, Jorg Buttgereit, Larry Cohen, Joe D'Amato, Ruggero

Deodato, Dwain Esper, Abel Ferrara, David Friedman, Lloyd Kaufman, Antonio Margheriti, Ted V. Mikels, Gary Graver, or Fred Olen Ray (to name only the ones that a five-minute Facebook request turned up), then it should be clear that there is a lot of work to be done.

Here, I will only discuss two filmmakers at some length, because of the totemic cult status they hold, and because their careers are symptomatic for how exploitation auteurs are usually studied: Roger Corman, the King of the B's, and Radley Metzger, the unsung hero of the sex film. Roger Corman has received several coronations as the most significant filmmaker in exploitation – someone whose image spans both the classical period (as a producer/showman) and the modern period (as a self-conscious auteur). With a career that runs from the 1950s onto the twenty-first century, and with more than 100 films to show as producer and/or director, there is certainly a quantitative wealth of material available. Scholarly consideration for Corman grew in the early 1970s, when his production companies were given extra attention through the mainstream success of directors he'd been the first to give a chance in the craft (see Dixon 1976). Since then, there has been a steady stream of studies. The first kind focuses on his oeuvre, from an auteurist perspective. While there is a certain degree of auteur-celebration in these studies, they are also characterized by an unusual attention for logistics of filmmaking (instead of aesthetics). The second kind concentrates on Corman's efforts as a producer, with A.I.P., New World Pictures, Aries Films (in Latin America), and others (see Osgerby 2003, on A.I.P.'s biker films, and Falicov 2004, on Aries Films). The emphasis in these studies lies on the political economy, topicality, and reception of the films. In spite of the global recognition for Corman's contribution to American film in general, it is still indicative of the status of exploitation film that the majority of studies on Corman openly celebrate his achievements as a businessperson and mentor, yet remain underwhelmed when discussing the aesthetics and values of the films. The name of Metzger is often coupled to that of the better-known Russ Meyer: both have had parallel careers, starting in the late 1950s with nudie pictures, and gradually moving into bigger-budget R-rated softcore extravaganzas by the late 1960s. Like Meyer, Metzger also received some respect from the critical establishment in the early 1970s (see Corliss 1973 – in *Film Comment*!). Unlike Meyer, however, Metzger has been unable to sustain that reception. That is at least partly due to the move towards hardcore pornography. Under the pseudonym Henri Paris Metzger directed a handful of the most elaborately designed and narratively sophisticated hardcore porn films (see Servois 2009 on one of Metzger's most famous hardcore films, *The Opening of Misty Beethoven*). Metzger's career is also widely diverse. He was first and foremost a distributor, next a producer, and then a director. This has made scholars more reluctant to study his oeuvre through the lens of auteurism. Alternative lenses, such as camp, kitsch, and 'taste' have been used more frequently (see Gorfinkel 2002), often leading to a consideration of Metzger's aesthetics as 'Euro-chic'). Together, the perspectives of the iconoclastic art-rebel, the showman, and the pornographer with attitude, make up the composite image of the 'ideal' exploitation filmmaker.

That image also appears to be very male. Often rightfully derided as a masculinist enterprise, exploitation film nevertheless has some notable female auteurs. Scholarship on these filmmakers has been scarce, but since the 2000s there has been an increase in attention. As with other studies of exploitation film auteurs, much of the argument centers on the quest for a redeemable quality of an oeuvre. In the case of female exploitation filmmakers this ambiguity is compounded by several other factors. Often, it seems, discussions of women exploitation filmmakers suffer from short spans of attention, and from being pressed into frameworks that sees their work as symp-tomatic of political developments in cinema – thus denying them a specific identity within exploitation film. In addition, the comparatively short careers of women exploitation directors have made the adoption of auteurist approaches difficult. It has impacted, for instance, on the scholarship on Stephanie Rothman's work (see Cook 1985). Probably the most visible and consistently referenced female exploitation filmmaker is Doris Wishman, whose films with Chesty Morgan are frequently touted as exemplary of the ambiguities involved in women filming the exploitation of women (see Luckett 2003 and Modleski 2007). Other female auteurs who have more recently been put under academic scrutiny include Roberta Findlay (see Peary 1978, and discussed in this volume), Anna Biller (discussed separately later in this book), and Jen and Sylvia Soska (who are not only openly courting horror exploitation but also sports exploitation through their episodic work on wrestling and the WWE). Overall, however, female auteurs remain an under-investigated and fugitive subject in the study of exploitation film.

Exploitation sub-genres

One of the most effective ways of discussing exploitation film is by distinguishing various sub-genres.[2] Traditionally, this occurs through methods of textual analysis: the salient forms, styles, and themes of films are analyzed, and those films that share many components are grouped together and labeled as a genre. Often, contextual information, such as the film's place in history, its production history, and its director (and their intentions) are also used to arrive at such groupings. In the case of the exploitation film, where labeling a film as a certain kind of experience is important for marketing campaigns, and as a function of controversies and censorship, a myriad number of genre labels exist. Many of them overlap. In fact, for some genres (or sub-genres) there exist so many different names that a categorical overview is near impossible. This complexity is further complicated by the fact that several genres, of which the label continues to be used actually only exist(ed) as cycles or waves – in other words, they only occupied a place as a genre for a limited period. Several of the genres on which exist a high degree of consensus (both on their name and on their template) are surveyed elsewhere in this book because they supersede the limitations of exploitation film. Blaxploitation, horror, and Kung Fu or Martial Arts films of Asian heritage are amongst those. Sexploitation films are covered in the sections on gender and cult film. Next to these, labels exist such as Nazisploitation (covered valiantly by Magilow, Vander Lught, and Bridges 2012), the 'erotic thriller' (mostly following the templates set out by Gregory Dark, Zalman King, and the *Red Shoe Diaries* series, see Eberwein 1998; Andrews 2006), the 'sick film' (for which Pier Paolo Pasolini's *Salo*, 1975 became a template, see Church 2009), and the mondo and snuff film (pioneered by *Mondo Cane* of 1963 and immortalized by *Cannibal Holocaust*, by Ruggero Deodato 1979; see Brottman 2004 and Goodall 2006).

The majority of these sub-genres are the result of textual analysis. Blaxploitation, Nazisploitation, torture porn, and Mondo and Snuff Film, for instance, are the result of a grouping of modes of representation. So is the yo-yo cycle of films around women in prisons, a combination of naughty and nasty that received respectability thanks to the television series *Orange Is the New Black* (Netflix, 2013–). As this example shows, occasionally, contextual factors such as a sub-genre's cultural impact on female issues of representation have made a significant difference in the usage of a label. In the case of the Video Nasties (a grouping of films banned from video release in the United Kingdom in the early 1980s; see Egan 2007), context has virtually been the only factor in labeling. Additional complications arise when the terminology to denote exploitation genres is overused. 'Horror', for instance, contains so many films (strictly quantitatively speaking) and has been used so indiscriminately as a tag for exploitation that subdivisions have been designed to speak more specifically about the kind of exploitation these labels cover ('slasher,' 'softcore,' 'hardcore' or 'zombedy', for instance). The same applies to waves of exploitation films about monstrous animals, from rabbits (Bunny-sploitation, of which *Night of the Lepus* is an example) to sharks (*Sharknado*). As can be surmised from this last example, exploitation films that aim for these tropes are often produced as highly self-reflexive and tongue-in-cheek mockeries of mainstream films – in much the same way *Matinee* does.

Conclusion

'Exploitation,' like 'cult,' is a mobile carrier of meanings; both aim for provocation and do so in ways that refuse easy categorization. *Because* they explore, and exploit, morally contentious subjects through a mixture of hyperbolic and excessive aesthetics (that are sometimes intentional and sometimes accidental), they receive receptions that put them aside from mainstream circuits of culture, often relegated to niches in terms of distribution and exhibition – from which they attempt to escape by drawing undue attention to themselves (undue, that is, in the minds and eyes of guardians of moral decency and moderation). As this chapter has observed, there has been a gradual move, interrupted and complicated by ever-oscillating swings of 'coolness' and fashionable 'appropriation', of exploitation cinema towards a position where its place in commercial circuits of culture, and the film industry in particular, is earned, and respected, and where its existence is, most of the time, reluctantly tolerated.

While, ultimately, this gradual recognition has not neutered exploitation film, the fact that thanks to efforts by critics, curators, fans, filmmakers, and scholars exploitation film now has a history, an official narrative with heroes and survivors upon which it can reflect nostalgically, has legitimized it. The cult reception of many exploitation films, from the drugged teens warning film *Reefer Madness* to the drunk women in prison and Hans and Gretel hallucination *Freeway II: Confessions of a Trickbaby* (Bright, 1999), is testimony to that. Speaking of which: *Freeway II* is a sequel to *Freeway* (Bright, 1999). With John Landis in a cameo role as a judge, and Natasha Lyonne and Vincent Gallo as White Girl (a 'crazy serial killer girl') and Sister Gomez (a 'cult lord') respectively, running amok in rundown neighborhoods in Mexico, it is an unruly summary of the modern exploitation film. Given Landis' pedigree as a director, Gallo's reputation as a provocateur, and Lyonne's subsequent rise to mainstream stardom thanks to her roles in Netflix' women in prison drama *Orange is the New Black* and supernatural time-travel spiritual mystery *Russian Doll* (Netflix, 2019–), *Freeway II* is a pivotal film for illustrating where exploitation film sits as a type of cult cinema. After all, when Lyonne's *Russian Doll* character Nadia needs a secret password to unlock life's mysteries it is revealed as 'Jodorowsky's *Dune*.'

Notes

1 This chapter contains large sections that first appeared in Ernest Mathijs (2011), 'Exploitation Film' Oxford Bibliographies Online (www.oxfordbibliographies.com/) accessed 19 January 2019. We thank Oxford University Press and Dana Linken and Krin Gabbard for their generous permission to use these arguments in this context.
2 I wish to thank the hundreds of students of the University of British Columbia's long-running course Cult Cinema (FIST 300) for their contributions to exploring exploitation sub-genres as part of their assignments. Their ability to come up with sub-genres such as 'Nicholas Spark–sploitation' and 'Sharksploitation' (from *The Notebook* to *Sharknado*) is testament to the fertile ground of exploitation cinema. I also want to thank Vince D'Amato for his contribution to these sessions.

References

Andrews, David. 2006. 'Sex Is Dangerous, So Satisfy Your Wife: The Softcore Thriller in Its Contexts'. *Cinema Journal* 45.3: 59–89.
Brottman, Mikita. 2004. 'Mondo Horror: Carnivalizing the Taboo', in Stephen Prince, ed., *The Horror Film*. Piscataway, NJ: Rutgers University Press: 167–188.

Brown, William. 2017. 'Wakaliwood: Where Supercinema Meets Non-Cinema'. Online at: www. wjrcbrown.wordpress.com. Accessed 6 August 2019.

Cartmell, Deborah, Ian Q. Hunter, Heidi Kaye and Imelda Whelehan, eds. 1997. *Trash Aesthetics: Popular Culture and Its Audience*. London: Pluto Press.

Church, David. 2009. 'Of Manias, Shit, and Blood: The Reception of "Salò" as a "Sick Film"'. *Participations* 6.2. Online at: www.participations.org/Volume%206/Issue%202/church.htm. Accessed 6 August 2019.

Clark, Randall. 1995. *At a Theatre or Drive-In Near You: The History, Culture and Politics of the American Exploitation Film*. New York: Garland Publishing.

Cook, Pam. 1985. 'The Art of Exploitation: Or How to Get into the Movies'. *Monthly Film Bulletin* 52 (Dec.): 367–369.

Corliss, Richard. 1973. 'Radley Metzger: Aristocrat of the Erotic'. *Film Comment* 9.1 (Jan.–Feb.): 18–29.

Dixon, Wheeler Winston. 1976. 'In Defense of Roger Corman'. *Velvet Light Trap* 16 (Fall): 11–14.

Doherty, Thomas. 1984. 'The Exploitation Film as History: Wild in the Streets'. *Literature/Film Quarterly* 12.3: 186–194.

Doherty, Thomas. 1999. *Pre-Code Hollywood: Sex, Immorality and Insurrection in American Cinema 1930–1934*. New York: Columbia University Press.

Doherty, Thomas. 2002. *Teenagers and Teenpics: The Juvenilization of American Movies in the 1950s*. Revised and Expanded Edition. Philadelphia, PA: Temple University Press.

Eberwein, Robert. 1998. 'The Erotic Thriller'. *Post Script* 17.3: 25–33.

Egan, Kate. 2007. *Trash or Treasure: Censorship and the Changing Meanings of the Video Nasties*. Manchester: Manchester University Press.

Falicov, Tamara. 2004. 'U.S.-Argentine Co-Productions 1982–1990: Roger Corman, Aries Productions, "Schlockbuster Movies", and the International Market'. *Film and History* 34.1: 31–39.

Fenton, Harvey, ed. 2003. *The Flesh and Blood Compendium*. Guilford: UK: FAB Press.

Ferrer, Frank. 1963. 'Exploitation Films'. *Film Comment* 2.6 (Fall): 31.

Fisher, Austin, and Johnny Walker, eds. 2016. *Grindhouse: Cultural Exchange on 42nd Street, and Beyond (Global Exploitation Cinemas)*. London: Bloomsbury.

Goodall, Mark. 2006. *Sweet and Savage: The World Through the Shockumentary Film Lens*. Manchester: Headpress.

Gorfinkel, Elena. 2002. 'Radley Metzger's "Elegant Arousal": Taste, Aesthetic Distinction and Sexploitation', in Xavier Mendik and Steven Jay Schneider, eds, *Underground U.S.A.: Filmmaking Beyond the Hollywood Canon*. London: Wallflower Press: 26–39.

Hantke, Steffen, ed. 2007. *Caligari's Heirs: The German Cinema of Fear After 1945*. Metuchen, NJ: Scarecrow Press.

Harris, Sue. 2011. 'Sex, Comedy, and Sexy Comedy at the French Box Office in the 1970s: Rethinking Emmanuelle and Les Valseuses'. *Contemporary French Civilization* 35.1 (Winter/Spring): 1–18.

Hitchens, Gordon. 1964. 'The Truth, the Whole Truth, and Nothing but the Truth About Exploitation Films (Interview with Barry Mahon)'. *Film Comment* 3.2 (Spring): 1.

Hunt, Leon. 1998. *British Low Culture: From Safari Suits to Sexploitation*. London: Routledge.

Hunter, Jack, ed. 2002. *The Bad Mirror: Cult Exploitation, and Underground Cinema*. London: Creation Books.

Jancovich, Mark, Antonio Lázaro-Reboll, Julian Stringer and Andy Willis, eds. 2003. *Defining Cult Movies: The Cultural Politics of Oppositional Taste*. Manchester: Manchester University Press.

Klein, Joshua. 2000. 'Interview with Joe Dante', *AV Club* (29 Nov.): www.avclub.com/joe-dante-1798208125. Accessed 6 August 2019.

Landis, Bill, and Michelle Clifford. 2002. *Sleazoid Express*. New York: Simon & Schuster.

Lucas, Tim. 1990. *Video Watchdog: The Perfectionist's Guide to Fantastic Video*. www.videowatchdog.com/home/HomeNews2-old2.htm. Accessed 9 August 2019.

Luckett, Moya. 2003. 'Sexploitation as Feminine Territory: The Films of Doris Wishman', in Mark Jancovich, Antonio Lázaro-Reboll, Julian Stringer and Andy Willis, eds, *Defining Cult Movies: The Cultural Politics of Oppositional Taste*. Manchester: Manchester University Press: 142–156.

Magilow, Daniel, Kristin Vander Lugt and Elizabeth Bridges, eds. 2012. *Nazisploitation! The Nazi Image in Low-Brow Cinema and Culture*. New York: Continuum.

Mathijs, Ernest, and Xavier Mendik, eds. 2004. *Alternative Europe: Eurotrash and Exploitation Cinema Since 1945*. London: Wallflower Press.

Mathijs, Ernest, and Xavier Mendik, eds. 2008. *The Cult Film Reader (Foreword by Roger Corman)*. Maidenhead: Open University Press.

Mathijs, Ernest, and Jamie Sexton. 2011. *Cult Cinema*. New York: Wiley-Blackwell.

Mathijs, Ernest. 2011, 'Exploitation Cinema', in Krin Gabbard, ed., *Oxford Bibliographies Online: Film and Media*. New York: Oxford University Press. http://aboutobo.com/cinema-and-media-studies/. Accessed 9 August 2019.

McCarty, John, ed. 1995. *The Sleaze Merchants: Adventures in Exploitation Filmmaking*. New York: St. Martin's Press.

Mendik, Xavier. 2010. 'Body in a Bed, Body Growing Dead: Uncanny Women in Joe D'Amato's Italian Exploitation Cinema', in Robert Weiner and John Cline, eds, *Cinema Inferno: Celluloid Explosions from the Cultural Margins*. Lanham, MD: Scarecrow Press: 124–141.

Mendik, Xavier, and Graeme Harper, eds. 2000. *Unruly Pleasures: The Cult Film and Its Critics*. Guilford: UK: FAB Press.

Mendik, Xavier, and Steven Jay Schneider, eds. 2002. *Underground U.S.A.: Filmmaking Beyond the Hollywood Canon*. London: Wallflower Press.

Modleski, Tania. 2007. 'Women's Cinema as Counterphobic Cinema: Doris Wishman as the Last Auteur', in Jeffrey Sconce, ed., *Sleaze Artists: Cinema at the Margins of Taste, Style and Politics*. Durham, NC: Duke University Press: 47–70.

Nakahara, Tamao. 2004. 'Barred Nuns: Italian Nunsploitation Films','in Ernest Mathijs and Xavier Mendik, eds, *Alternative Europe: Eurotrash and Exploitation Cinema Since 1945*. London: Wallflower Press: 124–133.

Osgerby, Bill. 2003. 'Sleazy Riders: Exploitation,"Otherness," and Transgression in the 1960s Biker Movie'. *Journal of Popular Film & Television* 31.3 (Fall): 98–108.

Peary, Gerald. 1978. "Woman in Porn: How Young Roberta Findlay Grew Up and Made Snuff." *Take One* 6.10 (Aug.–Sept.): 28–32.

Ruétalo, Victoria, and Dolores Tierney, eds. 2009. *Latsploitation, Exploitation Cinemas and Latin America*. London: Routledge.

Santos, Alessandra. 2017. *The Holy Mountain*. New York: Columbia University Press.

Schaefer, Eric. 1999. *'Bold! Daring! Shocking! True!' A History of Exploitation Films, 1919–1959*. Durham, NC: Duke University Press.

Sconce, Jeffrey. 2003. 'Esper, the Renunciator: Teaching "Bad" Movies to Good Students', in Mark Jancovich, Antonio Lázaro-Reboll, Julian Stringer and Andy Willis, eds, *Defining Cult Movies: The Cultural Politics of Oppositional Taste*. Manchester: Manchester University Press: 14–34.

Sconce, Jeffrey ed. 2007. *Sleaze Artists: Cinema at the Margins of Taste, Style and Politics*. Durham, NC: Duke University Press.

Servois, Julien. 2009. 'La pornographie comme genre cinematographique: De quoi le porno est-il l'histoire: Misty Beethoven', in *Le cinéma pornographique: Un genre dans tous ses états*. Paris: Librairie Philosophique J. Vrin: 47–77.

Sheridan, Simon. 2001. *Keeping the British End Up: Four Decades of Saucy Cinema*. London: Reynolds & Hearn.

Smith, Adrian-Luther. 1997. *Delirium: A Guide to Italian Exploitation Cinema: 1975–1979*. London: Media Publications.

Syder, Andrew, and Dolores Tierney. 2005. 'Importation/Mexploitation, or, How a Crime-Fighting, Vampire-Slaying Mexican Wrestlet Almost Found Himself in an Italian Sword-and-Sandals Epic', in Steven Jay Schneider and Tony Williams, eds *Horror International*. Detroit, MI: Wayne State University Press: 33–55.

Tierney, Dolores. 2004. 'José Mojica Marins and the Cultural Politics of Marginality in Third World Film Criticism'. *Journal of Latin American Cultural Studies*, 13.1: 63–78.

Upton, Julian. 2001. 'Poverty Row, Wardour Street: The Last Years of British Exploitation Cinema'. *Bright Lights Film Journal* 33. Online at: https://brightlightsfilm.com/poverty-row-wardour-street-last-years-british-exploitation-cinema/#.XLhovy-ZOfQ. Accessed 6 August 2019.

Weldon, Michael. 1996. *The Psychotronic Encyclopedia of Film*. New York: Ballantine Books.

2

UNDERGROUND FILM AND CULT CINEMA

Glyn Davis

Ron Rice's film *The Queen of Sheba Meets the Atom Man* (1963/1982) was planned as a lengthy epic but was left incomplete at the time of Rice's death. Rice, born in 1935, made only a few films during his lifetime, his career prematurely cut short by bronchial pneumonia in 1964. Taylor Mead, one of *The Queen of Sheba*'s lead actors, eventually edited it into a final form and added a soundtrack of classical, country, pop and rock music in 1982. Mead plays an impish innocent who wanders around a number of New York locations; Winifred Bryan stars as an often-naked odalisque with a penchant for alcohol. The film exhibits many of the markers of cult cinema. First, although low-resolution bootlegs of the film can be found online, *The Queen of Sheba* is difficult to source in a high-quality format; limited availability and scarcity can often contribute to a film's cult status. Second, as with the foci of various forms of cult practice and behaviour, Rice's film has a small but passionate and devoted audience (mainly scholars of experimental film and fans of 1960s avant-garde cinema). Third, as a film that was left unfinished and which was only forged into one possible edit years later, *The Queen of Sheba* displays the 'organic imperfections' and 'glorious ricketiness' that Umberto Eco identifies as core characteristics of the cult object (Eco 1987: 198). Fourth, Rice's premature death adds to the film's potential cult value, its role as a marker of lost opportunities: cult appreciation has a tendency to flower around actors and directors who die young. Other factors could be added here: even the film's title makes it sound like an example of cult cinema, a trashy piece of exploitation fare in which actors in rubber suits battle each other in a generic Midwestern town.

However, *The Queen of Sheba Meets the Atom Man* (and, indeed, Rice's career more broadly) is rarely, if ever, discussed in accounts of cult cinema. Rather, it is most often framed as an example of underground cinema. Rice made his first film *The Flower Thief* (1960) – also starring Taylor Mead – on the west coast of the United States. That film was a key contribution to the flourishing of 'Beat cinema', a movement that was, for some film historians, the first phase of underground cinema history. By the time of *The Queen of Sheba* Rice had moved to New York and was socializing with pivotal underground film figures such as Jack Smith, who makes a cameo appearance in the film. Rice and *The Queen of Sheba* both feature in seminal texts on underground film, including books by Sheldon Renan (1967), Parker Tyler (1974) and P. Adams Sitney (2002).

Does the lack of attention to Ron Rice and *The Queen of Sheba Meets the Atom Man* in texts on cult cinema reveal some sort of cleft – categorical, conceptual, definitive – between cult film and underground cinema? This chapter will argue the opposite: it will examine the landscape of underground cinema as a distinct field, identify a number of key connections and overlaps with cult film, and reveal ways in which the categories sometimes blur together.

A map of the underground

Like cult cinema, definitions of underground film are complex, multifaceted, and contested. The contestation arises from differing uses of the term: it is sometimes deployed as a synonym for experimental or avant-garde film of any hue; at times it is used to refer to films that test the limits of sex, violence, morality or taste; it is also employed more specifically in relation to a particular period in the history of avant-garde American filmmaking. The latter is the main form in which underground film tends to be identified, historicized and analysed, and therefore the understanding that this chapter will adopt. Underground cinema briefly flourished in the United States in the late 1950s and throughout the 1960s. As a movement, it is often identified as having specific antecedents, particular historical moments when creative experimentation with the moving image blossomed productively: the proliferation of films made in the 1920s by artists associated with the Dada and surrealist movements including Luis Buñuel, René Clair, and Man Ray; 1940s experimental works by filmmakers such as Kenneth Anger, Maya Deren, Curtis Harrington, and Gregory Markopoulos who used the moving image to shape oneiric expressions of subjective experience. However, underground cinema had its own distinctive contours.

One of the earliest uses of the term 'underground' in relation to cinema was by the critic Manny Farber in 1957, although he used it to refer to low-budget adventure films by directors such as Raoul Walsh and William Wellman (Farber 1998). Sheldon Renan notes uses of the term in 1959 by journalist Lewis Jacobs and filmmaker Stan Vanderbeek, with the latter claiming that he coined the term 'to describe his films and those like them' (Renan 1967: 22). Jonas Mekas, in a 1976 catalogue essay for Paris's Centre Georges Pompidou, attributed the notion of an artistic underground to a 1961 speech given by Marcel Duchamp (see Suárez 1996: 81). Whatever the original source, the notion of a filmic underground gained currency and a notable level of cultural visibility throughout the 1960s.

Not only is the origin of the phrase 'underground cinema' open to question, but the chronological limits of the movement itself are debated. For David E. James in his book *Allegories of Cinema*, the history of underground cinema begins in 1959, with the release of Robert Frank and Alfred Leslie's Beat film *Pull My Daisy*, and ends in 1966 with screenings of Andy Warhol's *The Chelsea Girls* (James 1989: 94). Other authors do not include Beat cinema in their accounts and understandings of underground cinema and concentrate more centrally on the mushrooming of avant-garde filmmaking and film culture that took place in New York during the 1960s. For Juan Suárez, for instance, underground cinema starts in 1961, with the weekend midnight screenings of avant-garde films at the Charles Theatre in Manhattan, and ends in 1966 with *The Chelsea Girls* – and with Tony Conrad's *The Flicker*, which heralds the beginning of a new, formalist approach to making experimental cinema (Suárez 1996: 55). Dominique Noguez (1985) offers alternate boundaries: 1962 serves as an origin, as it was when Jonas Mekas first used the phrase 'underground cinema' in his writings, and 1968 as an end-point, as the year that Warhol directed his last films before handing the reins to Paul Morrissey.

However it is temporally framed, the realm of underground cinema reveals itself to be heterogeneous, lacking the cohesion of some film movements. The stasis of Andy Warhol's

Empire (1964), for instance, an eight-hour-and-five-minutes-long film of the Empire State Building, seems to have little in common with the campy, trashy tenor of Mike Kuchar's *Sins of the Fleshapoids* (1965). As Suárez writes, the underground 'constituted an anarchic, motley growth composed of many sensibilities, styles, and modes of production' (Suárez 1996: 55). Underground cinema is associated with a loose group of filmmakers that included Kenneth Anger, Stan Brakhage, Bruce Baillie, Bruce Conner, Ken Jacobs, George and Mike Kuchar, Marie Menken, Barbara Rubin, Jack Smith, and Andy Warhol. These filmmakers were never formally affiliated as a collective, and connections between them varied widely in form and valence. One central figure of notable significance to the field of underground cinema, however, was Jonas Mekas – poet, critic, agitator, distributor, promoter, filmmaker. Born in Lithuania in 1922, Mekas arrived in New York in 1949. Inspired by his viewing experiences at Amos and Marcia Vogel's Cinema 16 film society, Mekas began to curate screenings of avant-garde films and to write about cinema. He launched the journal *Film Culture* in 1955 – a publication identified by Gregory Smulewicz-Zucker as 'an early indication of Mekas's ambitious vision for cultivating new forums for the discussion and promotion of the understanding of film as an art form in the United States' (2016: xv). Mekas also started to write a column, 'Movie Journal', for the *Village Voice* in 1958, which he regularly used to discuss, draw attention to, and proselytize about avant-garde cinema. Mekas' advocacy for avant-garde film led to his involvement in distribution and exhibition: he collaborated in the 1962 establishment of the Film-Makers' Cooperative, an organization devoted to the distribution of cinema by avant-garde filmmakers, and was the founder of the Filmmakers' Cinematheque, an itinerant exhibition practice which eventually transformed into the more stable Anthology Film Archives in 1970. He was also a prolific filmmaker, with a predilection for making diary films such as *Walden (Diaries, Notes and Sketches)* (1968) and *Reminiscences of a Journey to Lithuania* (1971–1972).

Mekas was a pivotal figure in underground film history, as he provided the movement's directors with forms of institutional support, however short-lived: mechanisms for distribution, spaces for screenings, a film column raising awareness of their work. These all helped to nurture a sense of community and provide opportunities for underground directors to come into contact with each other's work. Andy Warhol, for instance, was a regular attendee of underground film screenings at the Bleecker Street Cinema and Gramercy Arts Theatre in 1963 (see Davis and Needham 2013: 14). Aside from these spaces or organizational contexts that afforded some degree of cohesion to the underground film scene, other connections between its disparate forms and instances can be identified – connections which are not easily separated from each other. First, as Sheldon Renan noted, these films were 'made for very little money, frequently under a thousand dollars' (Renan 1967: 17). Jonas Mekas for instance, writing in June 1963 in the *Village Voice*, revealed that Jack Smith's *Flaming Creatures* (1963) cost just $300 (Mekas 2016: 93). Production costs – on elements such as set design, costumes, lighting, film stock, cameras, and cast – had to be reduced to the bare necessities. Low budgets segregated underground filmmakers from commercial forms of cinema; scarcity of means afforded them a degree of creative freedom and inspired innovation. Second, underground cinema was a form of counter-cinema, purposefully setting itself against mainstream, commercial film. Its directors conceived of film as an art form. As Jared Rapfogel writes, underground filmmakers' 'methods were often radically different, but the goal they sought, both aesthetically and culturally, was a new freedom of expression liberated from inherited, conventional mores and forms' (Rapfogel 2012: 268–269). Although the aesthetics of underground films differed widely, the films were connected through their attempts to present audio-visual alternatives to the neat, glossy polish of mainstream studio product. Third, many underground films of the 1960s had political aims, intentions or messages. Juan Suárez highlights that the metaphor of 'the underground' connected avant-garde cinema of the 1960s 'to the culture of dissent in postwar America' (Suárez 1996: 82). Commentary about mainstream politics appeared, for instance, in underground films such as Andy Warhol's *Since* (1966), which re-staged the Kennedy assassination; Kenneth Anger's *Scorpio Rising* (1963), meanwhile, linked motorcycle gang behaviour to fascist belief systems; and *Flaming Creatures* challenged calcified norms relating to gender and sexuality, as well as censorship strictures.

For all of its diversity, then, underground cinema cohered around particular factors: low budgets and a related economy of means; an attempt to offer alternative aesthetic options to those of mainstream cinema; political impulses and intentions; and common opportunities for exhibition and distribution. Having outlined the specific contours of underground cinema as an identifiable phenomenon, the remainder of this chapter will move to examine potential bridges and links between the realms of underground cinema and cult film.

Mind the gap

In the chapter on underground and avant-garde cinema in their 2011 book on cult cinema, the editors of this volume point out that, despite the seeming gap between underground cinema and cult film, 'these two spheres commonly intersect' (Mathijs and Sexton 2011: 155). They point out, in particular, that 'a number of key films belong to both domains', and that certain viewing contexts associated with underground cinema 'became important sites in which some cult films established their reputations' (ibid.); they also trace a number of other vital links. Taking Mathijs and Sexton's observations as a starting point, I want to identify and briefly discuss four ways in which cult film and underground cinema can be identified as formally or conceptually connected to each other. The account presented here is far from exhaustive but serves to highlight some vital links.

One: Exhibition

The Charles Theatre, located at 12th Street and Avenue B in New York, began hosting midnight screenings of films late in 1961 and continued to do so throughout much of 1962. Although the Charles screened a variety of films in this slot, underground films were part of the ongoing programme. Mainly, the screenings focused on the work of one director: on 29 and 30 December 1961, for instance, there was a Marie Menken retrospective. Jonas Mekas, who was involved in organizing some screenings at the Charles, often reviewed the midnight shows in his *Village Voice* column. In January 1963, Mekas began organizing Monday night midnight screenings at the Bleecker Street Cinema, but these came to an abrupt end after several months. 'The truth is', Mekas wrote in his 'Movie Journal' column in June 1963, 'we have been thrown out. The Bleecker Cinema people did not like our movies. They thought the independent cinema was ruining the "reputation of the theatre"' (Mekas 2016: 93).

Midnight screenings were not new in 1961, but they became a more prominent part of the cinema landscape throughout the 1960s – and especially into the 1970s, when a number of New York cinemas began programming material in midnight slots. As Mathijs and Mendik note, the midnight movie phenomenon enabled the showing of films 'unsuitable to be programmed at other times (too risky for regular evenings, too shocking for matinées)' (2008: 167–168); midnight screenings thus became 'an eclectic network for audiences craving unusual, subversive films, and anything daylight shun' (ibid.: 168). In terms of the history of cult cinema, this reached its peak in the 1970s with showings of particular films that generated devoted repeat-viewing fan audiences, including *El Topo* (Jodorowsky, 1970), *Pink Flamingos* (Waters,

1972), *The Rocky Horror Picture Show* (Sharman, 1975), and *Eraserhead* (Lynch, 1977). A screening format that had associations with underground cinema in the 1960s, then, became a key component of cult film exhibition and consumption in the following decade. A further link can be made through the notion of political dissent. Hoberman and Rosenbaum note in their book *Midnight Movies* that there was an anti-establishment aspect to many of the 1970s cult films screened in midnight slots: their explicit content and examinations of dissident morality seemed to square with the political turmoil affecting the United States at the time (Hoberman and Rosenbaum 1991: 112). As already noted, the same could be said of some of the underground films screening in similar timeslots in the 1960s.

Aside from midnight screenings, across the 1960s venues that showed underground films would often simultaneously programme other types of cinema. Art cinema, exploitation movies and underground films would be advertised alongside each other in the press; instances of all three challenged what could be legally shown on screen, further eroding the lines between them. As Mark Betz writes, 'these films at times shared not only the same representational codes of marketing and the same police lockup shelves, but also the same exhibition space and quite heterogeneous audiences' (Betz 2003: 219). Due to their risqué content and flouting of principles of decency, as well as their resistance to Hollywood standards of quality and finish, a significant number of these films have acquired cult standing. The exhibition spaces in which these films were encountered, then, facilitated the acquisition of cult status by some underground films, and smudged any pencilled-in boundaries between underground cinema and other forms of independent, experimental and risky work.

Two: Transgression

Underground films are often associated with transgression, at the level of aesthetics, form and depicted content. Their low budgets often conferred on them an appearance of amateurism. Sound and image quality could be rough: one reel of Warhol's film *Poor Little Rich Girl* (1965), for instance, was recorded out of focus. Acting styles often ran counter to mainstream norms; improvisation was regularly favoured over careful scripting and rehearsal. Edits might be jarring. Soundtracks could be dubbed on later, as with Rice's *The Queen of Sheba*. Jonas Mekas was a supporter of such amateur stylistics: as Paul Arthur notes, Mekas linked 'the excitement of new cinematic forms with a repudiation of "professionalism" and economic domination' (Arthur 2005: 18). The transgression of the underground also manifested in other ways, challenging dominant film form: some films pared back content to a minimum, as with Warhol's early minimalist works such as *Sleep* (1963); some of the films were extraordinarily long, unbearable to sit all the way through, such as *Empire*; there were experiments with superimposed projection like Barbara Rubin's *Christmas on Earth* (1963) or dual-screen projection such as *The Chelsea Girls*.

Underground film's transgression also incorporated taboo-breaking content. Casual drug use was depicted, and language that could offend was not avoided. Nudity regularly featured, as did sex. The sex was explicit, non-idealized, and took various forms, including but not limited to heteronormative couplings. This occasionally landed some of the films in trouble. *Scorpio Rising* was accused of obscenity and tried in a Los Angeles court due to its inclusion of a few frames of an erect penis. *Flaming Creatures* features a number of characters whose gender and sexuality is ambiguous; the film includes a rape/orgy sequence. In March 1964, a screening of the film at the New Bowery Theatre organized by Jonas Mekas and the filmmakers Ken Jacobs and Florence Karpf was raided by police; all three organizers were arrested. Following legal wrangles, the film was eventually banned in the State of New York and subjected to a Senate investigation. Throughout the 1960s, screenings of *Flaming Creatures* across the United States were repeatedly cancelled or raided. Juan Suárez argues that *Flaming Creatures* was deemed especially troubling and transgressive due to its 'collapse of sexual distinctions': 'all characters behave in blissful oblivion of traditional alignments of anatomy and gender roles' (Suárez 1996: 185).

Cult cinema is, similarly, regularly associated with transgression. This may take the form of extreme violence or gore, such as with *The Texas Chainsaw Massacre* (Hooper, 1974) or *The Evil Dead* (Raimi, 1981). It might involve a level of erotic or sexual content that would not usually be permitted by mainstream cinema, as in Doris Wishman or Russ Meyer films. It may transgress moral boundaries by depicting acts and behaviours deemed objectionable – as with Divine's consumption of a dog's freshly deposited faeces in *Pink Flamingos*. Like underground cinema, the transgression can also be aesthetic: a film's failure to adhere to norms of mainstream quality and skill may facilitate its embrace as a cult object. Tommy Wiseau's film *The Room* (2003) is clumsily assembled on its meagre budget, and the sets, acting, and editing of Edward D. Wood Jr's *Plan 9 from Outer Space* (1959) are notably sloppy, but both have notable cult followings. Cult audiences and underground film audiences, then, may relish amateurishness, or at least welcome an alternative to the limited vocabulary of mainstream, commercial film.

There are limits to the transgression of underground film and cult cinema, of course. The underground of the 1960s did not entirely reject the mainstream; indeed, it often displayed a willing engagement with elements of popular culture. The Kuchar brothers paid tribute to Hollywood melodrama and science-fiction with their campy, Pop-inflected pastiches. Jack Smith wrote of his adoration of the Hollywood actress Maria Montez and fabricated his own low-budget version of cinematic glamour in his mouldy fables. Warhol was infatuated with Hollywood and its stars, and organized his studio, the Factory, to operate like a mechanical, industrial production-line. For all of underground cinema's political dissidence, then, many of its filmmakers remained captivated by the lure of the silver screen (a captivation that often took the form of cult-like obsession). As David E. James writes, 'The form of underground film as subcultural production is … determined by its functions as "protest" film and as intertextual dialogues with Hollywood; even at its most liberated, these functions are found' (James 1989: 99–100). There are similar limitations with cult cinema. Barry K. Grant has noted the ability of cult films 'to be at once transgressive and recuperative, in other words, to reclaim that which they violate' (Grant 2008: 78). Despite their marginal cultural position, away from the conventional, normative mainstream, the politics of many cult films are conservative, their content serving to shore up racist, colonialist, sexist and homophobic attitudes. Many sit comfortably within existing generic formations, rather than offering radical shake-up. For Grant, even those cult films which feature transgressive elements – his example is *The Rocky Horror Picture Show* – tend to recuperate them through a process of Othering, positioning those components as the monstrous, to be rejected and dismissed. Cult and underground cinema, then, are far from being utopian playgrounds for the liberal, or free zones of expression offering correction or alternative to the oppressive norm.

Three: Gender

The history of underground cinema is largely one of men making films. The occasional female filmmaker such as Marie Menken or Barbara Rubin managed to make space for themselves within the movement, but they were exceptions. The small number of such women reveals the extent to which female artists wanting to work with film in the 1960s had a more complex relationship to the means of production than men, or were relegated to marginalized positions, even as the fight for women's rights gathered a new force and visibility throughout the decade. Historical accounts of this era are also limited and partial: women's contributions to underground cinema have, on the whole, only received slight attention from critics, theorists and curators. Ara Osterweil has written, for instance, of the difficulties of tracking down detailed accounts of Rubin's life: she 'exists only in fragments', brief references or glimpses (Osterweil 2014: 26).

These sexist and misogynist forces of omission, occlusion and erasure are marginally countered by the fact that a notable number of underground directors were queer, and committed to filming dissident forms of sexuality; and by the opportunities in front of the camera afforded for women by some underground directors. Richard Dyer notes that the underground 'provided a space and an opportunity for gay men and… lesbians to represent themselves in films in a way that mainstream filmmaking (where many covert lesbians and gay men worked) did not' (Dyer 1990: 104). Kenneth Anger, Jack Smith, the Kuchar brothers and Andy Warhol all created films in which queer bodies or subjectivities appeared on screen, or which exuded a queer sensibility through the promotion of a camp register or trash aesthetic (the lesbians that Dyer mentions are a little more elusive). Women were regularly given prominent or lead roles in underground films; their directors worked to upend or transform normative ideals of glamour and beauty. Warhol, in his book *The Philosophy of Andy Warhol*, compared two types of people, 'Beauties' and 'Talkers', expressing a preference for the latter: 'To me, good talkers are beautiful because good talk is what I love' (Warhol 1977: 62). For Warhol, the most attractive and magnetic stars were those with the ability to converse, to declaim, to control a space or interaction with their words. Several of Warhol's most memorable performers were women who could talk at great length when the camera was turned on them: Viva, Ingrid Superstar, Brigid Berlin.

Cult cinema is also often seen as a predominantly male field. Many of the spaces associated with cult cinema, such as the midnight movie theatre auditorium, the video or DVD collector's store, or the fan convention, are predominantly gendered as masculine. The genres most often linked with cult cinema – science fiction, horror, sexploitation, erotica, fantasy, martial arts – are seen as mainly male preserves. Publications focused on cult cinema may exclude women through their sexist and misogynist imagery as well as their obsession with trivia; the collecting culture that circulates around cult film is notably masculine in form. In an essay on 'the masculinity of cult', Joanne Hollows has highlighted that mainstream mass culture is often culturally and discursively constructed as feminine, with the realm of the cult positioned as its heroic masculine antithesis. Within this gendered positioning of the mass against the marginal, 'cult would seem to reproduce existing power structures rather than simply challenge them' (Hollows 2003: 37). Female fans of cult cinema do of course exist, and specific films have significant female cult followings. These phenomena remain on the periphery of cult film culture, however, and have only recently begun to attract sustained academic attention.

Four: Stardom

A further key connection between cult cinema and underground film is that both have fostered their own circuits and instances of stardom that operate counter to the mainstream's nurturing and promotion of a particular roster of highly paid mass-appeal actors. Indeed, cult stars will often reject, or work against, characteristics associated with the mainstream film star: the embodiment of normative ideals of beauty, expressions of naturalistic or realistic acting ability, an association with heroic and sympathetic characters. With cult cinema, these actors may make their contributions in low-to-medium-budget genre cinema, accruing a fanbase through their commitment to the lowbrow and a consistent screen persona with recognizable quirks: Robert Englund, Michael Ironside, Sylvia Kristel, Christopher Lambert, Ingrid Pitt. Alternatively, their cult status may come from long-term collaborations with directors of cult cinema: John Waters' regular troupe of actors for instance, known as the 'Dreamlanders', included Divine, David Lochary, Edith Massey, Cookie Mueller, and Mink Stole. Cult stars may also build a reputation and devoted audience via performances in more mainstream cinema, performances marked by a dissonant register that makes them stand out from the rest of the cast: Martin Donovan, Crispin Glover, Udo Keir.

In the 1960s, underground film directors fostered their own stables of performers. Jonas Mekas, writing in 1964, noted that underground cinema 'is developing a new set of stars and is, in great part, a star cinema' (Mekas 2016: 128). These performers were identified as 'all talented, intense, obsessed and possessed, each one with a completely different world which they impose upon the films in which they appear' (ibid.: 129). Mekas provided a list of these performers, which included Taylor Mead, Beverly Grant, Winifred Bryan, Naomi Levine, and John Giorno. He singled out the contribution that Mead made to *The Queen of Sheba Meets the Atom Man*, comparing Mead's performance to 'the best work of Chaplin, Keaton, or Langdon' (ibid.: 128). Perhaps the clearest attempt by an underground filmmaker to construct their own roster of stars was Andy Warhol's assemblage of performers at the Factory. Warhol understood the cult adoration of film stars: he collected autographed photographs of stars as a child and had a particular fascination with Shirley Temple; his early 1960s screen-prints of stars including Troy Donahue and Liz Taylor commented on the power of the mechanically reproduced portrait as an object of seduction and infatuation. Despite this fan's understanding, Warhol's attempts to manufacture stardom with his films were only partially successful. He tried to fabricate a following for Edie Sedgwick, for instance, casting her as the lead in a number of films in 1965 and 1966, but her cult stardom only began to seriously bloom after her early death at the age of 28 in 1971.

Cult cinema stars and underground stars are connected through their lack of mobility. Carving out a space for themselves within their particular fields of practice, they very rarely achieve circulation and recognition beyond those spheres. Divine, despite a wider level of cultural recognition through his music, stage performances, and chat-show appearances, made films almost exclusively with John Waters, ignored by mainstream cinema; Edie Sedgwick did not move beyond the underground. There are exceptions: Mary Woronov began her career as an actress at Warhol's Factory, before moving into independent, exploitation and genre cinema, whereas Joe Dallesandro transitioned from modelling to making films with Warhol, after which he moved into starring in generic fare for European and American directors, with the occasional appearance in an art-house movie. In general, however, the limited movement of cult and underground stars serves to reveal the boundaries of specific film cultures which, in other ways, are often permeable.

Taking into consideration all of the connections between cult film and underground cinema that this chapter has raised, the conundrum with which it began remains. Why is Ron Rice's *The Queen of Sheba Meets the Atom Man* not a cult film? Ultimately, of course, any particular film's status as a cult object is dependent on an audience embracing it, transforming it through their adulation and devotion. Rice's film is known predominantly by scholars of experimental and underground cinema, some of whom (myself included) have a marked passion for its rich performances and an appreciation of its ramshackle form. A broader cult following has failed to materialize, however; perhaps the film is not transgressive enough in its content or remains too esoteric. For all of the links between cult and underground cinema, the two remain distinct formations.

References

Arthur, Paul. 2005. *A Line of Sight: American Avant-Garde Film Since 1965.* Minneapolis: University of Minnesota Press.

Betz, Mark. 2003. 'Art, exploitation, underground', in Mark Jancovich et al., eds, *Defining Cult Movies: The Cultural Politics of Oppositional Taste.* Manchester: Manchester University Press: 202–222.

Davis, Glyn, and Gary Needham. 2013. 'Introduction', in *Warhol in Ten Takes.* London: BFI: 1–45.

Dyer, Richard. 1990. *Now You See It: Studies in Lesbian and Gay Cinema.* London: Routledge.

Eco, Umberto. 1987. 'Casablanca: Cult Movies and Intertextual Collage', in *Travels in Hyperreality.* London: Picador: 197–211.

Farber, Manny. 1998. 'Underground Films' in *Negative Space: Manny Farber on the Movies.* New York: Da Capo Press: 12–24.

Grant, Barry K. 2008. 'Science Fiction Double Feature: Ideology in the Cult Film', in Ernest Mathijs and Xavier Mendik, eds, *The Cult Film Reader.* Maidenhead: Open University Press/McGraw-Hill: 76–87.

Hoberman, Jim, and Jonathan Rosenbaum. 1991. *Midnight Movies,* second edition. New York: Da Capo Press.

Hollows, Joanne. 2003. 'The Masculinity of Cult', in Mark Jancovich et al., eds, *Defining Cult Movies: The Cultural Politics of Oppositional Taste.* Manchester: Manchester University Press: 35–53.

James, David E. 1989. *Allegories of Cinema: American Film in the Sixties.* New York: Princeton University Press.

Mathijs, Ernest, and Xavier Mendik. 2008. 'Section 2: Cult Case Studies: Introduction', in *The Cult Film Reader.* Maidenhead: Open University Press/McGraw-Hill: 163–172.

Mathijs, Ernest, and Jamie Sexton. 2011. *Cult Cinema: An Introduction.* Malden, MA: Wiley-Blackwell.

Mekas, Jonas. 2016. *Movie Journal: The Rise of the New American Cinema, 1959–1971,* second edition. New York: Columbia University Press.

Noguez, Dominique. 1985. *Une renaissance du cinéma: Le cinéma "underground" américain.* Paris: Klincksieck.

Osterweil, Ara. 2014. *Flesh Cinema: The Corporeal Turn in American Avant-garde Film.* Manchester: Manchester University Press.

Rapfogel, Jared. 2012. 'American Underground Film', in Cynthia Lucia, Roy Grundmann and Art Simon, eds, *The Wiley-Blackwell History of American Film.* Chichester: Wiley-Blackwell: 267–289.

Renan, Sheldon. 1967. *An Introduction to the American Underground Film.* New York: E.P. Dutton.

Sitney, P. Adams. 2002. *Visionary Film: The American Avant-Garde, 1943–2000,* third edition. New York: Oxford University Press.

Smulewicz-Zucker, Gregory. 2016. 'Introduction to the second edition', in Jonas Mekas, *Movie Journal: The Rise of the New American Cinema, 1959–1971,* second edition. New York: Columbia University Press: ix–xxxvi.

Suárez, Juan A. 1996. *Bike Boys, Drag Queens, and Superstars: Avant-Garde, Mass Culture, and Gay Identities in the 1960s Underground Cinema.* Bloomington: Indiana University Press.

Tyler, Parker. 1974. *Underground Film: A Critical History.* Harmondsworth: Pelican.

Warhol, Andy. 1977. *The Philosophy of Andy Warhol: From A to B and Back Again.* New York: Harvest.

3

CULT-ART CINEMA
Defining cult-art ambivalence

David Andrews

Cult cinema is a super-genre whose participants fetishize the cultural illegitimacy of their own cult activities and forms, often wearing their "shame" as a badge of honor in cult contexts. In a sense, this illegitimacy lends these participants a narrow mystique with a restricted legitimacy. Because this legitimacy is only intermittently recognized outside the cult nexus, we may refer to it as "subcultural legitimacy." These assertions can help us understand cult cinema's complex overlaps with other fields. For example, cult cinema's intersection with art cinema produces "cult-art cinema." As a cult variety, cult-art cinema is striking in that it exemplifies the cult identity even as its manifest aspiration to high-art distinction threatens to erase that identity. At the same time, cult-art cinema's cult identity always calls into question its high-art distinction. This conflicting, often ambivalent nature is at the heart of cult-art cinema.

To understand this, we must be very careful in how we think about both cult cinema and art cinema. What is cult cinema, anyway? Is it, for example, more useful to think of it as a group of subcultural artifacts or as a group of subcultural processes? There are, after all, traditions for presenting cult cinema in both ways. For example, in their introduction to *The Cult Film Reader* (2008), Ernest Mathijs and Xavier Mendik seem to define cult cinema primarily as a set of movies:

> Cult films transgress common notions of good and bad taste, and they challenge genre conventions and coherent storytelling, often using intertextual references, gore, leaving loose ends or creating a sense of nostalgia. They have troublesome production histories … and in spite of often-limited accessibility, they have a continuous market value and a long-lasting public presence.
>
> (11)

There are, however, problems with presenting cult cinema as a group of movies. Even if cult fans, or "paracinephiles," seem mainly interested in the movies, there is nothing permanent about which movies are designated "cult movies." As a result, cult theorists often perform maneuvers similar to those made by aestheticians in the philosophy of art before the interventions of Morris Weitz and George Dickie: they define certain movies and certain types of movie as exemplifying the cult concept in a way that restricts what may and may not be called a "cult movie." In other words, these theorists promote the historical reality of *some* cult movies as the ahistorical essence of *all* cult movies. But this cannot work. Have *all* cult movies had "troublesome production histories"? Have *all* of them "challenge[d] genre conventions and coherent storytelling"? Even if they had, how would these facts restrict future usage of the concept?

A more serviceable approach is charted in *Defining Cult Movies* (2003). In introducing this collection, Mark Jancovich and his colleagues pursue a strategy of defining cult cinema in terms of "subcultural ideology":

> [T]he "cult movie" is an essentially eclectic category. It is not defined according to some single, unifying feature shared by all cult movies but rather through a "subcultural" ideology in filmmakers, films or audiences [that] are seen as existing in opposition to the "mainstream" … it is by presenting themselves as oppositional that cult audiences are able to confer value upon both themselves and the films around which they congregate.
>
> (2003: 1–2)

This definition is useful because it acknowledges the textual multiplicity and contingency of cult cinema but still manages to move beyond it, pursuing the sociological realities that unify the cult phenomenon. Through their ideas of cult adversarialism, Jancovich and his fellow editors see how cult participants re-value abject positions, achieving subcultural legitimacy through their opposition to the "mainstream." But we should be careful here, too, for this idea of cult adversarialism is easily overdone. As scholars have made clear, the cult nexus is not deeply militant in its opposition to dominant sectors like mainstream cinema or art cinema. This oppositionalism is often nominal, limited to subcultures or pursued as a marketing strategy only. What is more, cult cinema is not the only super-genre to have constructed itself as an adversary to a context-specific "mainstream." Art cinema as a whole has presented itself as adversarial, often by opposing the mainstream cinemas and cult cinemas that depart from pure-art values.

Which is to suggest that art cinema is as slippery and complex as cult cinema. If it is odd that cult cinema overlaps with a field that aspires to cultural legitimacy, it is equally odd that art cinema overlaps with a field that opposes this kind of legitimacy. What makes this oddity possible is the fact that art cinema is itself a flexible group of sociological processes and not an unchanging canon of masterpieces. The main difference between art cinema and cult cinema is ideological in nature. Art cinema subscribes to (mostly) dominant cultural ideologies, while cult cinema subscribes to (several) non-dominant ones. By looking at cult as an area of cinematic production and distribution that promotes non-dominant ideologies, we can avoid confusion with avant-garde cinema, which is a deeply adversarial sector of art cinema whose legitimacy, like that of cult cinema as a whole, is subcultural in nature – but whose values, unlike those of cult cinema, are dominant and traditional almost by definition.

The cult sensibility, as now constructed, does share some principles with high-art sensibilities. For example, both cult cinema and art cinema portray themselves as indie outsiders in an industry dominated by Hollywood – and both cinemas now seem equally disingenuous in making these claims. This common adversarialism is why it was often possible for tastemakers like Andrew Sarris, Susan Sontag, and Amos Vogel to refer to art-house tastes as "cult" tastes in the United States at least through the 1960s. But it is the differences between these cinemas that usually dictate our thinking about them. For example, the cult sensibility departs from art cinema's high-art values by *endorsing* an active audience. The art-house sensibility, by contrast, has never overtly embraced an active audience. The neo-Kantian ideal of aesthetic disinterest is the linchpin of most legitimate aesthetics, and this principle applies to film as well as to more traditional art forms. Practical understandings of "disinterest" usually equate it with "close attention," a viewing posture that aids immersion, allowing viewers to gather as much of a work's detail as possible. The ideal of disinterest is also useful to cultural authorities and to institutions in that it justifies and maintains social control; it has been thought that training people to adopt this posture cultivates everything from fair play to individual restraint in public places, like crowded museums and art houses. As a consequence, this ideal has been tied to notions of refinement and spirituality.

Cult consumption opposes this form of the aesthetic attitude. Indeed, this sort of consumption has been celebrated as a class-oriented rejection of the high-art posture. This rejection may be seen in the boisterous, populist behaviors that have often typified cult consumption in public. Thus, screenings of midnight movies like *Freaks* (1932), *Reefer Madness* (1936), *Mom and Dad* (1945), *Blood Feast* (1963), *El Topo* (1970), *The Rocky Horror Picture Show* (1975), and *The Toxic Avenger* (1984) have been known for the carnivalesque hullabaloo they have inspired in audiences. Cult audiences seem unified by their need to express themselves physically; they often seem most pleased if they can laugh without regard for appropriateness. It is no surprise, then, that this mode of consumption has alarmed traditional auteurs (see, e.g., Peter Greenaway), who have always argued that the aesthetic object should be the sole determinant of cinematic experience. The last thing that an auteur, in the classic sense, wants to do is to encourage viewers to seize control of the cinematic experience, which is one goal of cult cinema's egalitarian, often interactive modes of consumption.

Types, examples, and exclusions

As noted, a cult-art movie seems to have, or aspire to, two kinds of status: cult value and high-art value. This "quasi-legitimate" strain of cult movie may be identified the same way that we identify more legitimate art movies: by presenting evidence of auteurism and canonization. Here cult-art cinema creates special problems. Though paracinephiles have long sought to devise, in the words of Mathijs and Mendik, "an alternative canon of cinema, pitched against the 'official' canon" (2008: 6), we cannot assume that this canon amounts to cult cinema's high art. A canonical cult movie is usually considered a "classic," but these classics come in many varieties, most of which are *not* ascribed high-art value. This is true of Henenlotter's movies and Troma's many gross-out comedies; it is also true of individual American cult classics, from Herschell Gordon Lewis's aforementioned *Blood Feast* to John Carpenter's *They Live* (1988), Lloyd Kaufman's *Tromeo and Juliet* (1996), Jay Lee's *Zombie Strippers* (2008), and Raimi's *Evil Dead* movies (1981, 1987). As it turns out, the cult-cinema canon has relied on a variety of criteria, which are loose and derive from many quarters. Thus, cult cinema is rich, byzantine – and its canons are in rapid and continual flux.

Before emphasizing three intentional kinds of cult-art movies, I want to discount two unintentional kinds. The first type involves cult-art movies appropriated from other spheres. The cult canon has often included experimental cinemas, mainstream cinemas, and world cinemas that were initially made and celebrated far from cult cinema as we currently imagine it. Some of these films represent unintentional cult-art movies, like Robert Wiene's *Des cabinet des Dr. Caligari* (1919), Leni Riefenstahl's *Triumph of the Will* (1935), and David Lynch's *Eraserhead* (1976) as well as Luis Buñuel's *Un chien andalou* (1929); Riefenstahl's *Olympia* (1938); Orson Welles's *Touch of Evil* (1958); Jean-Luc Godard's *Le week-end* (1967); Stanley Kubrick's *A Clockwork Orange* (1971); Stan Brakhage's *The Act of Seeing with One's Own Eyes* (1971); David Cronenberg's *Videodrome* (1983), *Dead Ringers* (1988), and even *Crash* (1996); John Dahl's *The Last Seduction* (1994); the Coens' *Big Lebowski* (1998); and Richard Kelly's *Donnie Darko* (2001), to cite only a few. The overlaps with more legitimate cinemas in evidence in this list indicate that the cult sensibility has not been limited to movies that were inexpensive to make or that have only ever enjoyed a lowbrow status, which has been cult cinema's principal classification since the 1980s. Instead, cult tastes are *underground* tastes that may "cultify" any film so long as the process is directed by subcultural audiences who embrace subcultural values and modes of consumption. If we blend these ideas of cult with the understanding that cult auteurism is often unintentional, we can reconcile two seemingly divergent facts: on one hand, auteurs like Welles, Brakhage, and Kubrick were traditional auteurs whose main allegiance was to a traditional aesthetic; and, on the other, some of their movies have been praised as cult-art icons.

This kind of cult appropriation and elevation amounts to a populist intervention that forcibly reappraises a movie that may have failed in legitimate forums or that may have fallen out of favor with mainstream critics – a description that applies as readily to recent indie films like *The Last Seduction* and *Donnie Darko* as to Hollywood classics like *Touch of Evil*. *The Last Seduction* and *Donnie Darko* were both mid-budget indie art films that initially failed in legitimate channels: *The Last Seduction* at first failed to find a theatrical distributor, while *Donnie Darko* failed to earn back its production financing in its first go-round in theaters (Newman 2011, 211–213). But in both cases, these movies earned an underground cult following in their non-theatrical releases that gave them a chance for a successful re-release in theatrical art houses, which in turn allowed them to earn even more money in their subsequent releases to ancillary windows. It is as if the people spoke – and though their voice has always been deemed "illegitimate" in legitimate sectors, it lent these films an unintentional cult status that led to box-office successes and to positive reappraisals by traditional critics, ironically salvaging their legitimacy.

The second type of cult-art movie that we should put to the side is the kind of cult movie that results from the fetishization of directorial incompetence, that is, "badfilm." There is nothing wrong with celebrating "bad" movies. But we must understand what we are doing when we call bad movies "auteur movies." Auteurism implies control, purity, and intentional aspiration – and cult auteurism implies these notions as much as any other auteurism. Thus, it is possible to modify existing auteur methods to identify cult-art cinema and cult-art movies. But we can only rarely construct cult auteurism and the cult-art movie in terms of the bad movie, which is a pleasurable failure, a *tour de force* of ineptitude. This cult tradition is most often a sign of an unintentional, or an accidental, auteurism that is an effect of promotion and consumption.

Of course, some campy cult movies that qualify for so-bad-they're-good status have been made that way on purpose. Here we might consider Russ Meyer's *Mudhoney* (1965), Jess Franco's *Vampyros Lesbos* (1971), John Waters's *Pink Flamingos* (1972), Nobuhiko Obayashi's *House* (1977), the transgressive shorts that Richard Kern made between 1983 and 1993, Rodriguez's *Planet Terror* (2007), Anna Biller's *Viva* (2007), and so on. The bad movie and cult auteurism clearly go together here, for the intentional camp irony of such works indicates that we should not call them "bad" in any straightforward sense; rather, they seem rich in complex effects that their creators intended. Although we may be able to align such movies with the cult of pleasurable bad taste, we cannot align them with directorial ineptitude – for their directors found a way to do what they wanted to do within their particular constraints. But the more common kind of bad movie – where camp laughter seems to work against directors, not with them, and where the irony is a function of the viewers and their environment – does not exemplify the auteur ideal in any sense. In this case, the "authorship of the aura" is more properly attributed to the audience and not to the director.

One of the problems here is that intentional badness is typically disowned by bad cult directors. Certainly, the first generation of bad cult directors – individuals like Wood, Doris Wishman, Larry Buchanan, and Andy Milligan, who have all been celebrated in critical forums as intentional auteurs – did not fetishize their own incompetence. Indeed, there is often little evidence beyond these directors' embrace of what others have defined as their "trashy" aesthetics to support the idea that they were trying to make pleasurably horrid movies. For the most part, then, their auteurism is a product of cult consumption, not of cult production – which means they are better positioned as significant "failures" whose technical and stylistic incompetence influenced later directors, like Jim Wynorski and Henenlotter. But not even the later directors have consistently promoted themselves in terms of an ironic camp control that may function as a subculturally legitimate sign of auteurism. They might label themselves "unimportant" and glorify bad taste and cheap things, but they rarely take any explicit pleasure in the bad cinematic qualities imparted by their own incompetence. Bad auteurs become bad auteurs, it seems, almost despite themselves, with their very authoritative ineptitude a product of certain styles of cult consumption and evaluation. This dynamic reminds us of cult cinema's audience-driven ethic. But it is so far from the traditional that it is worth asking whether the idea of the unintentional bad auteur makes sense in broader contexts.

As noted, regarding intentional cult-art movies, there are at least three main types to consider. What unifies these three types is their ambivalence about their cult identity, an ambivalence that seems to be a function of their makers' high-art aspirationalism – which is forever qualified, it appears, by their cult identity. Perhaps the best example of this ambivalence involves new cult movies that have *too much* legitimacy as a result of their provenance. This phenomenon is most evident on the festival circuit, where Bong Joon-ho, Tomas Alfredson, Tarantino, Park Chan-wook, Lars von Trier, and others have released movies that might well be classified as cult-art films. In their production values, distribution, and overall prestige, movies like Bong's moody toxic-creature film *The Host* (2006), Alfredson's equally moody vampire movie *Let the Right One In* (2008), Tarantino's riotous Nazi-revenge picture *Inglourious Basterds* (2009), Park's vampire comedy *Thirst* (2009), and von Trier's torture-porn meditation *Antichrist* (2009) are all first and last traditional art films. They have won awards, critical acclaim, and global distribution through their mastery of the devices of traditional art films and through the reputations of their makers. Indeed, these directors are all veterans of the festival circuit, where they have served on juries and have made regular appearances at Cannes. The thing that distinguishes their new movies as *cult*-art movies, then, is their generic content: the severed body parts, the chills and thrills and spasms of violence, the monsters. Or, in a different sense, what has made all these movies cult-art movies is that their genre-coded materials are still not always accepted by traditionalists. Indeed, though horror and sex have long been regular parts of traditional festivals, horror films and sex films continue to face resistance on the circuit from the most conservative cinephiles and critics. There is, then, still an argument for labeling these art films "cult" movies on a formal basis alone, even if they remain highly distinguished cult productions that are more legitimate than illegitimate. But this argument is, I believe, fading, for other equally traditional critics have recently been depicting cult violence as more of the same, perceiving in it the tedium of art-world tradition. When the critics and institutions have been all converted, these art films won't be able to function as cult movies at all.

A more sustainable, albeit still ambivalent, cult-art identity is evident in the quasi-legitimate films of auteurs like Mario Bava and Dario Argento and Johnnie To, most of whose work has been released through illegitimate cult-movie mechanisms and not through legitimate art-film mechanisms – but whose work has since then gathered acclaim in both illegitimate *and* legitimate circles. Here we might want to step back and think about the cult nexus as a loose collection of low-budget genres that in the United States has for the past thirty years actively promoted itself as a "cult" area. Given how accepted this practice has become, with whole institutions being devoted to this idea of a low-budget cult sector of movie-making, we might well say that *all* the movies produced in these illegitimate spheres have some loose claim to the label "cult movie" just as a movie that manages to navigate its way through legitimate festival channels has some automatic claim to the label "art film." Needless to say, cult movies that arrive through these means have not earned any cult *classic* status, let alone any high-art status – but they are free to begin earning this status subculturally. Thus, cult auteurs, like traditional auteurs, first seek praise for their movies through critics, viewers, and institutions, albeit in channels defined as illegitimate. Indeed, the most respected films of many auteurs currently deemed "quasi-legitimate" (including Bava, Corman, Meyer, Koji Wakamatsu, George Romero, Radley Metzger, Wes Craven, The Mitchell Brothers, Wakefield Poole, Gerard Damiano, Tobe Hooper, Just Jaeckin, Obayashi, Argento, Tinto Brass, John Woo, Andrew Blake, Takashi Miike, To, Eli Roth, Nacho Cerdà, and others) were shortly after their production often identified with their illegitimate cult auteurism and their illegitimate embrace of genre-branded materials and genre-branded distributions. But as these movies achieved classic status within cult, the trend over time has been for them to become detached from their original distribution channels, freeing them to develop new affiliations with more legitimate institutions, including art-cinema institutions. Hence, legitimate forums like film festivals, museum archives, repertory theaters, and crossover magazines like *Sight & Sound* have often been among the first forums to promote the canonical value of these movies and directors at the cultural level.

If we made a list of admired movies by these and other quasi-legitimate auteurs, we would find many cult classics that have been admired culturally and/or subculturally for their aesthetics, their contributions to the art of cinema. They include *Black Sabbath* (1963), *The Evil Eye* (1963), *Blood and Black Lace* (1964); *The Masque of the Red Death* (1964); *Faster, Pussycat! Kill! Kill!* (1965); *Secrets Behind the Wall* (1965); *Night of the Living Dead* (1968); *Camille 2000* (1969) and *The Opening of Misty Beethoven* (1975); *Last House on the Left* (1972); *Behind the Green Door* (1972); *Bijou* (1972); *The Devil in Miss Jones* (1973); *The Texas Chainsaw Massacre* (1974); *Histoire d'O* (1975); *House* (1977); *Suspiria* (1977) and *Tenebrae* (1982); *La chiave* (1983); *The Killer* (1989) and *Hard Boiled* (1992); *Paris Chic* (1997) and *Hard Edge* (2003); *Audition* (1999); *Fulltime Killer* (2001) and *Breaking News* (2004); *Hostel* (2005); and "Aftermath" (1994) and *The Abandoned* (2006). In addition to these quasi-legitimate classics, we could add the Hollywood classics of cult directors like Samuel Fuller, including *Shock Corridor* (1963), *The Naked Kiss* (1964), and *White Dog* (1982), and the high-art canons of cult Hollywood genres, such as film noir. Indeed, we could even add the slashers and torture-porn movies that have recently arrived from France, such as *Dans ma peau* (2002), *Haute tension* (2003), *Frontière(s)* (2007), *À l'intérieur* (2007), and *Martyrs* (2008), along with certain Japanese pinks, including *The Glamorous Life of Sachiko Hanai* (2004). Praised as auteur vehicles and lumped into movements (e.g., the "New Wave of French horror" and the "pink nouvelle vague"), these films are quasi-legitimate examples of cult-art cinema. When we add them and other cases to our idea of art cinema, we re-orient traditional ideas of the genre, expanding it quantitatively and qualitatively. However, in making these additions, we must remember that it is legitimate critics who have always been most responsible for the elevation of these movies. It was, for example, legitimate critics from forums like *Sight & Sound* or *The Village Voice* who most directly canonized the "high end" of film noir by praising films like Jacques Tourneur's *Out of the Past* (1947) over more lowbrow noir classics like Edgar G. Ulmer's *Detour* (1945).

But there is one final type of cult-art movie, one that does not rely on legitimate critics for its status – for a cult-art movie does not have to be recognized by outsiders in order to function as art cinema *within* a cult subculture. Cult promoters, cult critics, and cult institutions are more than capable of making value distinctions among cult movies on their own. To get a sense of the true scope of cult cinema *and* art cinema as super-genres, then, we must acquaint ourselves with sectors that legitimate critics rarely, if ever, visit. For example, if we looked at contemporary American softcore, we would find a cult auteur like Tony Marsiglia, whose value was once beyond dispute according to sites like b-independent, Softcore Reviews, and Alternative Cinema. As a result, we would have to integrate ultra-low-budget, cult-softcore movies like *Lust for Dracula* (2004), *Chantal* (2006), and *Sinful* (2007) into our notion of art cinema. We would also have to add a number of very different auteur vehicles, like Tom Lazarus's corporate-softcore films, *Word of Mouth* (1999) and *House of Love* (2000). From there, we could move to Spanish exploitation and look at the work of independent horror auteur Franco, whose output is often praised in cult circles but rarely recognized outside them. Franco's low-budget films, though often exceptionally confusing, have achieved a patina of the personal through the passage of time and their insistent swirls of psychosexual incoherence. Or we might study American hardcore by looking at single videos, like Gregory Dark's *New Wave Hookers* (1985), or entire *oeuvres*, like that of Michael Ninn. Indeed, as a subculture, the adult industry seems to value Ninn movies like *Latex* (1995) over the "prestige" hardcore of the much higher-profile Blake.

These lists could go on indefinitely. Though it is helpful to compile such lists in untraditional contexts where high-profile institutions have yet to clarify the kinds of directors and movies that count as high culture, we needn't enumerate every auteur and "masterpiece." Nor do we need to perform formalist inquiries, surveying cult cinema for traditional art-film techniques (like disinterested stylization, deep focus, the long take, the tracking shot, and slow pacing) or relevant cult mutations of these accepted techniques. Cult-art movies clearly exist, as certified by the fact that movies in so many low forms – including the Italo-Spanish spaghetti western, the Japanese pink, the Italian giallo, the British Hammer film, the American torture-porn movie, and the Hong Kong martial-arts film, to name just a few – have functioned as high art in the subcultures that have grown around them. When made, circulated, and praised with flair, these cult-art movies have even generated a qualified status outside of those subcultures.

References

Jancovich, Mark, et al. 2003. "Introduction," in *Defining Cult Movies*. Manchester: Manchester University Press: 1–13.

Mathijs, Ernest, and Xavier Mendik. 2008. "Editorial Introduction: What Is Cult Film," in *The Cult Film Reader*. New York: Open University Press: 1–11.

Newman, Michael. 2011. *Indie: An American Film Culture*. New York: Columbia University Press.

4

"IT HAPPENS BY ACCIDENT"

Failed intentions, incompetence, and sincerity in badfilm

Becky Bartlett

Introduction

Badness is a well-established characteristic of cult cinema. Although cult films are frequently thematically or aesthetically innovative, they can also be bad – even simultaneously (Mathijs and Mendik 2008: 2). Badness can manifest in various, sometimes overlapping ways: cult films can be aesthetically or morally bad, critically disreputable or in "bad taste," or belong to "illegitimate" genres like pornography. With cult films traditionally positioned in opposition to the "mainstream," badness can be transgressive, challenging standards and conventions of taste, style and quality. This chapter examines films that are identified, distinguished, and potentially valued for their incompetence and technical failure – a category known as badfilm. This is less a thematic category than a stylistic one, with films appreciated for deviance born from a "systematic failure … to *obey* dominant codes of cinematic representation" (Sconce 1995: 385). Badfilms are those in which viewers can recognise, or claim to recognise, the failed intention to achieve certain standards of cinematic representation.

Although theoretically the failure to achieve the desired result is not restricted to any particular type of cinema, only a small proportion of badfilms have gained cult status, becoming known as the "worst films of all time." These are often, but not exclusively, low-budget American science-fiction and horror films, particularly from the 1950s and 1960s. As a period in which classical Hollywood style was the dominant narrative form, bad movie fans can identify the failure to achieve such standards with relative ease through a familiarity with categorical and stylistic conventions that were prevalent then and continue to be commonplace today. It was also a period of significant change for the industry and several factors, including the collapse of the studio system, enabled independent filmmakers like Edward D Wood Jr (*Plan 9 From Outer Space*, 1956), Vic Savage (*The Creeping Terror*, 1964), Coleman Francis (*The Beast of Yucca Flats*, 1961), and Phil Tucker (*Robot Monster*, 1953) to flourish on the fringes of Hollywood. These filmmakers, and others, are today celebrated for their failures. Although immediately recognisable as films of a certain time and place, their badness remains as visible as ever. Furthermore, historical and contemporary badfilms can be, and are, analysed in similar ways; internal incoherence and consistently inconsistent style due to failed intentions are not restricted to a specific time or place.

Critical and historical perspectives

Badfilm appreciation can be traced back to the Surrealists, who believed the "worst" films could also be sublime. Although Pauline Kael, writing in the 1960s, lamented the critical prioritisation of "art" films, arguing that "most of the movies we enjoy are not works of art" (1969/ 1994: 89), cult appreciation for bad movies was not truly visible until *The Fifty Worst Films of All Time* (Medved and Medved 1978) and its influential successor, *The Golden Turkey Awards* (1980). Echoing Kael, the authors observe that "people show greater enthusiasm in laughing together over films they despise than in trying to praise the films they admire," adding "absolutely anyone can recognise a lousy film when he [*sic*] sees one" (1978: 9).

The "awards" format adopted by the Medveds is typical of fan-authored bad movie literature, allowing a broad selection of films to be included within a single text. Like cult cinema generally, definitions of bad movies are vague. While some authors provide lists of examples (Sconce 1995) or different categories of badness (Medved and Medved 1980; Sauter 1995), badfilms also feature in "trash," "psychotronic," or "cult" encyclopaedias and reference guides (Peary 1981; Weldon 1983; Juno and Vale 1986). The search for the "worst film of all time" continues to this day. This may be a personal endeavour (Adams 2010) or a relatively large-scale, publicised event such as the Golden Raspberry Awards (Razzies), which tends towards big-budget Hollywood films deemed "undeserving" of box office success. IMDb's Bottom 100, meanwhile, is based on user ratings and features a combination of established badfilms and an ever-changing selection of contemporary titles that are predominantly American, Turkish, or Indian productions.

Extrinsic factors, including a film's existing reputation, its availability, and the viewer's individual position can affect how badness is interpreted and understood. Mark Jancovich, for example, argues the eclectic selection of films featured in *Incredibly Strange Films*, as well as the authors' fan status, led to frequently contradictory reading strategies being employed, with the films discussed in terms ranging from "virtual contempt" to "patronising affection" and "awe-filled admiration" (2002: 314). This inconsistency is typical, indicating the diversity of both cinematic badness and subsequent cult appreciation.

Taste, constructed and influenced by factors including social status, education, and cultural capital (Bourdieu 1984), and subjectivity also play a role in badfilm appreciation. Valuing badness can appear to challenge the established taste culture: Mathijs writes, for example, that "when bad films are hailed – tongue in cheek or not – as masterpieces … notions of what counts as 'good' are problematized" (2009: 366; see also Sconce 1995). MacDowell and Zborowski offer a "flat repudiation" of this position, arguing that describing badfilms as masterpieces "can only *ever* be on some level 'tongue in cheek,' and, thus, scarcely threatening to even the most traditional standards of aesthetic evaluation" (2013: 23). The Medveds, for example, discuss their bad movie fandom in terms implying taboo activities, but rarely suggest radicalism: as Jancovich notes, they more often support the established taste culture than oppose it (2002: 313). The Medveds are deviants only in that they get a "kick" out of watching bad movies, indicating a distinction between *identifying* badness and *valuing* it. However, rather than reject Mathijs' claim entirely, I suggest some clarification is required. His comments refer to the broad category of bad films, which here includes the varied output of Doris Wishman, Mario Bava, and Todd Haynes, among others. MacDowell and Zborowski, meanwhile, are discussing badfilms, those specifically characterised and identified by technical incompetence and failed intentions. This small but significant distinction indicates the importance of acknowledging the variety of ways in which badness is identified and analysed.

J. Hoberman's article, "Bad Movies," represents an early attempt to identify films that "transcend taste and might be termed *objectively bad*" (1980: 8). An objectively bad movie, he argues, draws the viewer's attention away from its plot to its construction, with the visible artifice of the filmmaking process creating a heightened sense of realism. Crucially, this dismantling of the diegesis is unintentional, caused by the failed attempts to reproduce "institutional modes of representation" (1980: 8). Hoberman proposes the "best" bad movies are made in restrictive conditions, often rooted in exploitation, and contain auteurist signatures that enable the viewer to identify, or claim to identify, a filmmaker's sincere determination to complete their film against all odds. Although weakened by a failure to adequately consider the impact of intention (1980: 22), Hoberman's claims regarding the "best" bad movies still resonate – many cult badfilms meet his criteria, suggesting both a certain mode of production likely to result in objective badness, and a specific mode of reception created as a result.

Badfilm fandom became more visible throughout the 80s and 90s, due largely to the Medveds' books and, later, the cult television programme *Mystery Science Theater 3000* (1988–1999). As well as providing audiences an opportunity to experience films they may have only read about before, *MST3K*'s format created the illusion of a shared viewing environment (a diegetic audience and the viewer watching television at home) and directed viewers towards a specific reading of the films that prioritised the identification, and subsequent mocking, of badness. This appreciation is described as "cinemasochism," whereby fans find "pleasure in cinema others have deemed too painful to endure" (Carter 2011: 102). Cinemasochism, like Sconce's "paracinema" (1995), is an ironic reading strategy not dissimilar to Susan Sontag's conception of camp (1966/1999), which champions artifice and exaggeration, and celebrates badness, particularly when it appears to be naïve or unintentional.

Although Sconce describes paracinema as an "elastic textual category" (1995: 372), it is best thought of as a particular interpretive strategy adopted by cult fans who position themselves in opposition to "mainstream" tastes; like camp, there is a distinction between paracinematic films and paracinematic sensibilities. Sconce initially proposes (1995: 387) that the paracinematic audience is "the one group of viewers that does concentrate exclusively on the 'non-diegetic aspects of the image'." In subsequent work, however, he argues badfilms "compel *even the most complacent viewer* into adopting a reading position marked by that rare combination of incredulous amazement and critical detachment [my emphasis]" (2003: 21), suggesting this is not necessarily a strategy employed by viewers but one encouraged by the films themselves. Badfilms can be "thought-provoking, if only because you were made to wonder how they'd ever been made" (Adams 2010: 4). Faced with such overwhelming failure and incompetence, viewers are thus encouraged to look beyond the filmic text as a way of understanding what they are witnessing.

In academia, badfilms are firmly positioned within cult studies. Consequently, the emphasis has been on the audience, with textual analysis largely being left to fans. Perhaps the characteristics of badfilm are simply so obvious that they have been taken for granted within scholarly writing. However, although some fans are capable of employing a range of sophisticated reading strategies, fan-authored literature tends to comprise synopsis-based reviews rather than detailed analysis, and not all the information is reliable. For example, William Routt identifies some of the erroneous or misleading claims made about Wood and his films (2001: 3), acknowledging the irony that "criticism that depends so strongly on the identification of gaffes should itself be so riddled with them." The academic tendency towards reception studies is understandable – the value of badfilms is most obviously located in the ways cult fans use the texts – but Justin Smith suggests the critical task for the academy now "must be to see if it is possible to find textual evidence for cult affiliation" (2013: 109). The focus on reception means there have been few attempts to analyse how badness is identified and how it functions within the text.

Recent efforts to address these gaps tend to focus on films that are "so bad they're good," a phrase effectively demonstrating the tensions so often at play in simultaneously recognising, valuing, and enjoying badness. Taken literally, "so bad it's good" is problematic and paradoxical, but it is generally understood that "good" in this context is "almost exclusively used to refer to how humorous something is, as opposed to any other laudable artistic qualities" (McCulloch 2011: 195). MacDowell and Zborowski propose "so bad it's pleasurable" as a more accurate description, arguing this "does justice to the fact that no claim is being advanced for a text's intrinsic value … but rather its potential instrumental value as an object of fascination or fun" (2013: 17). Similar assertions can be found elsewhere. Hoberman suggests the Medveds' initial "worst films" selection did not develop cult status because "few are bad enough to be pleasurable" (1980: 9), while Sconce distinguishes between the "paracinematic pleasure" a film like *Glen or Glenda* (1953) can evoke and Larry Buchanan's "bleak and sombre" films that induce only a "profound feeling of desperation, anxiety and terminal boredom" (1995: 389–390).

Although Sconce does not explicitly use the term, his descriptions indicate the distinction between films considered to be "so bad they're good" and films that are "*just* bad," the former a pleasurable experience, the latter not. The challenge is to consider what textual characteristics might result in a film being considered "so bad it's good/ pleasurable." Focusing on the "so," MacDowell and Zborowski argue it can be "strange, entertaining, and perversely thrilling simply to experience such an overwhelming quantity of failed intentions" (2013: 18), suggesting there is evidence of so *much* badness. A pleasurable badfilm is also one where the badness is so *obvious*. Badfilms expose incompetence and failure in a multitude of ways. Individual elements fail to convince and fail to support one another, indicating the films contain so *many different kinds* of badness. Badfilms most likely to be championed as "so bad they're good" are those in which badness is excessive, obvious, and varied. Films that are "just bad," in contrast, are often characterised by a leaden pace and lack of excess. This can be interpreted as absence of effort or ambition (see Sontag 1966/1999: 283), which further hinders their potential to be transformed into objects of fun.

Over the years several films, including *The Room, Troll 2* (1990), and *Plan 9,* have been declared the "best-worst" movie: the ultimate "so bad it's good" experience. Most badfilm fans probably have their own, inherently personal choice of "best-worst" film and could convincingly justify their selection. As "so bad it's good" suggests, the greater the evidence of technical failure, the greater the potential for enjoyment. However, attempts to provide textual evidence for what is ultimately a taste judgement can be limited by the subjective nature of the filmic experience. Whether a film is described as "so bad it's good" or "so bad it's pleasurable," the underlying assumption is that it *is* pleasurable. The textual excess of films considered to be "so bad they're good" does have other potential value, however. The overwhelming failure in *Maniac* (1934) leads Sconce (2003) to argue for the pedagogical value of badfilm, for example. Furthermore, if future investigations are to explore how failure functions within the text, "so bad they're good" films can be particularly productive because they represent some of the most extreme, excessive, and obvious examples of incompetence.

This does not mean that declaring a film to be bad is only ever a subjective evaluation: it is possible to distinguish between identifying badness and valuing it. Identifying failure – recognising a schism between the attempts to achieve certain results and the results themselves – is less a matter of taste than context. By stating a film fails in its intended aims, we make no claims about its instrumental value. Furthermore, "one need by no means attach the value of 'good' to conventions in order to make a judgement of 'bad' when they appear to be striven for and missed" (MacDowell and Zborowski 2013: 16). Intentionality is a complex issue and central to the debate surrounding badfilm but has only recently been considered. The remainder of this chapter explores intentionality in more detail.

Intentionality and authorship

Badfilm literature indicates assumptions are frequently made regarding intentions. Alison Graham argues it is the "*appearance* of Wood's intentions that so engages cult audiences – the perceived distance ... between his desire to create compelling narratives and his inability to do so" (1991: 109). Sconce notes that counter-cinematic and paracinematic styles are distinguished from one another by the artistic intentions of the filmmaker, the former intentionally deviating from Hollywood classicism, the latter hindered by financial constraints and technical incompetence (1995: 384). Intention is crucial to badfilm identification precisely because "if we cannot assume that a film intended to achieve certain aims, then we cannot deem it 'bad' for failing in those aims" (MacDowell and Zborowski 2013: 5). Intention allows us to distinguish between "bad" films and badfilms – the former deliberately ironic, the latter not. Indeed, "bad" films, such as Larry Blamire's *Dark and Stormy Night* (2009), often demonstrate an acute knowledge of filmmaking conventions by intentionally flouting them for comic effect. The "badness" in such films is often well judged, with "bad" moments fully supported by the other elements, carefully placed to be most effective, and subtly acknowledged within the diegesis. The film's textual qualities, therefore, encourage the audience to adopt an ironic viewing position.

Badfilms, in contrast, expose the failed intention to achieve certain standards. Examples of unintentional badness include: the fragmentation of the landscape in *The Beast of Yucca Flats*, rendering an important chase sequence entirely incomprehensible; the voice-over narrator's claim that a victim was "horribly mangled" moments before the unblemished body is revealed in *Monster A-go Go* (1965); *Plan 9*'s UFOs wobbling across the screen on strings while accompanied by sound suggesting a smooth journey (and none of the characters remarking on the bizarre flight pattern). These moments, unsupported by the other filmic elements, limit the narrative's immersive potential and draw attention to the film's construction instead.

Reflecting on the complex concept of intention invites consideration of both how intentionality is identified and who, or what, is the subject of intention. The incompetence (failed intention) of badfilm is generally attributed to the filmmaker and, specifically, the director. Auteurist interpretations often underpin cult appreciation: Juno and Vale argue that badness is often the consequence of a "single person's individual vision and quirky originality," and evidence of creative, improvised solutions to problems largely caused by budgetary restrictions (1986: 5). Although the various duties undertaken by filmmakers like Ed Wood, Tommy Wiseau, or Sam Mraovich make claims of authorship more persuasive – Mraovich has twelve credits in *Ben & Arthur* (2002) including director, editor, producer, scriptwriter, and lead actor – auteur theory is not without its critics. Routt criticises how it has been applied to Wood's filmography, for example, challenging the assumption that the "gap between intention and act is apparent only in what is bad about Wood's movies" (2001: 8) and suggesting the filmmaker's life, particularly his transvestism and alcoholism, is used in a "kind of bonehead auteurist fashion where the badness of the life is taken as evidence for the badness of the work" (2001: 2).

MacDowell and Zborowski provide the most comprehensive examination of intentionality in badfilm to date, and suggest it is not always beneficial to look to the filmmaker as a source of intention. They argue such an approach, "if offered in full earnest, could still capture only (a) what an author remembers intending, (b) what s/he intended consciously, and (c) what s/he is capable of articulating about his or her conscious intentions" (2013: 6). Furthermore, badfilm fans generally prioritise the perceived visibility of failed intentions within the film text even if the filmmaker's stated intentions appear to contradict the filmic evidence. Despite producer Sam Sherman claiming *Blood of Ghastly Horror* (1967), an incoherent film comprising several unrelated, uncompleted narratives, *wasn't designed* to make any sense (Konow 1998: 115), and

Wiseau now maintaining *The Room* was always intended to be a black comedy, these claims are largely ignored by badfilm fans. It is only by assuming badfilms are *not* intended to be parodies or comedies that the audience is able to laugh at them in the way they so regularly do (MacDowell and Zborowski in McCulloch 2011: 196).

Comparing contemporary cult badfilm *Birdemic: Shock and Terror* (2010) and its sequel *Birdemic 2: The Resurrection* (2013) demonstrates how issues of intention and authorship can be further complicated if filmmakers embrace their films' cult status. *Birdemic*, a tribute to Hitchcock's *The Birds* with a strong environmentalist message, is incompetent throughout. The narrative structure and pace is inconsistent and incoherent, sound editing is terrible, dialogue is stilted and poorly delivered, acting is wooden, and the attacking eagles and vultures are unconvincing, barely-moving GIFs. The film's tiny budget is revealed in every scene, exposed through writer-director-producer James Nguyen's attempt to tell a story that far outreaches his ability. *Birdemic* is demonstrably, objectively bad, its failed intentions unavoidably apparent.

Nguyen often appears resolutely oblivious to the reason for *Birdemic*'s cult success and the ironic temperament underpinning many of the questions posed to him in interviews (e.g., Eggertsen 2011), but concedes that "you cannot intentionally go out and make a cult movie. … It happens by accident" (2011). More accurately, however, it is not possible to make a badfilm – a film characterised by failed intentions. Nonetheless, *Birdemic 2* is a blatant attempt to capitalise on the cult popularity of *Birdemic*, with its "success" depending on its ability to "replicate the 'failure' of its predecessor and evince the same essential authentic sincerity" (Hunter 2014: 490). However, although *Birdemic 2* is generally as cheap-looking and incompetent as Nguyen's initial effort, the "authentic sincerity" is called into question precisely because it replicates, repeats, and exaggerates the original film's failure. There is no evidence of any attempt to improve. As one reviewer on IMDb writes, "this movie is trying way too hard to be as terrible as the first one, and that effort completely ruins it. You can't intentionally repeat accidental mediocrity" (Debtman 2013). Further complicating matters, not all reviewers agree: there are as many celebrating *Birdemic 2*'s incompetence as those lamenting the film's lack of originality and intentional badness.

Figure 4.1 *Birdemic: Shock and Terror*'s objectively bad aesthetics (Nguyen, USA, 2010). Expedition Films/Moviehead Pictures

Figure 4.2 One of several attempts to replicate failure in *Birdemic 2: The Resurrection* (Nguyen, USA, 2013). Got A Fish Productions/Moviehead Pictures

The mixed reception of *Birdemic 2* challenges Sontag's claim that the "one doesn't need to know the artist's private intentions. The work tells all" (1966/1999: 282), indicating that the viewer's knowledge, or lack thereof, of *Birdemic* impacts their understanding and identification of intentionality. Films are rarely viewed in isolation, and it is precisely this fact that enables incompetence to be identified. Building on Umberto Eco's concept of the "intention of the text" and the importance of context, MacDowell and Zborowski argue that our sense of the "intention of the text" is guided by its "relationship with pre-existing cultural forms and genres, and their attendant conventions. Such a relationship will often facilitate identification of, at a minimum, a text's categorical intentions" (2013: 8). *Birdemic's* categorical context strongly suggests it intends to be a horror-romance that adheres to the standards of cinematic representation and realism established in the classical continuity system. For the informed viewer however, the categorical context of *Birdemic 2* necessarily includes its predecessor, enabling it to be identified as a far more self-conscious, albeit still ineptly constructed, effort. Whereas *Birdemic* reveals the sincere, earnest intention to be *good*, its sequel reveals the attempt at parody (rather than homage) and the intention to be *cult*. This echoes Sontag's concepts of "naïve" and "deliberate" camp: just as naïve camp is "satisfying" because it reveals a "seriousness that fails," (2009: 283) unselfconscious badfilms expose the failed intention to be *taken seriously*.

Extratextual information

Although attributing intentionality to the text rather than the author, as per Eco, has its benefits, the two sources are used interchangeably. Hunter, for example, argues that although contemporary "exploitation" films like *Snakes on a Train* (2006) are bad, "their intention is never, exactly, to be 'good'" (2014: 483); later he describes the viewing experience of watching badfilms as going "against the grain of the director's legible intentions" (489). This indicates intentionality may be variously attributed to both/either film and filmmaker. The distinction between authorial and textual intent often appears to be related to the levels of extra- and inter-textual information at the viewer's disposal. This represents a challenge to Eco's approach, which discourages looking beyond the text, and aligns badfilm fans with Richard Rorty's pragmatic assertion that *any* reading of a text will inevitably be influenced by other information at the reader's disposal (1992: 105). In the case of older, less established badfilms from the 1950s and 1960s, for example, a lack of information about filmmakers or production conditions can encourage intentionality to be repositioned onto the film texts instead of an author.

Discussing the pedagogical potential of badfilm, Sconce claims that an advantage of a badfilm like *Maniac* (1934) is that it "carries none of the critical baggage of a *Citizen Kane* nor the weighty reputation of ... [a] director whose popular persona precedes the consumption of their work" (2003: 20). However, assuming contemporary audiences watch badfilms without any knowledge of their reputation is problematic, particularly in the age of the internet. Inevitably, extratextual information (whether accurate or not) can impact how informed viewers understand and approach film texts. This can be beneficial: Ed Wood was initially voted "worst director of all time" but, despite the incompetence of his early films, "the critical discourse ... surrounding Wood has since shifted from bemused derision to active celebration" (Sconce 1995: 387–388). Wood is now considered a "unique talent" rather than a "hack" (388) and, as a result, certain films of his – notably *Glen or Glenda* – are discussed in far more sympathetic and interpretive ways than many other badfilms. As Robert Birchard has pointed out, however, the various texts surrounding Wood's films have "created a highly romanticised fable that prints legend with just enough verisimilitude to suggest it's all true" (1995: 450). Arguably, the amount of extratextual information available, and the way information has been used to appropriate and re-evaluate his films, is "unique," rather than the contents of the films themselves.

The cult interest in certain contemporary badfilms, such as *The Room* and *Birdemic*, as well as the fact that the filmmakers are still alive, willing to be interviewed, and have embraced their films' cult status, leads to greater availability of extratextual information. However, such information, whether about "classic" or contemporary badfilms, is not always reliable. *The Disaster Artist*, an account of *The Room*'s production co-written by actor Greg Sestero that inspired the Oscar-nominated biopic of the same name (Franco, 2017), effectively paints a picture of the filmmaker not dissimilar to the "romanticised fable" surrounding Wood. There are also numerous anecdotes used to understand badfilms that are directly contradicted by other trivia or by the film text itself. The jerky, disjointed editing in *Manos: The Hands of Fate* is still explained by a claim that the camera used could only shoot thirty-two seconds of footage at a time, despite at least two shots in the film being more than double this length. It is unlikely that Vic Savage really dropped *The Creeping Terror*'s sound reel in Lake Tahoe, but the story is still used to explain the film's excessive voice-over narration. As Mathijs notes, "the longer a film's reputation chronology becomes, or the longer its public visibility lasts (even if only in small fan communities), the more important extrinsic references ... become in determining the meaning of a film and its reputation" (2005: 467). This, of course, does not mean the information at our disposal should be ignored. However, because the reputations of certain badfilms can result in a situation in which existing *claims* of badness replace detailed examination of *evidence* of badness, we should interrogate and challenge extra- and inter-textual information by returning to the film texts themselves: to use extrinsic references to inform, rather than influence, how badfilms are read.

Conclusion

Watching a film that contains such overwhelming failure and ineptitude is frequently an unsettling experience, one that raises more questions than provides answers. How did a film so obviously terrible get made? How did it get released? Why would a filmmaker not only endorse and promote such a mess, but be proud of it? Furthermore, why is excessive, extreme failure so often a pleasurable experience; what makes a film "so bad it's good"? Badfilm appreciation often begins with these questions, with the viewer desiring to explain what they have witnessed, to find a way of rationally understanding what is often an irrational, incoherent product. The starting position accepts the films are intrinsically, demonstrably bad. From here, individual taste determines our response to the films, which, because of their inherent incoherence and inconsistent style, can be ambiguous enough to allow for a multitude of interpretations. Badfilms can be appropriated as accidental art, as *Glen or Glenda* is today; they can be viewed as evidence of entrepreneurial graft and auteurist determination; they can reveal modes of production that are otherwise concealed in "good" films; they can be dismissed as "trash," referenced only because they represent one end of the quality spectrum. The value and reception of badfilms is necessarily subjective, but the film text itself remains constant.

As interest in bad films – and badfilms – has increased, several useful avenues for further investigation have opened. Hunter, for example, relates badness to the "abject" and suggests a "phenomenology of bad film" might exist. This approach considers the paradoxical claims of badness-as-goodness in terms of experience, and indicates a way to conceive of a shared understanding of badness despite difference: "bad films, *both aesthetically incompetent and morally suspect ones*, can be genuinely disconcerting, for they enable entry into imaginative worlds where the usual criteria no longer seem to apply [my emphasis]" (Hunter 2014: 498). Alternatively, approaching the subcategory of badfilms from a position that addresses failed intentions shifts the core of the debate from reception back to the text itself. The narrative and stylistic incoherence and inconsistency of badfilms is revealed in strange and unusual ways that are distinct and different from both mainstream and art cinema precisely due to the appearance of failed intentions. Furthermore, MacDowell and Zborowski suggest that studying badfilm "forces us to return with renewed vigour and evidence to still-vital issues for aesthetics that we can often complacently presume to move beyond" (2013: 24). When considering cult's increasing commercialisation, leading to films that blur the line between "badness" and badness (the former intentional, the latter not), it has become necessary to further interrogate our understanding of subjective and objective badness including, though by no means limited to, failure and incompetence.

References

Adams, Michael. 2010. *Showgirls, Teen Wolves and Astro Zombies: A Film Critic's Year-Long Quest to Find the Worst Movie Ever Made*. New York itbooks.

Birchard, R. S. 1995. "Edward D Wood Jr – Some Notes on a Subject for Further Research," *Film History*, 7: 450–455.

Bourdieu, Pierre. 1984. *Distinction: A Social Critique of the Judgement of Taste*, translated by R. Nice. London: Routledge & Kegan Paul.

Carter, David Ray. 2011. "Cinemasochism: Bad Movies and the People Who Love Them." In Weiner, R. G., and Barba, S. E., eds, *In the Peanut Gallery with "Mystery Science Theatre 3000': Essays on Films, Fandom, Technology and the Culture of Riffing*. Jefferson, MD: McFarland: 101–109.

Debtman. 2013. "You Can't Intentionally Repeat Accidental Mediocrity," *IMDb*. www.imdb.com/title/tt1674047/reviews?ref_=tt_ql_3 (accessed 14 December 2015).

Eggertsen, Chris. 2011. "Special Interview: 'Birdemic: Shock and Terror' Director James Nguyen!!' *Bloody Disgusting*. http://bloody-disgusting.com/interviews/23593/special-interview-birdemic-shock-and-terror-director-james-nguyen/ (accessed 3 May 2016).

Graham, Allison. 1991. "Journey to the Center of the Fifties: The Cult of Banality'. In Telotte, J.P., ed., *The Cult Film Experience: Beyond All Reason*. Austin: University of Texas Press: 107–121.

Hoberman, J. 1980. "Bad Movies," *Film Comment*, 16.4: 7–12.

Hunter, I. Q. 2014. "Trash Horror and the Cult of the Bad Film." In Benshoff, H. M., ed., *A Companion to the Horror Film*. Chichester: Wiley-Blackwell: 483–500.

Jancovich, Mark. 2002. "Cult Fictions: Cult Movies, Subcultural Capital and the Production of Cult Distinctions," *Cultural Studies*, 16.2: 306–322.

Juno, Andrea and Vivian Vale. eds. 1986. *RE/Search # 10: Incredibly Strange Films*. San Francisco: RE/Search Publications.

Kael, Pauline. 1969/1994. "Trash, Art, and the Movies." In *Going Steady: Film Writings 1968–1969*. New York: Marion Boyars: 87–129.

Konow, David. 1998. *Schlock-o-Rama: The Films of Al Adamson*. Los Angeles: Lone Eagle.

MacDowell, James and James Zborowski 2013. "The Aesthetics of "So Bad It's Good": Value, Intention, and The Room," *Intensities*, 6, Autumn/Winter. http://intensitiescultmedia.com (accessed 15 March 2016).

Mathijs, Ernest. 2005. "Bad Reputations: The Reception of "Trash" Cinema," *Screen*, 46.4: 451–472.

———. 2009. Review, *Screen*, 50.3: 365–370.

Mathijs, Ernest and Xavier Mendik 2008. "Editorial Introduction: What Is Cult Film?' In Mathijs, E., and Mendik, X., eds, *The Cult Film Reader*. Maidenhead: McGraw-Hill/Open University Press: 1–11.

McCulloch, Richard. 2011. "'Most People Bring Their Own Spoons': The Room's Participatory Audiences as Comedy Mediators," *Participations*, 8.2: 189–218.

Medved, Harry and Michael Medved 1978. *The Fifty Worst Films of All Time (And How They Got That Way)*. London: Angus & Robertson.

———. 1980. *The Golden Turkey Awards: The Worst Achievements in Hollywood History*. London: Angus & Robertson.

Peary, Danny. 1981. *Cult Movies*. New York: Delacorte.

Rorty, Richard. 1992. "The Pragmatist's Progress'. In Collini, S., ed., *Interpretation and Overinterpretation*. Cambridge: Cambridge University Press: 89–108.

Routt, W. D. 2001. "Bad for Good," *Intensities*, 2, Autumn/Winter. www.intensities.org/Issues/Intensities_Two.htm (accessed 15 March 2016).

Sauter, Michael. 1995. *The Worst Movies of All Time Or: What Were They Thinking?* New York: Citadel Press.

Sconce, Jeffrey. 1995. "'Trashing' the Academy: Taste, Excess and an Emerging Politics of Cinematic Style," *Screen*, 36.4: 371–393.

Sconce, Jeffrey. 2003. "Esper, the Renunciator: Teaching 'Bad' Movies to Good Students." In Mark Jancovich, Antonio Lázaro-Reboll, Julian Stringer, and Andy Willis, eds, *Defining Cult Movies: The Cultural Politics of Oppositional Taste*. Manchester: Manchester University Press: 14–34.

Sestero, Greg, and Tom Bissell. 2013. *The Disaster Artist*. New York: Simon & Schuster.

Smith, Justin. 2013. "Vincent Price and Cult Performance: The Case of Witchfinder General'. In Kate Egan and Sarah Thomas, eds, *Cult Film Stardom*. London: Palgrave Macmillan: 109–125.

Sontag, Susan. 1966/1999. "Notes on Camp." In *Against Interpretation and Other Essays*. London: Penguin Classics: 275–292.

Weldon, Michael. 1983. *The Psychotronic Encyclopedia of Film*. London: Plexus.

5

CULT HORROR CINEMA

Steffen Hantke

Horror and cult cinema: Kindred spirits

Although the concept of cult cinema did not exist during the early years of cinema, the genre of the horror film would emerge with a strong affinity to the practices, preferences, and affective aesthetics of cult cinema at large. As genre conventions would begin to solidify, horror's interest in the transgressive aspects of culture – from the bodily manifestations of death and disease, to the spiritual burdens of sin and taboo – would lock it into an antagonistic or even subversive relationship to the ideological mainstream of the national culture that produced it. Thus, horror's affective aesthetic would plant it firmly within the small group, together with melodrama and pornography, of what Linda Williams has so aptly named "body genres." Their emphasis on the viewer's visceral reaction distances horror from the contemplative, analytical audience response predicated upon that safe sense of voyeuristic detachment that makes up the standard viewer position of so much narrative cinema. Instead, horror retains an immersive, or even assaultive grasp upon its audience, a claim akin to that of an earlier "cinema of attractions" that had not yet fully established the rules of narrative cinema. An oddly raw and atavistic cinema amidst well-mannered genres, horror film has always been demonstratively raunchy, vulgar, tasteless, offensive, and scandalous. Together with pornography, it has been the genre most frequently targeted by the censor, its shoddiest products snipped and cut and edited for content as often as its acknowledged masterpieces – a status the genre claims as a badge of honor whenever given the chance.

Nowhere does the potential for horror film to be produced and consumed as cult cinema emerge more clearly than in the genre's embrace of an antagonistic stance toward the cultural mainstream: its dislocation within clear classificatory frameworks, its embrace of taboo subject matter, its abandonment of the rules of polite representational restraint, and its affective aesthetic. This applies both to the films that qualify as entries into the genre, as it does to a number of directors – and, to a lesser extent, to stars and technicians (like writers, composers, make-up experts, and cinematographers) – who make up a canonical body of "horror auteurs" said to represent the best or purest iteration of the genre. It is at the nexus of this fetishization of aesthetic, affective, and ideological qualities, and their projection onto equally fetishized films and their makers, that cult horror operates. The nature of these operations may vary; the element of "cult" may be defined by practices of production or reception, by authorial self-representation or marketplace presence. It may be contested among specific demographic audiences vying for (sub-) cultural capital. But in the final instance, there is an insistence that cult horror takes place outside the mainstream – that it distinguishes itself from the smooth, slick products of commercial filmmaking. Since this type of filmmaking is practically synonymous with Hollywood, the following examination of cult horror will focus specifically on American cinema, and on a period of historical transition when margin and mainstream were undergoing radical changes.

Playing both ends against the middle: The politics of cult horror

What complicates the horror genre's broad and somewhat self-aggrandizing account of its own anarchic powers to critique, challenge, and undermine the cultural mainstream is the fact that horror films, much like any other popular genre, come in both progressive and conservative political shades. In its treatment of non-normative, unruly, monstrous bodies, for example, horror films can go either way, embracing or destabilizing the status quo. On the conservative end of the spectrum, horror's narrative options include stories that begin with a world balanced in perfect harmony, which is then destabilized by the intrusion of the monstrous or abject, but ultimately returned to the status quo. On the other end of the spectrum are stories that destabilize their diegetic world yet embrace this destabilization – either at the outset of the narrative, when they show that the world was never too stable to begin with, or that a return to the status quo is not desirable, or when, at the point of closure, they reject stability altogether – and thus ultimately argue for the benefit or even the need for destabilization. The monstrous has its part to play in this narrative as well – whether it is entirely other, or whether it entertains covert relationships with the self, it always shapes critical discussion about horror's political stance. Whatever the nature of the monstrous might be that is condemned or celebrated, whatever transgressive weight the horror film shoulders along the way to this final narrative destination: it registers in the context of the narrative telos. Even as a genre on the margins of the culture, horror's ideological flexibility testifies to the fact that there is a margin both on the left and the right.

Just as horror's political agenda stretches from left to right despite the genre's inherently transgressive potential, so horror's claims to cultural capital stretch from the mainstream to the margins. If it is true that the connection between horror's inherent transgressiveness accounts quite comfortably for horror films pushing beyond the boundaries of mainstream taste – directed by highly idiosyncratic auteurists, produced on shoestring budgets, and thus attracting small and highly specialized audiences: all preconditions for horror films to identify with the practices of cult cinema – then it follows that horror films in the mainstream are somewhat harder to account for. Fans of the horror film genre might suspect that a mainstream horror film's inclusiveness, its appeal to a mass audience beyond fandom, must be achieved by, paradoxically, compromising on exactly that transgressiveness which defines the appeal of its genre in the first place. Other genres, like melodrama or the Western, cannot "sell out" – horror can. A studio-produced horror film like *The Silence of the Lambs* (Jonathan Demme, 1991) can enjoy a high degree of popularity, but its claim to cult horror credentials is far more difficult to establish than those of relatively obscure fan favorites produced outside the studio system, like *Carnival of Souls* (Herk Harvey, 1962) or *Blood Feast* (Hershel Gordon Lewis, 1963).

For exactly this reason, canonicity proses problems for horror films positioning themselves in relationship to the concept of cult cinema. Commercially speaking, horror films have operated quite successfully within the cultural mainstream. With box office numbers at respectable blockbuster levels, films like *The Sixth Sense*, *Jaws*, *I am Legend*, *What Lies Beneath*, *The Blair Witch Project*, and *The Exorcist* qualify unquestioningly as mainstream cinema.[1] All of these films feature major stars or ostentatiously display the latest technological effects or high production values.

By and large, they are smooth and polished, competently or even masterfully directed, based on commercially successful source material, and their success at the box office is in no small part the result of expensive marketing campaigns. An exception in this lineup could be made for *The Blair Witch Project*. But even in this case – a film for which the marketing campaign quite consciously tried to generate a reputation as cult horror (conveniently underscored by the film's low budget and cheap found-footage aesthetic) – the mainstream appeal and commercial success interferes with the credibility of its so obviously manufactured cult status. As the case of *The Blair Witch Project* demonstrates, cult horror is defined clearly enough to be commercially appropriated – by way of a logic that can be commercially viable while being oddly oxymoronic and self-defeating in every other respect.

Margins and mainstream: The horror film canon and cult horror

Those engaged in the compilation of a horror film canon do not seem fazed by cult horror's entanglement in these complex interactions between margin and mainstream. Kendall R. Philipps, for example, in his book *Projected Fears* (2005), assembles nine canonical horror films well-known beyond horror fandom: *Dracula* (Tod Browning, 1931), *The Thing from Another World* (Christian Nyby, 1951), *Psycho* (Alfred Hitchcock, 1960), *The Exorcist* (William Friedkin, 1973), *The Texas Chainsaw Massacre* (Tobe Hooper, 1974), *Halloween* (John Carpenter, 1978), *The Silence of the Lambs* (Jonathan Demme, 1991), *Scream* (Wes Craven, 1996), and *The Sixth Sense* (M. Night Shyamalan, 1999). While only two of the top grossing horror films of all times mentioned earlier have found their way on to Philipps' list, all ten films are well known and have enjoyed considerable commercial success. Undoubtedly, these films are part of mainstream culture: one is made by a director with unrivalled artistic credentials (*Psycho*), another garnered a rare Academy Award for Best Picture (*The Silence of the Lambs*), and two initiated massively successful franchises (*Halloween* and *Scream*). Philipps' intention to demonstrate the cultural relevance of each film in its historical and social context further emphasizes the high degree of cultural capital with which he invests these films. Past their commercial viability, these films matter: to the history of the genre and, more importantly, to the cultural history of the United States.

The moment in Philipps' canonical layout when mainstream and margin operate side by side comes with the chapters about the 1960s and the 1970s. Here, he lines up *Night of the Living Dead,* directed on a shoestring budget by a completely unknown maker of industrial safety films, directly following Hitchcock's masterpiece *Psycho*; then he assembles *The Exorcist*, the very definition of a well-made film by a master craftsman and auteur of New Hollywood cinema, cheek to jowl with *The Texas Chainsaw Massacre*, a sloppy, unruly, anarchic B-movie by another complete unknown. The fact that Philipps orchestrates this odd convergence of margin and mainstream in the horror film canon around the late 1960s and into the 1970s is no coincidence. Something is happening at this time which goes directly to the assumption that the horror genre operates essentially in an antagonistic relationship to the cultural mainstream, and that cult horror represents the purest, most transgressive expression of this antagonistic relationship. True or not, these assumptions about the horror genre emerge from a specific historical moment – and with it the basic shape of cult horror as a subcategory of the genre at large.

New Hollywood, neo horror

Philipps' canonical lineup ties horror to the emergence of New Hollywood in the 1960s, a cultural shift described by Peter Biskind as an era of unprecedented maturity and artistic achievement within the context of Sixties Counterculture. Biskind celebrates the post-classic filmmaking scene which "produced a body of risky, high-quality work," which was "character-, rather than plot-driven, that defied traditional narrative conventions, that challenged the tyranny of technical correctness, that broke the taboos of language and behavior, that dared to end unhappily" (Biskind 1998: 17). As New Hollywood films appear to sneer at their studio predecessors (Harris 2008: 1), their "nervous, rootless, [and] hip" (3) aesthetics would carry more subcultural than cultural capital, laying the groundwork for cult practices to emerge around their production and consumption.

As if to confirm Biskind's vision of New Hollywood being imbued with the "flavor of countercultural resistance" (Mathijs and Sexton 2011: 196), the horror film would acquire a new maturity that would distance it from its reputation of catering primarily to an audience of teenagers. Nowhere is this shift more impressively illustrated than in Roger Ebert's review of *Night of the Living Dead* (George Romero, 1968). After some initial cheerful screaming, Ebert reports, "the mood of the audience seemed to change. Horror movies were fun, sure, but this was pretty strong stuff. There wasn't a lot of screaming anymore; the place was pretty quiet" (Ebert 1969). Eventually, there would be almost complete silence:

> The movie had stopped being delightfully scary about halfway through, and had become unexpectedly terrifying. There was a little girl across the aisle from me, maybe nine years old, who was sitting very still in her seat and crying. I don't think the younger kids really knew what hit them.
>
> (Ebert 1969)[2]

Ebert's review provides a vivid insight into Romero's ability to actualize exactly that inventory of aesthetic features Biskind praises as signs of maturity among New Hollywood filmmakers.

Of course, there had always been exceptions to this rule of polite restraint on the part of horror films, even those designed for teenagers. Exploitation films like those of Herschel Gordon Lewis, for example, would operate in the same transgressive territory as *Night of the Living Dead*, and had done so before Romero would unleash his zombies upon American cinema. But none of Lewis' films would have had a reviewer of Ebert's caliber even attending a screening. While Romero would become culturally visible as a maker of horror films that carried subcultural capital (a critical term introduced into the debate of popular culture by Sarah Thornton, extending Bourdieu's standard terminology) into the mainstream, Lewis would remain a more strictly marginal figure, his joyful splatter aesthetic permanently segregated from mainstream horror just as his films would never play outside of grindhouses and drive-ins (Thornton 1996: 98–105). To the extent that both filmmakers can lay claim to a "defiance of industry routines and practices" (Mathijs and Sexton 2011: 195–196), which invests their work with the "flavor of countercultural resistance" (196), both are open to be appropriated to the ranks of cult horror by audiences recognizing their shared transgressive aesthetic.

Cult horror films like *Night of the Living Dead*, which were to emerge from this infusion of New Hollywood maturity into the horror genre, would prove themselves adept at creating memorable images that borrowed from Lewis' splatter film aesthetics. From the little girl gleefully disemboweling her mother with a trowel in *Night of the Living Dead* (George Romero, 1968), to the majestic full frontal slow-motion shot of a human head exploding in *Scanners* (David Cronenberg, 1981), or the brutal rape and shooting of Mari Collingwood in *Last House on the Left* (Wes Craven 1972): neo horror would position itself carefully and ambiguously between aesthetic and social categories the way early horror films had. Often the films would look rough and cheap, adopting (by choice or necessity) the low-budget aesthetic of exploitation films. Unlike the adolescent desire to shock and jeer at mainstream prurience on display in exploitation films, they would come with a carefully calibrated self-awareness (something critic Philip Brophy has

Figure 5.1 "That's disgusting": Horrality in *The Fly* (Cronenberg, USA, 1986). SLM Production Groups/ Brooksfilms

famously named "horrality") and often show the hand of a masterful director at the helm. Both the stylistic and auteurial variety of neo horror, as well as its various internal ambiguities, rifts, and ruptures would provide ample traction for the attitudes, standards, and practices of cult cinema.

Three exemplary careers: The mainstreaming of neo horror

As much as *Easy Riders, Raging Bulls* celebrates New Hollywood for its maturity and creativity, Biskind also provides a compelling narrative for the end of this creative boom at the turn of the 1970s to the 1980s. According to this narrative of the rise and fall of New Hollywood, the end of mature, aesthetically challenging American cinema would come with the arrival of the 1970s blockbuster aesthetic. Its premier practitioners – Steven Spielberg and George Lucas – would be two of the directors who had initially been fellow travelers of the 1960s' and 1970s auteurists. In defiance of their roots, however, they would turn away from their generation's artistic ambitions. At their behest, Hollywood would ratchet back to the loud and noisy kiddie fare of their own childhood – a childhood spent at movie matinees and in front of the television set (showing, in no small measure, old horror films). With its insistence that "maturity" would be the core value of a new American filmmaking – its absence in much of classical Hollywood, its emergence in New Hollywood, and its loss with the rise of Lucas and Spielberg – Biskind's narrative ends with the admission of artistic and commercial failure that echoes *Easy Rider*'s somber farewell to countercultural optimism: "We Blew It."

Biskind's narrative of the rise and fall of New Hollywood is so compelling that the career paths of the most significant horror film auteurs of the 1960s and 1970s fit right in with the failure of mainstream Hollywood to retain or expand its cultural capital. Except for the few notable exceptions of New Hollywood directors who would "go slumming" in the horror film genre – Polanski with *Rosemary's Baby*, Kubrick with *The Shining*, and Friedkin with *The Exorcist* – the new horror film that was developing on a parallel track at the same time did not have much in terms of cultural capital to risk and gamble away. Mainstream directors would incur "notoriety through association with this supposedly dissolute genre" (Kooyman 2014: 6), while directors angling for cult credentials would appropriate and harness this notoriety "as a promotional and self-fashioning device to boost their counter-culture cache" (Kooyman 2014: 7). When the counter-culture of the 1960s would reshape the mainstream, the horror film was to acquire cultural capital in abandoning classic Hollywood horror and pushing out to the cultural margins – cultural capital it was to lose again by going mainstream and selling out.

One director who features prominently on Kendall Philipps' canonical list, Tobe Hooper, fits Biskind's narrative particularly well. A complete unknown, Hooper burst onto the scene in 1974 with *The Texas Chainsaw Massacre*. The film would set a standard for Hooper's entire subsequent career that the director would always be trying to live up to. Hooper's low-budget follow-up, *Eaten Alive* (1976), did not hit the nerve of its time like its predecessor did, as much as both films resemble each other in terms of their rough, unpolished aesthetic. Hooper's greatest commercial success would come with *Poltergeist* (1982), a slick, polished production so unlike *The Texas Chainsaw Massacre* that the persistent questions raised about its troubled authorship already signal Hooper's problems in sustaining his early cult credentials.[3] Carrying much of Spielberg's blockbuster aesthetic over to his next large project, Hooper went on to direct *Lifeforce* (1985), a film generally considered to be one of the worst horror films of all times.[4] Since *Lifeforce* relentlessly foregrounds high production values, which stand in contrast to the director's early low-budget aesthetics, it is hardly surprising that advertising posters for the film listed Hooper as the creator of *Poltergeist*, omitting any mention of *The Texas Chainsaw Massacre*. Some of Hooper's notable subsequent films have revisited the 1950s – a nostalgic point of reference for Spielberg's brand as director and producer during this period as well. Hooper's remake of William Cameron Menzies' *Invaders from Mars* (1986), as well as *Spontaneous Combustion* (1990), rework genre tropes with intelligence and critical self-consciousness, but constitute valuable contributions to the horror film canon in neither mainstream nor margin. In its oscillation between margin and mainstream, Hooper's career stands as an example of early cult horror credentials, translated into a mid-career move toward the mainstream, and a period lasting until Hooper's death in 2017 during which none of his films would succeed in resolving the tension between margin and mainstream and granting Hooper a legacy as a maker of commercially successful horror or an auteurist creator of cult horror.

Following a similar arc as Hooper's, the career of Joe Dante has been shaped by the influence of Steven Spielberg as well. First off, though, Dante began his directorial career under the tutelage of producer Roger Corman. A low-budget response to Spielberg's *Jaws*, the campy *Piranha* (1978) immediately placed Dante in the antagonistic relationship to the mainstream. *The Howling* (1981) confirmed his status, just as the film took its place among cult horror favorites. The move from margin to mainstream, however, happens with *Gremlins* (1984), which fits the model of commercial filmmaking as much as Hooper's *Poltergeist* did. Not surprisingly, Spielberg served as executive producer. Unlike *Lifeforce*, *Gremlins* turned out to be commercially successful. Despite the film's grimmer, more pessimistic aspects, it is still largely considered family entertainment. Much like Hooper, Dante would go on to "crafting populist fare for Spielberg" (Kooyman 2014: 138) and reworking horror film tropes associated with the 1950s with his contributions to the 1980s reboot of *The Twilight Zone* (1985) and *Amazing Stories* (1986).

Another director whose career fits Biskind's narrative, albeit more loosely, is David Cronenberg. Affectionately dubbed by cult horror fans the "Baron of Blood," the Canadian director made a name for himself with a number of low-budget films – *Shivers* (1975), *Rabid* (1977), *The Brood* (1979), and *Scanners* (1981). Hollywood would come calling with *The Dead Zone* (1983), produced by Dino DeLaurentiis and distributed by Paramount. Based not on

Figure 5.2 Transgressiveness in the mainstream: *Gremlins* (Dante, USA, 1984). Warner Bros/Amblin Entertainment

original source material like all of Cronenberg's previous work, the film tried to cash in on the massive commercial success of writer Stephen King. Although *The Dead Zone* was not an outright failure, it remains a weak film, especially when compared to *The Fly* (1986), which enabled Cronenberg to work out tensions between his own auteurist visions and the demands of mainstream filmmaking. Subsequently, Cronenberg would succeed in negotiating a place for himself between mainstream and margin based on – or paid for by? – his gradual abandonment of genre conventions in favor of a unique auteurist vision.[5]

For a career untouched by Spielberg, one might turn to George Romero. Following the cult success of *Night of the Living Dead* (1968), Romero would go on for a while to make films with considerable subcultural cache, like *The Crazies* (1973) and *Martin* (1977). Even *Knightriders* (1981), a film outside the horror genre, would attain cult status. With its enlarged budget but sustained low-budget aesthetic, *Dawn of the Dead* (1978) still registers essentially as a cult film. Romero's commercial recognition would eventually come with the attempt to link his work with the mainstream success of Stephen King – first in *Creepshow* (1982), then again in *The Dark Half* (1993). As in the case of Cronenberg, Romero's collaboration would produce respectable and moderately successful films, although neither film would live up to the expectations raised around the director's relationship, established early on, to the subcultural capital of cult horror. By the time of his death in July of 2017, Romero would be remembered almost exclusively as the director of *Night of the Living Dead*.

Conclusion: The beginning and the end of cult horror

Produced in the margins of the culture, the more notable neo horror films would launch their directors into the cultural mainstream where, re-contained by a more restrained aesthetic and ideological framework, they would participate in the integration of the horror film into the broader cinematic canon. The conceptual mapping of horror would help to re-assess the potential of films preceding the 1960s and 1970s, a process leading to forgotten, neglected, or dismissed filmmakers and their films to be read and consumed as cult horror. It would also work as a category to be taken into consideration in the conceptualization, production, and marketing of films. Dwain Esper or Herschel Gordon Lewis never set out to make a cult horror film, and neither did Romero, Hooper, or Cronenberg. But contemporary filmmakers might. And 1970s neo horror showed them how. Cult cinema, it turns out, defines a quality that can be extracted, reproduced, and transferred. Cult horror will have to plot a course past this erosion of countercultural authenticity. If cult horror wants to avoid degenerating into an exercise in nostalgia for neo horror's greatest hits, it will have to reclaim cult cinema's risky "instability" not as "evidence of its redundancy as a valid concept" (Mathijs and Sexton 2011: 1) but as evidence of its capacity to evolve and adapt.

Notes

1 The tallying up of box office grosses vary slightly depending on accounting rules. While there is a consensus that *The Sixth Sense* earns the title as the highest grossing horror film so far, with *Jaws* as a close second, Christina Austin lists *Ghostbusters* and *The Exorcist*, respectively, in third and fourth place, while Hayley Cuccinello lists *I Am Legend* and *War of the Worlds* as bumping *The Exorcist* to fifth place on their lists. For a full list, see Cuccinello, *Forbes* (2015), and Austin, *Fortune* (2015). Entries in both lists also testify to the classificatory problems in defining what is and is not a horror film.
2 Ebert also points out a significant factor that would change around the time Romero's film was released, a factor of specific significance to the horror film:

> The new Code of Self Regulation, recently adopted by the Motion Picture Assn. of America, would presumably restrict a film like this one to mature audiences. But 'Night of the Living Dead' was produced before the MPAA code went into effect, so exhibitors technically weren't required to keep the kids out.

(Ebert 1969)

3 Andrew M. Gordon concludes that *Poltergeist* is "undeniably a Spielberg film because it has all the earmarks of one" (2008: 94), a conclusion supported by remarks by *Poltergeist* DP Matthew Leonetti. See Wamper (2017).
4 Considering that Ridley Scott had been "watching Tobe Hooper's *Texas Chainsaw Massacre*, and was aiming for the same bone-at-breaking-point tone" in preparing *Alien* (Shone 2004: 92), it is ironic that a director other than Hooper would succeed in marrying cult horror and mainstream success by learning from Hooper.
5 It is no coincidence that, as a member of a roundtable conversation with John Landis and John Carpenter, Cronenberg is the only one who disavows his link to the horror genre. For the full roundtable, see "FEAR ON FILM: Landis, Carpenter, Cronenberg" (1982).

References

Austin, Christina. 2015. "These Are the Top Grossing Horror Movies of All Time." *Fortune*, October 29. Accessed 15 May 2015. http://fortune.com/2015/10/29/top-grossing-horror-movies.
Biskind, Peter. 1998. *Easy Riders, Raging Bulls: How the Sex 'n' Drugs 'n' Rock 'n' Roll Generation Saved Hollywood*. New York: Simon & Schuster.
Cuccinello, Hayley C. 2015. "15 Highest Grossing Scary Movies of All-Time." *Forbes*, October 27. Accessed 15 May 2015. www.forbes.com/sites/hayleycuccinello/2015/10/27/15-highest-grossing-scary-movies-of-all-time/#ae2bb9256b84.
Ebert, Roger. 1969. "Review of *Night of the Living Dead*." Accessed 18 May 2015. www.rogerebert.com/reviews/the-night-of-the-living-dead-1968.
"FEAR ON FILM: Landis, Carpenter, Cronenberg." 1982. YouTube. Accessed 19 May 2015. www.youtube.com/watch?v=F9VfvUVrlgs.
Gordon, Andrew M. 2008. *Empire of Dreams: The Science Fiction and Fantasy Films of Steven Spielberg*. New York/Toronto: Rowman & Littlefield.
Harris, Mark. 2008. *Pictures at a Revolution: Five Movies and the Birth of the New Hollywood*. New York: Penguin.
Kooyman, Ben. 2014. *Directorial Self-Fashioning in American Horror Cinema: George A. Romero, Wes Craven, Rob Zombie, Eli Roth, and the Masters of Horror*. Lewiston, NY: Mellen Press.

Mathijs, Ernest, and Jamie Sexton. 2011. *Cult Cinema: An Introduction.* Malden: Wiley Blackwell.

Philipps, Kendall R. 2005. *Projected Fears: Horror Films and American Culture.* Westport, CT: Praeger.

Shone, Tom. 2004. *Blockbuster: How the Jaws and Jedi Generation Turned Hollywood into a Boomtown.* New York: Simon & Schuster.

Thornton, Sarah. 1996. *Club Cultures: Music, Media and Subcultural Capital.* Hanover, CT: Wesleyan University Press.

Wamper, Scott. 2017. "New Claims Suggest that Spielberg Really Did Direct *Poltergeist.*" *Birth. Movies.Death.* July 17. Accessed 23 March 2016. birthmoviesdeath.com/2017/07/17/new-claim-suggests-that-spielberg-really-did-direct-poltergeist.

6

CULT SCIENCE FICTION CINEMA

Mark Bould

Although science fiction (sf) – and numerous specific sf texts, authors, artists and directors – has attracted major fan followings, and many cult movies are also sf movies, there is surprisingly little critical work on sf as a cult phenomenon. Historically, from the perspective of sf studies, this is understandable, if hardly defensible. In the pages of the pulp and digest magazines which dominated the development of American sf from the 1920s until the 1960s, and in its organised fandom, and in the first academic journals and monographs devoted to the genre,[1] sf criticism was engaged in a cultural battle to demonstrate the genre's significance, seriousness and worthiness. Repeatedly this was accomplished by identifying some variety of sf (e.g., cosmic horror, planetary romance, science fantasy) as a debased and inferior version of the 'real' thing, and by differentiating sf from horror and fantasy. For example, in 1941, Wilson Tucker coined 'space opera' as a pejorative term – echoing soap opera and horse opera – to describe the 'hacky, grinding, stinking, outworn, spaceship yarn[s]' (Prucher 2007: 205) filling the pages of some sf pulps; three decades later, Darko Suvin insisted that the 'commercial lumping' of H.P. Lovecraft and other fantasy 'into the same category as SF is ... a grave disservice and rampantly socio-pathological phenomenon' (1979: 9).[2] Sf in all other media forms – comics, games, toys, radio, movies, television – was likewise treated as inherently lesser than prose sf. For example, Carl Freedman (1998) argues that the very nature of cinema means that, with the sole exception of *2001: A Space Odyssey* (Kubrick, 1968), no film can truly be sf (his logic is flawless, his premises less so). Consequently, and with some exceptions, sf studies did not engage seriously with film until the 1990s; even now, apart from *Science Fiction Film and Television*, Anglophone sf studies journals continue to privilege prose fiction, with less than ten per cent of their articles focusing on other media. Little wonder then that, when it comes to movies, sf studies has largely neglected a discourse as seemingly disreputable as 'cult'.

Despite sf's traditional coding as a masculine genre, film studies was slow to treat it seriously – partly because of its associations with spectacle, fantasy and juvenile audiences, and partly because sf is not as susceptible as westerns and crime movies to iconographic and structuralist theorisations of genre. Furthermore, sf has been rather a spectral presence in cult movie studies. Often acknowledged but only occasionally glimpsed, cult sf movies that are not *The Rocky Horror Picture Show* (Sharman, 1975) are rarely treated in detail.[3] This general neglect might also arise from cult movie studies' own anxieties about and cultural politics of legitimation.

With the study of horror films already relatively well established, cult movie studies had critical-theoretical resources to draw upon. Furthermore, with genre cinema's 'reimagining of … tropes through a more visceral and realistic style' not only 'challenging audiences with graphic nihilistic and often brutal imagery' but also blurring – or splattering – distinctions between sf and horror in the 1970s (Abbott 2015: 53), critical discussions of films by George Romero, Larry Cohen and David Cronenberg often downplayed their science-fictionality to treat them as horror movies. This tendency extended through the subsequent rise of video and of such directors as Stuart Gordon, Frank Henenlotter and Brian Yuzna. Consequently, there was a risk that the disreputable aura of low-budget, marginal or gory horror, which cult film studies could use to cultivate its own outsider 'bad-boy' status,[4] might evaporate in the face of an sf cinema whose growing budgets and increasing pop-cultural centrality made it just a little too respectable.

Arguably, cult film studies' spectralisation of sf is coming to an end. The first textbook on cult cinema devotes a chapter to the genre, there is now an edited collection about cult sf movies, and six of the first twelve *Cultographies* published since 2007 treat sf films.[5] However, that sextet of films also reinforces sf's spectralisation. It is unclear how many would regard *Bad Taste* (Jackson, 1987), *Donnie Darko* (Kelly, 2001), *Frankenstein* (Whale, 1931) and the inevitable *Rocky Horror* primarily as sf films, and while few would dispute that *Blade Runner* (Scott, 1982) and *They Live* (Carpenter, 1988) are sf, the former is equally significant as neo-noir and the latter, which nods heavily to the western, is as much a conspiracy thriller and an action movie. Once more, sf is glimpsed only to fade away, but this sense of elusiveness opens up useful ways to think about some of the appeals of cult cinema.

Jeffrey Weinstock identifies three kinds of fan activity in *Rocky Horror*'s audience participation repertoire. Predictive responses consist of phrases or sentences shouted out in the gaps between lines of dialogue, to which the subsequent line then appears to respond. Reactive responses are shout-outs that deliberately and humorously misconstrue. Simultaneous responses include throwing rice during the wedding scene and singing and dancing along with the film. Predictive and reactive responses interrupt the film, disrupt conventional processes of cinematic identification, and create ironic distantiation. They block interpellation and unsuture the subject, lending audiences a sense of mastery over the film, since it 'appears powerless to resist' and 'subject to [their] commands' (2007: 48). In contrast, simultaneous responses demonstrate not the desire to control the film, but 'to "be" the film, to dissolve the boundaries between the cinematic world … and the real world … and to "submit" to the film' (41). Of course, the film itself remains indifferent to these antics, prompting cult fans sadistically to denigrate it and compulsively to return and repeat the experience.

The cinema culture that enabled such experiences has more or less passed, giving rise to other modes of attempted mastery and immersion. Just as the VCR and video cassette began to overcome the issue of cult movie scarcity, so they – and subsequent domestic viewing apparatuses – also transformed viewing situations and practices. The problem of *getting* a cult movie has changed. It has shifted from gaining access to a screening, to a midnight crowd and to ancillary information through magazines and books, and become more strongly about accumulating and mastering detail through repeated viewings with the aid of pause and rewind and zoom functions, alongside print and electronic sources. However, cult aficionados typically use this stock of knowledge not to pin down a singular meaning, but to approach the film in a condition that enables its meaning to remain open and thus capable of generating an endless, shifting engagement (Hills 2011: 8). To sustain such activity, the films themselves must 'contain gaps, irresolutions, contradictions, which both allow and invite fan productivity' (Fiske 1992: 42). Such gaps range from the contradictory information and fractal design of *Blade Runner* to the sorts of metadiegesis 'industrially normalised by latter-day convergence cults'

(Hills 2011: 15) and typically developed through such transmedia sf franchises as the *Star Wars*, Marvel and DC universes.

Repeated and prolonged engagement is also invited by puzzle films, the characteristics of which, according to Barbara Klinger, include:

> a complex, atypical, multilayered narrative (that experiments with temporal order, for example); a confusion of objective and subjective realms; a visually dense style; an ending that depends upon a reversal or surprise that makes viewers reevaluate their experience with the text; and the presence of an initially occult meaning that requires re-viewing to uncover the text's mysteries.
>
> (2006: 157; cf Elsaesser 2009)

She mentions only two sf puzzle movies – *2001: A Space Odyssey* (Kubrick, 1968) and *The Matrix* (Wachowski siblings, 1999) – but there are many more. They often feature time-travel, multiple realities, multiple personalities, obscured histories and/or parallel universes, as in *Videodrome* (Cronenberg, 1983), *eXistenZ* (Cronenberg, 1999), *Cypher* (Natali, 2002), *Primer* (Carruth, 2004), *Timecrimes* (Vigalondo, 2007), *Fish Story* (Nakamura, 2009), *Mr Nobody* (Van Dormael, 2009), *Detention* (Kahn, 2011), *Looper* (Johnson, 2012), *Upstream Color* (Carruth, 2013), *Predestination* (Spierig brothers, 2014) and *The Signal* (Eubank, 2014). Some of them fascinate through their intricacy, the rigour and neatness of their structure; some through the ways in which these qualities fail; and others through the impossibility of resolving their ambiguities. What they and the other varieties of open(ed) films have in common is their invitation to the audience's 'creative readiness' and 'heuristic hope' (Hills 2011: 11). They appeal to an epistemophilic desire to know and thus to master that ultimately can never be fulfilled. As with the audience responses Weinstock describes, puzzling away at puzzle movies performs 'the failure of not only [the cultists'] desires, but of cinematic desire in general' (2007: 40).

Let us now turn to three related cult sf movies which model these desires through the quest for some great whatsit, some *objet petit a*, in the city on the edge of a civilisation turning back on itself: Robert Aldrich's *Kiss Me Deadly* (1955), Alex Cox's *Repo Man* (1984) and Richard T. Kelly's *Southland Tales* (2006). Each of them has the textual fractures and kind of chequered history that leads to cult appreciation. *Kiss Me Deadly*, which was denounced by the Kefauver Commission, opens with famously mismatched shots and soundtrack, and for decades circulated with a truncated, bleaker ending. Universal shelved *Repo Man* after a handful of poor screenings, and only released it because the soundtrack album was doing so well for another division of the company. Cox scripted a sequel he could not get made, which eventually became the graphic novel *Waldo's Hawaiian Holiday* (2008), and his thematically related non-sequel *Repo Chick* (2009) was subject to a cease-and-desist order from Universal, who were finally releasing the unrelated *Repo Men* (Sapochnik, 2010). The $17 million *Southland Tales* suffered a disastrous reception at Cannes, where a 160-minute rough cut with incomplete special effects was in competition for the Palm d'Or. Kelly cut 25 minutes from it in exchange for funding to complete the effects, and it eventually took less than $400,000 at the global box office. Kelly's plan for six prequel graphic novels, to be published at monthly intervals before its release, was also cut back, to just three volumes.

Kiss Me Deadly

I first encountered *Kiss Me Deadly* as a geeky teen, reading Phil Hardy's *The Aurum Film Encyclopedia: Science Fiction* (1984) from cover to cover. That is, I first encountered it as an sf film, not as a film noir. Hardy's scant paragraphs do not make clear why it should be considered sf, although they point to its apocalyptic conclusion and the replacement of the narcotics in Mickey Spillane's 1952 source novel of the same name (give or take a comma) with stolen nuclear materials.[6] This zone of heuristic uncertainty – *Kiss Me Deadly* did not sound much like an sf film, but was listed as such in an apparently authoritative source – did not collapse when I saw the movie a few years later. Despite intuiting the rightness of the claim that this most noirish of noirs is also an sf movie, I was left puzzled and puzzling. And since I lack the quick wits of Ralph Meeker's lunk-headed Mike Hammer – who somehow navigates the improbable connection between an about-to-be-murdered woman's plea to be remembered and the 'clue' hidden in Christina Rossetti sonnet 'Remember' (1862)[7] – it took me repeated viewings over several years to grasp the film's profound science-fictionality.

If, as William Gibson is reputed to have said, 'the future is already here, it's just not very evenly distributed', then we 'must be able to comprehend the present as a becoming' (Lukács 1971: 204), to see within it not only potential futures but also the systems of power which sustain that uneven distribution. *Kiss Me Deadly*'s science-fictionality stems, then, from its depiction of a mid-1950s LA in terms of the maldistributed futurity intrinsic to a capitalist economy. Hammer lives in a world in which chunks of the future are already embedded; his Wilshire Boulevard *Playboy* bachelor pad comes complete with a wall-mounted, reel-to-reel telephone answering machine, a television that looks like the sleek offspring of a jukebox and Robbie the Robot, and lampshades that resemble flying saucers.[8] Such commodity futurity is emphasised in the contrasts between his lifestyle and the depressed dwellings, battered belongings and shabby clothing of truck-driver Harvey Wallace (Strother Martin) or down-on-his-luck opera singer Carmen Trivago (Fortunio Bonanova). Although the mobster Carl Evello (Paul Stewart) is much wealthier than Hammer, his mansion belongs to an older era; the dully representational art on his walls tie him to an outmoded past, especially in comparison to the modernist works in Hammer's apartment, laden with a futurity implied by the as-yet unsold contemporary works in William Mist's gallery.

As the withering assessment of Hammer's narcissistic disconnection offered by Christina (Cloris Leachman) after just a few minutes in his company implies, he treats his body as an extension of his Jaguar XK120 convertible. His corporeal maintenance and grooming – a cyborgic veneer over his sadistic brutality – is central, so Interstate Crime Commissioners suggest, to his business as a 'bedroom dick': he honeytraps wives, uses his secretary/girlfriend Velda (Maxine Cooper) to honeytrap their husbands, and then plays them off against each other. In this, all social relations, however intimate they might otherwise be, are reduced to the cash-nexus, to 'naked self-interest' and 'callous "cash payment"': 'the most heavenly ecstasies' are 'drowned … in the icy water of egotistical calculation'; 'personal worth' is 'resolved … into exchange value'; and 'the family relation' is 'reduced … to a mere money relation' (Marx and Engels 1967: 82). Introjected from the future back into the bedrooms of 1950s Los Angeles is the logic of a more thoroughly ubiquitous capitalism. Out on the edge of the continent, where there is no longer a physical frontier, Hammer pursues the great whatsit with all the machinic stupidity of an early model Terminator.

Throughout the film, female characters are reduced to sex – often parodically, as when Gabrielle aka Lily Carver (Gaby Rodgers) and Friday (Marion Carr) throw themselves, with excessive implausibility, into Hammer's arms – or to their ability to exchange sex, or the promise of it, for material reward. Like commodities, they are presented as always available to the senses and for consumption, always promising, and of course always failing, to fulfil desire.[9] This is echoed in two of mythological allusions – 'Pandora's box' and 'the head of the Medusa' – the preposterous Dr Soberin (Albert Dekker) uses to describe, and thus not describe, the container of stolen nuclear materials. Images of female sexual difference and lack, they evoke desire and provoke castration anxiety as well as reiterating the lure and inevitable disappointment of the commodity.[10]

Repo Man

If I cannot recall exactly when I first saw *Kiss Me Deadly*, I do remember rewatching it on BBC2 on 12 September 1994. Alex Cox's introduction to it, the final film in his seven-year tenure as BBC2's *Moviedrome* host, ended: 'There are those who say the plot of *Kiss Me Deadly* has been lifted for various films. Among them, *Repo Man*.' As with Aldrich's film, I first encountered Cox's directorial debut in ancillary material – a bootleg tape of the soundtrack album, featuring not only Iggy Pop but Black Flag (love), Circle Jerks (like), Suicidal Tendencies (take or leave) and other, lesser lights and lighter lessers from the US hardcore punk scene. For a working-class kid in a provincial forces town in the era of the New Romantics, such music, virtually unattainable, was a lifeline – another great whatsit. When I saw the film a couple of years later (on a pirated VHS with dodgy sound), I felt something vast and inexplicable – but very important – at the moment when Otto (Emilio Estevez) gets up from the LA dust and starts to sing Black Flag's 'TV Party'. The track has already played in a party scene, just after some uncredited Minor Threat (love), but at that moment, when Otto chooses it in particular, it was as if someone understood what this sound from another time and place could mean.

While Aldrich reorients *Kiss Me Deadly* towards the future by relocating it from New York to LA, Alex Cox uses LA to reveal the grim neoliberal future already unfurling in the 1980s. *Repo Man*'s opening credits play over an animated road map, green graphics on a black backdrop, flickering and jolting and changing scale as it charts the path of scientist J. Frank Parnell (Fox Harris) westwards along, of course, Route 66, from Los Alamos through New Mexico, Arizona and Nevada towards California. This trajectory not only repeats the path of Aldrich's great whatsit, bringing the nuclear threat – or is it aliens recovered from a crashed UFO? – into the heart of the metropolis, but also underpins the film's hollowing out of the mythology of the American west. For example, after whatever is in the trunk of Parnell's Chevy Malibu vaporises a highway patrolman (Varnum Honey), the opening scene ends with a tuneless rendition of 'Oh, My Darling Clementine', the 1884 ballad about the 1849 California Gold Rush which opens John Ford's similarly-named 1946 western (seemingly unaware that it was actually a parody of such western folksongs). The film cuts to a Pik'n'Pay supermarket in LA, where shelf-stacker Otto is fired for absurdly petty reasons. The security guard (Luis Contreras) unnecessarily draws his revolver and, before reholstering it, just as unnecessarily twirls it like a gunfighter. Elsewhere, the film alludes to *Taxi Driver* (Scorsese, 1976), itself a disillusioned rewrite of the already-bleak *The Searchers* (Ford, 1956), but instead of Scorsese's Catholic vision of the nocturnal city as an inferno, *Repo Man* presents us with the dry, dusty, sun-worn desert of the real. The sublime landscapes of the American west is reduced to junkyards and convenience stores, tabloids and televangelists, homelessness and debt – a place where it is possible for Kevin (Zander Schloss), fired from Pik'n'Pay just for being Otto's friend, to imagine that becoming a fry cook will be the key to geographical and social mobility. Some 90 years after the closing of the American frontier, this is what has been wrought, not the democratic egalitarianism that Frederick Jackson Turner claimed, but alienated, monadic individuals, held together by the most tenuous of social bonds and by the economic fetters of late capitalism. In this immiserated LA, it is no longer clear where futurity resides; like capital, it is concentrated elsewhere.

Repo Man's ironic deflation of American mythology is best captured by Bud (Harry Dean Stanton), Otto's repo man mentor. In 'The Simple Art of Murder' (1944), Raymond

Chandler described the hard-boiled private detective as an incorruptible man, lonely and proud, with an unassuming sense of honour and justice, who walks down the mean streets of a world so unfragrant that corruption and violence are the norm. If Spillane's Mike Hammer, revealed as a crypto-fascist bully by Aldrich, is the mutant progeny of Chandler's Philip Marlowe, Bud is an equally if differently damaged descendent. He has utterly internalised the demands of capital. He advocates semiotic intimidation (dressing like a detective) and amphetamine use, both of which serve to maximise the surplus value that can be extracted from his labour, while preferring to be paid a commission rather than a regular wage, which reduces the amount of actual labour for which his employer must pay. He also decries the evils of carpooling and argues that 'credit is a sacred trust; it's what our free society is founded on'. Driving the streets at night, he evinces 'the Repo Code', which is not a code so much as a series of boasts about the proficiency with which he performs his otherwise thankless role. The nearest he comes to articulating a moral precept is the injunction: 'Thou shalt not cause harm to any vehicle nor the personal contents thereof, nor through inaction let that vehicle or the personal contents thereof come to harm'. Whatever grandiosity this pseudo-archaic, pseudo-forensic language lends his quietly desperate efforts to construct his labour as somehow noble and epic is undermined by its obvious echo of the first of Isaac Asimov's three laws of robotics: 'A robot may not injure a human being or, through inaction, allow a human being to come to harm'.

In *Repo Man*'s LA, the only share of the maldistributed future available is this kind of intensified reduction of the self to one's labour power. There are no pocket-utopias of commodities or – with one fleeting exception – libidinal fulfilment dotting this landscape. Bud pursues the Chevy Malibu not for the car itself or for the mystery it contains, but for the $20,000 bounty placed on it by the covert Department of Investigation, with which he hopes to open his own repossession business. All of his dreams for the future are bound up in the system of credit – that is, debt – and upon individual's defaulting on repayments in sufficient numbers that he can carve out a space in which to compete for potential profits. It is the film's most brilliantly proleptic move, its most science-fictional moment of extrapolation. Contrary to Bud's ahistorical perception of credit, his chances of long-term success would rest largely on neoliberalism's massive expansion, then still in its early stages, of consumer credit. It would depend on a future much like our present coming into being, a future in which 'U.S. household debt is now estimated at on average 130 percent of income' (Graeber 2011: 379; cf Lazzarato 2012).

In the final moments of the film, however, the Chevy becomes something other than a business opportunity. Bud, who is dying from a gunshot wound, and Otto climb into the eerily glowing car, and it rises into the night sky, taking them on a joyride over the LA and then apparently jumping into hyperspace. As an image of transcendence it is simultaneously utopian and absurd: a slingshot out of the perpetual and perpetuated present, a potential break with the already existing future that is locked into place by the mechanisms of credit and debt, but also, as the film well knows, no kind of solution at all.

Southland Tales

I first saw *Southland Tales* on DVD in the second week of May 2008; I had just come back from a conference in California, a coincidence that prompted an overly excited exclamation when Dwayne 'The Rock' Johnson stood in exactly the same spot in Venice Beach's Small World Books where just a few days earlier I had been.

Kiss Me Deadly plays on TV screens in the background of various scenes, and Kelly's film is full of allusions to it: Starla Van Luft (Michelle Durret) urges Boxer Santaros (Dwayne Johnson) 'remember me'; there are even characters called Dr Soberin (Curtis Armstrong) and Kefauver (Lou Taylor Pucci). It borrows elements of its conclusion from *Repo Man*, and like Cox's film it nods frequently to the work of Philip K. Dick. The generic products lining the shelves of *Repo Man* – culminating in a tin labelled 'FOOD' and a six pack of 'DRINK' – 'present a culture whose identical and homogenized nourishment belies its cosmetic diversification and fragmentation' (Sobchack 1991: 245). They are also inspired by conceits that Dick deployed in *Time out of Joint* (1959), *The Three Stigmata of Palmer Eldritch* (1965) and *Ubik* (1969) to underscore the manipulative instrumentalism and empty promises of commodity culture. In *Southland Tales*, Zora (Cheri Oteri) is only one letter away from *Blade Runner*'s Zhora (Joanna Cassidy), and when policeman Bart Bookman (Jon Lovitz) says, with mock remorse after gunning down two people, 'Flow my tears', he enacts the title of a 1974 Dick novel.[11] Beyond such allusions, the film is full of Phildickian moments, such as the sequence in which Ronald Taverner, posing as his twin brother Roland Taverner, realises his reflection in the bathroom mirror has gone out of synch with his movements. It later transpires that they are not actually twins, but – of course – two versions of the same person caused by a rift in space-time. Boxer Santaros, adversely affected by the same phenomenon and the subject of a complex, multilayered conspiracy, begins to confuse himself with Jericho Cane, the protagonist of a screenplay he has written (or, rather, has been led to believe he has written). Late in the film, he meets Simon Theory (Kevin Smith), who confirms that the ridiculous screenplay is only superficially a work of fiction; in fact, it reveals the truth of the impending apocalypse. The meeting, however, yet of course, might be just an hallucination.

In contrast to *Repo Man*'s enervated and decrepit desert of the real, *Southland Tales* is set in an extended hyperreal present in which it is utterly natural for porn star Krista Now (Sarah Michelle Gellar) to develop a personal brand that includes lines of jewellery, clothing and perfume, an energy drink, a debut album and single called 'Teen Horniness is Not a Crime', and a 'topical discussion chat reality show' in which she and other performers chew over such pressing issues as 'abortion, terrorism, crime, poverty, social reform, quantum teleportation, teen horniness and war'. In this Baudrillardian very-near future, cameras and screens are a constant, mediating present, often poised between diegesis and extra-diegetic exposition. It is through a domestic video camera that we learn of the terrorist nuclear attacks on Abilene and El Paso three years earlier, but this footage flows into the broadcast news media through which we learn that, in response, citizens now require visas to cross the newly-militarised borders between states; that government agencies have taken control of the internet; that surveillance is almost ubiquitous; and that, alongside this intensified suppression of domestic civil liberties, the United States has expanded and escalated its wars in the middle east – so much so that 'the war machine is running out of gas', prompting the quest for an alternative energy source, such as Fluid Karma, a kind of wireless electricity developed by the wizard Baron von Wesphalen (Wallace Shawn) that utilises quantum entanglement to operate at a distance. This imaginative conceit, this new great whatsit, crystallises a deeper and hitherto unrecognised connection between the three films.

Kiss Me Deadly, obsessed with automobiles and nuclear power, was made around one of the times from which the anthropocene – the period of time in which human activity has altered significant geological conditions and processes – is sometimes dated: the global spread of carbon isotopes from the Trinity nuclear tests of 1945 and postwar consumerism's expansion of petroculture, particularly through the mass production of plastics.[12] *Repo Man* is also centred on the expansion of car culture and atomic weapons.[13] Towards the end of the film, Parnell tells Otto about a scientist who was driven mad by working on the neutron bomb because it is so immoral. He had to have a lobotomy, as a result of which the hemispheres of his brain are now fundamentally at odds with each other, but at least he is able to continue his work.

Parnell is clearly talking about himself, or at least one half of his brain is. *Southland Tales* brings this anthropocene unconscious to the surface, as sf is so well-equipped to do, and offers a pair of solutions. On the one hand, there is Fluid Karma, which like all such technological fixes cascades consequences and new problems in need of fixes (see Foster et al.). There is talk of a mysterious red substance now washing up on California's shores, and of the Earth's rotation slowing down by tiny daily increments (the latter might just be in Boxer's screenplay, rather than reality, but in this hyperreality who can tell the difference?). On the other hand, there are two potential slingshots into transcendence. As the climax approaches, and as if in response to the film's frequent references to the Book of Revelation, Boxer's back tattoo of Jesus begins to bleed like a stigmata; but just as this bloody Christ seeps into visibility through his immaculate white shirt, Boxer – and everyone else aboard the mega-zeppelin – is killed by a missile strike. It was just a momentary misdirection. The Rock cannot save us; he is not the new messiah. For that, we must look elsewhere, to – in the words of Pilot Abilene (Justin Timberlake) – 'Roland Taverner from Hermosa Beach, California'. In the back of an ice cream truck flying, like *Repo Man*'s Chevy Malibu, over LA, Ronald and Roland forgives himself, and in doing so triggers some kind of mystical renewal, the nature and consequences of which go undepicted. As with *Repo Man*, this utopian passage is absurd, and no kind of solution at all.

Initially, it invites frustration and disappointment because, while fulfilling the formal function of a conclusion, it remains desperately inconclusive. However, for a film whose 'compositional logic ... is paratactic and additive', refusing 'conventional film syntax' and 'hierarchical organization' of its elements, and refusing 'linear causality' and 'action grounded in character', in favour of a network of 'correspondences and connections', 'juxtaposition[s], dreamlike free association[s]' and proliferating 'referential feedback loops' (Shaviro 2010: 70–74), what other choice could there be? Indeed, the film's recurring inversion of the final stanza of T.S. Eliot's 'The Hollow Men' (1925), promising that the world will end not with a whimper but a bang, presages precisely such a termination. There is no other way for the film plausibly to wind up. It must just stop. While the film's dispersed and ambient narrative, and its proliferation of screens, tend 'to dissolve the boundaries between the cinematic world ... and the real world' (Weinstock 2007: 41), the conclusion reinforces the contrary effect of alienation and desuturing that viewers seeking a more conventional cinematic experience might have felt throughout. Either way, the cult viewer's epistemophilia – and 'cinematic desire in general' (40) – fail.

But still we return.

After all, the great whatsit is still out there. Always.

Notes

1 For example, *Extrapolation* (1959–) and *Science Fiction Studies* (1973–), and Suvin (1979).
2 As Roger Luckhurst (1994) argues, sf is continuously constituted by legitimation crises, from the canonisation of certain magazines over others (in the 1940s, John W. Campbell's *Astounding* over Macolm Reiss's *Planet Stories* or Raymond Palmer's *Amazing*), through battles in the 1960s and 1970s over New Wave sf and in the 1980s over cyberpunk, through the development of slipstream as a boundary discourse (see Frelik 2011), to the Rabid Puppies' recent efforts to subvert the Hugo Awards through nomination- and voting- slates (in order to promote the often right-wing futuristic military adventure fiction they prefer, and some of them write and publish, and thus to save the genre from the malign influence of a cabal of 'social justice warriors' and literati who are just plain ruining it for everyone else). In the case of cult movies, similar dynamics and hierarchies are observed in audience differentiations between established and uninitiated viewers of *Rocky Horror*, early adopting and post–*Lord of the Rings* fans of *Bad Taste*, those who prefer the more ambiguous original version to the explication-heavy director's cut of *Donnie Darko*, and the masculinised connoisseur rather than the feminised mass audience of cult blockbuster *Star Wars* (see, respectively, Weinstock 2007, Barratt 2008, King 2007, and Hills 2003).

3 See, for example, Telotte 1991, Harper and Mendik 2001, Jancovich et al. 2003, Mathijs and Mendik 2008.
4 See Hollows 2003 and Read 2003.
5 See Mathijs and Sexton 2011, Telotte and Duchovnay 2015, King 2007, Weinstock 2007, Barratt 2008, Hills 2011, Horton 2014 and Wilson 2015.
6 The rather different description in Hardy's belated companion volume on gangster films offers some oblique clues in its evocation of post-nuclear abstraction and paranoia.
7 In the novel, the clue that the murdered woman swallowed the key is much more straightforward, a note that reads '*The way to a man's heart—*' (118).
8 On the *Playboy* bachelor pad, see Cohan 1997: 267–275. On the significance of lampshades, see Bould 2015.
9 The unnamed caretaker's wife (Jesslyn Fax) at Christina's apartment building and the taciturn manager (Marjorie Bennett) at Carmen's residential hotel offer important contrasts. They both perform the kinds of domestic labour that is typically unwaged and treated as an external in economic calculations, in the former case brought close to, and in the later transformed into, waged labour. Treated as grotesques rather than erotic objects, they promise neither sexual nor domestic fulfilment while clearly also working to create commodified simulations of the latter for residents.
10 Such a mapping together of nuclear materials and female sexuality is not uncommon in the decade following the Hiroshima and Nagasaki bombings, when American culture seemed uncertain whether it should instead focus on the utopian possibilities of the atom. In 1945, *Life* described model and actress Linda Christian as 'the anatomic bomb'; the following year, the two-piece swimsuit was named after the Bikini Atoll, a site of US nuclear weapon tests; and in 'Thirteen Woman (And Only One Man in Town)' (1954), Bill Haley was capable of finding among the glowing wreckage of an H-bomb attack a libidinal utopia in which sundry women euphemistically butter his bread and sweeten his tea.
11 *Flow My Tears, the Policeman Said*, the protagonist of which is called Jason Taverner.
12 Some suggest the anthropocene coincides with more or less the entire Holocene epoch (i.e., the last 12,000 years, since the Neolithic or Agricultural revolution); more commonly it is dated from the late eighteenth century turn to coal and steam power, which led to the industrial revolution and the later oil economy.
13 Until late in the shoot, the film was supposed to end with the Chevy's trunk being opened and the ensuing nuclear blast engulfing LA. Executive producer Mike Nesmith abruptly told Cox and his producers, Peter McCarthy and Jonathan Wacks, to change the ending, although none of them seem sure of who actually wrote it; in interview, they each always attribute it to one or more of the others.

References

Abbott, Stacey. 2015. '"It's Alive!":' The Splattering of SF Films'. *Science Fiction Double Feature: The Science Fiction Film as Cult Text*. Ed. J.P. Telotte and Gerald Duchovnay. Liverpool: Liverpool University Press: 53–67.
Barratt, Jim. 2008. *Bad Taste*. London: Wallflower Press.
Bould, Mark. 2015. 'The Coy Cult Text: *The Man Who Wasn't There* as Noir SF'. *Science Fiction Double Feature: The Science Fiction Film as Cult Text*. Ed. J.P. Telotte and Gerald Duchovnay. Liverpool: Liverpool University Press: 38–52.
Cohan, Steven. 1997. *Masked Men: Masculinity and the Movies in the Fifties*. Bloomington: Indiana University Press.
Elsaesser, Thomas. 2009. 'The Mind-Game Film'. *Puzzle Films: Complex Storytelling in Contemporary Cinema*. Ed. Warren Buckland. Malden: Wiley-Blackwell: 13–41.
Fiske, John. 1992. 'The Cultural Economy of Fandom'. *The Adoring Audience: Fan Culture and Popular Media*. Ed. Lisa Lewis. London: Routledge: 30–49.
Foster, John Bellamy, Brett Clark and Richard York. 2010. *The Ecological Rift: Capitalism's War on the Earth*. New York: Monthly Review Press.
Freedman, Carl 1998. 'Kubrick's *2001* and the Possibility of a Science-Fiction Cinema'. *Science Fiction Studies* 75: 300–318.
Frelik, Paweł. 2011. 'Of Slipstream and Others: SF and Genre Boundary Discourses'. *Science Fiction Studies* 113: 20–45.
Graeber, David. 2011. *Debt: The First 5,000 Years*. Brooklyn: Melville.

Hardy, Phil, ed. 1984 *The Aurum Film Encyclopedia: Science Fiction*. London: Aurum.
———. 1998. *The Aurum Film Encyclopedia: Gangsters*. London: Aurum.
Harper, Graeme, and Xavier Mendik, eds. 2001. *Unruly Pleasures: The Cult Film and Its Critics*. Guildford: FAB Press.
Hills, Matt. 2003. '*Star Wars* in Fandom, Film Theory, and the Museum: The Cultural Status of the Cult Blockbuster'. *Movie Blockbusters*. Ed. Julian Stringer. London: Routledge: 178–189.
———. 2011. *Blade Runner*. New York: Wallflower/Columbia University Press.
Hollows, Joanne. 2003. 'The Masculinity of Cult'. *Defining Cult Movies: The Cultural Politics of Oppositional Taste*. Ed. Jancovich et al. Manchester: Manchester University Press: 35–53.
Horton, Robert. 2014. *Frankenstein*. New York: Wallflower/Columbia University Press.
Jancovich, Mark, Antonio Lázaro-Reboll, Julian Stringer and Andy Willis, eds. 2003. *Defining Cult Movies: The Cultural Politics of Oppositional Taste*. Manchester: Manchester University Press.
King, Geoff. 2007. *Donnie Darko*. London: Wallflower Press.
Klinger, Barbara. 2006. *Beyond the Multiplex: Cinema, New Technologies, and the Movies*. Berkeley: University of California Press.
Lazzarato, Maurizio. 2012. *The Making of Indebted Man*. Trans. Joshua David Jordan. Los Angeles: Semiotext(e).
Luckhurst, Roger. 1994. 'The Many Deaths of Science Fiction: A Polemic'. *Science Fiction Studies* 62: 35–50.
Lukács, Georg. 1971. *History and Class Consciousness: Studies in Marxist Dialectics*. Trans. Rodney Livingstone. London: Merlin Press.
Marx, Karl, and Friedrich Engels. 1967. *The Communist Manifesto*. Trans. Samuel Moore. London: Penguin.
Mathijs, Ernest, and Xavier Mendik, eds. 2008. *The Cult Film Reader*. Maidenhead: Open University Press.
Mathijs, Ernest, and Jamie Sexton. 2011. *Cult Cinema*. Malden: Wiley-Blackwell.
Prucher, Jeff, ed. 2007. *Brave New Words: The Oxford Dictionary of Science Fiction*. Oxford: Oxford University Press.
Read, Jacinda. 2003. 'The Cult of Masculinity: From Fan-boys to Academic Bad-boys'. *Defining Cult Movies: The Cultural Politics of Oppositional Taste*. Ed. Jancovich et al. Manchester: Manchester University Press: 54–70.
Shaviro, Steven. 2010. *Post Cinematic Affect*. Winchester: Zero.
Sobchack, Vivian. 1991. *Screening Space: The American Science Fiction Film*. New York: Ungar.
Spillane, Mickey. 1975. *Kiss Me, Deadly*. London: Corgi.
Suvin, Darko. 1979. *Metamorphoses of Science Fiction: On the Poetics and History of a Literary Genre*. New Haven, CT: Yale University Press.
Telotte, J.P., ed. 1991. *The Cult Film Experience: Beyond All Reason*. Austin: University of Texas Press.
Telotte, J.P., and Gerald Duchovnay, eds. 2015. *Science Fiction Double Feature: The Science Fiction Film as Cult Text*. Liverpool: Liverpool University Press.
Weinstock, Jeffrey. 2007. *The Rocky Horror Picture Show*. London: Wallflower Press.
Wilson, D. Harlan. 2015. *They Live*. New York: Wallflower/Columbia University Press.

7

CULT COMEDY CINEMA AND THE CULTIC, COMIC MODE

Seth Soulstein

"Cult films," note the editors of *Cinéaste*'s special issue on cult film, "make us feel less alone in the dark" (Lucia and Porton 2008: 6). Consistently, attempts to distinguish cult films from any other film emphasize the "phenomenal" and "collective" (Mathijs and Sexton 2011: 17–19) nature of the cult film viewer's experience. There is a similar powerful force that binds audiences together, generating an embodied, collective experience of community that cuts through darkness: laughter. It would follow, then, that the quintessential genre for cult film enthusiasts, the niche within the niche, would be comedy. Indeed, in his 1932 essay "Film Cults," often considered to be the starting point of the scholarly and critical analysis of cult cinema, Harry Alan Potamkin locates the beginning of cult film spectatorship in the French fascination with American slapstick comedy, stating early on, for example, that "[Charlie] Chaplin was the key cult" (Potamkin 2008: 26). Yet, setting aside the wide array of film genres that don't seem to consistently generate cult followings – Westerns, romances, bio-pics, and so on – comedy is often the most overlooked genre in studies of cult cinema and in the inevitable "Top __ Cult Films" lists. Two notable lists, separated by three decades, Danny Peary's *Cult Movies: The Classics, the Sleepers, the Weird, and the Wonderful*, and Ernest Mathijs and Xavier Mendik's list in *100 Cult Films*, for example, each boast less than ten comedies in their hundred-film lists (five and six, respectively, by my count, though this is somewhat difficult to discern – a phenomenon we will discuss further on). Furthermore, academic monographs and anthologies devoted to cult film, such as *Cult Cinema: an introduction* (Mathijs and Sexton) or *Sleaze Artists: Cinema at the Margins of Taste, Style, and Politics* (Sconce), have chapters devoted to specific genres, such as horror and sci-fi – but never to comedy. Why is it so difficult to find comedies represented in such cultographies? Does something about the genre itself subvert or otherwise defy categorization as cult? Are cinephiles unable to form the same level of attachment or religious devotion to simply funny flicks? Comedies are often overlooked in academic and critical approaches to not only film, but television, theatre, literature, etc.; is comedy too low an art form for even the cultists – supposed celebrants of the "cheap," the "bad," or the "low" – to respect? Or, conversely, is it not low enough? To attempt to answer these questions, it will be helpful to go back to the origins of Western cult behavior and examine the comic stamp within it.

While sociologist Emile Durkheim is often mentioned as one of the originators of the term "cult" as it is used today (Hills 2009); Mathijs and Mendik 2008), cult behavior of course existed well before the modern moment. One of the earliest "cults" in the western world was the ancient Greek cult in honor of the god Dionysus. Dionysus (a.k.a. Bacchus), the god of wine and revelry, was associated with "darkness, nocturnal drinking bouts, and the loss of mental clarity in moments of collective emotion, with the loss of boundaries around the self experienced in a crowd and the hiding of self behind a theatrical mask" (Wiles 2000: 7). These associations fit neatly into the framework of the carnivalesque, as described centuries later by Mikhail Bakhtin. Bakhtin sees carnival celebration – the regular, temporary suspension of normative hierarchies and customs – as an essential component of any culture, existing outside of officialdom and shaped according to a pattern of play – and most importantly, inherently linked with comedy and the comic. "[C]arnival is the people's second life," he notes, "organized on the basis of laughter" (Bakhtin 1984: 8), represented by clowns and fools. Bakhtin's concept of carnival laughter, as Domnica Radulescu points out, is not "superior, sarcastic, distanced laughter … but a laughter which brings people together and blurs differences" (Radulescu 2012: 33).

In honor of Dionysus, ritual celebrations were held four times a year, centering on performance – specifically, comedic performance. A through line in many analyses of cult film consumption is its ritual nature; "cult cinema reception relies on ritualized manners of celebration" (Mathijs and Mendik 2008: 4), note Mathijs and Mendik, echoing Walter Benjamin's assertion that "the earliest art works originated in the service of a ritual … it is significant that the existence of the work of art with reference to its aura is never entirely separated from its ritual function" (Benjamin: 33). Performance scholar and anthropologist Richard Schechner sees ritualized performance extending back to the Paleolithic era, all the time with a clear distinction between theatrical performance (classified as entertainment) and ritual performance (classified as efficacy). He charts key characteristics of theatre/entertainment as, among others, "individual creativity; audience watches; audience appreciates," while ritual/efficacy is characterized by "collective creativity; audience participates; audience believes" (Schechner 1994: 622). Cult films depend on audience participation and collective creativity; J. Hoberman, for example, explains, "[a] cult film is created by its audience. The audience 'remakes' the movie – sometimes, especially these days, literally" (Briggs et al. 2008: 44). And the mantra of "paradigmatic cult film" (Wood 1991: 156) *Rocky Horror Picture Show*, "Don't dream it, be it" is the perfect distillation of the difference between an audience appreciating vs. believing in the cult experience. In ancient Athenian culture, "[T]here is no clear dividing line between theatre and ritual," notes Wiles; "[a] comic performance was itself a competitive ritual performed in honour of the god Dionysos" (Wiles 2000: 29). Thus the plays of comic playwrights, such as Aristophanes and Menander, became the centerpieces of larger ritual, comic celebration – much like the celebration around a screening of *The Room* today does not entirely begin and end with the film's opening and closing credits.

Scholars of comedy tend to locate a bridge between ancient comedy and the comedy of the twentieth and twenty-first centuries in the *commedia dell'arte* of Renaissance Italy and elsewhere in Europe. During this time, small troupes of comedic performers traveled throughout much of Western Europe, putting on performances that were part-improvised and part-scripted, anchored by scenarios that described the various *lazzi* (comic "bits") that made up a performance. A visit from a *commedia* troupe, with its promise of social satire, comic inversions and structured chaos, punctuated the year in the same manner as other Bakhtinian carnival ceremonies and rituals do.

Besides the *zanni*, or general masked clown characters that intermingled with unmasked main players and often instigated or complicated the comic action (from whence the term "zany" comes), several stock characters populated the comic scenarios. Audiences knew what to expect when attending a *commedia* performance, which was famous for its *tipi fissi*, or fixed parts, "in which roles often became inseparable from the person of the performer her/himself" (Radulescu 2012: 23). As a result, performers such as Isabella Andreini and Caterina Biancolelli became not only renowned throughout the comedy connoisseurs of Western Europe as top-tier comic figures, but became a part of the form itself; the roles they always played onstage – Isabella and Columbina, respectively, for Andreini and Biancolelli – became stock characters in every *commedia* scenario, with stock gestures, postures, and vocal patterns that came not from thin air, but rather that can be mapped back on to the bodies of the original performers themselves. Richard Andrews argues that the non-masked roles could arguably be considered "masked" as well, in that "they had a fixity in their appearance and personality which was instantly recognizable" (Scala and Andrews 2008: xix). A commedia character need not always be exactly the same depending on the scenario, or express the same emotions, but did always work within a framework of signs, signals, and gestures particular to his or her comic persona. This holds true to the stock characters such as Isabella, and the performers who played them, who typically embodied only one character consistently throughout their career.

Andrews sees this "masks without masks" (Scala and Andrews 2008: xx) tradition as repeating itself in early silent comedy; Chaplin's "Tramp" and Keaton's "Stone Face" characters, for example, followed each actor from film to film, complete with a set of gestures, postures, and so forth. This is not the only device brought from commedia to silent film comedy – a large, noise-making stick was carried by one of the clown characters (either a *zanni* or a stock character, Arlecchino); it was used as a noise-maker to punctuate jokes and comedic bits, and also to beat other characters, upping the physical comedy and cartoon violence – a literal slap-stick. The "masks without masks" phenomenon of comic personas "sticking" with an actor across performances – more recently referred to as "comedian comedy" (Seidman 1981; Jenkins 1992; Karnick and Jenkins 1995; Neale 2000) – is seen as continuing in films made to this day. When we go to see a film starring Steve Martin or Robin Williams, Rowan Atkinson or Melissa McCarthy (although notably, these comedians are overwhelmingly male) we often expect their characters to bring a familiar bag of tricks, facial expressions, and so on: a consistent comic persona that travels across and through a comedian's filmography. As Geoff King describes it, in reference to contemporary film comedy, "[t]he existing comic persona of the star is used to shape the fictional character" (King 2006: 33) – again, much like the *commedia* character Isabella was shaped explicitly around comic star Isabella Andreini. Yet it was in early twentieth century silent film that comedian comedy most notably became intertwined with a certain subset of film comedy. It is important, for our purposes, to acknowledge this tradition's intertwining with cult film spectatorship:

> For a segment of cult fans, repetitive performances can provide pleasure rather than suggesting a lack of range. Pleasure can arise from viewing the same persona manifest itself in different filmic environments, in which subtle differences and qualities can be identified by avid, invested audiences. Certain actors become particularly cherished for acts or traits that evidence an identifiable style, a kind of authorial trace that they leave upon the films they appear in.
>
> (Mathijs and Sexton 2011: 83)

Stock/recurring characters are simple building blocks in the process of intertextual referencing – a common feature of cult film appreciation. In this context, then, it is no wonder that, as Potamkin put it, "along came Charlie" (Potamkin 2008: 26).

"[C]ult appreciation exploded as a tactical response to the very growth of mass culture," claims Greg Taylor, "the cultist identifies and refuses 'mass' taste by developing a resistant cult taste for more obscure and less clearly commodified cultural objects" (Taylor 1999: 15). In the early days of film's presence in/as mass culture, two characters achieved a global presence like none other: Mickey Mouse and Charlie Chaplin. Both had mass appeal (and simply recognition), and both had a smaller subset of cultists approaching and appreciating their films in a different manner than the mainstream. As many scholars on cult argue (Waller 1991; Sconce 2007; Taylor 2007; Martin 2008), it might be Chaplin's very "mainstream" nature that opened him up to the kinds of "oppositional" viewing that some find common in cult spectatorship. "The cultist love of a film," notes Adrian Martin, for example "is all about taking what is deemed of little or no value by society at large, and then reinventing it magically, as a site of extracurricular 'surplus value' – a cult movie is a 'value-added' object" (Martin 2008: 40). Chaplin's (as well as Mickey's) wide appeal also made him a cheap commodity; cultists, such as members of the French avant-garde, then mined his comedic products to create deeper/alternative meanings. This approach soon spread to other American slapstick comics, like Buster Keaton. As a result, figures like Keaton and Chaplin became "cult before cult was cool" (Gorfinkel 2008: 34).

One particularly noteworthy group that formed a cult around American slapstick are the Surrealists. They wrote extensively on their adoration for, and consumption of, American silent comedy – which gives us an excellent window into the motivations behind, and the methods of, their cult spectatorship. The factory-like production of silent comedy shorts, notes Richard Maltby, "with no deference to tradition or hierarchies of taste," led them to be received as "unself-conscious, underdetermined, spontaneous, authentic, primitive" (Maltby 2011: x): exactly what the Surrealists, with a fascination with dreams and rejection of logic, would find attractive. The speed with which production happened, and the shoestring budgets with which many such films were produced, increased their cult appeal as well, given, as is often argued, the cultist's disdain for normative taste categories. "What the film cultist embraces is a form that, in its very difference, transgresses, violates our sense of the reasonable. It crosses boundaries of time, custom, form, and – many might add – good taste" (Telotte 1991: 6). In this instance, the form the Surrealists celebrated – comedy films made for mass consumption – was also readily eaten up by mainstream audiences. The manner in which they enjoyed the films, however, taking "low" comedy and giving it the scrutiny and embedding it with layers of meaning usually reserved for more "artistic" fare, brought their consumption into the territory of the cultist.

The Surrealists started film clubs, arranged screenings both private and public, and wrote essays and odes all in honor of Keaton and Chaplin, and later Harry Langdon. "Films are the only film school" (Aragon 2000: 52), wrote early Surrealist Louis Aragon in a 1918 essay. They immersed themselves in American comedy film, eventually making their own, thick with references, homage, bricolage, and other intertextual nods to the objects of their appreciation (Soulstein 2013). In doing so, they embarked on a project of "cult connoisseurship" (Mathijs and Sexton 2011: 50); an attempt at "a cultivated response to a noncultivated culture (that is, a culture with little legitimacy)" (Le Guern 2004: 8). Mabel Normand, Louise Fazenda, Fatty Arbuckle, and Fay Tincher were all stock players in the comic reels of the time, and regularly had pages devoted to them in popular contemporary magazines such as *Photoplay* – and all had alternative, deeply devoted audience groups whose adoration came to form ritual, cult appreciation. While these performers all had very different styles and intentions with their work, they all orbited around a similar comic impulse, best articulated by French philosopher Henri Bergson (Bergson, Brereton, and Rothwell). Langdon claimed, channeling Bergson in a 1927 essay in *Theatre Magazine*, that "[t]he four greatest stimuli to laughter are rigidity, automatism, absentmindedness and unsociability" (Langdon 1995: 234). While the slippage between man and machine, and dream-like state of absentmindedness were of particular interest to the Surrealists, the unsocial/anti-social, anti-authoritarian nature of these comedians (see Fay Tincher's *Rowdy*

Ann, for example, for evidence of the complete disregard for etiquette, taste, and social norms of such comedies) made them especially appealing to a variety of cult audiences.

So, we return to the question that ultimately animates this essay: why, if comedy was such a keystone in our earliest understanding of what made a film a "cult" film, why does it seem so underrepresented in more contemporary cultographies, as well as academic explorations of cult cinema? One possible response is that there simply have been less and less comedies over the past hundred years that hit that special matrix of affective/intertextual qualities that allow them to garner a cult audience. If we are to take history as any example, then it makes sense that cult comedies have been films that loosely adhere to the structures of *commedia* or Ancient Greek comedy. Cult films like *Man Bites Dog*, *Animal House* and *Harold and Maude* fit the Bergsonian (Langdonian?) antisocial mold, while *Monty Python's The Meaning of Life*, with its infamous, morbidly obese Mr. Creosote, "a classic manifestation of the Bakhtinian grotesque body" (King 2006: 77) – interspersed with transgressive menstruation humor – is a grotesque carnival of a film. Other Monty Python films, as well as films like *Kentucky Fried Movie* or *Airplane!*, feature largely distinct scenes or bits, breaking with the conventions of narrative cinema and instead following in the *lazzi* tradition of *commedia*; this is perhaps another reason why sketch comedy often garners cult followings, and why silent film shorts generated cult appeal as well. We have mentioned the "oppositional" spirit often linked to cult film, which Gregory A. Waller sees as manifesting in both social/normative transgression (featured in films like *Caddyshack*, *Fritz the Cat*, or *Revenge of the Nerds*) as well as in parody of the film form itself (*Blazing Saddles*, *This is Spinal Tap*) (Waller 1991: 181). Perhaps humor on film has ultimately become less transgressive/oppositional – as Damien Love recently noted, "[t]he Jock joshing of American Pie and its ilk is antithetical to [John] Waters' unabashed celebration of the excluded underclass outsider" (Love in Briggs et al. 2008: 45). Alternatively, perhaps our sensibilities have become dulled to what once was seen as transgressive. When transgression becomes the norm, it is no longer transgressive; in other words, when the carnival is every day, it is no longer a special, set-aside ritual – it is simply banal. Matt Hills suggests complicating the dichotomy of the categories of "trash" and "legitimate" films, and instead "considering the ways in which they act in concert to exclude certain types of pop culture as 'mainstream' sleaze rather than sleazy art" (Hills 2007: 220). Is what was once low-class now just "mainstream sleaze?" Greg Taylor notes the tradition of cultism's "canon discernment and oppositional upheaval – the conferring of aesthetic special-ness on unlikely artifacts" (Taylor 2007: 259); maybe comedy films just don't seem that unlikely. We noted earlier the appeal, à la Adrian Martin, of cult film as a "value-added" product, and it simply might be too hard to add value to films that already have a sort of self-canceling nor-mative transgression, Stuart Hall's "double movement" of "containment and resistance," (Hall) baked in.

A final option is also a potentially less nihilistic one. Geoff King proposes that comedy in film might be best understood not as a *genre*, but as a *mode* (King 2006: 2). Might comedy as a genre be so underrepresented in cult film because it is so prolific as a mode? It does seem that the very techniques that often make a film garner a cult following – metacinema, pastiche, irony/parody, and so on – are also approaches embedded with a layer of comic meaning. Mathijs and Sexton, for example, suggest that Vincent Price's hammy style of acting in films like *The Tingler* and *House on Haunted Hill* can be viewed by cult audiences not as a failure, but as "an *alterna-tive* form of acting that contains more personality than many more respectable performances" (Mathijs and Sexton 2011: 82). We might, by this logic, view *The Tingler* as being at once a film in the horror genre and also one that has elements of comedian comedy – those elements being some of the very reasons that the film has cult appeal. Without Price's acting, the film loses a lot of its paracinematic address, its intertextual linkages to other Price films, and its heightened style. *The Tingler* might be considered a cult film then, precisely *because* of its comic element – though it is by no means a comedy. From the audience perspective, the same holds true. Janet Staiger proposes a useful way of exploring how an audience can make a film a cult film, with the example of her finding the comedy in an ostensibly un-funny film: *The Texas Chainsaw Massacre* (Staiger 2000). The same can be said for *The Room*, one of the largest cult film phenomena of the past decade: a film made without a trace of comedy in it, that is in fact so self-serious that it enabled an audience to make it a "value-added" experience, by adding a comic approach to their viewing ritual. The comic mode, applied by an audience to a banal film, made it a cult film.

"Comedy is drama with a kink," wrote Raymond Durgnat (Durgnat 1969: 2). From the Lumière Brothers' *L'Arroseur arrosé (The Sprinkler Sprinkled)*, often considered the first narrative film and precursor to countless "mischief gag" films, to *Rocky Horror Picture Show*, kinks have featured heavily in the history of oddball cinema – whether they be in hoses or in one's sexual predilections. *Rocky Horror Picture Show* is not a comedy, but without the "kink" that takes it away from being straight drama, or a straightforward genre flick, it very well might not be the quintessential cult film as we know it today. When we allow ourselves to see the comedic kinks in the genre films we acknowledge as cult cinema, it becomes clear that comedy is actually quite heavily featured as an element in their ranks. We would do well to expand on the scholarly literature of cult comedy not only by exploring more deeply films – and other media – that fall squarely within the genre of comedy, but also by examining what role, exactly, comedy – as well as laughter – plays in transforming any and all films into objects of cult interest.

References

Aragon, Luis. 2000. "On Décor." *The Shadow and Its Shadow: Surrealist Writings on the Cinema*. Ed. Paul Hammond. 3rd ed. San Francisco: City Light Books: 50–54.

Bakhtin, Mikhail M. 1984. *Rabelais and His World*. 1st Midland book ed. Bloomington: Indiana University Press.

Benjamin, Walter. 2008. "The Work of Art in the Age of Mechanical Reproduction." *The Cult Film Reader*. Ed. Ernest Mathijs and Xavier Mendik. New York: McGraw-Hill: 29–40.

Bergson, Henri, Cloudesley Brereton and Fred Rothwell. 2008. *Laughter: An Essay on the Meaning of the Comic*. Rockville, MD: Arc Manor. Print.

Briggs, Joe Bob, et al. 2008. "Cult Cinema: A Critical Symposium." *Cinéaste* 34.1: 43–50.

Durgnat, Raymond. 1969. *The Crazy Mirror: Hollywood Comedy and the American Image*. London: Faber and Faber.

Gorfinkel, Elena. 2008. "Cult Film or Cinephilia by Any Other Name." *Cinéaste* 34.1: 33–38.

Hall, Stuart. 1981. "Notes on Deconstructing 'The Popular.'" *People's History and Socialist Theory*. Ed. Raphael Samuel. London: Routledge: 227–240.

Hills, Matt. 2009. "Media Fandom, Neoreligiosity and Cult(ural) Studies." *The Cult Film Reader*. Ed. Ernest Mathijs and Xavier Mendik. New York: McGraw-Hill: 133–148.

———. 2007. "Para-Paracinema: The Friday the 13th Film Series as Other to Trash and Legitimate Film Cultures." *Sleaze Artists: Cinema at the Margins of Taste, Style, and Politics*. Ed. Jeffrey Sconce. Durham, NC: Duke University Press: 219–239.

Jenkins, Henry. 1992. *What Made Pistachio Nuts? Early Sound Comedy and the Vaudeville Aesthetic*. New York: Columbia University Press.

Karnick, Kristine Brunovska, and Henry Jenkins, eds. 1995. *Classical Hollywood Comedy*. New York: Routledge.

King, Geoff. 2006. *Film Comedy*. Repr. London: Wallflower Press.

Langdon, Harry. 1995. "The Serious Side of Comedy Making." *The Silent Comedians*. Ed. Richard Dyer MacCann. Methuchen, NJ: Scarecrow Press: 233–235.

Le Guern, Philippe. 2004. "Toward a Constructivist Approach to Media Cults." *Cult Television*. Ed. Sara Gwenllian Jones and Roberta Pearson. Minneapolis: University of Minnesota: 3–26.

Lucia, Cynthia, and Richard Porton. 2008. "EDITORIAL." *Cinéaste* 34.1 (Winter): 6.

Maltby, Richard. 2011. Foreword, in Peter Stanfield, *Maximum Movies–Pulp Fictions: Film Culture and the Worlds of Samuel Fuller, Mickey Spillane, and Jim Thompson.* New Brunswick, NJ: Rutgers University Press: ix–xii.

Martin, Adrian. 2008. "What's Cult Got to Do With It? In Defense of Cinephile Elitism." *Cinéaste* 34.1: 39–42.

Mathijs, Ernest, and Xavier Mendik, eds. 2008. *The Cult Film Reader.* Maidenhead: McGraw-Hill.

Mathijs, Ernest, and Jamie Sexton. 2011. *Cult Cinema: An Introduction.* Chichester: Wiley-Blackwell.

Neale, Stephen. 2000. *Genre and Hollywood.* London: Routledge.

Potamkin, Harry Alan. 2008. "Film Cults." *The Cult Film Reader.* Ed. Ernest Mathijs and Xavier Mendik. New York: McGraw-Hill: 25–28.

Radulescu, Domnica. 2012. *Women's Comedic Art as Social Revolution: Five Performers and the Lessons of Their Subversive Humor.* Jefferson, NC: McFarland.

Scala, Flaminio, and Richard Andrews. 2008. *The Commedia Dell'arte of Flaminio Scala: A Translation and Analysis of 30 Scenarios.* Lanham, MD: Scarecrow Press.

Schechner, Richard. 1994. "Ritual and Performance." *The Companion Encyclopedia of Anthropology.* Ed. Tim Ingold. New York: Routledge: 613–647.

Sconce, Jeffrey, ed. 2007. *Sleaze Artists: Cinema at the Margins of Taste, Style, and Politics.* Durham, NC: Duke University Press.

Seidman, Steve. 1981. *Comedian Comedy: A Tradition in Hollywood Film.* Ann Arbor, MI: UMI Research Press.

Soulstein, Seth. 2013. "Concrete Irrationality: Surrealist Spectators and the Cult of Harry Langdon." *Scope* no. 25. www.nottingham.ac.uk/scope/documents/2013/february-2013/soulstein.pdf. Accessed 6 August 2019.

Staiger, Janet. 2000. *Perverse Spectators: The Practices of Film Reception.* New York: New York University Press.

Taylor, Greg. 1999. *Artists in the Audience: Cults, Camp, and American Film Criticism.* Princeton, NJ: Princeton University Press.

———. 2007. "Pure Quidditas or Geek Chic? Cultism as Discernment." *Sleaze Artists: Cinema at the Margins of Taste, Style, and Politics.* Ed. Jeffrey Sconce. Durham, NC: Duke University Press: 259–272.

Telotte, J.P. 1991. "Beyond All Reason: The Nature of the Cult." *The Cult Film Experience: Beyond All Reason.* Ed. J.P. Telotte. Austin: University of Texas Press: 5–17.

Waller, Gregory A. 1991. "Midnight Movies, 1980–1985: A Market Study." *The Cult Film Experience: Beyond All Reason.* Ed. J.P. Telotte. Austin: University of Texas Press: 167–186.

Wiles, David. 2000. *Greek Theatre Performance: An Introduction.* Cambridge: Cambridge University Press.

Wood, Robert. 1991. "Don't Dream It: Performance and The Rocky Horror Picture Show." *The Cult Film Experience: Beyond All Reason.* Ed. J.P. Telotte. Austin: University of Texas Press: 156–166.

8

THE ITALIAN *GIALLO*

Alexia Kannas

Giallo means "yellow" in Italian, but in cult cinema discourses the term refers to a group of violent, highly stylized Italian crime films. The roots of this strange trajectory are literary. In 1929, Italian publishing house Mondadori released the first book in their series of pulp crime and mystery novels called *Il Giallo Mondadori*: the covers of the books in this mass-marketed series were predominantly yellow – a marketing ploy that was so successful, it meant that in Italian, the word *giallo* came to describe the crime/mystery genre as a whole. The first installments in this series were mostly translations of pulp crime novels by writers like Agatha Christie and Edgar Wallace. Film scholar Gary Needham tells us that the types of stories published as part of this original series were typically derived from two sub-genres of mystery fiction: British Sherlock Holmes-style "rational-deduction" stories and "quasi-fantastic murder mysteries" (2003: 135) modeled on the work of Edgar Allan Poe. The immediate popularity of the translated pulp fictions in Italy instigated a wave of similar series put out by Mondadori's competitors – many of which also utilized the yellow cover design – and it was not long before this new genre began to attract Italian writers who, for generic consistency, were often published using anglicized *noms de plumes*.

Because, as Mikel Koven points out, in Italian "the term *giallo* acts as a metonym for the entire mystery genre" (2), when Mario Bava's Hitchcockian murder mystery film *The Girl Who Knew Too Much* was released in 1962, it was described as a *giallo*. Cinematic *giallo* takes from Bava's film its basic narrative structure which involves a protagonist who assumes the role of amateur detective after becoming an eyewitness to a violent murder, which is invariably one of a series of killings by a perpetrator whose identity the amateur detective works to uncover. Much of what comes to be known as the *giallo*'s iconography is not developed until two years later, through the success of Bava's 1964 *giallo*, *Sei donne per l'assassino/Blood and Black Lace*. It is in this second film that the level of violence escalates and we are introduced to what will become an archetypal characterization of the *giallo* killer: a mysterious, faceless figure who wears a black coat, a wide-brimmed hat, and most famously, a pair of black leather gloves. Bava also instilled in this film a highly expressive and reflexive tendency, which became fundamental to the genre as it grew.

If Bava is responsible for establishing the codes of cinematic *giallo*, director Dario Argento is most often credited with their refinement and popularization. His 1970 film *L'uccello dalle piume di cristallo/The Bird with the Crystal Plumage*, which draws on Bava's use of stylized violence and the detection narrative, became an international success. This confirmation of the financial viability of the genre set off a wave of *giallo* film production in Italy, with many films being made relatively quickly and with fairly limited budgets.

While the term *giallo*'s broad use in Italy describes crime, detection and mystery narratives from *Murder She Wrote* to *Inspector Montalbano*, the particular conditions of production and exhibition in Italy at this time generated a group of films that, as critics and scholars have noted, seems to resist definition. *Giallo* films have been called "spaghetti nightmares", evoking their crossover with the horror film, and "Italian film noir", emphasizing their crime narratives and formal stylization (Bondanella 2001; Wood 2007). As a starting point, we can distinguish between two uses of the term that currently circulate: one connotes the broader Italian understanding of *giallo*, which refers to all mystery narratives both literary and cinematic, and the other refers to a critical category of films constituted primarily through English-language cult cinema discourses. This conceptualization is indebted to the particular stylization (and success) of *giallo* films by directors like Bava and Argento. When "*giallo*" is used in the context of cult cinema, it is typically this body of texts to which it refers.

Recognizing *giallo*

Although the group of films we might refer to as *giallo* is relatively finite, this does not mean that defining the parameters of the genre is any less complex. The *giallo* shares characteristics with a wide range of film categories and groups, from other Italian popular genres to European art cinema to Hollywood B-films. Some of the most commonly identified markers of the Italian *giallo* film include: the presence of an amateur detective and a traumatized killer, the stylization of violence and a tendency towards narrative incoherence.

For instance, one thing that sets the *giallo* apart from the Italian police procedural (*poliziotto*) is the fact that the key investigative perspective adopted is usually that of non-professional, who, in many cases, is drawn into the plot after becoming an eyewitness to the first murder (Koven 2006: 85). Many of the characters who become the *giallo*'s amateur detectives have occupations which require curiosity or creative thinking: they are journalists, artists and musicians, or – as in the case of Bava's first *giallo* – long time readers of pulp fiction crime novels. In each of their cases, processing the trauma of what they've witnessed is diverted into an obsession with making sense of what they saw. Caught up in a pathological drive to solve the case, the amateur detective frequently puts their life at risk, but is able to unravel the mystery in a way that the police cannot. In Bava's first *giallo*, teenager Nora Davis is in hot pursuit of the Alphabet Killer while the police mistakenly accuse her of alcoholism and then fall victim to her juvenile string and talcum powder trap. In Argento's *Profondo Rosso/Deep Red*, Marc Daly investigates a crumbling mansion concealing a horrific past while the police munch sandwiches and drink coffee from paper cups. Unlike the astute sleuth of traditional detection narratives, the *giallo*'s amateur detectives are everyday people; in this way, these protagonists inhabit the very world imagined by Walter Benjamin when he wrote that "in times of terror, when everybody is something of a conspirator, everybody will be in a situation where he has to play detective" (2003: 13).

Everyone is a possible suspect, partly because the *giallo* killer characteristically adopts a disguise that conceals their gender and other defining features. The noir-inflected sartorial choices of the killer in Bava's influential *Sei donne per l'assassino/Blood and Black Lace* established a kind of uniform for *giallo* killers to follow, consisting of a black wide-brimmed hat, dark raincoat and, most famously, black leather gloves. It is this combination, for instance, that in Argento's *Profondo Rosso/Deep Red*, both conceals the identity of Carlo's murderous mother and enables him to take her place as he tries to protect her. As audiences became more familiar with the genre's conventions, filmmakers introduced variations of the iconography established by Bava; in Carnimeo's *Perche quelle stran gocce di sangue sul corpo di Jennifer?/ The Case of the Bloody Iris*, for instance, we encounter yellow latex gloves, and in *Giornata nera per l'ariete/ The Fifth Cord*, white surgical gloves. The glove motif is given extra weight in Argento's *gialli* because the director himself wears them for the necessary shots, claiming in interviews that only he knows how to play the killer's hands correctly. However, as Koven points out, in a good number of *giallo* films, the killers do not conceal themselves at all (2006: 102); rather than a defining feature, then, the ubiquity of the killer's gloves in lists of *giallo* conventions reveals more about which films occupy privileged positions in the *giallo* canon. In other words, the codification of the *giallo* in cult film discourses draws on a relatively narrow selection of film texts.

The *giallo* killer's drive to commit murder is often inextricably linked to a past experience of violence and their stunted processing of this trauma furnishes them with a motive. In Sergio Martino's *I Corpi presentano trace di violenza carnale/ Torso* (1973), the killer murders women because he, as a child, witnessed his brother's death and holds a young girl responsible. In *Cosa avente fatto a Solange?/ What Have You Done to Solange?* (Massimo Dallamano, 1972), the killer is motivated by the need to exact revenge on those who have harmed his daughter. In Argento's films, this traumatic past is especially mythologized and aestheticized. Each time *Tenebre*'s killer retreats into his memories of the past, for instance, we find ourselves on a desolate beach where he suffers humiliating sexual rejection and physical violence at the hands of a mysterious woman and a group of young men; in one regression, she steps on the young killer's face, pushing the heel of her shiny red pump deep into his mouth.

The twisted motivations of *giallo* killers offer ample opportunity for the meticulously conceived methods of killing and inventive spectacular deaths, which form one of the key pleasures associated with the reception of *giallo* films in cult film contexts. As the precursor to the American slasher pic, *giallo* films are loaded with an array of sharp objects for the killer to slice or hack into their victims, including kitchen knives, pocketknives, razors, axes and syringes, but the killer's methods can put these implements to work in bizarre ways. In *Tarantola dal ventre nero/ Black Belly of the Tarantula*, for instance, the killer uses acupuncture needles and then a knife to mimic the way the black wasp kills tarantulas: after paralyzing his victims with the insect's venom, cuts open their bellies. The death of killer Marta (Clara Calamai) in *Profondo Rosso/ Deep Red* is particularly spectacular: when her pendent becomes caught in the ironwork of an old elevator, the film's amateur detective Marc sets the elevator in motion, causing it to decapitate her.

These violent set pieces can play a large part in fragmenting the structure of the *giallo* film, but the genre's characteristic disregard for continuity and linearity is evident outside of its spectacular deaths, too. In these films, point-of-view can oscillate between realistic and impossible perspectives and the collapsing of time and space through editing evokes formal strategies of experimental cinema. Despite expectations solicited from the audience via the crime narrative, the unmasking of the killer does not automatically imply a restoration of order. The distinctive and alienating tone that this formal play produces suggests that the *giallo* operates according to a particular internal logic, but their apparent incoherence has, historically, played a large part in the marginalization of *giallo* films as cheaply made schlock.

Reading *giallo*: *Filone*, vernacular, cult

Robbie Edmonstone (2008) suggests that popular genre films produced during this period in Italy cannot be organized neatly into genre-specific piles, because the conditions of production mean that particular characteristics – like the presence of "brutality" – flow laterally

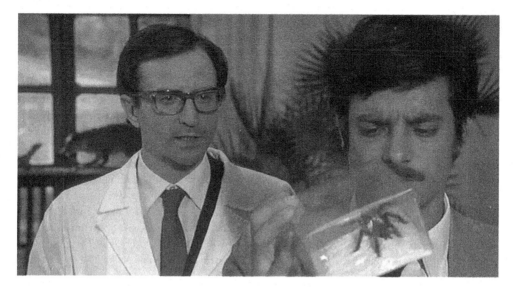

Figure 8.1   Inspector Tellini looks at a tarantula in *The Black Belly of the Tarantula* (Cavara, Italy/ France, 1971). Da Ma Produzione

across a range of film groups, from peplums to *gialli* to police procedurals. To counter this leakiness, recent scholarship on the *giallo* film has emphasized the use of the Italian term *filone*, instead of "genre", to describe this group of films. Meaning "vein", "streamlet" or "tradition", the term *filone* opens up flexibility to consider a wide range of films prone to consistent deviation from any established generic norm as nevertheless being part of the same discursive group.

Drawing on Christopher Wagstaff's work on the spaghetti western, *giallo* scholars have described how the three-tiered system of exhibition classes in Italy, made up of the *prima* (first), *seconda* (second) and *terza vision* (third-run cinemas) facilitated a tidal wave of *filone* production in the 1960s and 1970s. The *giallo filone* screened across these various levels, with films by well-known directors like Bava and Argento mingling with Hollywood releases and European art cinema in the *prima vision*, while a range of lower-budget *gialli* were made specifically for the second and third-run houses. As David Church argues, both Italian and international commercially successful films functioned as "triggers" for *filone* cycles, where "some *filone* capitalized on popular Anglo-American imports, some emerged after an Italian-made hit reinforced an Anglo-American one, and others were primarily imitative of homegrown Italian hits" (Church 2015: 5).

The concept of *filone* helps genre critics to acknowledge the complex relationships between both individual films and clusters, without having to commit wholly to a rigid set of classification rules to which the films often do not adhere. For instance, fan-authored lists of *giallo* films typically include Paolo Cavara's *La tarantola dal ventre nero/ The Black Belly of the Tarantula* (1972), despite the fact that its protagonist is a member of the police force, rather than the more typical amateur detective. As Koven points out, films that adopt the investigative perspective of the police are usually categorized as *poliziotto* (police procedurals) – another *filone* of the Italian popular cinema (2006: 7). But *Tarantola dal ventre nero/ Black Belly of the Tarantula* works in the tradition of the *giallo* by positioning Inspector Tellini (Giancarlo Giannini) as an outsider in the police force, while hitting other key *giallo* marks with its gloved and traumatized killer and Ennio Morricone score.

The surge of *giallo* film production was fed not only by Italian audiences' taste for murder and mystery, but by wider changes in international markets, too. Bolstered by financial aid designed to exert political control over the Italian film industry in the postwar period, the Italian system was primed to respond to the Hollywood production crisis of the 1950s, which sent smaller American distributers overseas in search of low-cost genre movies to fill screens in the nation's drive-ins and smaller cinemas. Stefano Baschiera and Franchesco Di Chairi explain how, because of this secondary market, the Italian genre film began to broaden the demographics it targeted, seeking not only to fulfill Italian audience expectations, but American and British ones as well (2010: 3). Baschiera and Di Chiara argue that this scenario resulted in certain strands of the Italian genre cinema of the 1960s and 1970s reflecting characteristics of transnational cinema; unlike Italian comedies and melodramas of this period, which characteristically work through traditions and tensions in national identity and culture, the *giallo* film's "Italianness" gives way to an indistinct and "vaguely Anglophone" milieu. The use of both Italian and foreign actors contributes to this, as well as international locations ranging from Athens (*La coda dello scorpione/ The Case of the Scorpion's Tail*, Sergio Martino, 1971) to Sydney (*La ragazza dal pigiama giallo/ The Pyjama Girl Case*, Flavio Mogherini, 1977).

Koven's book *La Dolce Morte: Vernacular Cinema and the Italian* Giallo *Film* employs the concept of *filone* in his argument for the *giallo* as an example of "vernacular cinema". Citing the conditions of production and exhibition in Italy during the 1960s and 1970s, Koven suggests that *giallo* films were designed to appeal specifically to the distracted gaze of second and third-run cinema audiences who talk, drink and smoke during film screenings while continually glancing away from, and then returning to, the screen. In this view, the poor reviews these films typically received on their theatrical releases in English-language reception contexts have missed the point: because *giallo* films were not designed to be consumed in the contemplative manner associated with art cinema, they cannot be productively analyzed using the same methods. He explains that "designating the film as vernacular cinema is a way of approaches genres, like the *giallo*, without adhering to the bourgeois criteria of classical narrative, intellectual abstraction, and elitist notions of 'the artistic'" (2006: 33).

While the vernacular cinema paradigm illuminates particularities of Italian audiences' spectatorial practices during this period, it also suggests that the key to understanding these films lies in this historically conceived, class-based, distracted relation to the screen. How then do we account for the popularity of *giallo* films with cult cinema audiences who are so often characterized as obsessive and detail-orientated consumers? One way would be to use a reception studies approach: this allows us to see how changing contexts facilitate shifts in textual meaning by acknowledging that different audiences watch *giallo* films in different ways. In his work on the exhibition of Italian horror films in the United States, for instance, Raiford Guins describes two distinct periods in this reception history alone: "The first period … is marked by the availability of Italian horror on videocassette, while the second period is distinguished by DVD's elevation to the preferred medium through which to experience Italian horror cinema" (2005: 17).

The availability of *giallo* films on home video facilitated a significant shift in the genre's cultural value from a cycle of films popular in Italy, to a style of brutal Italian horror that pushed the boundaries of acceptability and taste. Dubbed, reedited and cropped *giallo* video titles were first available to English-speaking markets during the pre-certification period, a time nostalgically evoked in paracinema and cult film magazines as a golden era of unregulated access to movies with unchecked levels of graphic violence and sexual content. But when moral panic around this new form of unregulated consumption of morally question-able content resulted in new censorship guidelines and unprecedented power for governing bodies, supply was cut off. The genre's use of stylized excessive violence was foregrounded as a defining feature when *giallo* titles by Argento, Bava, Lucio Fulci and Umberto Lenzi were categorized as harmful videotapes on the infamous 1983 "Video Nasties" list. Reflecting on this particular historical incident, Kate Egan sees the limited availability of affected video titles as a catalyst for the emergence of a taste culture built around a penchant for forbidden films (2007). In the years to follow, distributors would use strategies anchored in such moral panics to market full, "uncut" and "uncensored" *giallo* titles to audiences whose taste for illegitimacy generated a significant market.

It is worth pointing out that the *giallo*'s status as a bad object during this time had also to do with the video format itself. Kim Newman describes how the process of re-editing films for video distribution may have affected Italian cinema in particular, which he describes as being "uncomfortable on video". With the detail of their widescreen compositions lost through the use of pan and scan or careless telecine, the quality of many versions of *giallo* films cir-culating on video did not come close to that of their original theatrical release. "Combined with mostly indifferent dubbing and subtly unfamiliar narrative strategies", Newman writes, "… these squeezed and cropped films – they may have all the gore, but you only got half the image – seem alien artefacts" (1996: 140). But if, by celebrating its shock value, cult cinema discourse positioned the *giallo* film as a bad object, it also functioned to generate interest in and demand for this marginalized material.

Both the proliferation of online marketplaces and the DVD boom have drastically dismantled that sense of the *giallo*'s rarity and exclusivity fashioned by paracinema and cult audiences through years of collecting and discussion. Paradoxically, these enduring subcultural ideologies, which Mark Jancovich sees as emerging from a desire to "produce and protect a sense of rarity and exclusivity", have ensured distribution companies a ready and waiting audience for the multitudes of DVD releases (2002: 309). But this has also facilitated a new wave of interest in the *giallo*, offering unprecedented availability of films that are now marketed to a broader demo-graphic. While Guins argues that DVD technology helped to elevate the status of the *giallo* to "art-object", Church points out that, even now, many of the cheapest and most easily accessible DVD versions of *gialli* are poor quality transfers of heavily edited and censored prints of the original films (2015: 16). Still, the programming of *giallo* retrospectives at film festivals such as the Melbourne International Film Festival (2013) and film centers such as the Anthology Film Archive in NYC (2012), along with the recent surge of interest in *giallo* soundtracks and the inclusion of *giallo* films on university cinema studies courses, offers the genre new reception contexts that will continue to shape the meanings it produces.

Film noir, modernity, *giallo*

Some critics have seen the *giallo* as an Italian variant of *film noir*. Mary P. Wood argues that while the films make use of many of the stylistic conventions of *film noir*, "the simultaneous presence of visual excess and fantasy and the conventions of realist cinema" in the *giallo* problematizes this equation (2007: 238). Nevertheless, both terms do represent critical categories: just as *films noir* are understood to constitute a stylized subset of the Hollywood crime film constituted through French film criticism, English-language use of the term *giallo* in cult cinema discourse refers to a more specific (but permeable) canon of films. As with *film noir*, this classification process can be esoteric, relying less on sets of established rules or conventions, and more on a consistent tone, which, as Stephen Thrower notes, "is one of moral decay and cynicism, with ever more convoluted plots emphasizing morbid details in a Janus-faced world of paranoia and betrayal" (1999: 63). These films, as Wood points out, appropriate noir elements "to indicate dissatisfaction with official versions of events, and/or to evoke a dysfunctional world" (2007: 238), driven by what Koven suggests is the genre's "ambivalence toward modernity" (2006: 5). However, while *films noir* of the classical Hollywood period and Italian *gialli* made from the late 1960s onwards both offer dystopian views of the modern world, the *giallo's* engagement with modernity is irrevocably marked by its *lateness*.

The *giallo's* fascination with the conditions of late modernity means that it has a lot in common with art cinema produced during the same period, particularly in terms of the way it uses formal strategies of modernist cinema. But, while writers like James Naremore (1998) have explored *film noir* as a site of connection between modernism and popular culture, the *giallo's* complex relationship to modernist cinema is still relatively under-theorized. Mark Betz has suggested that the concept of the *filone*, with its lateral and multidirectional flow, might be used to help us understand "in stylistic as well as historical terms, the developments of art cinema in Europe in the postwar era and its confluence with what have previously been regarded as supplementary exploitation *codes* of *display*, of *content* and of *affect*" (Betz 2013: 513). As a starting point, we can observe that Italian *giallo* and art cinema productions often shared creative personnel: for instance, screenwriter Bernadino Zapponi worked on films by both Dario Argento and Federico Fellini, while cinematographer Vittorio Storaro who shot *The Bird with the Crystal Plumage* in 1970 and *The Fifth Cord* spent the time between shooting Bertolucci's films *Il conformista/The Conformist* (1970) and *Strategia del ragno/The Spider's Stratagem* (1970). Unsurprisingly then, we can often discern in *giallo* films qualities of modernist cinema such as reflexivity and abstraction, along with thematic preoccupations András Kovacs associates with modernism in European art cinema, including alienation and "disclosure of the idea of nothingness behind the surface reality" (2008: 203).

The typically privileged lifestyles of *giallo* characters furnish the films with a range of glamorous settings including hip parties, exotic holiday destinations and countless examples of late-modern architecture, but the *giallo's mise en scène* is generally disinterested in signs of everyday life. Homes are as sparsely furnished as hotel rooms and provide little comfort or sense of safety and action plays out in deserted warehouses, in sparsely furnished art galleries, on countless spiral staircases, in shadows and splatters of blood on crisp, white walls. These void-like, impersonal spaces recall Segfried Kracauer's description of the hotel lobby, a place he sees as both the definitive locale of the modern detective novel and a representation of modernity, where "togetherness has no meaning" (1997: 8).

Rupturing zooms, chromatic lighting and soundtracks with supernatural levels of agency offer an unrelentingly self-aware expression of the atomized existence that both lies at the existentialist core of *film noir* and is explored in European art cinema, but through the lens of the *giallo* genre's aggressive stylization, modernity balances precariously on the brink of a decadent collapse. Argento's 1982 *giallo Tenebre* includes a striking expression of this world's fragmentation and alienation in a two-and-a-half-minute, fetishistic close-up shot that traces the circumference of the apartment building of two victims, forcing the viewer to observe the magnified architectural detail of a modern home that cannot keep its occupants safe.

The *giallo's* absorption into the canons of cult cinema has helped to solidify a particular definition of the genre that pivots on the hyper-stylization associated with key *giallo* directors like Bava and Argento and has, more recently, inspired a recent wave of revisionist or neo-*giallo* films. One example is Hélène Cattet and Bruno Forzani's *The Strange Colour of Your Body's Tears*

Figure 8.2   Stylized murder in *Tenebre* (Argento, Italy, 1982). Sigma Cinematografica Roma

(2013), a film which cites the genre's iconography with such systematic fervor, that critic Jason Anderson suggests its opening sequence alone functions as "a primer on the semiotics of the *giallo* film" (2013: 45).

References

Anderson, Jason. 2013. "Black, White and Giallo," *CinemaScope* 56: 45.

Baschiera, Stefano and Francesco Di Chiara. 2010. "One Upon a Time in Italy: Transnational Features of Genre Production 1960s–1970s," *Film International* 8.6: 30–39.

Benjamin, Walter. 2003. "The Paris of the Second Empire in Baudelaire," in Howard Eiland and Michael Jennings, eds, *Selected Writings, vol. 4: 1938–1940*. Cambridge, MA: Harvard University Press: 3–92.

Betz, Mark. 2013. "High and Low and In Between," *Screen* 54.4: 495–513.

Bondanella, Peter. 2001. *Italian Cinema: From Neorealism to the Present*. 3rd ed. New York: Continuum.

Church, David. 2015. "One on Top of the Other: Lucio Fulci, Transnational Film Industries, and the Retrospective Construction of the Italian Horror Canon," *Quarterly Review of Film and Video* 32.1: 1–20.

Edmonstone, Robbie. 2008. *"Beyond "Brutality": Understanding the Italian Filone's Violent Excesses*. Doctoral diss., University of Glasgow.

Egan, Kate. 2007. "The Celebration of a 'Proper Product': Exploring the Residual Collectible through the 'The Video Nasty'," in Charles R. Acland, ed., *Residual Media*. Minneapolis: University of Minnesota Press: 200–221.

Guins, Raiford. 2005. "Blood and Black Gloves on Shiny Discs: New Media, Old Tastes, and the Remediation of Italian Horror Films in the United States," in Steven Jay Schneider and Tony Williams, eds, *Horror International*. Detroit, MI: Wayne State University Press: 15–32.

Jancovich, Mark. 2002. "Cult Fictions: Cult Movies, Subcultural Capital and the Production of Cultural Distinctions," *Cultural Studies* 16.2: 306–322.

Kovács, Andras. 2008. *Screening Modernism European Art Cinema, 1950–1980*. Chicago: University of Chicago Press.

Koven, Mikel J. 2006. *La Dolce Morte: Vernacular Cinema and the Italian Giallo Film*. Lanham, MD: Scarecrow Press.

Kracauer, Siegfried. 1997. "The Hotel Lobby," in Neil Leach and Helene Frichot, eds, *Rethinking Architecture: A Reader in Cultural Theory*. New York: Routledge: 50–62.

Naremore, James. 2008. *More Than Night Film Noir in Its Contexts*. 2nd ed. Berkeley: University of California Press.

Neale, Steve. 2002. *Genre and Contemporary Hollywood*. London: BFI Pub.

Needham, Gary. 2003. "Playing with Genre: Defining the Italian *Giallo*," in S.J. Schneider, ed., *Fear without Frontiers: Horror Cinema across the Globe*. 1st ed. Godalming: FAB: 135–144.

Newman, Kim. 1996. "Journal of the Plague Years," in Karl French, ed., *Screen Violence*. London: Bloomsbury: 132–143.

Thrower, Stephen. 1999. *Beyond Terror: The Films of Lucio Fulci*. Godalming: FAB Press.

Wagstaff, Christopher. 1992. "A Forkful of Westerns. Industry, Audiences and Italian Westerns," in Richard Dyer and Ginette Vincendeau, eds, *Popular European Cinema*. London: Routledge: 245–261.

Wood, Mary P. 2007. "Italian Film Noir," in Andrew Spicer, ed., *European Film Noir*. Manchester: Manchester University Press: 23–72.

PART II

Global and local cult cinema

Global and local cult cinema

In the early 1980s, Jonathan Rosenbaum and J. Hoberman, in an often quoted introduction to key midnight movies (a book that has become an exemplar for the study of cult cinema) warned against equating the release and reception of films in North America, and New York in particular, with these films' general presence on this planet. 'Midnight movies,' they wrote, 'were far from being an exclusively American phenomenon' (1983: 3). They dutifully extended the range to London and Paris. Ever since, that warning has been repeated (see, for instance, Mathijs and Sexton 2011, Sexton and Hills 2017, and Smith and Tierney 2020). Yet, even today, New York and 'the Upper West' remain the predominant touchstone for cult reputations – if not by assigning cult then by acting as its major imagined enemy. It wasn't until New York's *Harper's Magazine* paid attention to screenings of *The Room* (Wiseau, 2003) that had been going on for years elsewhere, that the film was considered a 'legitimate' cult film. And, as Rayna Denison points out in this section's chapter on Anime, it wasn't until the Japanese animation aesthetics' presence left the shores of Asia (and the hands of its diaspora) that it was being viewed as cult-ish.

This is not a problem unique to cult cinema, or its academic study. For decades, criticism has been directed at film culture, and at cinema studies, for its Western-centred lens. All too often, films' presences and status in Europe and North America were considered equal to their global value. No matter how hard theories of post-colonialism, Orientalism, and (g)localized studies of cinema tried to adjust the lens, its focus has been persistently Western. However, as corrections continue to push against that Western-centrism, and force that lens towards recalibrations, cult cinema has found itself pushing harder as well. True to its reputation, much of cult film has always tried to put itself outside any 'movement', marginal to any type of concerted effort towards 'whatever' program. In that sense, cult cinema is akin to what Dick Hebdige describes in *Subculture: the Meaning of Style* (1979) as a form of 'refusal' and 'resistance' – a punk attitude, if you will, or a 'sneer' (Hebdige's term) towards all attempts to rein in, from whatever angle, cult cinema. Equally true, this persistence of resistance may also prevent cult cinema from becoming a truly revolutionary force, and its transgression, as Barry Keith Grant (1991) notes, is often a 'safe' one, playing and colouring in the margins while not affecting social change. True too, much of cult cinema fails to be recuperated through lack of accountability or achievement progressive or reactionary, because it just doesn't sit well, and remains a misfit or embarrassment.

All that said, it is high time that cult cinema studies did start showing instead of assuming its existence outside the Westernized arenas of cultural debate. This section, therefore, problematizes the idea of 'place' in the study of cult cinema, by offering six chapters that are, at the same time, confirmations of how local and localized cult film cultures are of significance for any understanding of cult film in general, but also, how these film cultures never act insularly – they are always actions towards other places and instances, assertions of place, and reactions against imposed positions. Harry Benshoff revisits the arena of Blaxploitation film. This chapter is one of internal reexamination of assumptions, from within the inner bowels (the underbelly) of American culture. As issues of cultural identity, expression and frustration through aesthetics, and potential political power force themselves (again) onto the political agenda, an investigation of Blaxploitation is necessary, especially in a time when 'Black Lives Matter' movements, anniversaries of legendary Blaxploitation films such as *Ganja and Hess* (Gunn, 1973), *Sweet Sweetback's Badass Song* (Van Peebles, 1971), and repeated remakes (of *Shaft*, 1971) as well as rediscoveries of Afro-futurism abound.

Five chapters in this section place their focus outside Europe and North America. Denison discusses anime cinema not only as 'that type of animation' but also, and importantly, as a mode of viewing film, cultish-ly, to think with 'multiple categorical possibilities,' as the chapter puts it, as it makes English language and Japanese language understandings of terms confront each other. Language is place- and situation-specific, and this chapter stresses those conditions. Terminology and language are also the starting point of Babak Tabarraee's chapter on Iranian cult cinema. Like Denison, Tabarraee questions the usefulness of the word 'cult' (which has no equivalent in Farsi) in order to discuss films that share aesthetics and receptions, and he argues that such obstacles in themselves 'cultify' their discussion. Vibhushan Subba, in the chapter on Indian cult cinema, uses the large hegemonic structures of (and international misunderstandings about) Bollywood as a point of contention to discuss Bombay cult films, and exploitation films in particular – Bombsploitation as he calls it. Subba uses elements of aesthetics and budget to argue that this localized type of cinema usually escapes larger lenses. The chapters by Vibhushan and Tabarraee also illustrate the extent to which necessarily mobile understanding of the term cult can stimulate excavations of specific cult situations and locations (India and Iran). Orientalism looms large in such endeavours, and both Robyn Citizen, in a chapter that overviews key East Asian cult cinema, and Dolores Tierney, in a discussion that covers another large area, Latin America, point out that the very attempt to bring together films with cultist characteristics (in their make up or reception) from regions and times (not to mention political ideologies and cultural heritage – often tainted by colonial pasts) that are so vastly diverse is in and of itself a risky undertaking. Unless, of course, that impossibility to be 'placed' becomes the factor that brings the films together, one culturally shelter-less item next to another.

Finally, whether they explore small areas and places (inner cities, provinces, nations) or large masses of land and sea (continents and subcontinents, rims and coasts), the chapters in this section affirm that the films under scrutiny are *wild*, whatever the lens, in their efforts to express, represent, and reflect imaginations that are sometimes referred to as beyond human. This wilderness is reflected in anime and its unbridled robotic and cyber-imaginations, in the ghosts of Bombsploitation, and the philosophical and magical visions of Middle-Eastern and Latin American cult films – time travel, techno-warps, unnatural-looking environments, sublime deep space, endless marvel and wonder, blinding sunlight, magical realism, surrealism, or hallucinations included (all of it still infected by traditions of 'lensing' places that are brought about by mostly Western technology and aesthetic doctrines of taste and representation). Cult cinema from across the globe appears to allude to something beyond humans. Today's study of culture often tries to look beyond the human factor and action. Terms such as 'anthroposcene,' as an effort to carve (and therefore 'place') the arenas of human presence and intervention *anywhere*, exemplify that. The films in this section, by being different to pretty much anything else, may well also put cult cinema's *wilderness* on that map.

References

Grant, Barry Keith. 1991. "Science-Fiction Double Feature: Ideology in the Cult Film," in J.P. Telotte (ed.), *The Cult Film Experience: Beyond all Reason*. Austin: University of Texas Press, 122–137.
Hebdige, Dick. 1979. *Subculture: The Meaning of Style*. London: Routledge.
Mathijs, Ernest, and Jamie Sexton. 2011. *Cult Cinema*: New York: Wiley.
Rosenbaum, Jonathan, and J. Hoberman. 1983. *Midnight Movies*. New York: Da Capo Press.
Sexton, Jamie, and Matt Hills (eds). 2017. "Cult Cinema and the Transnational", *Transnational Cinemas* 8:1 (special issue). https://doi.org/10.1080/20403526.2017.1262504. Accessed 6 August 2019.

9

LATSPLOITATION

Dolores Tierney

Although one hears little about it, Latin America has an exceptionally diverse tradition of what could be called exploitation cinemas ranging from the 1950s vampire and wrestling/horror hybrid movies of Mexican director Fernando Méndez (*Ladrón de cadáveres/Bodysnatcher* 1956, *El vampiro/The Vampire* 1957) to more contemporary cult horror films like *La casa muda* (*The Silent House*, Gustavo Hernández, Uruguay 2010). When *Latsploitation, Exploitation Cinemas and Latin America* (Ruétalo and Tierney 2009) was first published, it represented a significant move forward in English language work on these exploitation cinemas. What made *Latsploitation* exceptional in terms of work on the region's cinema at the time was that, unlike most of the previous anthologies and continent-wide accounts of the region's different national filmmaking endeavours, the authors of its seventeen essays did not focus on mainstream, art or political cinemas, but instead took on the task of analysing and accounting for these almost completely critically neglected exploitation cinemas, arguing for their inclusion as part of a bigger regional "picture of film production, exhibition and circulation" (D'Lugo 2012: 592).[1] With respect to exploitation cinemas, *Latsploitation* filled a gap in the then burgeoning field of exploitation cinema studies, bringing the hitherto largely ignored diverse exploitation cinemas of Latin American into its frame of reference. As such, *Latsploitation* was the first book in English of its kind. In the years since its publication, "latsploitation" as a term has gained increasing currency in academic studies. The term appears as a stand-alone entry in Annette Kuhn and Guy Westwell's *A Dictionary of Film Studies* (2012), who define it as: "[A] distinctly Latin American variant of the exploitation film" (2012: 243). The term also appears in publications which seek to build on the *Latsploitation* anthology including Rosana Díaz-Zambrana and Patricia Tomé's Spanish-language anthology *Horrorfílmico: Aproximaciones al cine de terror en Latinoamérica y el Caribe* (2012).

The task of bringing together the incredibly diverse styles, genres (violence, gore, sexploitation, horror, science fiction and fantasy), production modes (independent video, low budget home video, big budget studio productions), exhibition sites (mainstream theatres, *los videohome/* home videos, local circuits, the US drive-in, Spanish language circuits in the United States) and different institutional statuses (independent, pirated, government funded) of exploitation cinemas in Latin America, under a single category "latsploitation" is by no means a small one. Nevertheless, the attempt to complete this task, has the effect of making visible as a collective the previously invisible histories, texts, and contexts of different exploitation films made both *by*

Latin Americans and foreign film producers (Roger Corman, Roberta and Michael Findlay) *in* Latin America. Following the coining of the term "Mexploitation" to refer to Mexican exploit-ation cinema (Greene 2005; Syder and Tierney 2005), the devising of the term "Latsploitation" carries with it the idea that exploitation cinemas in Latin America are specific enough to warrant their own category. Ruétalo and Tierney define the specificity of "latsploitation" as:

> an umbrella term that embraces a range of different production, generic, and textual strategies under some overarching shared characteristics and considerations [...] intended to underline the *difference* of Latin American exploitation cinema to the already quite elastic concept of exploitation cinema as it is understood (principally) in U.S. terms and to suggest that this difference has to do with the very different indus-trial organization and history of Latin American cinemas.
>
> (Ruétalo and Tierney 2009: 2–3)

Latsploitation as it is outlined here emphasizes Latin American cinema's historical and eco-nomic exceptionality and how this creates a different kind of exploitation cinema. The term also acknowledges the different criteria which determine a Latin American exploitation film and which set it apart from exploitation as it is understood in primarily US terms (Schaefer 1999). A loose definition of exploitation as a low budget, poor quality, alternative to mainstream filmmaking does not necessarily easily transfer to Latin America's different national filmmaking contexts where erratic funding and different economies of scale as well as differing levels of quality and the frequent absence of a defined mainstream mean that exploitation cinema is and has been much less clearly demarcated. In fact, in Latin America as Sergio de la Mora points out "boundaries between exploitation, mainstream and art cinema are more porous" and "some films simultaneously resid[e] in more than one of these categories" (2009: 258). As a result, local criticism in Latin America has almost never or in some cases rarely used the term exploitation, as a descriptive for the films which are now more commonly incorporated under a Latsploitation banner (De la Mora 2009: 247).

Latsploitation also carries with it negative associations. As with blaxploitation, there is an implied degradation of the subject matter: a belittling of Latin American locales through the perpetuation of continental and national stereotypes of the weird, the violent and the savage. It is precisely for these reasons that arbiters of national cinema in Latin America's different national contexts have largely chosen to disavow or dismiss the low brow, popular and often derivative cinemas which could be incorporated under the term latsploitation, preferring to stress instead art cinema and the political cinemas of the 1960s and 1970s (particularly of the New Latin American Cinema) which possess greater cultural capital and additionally present a much more preferable image of postcolonial artistic autonomy.[2] It is also possible however, as Rowena Santos Aquino points out, to consider how the coining of a term like latsploitation, may actually function on a socio-political level (Santos Aquino 2011: 26) to recuperate many of these films in a way that emphasizes their collective assertion of regional, national or local self-image. Work on *narcofronteriza* (drug/border) films like those starring the Almada brothers (Mário and Fernando) for instance, emphasizes how the border narratives of vintage exploitation films like *La banda del carro rojo* (*The Red Car Gang*, Rubén Galindo, 1976) have in the past and may still offer Mexican migrant workers in the United States, not just otherwise unavailable images of their experiences and economic struggles but also figure the US/Mexico border as a place of "opportunity and self-invention" (Ávalos 2009: 196).

Partly responsible for latsploitation passing into academic speak as an accepted term in the last decade, is the greater accessibility in Anglo and exterior markets beyond their target Latinx or Spanish-speaking audiences of the broad array of cinemas that fit within the category. Greater accessibility has made these cinemas more familiar objects of research in academic publications and of study on university courses both in Europe and North America.[3] During the late 1960s, 1970s, and the 1980s a number of exploitation cinemas could be consumed by Latinx audiences attending theatres in Spanish language circuits in different areas (the Southwest) and metropolitan centres of the United States (predominantly New York, Los Angeles, and New Jersey). Once these circuits closed the majority of Latin America's exploitation cinemas were only available outside Latin America via private collections (Agrásanchez), informal networks or specialist mail-order video companies with only certain genres (the *narcofronterizas*) more broadly available to rent and buy on VHS in predominantly Latinx communities. The advent of DVDs in the late 1990s and the wave of re-issuing of old titles that accompanied it, as well as the founding in the 2000s of video sharing sites like YouTube have facilitated the informal distribution of both classical and current Latin American exploitation films and made them more widely available both to popular audiences and exploitation film scholars. Indeed, as I have pointed out elsewhere, video sharing sites like YouTube represent precisely the kind of viewing platform suited to material perceived as being of "low" cultural capital like exploitation cinema. Films like *La mansion de la locura* (*The Mansion of Madness* Juan López Moctezuma, Mexico, 1973) or *La Llorona* (Ramón Peón, Mexico, 1933) can appear and remain on YouTube because, in their case, there are no MPAA studios or content owners scouring the internet to take down pirated material (Tierney 2014b). Many titles including *Santo contra los zombies* (*Santo versus the Zombies*, Mexico, Benito Alazraki, 1962) or *Fuego* (*Fire*, Argentina, Armando Bo, 1969) are available to purchase in subtitled versions on DVD in the US and Europe in such mainstream venues as Amazon, and in the US at Walmart and other supermarket chains, and also screened on local Spanish language television networks (Channel 62 in Los Angeles) and Spanish language cable channels (Galavision) (Madrigal 2010).[4]

For an Anglo audience, the growth in psychotronic and exploitation film culture during the 1980s, 1990s, and early 2000s (as per Mike Weldon's *The Psychotronic Encyclopedia of Film* [1986] and Pete Tombs *Mondo Macabro: Weird and Wonderful Cinema from Around the World* [1997]), the emergence of specialist mail-order video companies like Mike Vraney's Something Strange Video, Rhino and Sinister Video and also television programmes like *Mystery Science Theater 3000* and *Joe Bob's Drive-In* and *Monster Visions* also fuelled the availability, visibility and consequently the greater attention paid to Latin America's exploitation cinemas. Most recently, Latin American exploitation cinemas have achieved a level of cultural normality sufficient for some of their subgenres to be considered an accepted part of the global history of cinema and cited as indicative of various industrial processes. For instance, the cover of *Film Studies: A Global Introduction* (Davis, Dickinson, Patti and Villarejo 2015), features, not un-coincidentally, the original Spanish-language film poster of one of the same wrestling Santo movies, that is available to buy in subtitled version on Amazon, *Santo contra los Zombies*. Additionally, Glyn Davis et al.'s book offers the advent of the *lucha libre* (wrestling) genre as an example of how film production will often exploit a gap in the market. In this case, the one left in Mexican popular culture by the banning of Mexican wrestling from Mexican television screens in the 1950s and the subsequent development of films starring Mexican wrestlers (Davis et al. 2015: 160–161).[5]

The emergence of "latsploitation" however, as a new and discrete field of study, has not been completely without antecedents. In Latin American film studies, a greater interest in the kind of "low brow" and "vulgar" genres it encapsulates came out of the turn towards the popular of the late 1980s and 1990s led by Latin American film scholars like Ana M. López, Paulo Antonio

Paranaguá and others. In López' key articles such as "Celluloid Tears: Melodrama in the Classic Mexican Cinema" (1991) and "The Melodrama in Latin America: Telenovelas, Film, and the Currency of a Popular Form" (1985), there is a shift from privileging the obvious militancy of the New Latin American Cinemas of the 1960s and 1970s towards valuing the resistive possibilities and pleasures of classical popular genres like melodrama – redeeming them from the theoretical formations of the 1970s which had dismissed them as ideologically conservative and complicit with bourgeois ideology (Colina and Díaz Torres 1972: 14–16).[6] The study of Latin America's classical cinemas paved the way for the subsequent cultural studies approach to exploitation cinemas that challenged the inherent hierarchies of Latin American culture in which popular films, such as the low brow "India Maria" comedies starring and/or directed by Maria Elena Velasco, are disregarded, to assert instead that her films such as *Ni de aquí, ni de allá* (*Neither Here or There*, Velasco, 1987) are relevant in scholarship and worthy of academic analysis (Ricalde 2004: 200). *Ni de aquí, ni de allá* for instance, can be viewed as speaking to the migrant experience of "inbetweeness" in the United States, through a series of in jokes including the "coffee and donuts" which constitute the entirety of Maria's US diet because it's the only thing she knows to order in English (Rohrer 2017: 157–158).

As well as following this turn towards the popular in the study of Latin American cinemas, the study of its exploitation and related cinemas also takes its cue from the foundational studies of US and UK(-based) scholars, Eric Schaefer (1999), Joan Hawkins (2000), Jeffrey Sconce (1995, 2007), Mark Jancovich, Antonio Lázaro-Reboll, Julian Stringer and Andrew Willis (2003) writing on the similarly once marginal but now increasingly critically accepted US and European exploitation, trash, cult cinemas and their paracinematic reading protocols. Scholars writing on the pre-industrial experimental era of Mexican Cinema, or the horror/trash films of José Mojica Marins situate their approaches in work by Schaefer, Hawkins and others, whilst also underlining the differences in their objects of study resulting from Latin America's very different cinematic history (much later consolidation of industries and classical styles in Mexico, the contiguity of the avant garde film movement and trash aesthetics in Brazil). For instance, López' analysis of Juan Orol, René Cardona and José Bohr borrows Schaefer's concept of exploitation cinema as an "alternative cinematic practice grounded in spectacle" but emphasizes its later development in Mexico (1940s and 1950s versus the 1920s in the United States) and how certain directors acted as important precursors to many exploitation practices including foregrounding spectacle (2009: 15).

Although exploitation cinemas were and continue to be largely disavowed and/or discredited by local Latin American critics, the resurrection of exploitation cinema in English language also takes its cue from the few local critics, academics, preservationists and curators often working outside the range of texts canonized as part of national patrimonies who *have* been paying attention to the myriad of gore, horror, sexploitation, science fiction and fantasy films in their own national traditions; Argentine critic Diego Curubeto for instance, whose collection *Cine bizarro: 100 años de películas de terror, sexo y violencia* (Strange Cinema: 100 years of horror, sex and violent films, 1996) looks at a range of horror, sex, violent and exploitation films from all over the continent, spanning from the early sound era to the present; Mexican journalists Raúl Criollo, José Xavier Navar and Rafael Aviña whose *Quiero ver sangre: Historia ilustrada del cine de luchadores* (I want to see blood: An illustrated history of the wrestling film, 2011) gives an account of the wrestling film subgenre in Mexico between 1938 and 2011 and Brazilian journalists André Barcinski and Ivan Fanotti's *Maldito: A vida e o cinema de José Mojica Marins, o Zé do Caixão* (Damned: the life and cinema of José Mojica Marins, Coffin Joe, 1998) talks about Brazilian horror auteur José Mojica Marins' career as a filmmaker. Brazilian academic Alfredo Luis Suppia is also working in this field, seeking to define a tradition of Latin American science fiction and fantasy film (2013). In 2013 Mexican filmmaker Viviana García Besné, grandniece of Mexican producers of many films that could be classed as exploitation Memo, Perico y Pepé Calderón and great granddaughter of exhibition and distribution pioneer José Calderón set up the Permanencia Voluntaria in Tepoztlán, Mexico, to house and preserve the family film archive and also restore films which have been deemed "too low brow and commercial for preservation" (Horak 2015). Most recently, the Permanencia Voluntaria has (in collaboration with the Academy Film Archive in Los Angeles) restored *Santo y el cerebro del mal* (*Santo vs. the Evil Brain,* Joselito Rodríguez 1959) which was screened at the Berlinale in February 2018.

Another important beginning or antecedent to "Latsploitation" as a discrete field of study are the individual essays on Latin American exploitation cinemas in English language exploitation and/or horror anthologies as these begin the process of aligning these films within the parameters of exploitation, bad, trash and film culture as it has been principally understood in US and European terms. Colin Gunckle's essay on the Mexican Aztec horror films in Jeffrey Sconce's *Sleaze Artists: Cinema at the Margins of Taste, Style and Politics* (2007) for instance aligns the scenes of "human sacrifice, decaying corpses and maniacal scientists" prevalent in films like *El signo de la muerte* (*The Sign of Death,* Chano Urueta, 1939) and *La momia Azteca contra el robot humano* (*The Robot vs. the Aztec Mummy,* Rafael Portillo, 1957) with the reversals of dominant culture common in exploitation film (2007: 122). Andrew Syder and Dolores Tierney's essay on Mexican wrestling films in Steven Jay Schneider's *Horror International* (2005) thinks self-consciously about how we understand the terms of exploitation, pscyhotronic and paracinematic film culture in relation to these films as they shift in context from their original production in Mexico in the 1950s/1960s, to 1960s US midnight television and 1980s psychotronic film culture. These inclusions, together with standalone articles in a variety of journals (Ricalde 2004; Tierney 2004; Ruétalo 2004), represent the beginnings of interest in the field and help foment broader interest and generate more scholarship.

More recently positive signs of the growth of latsploitation include further focus on what have become the central texts of Latin American exploitation cinemas: Santo films (Hegarty 2013), Alejandro Jodorowsky's *El Topo* and the work of Mojica Marins (St George 2016) as well as opening out to embrace films beyond this non-canonical canon. Work in this area has included several studies of individual films, including a book on Jodorowsky's *The Holy Mountain* in the Cultographies series (same director but different film) by Alessandra Santos (2017) a monograph *Narcocinema: Sex, Drugs and Banda Music in Mexico's B-Filmography* by Ryan Rashotte (2015), Seraina Rohrer's *La India Maria: Mexploitation and the Films of Maria Elena Velasco* (2017) which explores the style, context and significance of one of Mexico's most popular (but critically derided) filmmakers and also Valentina Vitali's exploration of Mexican exploitation auteur Fernando Méndez in *Capital and Popular Cinema: The Dollars Are Coming* (2016).

Whilst the arbiters of dominant film culture in Latin America still do not embrace Latin America's exploitation cinemas[7] they are increasingly less marginalized in critical discourse and in canons as their aesthetics and associated subgenres shift more and more towards the mainstream. The successes of Mexican auteur Guillermo del Toro in fantasy, horror and science fiction (*Cronos* 1992, *Mimic* 1997, *The Devil's Backbone* 2001, *Blade II* 2002, *Hellboy* 2004, *Pan's Labyrinth* 2006, *Hellboy II: The Golden Army* 2008, *Pacific Rim* 2013, *Crimson Peak* 2015) and most recently with Oscars for Best Director and Best Picture at the 90th Academy Awards (*The Shape of Water* 2017) have substantially rehabilitated the critical disreputability of these genres and facilitated increased production in Mexico and the rest of Latin America. Del Toro's curatorial efforts, including financing the restoration of a thought lost (but also critically disavowed) adult version of a 1968 Mexican wrestling/science fiction film *El vampiro y el sexo* (*The Vampire and the Sex* René Cardona), have also contributed to the rehabilitation of exploitation (particularly horror and science fiction) and to the acknowledgement of its significance to Mexico's cinema history. Also of note in this recuperation of science fiction, horror and fantasy is the international festival Buenos Aires Rojo Sangre Festival de Cine de Terror, Fantástico y Bizarro (BARS) which has been running since 2000 and is now into its twentieth year. The work of Robert Rodriguez (*El Mariachi* 1993, *Desperado* 1996 and *Once Upon a Time in Mexico* 2004) has also increased the visibility and popularity of the *narco videohome*, aligning it with a US independent sensibility and helping it to acquire a legion of Anglo fans.[8]

Now that we are ten years on from the publication of *Latsploitation*, there are two new and related frontiers for the study of exploitation cinemas and its associated genres in Latin America. Firstly, the incorporation of Latsploitation cinemas like the videohome, the comedies starring Maria Elena Velasco as La India Maria, the "terrir" films of Brazilian director Ivan Cardoso and others into work on the emerging field of global cult cinema and secondly, and relatedly, questions about how to critically assimilate the concept of cult cinema into Latin American film cultures. Like "exploitation cinema", the term "cult film" (una película de culto) has not entered into common usage in local criticism in Latin America to date because "culto" most directly translates in Spanish as "cultured" or "educated", which most films of a "cult" nature in the Anglo meaning of the word are very far from being. Nevertheless, with these caveats, "cult" or "culto" is increasingly used in recent English and some Spanish language scholarship on the region's cinema as a descriptive for a broader spectrum of subgenres (trash, exploitation, horror) as well as a range of viewer practices and modes of consumption. Several essays in the *Latsploitation* anthology (2009) use the term cult; Josetxo Cerdán and Miguel Fernández Labayen outline the cult status of the work of Jodorowsky (2009), Antonio Lázaro-Reboll looks at the reception of Latin American exploitation cinemas in Spanish fan magazines as an example of "localized cult response" (2009: 38). In another anthology Kirsten Strayer identifies Mexican filmmaker Juan López Moctezuma's *The Mansion of Madness* (1973) as a "cult object" (2014: 110). Rosana Díaz-Zambrana and Patricia Tomé in *Horrorfílmico* call *The Vampire* (*El vampiro*; Mexico, Fernando Méndez, 1957) "el primer largometraje de culto" ("the first cult feature") (2012: 31). Most recently the Cuban zombiecom (zombie comedy) *Juan de los muertos* (*Juan of the Dead* Alejandro Brugués, 2011) has been called "a cult film hit" (Maristany Castro 2012). As I have rehearsed elsewhere in relation to exploitation cinema and its transition to a Latin American context, the new field of cult cinema presents a range of problems because Latin American film industries have followed very different paths to Hollywood and other dominant industries of the Global North. In addition to linguistic translations, in which "cult" and "culto" do not necessarily transfer straightforwardly, the cultural translation across borders of the terms that are part of cult analysis "subcultural ideology" or "subcultural value" and practices that are part of cult viewing protocols (talking back to the screen) associated with cult cinema in the United States and Europe is similarly not uncomplicated (Tierney 2014a: 132–133).

More work on the cross-border reception of cult and exploitation cinemas from Latin America, in the United States, Europe and other venues in the Global North is required in order to understand how cult functions in Latin American film cultures. This work has to recognize the potential for "colonialist" textual poaching, in which some metropolitan viewers may delight in the "zany" and "unfathomable" cultures of postcolonial nations, but at the same time do so without falling into an "exoticist assumption" or automatically categorizing *all* spectators of exploitation cinema or more specifically *all* "cultists" in the Global North as "white, straight, privileged males" and/or suggest they consume exploitation cinema made in the Global South in the same way (Sexton 2017: 9, 16). More work is also necessary on instances of cult consumption in Latin America (that sometimes centre on the same cult texts common in US and

European notions of cult such as *The Rocky Horror Picture Show, Casablanca, The Breakfast Club, Cat People*) to explore what it means for cult audiences in Latin America to consume texts from the North. What scholars of the new field of cult in latsploitation need to explore is whether these instances of cult consumption in Latin America shift the potential power dynamic of a metropolitan audience consuming the filmic products of the periphery when the process is reversed.

Notes

1 Lisa Shaw and Stephanie Dennison's *Popular Cinema in Brazil* is the exception amongst accounts of a Latin American national cinema, Brazil, devoting several pages both to horror auteur José Mojica Marins and to the *pornochancha* films that proliferated in the 1970s and 1980s (2004: 140–143, 149–178).
2 Representative of this privileging is how Mexican film historian, Emilio García Riera opens his prefatory essay to volume 14 of his encyclopaedic history of Mexican cinema by suggesting that the documentary made about the student protests at the National Autonomous University in Mexico City, *El grito* (*The Scream* Leobardo López Arretche) was the most significant film of 1968, and after it the most significant films were made by the auteurs of the nuevo cine (new cinema) movement, Jorge Isaac, and others (1995: 8).
3 A quick internet search reveals Latin American films appearing in various overviews of World Cult Cinema. For example, Mexican cult film *El Topo* (Alejandro Jodorowsky 1970) is programmed for a course on Global Cult Cinema at Kings College London, whilst the films of Brazilian horror director Zé do Caixão (Coffin Joe) are taught as the Latin American element on a course in Cult Cinema at the University of British Columbia in Canada.
4 That these films are now subtitled when through the 1960s, 1970s, 1980s and 1990s, they would have been dubbed to meet the needs of their drive-in, late night television or pyschotronic/paracinematic audiences signals a further shift in how these films are received and valued.
5 See Andrew Syder and Dolores Tierney (2005) for more on both the Mexican context and circulation of these films as well as their circulation on the North American drive in circuits and on late US night television in the 1960s.
6 See Paranaguá (1992, 1995).
7 A recent example of such a rejection includes the refusal in November 2017 by the director of Mexico's National Cinematheque Alejandro Pelayo to hold centenary celebrations and a retrospective homage for El Santo, Mexican wrestler and star of over eighty hugely popular films because his films are, in the words of Pelayo "very bad" (https://codigoespagueti.com/noticias/cultura/no-habra-homenaje-el-santo-en-la-cineteca-nacional-porque-sus-peliculas-son-muy-malas/). After a huge public outcry, it was made clear that this was Pelayo's opinion and not that of the Cinematheque and that there would be an homage to El Santo, but at the time of writing no dates have been given for any future season celebrating El Santo and his films (http://revesonline.com/2017/11/03/si-habra-homenaje-a-el-santo-en-la-cineteca-nacional/).
8 It's also worth pointing out various treatments of the narcocinema aesthetic in mainstream Mexican cinema; *El Infierno* (Luis Estrada, 2010) and Amat Escalante's *Heli* (2013).

References

Ávalos, Adán. 2009. "The Naco in Mexican Film: *La banda del carro rojo*, Border Cinema, and Migrant Audiences", in Victoria Ruétalo and Dolores Tierney, eds, *Latsploitation, Exploitation Cinemas and Latin America*. London: Routledge: 185–197.

Barcinski, André, and Ivan Fanotti. 1998. *Maldito: A vida e o cinema de José Mojica Marins, o Zé do Caixão*. São Paolo: Editora 34.

Cerdán, Josetxo, and Miguel Fernández Labayen. 2009. "Art Exploitation, Cool Cult, and the Cinema of Alejandro Jodorowsky", in Victoria Ruétalo and Dolores Tierney, eds, *Latsploitation, Exploitation Cinemas and Latin America*: 102–114.

Colina, Enrique, and Daniel Díaz Torres. 1972. "Ideología del Melodrama en el Viejo Cine Latinoamericano", *Cine Cubano* 74: 14–26.

Criollo, Raúl, José Xavier Navar and Rafael Aviña. 2011. *Quiero Ver Sangre: Historia ilustrada del cine de luchadores.* Mexico City: Universidad Nacional Autónoma de Mexico.

Curubeto, Diego. 1996. *Cine Bizarro: 100 años de películas de terror, sexo y violencia.* Argentina: Sudamericana.

Davis, Glyn, Kay Dickinson, Lisa Patti and Amy Villarejo. 2015. *Film Studies: A Global Introduction.* London: Routledge.

Díaz-Zambrana, Rosana, and Patricia Tomé. 2012. *Horrorfílmico: Aproximaciones al cine de terror en Latinoamérica y el Caribe.* San Juan: Isla Negra Editores.

De la Mora, Sergio. 2009. "'La ley me las paso por mis huevos': Isela Vega and Mexican Dirty Movies", in Victoria Ruétalo and Dolores Tierney, eds, *Latsploitation, Exploitation Cinemas and Latin America*: 245–257.

D'Lugo, Marvin. 2012. "*Latsploitation, Exploitation Cinemas and Latin America* Review", *Revista de Estudios Hispánicos* 3: 592–594.

García Riera, Emilio. 1995. *Historia Documental del Cine Mexicano*, vol. 14, Mexico: Universidad de Guadalajara.

Greene, Doyle. 2005. *Mexploitation: A Critical History of Mexican Vampire, Wrestler, Ape Man and Similar Films 1957–1977.* Jefferson, NC: McFarland.

Gunckle, Colin. 2007. "*El signo de la muerte* and the Birth of a Genre: Origins and Anatomy of the Aztec Horror Film", in Jeffrey Sconce, ed., *Sleaze Artists: Cinema at the Margins of Taste, Style and Politics.* Durham, NC: Duke University Press: 121–143.

Hawkins, Joan. 2000. *Cutting Edge: Art-Horror and the Horrific Avant Garde.* Minneapolis: University of Minnesota Press.

Hegarty, Kerry. 2013. "From Superhero to National Hero: The Populist Myth of El Santo", *Studies in Latin American Popular Culture* 31: 3–27.

Horak, Jan-Christopher. 2015. "Permanencia Voluntaria", UCLA Film and Television Archive Blog, August 28. www.cinema.ucla.edu/blogs/archival-spaces/2015/08/28/permanencia-voluntaria (accessed February 28, 2018).

Jancovich, Mark, Antonio Lázaro-Reboll, Julian Stringer and Andrew Willis, eds. 2003. *Defining Cult Movies: The Cultural Politics of Oppositional Taste.* Manchester: Manchester University Press.

Kuhn, Annette, and Guy Westwell. 2012. *A Dictionary of Film Studies.* Oxford: Oxford University Press.

Lázaro-Reboll, Antonio. 2009. "'Perversa America Latina': The Reception of Exploitation Cinemas in Spanish Subcultures", in Victoria Ruétalo and Dolores Tierney, eds, *Latsploitation, Latin American Cinema and Exploitation*: 37–54.

López, Ana M. 1985. "The Melodrama in Latin America: Telenovelas, Film, and the Currency of a Popular Form", *Wide Angle* 7.3: 4–13.

———. 1991. "Celluloid Tears: Melodrama in the Classic Mexican Cinema", *Iris* 13: 29–52.

———. 2009. "Before Exploitation: Three Men of Cinema", in Victoria Ruétalo and Dolores Tierney, eds, *Latsploitation, Latin American Cinema and Exploitation Cinemas*: 13–37.

Madrigal, Alex. 2010. "Millones de latinos compran narcopelículas", *El Universal.com.mx.* http://archivo.eluniversal.com.mx/espectaculos/96945.html (accessed July 1, 2017).

Maristany Castro, Carlos Eduardo. 2012. "'Juan of the Dead': The Making of a Cult Film Hit", *Cuba Art News*, March. www.cubanartnews.org/news/juan_of_the_dead_the_making_of_a_cult_film_hit_part_one-995 (accessed July 12, 2017).

Paranaguá, Paulo Antonio. 1992. *Le cinema Mexicain.* Paris: Centre Pompidou.

———. 1995. *Mexican Cinema.* London: BFI.

Rashotte, Ryan. 2015. *Narco Cinema: Sex, Drugs and Banda Music in Mexico's B-Filmography.* London and New York: Palgrave Macmillan.

Ricalde, Maricruz Castro. 2004. "Popular Mexican Cinema and Undocumented Immigrants", *Discourse* 26.1/2: 194–213.

Rohrer, Seraina. 2017. *La India Maria: Mexploitation and the Films of Maria Elena Velasco.* Austin: University of Texas Press.

Ruétalo, Victoria. 2004. "Temptations: Isabel Sarli Exposed", *Journal of Latin American Cultural Studies* 13.1: 79–85.

Ruétalo, Victoria, and Dolores Tierney, eds. 2009. *Latsploitation, Latin American Cinema and Exploitation Cinemas.* London: Routledge.

Santos, Alessandra. 2017. *The Holy Mountain.* London: Wallflower Press.

Santos Aquino, Rowena. 2011. "*Latsploitation, Exploitation Cinema and Latin America*", Review, *Scope: An Online Journal of Film* 21: 26–27.

Schaefer, Eric. 1999. *Bold! Daring! Shocking! True! A History of Exploitation Films (1919–1959)*. Durham, NC: Duke University Press.

Sconce, Jeffrey. 1995. "Trashing the Academy: Taste, Excess, and an Emerging Politics of Cinematic Style", *Screen* 36.6: 371–393.

———. 2007. *Sleaze Artists: Cinema at the Margins of Taste, Style and Politics*. Durham, NC: Duke University Press.

Sexton, Jamie. 2017. "The Allure of Otherness: Transnational Cult Film Fandom and the Exoticist Assumption", *Transnational Cinemas* 8.1: 5–19.

Shaw, Lisa, and Stephanie Dennison. 2004. *Popular Cinema in Brazil*. Manchester: Manchester University Press.

St George, Charles. 2016. "Brazilian Horrors: Past and Present", *Journal of Latin American Cultural Studies* 25.4: 555–570.

Strayer, Kristen. 2014. "Art, Horror, and International Identity in 1970s Exploitation Films", in Dana Och and Kirsten Strayer, eds, *Transnational Horror Across Visual Media: Fragmented Bodies*. New York: Routledge: 109–125.

Suppia, Luis Alfredo. 2013. "The Question for Latin American Science Fiction and Fantasy Film", *Frames Cinema Journal* (Special Issue "Mondo Pop: Rethinking Genre Beyond Hollywood") 6. http://framescinemajournal.com/article/the-quest-for-latin-american-science-fiction-fantasy-film (accessed July 2017).

Syder, Andrew, and Dolores Tierney. 2005. "Mexploitation/Exploitation: Or How a Crime-Fighting, Vampire-Slaying Wrestler Almost Found Himself in a Sword and Sandals Epic", in Stephen J. Schneider and Tony Williams, eds, *Horror International*. Detroit, MI: Wayne State University Press: 33–55.

Tierney, Dolores. 2004. "José Mojica Marins and the Cultural Politics of Marginality in Third World Film Criticism", *Journal of Latin American Cultural Studies* 13.1: 63–78.

———. 2014a. "Mapping Cult Cinema in Latin American Film Cultures", *Cinema Journal* 54.1: 129–135.

———. 2014b. "Reflections about Film Scholarship and the Internet", *In Media Res*. http://mediacommons.futureofthebook.org/imr/2014/11/17/reflections-film-scholarship-and-internet. Accessed 17 July 2017.

Tombs, Pete. 1997. *Mondo Macabro: Weird and Wonderful Cinema from Around the World*. London: Titan Books.

Vitali, Valentina. 2016. *Capital and Popular Cinema: The Dollars Are Coming*. Manchester: Manchester University Press.

Weldon, Mike. 1986. *The Psychotronic Encyclopedia of Film*. New York: Ballantine Books.

10

IRANIAN CULT CINEMA

Babak Tabarraee

Watching films can rarely be free of ideological and political connotations. This is especially true about Iran. A turbulent history of power struggles and contesting cultural policies in this country, at least since the Constitutional Revolution (1906–1909), has deeply engraved the sociopolitical contexts of film reception onto the usual currencies of cult cinema definitions. Mapping Iranian cult cinema, then, cannot be limited to (inter)textual analyses or audience-oriented surveys, especially considering that Iranian movie fans do not have the same venues of expression as their Western counterparts. A thorough consideration of the relationship between the systems of film production and the modes of their reception in each historical period can radically change current canonizations of the festival-favorite Iranian films and partly redress the mostly Anglo-Western scholarship on cult cinema. Obviously, such a task is beyond the scope of this short article. The following, therefore, should be read as a schematic depiction of an alternative film history, in a most condensed form.

During the reign of Reza Shah Pahlavi (1925–1941), only nine Iranian features were made in Iran and in India. Today, we only have access to two of these films, including a shortened version of the first Iranian talkie, *The Lor Girl* (Ardeshir Irani, 1932). Written by its migrated male star, Abdolhosein Sepanta, and directed by an Indian of Parsee descent in Mumbai, the historical records of *The Lor Girl*'s long and recurrent theatrical runs suggest that it might well have been the first Iranian cult film (Omid 1984: 40–42). The film's main plotline revolves around the relationship between a girl kidnapped by a Lor tribe (Golnar) and a government inspector fighting the bandits in the region (Jafar). They escape to India, and finally return to an apparently modernized Iran. Iranian film histories abound with accounts of the cinemagoers' obsession with *The Lor Girl*, including applauses while watching (Naficy 2011a: 237); anecdotes of repeat viewing to as many as seventy times (Khatibi 2001: 536); extensive recitations of its songs and quoting its lines in different cities;[1] and re-enactment of some of its scenes by the youth in family parties (Naficy 2011a: 240).

The technological novelty of sound film can only explain part of this unprecedented success. The collage-like form of *The Lor Girl* is reminiscent of Eco's oft-quoted textual criterion of a cult film: "it is not *one* movie. It is *movies*" (Eco 1985: 10). The makers of *The Lor Girl* re-appropriated the Orientalist overview of American Westerns and epic features and combined it with the performative traditions of Indian musical drama and Iranian picaresque folk tales and pastoral romance.[2] More importantly, the film's improbable plotline touched upon some crucial elements of the cultural metamorphosis that the Iranian urban middle classes were going through in the 1930s. The protagonists of the film, Jafar and Golnar, rarely miss a chance to emphasize the importance of national identity, Reza Shah's top-bottom model of modernization, themes of migration and return, and even the *à la mode* anti-Arab feelings of the time. These made *The Lor Girl* historically relevant and a strategic role model for a nascent industry. Many of the Iranian popular films of the next few decades, collectively known as *Filmfarsi*, deployed the formal strategies and moral suggestions of *The Lor Girl* (Baharlu 2003: 22). Moreover, the film continued to revive its popularity through several homages, including Manuchehr Qasemi's remake with the new title *Jafar and Golnar* (1970), Mohsen Makhmalbaf's post-modernist reincarnation of Golnar's scenes in *Once Upon a Time, Cinema* (1992), and Massoud Bakhshi's ironic refences to its soundtrack in his acclaimed docufiction, *Tehran Has No More Pomegranates* (2006). *The Lor Girl*'s continuous commemoration by the scholars of Iranian cinema outside Iran also makes it an object of transnational academic cult fandom.

The era of Reza Shah's son, Mohammad Reza Pahlavi (1941–1979) witnessed an increase in local production along with a relentless import of foreign films. Unlike what happened in many Western and Far-Eastern countries, however, the more susceptible genres to cult status, such as horror, Sci-Fi, and fantasies never found a reliable fanbase in Iran. Instead, with the advent and popularity of dubbing practice since 1946, different forms of foreign films shaped their own dedicated transnational audience (Baharlu 2006: 83–89). These included various genres of popular Indian melodrama and Hong Kong Kung-Fu films, American musicals re-composed with Persian lyrics, Italian sex comedies and Western Spaghettis, European art films, and renewed dubbed-versions of Hollywood classics. Many Iranian productions imitated the narrative formulae of these films to secure and develop their fanbase. Two films, in particular, were outstandingly successful. Siamak Yasemi's *Qarun's Treasure* (1965) initiated a new subgenre of *Filmfarsi* known as *film-e ābgushti* (stewpot film) (Naficy 2011b: 197). This dramedy is about a rich man who commits suicide but is rescued by a poor young man that turns out to be his long-lost son. The son rejects his father and all his fortune at first, but finally embraces his new identity, seemingly without changing his attitude toward bourgeoise. The expression *film-e ābgushti* refers both to the male bonding over a traditional, lower-middle-class dish of *ābgusht* (stewpot) as depicted in this film and present in the Iranian society in general, and to the mishmash of folk songs, sexy dances, unlikely combination of religious principles and drinking scenes, patriarchal values, and a happy-go-lucky attitude that seemed hopeful for upward social mobility, but also released its tensions. These were some of the reasons described for the film's phenomenal box-office success (Naficy 2011b: 199–200).

The other popular film of the time, *Qeysar* (Masoud Kimiai, 1969), was among the several pioneers of the so-called Iranian New Wave in the late 1960s and early 1970s. *Qeysar* is a cinematic *tour de force* of its titular protagonist's quest to take revenge from the three brothers responsible for raping his sister, killing his brother, and making his mother die of their grief. This film became the prototype of a trend of commercial films promoting individual protest, righteous violence, patriarchal values, and what some critics later denounced as a "completely traditional and reactionary view of social concepts" (Aghighi 2012: 104). *Qarun's Treasure* and *Qeysar* paved the way for waves of similar productions and made their stars pigeonholed in similar roles (Ejlali 2015: 179–181). While these two films and their stars were already representing certain cinematic and social subcultures in the 1970s, their development to a full-fledged cult status was completed after the 1979 revolution.

The Islamic Republic's antagonistic views toward West and what was conceived as Western-inspired cultural products soon led to a halt of film import and to the ban of many pre-revolutionary films and their stars. In the past four decades, domestic film-viewing in Iran has undergone a five-stage path. These include the introduction and instant popularity of Betamax and VHS systems (1979–1983), an official ban on videotapes combined with the emergence of a highly accessible underground market (1983–1994), the spread of computers and VCDs (since the late 1990s), prevalence of bootleg DVDs (since the mid-2000s), and finally, the Internet era with its easily downloadable digital files (since the late 2000s). Similar to the case of video nasties in the United Kingdom in the 1980s, this restrictive climate turned many average Iranian cinephiles into obsessive collectors (Egan 2007: 203). Trying to rebuild their own deprived private sphere, these individual archivists began to collect a broad variety of *Filmfārsi*, old and new Hollywood and Bollywood, and European art films. Acts of resistance, remembrance, or re-connection to an imagined global cinephilia might have been conducive to this kind of illegal, indiscriminate, and addictive film-collecting, at least until the age of the Internet.[3]

Despite the lack of an officially visible fandom and communal or participatory viewing possibilities, these new conditions of viewing turned certain popular stars of the pre-revolutionary films into new cult figures. The romantic films of Googoosh (a much loved pop singer who went into silence until her departure for the United States in 2000), the melodrama-with-happy-endings of Mohammad Ali Fardin (a former wrestling champion and the star of *Qarun's Treasure* and other stewpot *Filmfārsi* who remained in Iran until his death in 2000), and the failure-dramas of Behrouz Vossoughi (the star of *Qeysar* and many other New Wave films who left Iran for the United States during the revolution) became some of the most requested titles from the underground film-dealers.[4]

The case of Behrouz Vossoughi may serve as a telling example. His cinematic persona of a lonely, uncompromising, wounded hero who helplessly fought for his honor complied with both the underlying values of the revolution and the oppositional voices after the regime change. His many belligerent, angry, and overly masculine monologues continued to remain the *locus classicus* of colloquial statements of protests even among my own generation of *the children of the revolution*. Like some other national cult stars, the overwhelming presence of Vossoughi as the personification of the complexities of social mobility earned him a devoted fanbase despite his long years of absence from Iranian cinema screens.[5] This association becomes clear in one of the very few cases that Iranian film reviewers have written on a pre-revolutionary cult film: *The Beehive* (Fereydoun Goleh, 1975). Loosely inspired by Frank Perry and Sydney Pollack's *The Swimmer* (1968), this film is about a down-and-out ex-convict played by Vossoughi whose punishment of losing a gambling game is to drink in any bar in Tehran that the winner orders him, without paying for it. As a reviewer of the prestigious Iranian magazine, *Film Monthly*, asserted in 2013, the merciless image of Tehran and its class conflicts, crystalized in the rich-north/poor-south contrast, has been essential to the film's enduring cult status. However, at least half of this review is about the similarities and differences of Vossoughi's cinematic portrayals of alienated tough guys (Karimi 2013: 92–93).

The end of the Iraq-Iran war in 1987 and the changes in the Iranian supreme leadership in the following year promised a new era for the Iranian cinema. Internationally, the art films of humanistic auteurs, such as Abbas Kiarostami, became an indispensable part of festival circuits. Locally, the relative laxity of previous supervisions initiated a gradual reform in cultural policies and the film industry.[6] Generally considered as a cult film for the intelligentsia, *Hamoun* (Dariush Mehrjui, 1989) was one of the vanguards of this new era. Inspired by Søren Kierkegaard's philosophical treatise, *Fear and Trembling* (1843), and Saul Bellow's existential novel, *Herzog* (1964), the film depicts the midlife crisis of its antihero, Hamid Hamoun, who is a PhD candidate in humanities. Consumed by writing his dissertation on love and faith to Abraham, Hamoun is going through a painful divorce process and many financial difficulties. With its Felliniesque dream sequences and complex flashback-in-flashbacks, *Hamoun* may be the most recognizable example of a cult film to the Western audience. Its local status as a source of endless quotes within intellectual circles, however, lies in its incorporation of many intertextual and extratextual references to the books, poems, and conditions only too familiar to those recovering from the cacophony of a revolution and the disasters of a war. When *Hamoun*'s star died in 2008, a reformist writer in exile wrote:

> Hamoun to us was a lifestyle, an approach, a way of thinking and living. He read the same things that we did, had the same taste as we did, carried the same loves and hates as we did. We loved him, because he was our mirror reflection.
>
> (Nabavi 2008)

This deep connection later became the subject of a documentary (directed by Mani Haghighi in 2007) and a stage drama (written and directed by Mohammad Rahmanian in 2015), both titled *Hamoun-bāz-hā* [*The Hamooners*], about the experiential and extraordinary relationship of *Hamoun*'s fans to this film and its central character.

In the last years of Akbar Hashemi Rafsanjani's self-labelled "construction" age (1989–1997) and during Mohammad Khatami's "reform" government (1997–2005), socio-politically aware reconfigurations of pre-tested genres changed the conventional norms of film reception in Iran. Three modes of films developed new forms of audience engagements in these years. These were bitter films about rebellious youth, sophisticated romances, and comedic transgressions. Each of these non-campy trends, even the comedies, have generated extremely serious receptions. Parviz Shahbazi's *Deep Breath* (2002), for example, was about a rebellious young generation who was even deprived of voicing their protest. One of the film's main three characters refuses to eat until he dies. For unknown reasons, the actor of this role never appeared in another film. When he died ten years later, seemingly due to a gas leak in his apartment, critics began to assess the cultish popularity of his filmic character by exploring his transformation to a cinematic icon comparable to James Dean in the American culture ("Saeed Amini," mehrnews.com; Safarian 2013). Another youth favorite, Farzad Motamen's same-title adaptation of Dostoevsky's *White Nights* (2003), shifted its sentimental focus on a doomed love between a cerebral professor of literature and a helplessly romantic young woman claiming to be in love with another man. The senselessness of this relationship was doubly forbidden by the religious laws that do not allow for direct representation of physical love on Iranian screens. The critics and viewers were indifferent to the initial screening of the film at Tehran's Fajr Festival. But, soon, it turned into a romantic, yet erudite, cult film and one of the rare Iranian cases enjoying multiple special re-screenings in the following years (Motamen 2016).

Conforming to Barry Keith Grant's argument about the ideological double feature of cult films (2000: 15), the cult comedies of this period were simultaneously transgressive and recuperative. Moreover, the politically appropriable nature of these films added a layer of controversy to their official and public receptions. Bans, censorship, underground distributions, and final resurrections are elements shared between *Snowman* (Davoud Mirbaqeri, 1994) and *The Lizard* (Kamal Tabrizi, 2003). The former depicts a man's cross-dressing in order to obtain an American visa from the US Consulate General in Istanbul, Turkey. In the last act of the film, though, he falls in love, changes his mind, and decides to go back to Iran. After the Fajr Festival screening, *Snowman* was banned for three years because of crossing many religious and political red lines, while its VHS tapes became extremely accessible and popular in the underground market. Nonetheless, neither the film's conservative ending nor its far-reaching illegal distribution diminished the sensitivities about it. When it was finally released in 1997, rumors and reports spread about physical confrontations between the films' fans and Islamic revolutionary plainclothes.[7] So, despite its obvious message, watching *Snowman* became a symbol of cultural resistance.

The situation was even more complicated for *The Lizard*. This Iranianized version of Neil Jordan's *We're No Angels* (1989) is about a roughneck prisoner who escapes from jail by stealing a Shi'i cleric's clothes and maintaining this pretense in a small border town before getting arrested. Released only for four clamorous weeks in 2004, *The Lizard* became the highest-selling Iranian film up until that point and a cultural battleground for many prominent religious and political figures. The contrasting narratives about the film introduced it as a conformist, reformist, anti-cleric, transcendental, or a safety-valve device. Whatever the interpretations, it has survived as a controversial trope for the complex relationship between the Iranian society and its ruling theocracy.

Mahmoud Ahmadinejad's eight years of nationally conservative and internationally adventurous presidency (2005–2013), once again pushed for politicization of both cultural productions and receptions. Coincided with the technological revolution of the Internet and the ease of access to all kinds of films, Ahmadinejad's blatant support of a certain ideological cinema faced an equally strong resistance by films that were either produced in direct response to his policies or were received as such. The international success of Asghar Farhadi's films, for example, along with their emphasis on themes such as the importance of truthful conversations for reaching practical results, made them a national bulwark against the impositions of the officially sponsored pro-government films. The cult potentials of Farhadi's films have maintained their status even during the moderate government of Hasan Rouhani (2013-present), partly due to the ongoing national culture wars and partly because of the country's many unresolved economic and social problems. The symbolic value of quoting *About Elly* (2009) in friendly gatherings, referring to the Oscar of *A Separation* (2010) as a victory against Ahmadinejad's policies, and debates over the political nature of Farhadi's 2017 Oscar for *The Salesman* (2015) vis-à-vis the American travel bans for Iranian citizens are some possible components of the projection of cult values onto Farhadi's films. Only the passage of time, however, can tell us whether these films will enjoy a persistent celebration by their fans.

The many different definitions of cult films entail different approaches to their investigation. As Mathijs and Sexton have previously described, the American-centric studies on cult cinema have mostly been concerned with either films as texts, or viewers as subjects of research (Mathijs and Sexton 2011: 6–9). Here, I have suggested a broader historical approach, at least in the case of one national cult cinema, in which the sociopolitical contexts of film production and reception are deemed as important factors in a film's cult status as other textual and audience-based elements. A direct consequence of this approach can be reaching new histories of national cinemas. Furthermore, this article implicitly invites the readers to reconsider the concept of (cult) fandom as a communal activity. Participatory screening, for example, has not even been a possibility for many Iranian films that have otherwise enjoyed continuous and/or uncommon elevations. Indeed, there cannot be a cult film without cult fans. The manifestations of cult fandom, however, can take different shapes in different places and times, not necessarily following cosmopolitan rules.

Notes

1 Shoai (1976: 40) for example, talks about the quotability of the film among the citizens of Mashhad.
2 For an elaboration of the influence of Hollywood on the works of Sepanta, see Sadr (2006: 27–32).
3 There is an extensive literature on the relationship between collecting and power (e.g. Foucault 2004 and Derrida 1995), memory and symbolic values (e.g. Baudrillard 2002 and Geraghty 2014), and personal and collective identity (e.g. Martin 1999 and Klinger 2006).
4 Underground video dealers are one of the subjects of Blake Atwood's recent research on the informal media distribution in Iran, as presented in his conference paper at the 2018 SCMS Conference, and in his upcoming book on the issue. I should thank him for generously sharing his analytical findings with me for this chapter.

5 For an exemplar depiction of the relationship between cult stardom and sociopolitical contexts in a non-Western national cinema, see Lim (2004).
6 For a detailed analysis of these historical changes, see Atwood (2016: 14–23).
7 The most persistent myth has been about the attack of a group of plainclothes to a movie theater showing this film, leading to the miscarriage of a pregnant viewer. This rumor is still in circulation. See, for example, "*Boresh-hā," tabnak.ir.*

References

Aghighi, Said. 2012. "Iranian New Wave: 1969–1979," in Parviz Jahed, ed. *Directory of World Cinema: Iran.* Chicago: Intellect and University of Chicago Press: 102–111.

Atwood, Blake. 2016. *Reform Cinema in Iran.* New York: Columbia University Press.

Atwood, Blake. 2018. "Underground Video Dealers in Iran: Labor and Informal Media Distribution," Paper presented at the Society for Cinema and Media Studies Conference, Toronto, ON, March.

Baharlu, Abbas. 2003. "*Do Film va Hameh-ye Cinema-ye Iran* [Two Films and All of Iranian Cinema]." *Film Monthly*, 300 (May): 21–22.

Baharlu, Abbas. 2006. "*Dubleh beh Farsi, az Āqāz tā Emruz* [Dubbing into Persian, from the Beginning until Today]." *Ketāb-e Sāl-e Cinema-ye Iran 1384* [*The Annual Book of Iranian Cinema 2005*], 15: 74–96.

Baudrillard, Jean. 2002. *The System of Objects.* Translated by James Benedict. London: Verso.

"*Boresh-hā-yi az Film-e 'Ādam Barfi'* [Excerpt from the Film, *Snowman*]." *tabnak.ir.* Last modified 30 December 2017. www.tabnak.ir/fa/news/760091/. Accessed 15 March 2018.

Derrida, Jacques. 1995. *Archive Fever: A Freudian Impression.* Translated by Eric Prenowitz. Chicago: University of Chicago Press.

Eco, Umberto. 1985. "*Casablanca*: Cult Movies and Intertextual Collage." *SubStance*, 14.2: 3–12.

Egan, Kate. 2007. "The Celebration of a 'Proper Product': Exploring the Residual Collectible Through the 'Video Nasty'," in Charles R. Acland, ed. *Residual Media.* Minneapolis: University of Minnesota Press: 200–221.

Ejlali, Parviz. 2015. *Degarguni-e Ejtemā'i va Film-hā-ye Cinemayi dar Iran* [*Social Change and Narrative Features in Iran*]. Tehran: Agah.

Foucault, Michel. 2004. *The Archeology of Knowledge.* London: Routledge.

Geraghty, Lincoln. 2014. *Cult Collectors.* New York: Routledge.

Grant, Barry Keith. 2000. "Second Thoughts on Double Features: Revisiting the Cult Film," in Graeme Harper and Xavier Mendick, eds, *Unruly Pleasures: The Cult Film and Its Critics.* Surrey: FAB Press: 13–27.

Karimi, Iraj. 2013. "*Tehran-e Bi-Rahm* [Merciless Tehran]." *Film Monthly*, 458 (May): 92–93.

Khatibi, Parviz. 2001. *Khāterāti az Honarmandān* [*Memories from Artists*]. Edited by Firouzeh Khatibi. Tehran: Moin.

Klinger, Barbara. 2006. *Beyond the Multiplex.* Berkeley: University of California Press.

Lim, Bliss Cua. 2004. "Cult Fiction: *Himala* and *Bakya* Temporality." *The Spectator*, 24.2: 61–72.

Martin, Paul. 1999. *Popular Collecting and the Everyday Self.* London: Leicester University Press.

Mathijs, Ernest, and Jamie Sexton. 2011. *Cult Cinema.* Oxford: Wiley-Blackwell.

Motamen, Farzad. 2016. "*Az 'Shab-hā-ye Roshan' Motenafferam* [I Hate *White Nights*]." *banifilm.ir.* http://banifilm. ir/%D9%81%D8%B1%D8%B2%D8%A7%D8%AF-%D9%85%D9%88%D8%AA%D9%85%D9%86-%D8%A7%D8%B2-%D8%B4%D8%A8%D9%87%D8%A7%DB%8C-%D8%B1%D9%88%D8%B4%D9%86-%D9%85%D8%AA%D9%86%D9%81%D8%B1%D9%85/. Accessed 15 March 2018.

Nabavi, Ebrahim. 2008. "Hamoun *Mā Budim* [We Were Hamoun]." *roozonline.com.* www.roozonline.com/persian/opinion/opinion-article/article/-c84fe57d6c.html. Accessed 15 March 2018.

Naficy, Hamid. 2011a. *The Social History of Iranian Cinema. Vol. 1: The Artisanal Era: 1897–1941.* Durham, NC: Duke University Press.

Naficy, Hamid. 2011b. *The Social History of Iranian Cinema. Vol. 2: The Industrializing Years: 1941–1978.* Durham, NC: Duke University Press.

Omid, Jamal. 1984. *Abdolhosein Sepanta: Zendegi va Cinema* [*Abdolhosein Sepant: Life and Cinema*]. Tehran: Faryab.

"*Saeed Amini James Dean-e Cinema-ye Iran Bud* [Saeed Amini Was the James Dean of Iranian Cinema]." *mehrnews.com.* Last modified 6 November 2013. www.mehrnews.com/news/2170262/. Accessed 15 November 2018.

Sadr, Hamid Reza. 2006. *Iranian Cinema: A Political History.* New York: I.B. Tauris.

Safarian, Robert. 2013. "*Qodrat-e Āykon-hā-ye Cinema-yi* [The Power of Cinematic Icons]." *robertsafarian. com.* http://robertsafarian.com/?p=1956. Accessed 15 November 2018.

Shoai, Hamid. 1976. *Nāmāvarān-e Cinema dar Iran, Vol. 1: Abdolhosein Sepnta* [*Celebrities of Iranian Cinema: Abdolhosein Sepanta*]. Tehran: Self-published.

11

REBELS WITHOUT A CAUSE

The Bombay cult film

Vibhushan Subba

Fault lines

From avenging amazons in leopard print leotards to wild jungle fantasies with stuffed tigers, violated men in cheap Halloween costumes to super heroes with questionable abilities, from lusty dismembered ghosts with insatiable appetites to draculas with styrofoam wings, the universe of the Bombay low budget film runs silent, runs deep. For years these films have travelled along the mofussil circuits, drawing committed audiences in single-screen theatres, a scandalous, disreputable and degraded cultural object.

Existing in the margins of the Bombay film industry the Bombay exploitation film travels through informal circuits far removed from the standardized networks of a mainstream film. It is defined by an uncharacteristic operational mode deeply rooted in a framework of improvisation, shaped by unregulated economic relations and implemented by practices of distribution and exhibition suspended at the edges of legality. Bringing these films under one category is a self-defeating task brought upon by the sheer variety of genres and styles. It will not be an exaggeration to state that it is an extremely flexible category that cannot and should not be harnessed under one unifying label. The films that I am referring to are low budget Hindi films produced in Bombay and within this variegated and ambiguous territory such low genres as sexploitation, horror, soft-core jungle adventures, bandit films, cheap super hero spectacles, spy thrillers and murder mysteries co-exist together. This eclectic body of films is what I call 'Bombsploitation'. They are otherwise known as B-movies, B, C, D and Z grades, trashy films, sex films, adult films amongst other things.

The Bombsploitation film has followed a different route than its counterparts in the rest of the world. These exploitation films were not necessarily always part of a subcultural ideology with self-conscious cult materials or a strong contrarian desire but have travelled the interiors of India attracting audiences from the working class, migrant labourers and construction workers. So, there were no communities or film clubs built around these films, no cinephiliac circuits, no fanzines and of course no cult. Instead, these films flew under the radar as sleazy objects and circulated as a well-guarded 'public secret', which explains the vast silences that haunt these films with little mention in press and academia. As far back as the 1920s fantasy, stunt and action films drew committed audiences giving 'all-India super hits' like the 1924 fantasy film *Gul-e-Bakavali* (The Bakavali Flower, Kanjibhai Rathod) (Thomas 2014: 37). In the 1930s, action and stunt films continued to dominate under the aegis of the Wadia brothers and their production house Wadia Movietone movies. The Wadia brothers gave many sizeable hits like *Hunterwaali* (1935) and *Miss Frontier Mail* (1936), introducing Fearless Nadia who went on to become the stunt queen of the 30s raking in huge box office hits well into the forties. However, the stunt and action films remained dominant only in the B and C circuits (Thomas 2014: 10).[1] Through the forties and the fifties these films did mildly well surviving on remakes and rehashing of earlier films. It was not until the 1960s that action films produced on small budgets made a comeback in the form of sword and sandal epics like Dara Singh's *Samson* (Bhatt, 1964) and *Hercules* (Shriram, 1964) redolent of Italian peplums. However, it was in the late seventies and early eighties that these films turned to exploitation and waded into a landscape of 'sleaze', which made them disreputable and scandalous. The eighties enjoys a special place in the history of Indian cinema because this was the decade which saw the invasion of the video cassette.[2] This cassette culture had a transformational impact on the media landscape by opening up different avenues of exhibition like small video parlours and a change in consumption patterns was inevitable. Filmmakers and exhibitors believe that this decade gave birth to the trashy film as the middle classes chose to watch films in the comfort of their homes and left the theatres to the working classes. Since there was an endless demand for video, hiring out cassettes became a profitable business with even 'kirana merchants', 'paanwallahs' and 'petty shopkeepers' joining the fray to open makeshift libraries within the space of their tiny shops as side businesses (as reported in *The Times of India*, on 31 May, 1987). However, these low budget horror, sex and jungle adventures from that sleazy era are the very films that have been celebrated as cult within a small but growing community of fans. A wave of cinephiliac B-movie desire has erupted across social media platforms recently. Born largely within the networked environment of the internet, this vibrant community of B-movie cinephiles operating within the folds of the internet has revived the forgotten history and aesthetic of B-movies, horror and sexploitation films that sit at the bottom of the cinematic ecology in India reclaiming them as cult (Subba 2017). Changes in delivery platforms have resulted in changes in the constitution of audiences. As the internet opens up its informal archives to people from all walks of life the matter of placing these cult films in a specific context is further complicated. In many ways then, the small budget Bombay cult film occupies a liminal space in that it is neither mainstream nor pornography, something that is known and yet cannot be articulated.

The mutating form of Bombsploitation

The Bombay cult film's invisibility comes from the fact that the cult film enters arenas that other films are unable to and this affords the films a special charge. As a case study let us look at Harinam Singh's work. Singh's work remains unknown to most audiences. Working on abysmally low budgets, his films, if not a model of technique, are a miraculous supply of contorted narratives, improbable montages, curious hybridity, pop culture references and mysterious circumstances.

Consider for example, a film like *Shaitani Aatma* (*The Satanic Spirit*, 1998). Shyam, a beauty pageant coach finds a dedicated contestant in Mona. In the course of the training they fall in love with each other. As the training intensifies, Mona requests Shyam to train her friends who are all Miss India aspirants. In her absence, Mona's friends organize a 'kitty party' and the night quickly takes a wild turn. After several bottles of whiskey and staccato dancing their eyes fall on Shyam. The women take turns raping him and when they're done with him one of them clobbers him to death with a whiskey bottle. When Mona returns her friends tell her that Shyam had to leave for his village. As Mona dwells over her lover's mysterious disappearance,

Shyam returns as a disturbed spirit and picks off his murderers one by one. This simple rape revenge story unfolds like a non-linear nightmare played in reverse.

The film opens with a group of policemen outside a police station discussing the night that lies ahead. One of them whispers that something is amiss. A close-up of Shyam's eyes appears over which an ominous voice pronounces that the sky is moonless. A woman in a yellow sari wanders the night, anxious, scared, searching for Shyam. A tantrik meditates engulfed in billowing smoke and red gel, the voice re-iterates that it is indeed a moonless night, a night that belongs to the dead. Somewhere, a grave explodes; a corpse comes to life and wanders into the night. Elsewhere, patrolling policemen stumble onto a dead body in the jungle. A photograph of an ancient mansion appears briefly before leading us into a room full of dancing women. Someone watches them, an extreme close-up of an eye to be precise. The ancient mansion reappears and this time leads us to a woman in the shower. Flashes of lightning, close-up of approaching footsteps, a wolf howls in the distance, a ceiling fan grinds stale air, more footsteps, a man raping a woman in bed is cut with approaching traffic lights and a speeding ambassador, she screams, the car screeches to a halt, a snapshot hint of the mansion. As an eerie quiet settles and crickets burst into song, a man enters a room to find his daughter Chaya raped and murdered. We never see him again.

Shaitani Aatma breaks all conventions of plot development. Singh has little value for narrative elements, nuances or plot concerns. His films are pure spectacle unfolding shot by lurid shot. This is especially evident in his infamous film *Shaitani Dracula* (*The Satanic Dracula*, 2006) that is a cult favourite. In it Harinam, a six-hundred-year-old Dracula with a mission of spawning millions of draculas terrorizes a group of students who stumble into the forest that he inhabits. The entire film revolves around a variety of vampires and beasts chasing unsuspecting college victims in the forest, which suggests that Singh is no stranger to sparse plotlines. However, what sets *Shaintani Aatma* apart is its temporal complexities. After the opening, little effort goes into introducing the characters and the plotline. All we know is that there is someone out there killing women. The scenes move forward haltingly all the while intensifying the confusion. Thus, even as Mona has to negotiate mysterious murders, the occasional picnic to a haunted house, disbelieving and inefficient policemen she must also frequently encounter the memory, the images and the spectre of Shyam. In a telling scene, in the earlier part of the film, when we have little information about Mona and Shyam a group of guys confront Mona and tell her that they are suspicious of the coach (Shyam). Mona brushes them off and vouches for Shyam's innocence. In the following scene Mona and Shyam are seen romancing in the park professing their love for each other. Our heroine is then seen in a room drenched in red, twisting and turning as insomnia takes over. Next, she is seen wandering in the forest (the first shots from the film) singing a sad song and reminiscing good times with Shyam. It is only towards the end of the film when a tantrik coaxes the truth out of the spirit of Shyam that the storyline is revealed. All along the course of the film the audience is kept in the dark, questioning the identity of random characters and improbable scene developments. However, Singh manages to jog back and forth in time and with the help of songs and dream sequences he is able to weave immiscible times together where the past bleeds into the present and the present becomes the past. This departure from non-linear plotlines with scrambled continuity is a practice that most mainstream Bombay films stay away from. The Bombay cult film appropriates familiar tropes and formal elements from mainstream films, like the inclusion of the song and dance sequences, comedic subplots, social commentaries but recombines and reclaims them as its own. *Shaitani Aatma* inverts some familiar themes, devices and motifs that are deployed frequently in Hindi mainstream films. To begin with, mainstream films have exhausted the rape revenge story, but Singh uses this popular plotline and inverts it by introducing a male victim thereby opening up spaces that mainstream films have ignored. The exploitation of the male body, the evisceration of masculinity at the hands of a group of revelling and lustful women not only subverts the existing order but challenges and overturns the manner in which sexuality has been handled in mainstream films.

Singh also displays a special connection with the aural and the sonic with his fascination for the audio cassette and the tape recorder. In several of his films the tape recorder features regularly before special scenes. In *Khooni Dracula* (*The Bloody Dracula*, 1992-93), it appears in the disco scene minutes before the Dracula tries to mingle with the dancing crowd; in *Shaitani Dracula* (2006), when the attacks intensify Sheetal carries a tape recorder and wanders into the night to confront the Dracula; in *Shaitani Badla* (*Sinister Revenge*, 1993), it is part of the rape scene. However, he uses the aural space most interestingly in *Shaitani Aatma*. In a scene, almost an hour into the film, right before the entire truth is revealed, Mona lies on her bed tormented by her dreams. In a cut away, we see the audio tape recorder as the song 'Lag jaa gale' ('Come into My Arms') from the film *Woh Kaun Thi?* (*Who Was She?*) (Khosla, 1964) fills the room as Mona twists and turns into a feverish dream. The significance of the song is that it is from a gothic thriller where a doctor is tormented by the spectral presence of a ghostly and mysterious woman. Lata Mangeshkar, the singer that lends the voice has always been associated with the spectral giving voice to such haunting songs like, 'Aayega Aanewala' ('My Beloved Will Come'); songs that have featured in gothic and supernatural thrillers. For instance, in *Mahal* (*Mansion*) (Amrohi, 1949) the hero, lured by the provocatively intoxicating song 'Aayega Aanewala', meanders between the past and the present persistently pursuing a reunion with his ghostly lover. Singh uses this tradition and using the singer/songstress Lata's spectral voice to lure Mona out of bed towards Shyam who waits outside the house with outstretched arms. He lures her into the forest but her friends stop her from following him. Singh uses a popular gothic device of the spectral woman luring the hero into madness and destruction and turns it around; here the spectral lover is a man leading the woman into death and destruction. Marshalling a wide range of sources like horror, melodrama, romance, gothic supernatural thrillers, Singh's genre mixing and recombination gives birth to a unique aesthetic best described as 'patchwork aesthetic'. He rearranges, combines and recycles his own footage and *Shaitani Aatma* is a case in point where he poaches large chunks from his earlier films like *Shaitani Badla* and *Khooni Dracula*. Re-mastering his own texts Singh twists it to fit different contexts. For instance, the rape scene in *Shaitani Aatma* has been recycled from *Shaitani Badla* and many scenes of haunting have been used from his earlier film *Khooni Dracula*. It could be argued that the pressures of completing entire films in such short spans and non-existent budgets makes improvisation an imperative. In a discussion, Kishan Shah made it clear that the key to flourishing in a small budget world is speed. He went on to elaborate that he completes entire films within a span of fifteen days.

> From here I go to Silvassa in a bus with 20 people. So back and forth it costs us around 36,000. 5 girls, 3 guys, a mom and a dad, ten artists, 3 films can be made, the expense is the same no? … It is quite simple really because the subject is made like that – there are two bathroom scenes, two swimming pools, three bedrooms, four kissing scenes. Never go by the story, five lip to lip, and four songs will have sex. Simple!
>
> (Subba 2016)

Functioning largely on the fears and anxieties of the middle class the Bombay cult films purvey the forbidden spectacles that are otherwise considered taboo. Such themes like incest, infidelity, adultery, impotence and hypersexuality figure quite consistently. The re-imagination of the sanitized family space of the high popular and circumnavigating censorship anoints this 'bad

cinema' with both a cult status amongst its followers and a blanket of invisibility in the mainstream circuit. The family as a unit has always remained a universal anchor of traditionalism, cultural values, morality and stability in mainstream Hindi cinema. In the nineties, prised open by
a host of liberal reforms, the country was overwhelmed by a changing visual regime; the sheer
viscosity of a new and unfamiliar visual culture threw open the streets, the shopping complex,
the public places and the media landscape to boisterous advertising, new brands and commodities transforming the optical regime and the lives of the people. In this climate of uncertainty, the unit of the family grew into a refuge and sanctuary that pacified fears and assuaged
doubts and reservations. In cinema, enormous family dramas burst on the scene of which Sooraj
Barjatya's *Hum Aapke Hain Kaun* (*Who am I to You?*) (1994) was the first in a long line of family
dramas that followed. *Hum Aapke Hain Kaun*, a blockbuster, navigates the landscape of a happy
upper class North Indian family in the backdrop of a marriage. In Ranjani Mazumdar's words,

> Familial values of devotion, Hindu rituals, traditional costumes, and the moral uni-
> verse of the joint family saturate the rather thin story of the film. The film is dotted
> with innumerable characters that help construct the carnivalesque utopia of the great
> Indian family, in which conflict is minimal and the desire to be united is powerful.
>
> (2007: 122)

The family has been the central concern of Hindi cinema and it is the unit of the family that
is central to the Bombay sexploitation films but contrary to the mainstream Bombay film, here,
families are no markers of traditional values or devotion. Films like *Bedroom* (Shah, 2005) and
Angoor (*Grape*) (Shah, 2005) nuzzle the dark recesses of incest, *Ek Namard* (*An Impotent*) (Shah,
2004) descends into a tale of conjugal strain due to impotency, *Garam Padosan* (*Hot Neighbour*)
(Shah, 2006) explores adultery and infidelity and *Garam* (*Hot*) (Shah, 2005) traces the story
of Bobby, a hypersexual girl with an insatiable appetite for sex. *Garam* is the story of Bobby, a
hypersexual girl with an insatiable appetite for sex. Her world falls apart when she finds that
her husband is incapable of satisfying her as he is inexperienced and impotent. Driven by her
desires their family is torn apart when she travels from Bangkok to India and plunges into a
life of lust and reckless abandon. Most families in these sexploitation films are dysfunctional or
disintegrated. In place of morals and values espoused by mainstream cinema, there is infidelity
and incest. This is no utopia but a dark world spiralling into chaos and conflict. It holds on to
unit of the family as a central point of the film only to subvert them to expose those exertions,
the scarcities, the conflicts, those fissures that exist below and operate as secret and taboo.

Conclusion

The Bombay cult film is marginal in the routes that it negotiates, opening up alternative spaces
of exhibition. It has reached its audience through a variety of spaces: popping up in early
morning metropolitan shows, travelling through remote areas via tent and touring cinemas,
drawing committed audiences in mofussil and interior towns in run down theatres, appearing
in small video parlours and footpath stalls and now on the vast folds of the internet. It operates
on the edges of legality, often sidestepping censorship guidelines with its own ingenious devices
of improvisation like 'cut-piece', 'bits' and 'dupe'. A cut-piece or bits is a few feet of celluloid with pornographic or sexually explicit material that is furtively attached to a film being
projected. Since it can appear and disappear at will the filmmakers can use them at will in certain venues to complement their films. These little bits appear in smaller single screen theatres
during the screening of low-budget films and cannot be normally traced. The dupe is another

device in which filmmakers strike two different prints, the clean cut travels to the censors so that they can avoid extensive injunctions and the raunchy cut with explicit scenes travel to smaller exhibition sites and DVDs. These films are transgressive and challenge traditional conservatism by exploring themes that are largely ignored and neglected by mainstream films as has been discussed above. In *Maut* (*Death*) (Jeetu, 1998), the wronged spirit of a hypersexual girl murdered for her lusty ways sets out in search of a new body. The search leads the spirit to a hospital where it settles on a woman's corpse. However, moments before the spirit's arrival a worker at the hospital unable to suppress his fear hurriedly stitches the amputated remains of two accident victims. In his haste he unknowingly stitches the nether portions of a man to a woman's corpse creating a trans-body, which the spirit embodies. In the aftermath the female spirit realizes that she is now attracted to women more than men. The idea of a mutating body is a useful metaphor for Bombsploitation because like the hybrid body of *Maut*, the Bombay cult film is an object that is in a constant state of alteration. It appropriates, re-combines and cannibalizes different forms but it is not only a hybrid in a cultural genre mixing way but a body that experiences constant alteration because of the routes that it travels through, from the devices that it deploys to bypass censorship, by its changing form in different sites of exhibition. It is something that truly resists paraphrase.

Notes

1 A grade is generally the term given to a mainstream film with a decent budget and recognizable stars, films which circulate in the prestigious circuits of metropolitan cities. B and C grades are those circuits characterized by falling level of investments. These films do not have big stars and big production budgets and circulate in small towns and mofussil circuits. In terms of production the B-grade film would be fractionally considered better than the C-grade film. Using Andhra Pradesh as his site to track the circulation of Hong Kong action films in India, S. V. Srinivas (2003) distinguishes between A and B circuits of circulation. For Srinivas, the B circuit in India represents that segment of low investment distribution and exhibition where films enter non-metropolitan territories after they have traveled the more prestigious circuits. The distributors here pick up the cheapest films or reruns of older films since it is the concluding lap of distribution, those frontiers of the industry where incomes are so abysmally low that it is not viable for major players to operate (Srinivas 2003).
2 'In 1983 the government suddenly realized the spatial dangers of hundreds and thousands of VCRs that had been imported during the Asiad and also smuggled through different channels' (Sundaram 2010: 116). The 1980s saw the rise of cassette culture in India with the introduction of the VCR and the move of the Union government to allow the import of colour television sets and VCRs. Hundreds and thousands of VCRs found their way to India through legal and illegal channels during the Asiad games of 1982.

References

Mazumdar, Ranjani. 2007. *Bombay Cinema: An Archive of the City*. Minneapolis: University of Minnesota Press.

Srinivas, S.V. 2003. 'Hong Kong Action Film in the Indian B circuit'. *Inter-Asia Cultural Studies*, 4(1): 40–62.

Subba, Vibhushan. 2016. 'The Bad-Shahs of Small Budget: The Small-budget Hindi Film of the B Circuit'. *BioScope: South Asian Screen Studies*, 7(2): 215–233.

Subba, Vibhushan. 2017. 'Embalming the Obscure: The Rise of B-Movie Cinephilia'. *Studies in South Asian Film & Media*, 8(2), October: 89–107.

Sundaram, Ravi. 2010. *Pirate Modernity: Delhi's Media Urbanism*. London: Routledge.

Thomas, Rosie. 2014. *Bombay before Bollywood: Film City Fantasies*. Delhi: Orient Blackswan.

12

EAST ASIAN CULT CINEMA

Robyn Citizen

When it comes to international cult cinemas, the popular and obscure films of Hong Kong, Japan and recently South Korea, seem to take up a disproportionate amount of space in the canon. In addition to the relative accessibility of these films, the "West's" long history of political engagement through imperialism and/or military action with these nations have made them privileged sites for imagining and defining otherness.

By displacing otherness and exoticism onto The Orient/East, a conflation of discrete landscapes, traditions, languages and cultures, the West reflexively defines itself (Said 1978: 363). Thus, discourses of Orientalism are inevitable when it comes to the "cult" credentials and reception of Asian cinemas because, due to this history of misrepresentation, as Mathijs and Sexton state, "everything is 'other', everything is potentially marginal" (Mathijs and Sexton 2011: 154). However, invoking a dominant "West" also oversimplifies racial-cultural power dynamics down to geographic location and national identity, homogenizing both the population of the West and its fandom for Asian cult cinema. Many scholars have written about the whiteness of fan studies and the construction of fandom itself as a marginalized position that elides the ways in which individual fans may occupy multiple other marginalized identity categories (race, gender, sexuality, class, language, etc.) within fan cultures (Wanzo 2015; Warner 2015; Stanfill 2018). The history of Asian cult cinema reception intervenes into the construction of the Western cult film fan as predominately a white, cis-gendered heterosexual male, and focuses on how the subgenre is consumed and interpreted by members of groups subject to "internal orientalism", that is, black and immigrant diasporas who have been defined in opposition to normative "Western" identity (Wilson 1981: 59–69). In particular, the fandom in Western non-white diasporic communities for "Eastern" cultural products problematizes the concept of the "West" as a stable cultural identity and a holder of the gaze against "Eastern" foreign others.

The majority of this chapter focuses on Hong-Kong and Japanese films – the two pillars of Asian cult cinema. But before that, I would like to signal a few poignant characteristics these to two cinemas share with "other" Asian cult cinema, and its receptions. South Korean film has only recently emerged as a site of cult fandom since before the mid-1980s the country was under a dictatorship that monitored the content of local films and had a strict quota on the number of foreign films that could be imported and screened. Even as the restrictions began to relax under Chun Doo-hwan in the 1980s, the industry still privileged escapist narrative content and genre films that fell under the "3S" policy – sex, screen and sports. While this led to the production of horror and erotic films that typically comprise much of the cult cinema canon, few if any of these films were exported outside of the region and most are out of circulation today thus inhibiting the growth of cult fandom (Peirse and Martin 2013: 8). However, as scholar Jinsoo An claimed, the 1980s was also the decade in which Korean viewers became aware of foreign cult cinema through "Western 'midnight movies'" as well as the action cinema of Hong Kong, particularly John Woo films (An 2008: 325). It was not until 1999 that South Korea started to release its own films to the rest of Asia, Europe and North America that would acquire cult status, most notably *Nowhere to Hide*[1] (1999) *Oldboy* (2003) and a number of films by director Kim Ki-duk from 2000 to 2004 (Martin 2015: 149). *Oldboy*, Kim Ki-duk's film and the director himself have faced critiques by viewers and critics for their transgressive sexuality and violence. In *The New York Observer* in 2005, Rex Reed famously associated the most disturbing aspects of *Oldboy* with Korean culture itself,

> What else can you expect from a nation weaned on kimchi, a mixture of raw garlic and cabbage buried underground until it rots, dug up from the grave and then served in earthenware pots sold at the Seoul airport as souvenirs?

And Tony Rayns criticized the enthusiastic Western critical reception of Kim Ki-duk's *The Isle*, and *Spring, Summer, Fall, Winter ... and Spring*, blaming critics for mistaking Kim's provocative themes and images for depth and/or as representative of Korea. Underlying Rayns argument was the vague accusation of Orientalism, that this misrecognition was due to critics' ignorance of Korean culture and Kim's own self-orientalizing through films, which Rayns takes pains to point out, had been rejected by local critics and viewers.

The inability of foreigners to fully understand local culture, or representations thereof, actually was part of the plot in Indonesian cult films of the 1970s through early 1990s. Director H. Tjut Djalil was responsible for some of the most recognizable films in and after the golden age (1980–1986) of Indonesian horror cinema with *Lady Terminator* (1987) and *Mystics in Bali* (1981). The mixture of heavy-handed religious messages juxtaposed with sexually suggestive content, cheap special effects and overall tonal unwieldiness later helped Djalil's films appeal to cult film viewers abroad. In many of these films, the centuries-long history of Indonesian colonization by various European countries was distilled into white Western women scholars or urban Indonesian women associated with Western feminism, unleash chaos by intervening with local beliefs and spiritual traditions (Gladwin 2003). Even as the film narratives expressed anxiety around the influx of Western cultural values – most specifically around gender roles – they courted American video markets and strategically drew upon regional folklore such as the *penanggalan* that may be "exotic", transgressive and new to foreign audiences. This mixture of culturally specific elements with globally popular genres was greatly influenced by the regional examples set by the Japanese (who also ruled Indonesia during World War II) and the Hong Kong industry's horror and action film industry.

One of the stars of those Hong Kong action films, Bruce Lee, who also worked in Hollywood and American television, was vital to increasing the popularity of martial arts films around the world and to wider audiences than before. The fandom around Lee in black and brown working-class communities has been discussed by David Desser, Leon Hunt and Vijay Prashad as transnational and particularly racially diverse. Lee's mixed ethno-racial background, embrace of Western fashion, syncretic fighting styles in the form of Jeet Kune Do, and the liminal status of his parents' birthplace Hong Kong all contributed to his contested status. Lee's and other martial arts films found an audience in black and brown communities for reasons connected to political economy (the second-run theatres that played these films were often in lower income neighbourhoods) and geopolitics.[2] Thematically, blaxploitation and martial arts films share a structure, which allows the viewer to root for a non-white underdog/hero who successfully takes on the establishment, whether that be a colonial power or "the man". These films and their themes continue to resonate with members of the communities who grew up watching them in theatres. One notable example is RZA, a member of hip-hop group Wu Tang Clan, which was named in homage to the HK martial arts genre. RZA has stated that martial arts films, which often depicted Chinese villagers oppressed by state officials, were important to his identity, "Beyond the Kung Fu it was the reality of the situation that hit me. Growing up as a black kid in America, I didn't know that kind of story had existed anywhere else" (Harris 2018). He frequently tours theatres in North America live-scoring screenings of the Shaw Brothers *The 36 Chambers of Shaolin* (1978).

In fact, the central conflict and point of view from Lee's popular film *Fist of Fury* aka *The Chinese Connection* involved the brutality of Japan's occupation of China. This plot and the multicultural flair of Lee's last film *Enter the Dragon* were superimposed onto the cast and setting of a blaxploitation film in the 1985 film *The Last Dragon* (Michael Schultz). In its homage to Bruce Lee and his oeuvre, the film also explores the various Afro-Asian connections happening in New York City. *The Last Dragon* borrows the narrative core of many of Lee's films: a lone protagonist who eventually teams up with other racial outsiders against oppressors for violent retribution (Prashad 2001). Yet, *Dragon*, a comedy/action/musical hybrid designed mainly to be a vehicle for producer Berry Gordy's recording artists, takes a more depoliticized and lighthearted approach: depicting its villains as mildly troublesome, megalomaniacal gangsters, not vicious racist oppressors. Also, the racial dynamic of the protagonist, sidekick and villain have been inverted; here the protagonist is black, his sidekick is biracial Korean-Italian American, and the villains are white (Eddie Arkadian, a New Jersey Italian-American) *and* black American (Sho'nuff). More significant however is the way in which the two black characters are aligned with either China or Japan through visual iconography and characterization. Protagonist Leroy Green, known as Bruce Leroy throughout most of the film, studies Kung Fu, runs a martial arts studio where he espouses pseudo-Eastern aphorisms and spends his spare time in Chinese peasant clothes and a "coolie"[3] hat. Leroy's main villain is Sho'nuff, the head of a

Figure 12.1 Sho'nuff in the modified costumes of imperial Japanese iconography and Leroy in the iconic yellow jumpsuit of Bruce Lee from the film he was making before his death, *Game of Death*. Still from *The Last Dragon* (Schultz, USA, 1985). Delphi III Productions/Motown Productions

neighbourhood gang, who refers to himself as the "Shogun of Harlem". Sho'nuff's costumes in the film are an urban version of a samurai winged vest and *hakama* pants accessorized with images of the Imperial Japan flag. His hair is in a modified *chonmage* topknot as samurai wore in popular *jidaigeki* films.

That wartime era Japan is associated with oppressive violence in a film set in a 1980s primarily black neighbourhood, is a testament to fans' familiarity with the Japanese as villains in films like *The Chinese Connection* and the lingering memories of Japan's role in World War II. The more favourable view of the Chinese here overlaps with both Lee's heritage and the role of Mao's teachings in the Black Power movements that ultimately inspired blaxploitation cinema.

More recently, a core part of Asian cult cinema from Hong Kong has revolved around the films of John Woo – including *The Killer* (1989), *A Better Tomorrow* (1986), and *Hard Boiled* (1992). However, the "cult" aspect of their reception refers to the fanbase in the West since these were mainstream films, although not necessarily huge hits, in Hong Kong and across much of Asia. *The Killer* has been cited by Vibe magazine as 21st out of a list of 50 films to significantly influence hip hop music and culture ("Top 50 films that have influenced Hip-Hop" 2016). Both RZA and Raekwon, another member of the aforementioned Wu Tang Clan, have sampled heavily from *The Killer*'s scenes for songs and interludes. According to Jinsoo An, the reception of Woo's *The Killer* in Asia was quite different to that in the West. Woo's style is known for ballet-like action sequences with heavy use of slow motion and copious amounts of sentiment which led to their categorization as male melodrama or "heroic bloodshed" films (Hoover and Stokes 1999: 64). In places like Japan and South Korea, the film and Chow Yun Fat's performance were appreciated earnestly. In the West, poorly subtitled copies mangled what was already considered, according to the norms of Western masculinity, over-the-top, bordering on homoerotic sentiment (An 2008). Therefore, in the West the heroic bloodshed films were primarily appreciated for their cinematographic virtuosity, which has subsequently been very influential to North American action cinema, but narratively regarded as camp or ironically consumed as cult texts. Woo's films, hugely influential to American cult and genre films and filmmakers, particularly Luc Besson and Quentin Tarantino, are themselves examples of transnational influences. *The Killer* was famously inspired by Jean-Pierre Melville's *Le Samourai* (1967) which in turn, was inspired by *Harakiri* (Kobayashi, 1962) and other *jidaigeki* ronin films, providing a paradigmatic example of what critic Trifonova states as the "the geographically and temporally confused nature of cinephilia" (Trifonova 2006).

This brings us to the question of why Japanese films are the other pillar of Asian cult cinema canon and central among the figures who act as cultural gatekeepers and interpreters for other Western consumers of Asian cult. Once again Tarantino emerges here as someone associated with Chinese, Hong Kong and Japanese national cinemas and the cult film format by his stated fandom, casts, endless intertextual references and pastiches of familiar content and elements. Scholar Hiroki Azuma calls this tendency – the passive and isolated consumption of story and character elements focusing on endless intertextual recombination instead of narrative meaning – "database" culture, and claims that it is a characteristic of global postmodernity (Azuma 2009). But he also asks, "if the rise of otaku (postmodern database) culture is part of a global trend, why are we focused on Japanese things?" (ibid.: 11). For historical reasons of World War II, the Occupation, and the subsequent ally Japan occupies a unique and liminal place in the Western imaginary and East/West binary: East/Japan/West. In addition to the Orientalism that Said originally described, the outcome of global modernization has spawned techno-orientalist discourses (Morley and Robins 1996). In media representation, techno-orientalism uses futuristic high-tech images of Japan and the anachronistic images of feudal Japan that still widely circulate in Western imaginations and map them onto narratives in moments of cultural paranoia and anxiety, i.e., the 1980s Japan, Inc. panic. These narratives form two representational tropes: Japan-as-future and/or feudal-traditionalist Japan. The first depicts the Japanese as the collectivized automated Other (Japanoid, Japan Inc.), and Japan as a site of proliferating weird subcultures, kawaii and "cool" cultural products, and advanced technology (Ueno 1996). The latter emphasizes rigid social hierarchies including oppressive gender roles, ancient moral codes, and highly aestheticized cultural objects and spaces (Wagenaar 2016: 49). Clearly *Blade Runner* is an example of the former trope as it a maps Asian-ness, and Japanese-ness in particular, onto the dehumanized masses of a pathologically technological dysphoria. However, Japanese texts such as *Akira* (Otomo, 1988), *Tetsuo: The Iron Man* (Tsukamoto, 1989) and *Ghost in the Shell* (Oshii, 1995) also, intentionally or not, become part of this discourse contributing to representational patterns of Japan reimagining its own destruction, from the post-nuclear wrath of Godzilla to the white quasi-mushroom cloud destroying Neo-Tokyo in *Akira*. Films and subgenres – such as pinky violence and Japanese cyberpunk manga adaptations – that play off one or both of these tropes tend to invite cult reception and/or cult readings.

The pinky violence and *sukeban* (girl boss) subgenres are examples of how particular types of violence and sexuality arising from those broad tropes intersected to form categories that were at once mainstream – in that they were produced by major studios – yet, often thematically and formally transgressive. Meiko Kaji was one of the major cult figures to emerge from the latter subgenre. *Sukeban* films, centred on delinquent girl gangs, maintained "pinky" elements of eroticism but foregrounded themes common to *yakuza* films through the lens of female camaraderie, exploitation and discrimination. Unlike many typical female characters in other Japanese film genres including yakuza films, girl bosses were not resigned to their socially enforced gender role and expressed their agency through violent action. The mixture of Kaji's classic good looks, a cool aloofness usually reserved for male anti-heroes, and feral gaze made her a singular presence in the genre. Ethno-racial outsiders and biracial characters made appearances in pinky violence and sukeban films in a critique of the American occupation and hypocrisy, as well as Japanese ethnic parochialism. Kaji's starring role (although she was not top-billed) in the first hit series of the girl boss subgenre, the *Stray Cat Rock* films, involved her character falling in love with, befriending and defending biracial outsiders (Desjardins 2005: 60). In *Stray Cat Rock: Sex Hunter*, Mako (Kaji) and another member of her gang become romantically interested in mixed-race characters. The members of the male gang with whom they share territory, and who have unrequited feelings for the girls, vow to run "half-breeds" out of town but mainly target the half-black locals. The film explores the psychosexual effect of the Occupation and Westernization on Japanese masculinity – male protagonist Baron uses racialized violence and misogyny to hide his own sexual impotence and lack of social power in the Japanese mainstream. Kaji's detached charisma and iconic fashion quickly take centre stage in a vehicle originally designed to promote singer Akika Wada's career. Ironically, Kaji's own singing career would be what revived her career thirty years later when Quentin Tarantino's included her songs "Urami Bushi" and "Shura no hana" on the *Kill Bill* soundtrack. His claim that her star persona and incarnation as *Lady Snowblood* were main inspirations for The Bride also helped to revive interest in her career to a new generation both in Japan and cult fans in the West.

The numerous mentions of Quentin Tarantino show the importance of individual gatekeepers in "translating" the cultural cool of certain texts and figures to other audiences. The marketing of Nobuhiko Obayashi's *House* to Western cult audiences is an example of how more informal systems of fan "talk" are mobilized by cultural institutions to produce cult credibility. World War II and its aftereffects find a way into the narrative of *House* and featured prominently in its marketing together with the singular nature of the film's effects and the fact that Obayashi's then-seven years old daughter Chigumi supplied many of the ideas for the film.

In order to reproduce the "liveness" quality of cult reception, a screening tour of the film was planned at the NYAFF. The hosts read quotes from the filmmaker and others involved in the film who claimed that, at the time, even they felt like they were making nonsense. Furthermore, the Japanization of the word *House* was retained so that when the film screened at the festival it was initially spelled *HAUSU* on posters.

House was picked up by Janus films, typically a distributor of art films, and the film was intended for Criterion's new Eclipse DVD brand, created to be a subsidiary that would specialize in cult films. *House,* and Obayashi's reputation, had been circulating among the "grey market" and cult fans for a while. *House* was a commercial hit but, like *Realm of the Senses*, too transgressive and bizarre to be recuperated even by local audiences as anything but radically other (Wilentz 2009). When Eclipse's branding changed, *House* was released on Criterion. Arguably, the success of *House* for Criterion, in addition to the Nikkatsu Noir series on Eclipse, opened the door for other non-art cult classified films to be released on this line. It was followed by the *When Horror Came to Shochiku* series, which featured films that can only really be appreciated through a cult reading. To put the novelty of this acquisition into some perspective, it is worth noting that *House* received a Criterion treatment *before* widely acknowledged cult classic *Godzilla*. This cult to mainstream crossover was part of a larger pattern that unfortunately endangered early distributors of cult films such as Synapse, Something Weird Video and now-defunct Tartan Asia Extreme. These companies did not always have the capital for extensive remastering, restorations and DVD extras or commentary. Ultimately, this process elides perceived divisions between elite cinephiles and fan cult viewers, continuing the intermeshing of high and low cultures that is the hallmark of postmodernism.

Finally, the film that I keep coming back to which seems to combine this undermining of the "West" as holder of the gaze, its incorporation of a pre–World War II mass cult literary trend and the burgeoning cyberpunk, its imagining of Japan's destruction in a collision of its materialist industrial past, rapid technological advancement and globalization, is *Tetsuo: The Iron Man*. Aspects of *Tetsuo*'s visuals can be traced back to Japanese radical theatre traditions and ero-guro-nansensu or Erotic Grotesque Nonsense, a modernist movement between the Taisho Era (1912–1926) and Imperial Japan. This was not a fringe cult but a mass aesthetic movement distributed in comic revues, literature and popular magazines. The elements are comprised of the following sentiments:

1. Erotic – the corporeal, bestiality, freakery, human-machine pairings;
2. Grotesque – the malformed, deviant, uncanny, mentally ill and the non-normative human body;
3. Nonsense – slapstick humor, irony, carnivalesque, decadence.

Edogawa Rampo, a pseudonym for Hirai Tarō, based the *katakana* pronunciation of Edgar Allan Poe's name, became the primary literary figure associated with this movement. His ero-guro novel *The Strange Tale of Panorama Island* was loosely adapted into Teruo Ishii's *Horrors of Malformed Men* (1969), which had the unusual distinction of being banned after its theatrical run was completed (Macias 2001: 189). *The Horrors of Malformed Men* may otherwise be a foot-note in Japanese cult cinema history if it did not feature the infamous dancer and co-creator of the *butoh* dance style, Tatsumi Hijikata. *Butoh* was created as a reaction to the overly mannered and Western dance forms that had become popularized in Japan. In the postwar landscape of political resistance, *Butoh*'s slow motion controlled but primal movements depicted the transformation or hybridization of the human body with other forms. The choreography was a grotesque meditation on death, decay, sexuality – simultaneously a defamiliarization of the body through a deconstruction of the beautiful or sacred body, and an exploration of the "natural"

Figure 12.2   Hijikata as Jōgorō Komoda using the butoh movements that he pioneered in service of the film's thematic freakery. Still from *Horrors of Malformed Men* (Ishii, Japan, 1969). Toei Company

body. *Butoh* moments and ethos would become incorporated into the visuals of *Tetsuo*, with the slow morphing of the protagonist into a metal man, and later into films of the J-horror genre.

Thus with this tropic combination of "weird" Japan (narrative content, ero-guro, *butoh*, Hijikata himself) plus a period setting (Taisho era – traditional costuming and rural settings), *The Horrors of Malformed Men* was recuperated as a precursor to both the pinky violence and J-horror genres and earned a mass market DVD release by North American-based Synapse Films (Macias 2001: 189–190).

If *butoh* is about acknowledging the permeability of the body and the desire to return to an undifferentiated state of co-mingling with others and the environment in which we live then it provides a convenient metaphor for the, at times violent and haphazard exchange of cultures and populations in the era of globalization. As Annalee Newitz noted,

> Tetsuo's sexuality ... represents both the physical and cultural alterations we associate with cross-national – and multi-cultural – relations. That it is both ironic and ugly drives home the point that what we have here is a series of critical looks at American culture.
>
> (1995: 10)

Perhaps corroborating Newitz's assessment is a brief shot in the film focusing on photographs of athletes that the Iron Man has taped up; one in particular is of a black runner in a race.

It stands out precisely because it is one of few organic images in a sea of other metallic artefacts and props. Given the emphasis on black physical virtuosity in American racial discourse, which has been exported around the world via cultural products and media texts[4], in this moment the film's broader theme of merging man and machine towards the logical endpoint of "industrial dehumanization", draws upon a foreign ethno-national image reservoir (ibid.). Should Tetsuo's ambition to physical transformation be interpreted through the lens of national identity or include racial identity as well? Is the aspect of American culture being critiqued

117

Figure 12.3 This image of a black track and field athlete hangs on Tetsuo's wall. Still from *Tetsuo: The Iron Man* (Tsukamoto, Japan, 1989). Japan Home Video/K2 Spirit/Kaiyu Theater/SEN

multiculturalism itself, or the hypocrisy in this multicultural ideal based on the persistence of its racialized policies, or simply the fact that it is perceived as yet another American value that is being imposed on Japan? Although *Tetsuo* does not have a documented fan culture among people of colour in the West in the same way that Bruce Lee and Hong Kong action/martial arts films do, the aforementioned shots are one example of how an Asian cult film – by virtue of its textual openness and cross-cultural references – may provide an interpretive access point and textual pleasures for viewers along different axis of identity, including those in diasporas experiencing "internal orientalism".

Along these lines Takashi Miike is also an interesting object of study in Japanese cult fandom. Although he came up through the struggling Japanese studio system as an apprentice of Shohei Imamura, Miike began to get recognized for his genre work in the V-cinema (direct-to-video) industry in which young filmmakers could produce films quickly without studio interference. With the release of the three films that would form his "Black Society Trilogy" – *Shinjuku Triad Society* (1995), *Rainy Dog* (1997) and *Ley Lines* (1999) – Miike garnered comparisons to Kinji Fukusaku yet developed the unique thematic concerns that shaped his cult auteur status. Miike depicts a remarkably heterogeneous Japan with mixed-race protagonists, transgressive violence and sexuality usually with female prostitutes and impotent or perverted men, black comedy and generic hybridity. The fact that Miike himself cut a punk-ish figure, with his dyed buzzcuts, graphic T-shirts and a professed love for motorbikes and rock 'n' roll, contributed to the iconoclastic persona. After the release of *Audition* (1999) and its reported audience walkouts, and the even more controversial *Ichi the Killer* (2001), Miike was regarded as the "godfather" of ultraviolent extreme cinema by vocal admirers Quentin Tarantino and Eli Roth. Miike was well-known enough by certain audiences to merit a cameo in Roth's *Hostel* (2005) as a satisfied customer of the torture hotel.

Along with certain Japanese New Wave and *taiyozoku* films, Asian cult films have arguably provided a way for the "East" to return a critical, exoticizing gaze to the West, and some of the starkest examples are its depictions of marginalized communities in the West. This critical gaze encompasses the liberated Western women scholars in Indonesian cult films, to athlete Jim Kelly's transplanted blaxploitation character as Bruce Lee's sidekick in *Enter the Dragon*, to Tetsuo's "ugly" metallic miscegenation symbolic of multicultural ideology, to the recent *Vampire Girl vs. Frankenstein Girl* (2009) using blackface makeup on its *ganguro* girl characters, to the startlingly multi-ethnic Japan of Takashi Miike films (ibid.). Yet, the films from Miike and Kim Ki-duk that take a sympathetic look at the lives of half-black American protagonists who struggle against discrimination, *Address Unknown* and *Blues Harp* respectively, are among the most overlooked parts of their oeuvres in terms of critical and cult reception. Both films contain narrative and thematic content that may favour cult readings – a critical engagement with the local and American systems of status-quo, they are told from POV of cultural outsiders, contain transgressive violence and have limited distribution. While not every film with some cult elements will be labelled as such, it is worth noting the interplay of subnational and international cultural and political practices at play in what type of content in Asian films is defined as difficult, transgressive and rebellious and what is the limit case of otherness when it comes to cult status and consumption.

Notes

1 Director Lee Myung-se is somewhat of a singular example in South Korea cinema. His films often have polarizing receptions, not due to transgressive subject matter but stylistic choices including the incorporation of animation, step-process slow motion and other visual techniques used to deconstruct expectations in genres such as romantic comedies and action films. It is interesting that his work has not received more attention in cult cinema.
2 Soldiers, who were disproportionately of colour, came home from wars in Asia having been personally exposed to these cultures and populations.
3 The slur "coolie" used for Asian workers became identified with the conical hats worn by rice paddy workers in East and Southeast Asia. The slur is used here quoting the way that characters in the film referred to it.
4 John G. Russell's work traces how Western racial discourses have been adapted and incorporated into various aspects of Japanese literary and popular culture. I wrote about this process as its represented in Japanese cinema from the postwar era to the mid-1990s in "Projecting Blackness: Japan's Cinematic Encounters with the black-American Other", PhD dissertation (New York University, 2015).

References

An Jinsoo. 2008. 'The Killer: Cult Film and Transcultural (Mis)Reading', in E. Mathijs and X. Mendik, eds. *The Cult Film Reader*. New York: McGraw-Hill/Open University Press: 320–327.
Azuma, Hiroki. 2009. *Otaku: Japan's Database Animals*. Minneapolis: University of Minnesota Press.
Desjardins, Chris. 2005. *Outlaw Masters of Japanese Film*. New York: I.B. Tauris.
Gladwin, Stephen. 2003. 'Witches, Spells and Politics: The Horror Films of Indonesia', in S.J. Schneider, ed. *Fear Without Frontiers: Horror Cinema Across the Globe*. England: FAB Press: 243–254.
Harris, R.L. 2018. 'Wu-Tang's RZA Brings the 36th Chamber of Shaolin to Toronto', *Hip Hop Canada*. Retrieved from: www.hiphopcanada.com/rza-toronto-36th-chamber. Accessed 03 September 2018.
Hoover, M., and Stokes, L.O. 1999. *City on Fire: Hong Kong Cinema*. New York City: Verso.
Macias, Patrick. 2001. *TokyoScope: The Japanese Cult Film Companion*. San Francisco: Cadence Books.
Martin, Daniel. 2015. *Extreme Asia: The Rise of Cult Cinema from the Far East*. Edinburgh: Edinburgh University.
Mathijs, Ernest, and Sexton, Jamie. 2011. *Cult Cinema: An Introduction*. Chichester: Wiley-Blackwell.
Morley, D., and Robins, K. 1996. *Spaces of Identity*. London: Routledge.
Newitz, Annalee. 1995. 'Magical Girls and Atomic Bomb Sperm: Japanese Animation in America', *Film Quarterly*, 49 (August): 10.

Peirse, Alison, and Martin, Daniel, eds. 2013. *Korean Horror Cinema*. Edinburgh: Edinburgh University Press.

Prashad, V. 2001. *Everybody Was Kung Fu Fighting: Afro-Asian Connections and the Myth of Cultural Purity*. Boston: Beacon Press.

Said, Edward W. 1978. *Orientalism*. New York: Pantheon Books.

Staff. 2006. 'The 50 Films That Shaped Hip Hop', *Vibe* (April): 122–129. Retrieved from: https://books.google.ca/books?id=-CYEAAAAMBAJ&pg=PA122&hl=en#v=onepage&q&f=false. Accessed 25 August 2018.

Stanfill, M. 2018. 'The Unbearable Whiteness of Fandom and Fan Studies', in P. Booth, ed. *A Companion to Media and Fan Studies*. Hoboken: Wiley-Blackwell: 305–317.

Trifonova, T. 2006. 'Cinematic Cool: Jean-Pierre Melville's *Le Samourai*', *Senses of Cinema*, issue 39. Retrieved from: http://sensesofcinema.com/2015/cteq/samourai. Accessed 03 August 2018.

Ueno, T. 1996. 'Japanimation and Techno-Orientalist: Japan and the Sub-Empire of Signs', *Yamagata International Documentary Film Festival*. Retrieved from: www.yidff.jp/docbox/9/box9-1-e.html. Accessed 29 May 2018.

Wagenaar, W. 2016. 'Wacky Japan: A New Face of Orientalism', *Asia in Focus*, issue 3 (Summer): 49.

Wanzo, R. 2015. 'African American Acafandom and Other Strangers: New Genealogies of Fan Studies', *Transformative Works and Culture*, no. 20. Retrieved from: https://doi.org/10.3983/twc.2015.0699. Accessed 13 September 2018.

Warner, K.J. 2015. 'If Loving Olitz Is Wrong, I Don't Wanna Be Right', *The Black Scholar*, 45.1: 16–20.

Wilentz, D. 2009. 'Hausu Party', *Brooklyn Rail*. Retrieved from: https://brooklynrail.org/2009/06/film/hausu-party. Accessed 01 August 2018.

Wilson, Ernest J. 1981 'Orientalism: A Black Perspective', *Journal of Palestine Studies*, 10.2: 59–69.

13

ANIME IS (NOT) CULT

Gainax and the limits of cult cinema

Rayna Denison

It should be easy to talk about anime as cult cinema. Few media are so obviously open to cult readings, and it is hard to deny the multiplicity of anime's cult signifiers: from its textual connections to already 'cultified' genres like pornography, science fiction and horror (Jancovich et al. 2003), through to its subaltern spread thanks to transnational grassroots fan communities (Hills 2002), and on through to regular commentary about the liminal and socially transgressive nature of anime's texts and, sometimes, its fans (Mathijs and Sexton 2011: 6–7). Big films like *Akira* (Katsuhiro Ōtomo, 1989) were hailed as cult as soon as they were released (Denison 2015) and have since been credited with the birth of anime fandom in places like the United Kingdom. So why then is the title of this chapter, 'Anime Is (Not) Cult'?

One reason is that the discussions of anime's relationship to cult are surprisingly few in number, so anime's cult-ness has yet to be fully explored. Furthermore, anime is not *always* cult. Brian Ruh eloquently makes this argument in one of the few extended accounts of anime's relationship to the cult category:

> While specific anime texts can fit into the cult category, the cult's emphasis on formal elements of the individual text means that anime as a whole cannot be considered cult. Nor, for that matter, can any other category or genre … . [A]nime fandom encompasses texts that can be considered cult and those that cannot. (There is no separate fandom for cult anime texts – *Evangelion* fandom cannot be separated from anime fandom in the same way that *Star Trek* fandom can be considered separately from general science fiction fandom). As a result, the cult aspects of certain prominent texts like *Evangelion* can expand to give all anime texts something of a cult sheen, which has the effect of helping anime texts travel translationally within established fan circles.
>
> (Ruh 2013: 9)

Ruh's exploration of the way cult discourses in Anglo-American scholarship intersect with anime's texts and franchises demonstrates how important it is to think beyond monolithic understandings of anime and cult alike; to see multiple categorical possibilities in their variety. However, I think that some clarification of Ruh's position is important, perhaps especially regarding the textual definition of cult anime and the tribalism within anime fandom (and academia). Anime, I argue, is often not 'cult' because other categories are used in place of that term; cult itself may not be a universal category.

Reflecting this observation, therefore, this chapter is titled 'Anime is (not) Cult' in order to denote a subcultural Shibboleth. For English-speaking fans of Hideaki Annō's *Neon Genesis Evangelion* (*Shin seiki Evangerion*, 1995–1996), the title of this chapter will be an obvious pun on the subtitles of Annō's Rebuild of Evangelion films (starting in 2007, there are currently three films, and a fourth is planned). But *only* for those fans who speak English. In Japanese, the subtitles of these films play on a *gagaku* (traditional music) structure: *jo-ha-kyū* (translated as: 'beginning, break, quickening'), which describes different parts of a performance (Kamen 2011: 10); whereas, in English, the first film's title was *Evangelion: 1.0 You Are (Not) Alone* (as tweaks were made for the home video market, the film's number has changed, and by its recent DVD release it had become *Evangelion: 1.11 You Are (Not) Alone*). Consequently, the Shibboleth only works for those who are aware of the history of these films in their English translations, much as the term 'cult' tends to be used more in the context of English-language scholarship than in Japanese. In this chapter, I argue that there is a dissonance between how fandom and cult in anime is discussed by scholars in English, and how Japanese scholars use terms like otaku and *ippanjin* (the general public).

As this suggests, the present moment marks a growing gap between scholars about how to conceptualize anime consumers. There are those who, like Henry Jenkins and Matt Hills, have come to the subject from fan studies, and have focused on a growing transnational *fandom* around anime (see also, work on fansubbing by Denison 2011; Lee 2011). This face of anime consumption has been at least partially incorporated into fan studies through discussions of a transnational 'pop cosmopolitanism' (Jenkins 2006). Perhaps the most important feature of this work is the way it divorces anime fan practices outside Japan from those undertaken within anime's domestic context (Hills 2002, 2017).

On the other side of the debate is a growing group of scholars, mainly from Japan, whose work is being translated and taken up within Anglophone scholarship. This second group uses the term 'otaku' as their central concept. Introduced in the mid-1980s, initially observed in use as an inter-community greeting (*otaku*, literally 'your house', being a polite form of 'you' in Japanese), Japanese theorists have now built a body of theory conceptualized from this domestic perspective on anime consumers. Recently, otaku has also increasingly been used to describe anime fandom's globalizing spread (Itō et al. 2012; Azuma 2009; Ōtsuka 2015). I am aware that I am drawing rather bold lines between the two groups, and that scholars like Sandra Arnett (2014) and Matt Hills (2017) have taken much more nuanced positions. Nevertheless, the discursive poles of anime fan studies and otaku studies stand apart, and this growing division is important because anime's cult categorization rests in the heart of this debate.

The frames we put around anime matter because they work to maintain and police the boundaries between otherwise cognisant groups of people, academic disciplines and cultural concepts that could usefully inform one another. The transcultural dimension of anime's consumption is the most contested because, as anime fandom has expanded beyond Japan, it has taken on many guises. There is a tendency on both sides of the debate to emphasize the differences between these fan communities rather than what Hills calls their homologies (2017). This is all the more important to studies of cult and anime because, as Hills asserts:

> Transnational cult is imagined … as attracting and organizing its own distinctive communities, brands and specialisms, rather than as a bridging of cultures that misrepresents 'authentic' Japanese culture or that seeks to attain some version of transcultural 'authenticity'.
>
> (2017: 84)

If transnational cult is transnational because of its generation of *new* cultural understandings and activities, then it cannot act as a salve to the discursive split between the United Kingdom/United States and Japan-centred debates about anime's cult status, or indeed regarding how to understand anime's (cult) consumers. However, in her book, *Anime Fan Communities: Transcultural Flows and Frictions*, Sandra Arnett has gone a considerable way towards squaring this circle. Like Hills, Arnett calls for a comparative historical approach that would 'understand how today's anime fan communities work to build global connections' (2014: 1). In this her position is similar to that of Patrick Galbraith et al., who argue for a 'focus on the activity in question' rather than assuming a taxonomic approach to understanding cult consumers (10). Therefore, rather than asserting status from without, we can investigate perceptions of anime as activities *within* communities. In this chapter, therefore, I want to examine a specific case of transnationally shared anime culture and investigate how it has been continually re-constructed as (not) cult (Hills 2017).

To do so, I am taking a view of anime and cult that goes against the grain of cult cinema studies: an industrial one. Most definitions assert cult status through attention to facets of texts, exhibition and reception (Jancovich et al. 2003; Mathijs and Sexton 2011; Hills and Sexton 2017). Industry, where invoked, has tended to wear one of two faces: either that of the auteur or the distributor. In the former instance, for example, David Andrews argues for two versions of the cult auteur, one intentional and the other less so, as a means to suggest connections between art cinema and cult cinema (2013). The transnational assertion of cult status, however, often resides in the hands of distributors, who have been judged as appending the moniker of cult to films with little care for their original meanings (Imanjaya 2009; Tierney 2014). Dolores Tierney, in a rousing defence of Latin American cinema, for example, labels distributors' sometimes callous approach to cultifying Latin American cinema as little more than 'cult colonial appropriation' wherein 'a potentially dominant group ... thrills in seeing the culture of the peripheries failing to copy the culture of the centre' (131). Taking her admonition seriously means thinking not just about authorship and reception of cult cinema, but about the way industry shapes the texts we see.

I want to try to bring these various strands of theory together in this chapter by invoking a company that has been at the heart of anime's transnational cultification debates since the 1980s: Gainax. Gainax has a substantial claim to the status of cult company, or otaku company, depending on how its history is read. I will examine specific moments in Gainax's history in order to think through the relationship between industry and the production of 'cult' anime. In this way, I hope to emphasize a different dimension of cult cinema to that previously studied in relation to anime, one which has ramifications for our understanding of how cult operates within transnational cinema studies.

Gainax and the creation of cult anime

How can a company like Gainax help us think across the divides between 'fan' and 'otaku' theories and their relationship to cult media? Mizuko Ito's introduction to the book *Fandom Unbound: Otaku Culture in a Connected World* (2012) clarifies the split:

> In Japan, much of manga and anime is associated with mainstream consumption; otaku must therefore differentiate themselves from *ippanjin* (regular people) through a proliferating set of niche genres, alternative readings, and derivative works. In the United States, the subcultural cred of anime and manga is buttressed by their status as foreign 'cult media'.
>
> (xvii–xviii)

From Ito's point of view, then, anime is only cult outside Japan. But, there is already shared ground in the way she invokes 'regular people' as a corollary of cult media's 'mainstream' antithesis (Jancovich et al. 2003). Matt Hills' argues that, instead of reading cult and mainstream as a binary opposition, it would be more useful to consider how these terms might 'intersect' (2010). Thinking more about how cult and mainstream operate along a sliding scale from the commercial centres of cultural production to their liminal outskirts allows me to question what the two concepts mean in differing national contexts of production and consumption. Analysing these terms relationally also allows me to introduce other, comparative terms, when and where relevant. I would note, additionally, that if liminality provides the cultural ground for otaku and their cultures in Japan, then a company built out of those cultures would provide a good starting point from which to reconsider the shared grounds of the debate. Gainax is one such company.

According to Yasuhiro Takeda's *The Notenki Memoirs* (2002, translated into English in 2005: 90–93), Gainax was formed on Christmas Eve 1984, capitalized by a company called General Productions and specifically created in order to make an anime film called *Royal Space Force: The Wings of the Honneamise* (*Ōrisu Uchūgun: Oneamisu no Tsubasa*, Hiroyuki Yamada, 1987). However, by the time this team incorporated Gainax, the founders had already been working together for several years. Famously, Toshio Okada and Yasuhiro Takeda had been involved with their university science fiction fan clubs and had become interested in organizing conventions. This led to an encounter with university students who could animate – Hideaki Annō, Hiroyuki Yamada and Takami Akai – who were convinced to produce amateur, short, animated opening films for the Daicon III and IV conventions in Ōsaka (Takeda 2005; Condry 2013). These arrangements also led to Okada and Takeda separately setting up General Productions (to produce amateur merchandise) and, a short while later, Daicon Films. Therefore, by the time Gainax was founded, these amateur fan-producers had already begun to professionalize, and were already experienced leaders within the Japanese fan communities for science fiction and anime.

Ian Condry's rather celebratory response to the Takeda's history of Gainax declares that:

> The Gainax story shows how a group of devoted fans managed to turn their fan activities – notably science fiction conventions and the contacts and networks they developed through them – into a business enterprise that, although it did not make much money [before *Evangelion*], managed to sustain itself through the force of the personalities of those involved.
>
> (2013: 133)

This is problematic, not least because Condry fails to engage with the dysfunction that engendered Gainax's lack of initial commercial success. Especially important were the clashes between those 'forceful' personalities that led to Okada leaving the company in the early 1990s. In addition, this version of Gainax's history is itself questionable, as shown by Jonathan Clements, who contends:

> We might also note that such a chronology of fans turning professional might reflect the self-commemoration of the Gainax studio. Although Gainax has now been an established corporation for a quarter of a century, its contemporary publicity still regularly returns to a self-image of a collective of fans made good.
>
> (2013: 172)

Aggrandizing – and possibly apocryphal – though the Gainax foundation narrative may be, it does reveal an important potential cult aspect to the early life of the studio. The early amateur works produced by Yamada, Annō and others for the Daicon conventions are examples of non-standard and non-industry animation production intended for 'cult' consumption by fans. Clements argues that Daicon Film's production of video tape copies of their short films, sold after the conventions, may also be a precursor to the Original Video Animation (OVA) market that would later give rise to anime's 'cult' reputation in the United Kingdom and the United States (2013: 172). In this way, the pre-Gainax Daicon Films company was at the technological liminal edge of anime production; they retained in their way of making films and using technology, many of the signifiers of cult, even if they were more commonly associated with amateur, rather than cult production in this period.

Gainax's liminal cultural status seems also to have necessitated an interest in transnational fan markets for its products. Gainax was one of the earliest anime companies to show a determined interest in the overseas markets for anime, particularly the US market. For example, Okada and Takeda set up General Productions USA in 1989, spear-headed by Lea Hernandez, a US anime fan and manga-inspired comic book artist (Patten 2004: 39; Hernandez 2013–14). In Japan, General Productions was a maker of amateur-produced 'garage kits' – polyresin vinyl figures and props from anime and *tokusatsu* (sfx) television shows (Clements 2013: 171). With General Productions USA, the idea was to provide these kits as mail-order products for fans. Hernandez's web comic, written over 20 years after the fact, details the rise and fall of General Productions USA, which shuttered its doors in 1991 (Hernandez 2013–14). Both Fred Patten (2004) and Hernandez claim that the company's failure was caused by the long delays in getting new anime (and attendant merchandise) to the United States from Japan, causing General Productions USA to be out of step with the North American fan market.

At roughly the same time, however, Gainax was becoming a brand name familiar to US fans. Gainax became known for their involvement with Toren Smith in the production of the first ever anime convention in the United States: AnimeCon '91. Patten explains that Gainax were part of the committee 'of fans' and that they arranged 'for the attendance of many popular anime and manga creators as AnimeCon's guests, including Hideaki Anno, Johji Manabe, Haruhiko Mikimoto, Yoshiyuki Sadamoto and Kenichi Sonoda. ... The attendance from throughout North America is over 1,700' (Patten 2004: 41). Patten also notes that one of the first anime released on home video in the United States was Gainax's *Gunbuster* (*Toppu wo nerai!, Aim for the Top!*, Hideaki Annō, 1988–1989). Originally a six-part OVA series, released directly to home video in Japan, *Gunbuster* was another way that Gainax's Okada and Takeda targeted, and attempted expand, the US fan market for anime. Gainax's proactive courting of the US market for anime fans was therefore fundamental to the instantiation of gathering spaces specific to anime fandom. Through their convention work in the United States, General Productions and Gainax seem to have been attempting to foster good-will for their company and products, as seen in the appearance by Hideaki Annō at AnimeCon.

Gainax, therefore, was not just producing anime that would later take on cult resonances, it was actively producing and promoting a transcultural market and fandom for its anime film and television texts. I argue, therefore, that Gainax's transnational presence in the early years of anime fandom worked to shape that fandom from the inside out, creating overlaps between the celebration of anime texts within what would become cult fan spaces in the United States, and otaku spaces in Japan. But, Gainax's early experiences also demonstrate moments of cultural misapprehension between Japanese companies and the US fans that they were courting, seen in the failure of General Productions USA. By trying to create a fanbase born out of existing Japanese fan networks and extending them to the United States, Gainax positioned itself at the forefront of anime's transnational cult development, consistently looking to grassroots fandom for support and status. Gainax therefore offers more than a passive example of homologous cult reception; in its early years, Gainax was an active producer of 'cult' consumption inside and outside Japan.

Gainax, Toshio Okada and Otakuology

Gainax therefore provides a useful starting point for conceptualizing notions of anime's early subcultural status in Japan (through its early amateur/fan productions) and in the United States (through convention organization and early entry into the home video market). As those markets matured, and the company professionalized, one of the most significant changes at Gainax was the departure of founder Toshio Okada. Okada, according to Takeda's memoirs, was essentially pushed out of Gainax, where he was well-known for having outlandish ideas that failed to gel with those of the creative personnel around him (2005).

Okada's departure took place shortly after the production of Gainax's OVA *Otaku no Video* (Takeshi Mori, 1991), which Okada had co-written with Hirokyuki Yamada. Once more, in *Otaku no Video* the history of Gainax is replayed working to assert the company's credentials as fan-production, or otaku work. At times, the OVA even shades into a postmodern meta-promotional text for General Productions and Gainax. *Otaku no Video* relates the story of two otaku friends who move from fandom, to amateur production, to professional anime production success. This narrative is intercut with live-action documentary-style 'interviews' with a range of Japanese otaku characters. The film is therefore Gainax's most overt statement about otaku in Japan. The anime sequence's main character, Ken Kubo, declares himself to be the *'otakingu'* (Otaku King) as he seeks to make his new company 'Grand Prix' (modelled after General Productions) a success. Mirroring the reported history of General Productions and Gainax, the video highlights the necessity of transmedia production to the survival of the nascent anime studio, and it explores the necessity of fans turning prosumer in order to get the media they desire. In doing so it offers a playful, but not always positive, commentary on otaku (for example, one documentary otaku 'character' masturbates on screen and another admits to stealing cells from anime studios). Primarily, however, *Otaku no Video* helps to further mythologize the 'Gainax narrative' discussed by Clements, placing an only slightly altered version of Okada at the heart of that success story.

Okada, on his departure from Gainax, reinvented himself as one of the earliest proponents of *otaku bunka ron* (otaku cultural discourse, often alternatively called *otakugaku*, or otakuology). Okada took on a lecture series at the Tokyo University in the mid-1990s, where he attempted to combat negative Japanese media hysteria around otaku that had formed in the wake of the arrest and trial of 'otaku' Tsutomu Miyazaki (who had abducted, molested and murdered young girls; for more on the furore that this event raised, see: Kinsella 2000). Thomas Lamarre has commented that:

> otaku bashing made the term so popular that Okada could use it to garner attention, titling himself 'Otakingu' or the King of Otaku ... . This at times almost smacks of parody, as in his *Otaku no Video*, but it also was a political move made with the full expectation of media response.
>
> (in Galbraith and Lamarre 2010: 363)

Lamarre's assertion that Okada might not have been entirely serious in his analysis of Japanese otaku is echoed elsewhere. Eiji Ōtsuka, another central figure in the otaku studies field, has gone so far as to claim that he sees no value in discussing otakuology: 'I myself just cannot be interested in contemporary 'otaku' theory, which is a discourse that in the past we engaged in as a 'joke' and now is an un-self-aware Sokal-like recapitulation' (2015: xxii). Ōtsuka is arguing that the early and foundational work he, and people like Okada, undertook was intended as a tongue-in-cheek stab at the legitimacy of philosophical approaches within the Japanese academy. However, he laments that the joke is lost on contemporary scholars, who are determined to seriously engage in otaku studies. I suspect that the 'joke' may be partially on Ōtsuka, particularly when considering the global rise in fan studies over the last two decades; but, joke or not, Okada and Ōtsuka have created a slippage between the concepts of cult media studies and otakuology in Japan.

Okada is the more difficult of the two to position regarding the relationship between cult and otaku studies. In his earliest book on otaku, Okada specifically attempts to differentiate between US and Japanese contexts, stating: 'Let me make this absolutely clear: Otaku culture is not subculture' (translated and reprinted in 2015: 94). In particular, in this work, Okada differentiates the purpose and function of the otaku from that of other kinds of anime consumption by saying that otaku are, in essence, connoisseurs. He claims that the otaku's importance should be judged on their ability to have 'perfectly acquired otaku knowledge to appreciate works' (2015: 97) and he goes on to argue that: 'these actions are not meant for him [the otaku] alone, but are also in the interest of cultivating creators, and ultimately contributing to otaku culture as a whole. Otaku understand this point' (2015: 97–98). In this reading of otaku, their significance comes from their ability to communicate with those in the creative industries, and not in ancillary production. In this way, despite using different terms, Okada's position on the otaku is similar to Matt Hills's assessment of the reciprocal relationship between the 'cult' fans of *Dr. Who* and their influence on the show's creators (2010).

Okada also asserts that, in the darker days of the otaku in the early 1990s, transnational fandom helped to recuperate the meanings of anime in its domestic market. 'In Japan, there is a persistent image of *otaku* as gloomy, ugly and without friends. Overseas, however, *otaku* are accepted as something COOL' (quoted in Okada 2015: 168). Just as Gainax worked to build the US fandom for anime, by the 1990s Okada was using the perceptions of those fans as a means to support his subsequent scholarship. This makes it less likely that otakuology was intended as a joke, as reading it humorously would delegitimize Okada's position within industry and academia. Okada openly acknowledges the importance of US fans, as 'foreigners who were into anime', saying that they 'served to relativize the weirdness of those of us who live in Japan' (2015: 170). In this way, Okada has used the overseas otaku to reclaim positive – though liminal or cult – associations for the domestic Japanese otaku, fostering transcultural associations between the two groups.

Furthermore, Okada's recent book *Otaku wa sude ni shindeiru* (*Otaku are Already Dead*, 2014) functions, in part, as a seemingly serious call to arms; as an attempt to shock the current generation of Japanese fans into returning to the prosumer ways of their forebears. In this book, Okada departs from his earlier positive position on otakuology to note that the shifting generations of otaku in Japan have increasingly moved into the realms of generalized consumption and away from medium-specific understandings of anime's place within Japan's media networks. In essence, he argues that the current otaku is moving ever farther away from what Matt Hills conceptualizes as the active cult fan (2002). As Patrick Galbraith *et al.* note, however, 'it is difficult to plot Okada's position in the social construction of '*otaku*', because he is variably oriented to the term and says different things about it to different people at different times (and even in the same publication)' (2015: 12). I would agree but argue that Okada has become one of the leading figures in otakuology precisely because of his vagueness. Okada remains vague because he relies on his industrial experience with Gainax to authenticate his explanations of the otaku community across history. Okada's work throws the mobility of this signifier into relief at the same moment that it concretizes the separate communities who recognize the term.

The elasticity of the term otaku in these examples supports Patrick Galbraith *et al.*'s claims that 'nothing about 'otaku' can be taken for granted' (2015: 1). Okada's connection to Gainax, its cultifying practices and the mythologization of the company makes his presence within these debates all the more significant, as a former otaku-producer-turned-scholar. If the (former) Otaku King's writings tell us anything, it is that there is a deep connection in Japan between industry and those they serve. The fundamental perceptions of both the cultural industries and their consumers might shift with the prevailing media winds in Japan, but the existence of a transcultural fandom/otaku-dom has allowed those meanings to be negotiated and rehabilitated over time.

Okada's unstable positioning within the history of otaku in Japan reflects some of the shifts in the culture itself, from liminal amateur production to institutionalization within the Japanese academy. Okada is a long-standing player in all of the worlds of anime, from the domestic to the transnational, from the otaku to the international fan, and from fandom and cult media studies to otakuology. While we may not be able to take anything in these debates for granted, Okada offers a set of discourses worthy of analysis because of the way companies, key figures and fans have become interconnected over the decades since Gainax's formation. Cult, transnational fandom and otakuology could, therefore, be read as relational terms close to the liminal end of the sliding scale between the cult and mainstream inside and outside of Japan.

Conclusion

However, as these debates demonstrate, discussing anime's connection to cult cinema is easy and simultaneously well-nigh impossible. The sheer layering of hierarchical concepts involved in the invocation of cult across different cultural concepts and time makes it incredibly hard to see the cult anime for the otaku. Many of the works surveyed for this chapter see otaku as just one specialized type of prosumer. These otaku may produce texts that later become cult, but their own status as fans suggests a cult design to their creation (see: Lamarre 2006 and Hills 2010 for more). The problem is that terms are not discrete, and instead the meanings of each bleed into the debates and discussions being had about the others. Fan studies approaches to anime differ but overlap with those of otakuology, and the discussion of Gainax reveals how corporations can be built upon otaku identities. There are ideological reasons, from nationalism to anti-Orientalism, for the potential adoption of phrases like 'otaku mode' or 'otaku subculture' over 'cult fandom' in relation to anime (see: Galbraith and Lamarre, 2010), but none of these offer a precise alternative to the concept of cult itself. Moreover, the uses to which otaku is put as a term in Japan are not readily agreed upon, any more than fans themselves are consistent in their uses of the term inside and outside of Japan.

So, Gainax's anime have become entangled in a complex set of debates about fandom and consumption, almost all of which nod towards a relationship with cult cinema. And yet, these debates are so heated and new that, as yet, there has been little agreement about when, or which aspects of, anime might generally be considered 'cult'. Some, like Ito, would argue that cult is something that happens to anime in the United States and other Anglophone nations, with the implication being that it has less relevance in Japan. However, to argue that cult has no place in Japanese anime culture would be to radically overstate the distinctiveness of Japan's anime fandom and subcultures, and to miss the liminal prosumer tendencies amongst the otaku.

This is my main reason for wanting to analyse an example in this chapter that is not exclusively 'Japanese'. Gainax has a long history of looking beyond the Japanese market, and particularly of looking towards the US market, for consumers. Gainax have helped to inculcate the very cult fandom that Okada would go on to cite when he tried to restore the positive image of the otaku in Japan. Moreover, Gainax-as-cult-company demonstrates that the connections between fans and producers are closer than we allow if we only look to film texts or audiences for the meanings of cult media. Perhaps the most useful importation from Okada's otakuology into our understanding of cult fandom might well be his acknowledgement of the reciprocal relationship between active fan connoisseurs and those producing anime. Likewise, the closing down of the conceptual gaps between industrial and fan productions, seeing them not as primary and ancillary works, but potentially as commingled notions, might help to shift us towards the kinds of comparative histories of practice that Arnett and Hills have called for in their studies of anime fandom.

Gainax, as a company born from otaku, and making products for otaku at home and abroad, has therefore helped to create an understanding of anime as cult. From their status as otaku-fan creators, to their early adoption of video technologies, to their self-parodying texts, the early history of Gainax is almost tailor-made for a cult analysis. Consequently, if 'cult' anime is not a term in very wide usage today that may simply be because we have yet to decide what to call it. Gainax, however, has long embedded the idea of the otaku and cult into its transcultural practices, making them into a pioneering cult anime company.

References

Andrews, David. 2013. 'Losing the Asterisk: A Theory of Cult-Art Cinema', in *Theorizing Art Cinemas: Foreign, Cult, Avant-Garde, and Beyond*. Austin: University of Texas Press: 95–113.

Arnett, Sean. 2014. *Anime Fan Communities: Transcultural Flows and Frictions*. New York: Palgrave Macmillan.

Azuma, Hiroki. 2009. *Otaku: Japan's Database Animals*, trans. Jonathan Abel and Shion Kono. Minneapolis: University of Minnesota Press.

Clements, Jonathan. 2013. *Anime: A History*, London: BFI Palgrave.

Condry, I. 2013. *The Soul of Anime: Collaborative Creativity and Japan's Media Success Story*. Durham, NC: Duke University Press.

Denison, Rayna. 2011. 'Anime Fandom and the Liminal Spaces between Fan Creativity and Piracy', *International Journal of Cultural Studies* 14(5): 449–466.

Denison, Rayna. 2015. *Anime: A Critical Introduction*. London: Bloomsbury.

Galbraith, Patrick W., and Thomas Lamarre. 2010. 'Otakuology: A Dialogue', in Frenchy Lunning, ed., *Mechademia: Fanthropology*, vol. 5. Minneapolis: University of Minnesota Press: 360–374. Accessed June 2019.

Galbraith, Patrick W., Thiam Huat Kam and Björn.- Ole. Kamm. 2015. 'Introduction: "Otaku" Research: Past, Present and Future', in Patrick W. Galbraith, Thiam Huat Kam and Björn.- Ole. Kamm, eds, *Debating Otaku in Contemporary Japan: Historical Perspectives and New Horizons*. London: Bloomsbury: 1–18.

Hernandez, Lea. 2013–14. *Bani Garu*, http://boingboing.net/2013/10/23/bani-garu-problems-from-the-s.html. Accessed June 2019.

Hills, Matt. 2002. *Fan Cultures*. London: Routledge.

Hills, Matt. 2010. *Triumph of a Time-Lord: Regenerating Doctor Who in the Twenty-First Century*. London: IB Tauris.

Hills, Matt. 2017. 'Transnational Cult and/as Neoliberalism: The Liminal Economies of Anime Fansubbers', *Transnational Cinemas* 8(1): 80–94.

Hills, Matt and Jamie Sexton. 2017. 'Editorial Introduction: The Multiplicities of Transnational Cult – Intersecting with(in) Reason', *Transnational Cinemas* 8(1): 1–4.

Imanjaya, Ekki. 2009. 'The Other Side of Indonesia: New Order's Indonesian Exploitation', *Colloquy Text, Theory, Critique* 18: 143–159.

Jancovich, Mark, Antonio Lázaro-Reboll, Julian Stringer and Andy Willis, eds. 2003. *Defining Cult Movies: The Cultural Politics of Oppositional Taste*. Manchester: Manchester University Press.

Jenkins, Henry. Bloggers. 2006. *Fans, Bloggers, and Gamers: Exploring Participatory Culture*. New York: New York University Press.

Kamen, M. 2011. 'Advancing Ever Onwards', *Neo* 84 (June): 8–13.

Kinsella, Sharon. 2000. *Adult Manga: Culture and Power in Contemporary Japanese Society.* London: Routledge.

Lamarre, Thomas. 2006. 'Otaku Movement', in Tomiko Yoda and Harry Hartunian, eds, *Japan After Japan: Social and Cultural Life from the Recessionary 1990s to the Present.* Durham, NC: Duke University Press: 358–394.

Lee, Hye-Kyung. 2011. 'Participatory Media Fandom: A Case Study of Anime Fansubbing', *Media, Culture and Society* 33(8): 1131–1147.

Mathijs, Ernest and Jamie Sexton, eds. 2011. *Cult Cinema.* Malden, MA: Wiley-Blackwell.

Okada, Toshio. 2014. *Otaku wa sudeni shindeiru (Otaku/You Are Already Dead).* Tokyo: Rocket.

Okada, Toshio. 2015. 'Introduction to Otakuology', in Patrick W. Galbraith, Thiam Huat Kam and Björn.- Ole. Kamm, eds, *Debating Otaku in Contemporary Japan: Historical Perspectives and New Horizons.* London: Bloomsbury: 89–102.

Ōtsuka, Ejii'. 2015. 'Otaku Culture as 'Conversation Literature'', in Patrick W. Galbraith, Thiam Huat Kam and Björn.- Ole. Kamm, eds, *Debating Otaku in Contemporary Japan: Historical Perspectives and New Horizons.* London: Bloomsbury: xiii–xxix.

Patten, Fred. 2004. *Watching Anime, Reading Manga: 25 Years of Essays and Reviews.* Berkeley, CA: Stone Bridge Press.

Ruh, Brian. 2013. 'Producing Transnational Cult Media: *Neon Genesis Evangelion* and *Ghost in the Shell* in Circulation', *Intensities: The Journal of Cult Media* 5 (Spring/Summer): 1–22.

Takeda, Yasuhiro. 2005. *The Notenki Memoirs: Studio Gainax and the Men who Created Evangelion*, trans. ADV Manga. Houston, TX: AD Vision.

Tierney, Dolores. 2014. 'Mapping Cult Cinema in Latin American Film Cultures', *Cinema Journal* 54(1): 129–135.

14

BLAXPLOITATION FILMMAKING

Harry M. Benshoff

The controversial term "blaxploitation filmmaking" refers to hundreds of motion pictures made in the United States circa the early 1970s that featured proud and defiant African American protagonists. Some of the better known blaxploitation titles include *Shaft* (1971), *Super Fly* (1972), *The Mack* (1973), *The Black Godfather* (1974), and *Coffy* (1975). The term blaxploitation is a portmanteau word combining "black" and "exploitation," and most blaxploitation films do fit a loose definition of exploitation filmmaking in that they were often raw and cheaply made films containing plenty of sex and violence. (The origins of the term itself – around the controversy caused by *Super Fly* in 1972 – is explored in Koven 2010: 9–13.) Blaxploitation films were also exploitative in the sense that they exploited a new era of African American rebellion, social consciousness, and cultural presence. Other critics and historians have suggested that the films literally exploit the black community, in that many of them feature what some critics deem to be "negative" images of African Americans, such as pimps, gangsters, and prostitutes. And of course much of the money made from these films flowed back into white Hollywood. So while blaxploitation films were popular with many younger and urban African American audiences, other middle class critics – perhaps most famously black psychiatrist Alvin F. Poussaint (1974) – decried the films for portraying blacks as "violent criminal sexy savages."

In truth, many of the films do depict angry, violent, and/or sexually adventurous protagonists (both intra- and interracially), images antithetical to those found in earlier Hollywood films dealing with African Americans and African American issues, such as the social problem films of the late 1940s (*Pinky, Lost Boundaries, Intruder in the Dust* [all 1949]) or the soft-peddled, de-sexed Sidney Poitier vehicles of the mid-1960s (*Lilies of the Field* [1963], *A Patch of Blue* [1965], *Guess Who's Coming to Dinner* [1967]). As Josiah Howard puts it, Poitier's films "never adequately addressed or displayed the frustration, disappointment and/or out-and-out anger that was so much a part of the 1960s African-American experience" (2008: 9). It may easily be argued that these earlier films were made to appeal to white audiences; conversely, blaxploitation films represent the first time that Hollywood it put its fantasy-creating machinery to work for the black spectator. Blaxploitation filmmaking allowed for a range of more fully realized African American characters in triumphant narratives that often celebrated violent retribution against (more or less explicit) white supremacy. Black audiences enjoying blaxploitation films got to see black protagonists "kick whitey's ass" – and get away with it – for the first time in American film history. Arguably, this vicarious thrill is at the heart of the filmic phenomenon.

Some critics and film historians refer to blaxploitation as genre. I would like to argue against that view, chiefly for the primary reason that blaxploitation filmmaking contains (or exploits) many different genres. Although many of the best known films are gangster or crime dramas set in urban milieus like those mentioned above, there are also blaxploitation westerns (*Buck and the Preacher* [1972], *Adios Amigos* [1976]), blaxploitation horror films (*Blacula* [1972], *Sugar Hill* [1974]), blaxploitation musicals (*Sparkle* [1976], *Car Wash* [1976]), and even more "respectable" blaxploitation comedy-dramas like *Claudine* (1974) and *Cooley High* (1975). Furthermore, blaxploitation films contain elements common to other exploitation genres of the era, including women-in-prison films, kung-fu movies, biker films, revenge thrillers, and even late-period spaghetti westerns as in a film like *Take a Hard Ride* (1975). Therefore, instead of thinking about blaxploitation filmmaking as a genre in and of itself (with a stable iconography and consistent thematic meanings), it is perhaps more productive to consider it a filmic *movement*. Unlike genres, which tend to exist across decades, cinematic movements are circumscribed by – arising within and then declining within – a specific historical era. For example, the French New Wave (itself containing many different types of genre films) is usually understood as a movement of films reflective of post-World War II French culture, including intellectual trends such as existentialism and cinephilia, and made possible via financial opportunities afforded by the French government (all of which allowed young cinephiles like François Truffaut and Jean-Luc Godard to make their first feature films). Similarly, blaxploitation films arise and decline within a specific era due to contiguous social issues (the rise of Black Nationalism, the violent rhetoric of the Black Power movement and actual racial violence in the streets), industrial contexts (the scrapping of the Hollywood Production Code, a desperate try-anything approach in a floundering film business facing years of audience apathy and near-bankruptcy), and even distribution-exhibition contexts (as white audiences fled to the suburbs, large urban theaters built in previous eras realized the need to target black audiences). Approaching blaxploitation filmmaking as a historically contextual movement allows critics and historians to see it as a complex and highly diverse set of films (which it is), whereas calling it a genre perhaps suggests a consistent (and simplistic) unity.

Contra Ed Guerrero (in his otherwise superlative overview of the phenomenon), blaxploitation filmmaking is comprised of far more than "sixty or so Hollywood films" (1993: 69). Although some blaxploitation films were distributed by major Hollywood studios (MGM, Warner Bros., Paramount), many more were distributed by minor outlets like American International Pictures (AIP), Dimension, and New World Pictures. Still others were independently produced and distributed outside the usual Hollywood channels; as such, some blaxploitation films have big budgets and glossy production values, while others are strictly bargain-basement fare. Some blaxploitation films were written and directed by African American filmmakers (Melvin Van Peebles, Gordon Parks, Bill Gunn), while others were written and directed by white men who also worked in other exploitation genres (Jack Hill, Al Adamson, Larry Cohen). While it is tempting to argue that blaxploitation films made by African Americans tend to contain a harsher critique of white supremacy than those made by their white counterparts (or those made by major Hollywood studios), one should resist that reductive temptation. Many if not most blaxploitation films contain both racist *and* anti-racist themes and imagery, as well as problematic depictions of class, gender, and sexuality. I have argued elsewhere that blaxploitation films need to be examined on an individual basis and against the generic norms with which they engage (Benshoff 2000). At their best, blaxploitation films critique police corruption and brutality, dramatize black activism, showcase and celebrate black culture (especially music and fashion), and foreground the structural ills of the ghetto like poverty, crime, and drugs. At their worst, blaxploitation films re-circulate offensive stereotypes such as the Brutal Black Buck (Bogle

2016: 209–221), and make light or even mockery of serious social issues. Doubtless this is part of their ongoing camp and cult appeal – delight in their often crude excesses, as well as nostalgia for a less "politically correct" era, all combined with a taste for bad, schlocky "paracinema." (For more on the politics of paracinema and "retrosploitation," see Sconce [1995], and Church [2015].) Indeed, approaching blaxploitation as a movement (rather than a genre) allows our current interest in it to be understood as one particular form of retrosploitation: blaxploitation films originally existed in the early 1970s, faded from memory in the 1980s, only to be rediscovered by cultists (and cult filmmakers like Quentin Tarantino) in the 1990s.

Ed Guerrero (1993) suggests the high point of blaxploitation occurs with the production and reception of three key films: Melvin Van Peebles independent hit *Sweet Sweetback's Baadasssss Song* (1971), and the Hollywood hits *Shaft* (MGM) and *Super Fly* (Warner Bros.). Each film contains a swaggering macho black protagonist who is defiant, violent, street-smart, and hypersexualized (hence Bogle's assertion that these films recirculate the black buck stereotype). However, that type of black male character had been increasingly appearing in films prior to the release of *Sweet Sweetback*, as in the (albeit supporting character) roles played by ex-football film star Jim Brown in films like *The Dirty Dozen* (1967), *Ice Station Zebra* (1968) and *100 Rifles* (1969). (As blaxploitation filmmaking hit its peak around 1972–1973, Brown would be joined onscreen by other athletes-turned-actors including Fred Williamson, Jim Kelly, and Rosie Grier.) Similarly, Blaxploitation's giddily violent retributive aesthetic is definitely sounded at least a year before *Sweet Sweetback* in *The Liberation of L. B. Jones* (1970) when Yaphet Kotto, playing a black activist, tosses a white racist cop into a hay baling machine. Other films from the late 1960s explore racial issues in America from various hip or edgy perspectives. *Putney Swope* (1969) was a satire about a black man who takes over a white advertising agency. Melvin Van Peebles directed the Columbia Pictures release *Watermelon Man* (1970), a comedy about a white man who wakes up one day to discover he has become black. Other films written and/or directed by black men in these years include the nostalgic and autobiographical *The Learning Tree* (1969, written and directed by Gordon Parks) and Ossie Davis's crowd-pleasing buddy action-comedy *Cotton Comes to Harlem* (1970), based on the novel by Chester Himes. All of these films contributed to the blaxploitation aesthetic in various ways, several years before the term was coined.

However, for most film historians, it was the phenomenal independent success of *Sweet Sweetback's Baadasssss Song* in 1971 that truly defined the blaxploitation aesthetic. Melvin Van Peebles's "one man show" – he is credited as its star, producer, director, writer, editor, and even wrote some of its music – cost a half a million dollars to make and reaped ten million dollars in its first year of release (Guerrero 1993:86). Huey Newton, the leader of the Black Panthers, called it "the first truly revolutionary Black film made" (quoted in Guerrero 1993: 87). Formally, the film is almost avant-garde in its visual style (jump cuts, superimpositions, split screens, flares, vibrant color solarization) while its narrative is fairly minimalist. At the start of the film Sweetback (Van Peebles) is working in a bordello performing in a live sex show; his boss sends him off with two cops who are looking to show their superiors that they have a suspect in custody for an unrelated crime (any black suspect will do). When the two cops arrest and then brutally beat a black activist named Mu-Mu, Sweetback snaps and murders them both. For the rest of the film Sweetback runs in a picaresque manner south to the Mexican border, encountering assorted gamblers, pimps, corrupt preachers, whores, migrant farm workers, and more. He saves himself from a white motorcycle gang by sexually satisfying their female leader and rapes a woman at knife point at a hippy be-in (to evade police). Eventually Sweetback makes it to Mexico alive, after killing three hound dogs freed to hunt him down, and a superimposed title ends the film: "A Baadasssss Nigger is Coming to Collect Some Dues." Simultaneously raw and sophisticated, sexually provocative and defiant, *Sweet Sweetback's Baadasssss Song* arguably created the blaxploitation "formula" that would endure for several years: a violent sexually charged black man takes on a corrupt racist society and triumphs against it. (It should be noted that critiques of *Sweetback*'s sexist sexual politics were first sounded upon its original release [Bennett 1971] and have continued to the present day.)

Two of the best known blaxploitation films, *Shaft* and *Super Fly*, are Hollywood iterations of the *Sweet Sweetback* formula, and both were equally successful at the box office: *Shaft* cost a little over one million dollars and made 11 million in its first year. Similarly, *Super Fly* cost a half of a million dollars and made 12 million in its first year (Guerrero 1993: 92, 95). Importantly, both films were directed by black men, Gordon Parks Sr. and Gordon Parks Jr., respectively; they were also scored by popular black musicians. Isaac Hayes won an Oscar for his "Theme from *Shaft*," while Curtis Mayfield's soulful score for *Super Fly* out-grossed the film itself. Being Hollywood films, *Shaft* and *Super Fly* contain less of the raw anguish and X-rated sexuality of *Sweet Sweetback's Baadasssss Song*. They are also more generically formulaic. *Shaft* is a police drama starring Richard Roundtree as the titular detective John Shaft, while *Super Fly* is a gangster film about a charismatic drug dealer played by Ron O'Neal. Both films gave immediate rise to sequels, including *Shaft's Big Score* (1972), the globe-hopping James Bond-inspired *Shaft in Africa* (1973), seven *Shaft* TV movies (1973), and *Super Fly TNT* (1973). Everyone inside Hollywood (and on its fringes) wanted a piece of the action, and 1973 proved to be blaxploitation's "banner year ... judging by the numbers of films released" (Howard 2008: 13). It was also the year the industry had to answer its fiercest critics: middle class African American civil rights groups.

As mentioned at the start of this entry, not everyone found blaxploitation films harmless, "empowering" action-oriented entertainment. As early as 1972, Junius Griffin, head of the Los Angeles chapter of the NAACP, said in a *Newsweek* interview that "We must insist that our children are not exposed to a diet of so-called black movies that glorify black males as pimps, dope pushers, gangsters and super males with vast physical prowess but no cognitive skills" (quoted in Howard 2008: 12). Griffin was joined by other civil right activists including Jesse Jackson, black industry professionals like Tony Brown, and psychiatrist Alvin F. Poussaint in denouncing what they felt were blaxploitation films' degrading depictions of women and violent, hypersexualized, criminal men. The Coalition Against Blaxploitation (CAB) was briefly formed at this moment in time, headed by Junius Griffin and comprised of representatives from civil rights groups like the NAACP, CORE (Congress of Racial Equality), and SCLC (Southern Christian Leadership Conference). One of CAB's goals was to rate films based on their "negative" versus "positive" images of black people (Howard 2008: 13). Today we recognize that one viewer's positive image may be another's viewer's negative one, and vice versa: is *Blacula* the story of an avenging crusader or an evil monster? That methodological error aside, CAB was quickly undone by the voices of the many actors, writers, directors, and musicians working in blaxploitation films, filmmakers who wanted the work and who were earning a good living from it. Soon the protests quieted, and the movement began to diversify generically, before eventually withering away by the end of the decade.

Two new trends exemplify the blaxploitation films made between 1973 and 1976: the casting of women as strong black avenger figures, and the increased presence of martial arts. (Kung fu films like *Enter the Dragon* [1973] were almost as successful in urban theatres as were blaxploitation films.) Both trends may have been industry attempts to placate groups like CAB, by placing women in the formerly male avenger role, and moving away from gangster-style gun violence. However, both attempts were a bit disingenuous – in that martial arts fighting only theatricalizes and prolongs scenes of violence and that blaxploitation's new female action stars (most notably Pam Grier and Tamara Dobson) were exploited by the entertainment industry as much for their sex appeal as for their acting abilities. Dobson had been a fashion model and Grier had won beauty contests that first brought her to Hollywood, where she appeared as a supporting character in a string of low budget women-in prison films for Roger Corman's New World Pictures such as *The Big Doll House* (1971), *The Big Bird Cage* (1972), and *The Arena* (1973). Pam Grier's breakthrough came when she moved to AIP and starred in the vigilante action film *Coffy* (1973, written and directed by Jack Hill). The film was a huge hit and followed by the nearly identical and just as popular *Foxy Brown* (1974, also written and directed by Jack Hill). In both films Grier's character is out for revenge against corrupt white gangsters (who have killed her sister in *Coffy* and her boyfriend in *Foxy Brown*.) In both films the villains are organized criminals who run drugs and prostitution rings, their various depraved minions, and the white powers structures that tacitly enable them; in defeating these empires Coffy/Foxy uses her sexuality, her wits, and all sorts of weapons, from shotguns, to automobiles, to razor blades, and even a coat hanger. *Foxy Brown* ends memorably when Foxy presents the female gangster Miss Katherine with a Mason jar containing Miss Katherine's lover's genitals.

Pam Grier starred in two more similar blaxploitation vehicles for AIP, *Friday Foster* and *Sheba Baby* (both 1975), but each produced diminishing returns at the box office. Like many of the male blaxploitation stars of the 1970s, Grier was not in much demand in 1980s Hollywood, and found only sporadic work in supporting character parts. She returned to some degree of prominence during the 1990s with the revival of interest in blaxploitation filmmaking. She played small character parts in Mario (son of Melvin) Van Peebles's black western *Posse* (1993), and in the Tim Burton retrosploitation science fiction film *Mars Attacks!* (1993). She played the female lead in the retro-blaxploitation action film *Original Gangstas* (1996), along with fellow blaxploitation stars Jim Brown, Fred Williamson, Richard Roundtree, and Ron O'Neal. Most notably, her 1997 starring vehicle *Jackie Brown*, written and directed by Quentin Tarantino, was a homage to her star persona in films like *Coffy* and *Foxy Brown*.

The other female blaxploitation star who arose in the mid-1970s was former model Tamara Dobson, who starred as a very fashionable secret agent in *Cleopatra Jones* (1973) and *Cleopatra Jones and the Casino of Gold* (1975), both released by Warner Bros. Both films show the encroaching influence of kung fu on blaxploitation filmmaking in these years – Cleopatra practices martial arts, has two black karate experts as her sidekicks, and in the second film travels to Hong Kong to rescue two male secret agents. Intriguingly, in both films Cleopatra's arch opponent is a white lesbian gangster, played by Shelley Winters in the former and Stella Stevens in the latter. In more recent years, feminist and queer film theorists have found much of interest in blaxploitation's representation of women and sexual minorities. Studies by Yvonne D. Sims (2006) and Mia Mask (2009) explore the intersectionality of race and gender in black female action films and in the films of Pam Grier in particular. In another important piece, Joe Wlodarz (2004) explored the ramifications of "Queer Blaxploitation," noting that the films' frequent queer characters work to unsettle (as well as uphold) dominant notions of black masculinity. On a basic level, much of this research underlines the fact that B and exploitation films often contain non-dominant images of women and sexual minorities, whether they be Grier and Dobson's violent (albeit sexualized) avengers, or the interracial gay couples found in *Blacula* and the Redd Foxx vehicle *Norman … Is That You?* (1976). It might also be worth noting that black women were portrayed as violent avengers almost twenty years before white women were in films like *Thelma and Louise* (1991). Is this perhaps because within the racist imaginary black women are figured as closer to the animalistic physical body than the pure spirituality associated white women? Whatever the complex reasons, it is safe to say that twenty-first-century scholars will continue to find blaxploitation filmmaking a rich medium within which to explore historical constructions of race, gender, sexuality, class, as well as the broader contours of American film history. Films that were once dismissed as trash by white and black critics alike continue to constitute a rich a field of study for contemporary scholars.

Case studies: Two late-period independent blaxploitation films

Written, directed and produced by three white men (George Armitage, William Witney, and Gene [brother-of-Roger] Corman) for New World Pictures, *Darktown Strutters* (1975, aka *Get Down and Boogie*) exemplifies the more depoliticized and potentially offensive trends found in some blaxploitation films. Ostensibly a comedy about an outlandishly garbed female biker gang and their corresponding partners in a male biker gang, the film centers on Syreena (Trina Parks) who is searching the city for her missing mother, Cinderella (Frances Nealy). Her search eventually leads her to a corrupt white BBQ rib magnate named Commander Louisville Cross (costumed like Kentucky Fried Chicken spokesman Colonel Sanders), who lives on a plantation estate complete with cotton fields and a watermelon patch. With his KKK henchmen, Cross plans to use black women's bodies to help clone prominent black citizens, turning them into slaves instead of community organizers. Within this barely disguised allegory for the holocaust of slavery, the film attempts to wring comedy out of the sort of shtick AIP loaded into its beach party movies ten years earlier: whacky characters and costumes, impromptu music-and-dance numbers and pie-fight set pieces, kooky sound effects and Spike Jones-style music, and fast-motion car chases with Keystone-like cops (one of whom is played by AIP stalwart Dick Miller). It also contains a black face minstrel show, jokes about rape, jokes about abortion, jokes about lynching, jokes about black kids selling drugs, and jokes based on black men being drug addicts, thieves, pimps, welfare dependents, shoeshine boys, sexual disease carriers, and gorillas. In one particularly tone-deaf vignette, a white policeman applies black face and dons a dress in order to catch a "white female rapist on the loose [who] preys on black male faggots"; he is immediately shot to death by the white policemen whose "ghetto alert map" and "nigger alarm" has indicated his presence in the station.

Yes, the film also satirizes its white police officers, but how funny any of these jokes would have been to audiences in 1975 (or today) remains open to investigation. With Cross himself climactically dressed as a pig and the KKK treated like rejects from Eric Von Zipper's gang in any number of *Beach Party* movies (1963–1966), the film is an attempt to be a hip "insult everyone" scattershot comedy. But given the way it stereotypes black men, laughs about violence directed at queers of color, and jokingly represents black women's bodies (mis)used by the white power establishment – Cross's organization drugs and rapes black women and its cloning device is figured as a huge mechanical black woman named Annie – it ultimately trivializes serious issues of racial and sexual exploitation. The film may have been part of the trend to have black women take center stage in blaxploitation films, but in this case Syreena's story fails to overcome the white male biases within which it is figured.

Abar, The First Black Superman (1977, aka *In Your Face*) is a very different type of blaxploitation film. From Mirror Releasing, *Abar* was the only film ever written and produced by James Smalley, and the only film ever directed by Frank Packard. (I could not locate any information on the race or industrial context/s of these men.) However, unlike *Darktown Strutters*, *Abar* appears to be much more a labor of love (literally), liberally invoking the speeches, images, and philosophies of Martin Luther King throughout its running time. To some extent, it recalls both the aesthetic limitations and the earnest Christianity of Spencer Williams's 1940s "race movies." The plot concerns kindly black Dr. Kincade (J. Walter Smith), who develops a serum that can turn a human being into a superhuman, but that plot is almost secondary to the film's depiction of the racist hatred faced by Dr. Kincade, his wife, and their children when they move into a white middle class suburb in Southern California. The film offers no sugar coated version of this abuse: the Kincades receive verbal taunts from the neighbors (who first mistake Dr. Kincade and his wife for a butler and maid), endure vandalism, threats of harm towards them and their relatives, a dead and gutted cat hung on their front porch, attempts by their local home owner's association to buy them out of their new home, and even murder when a city official deliberately runs down and kills the Kincade's son.

The Kincades reluctantly accept the help and protection of Abar (Tobar Mayo) and the Black Front of Unity, his activist group from South Central Los Angeles. Abar's voice speaks the grievances of the ghetto (visualized in a powerful location-shot montage sequence), while also critiquing corrupt black politicians, racist white policemen, and even Dr. Kincade's decision to flee from the ghetto into a white middle class neighborhood (ostensibly so he can finish his scientific research). Both Dr. Kincade and Abar embody Martin Luther King's philosophy of non-violent social change: despite the terror his family is subjected to, Dr. Kincade explains to his children that racists are "people with broken minds and broken hearts." When Abar finally drinks the potion that makes him invincible, he sees a vision of Jesus Christ, and develops newfound psychic powers – which he explains as an awakening in his mind of an "ancient wisdom" of "Divine origin." He begins to redress both black and white crimes not with violence, but through transformation. In the climactic sequence, Abar appears in a blue suit, red shirt, and a tie adorned with white crosses; via his newfound powers, he makes black on black crime in the ghetto reverse itself and turns a street corner of drinking/gambling/pot-smoking youths into college graduates. With a sort of Divine wind that would not be out of place in any Biblical epic, Abar visits curses of snakes, rats, and bees on the Kincades' middle class neighbors, who quickly realize the error of their ways. One of the most racist housewives even admits that her hatred stems from the fact that she herself is a black woman passing for white, and the film ends with yet more words from Martin Luther King's "I Have a Dream" speech.

Conclusion

As the blaxploitation era was winding to a close, Rudy Ray Moore, a comedian who became famous performing on the "Chitlin Circuit" of African American theatres and nightclubs, produced and starred in Generation International Pictures *Disco Godfather* (1979, aka *Avenging Disco Godfather*). Moore's films (which also include *Dolemite* [1975] and *Petey Wheatstraw* [1977]) were generally based on his rapping, signifying, bigger-than-life stage routines, and his "Disco Godfather" Tucker fills that bill quite nicely: Tucker is a flamboyant ex-cop and nightclub owner determined to take down the gangsters pushing PCP ("angel dust," and/or "wack") to the kids in his community. As such, *Disco Godfather* is a compendium of common blaxploitation tropes: outlandish fashions, night club scenes with music and dancing (even a "roller boogie"), a plot about drugs in the ghetto, black activists, corrupt policemen and politicians, kung fu fighting, and even monstrous demons (visualized as the bad trips of the drug addicts). But by 1979, the formula had gotten stale, and Hollywood insiders as well as independents were shying away from making blaxploitation films. Compared to the 1970s, the film industry of the 1980s mostly turned its back on black films, black themes, and in many cases black filmmakers. Only with the mid-decade success of Steven Spielberg's *The Color Purple* (1985) and the rise of Spike Lee (beginning with *She's Gotta Have It* [1986]) would black participation in American filmmaking once again start to rise, albeit slowly.

Ed Guerrero argues that blaxploitation audiences paid Hollywood a lot of money when the industry needed it most, during the financially lean years of the late 1960s and early 1970s

(1993: 105). However, he also notes that black audiences were equally interested in the decade's nostalgic Hollywood blockbusters (films like *The Godfather* [1972], *Jaws* [1975], *Rocky* [1976], and *Star Wars* [1977]), films that were quickly defining the "New Hollywood." The majors no longer needed to cater to black audiences, and independent exploitation filmmakers found new genres to exploit, such as the slasher film. The relative flop of the big-budget musical *The Wiz* (1978) may have also soured Hollywood on black movies of any size. Despite the presence of black stars like Michael Jackson, Diana Ross, and Lena Horne, *The Wiz* was a dreary affair directed by gritty urban realist Sidney Lumet – a man who had never directed a musical before. What were they expecting? Still, blaxploitation filmmaking gave work and exposure to many African American actors, writers, directors, and musicians during the brief years that it flourished. The movement produced a wide range highly diverse films, many of which are still waiting to be discovered by cultists and scholars alike.

References

Bennett, Lerone. 1971. "The Emancipation Orgasm: Sweetback in Wonderland," *Ebony*, 26 (September): 106–116.
Benshoff, Harry. 2000. "Blaxploitation Horror Films: Generic Reappropriation or Reinscription?," *Cinema Journal*, 39.2 (Winter): 31–50.
Bogle, Donald. 2016/1973. *Toms, Coons, Mammies, Mulattoes and Bucks: An Interpretative History of Blacks in American Films, Fifth Edition*. New York: Bloomsbury.
Church, David. 2015. *Grindhouse Nostalgia: Memory, Home Video and Exploitation Film Fandom*. Edinburgh: Edinburgh University Press.
Guerrero, Ed. 1993. "Chapter Three: The Rise and Fall of Blaxploitation," in *Framing Blackness: The African American Image in Film*. Philadelphia, PA: Temple University Press: 69–111.
Howard, Josiah. 2008. *Blaxploitation Cinema: The Essential Reference Guide*. Surrey, England: FAB Press.
Koven, Mikel J. 2010. *Blaxploitation Films*. Harpenden: Kamera Books, 2010.
Mask, Mia. 2009. *Divas on Screen: Black Women in American Film*. Champaign, IL: University of Illinois Press.
Poussaint, Alvin F. 1974. "Cheap Thrills That Degrade Blacks," *Psychology Today*, 7 (February): 22–26.
Sconce, Jeffrey. 1995. "'Trashing' the Academy: Taste, Excess, and an Emerging Politics of Cinematic Style," *Screen*, 36.4: 371–393.
Sims, Yvonne D. 2006. *Women of Blaxploitation: How the Black Film Heroine Changed American Popular Culture*. Jefferson, NC: McFarland.
Wlodarz, Joe. 2004. "Beyond the Black Macho: Queer Blaxploitation," *Velvet Light Trap*, 53 (Spring): 10–25.

PART III

Critical concepts

Critical concepts

Studies of cult cinema have, like any other type of academic subject, led to a proliferation of critical concepts in order to probe and better understand this phenomenon in all of its complexity. This chapter focuses on of some particularly notable critical concepts that have been mobilised frequently within studies of cult cinema. While there are chapters in other sections of this volume that utilise critical concepts, the chapters in this section home in on a particular concept and shed light on it in relation to the development and understanding of cult cinema. Many of these concepts have been discussed prominently within cult cinema research.

Brenda Austin-Smith surveys the issue of gender and cult cinema, which has led to a number of debates. There have been critiques of the masculine biases and tastes related to cult cinema, as argued by Hollows (2003) and Read (2003). Austin-Smith outlines these arguments and, while agreeing to an extent nevertheless adds nuance to the claims of Hollows; for example, discussing Hollows' contention that cult cinema is exclusionary towards the feminine, she probes the spaces it opens up for females who watch as 'one of the boys' and who distance themselves from stereotypically 'girly' pleasures. Austin-Smith also looks into other areas of cult cinema in relation to gender, such as underrepresented female auteurs, as well as exploring the complexities of viewing positions which are often condemned as only offering masochistic positions for female audiences.

Renee Middlemost looks into the concept of nostalgia in relation to cult. Nostalgia has been a recurring theme within elements of cult cinema culture and cult cinema viewers are often nostalgic in various ways. As Middlemost argues, cult viewers can be nostalgic for films of the past and be nostalgic for cinema-going experiences of the past; cult films themselves may feature nostalgia as a theme, while repetition and repeat viewing – often associated with cult audiences – are also included. Middlemost looks at some ways in which nostalgic cults can emerge, firstly in her consideration of seasonal cult films – particularly Christmas – in which films air repeatedly on television during particular seasons and can therefore be linked to personalised and partly ritualized screenings. In her next case study, she examines the concrete example of a cult film group in Sydney, who evidence nostalgic tendencies in film tastes as well as tech-nostalgia in preferences for outmoded screening formats such as 16mm and Scoptines.

Middlemost argues that such nostalgic tendencies can be considered as (nostalgically) reviving a form of sociality that has been lost within the modern world.

In Anna Powell's chapter, the concept of spirituality is examined. The term 'cult', of course, stems from religion, and discussion of cult film audiences in relation to religion and spirituality has been common (e.g. Hoberman and Rosenbaum 1991; Lavery 1991; Hills 2002). Powell in her chapter focuses on a specific dimension of spirituality: the occult. Considering the ways in which the emergence of cult cinema has often been perceived in relation to the American counterculture, and the huge revival of the occult within that counterculture, Powell's focus is particularly pertinent, and she looks into the overlaps between the occult and cult film, as well as discussing a number of prominent occult films and filmmakers which have themselves become cult objects. A key figure in this discussion is Kenneth Anger, whom Powell describes as the 'oc/cult auteur *par excellence*'. Discussing the relations between the occult, and the cult audience, Powell outlines the mysterious allure of cinema – which she equates with magic – and the parallels between cult cinema and the occult such as secret knowledge, and rare and unusual interests shared amongst initiates.

Thomas Joseph Watson investigates the concept of transgression in his chapter, which as he notes has frequently been applied to cult cinema. Watson begins by providing some nuance to the definition of transgression, distinguishing it from the closely related notion of subversion. He further argues that we should avoid fixed, transhistorical theories of transgression in favour of context-dependent analyses linked to shifts in morality and legality. Watson then discusses how transgression can feed into cult cinema on different levels, as something within the film text as an aesthetic component, but also as something extra-textual, particularly apparent when communities can form around obtaining films that have been deemed transgressive, or on a more personal level through specific viewers 'testing themselves' through engaging with challenging material.

Watson inevitably discusses issues of censorship in relation to transgression and censorship is looked at in further detail in the final chapter of the section by Emma Pett. Pett addresses a number of more recent developments in detail through looking at two regulatory bodies, the BBFC (British Board of Film Classification) and the MPAA (Motion Picture Association of America). While both of these bodies have been seen as moving towards a more liberalized agenda overall, Pett argues that in actual fact in some areas they have tightened regulatory policies, and this is particularly the case regarding marginalized films and other online media. Noting how both organisations are linked to mainstream culture, she further contends that they actually play a role in the formation of new cult communities through their roles as cultural taste guardians. While it may now be easier to access prohibited texts than it once was, the proliferation of different versions and ideas as to whether certain films are considered acceptable or unacceptable lead to new forms of subcultural distinction emerging. Pett therefore disputes the oft-cited cliché that the increased accessibility of films via digital, networked platforms renders cult cinema a thing of the past.

References

Hills, Matt. 2002. *Fan Cultures*. London: Routledge.
Hoberman, J., and Jonathan Rosenbaum. 1991. *Midnight Movies*, second edition. New York: Da Capo.
Hollows, Joanne. 2003. 'The Masculinity of Cult,' in Mark, Jancovich, Antonio Lázaro-Reboll, Julian Stringer, and Andy Willis, eds, *Defining Cult Movies: The Cultural Politics of Oppositional Taste*. Manchester: Manchester University Press: 35–53.

Lavery, David. 1991. 'Gnosticism and the Cult Film,' in J.P. Telotte, ed., *The Cult Film Experience*. Austin: University of Texas Press: 187–199.

Read, Jacinda. 2003. 'The Cult of Masculinity: From Fan-Boys to Academic Bad-Boys,' in Mark Jancovich, Antonio Lázaro-Reboll, Julian Stringer, and Andy Willis, eds, *Defining Cult Movies: The Cultural Politics of Oppositional Taste*. Manchester: Manchester University Press: 54–70.

15

CULT CINEMA AND GENDER

Brenda Austin-Smith

What do cult films show and say about gender? Do they use conventional representations in order to perform the textual transgressions they are defined by and celebrated for? Or do cult films, and the practices that sustain their circulation, thumb a collective nose at gender as another oppressive way of organizing social life? To look at cult film and gender means looking not just at texts, but also at audiences. Who are these people, and what are they doing with these films? Are cult audiences a vanguard of revolution, or are their peculiar film attachments symptoms of reaction to the emergence of feminist and queer gender critiques? What follows is an overview of debates about gender representation and viewing possibilities generated by the growth of scholarship on cult film and cult consumption, and a brief tour of the complicated cult landscapes of production and reception.

The hallmarks of canonical cult cinema are very familiar to us by now: narrative weirdness, an air of rebellion, and arcane or strange content are all typical of cult, as is a winking, self-aware stance in relation to genre. For all of their apparent resistance to conformity, however, many claim that cult films tend to observe or recuperate distressingly conservative representations of gender and sexuality, opting for transgressive gestures that flout limits on the depiction of straight sex, for example, rather than exploding gender categories or championing queer pleasures as something other than ephemeral. This has been true of both grubby and glamorous examples of cult film. As Elena Gorfinkel (2008: 34) writes of both high and low cultural manifestations of the cult impulse,

> The art house, while championing continental esthetics and highbrow tastes, also gained a tacitly prurient appeal, a place where, according to exploitation producer David Friedman, "the cold beer and greaseburger gang" could rub shoulders with the "white wine and canapés crowd," in the interests of seeing exposed female flesh.

And as Ernest Mathijs and Jamie Sexton observe, the associations of cult cinema with a male viewer of a certain age, has meant that sexual content has often taken a conventional form, intensifying rather than questioning the norms of cinematic depictions of gender. For these reasons, many associate cult cinema with a philosophy of transgression that sees the elimination of restraint (on depictions of sexualized violence against women, for example) as a sign of political and aesthetic progressiveness, expressed, for example, in Steve Chibnall's celebration of "the rejection of censorship for adult viewers" (Chibnall 1998: 85). Whether defined primarily as a genre, or as a set of ritualized practices that coalesce around a group of privileged texts, the term "cult film" is one used most often in relation to the cinephilia of young straight, white men.

In her influential essay "The Masculinity of Cult," Joanne Hollows traces the attraction of the term "subculture" for film fans seeking an identity positioned in opposition not just to mainstream commercial films, but also to the majority of young people around them, who are imagined as conformist and false in relation to the cult film fan's fierce, unvarnished authenticity. The association of mainstream cinema with weakness, prudishness, and cowardice all work to feminize it, adding to the appeal of "cult film fan" as an identity attractive to spectators who see themselves as rebel figures when they watch objectionable films. What Hollows calls the "strategies of exclusivity" in the formation of cult fan identity – the "dare you to watch this" practices that demand "hardness" and stamina in the face of gory displays, for example – don't just work to distance the cultist from typical viewers, but can also work to shut out actual women from the "boyzone" of cult film enthusiasts (Hollows 2003: 45). The assertively heterosexual cast to such demonstrations of conventional masculinity also leaves out, at least implicitly, the viewing practices of many men who identify as queer rather than straight.

There are other ways of describing and experiencing films according to other cinephilias, however. Hollows writes about the exclusion of films such as *Titanic* from the realm of cult, in part because of its mainstream success, but also because of the legions of female fans who made films like it so successful (Hollows 2003: 38), and whose gendered presence is in some quarters regarded as the negation of the cult experience (as if women spectators exerted an emasculating force when acknowledged as audience members).

One of the boys

In their influential essays, both Joanne Hollows and Jacinda Read characterize cult film viewers and scholars as gendered in their assumptions and practices. Their critiques of cult film's default masculinity also, however, insist on space for women in cult. Both take pains to argue that there is nothing essentially male about cult film viewership or scholarship, and both detail the character of female participation in the cultures of cult. One sign of this participation is women's self-conscious embrace of cult's masculinized practices and attitudes. Female spectators of canonical cult can, for example, watch film as "one of the boys," in critic Sarah Thornton's words (Thornton 1995: 104). Watching cult films as "one of the boys" can appeal to female spectators for a lot of reasons. This cultural identity can help justify an interest or pleasure in violent or taboo images often regarded as unseemly in women. Such a viewing identity also allows some women viewers to distance themselves from all that is devalued as 'girly,' and in so doing, to claim and experience the kind of aesthetic credibility often awarded to cult subcultures, even temporarily (Hollows 2003: 39). In practical terms, it can also provide company (and implied protection) for attendance at the "sleazo" sites of midnight screenings that Hollows describes as one of the celebrated geographies of cult that has sometimes excluded women viewers (Hollows 2003: 42). I would add that watching as "one of the boys" also allows women to manage whatever discomfort might arise from the coincidence of cult films and porn, providing a space from which to ignore, mock, or enjoy material that might otherwise create more of an issue were they to claim its pleasures more publicly. Watching as "one of the boys" is what Mathijs and Sexton call a "hidden strategy of cult enjoyment" (Mathijs and Sexton 2011: 116).

While Hollows' essay focuses on cult spectators, Read's essay turns to the cult scholar, examining the sexual politics of those who claim a minority or outsider identity for themselves as academic fans of cult cinema. These are the critics who, Read claims, adopt and announce their attachment to "paracinema" (Sconce 1995) as a way of forestalling feminist criticism of their viewing pleasure. These academics proudly brandish a 'politics of incorrectness', which "simultaneously acknowledges and disavows both feminine competencies and feminist politics" (Read 2003: 62). For Read, the masculinity of cult finds its academic counterpart in scholars who use their awareness of cult's gender problematics in order to revel in the pleasure these incorrect texts provide, casting themselves as academic minorities whose outsider status in the thoroughly feminized and feminist world of academia deserves recognition and protection, since he (and the examples she provides are both male) is brave enough to come forward as a 'delinquent misreader' (Read 2003: 65). This move is akin to the "insulation trajectory" theory whereby fans acknowledge criticism of a revered film or director without altering the strength of their initial fan attachment (Hunter 2010).

Rebecca Feasey's study of Sharon Stone extends the utility of the "one of the boys" identity to the manoeuvres of cult actresses in ways that address the ambivalence with which the sexualized female stars of cult films (Elizabeth Berkley of *Showgirls*, Sylvia Kristel of *Emmanuelle*) are regarded by fans. Stone is a subject – and target – of analysis in the collection *Bad Movies We Love*, in which she appears as a figure of ridicule, both for her apparent willingness to appear nude early in her onscreen career, and for her later attempts to establish a career as a serious actor with more than erotic thrillers to her name. As Feasey observes, she is both criticized for the roles she plays in borderline exploitation films (as if she had total control over the parts), and then mocked for her presumption when she takes roles that emphasize something other than her body. Feasey contends that Stone reclaims a sense of agency in the collection's foreword, something she was invited to write by the authors. There, Stone at first adopts a self-deprecating tone, seemingly in accord with the treatment of her star-image by the authors. But over the course of her introduction, Stone performs a verbal "sleight of hand," adopting an ironic stance in relation to her own performance history, joining in on the joke, and slyly undercutting the condescending tone of the writers. Stone achieves this control over her presentation only through distancing herself "from her own femininity ..." thus becoming "one of the boys" in the contemplation of her own career (Feasey 2003: 182).

Women and/as cult directors

Toward the end of their chapter on "The Cult Auteur," Mathijs and Sexton address the paucity of women in the pantheon of celebrated cult directors, noting that only a few, such as Dorothy Arzner and Ida Lupino, have secured that status through their work in Hollywood. Arzner's film *Dance, Girl, Dance,* a flop after its 1940 release, gained cult traction in the wake of 1970s and 1980s feminist film criticism, especially for a scene in which Maureen O'Hara's character Judy stops a performance, walks to the edge of the stage, and tears into the heckling crowd of (mostly male) audience members. Judy confronts the hypocrisy of the men – both working and upper-class – who have come to taunt and ogle the women onstage, and ends her spirited tirade with a reminder that that the wives and daughters to whom they return "see through you just like we do." To watch and hear a character explicitly voice a challenge to the power of the male gaze – as if inspired by the theory of Laura Mulvey – within the diegetic world of a Golden Age film was, and still is, a thrilling filmic moment.

Lupino's cult appeal stems from her career move from actress to writer-director, the controversial topics of her films (bigamy, for example), and her determination to make the most of sets, outdoor locations, and personal acquaintances who could be pressed into acting. All this is typical of low-budget directors associated with cult, but Lupino's still muted reputation seems out of synch with her cult auteur credentials. In a recent article on *Outrage*, Lupino's portrait of a woman's trauma and isolation in the aftermath of sexual assault, *New Yorker* critic Richard Brophy ties the film's depiction of masculine violence, whether explicit or subtle, to current analyses of rape culture. Although dramatic, *Outrage* is nothing like the typical exploitative rape-revenge film. Although the film itself is obscure enough to draw the attention of cult collectors inspired by the inaccessibility of an independent Hollywood era low-budget black-and-white film directed by a woman, its seriousness and compassion still position the film outside the margins of cult's boy's club, and place it more firmly in the realms of an expanded cult cinema in which perspectives of women have a place.

Women like Stephanie Rothman, Catherine Hardwicke and Kathryn Bigelow are all well-regarded as directors, but as Mathijs and Sexton point out, are denied status as cult auteurs for reasons that include their close production associations with figures like Roger Corman, or their work across a variety of genres that never coalesces, in the responses of viewers, into a cohesive, auteurist oeuvre (Mathijs and Sexton 2011: 74). Not so Doris Wishman, "the female Ed Wood" (Mathijs and Mendik 2011: 57) who forged a strange and ambitious career in the sexploitation and "roughie" film business over thirty years of work. Mathijs and Sexton mention Wishman as a director whose position in the sexploitation world animates passionate debates about the ambiguous status of women in cult production (Mathijs and Sexton 2011: 74). But scholars like Moya Luckett, Tania Modleski, and Rebekah McKendry have all found in Wishman's catalogue something worthy of attention. While Modleski maintains that Wishman's work cannot be completely rehabilitated because of its traffic in sexualized violence against women (Modleski 2007: 49), Luckett and McKendry take a slightly different view. Referring to her as "the most prolific woman director of American film in the sound era" (2003: 142), Luckett stresses the feminine character of low-budget sexploitation film-making, and points to how often Wishman's films connected salacious locales (of the nudist camp for example), to the female protagonist's wish for a more fulfilling life and career, a vague narrative tendency that found its "fantastic limits" in *Nude on the Moon*, which depicts the orb as "harmoniously ruled by naked women" (Luckett 2003: 144). Both Luckett and McKendry also note the distinguishing quirks of Wishman's roughie films, set in city spaces, in which women confront the multiple dissatisfactions of heterosexual relationships. In these films, perversely motivated cutaways, monotone dialogue delivery, and a reliance on stereotypical characters (often unnamed) adds up to a curious aesthetic that foregrounds women's sexual frustration and all around repression (McKendry 2010: 66). Though women in films like *Bad Girls Go to Hell*, *My Brother's Wife*, and *Too Much Too Late* are physically brutalized by men and exploited, in the end they triumph, and the men who are narratively responsible for their descent into vice usually die. Watching Wishman's films brings to my mind a few more things that argue against a too-quick dismissal of them: one is that a considerable number of her roughies feature scenes of couples embracing, caressing, and of men kissing women's necks and bellies, gently erotic details surprising to encounter, given the tendencies of the genre. The other, prompted by McKendry's analysis of Wishman's weird editing style, catatonic actors and stock characters, is that the film most reminiscent of Wishman's in its depiction of female repression and sudden violence, is Chantal Akerman's *Jeanne Dielman*, a canonical work of woman's experimental cinema. Though these two directors are distinguished on the surface by many things (budget, language, artistic context), there is a flicker of resemblance between their filmic concerns that is worthy of consideration.

Genres and genders

Horror, pornography, and melodrama, the "body genres" (Williams 1991) that elicit physiological responses from viewers, are among the most favoured in cult film circles, and with each come gendered assumptions about their aesthetic qualities and appeal to spectators. In keeping with the masculinized cast of cult, the violence and shock of certain kinds of films – especially horror and gore – are prized as supreme experiences by many male cult fans. Describing his own shift in fandom from *Dr. Who* to British horror, Matt Hills remembers the moment as part of a vague personal association of *Dr. Who* with "'failed' or inadequate masculinity," while horror "provided a clearer sense of 'enduring' masculinity and an imagined 'toughness'" (Hills 2002: 85). This illustrates perfectly the "anxieties of cult consumption" that shape the reception of cult film (Mathijs and Sexton 2011: 110). But horror's treatment of gender is less tractable than its narrative conventions suggest. Many see cult horror films as essentially conservative in their plots and gendered imagery. Women and girls are the prey of masculine monsters; sexually active female adolescents are the inevitable victims of the serial killer, and subject to attacks that take up more screen time, and cause more character distress, than those visited upon male characters. Within this general group of horror films, and among those popular in the cult of horror period of the 1970s and 1980s (Mathijs and Sexton 2011), there is another category of films that have achieved cult status because they focus so single-mindedly on torture, bodily dismemberment, rape, and physical desecration. Depictions of gender-based violence in these cult films are difficult to rescue from charges of misogyny, although histrionic performances enable a cult text like *Blood-Sucking Freaks* to claim redemptive status as satire or exploitation at the very same time that it offends.

Criticism of horror has by extension suggested that taking pleasure in films like *Friday the 13th*, or *Halloween* is indefensible, especially for women, who are theorized as occupying psychological viewing positions as either perpetrator-identified sadists, victim-identified masochists, or something that oscillates between these states (Hansen 1991; Berenstein 1996). In *Phantom Ladies: Hollywood, Horror and the Home Front*, Tim Snelson puts the case this way:

> Film scholars continue to struggle in explaining the relationship between women and horror. Following a tradition of psychoanalytically informed feminist film theory, most accounts rely on the assertion that the horror spectator is typically positioned as male and that the genre is founded upon the subjugation of women; female horror spectatorship is best a displeasurable and at worst an untenable textual position.
>
> (Snelson 2015: 2)

Taking up Laura Mulvey's work on the male gaze, scholars like Linda Williams, Carol Clover, and Barbara Creed have all theorized an array of "looks" in horror in connection to women in the diegesis, and in the audience. Referring to men and boys daring to look at images of horror, while women and girls cover their eyes, Williams asks rhetorically why this refusal to look at the screen is a surprise, given that a woman watching a horror film is asked to "bear witness to her own powerlessness," and in any case, has "so little to identify with on the screen" (Williams 1984: 63). Countering this claim that women avoid images of horror is research by Brigid Cherry and Amy Vosper, who have conducted audience studies of female spectatorship of cult horror films and discovered women and girls who express persistent pleasure in watching horror films. Cherry finds that female viewers "refuse to refuse to look" when watching horror and suggests that women's identification with Clover's "Final Girl" may be one of many ways to delight in the genre. It is also possible that female fans of the genre, familiar with its tropes of clueless girls insisting on acting in obviously stupid ways ("I'm going downstairs to see what's making that noise!") celebrate the dispatching of such empty-headed characters out of sheer irritation. Interesting to note is that Snelson's historical investigation of women viewers of 1940s horror film suggests that the kinds of horror women enjoyed most in that period were atmospheric, Gothic-themed films, something that both Cherry and Vosper also report in their work on contemporary viewers. It is not that female viewers necessarily dislike or can't abide explicit violence, writes Vosper, but that they prefer their gore integrated into a "cerebral" and intellectually stimulating storyline (Vosper 2014).

Though Gaylyn Studlar chides midnight movies like *Pink Flamingoes* and *The Rocky Horror Picture Show* for their recuperations of gender divisions, even as they animate visions of "perversely erotic freedom" through their outrageous characters (Studlar 1991: 153), it is worth considering degrees of sexual self-awareness between and among monsters in horror films. Monsters in *The Mummy, King Kong*, and any number of horny alien films may be attracted to the women they kidnap, but their mechanical behaviour speaks to drives rather than charm and makes running away the narrative choice of everyone they approach. No hero or heroine would willingly remain within grabbing range of these creatures. But the gendered dimensions of cult films like *Rocky Horror* and *Ginger Snaps*, for example, featuring characters that revel in their transformations, emphasize the sexualized charisma of the monster, as well as the pleasure the monstrous character takes in that power. The werewolf's bite supercharges the effects of puberty in Ginger, making it virtually impossible for boys in her school not to respond to her aggressive allure as she catwalks along the hallways of her school. And Frank'n'Furter's grand entrance from the slowly descending elevator in *Rocky Horror* remains a powerfully erotic display that is impossible for anyone in the frame, and many in the audience, to resist.

For all the gender fluidity that characterizes theories of cult viewers of horror, specific attention to queer characters in, and viewers of, horror concentrates on vampire films such as *Daughters of Darkness, The Velvet Vampire, The Hunger*, and *Interview with the Vampire*, rather than on slasher, serial killer, or other canonical cult films. Scenes of same-sex attraction and elements of sexsploitation in the often art house production values of these films have propelled them to cult status, and has attracted analyses focused on the structural queerness of the monster as a presence that invokes fear, hatred, and persecution, as well as fascination and attraction on the part of both characters and spectators. Invoking the tradition of carnival as theorized by Mikhail Bahktin, Harry Benshoff argues that while monsters in horror film speak to the outsider status of queer spectators, identifying with the monster offers all viewers, straight or gay, the temporary delight associated with "the lure of the deviant" (Benshoff 1997: 13). Nevertheless, he writes, "Queer viewers are ... more likely than straight ones to experience the monster's plight in more personal, individualized terms" (Benshoff 1997: 13).

Despite its strong associations with queerness, the vampire horror film takes a cishet turn in *Twilight*, a film whose reception has ignited debates about the cultural status of the (presumably) teen girl viewer as much, or more than, the quality or significance of the film itself. Lisa Bode's analysis of film reviews of *Twilight* reveals that negative reviews of the film included more critical language used to describe the audience for the film (Bode 2012: 64). Whether intently focused on the screen, or shrieking at the sight of Edward sparkling in the sun, for some reviewers the teen girl is always on the wrong side of cult culture.

M and Ms

Sure, a traditional romantic comedy or a drama may be *somewhat amusing*, but once it's over, it's just as easily forgotten. ... those movies aren't entertaining at all. ... And what's worse, they lack balls.

(Gore 2010: ix)

This comically energetic dismissal of tame movie choices by Chris Gore provides a hyperbolically suitable entrée to the discussion of film genres with significant cult followings, for whom the audience is assumed to be largely (but not exclusively) straight women and girls: musicals and melodramas. Ian Conrich's observation that musical performance in cult films is often a "knowing perversion of the cultural values, performances, subjects and utopian aspects of the classical musical film" (Conrich 2006: 116) fits the rowdiness of cult musicals like *Rock 'n' Roll High School*, and the parodic qualities of *The Happiness of the Katakuris*. Similarly, the appeal to nostalgia of musicals like *Singin' in the Rain* map onto assumptions about the feminized audiences for these films, even though their karaoke versions have successfully traded on a broader appeal. This is why auto-ethnographic studies such as Garth Jowett's of what watching Hollywood musicals of the 1950s meant to him as "a heterosexual male in the last half of this century" are so critical (Jowett 2001: 149). Jowett describes childhood dancing in front of his parents' mirror, his mother's abiding love for the movies, and his conviction that the singing and dancing men of his most cherished musicals "are at the heart of the true masculinity I know" (Jowett 168).

It is, finally, hilariously ironic that melodramas elicit from some viewers the kind of disgust and resistance one would expect in response to cult practices in which machismo is achieved and sustained by watching the goriest cinematic scenes imaginable. Hollows, for example, quotes an interview in which a cult filmmaker declares that he's seen everything, but that he "can't sit through" the television serial melodrama *Dynasty* (Hollows 2003: 37). As a thoroughly feminized genre, classical and contemporary melodramas such as *Dark Victory*, *Stella Dallas*, *Beaches*, and *Steel Magnolias* have been subject to strong critiques from feminist film theorists for their conventional plots and stereotyped portrayals of women who sacrifice everything for love and family, even if it means, in the case of Bette Davis in *Dark Victory*, dying alone at home because you don't want to interfere with your husband's attendance at a medical conference. But in these films women viewers find images of themselves – often, in fact, in emotionally charged close-ups – and are in every way central to the storyline. Although the emotional travails they endure are structurally reminiscent of the physical threats and injuries sustained by female victims of horror in that they are often repetitive, prolonged, and undeserved, they arise from domestic situations familiar to viewers rather than from encounters with reincarnated masked murderers. The suffering that heroines of melodrama experience is as intense as that of any action hero, but it is psychological, internal, and registered in facial expressions that communicate their pain in tears, and that at other moments embody anguish too wrenching for full articulation. The stoicism of female characters in melodrama, compelled by ethical or situational concerns to quell their voices (like Kay Francis in *Confession*) saturates the genre with determined silence befitting tales of torture victims who refuse to give up information. That melodramas are more likely to be mocked for traits of excess and incredibility than are horror films, is another example of cult's valourization of emotions like shock and fear, and its apparent unease with emotions like extreme sadness. Nor are the cultish activities of repeat viewing, memorization of lines, and imitation alien to viewers of melodrama, as Helen Taylor's study *Scarlett's Women*, and my own research on women spectators of Hollywood melodrama, whose relationships with these films and their character-heroines manifest as "a willed and durable enterprise of self-fashioning make clear" (Austin-Smith 2007: 143-156).

Filmed images of gendered beings are fixed and permanent in ways that the reception and creation of meaning from those images can never be. Influenced, shaped and qualified by contexts, and by multiple adoptions and rejections of identification, cult cinema is shot through with recuperative, redemptive, and evasive strategies of production and viewing. It is not that cult film's treatment of gender is resistant to analysis, but that the art of cult film is an experience rather than a problem. Its troubling and fascinating contours will continue to be described, and with good fortune, the debates will continue.

References

Austin-Smith, Brenda. 2007. "Memory, Affect, and Personal Modernity: *Now, Voyager* and the Second World War," in Tina Mai Chen and David Churchill, eds, *History, Film, and Cultural Citizenship: Sites of Production*. New York: Routledge, pp. 143–156.

Benshoff, Harry. 1997. *Homosexuality and the Horror Film*. Manchester: Manchester University Press.

Berenstein, Rhonda. 1996. *Attack of the Leading Ladies: Gender, Sexuality and Spectatorship in Classic Horror Cinema*. New York: Columbia University Press.

Bode, Lisa. 2012. "Transitional Tastes: Teen Girls and Genre in the Critical Reception of Twilight," in Julia Vassilieva and Constantine Verevis, pp. 63–75.

Brody, Richard. 2014. "Movie of the Week: *Outrage*," in *The New Yorker*, October 9. Online: www.newyorker.com/culture/richard-brody/movie-week-outrage. Accessed 15 June 2017.

Cherry, Brigid S. 1999. "Refusing to Refuse to Look: Female Viewers of the Horror Film," in Melvyn Stokes and Richard Maltby, eds, *Identifying Hollywood's Audiences*. London: BFI Publishing, pp. 187–203.

Cherry, Brigid. 2009. *Horror*. London: Routledge.

Chibnall, Steven. 1998. *Making Mischief: The Cult Films of Pete Walker*. Guildford: FAB Press.

Cline, John and Robert. G. Weiner, eds. 2010. *From the Arthouse to the Grindhouse: Highbrow and Lowbrow Transgression in Cinema's First Century*. Lanham, MD: Scarecrow Press.

Clover, Carol. J. 1992. *Men, Women and Chainsaws: Gender in the Modern Horror Film*. Princeton, NJ: Princeton University Press.

Cornich, Ian and Estella Tincknell, eds. 2006. *Film's Musical Moments*. Edinburgh: Edinburgh University Press.

Creed, Barbara. 1993. *The Monstrous Feminine: Film, Feminism and Psychoanalysis*. Abington, PA: Routledge.

Feasey, Rebecca. 2003. "'Sharon Stone, Screen Diva': Stardom, Femininity, and Cult Fandom," in Mark Jancovich, Antonio Lázaro-Reboll, Julian Stringer and Andy Willis, pp. 172–184.

Gorfinkel, Elena. 2008. "Cult Film or Cinephilia by Any Other Name," *Cineaste*, 34.1, pp. 33–38.

Gore, Chris. 2010. "Foreword," in John Cline and Robert G. Weiner, eds, *From the Arthouse to the Grindhouse*, pp. ix–x.

Hansen, Miriam. 1991. "Pleasure, Ambivalence, Identification: Valentino and Female Spectatorship," in Christine Gledhill, ed., *Stardom: Industry of Desire*. London: Routledge, pp. 262–286.

Hills, Matt. 2002. *Fan Cultures*. London: Routledge.

Hollows, Joanne. 2003. "The Masculinity of Cult," in Mark Jancovich, Antonio Lázaro-Reboll, Julian Stringer and Andy Willis, pp. 35–53.

Hunter, Russ. 2010. "'Didn't You Used To Be Dario Argento?': The Cult Reception of Dario Argento, in William. Hope, ed., *Italian Film Directors in the New Millennium*. Cambridge: Cambridge Scholars Press, pp. 63–74.

Jancovich, Mark, Antonio Lázaro-Reboll, Julian Stringer and Andy Willis, eds. 2003. *Defining Cult Movies: The Cultural Politics of Oppositional Taste*. Manchester: Manchester University Press.

Jowett, Garth. 2001. "'Real Men Don't Sing and Dance': Growing Up Male with the Hollywood Musical – A Memoir," in Murray Pomerance, ed., *Ladies and Gentlemen, Boys and Girls: Gender in Film at the End of the Twentieth Century*. Albany: State University of New York Press.

Luckett, Moya. 2003. "Sexploitation as Feminine Territory: The Films of Doris Wishman," in Mark Jancovich, Antonio Lázaro-Reboll, Julian Stringer and Andy Willis, pp. 142–156.

Mathijs, Ernest and Jamie Sexton, eds. 2011. *Cult Cinema: An Introduction*. Chichester: Wiley-Blackwell.

Mathijs, Ernest and Xavier Mendik, eds. 2011. *100 Cult Films*. London: Palgrave Macmillan.

McKendry, Rebekah. 2010. "Fondling Your Eyeballs: Watching Doris Wishman," in John. Cline and Robert. G. Weiner, pp. 57–74.

Modleski, Tania. 2007. "Women's Cinema as Counterphobic Cinema: Doris Wishman as the Last Auteur," in Jeffrey Sconce, *Sleaze Artists*, pp. 47–70.

Mulvey, Laura. 1975. "Visual Pleasure and Narrative Cinema." *Screen* 16.3, pp. 6–18.

Read, Jacinda. 2003. "The Cult of Masculinity: From Fan-Boys to Academic Bad-Boys," in Mark Jancovich, Antonio Lázaro-Reboll, Julian Stringer and Andy Willis, pp. 54–70.

Sconce, Jeffrey. 1995. "'Trashing' the Academy: Taste, Excess, and an Emerging Politics of Cinematic Style," *Screen*, 36.4, pp. 371–393.

Sconce, Jeffrey. ed. 2007. *Sleaze Artists: Cinema at the Margins of Taste, Style, and Politics*. Durham, NC: Duke University Press.

Snelson, Tim. 2015. *Phantom Ladies: Hollywood, Horror and the Home Front*. New Brunswick, NJ: Rutgers University Press.

Studlar, Gaylin. 1991. "Midnight S/Excess: Cult Configurations of 'Femininity' and the Perverse," in J.P. Telotte, ed., *The Cult Film Experience.* Austin: University of Texas Press, pp. 138–155.

Taylor, Helen. (1989) *Scarlett's Women:* Gone With the Wind *and Its Female Fans.* New Bunswick, NJ: Rutgers University Press.

Telotte, J.P, ed. 1991. *The Cult Film Experience: Beyond All Reason.* Austin: University of Texas Press.

Thornton, Sarah. 1995. *Club Cultures: Music, Media, and Subcultural Capital.* Cambridge, UK: Polity Press.

Vassilieva, Julia and Constantine Verevis, eds. 2012. *After Taste: Value and the Moving Image.* New York: Routledge.

Vosper, A J. 2014. "Film, Fear and the Female." *Off Screen*, 18.6/7. Online: http://offscreen.com/view/film-fear-and-the-female. Accessed 15 June 2017.

Williams, Linda. 1984. "When the Woman Looks," in Mary Anne Doane, Patricia Mellencamp, and Linda Williams, eds, *Re-Vision: Essays in Feminist Film Criticism.* Los Angeles: University Publications of America, pp. 83–99.

Williams, Linda. 1991. "Film Bodies: Gender, Genre, and Excess," *Film Quarterly*, 44.4, pp. 2–12.

16

CULT CINEMA AND NOSTALGIA

Renee Middlemost

Cinema going is irrevocably tied to the past and, as such, our memories of past cinema attendance, and understanding of the discourses of cinema spectatorship are brought with us each time we step into a theatre. There have been few studies surveying the connection between cult film and nostalgia, despite the depth of research regarding nostalgia within film studies more generally (le Sueur, 1977; Jameson, 1998; Dika, 2003; Cook, 2005; Sprengler, 2009). This chapter will consider nostalgia and its relationship to cult film, in particular the viewing of Hollywood classic film on college campuses, seasonal cult films, and finally, a brief case study of the way that nostalgia and longing structure the practices of cult film audiences in Sydney, Australia. The case study illustrates how this group is influenced by nostalgia for the cinema going practices of the past, and subsequently, how they create traditions around seasonal cult films unique to the group. Therefore, this chapter will examine how cult films are viewed, valued and enjoyed by audiences and how their viewing practices articulate both a nostalgic yearning for the past, and a way to express one's (fan) identity into the future.

In order to establish the correlation between cult film fans, nostalgia and longing, the use of the term 'nostalgia' must be considered in this context. Urban (2007, 325) suggests that the modern usage of nostalgia is one where memories are reflected upon as pure and idealised, and as such, the resultant sense of longing is for an inaccurate recollection of the past. Although nostalgia is no longer thought of as a medical term, the connection to the idea of home and longing persist. As DeFalco states:

> Nostalgia (from [the Greek word] *nostos*- return home, and *algia*-longing) is a longing for home that no longer exists or has never existed. Nostalgia is a sentiment of loss and displacement ... the evolution of the term to its current meaning of a more general "longing for the conditions of a past age" ... that is, the nostalgic object's shift from place to time – make the object of desire irrecoverable, producing an inevitably frustrated longing.
>
> (2004, 27)

The nostalgic tendency of cult audiences is reflected upon by Mathijs and Mendik who suggest:

a core feature of many cult films is their ability to trigger a sense of nostalgia, a yearning for an idealised past. The nostalgia can be part of the film's story ... But most likely it is an emotional impression.

(2008, 3)

Thus, I would argue that nostalgia is felt more strongly by cult film fans and this nostalgia manifests in several distinct forms. These are:

1. nostalgia for films of the past
2. nostalgia as a theme within film texts, and an attraction to said;
3. repetition and repeat viewing; and
4. nostalgia for the cinema going experiences of the past as an event, which can also include a type of 'tech-nostalgia' for screening in outdated formats (16mm; VHS) and collections of these.

It is possible to regard the repeat viewing of Hollywood classic films and seasonal cults as a type of retreat from the modern world; a longing for a simpler time, for a non-existent past. This trend is revealed in the screening of Hollywood classic films as part of college life in the United States.

"Play it again, Sam"[1]: College film screenings

College film societies have played an enduring role in campus life as a means to relax and socialise with other students. Given the primarily youth demographic of college students, one would not necessarily consider campus film societies to be prone to bouts of nostalgia; yet there is emerging evidence (though few formal studies) regarding the role of nostalgic film screenings on campus, particularly classical Hollywood films.

One such campus with an enduring tradition of screening classic Hollywood films is Harvard University. The original founders of The Brattle Theatre (located in Harvard Square) utilised the cinema as a repertory theatre for repeat screenings of art house and obscure films – operator Marianne Lampke says their provocation was to: "... bring movies back. It introduced these old films to a whole new generation" (Mazur, 2013, 1). Given Harvard's reputation as America's oldest tertiary institution, and one steeped in tradition, it is perhaps unsurprising that it also has a long history of screening classical Hollywood cinema, in particular *Casablanca* (1942), identified by Eco (1987) as the cult film par excellence. Harvard screenings of *Casablanca* began upon its release in 1942. In the mid-1950s, the theatre initiated the yearly Humphrey Bogart film festival in the week before Harvard exams, with *Casablanca* the headline feature, offering students an opportunity to take a break from their studies. Creative director of the Brattle, Ned Hinkle recalls the high level of audience participation during screenings, most notably when the sound system malfunctioned, and the audience call back continued unfettered from the original. He also states that audience members would attend in costume, and even occasionally propose marriage, calling it the "... original *Rocky Horror Picture Show*" (Mazur, 2013, 1). This type of audience interaction is a key feature and attraction of both enduring cult films such as *The Rocky Horror Picture Show* (1975) and emerging cult films such as *The Room* (2003).

From 2001 onwards, screenings of *Casablanca* at Harvard were transferred to Valentine's Day, a custom that remains today. The Valentine's Day screening of *Casablanca* is imbued with the seasonal, and the cult; by being regularly screened at the same time of year, the screening, in addition to the filmic content, becomes a tradition infused with feelings of nostalgia. Perhaps the most significant factor in screening Hollywood classics such as *Casablanca* on campus is the separation between the time of release and the age of the audience, which raises the question – how, or can one be nostalgic for a time before they were born? Emma Pett (2013) addresses this issue in her research on the campus film screening of *Back to the Future* (1985) at Aberystwyth University in Wales. Her study found that despite being too young to have seen *Back to the Future* when it was initially released in cinemas, nostalgia in various forms was cited as a key reason for the students' enjoyment of the film. Noting the "cultic sensibility" of other 1980s films that were set in the 1950s (*Peggy Sue Got Married* (1986); *Dirty Dancing* (1987) to which Mathijs and Sexton (2011, 186) refer, Pett stresses the curious nature of a stated 'nostalgia' for a film released before one's birth. Citing Grainge (2000), she interrogates how her audience define nostalgia, suggesting that: "… the development of nostalgia as a cultural style reflects a new ability to re-view and renegotiate media texts that is specific to the late twentieth century" (Pett, 2013, 188). Speaking to this ability to re-view and renegotiate media texts in particular cultural conditions, Pett states: "… the nostalgic value associated with *Back to the Future* appears to be linked to childhood memories of watching the film on television or video" (2013, 189) a substantial finding which correlates not only with Klinger's (2006, 2010) work on repeat viewing and nostalgia but also to rituals inherent in viewing seasonal cult films. Whilst *Back to the Future* is not part of Hollywood classical cinema as such, Pett's study of university audiences and how they engage with nostalgia through film texts provides a clear impetus for further studies of this kind.

"It's the most wonderful time of the year"[2]: Seasonal cults

The second trend that illustrates the nostalgic appeal of cult film relates to the repeat viewing of certain films at specific times of year, or 'seasonal cults'. Writing this chapter immediately prior to Christmas allows one to indulge some reflexivity upon the practice of (re-watching) Christmas films. This re-watching allows one not only to nostalgically relive childhood and the associated family traditions but offers a means to counter the cynicism analogous with the commercialisation of the holidays. Mathijs (2010, 2) describes the seasonal cult as: "… the fervent cultism around specific, recurrent periods and dates in the year linked to cultist receptions – and to specialist television programming". The dates most likely to arouse this seasonal nostalgia for classics are Halloween, Christmas (or as discussed in the previous section examining *Casablanca*) Valentine's Day.

Mathijs links the seasonal viewing of specific films such as *It's a Wonderful Life* (1946) and *Meet me in St. Louis* (1944) to the tendency for these to be broadcast repetitively each year. Personal observation shows that yuletide screenings on free to air television in Australia extend, and tend towards more modern Christmas films, in contrast to the classical Hollywood films cited by Mathijs. *National Lampoon's Christmas Vacation* (1989) is screened yearly (either on Christmas Eve, or Christmas Day), and more recent additions *Elf* (2003) and *Love, Actually* (2003) have also been screened repeatedly prior to Christmas (see Dale, 2014). On pay television seasonal viewing extends to include not only Christmas films, but marathons of the entire series of *The Simpsons*.

Petersen (2013) similarly focuses on the implication of repeat screenings/viewings of modern Christmas films in an incisive article discussing her love/hate relationship with Christmas films (specifically, *The Family Stone* (2005).[3] In this article, she discusses Christmas as an ideological construct, and therefore the way Christmas films function to represent: "… 'Christmas' as a nourishing essential event" (Petersen, 2013, 1). In her eyes, once the film migrates to television, and becomes a repeat viewing event, the film itself becomes part of the Christmas ritual; because while our own unresolved Christmas problems remain, we can: "…retreat to watch others grapple with – and crucially, successfully address – those same problems. We feel better not because our Christmas woes have been solved, but the movie suggests they are, ultimately, solvable" (Peterson, 2013, 1).

Whilst Petersen acknowledges the many flaws of *The Family Stone*, and indeed Christmas films in general, she concludes that although these films are directed at a wide audience, their purpose lies in: "… how we watch them, and with whom – and how they, and their reductive yet charismatic messages incorporate themselves into an understanding of our own Christmases" (2013, 4). In light of Petersen's discussion, it is possible to suggest that the nostalgia felt when viewing seasonal cult films functions in two crucial ways. Nostalgia is present both within the text – the longing for times past and faraway places (particularly home, e.g. *The Wizard of Oz*, *Meet Me in St. Louis*, *A Christmas Carol*) – and felt by the audience when re-watching the film at the same time each year. For Mathijs the link between nostalgia, seasonal cults and Christmas in particular is clear:

> The time of year is right … the festive and repetitive nature of the holiday season with its recurrent parties, gifts, banquets, dinners and functions; its highly ritualised markings of the passage of time; the interruption of academic and school years for a pause in the rational pursuit of progress and education; the change in the rhythm of economic activity…; the overall presentation of the period as a time for family, friends, and small communities to renew their bonds; the fore-fronting of traditional and shared values; and the historical religious inspirations of the celebrations … all of these imbue this period with an atmosphere in which cultism is likely to flourish.
>
> (2010, 3)

In continuing his argument Mathijs suggests that films that provoke a yuletide cult 'transcend cynicism'[4] (2010, 5) and it is perhaps this observation that is central to appreciating their nostalgic appeal. Jancovich (2011, 92) also reflects on the tendency of cinema audiences to value the ritual of cinema attendance with family and friends (particularly at certain times of the year) over the film itself, and discusses how Christmas films are activated as a tool of: "…getting into the spirit of the holidays". Of greater significance is Jancovich's observation that:

> At Christmas, people will often see films that one would not see at any other time of the year, in which the film and the holiday become associated with the indulging of a specific emotion that would be seen as inappropriate at any other time of the year. It is even the case that certain films have become Christmas rituals themselves.
>
> (2011, 92)

Both Peterson and Jancovich reinforce Mathijs' argument regarding the function of seasonal cult films. By suspending one's typical tastes and critiques, cynicism can be transcended in favour of ritual and social bonding. In this way, the ritual bonding over these films functions as an extension of the season itself.

In a modern, insecure world Bauman (2001) believes our nostalgic longing for simple, often home based, pleasures is a response to jarring world events such as 9/11; therefore the suspension of cynicism, and feeling of comfort that manifests from re-watching (seasonal) cult films, is central to their appeal. For Bauman, globalisation has created a greater desire for community, and he refers to community as a kind of 'paradise lost' – an idea or a kind of world that is lost, and for which people yearn (2001, 3). For the organisers of cult film events in Sydney, Australia, nostalgia, and the desire to create a community of likeminded fans required the invention of their own screenings. These nostalgic tendencies, and the inherent contradiction of longing for an imagined past, are illustrated in the following case study of Australian cult film audiences.

"A good many dramatic scenes begin with screaming"[5]: Australian cult film audiences

Repeat viewings and seasonal cult screenings are just some of the rituals embedded in the experience/fannish behaviour of the cult film group I attend in Sydney, Australia. This part of the chapter brings together the recurring themes emerging from my research with Australian organisers and audiences of cult film– that is, the idea of cult groups as a form of community, and the feeling of nostalgia or longing for films, objects and activities of the past. In exploring these themes, it is apparent that cult film screenings occupy a unique position between the private and the public; and between the past – and the future. Whilst these cult groups display a distinct 'techno-nostalgia' and preference for the use of 'old' technology, access to the Internet provides benefits in the form of access to lost films, and keeping their group informed of forthcoming events.

For the interview candidates in my study, the desire to collect films from the past and gain a wider audience for these texts is tied to feelings of longing and nostalgia. Jaimie and Aspasia Leonarder (aka Jay Katz and Miss Death) are the organisers of Cult Cinema Tuesday night, which operated for a decade (2001–2011) at the Annandale Hotel, Sydney. They have also facilitated informal cult film screenings several times a week (at their home cinema, the Mu-meson Archives) for two decades, as well as guest screenings at numerous film festivals in Australia; in addition to hosting The Sounds of Seduction, Viva La Vinyl, and The Experiment clubs (showcasing classic vinyl albums, and local entertainers) and Miss Death's Stitch and Bitch craft group.

Organising cult film screenings and other 'outdated' social activities has a link not only to nostalgic longings for the film-going of the past but may also be interpreted as a longing for a type of home or belonging. Seiden suggests that the longing for home is a longing: "… to repair two kinds of separations – one in place, one in time. A home lost to time is no longer there and cannot be" (2009, 195). It would seem, then, that the longing for home is also a longing for a place with is 'othered' – for an idealised, or 'imaginary place' that exists only in the past, at a specific moment in time. For Seiden, no word other than 'home' is capable of catching the:

> associations, the mixture of memory and longing, the sense of security and autonomy and accessibility, the aroma of inclusiveness, of freedom from wariness. … Home is a concept, not a place; it is a state of mind where self definition starts.
>
> (2009, 191)

By presenting screenings in their home, I would suggest that Australian organisers Jay Katz and Miss Death are providing not only 'another space' or heterotopia as Foucault (1986) suggests, but another kind of home for the audience. Here, their audience is able to enjoy the comforts of home, with the benefits of socialising with a like-minded group; this, in turn leads to a feeling of community.

Pickering and Keightley (2006) propose an articulation of nostalgia that is applicable to its manifestation within cult film groups. Whilst they suggest that a condition of modernity is a feeling of loss, it is their contention that nostalgia should be:

reconfigure [d] ... in terms of a distinction between the desire to return to an earlier state or idealised past, and the desire not to return but to recognise aspects of the past as a basis for renewal and satisfaction in the future.

(Pickering and Keightley, 2006, 921)

The feelings of nostalgia amongst cult groups can be interpreted in this fashion, as this type of nostalgia draws upon the beneficial aspects of the past and configures them to meet the needs of the self or the group in the present. For cult groups: "Nostalgia ... recognises the value of continuities in counterpart to what is fleeting, transitory and contingent" (Pickering and Keightley, 2006, 923). The established pattern of activities that occur at the same time, and venue each week can be said to provide a touchstone, or a type of home for members of the Annandale cult film group, who may not experience this sense of belonging outside of the fan cluster.

The Annandale organisers emphasised their nostalgic feelings towards the film viewing of their past, and long to incorporate these viewing practices into the current audience paradigm. In this group, the organisers are emphatic when they explain their primary motivation for organising the screenings is their longing for cinematic practices of the past, and desire to create a sense of community around their screenings. By organising screening events, they intend to recreate the old-fashioned notion of a 'complete night of entertainment' that was popularised during the peak of the drive-in cinema. The organisation of screening events such as the double feature illustrates a desire to recreate childhood memories of Sunday afternoon matinees through screenings of their own. Jay Katz speaks of his frustration as a teenager that the matinee programs he had so relished as a child had disappeared, and his sense of loss motivated the creation of his own events that offer a full program of entertainment to the public. Being unable to purchase their own cinema, he and Miss Death decided the best way to keep this tradition alive was to conduct screenings in their own home. By fashioning screenings into an inclusive event, audiences are engaged and motivated to attend regularly, for as the organisers state 'community is at the centre of everything we do' (Katz and Death, personal communication 2014). Miss Death explains that, as organisers, eventually they get to know the people who attend the events and hopefully [the audience members] begin to feel like they belong, suggesting Percival's findings that screenings like these are: "...almost like creating a village in the middle of a very large city" (Percival 2007, 26). To open up one's private space in this way is no small task. As these statements indicate, a feeling of nostalgia, and regret that the film going practices of the past have been lost, are a powerful motivator for people to begin their own screenings.

For these cult organisers there is also a relationship between lost films and lost technology – there is a feeling that both are worthy of a 'second life' (Telotte, 1991, 7) and need simply to be exposed to an audience. This tendency suggests nostalgia not only for lost films, but technology of the past – a 'techno-nostalgia'. Cult screenings represent an opportunity not only to screen and celebrate the films of the past, but also the technology (16mm film and projectors, Scopitone jukebox video clips, and videos) and film experiences of the past – such as double or triple features, late night screenings, and a 'full night of entertainment' with shorts, previews of future films to be screened and cartoons shown before the feature. The nostalgia for eras gone by is also evident in the collections, and style of both cult film organisers and fans. At the Mumeson Archives, evidence of this collecting is visible throughout the screening area, where Jay Katz and Miss Death display and store thousands of reels of 16mm film, film projectors, books and other items such as collectable cards and figurines of pinup icons such as Bettie Page, Lili St. Cyr, Gypsy Lee Rose and Tempest Storm. A preoccupation with the past is also visible in the way audience members dress, with a particular emphasis on vintage fashion from the 1950s-60s, and traditional tattoos.Whilst these clothing styles and activities are popular with many people, it is noteworthy as further visual manifestation of nostalgia in a group that attempts to recreate the film viewing practices of the past.

In terms of ritual and seasonal screenings of cult films, the expanse of occasions for repeat screenings favoured by the Annandale group are distinct from those identified within Mathijs' research.This group typically includes a regular 'seasonal' film screening around Australia Day (January), Valentine's Day, Easter, Mother's Day (May), Halloween and Christmas; however, the film being screened tends to differ each year. Rather than re-watching classic Hollywood films, or established cult films, this group has matched cult films to various holidays (often featuring crowd favourite actors such as Bette Davis and Donald Pleasance, or themes, such as killer animals). Recent examples have included: Australia Day – *The Man from Hong Kong* (1975); Easter – *Night of the Lepus* (1972); Mother's Day – *The Anniversary* (1968); Halloween – *Halloween* (1978); Christmas – *Wake in Fright* (1971); *Jack Frost* (1997); *Black Christmas* (1974). These seasonal events are often double features, and greater attendance can be expected as they typically coincide with a public holiday.

In scheduling these repeat screenings at significant times of year the Annandale group creates its own traditions (for example, Christmas screenings usually feature festive snacks and gift giving). Repeat viewings of favourites also 'builds in' nostalgia amongst members who remember past seasonal screenings, as well as increasing anticipation for future screenings. Films that have gained large audiences in the past or are a 'favourite' (of either the organisers, or regular attendees) are also featured yearly as another form of seasonal cult. Favourites are scheduled as a monthly series, playing every Tuesday; e.g. Larry Cohen month, featuring the *It's Alive* (1974–1987) series and *Q: The Winged Serpent* (1982); these replays of favourites represent another form of 'seasonal' cult exclusive to the group.

The Annandale group also enacts nostalgia for other forms of social engagement despite a preoccupation with the screening practices of the past. This tendency differs from existing accounts of cult film and nostalgia, which are primarily concerned with repeat viewing, or nostalgia amongst audiences for the film text. Screenings in Sydney have also expanded to include other activities harkening back to a nostalgic, idealised past of community engagement such as a monthly craft afternoon and retro discos (often these are also seasonal cult events focused on significant dates such as Halloween, Christmas Eve or New Year's Eve).The Annandale cult film group intends to elevate activities (such as go-go dancing and knitting) and technology (16mm film, vinyl records) that have been abandoned by society at large.The organisation of a monthly craft group represents the desire of organisers for time set aside to catch up with friends, and to create something lasting, as a form of consumer resistance. As several sources suggest (Bauman, 2001; Delanty, 2003), community itself is a nostalgic concept, based on romantic ideas of a lost utopia or a time where society was more cohesive and connected. It seems that cult film groups, as well as activities such as the knitting group and discos established by cult film organisers, are part of a broader trend towards valuing the past.

The assertion made by Australian organisers – that cult film fandom is a *shared* experience – has historically been problematised in terms of gatekeeping and collecting (Sconce, 1995) or unequal access for female fans (Hollows, 2003; Read, 2003). This case study challenges long held stereotypes about fandom, in favour of a more nuanced analysis of individual groups. Whilst acknowledging these tendencies, Katz and Death posit that cult fandom need not be a closed group that forms in response to rejection or 'outsider' status during one's youth; instead, they suggest that nostalgia for the cult films, and screening styles of the past, can open a dialogue amongst audience members. Participation with the action on screen (in the style of *The Rocky Horror Picture Show*) can lead to engagement between members of the audience; thus, connections are forged with strangers through the medium of cult film. From this participation it can be suggested that a type of 'interpretive community' is formed and as Staiger (2000) has described, a process of exchange begins – trading of films and other artefacts, and socialisation outside of the screenings. The type of hub that is created by coordinating regular and seasonal screenings evokes nostalgia for a time when audiences were imagined to be more connected with one another. For the Annandale group, cult screenings are a way of reviving the style of sociality and viewing experience of the drive-ins and picture palaces of the past.

The influence of nostalgia on cult film audiences is clearly illustrated when examining the three examples covered in this chapter: on campus screenings of classical Hollywood film, seasonal cult viewing, and cult screenings in Sydney, Australia. The role of the audience in creating and maintaining film cults is highlighted through the screening and celebration of both classic and discarded films, and the nostalgic revival of practices which have also been set aside. Practices such as re-watching classic films in the cinema or watching seasonal cult films with loved ones are essential to the formation of a living community; that is – engagement with one another. This engagement, and the creation of a community in miniature, reveals that the word 'cult' cannot only exist as a text or genre; it encompasses so much more.

The rearticulation of cult film audiences as a type of community motivated by nostalgia, represents a way forward for research into cult film. My experience of cult film groups in Australia is that they are primarily concerned with the building of community, coupled with a nostalgia for the sociality and film viewing practices of the past. In these examples it is clear that the film itself is secondary to the 'experience' of viewing with loved ones or fellow fans – that the film is merely an entry point to something more. Ultimately, it is not just about the films, but a desire to connect, to create a group, where before there was only solitary fandom.

Notes

1 Further extending Eco's (1987, 198) point regarding the "glorious ricketiness" of *Casablanca* is the fact that one of its most oft quoted lines "Play it again, Sam" is actually a misquote. The line in the film is actually "Play it, Sam" (see Menand, 2007).
2 "It's the most wonderful time of the year" (1963).
3 Petersen's (2013) analysis of *The Family Stone* is based on an earlier article featured on *The Hairpin*, where Finger (2011) analyses his own love/hate relationship with 'his' Christmas movie, *Love, Actually*. Finger's taxonomy breaks down each of *Love, Actually*'s subplots, dividing what he hates (almost entirely narrative and ideological problems) and what he loves (almost entirely affective traits).
4 Whilst the films discussed by Mathijs may transcend cynicism, other Christmas cult favourites deliberately provoke a cynical response. These include horror films such as *Christmas Evil* (1980) and *Silent Night, Deadly Night* (1984) and cynical comedies such as *Bad Santa* (2003) and (arguably, a cult film set at Christmas) *In Bruges* (2008).
5 *Barbarella* (1968, Roger Vadim).

References

Bauman, Zygmunt. 2001. *Community: Seeking Safety in an Insecure World*. Cambridge, UK: Polity Press.
Cook, Pam. 2005. *Screening the Past: Memory and Nostalgia in Cinema*. London: Routledge.
Dale, David. 2014. "The Ratings Race: *Love, Actually* Is Australia's Favourite Movie, in December at Least". *The Sydney Morning Herald*. December 30. www.smh.com.au/entertainment/tv-and-radio/blogs/the-tribal-mind/the-ratings-race-love-actually-is-australias-favourite-movie-in-december-at-least-20141207-3m0u9.html (accessed 2/12/15).
DeFalco, Amelia. 2004. "A Double-Edged Longing: Nostalgia, Melodrama and Todd Haynes' Far From Heaven," *Iowa Journal of Cultural Studies*, 5 (Fall): 26–39.
Delanty, Gerard. 2003. *Community*. London: Routledge.

Dika,Vera. 2003. *Recycled Culture in Contemporary Art and Film*. Cambridge: Cambridge University Press.

Eco, Umberto. 1987. *Travels in Hyperreality*. London: Picador.

Finger, Bobby. 2011. "Hate, Actually," *The Hairpin*, 9 December. http://thehairpin.com/2011/12/hate-actually/ (accessed 2/12/15).

Foucault, Michel. 1986. "Des Espaces Autres (Of Other Spaces)," translated by J. Miskowiec, *Diacritics*, 16.1 (Spring): 22–27.

Grainge, Paul. 2000. "Nostalgia and Style in Retro America: Moods, Modes and Media Recycling," *Journal of American Popular Culture*, 23.1: 27–34.

Hollows, Joanne. 2003. "The Masculinity of Cult". In Mark Jancovich, Antonio Lázaro-Reboll, Julian Stringer and Andy Willis, eds, *Defining Cult Movies: The Cultural Politics of Oppositional Taste*. Manchester: Manchester University Press: 35–53.

Jameson, Fredric. 1998. *Postmodernism and Consumer Society in the Cultural Turn: Selected Writings on the Postmodern*. London: Verso.

Jancovich, Mark. 2011. "Time, Scheduling and Cinema Going," *Media International Australia*, 139 (May): 88–95.

Klinger, Barbara. 2006. *Beyond the Multiplex: Cinema, New Technologies and the Home*. Berkeley: University of California Press.

Klinger, Barbara. 2010. "Becoming Cult: *The Big Lebowski*, Replay Culture and Male Fans," *Screen*, 51.1 (Spring): 1–20.

le Sueur, M. 1977. "Theory Number 5: Anatomy of Nostalgia Films: Heritage and Methods," *Journal of Popular Film*, 6.2: 187–194.

Mathijs, Ernest. 2010. "Television and the Yuletide Cult," *Flow TV*, 11.5. http://flowtv.org/2010/01/television-and-the-yuletide-cult-ernest-mathijs-the-university-of-british-columbia/ (accessed 13/7/15).

Mathijs, Ernest and Xavier Mendik. 2008. "Editorial Introduction: What Is Cult Film?". In Ernest Mathijs, and Xavier Mendik, eds, *The Cult Film Reader*. Maidenhead: Open University Press: 1–24.

Mathijs, Ernest and Jamie Sexton. 2011. *Cult Cinema: An Introduction*. Chichester: Wiley-Blackwell.

Mazur, Rebecca J. 2013. "Past Tense: The Brattle Theatre". *The Harvard Crimson*. February 14. www.thecrimson.com/article/2013/2/14/brattle-theater-past-tense/ (accessed 10/8/15).

Menand, Louis. 2007. "Notable Quotables: Is There Anything That Is Not a Quotation?". The New Yorker. February 19. www.newyorker.com/magazine/2007/02/19/notable-quotables# (accessed 2/12/15).

Percival, Bob. 2007. "Archivists on the Edge," *Real Time Arts,* 79 (June–July): 27. www.realtimearts.net/article/issue79/8597 (accessed 2/7/09).

Petersen, Anne Helen. 2013. "The Christmas Movie: A Hate/Need Relationship," *LA Review of Books – Blog*, December 10. http://blog.lareviewofbooks.org/deartv/christmas-movie-hateneed-relationship/ (accessed 1/11/15).

Pett, Emma. 2013. "'Hey! Hey! I've Seen This One, I've Seen This One. It's a Classic': Nostalgia, Repeat Viewing and Cult Performance in *Back to the Future*," *Participations*, 10.1: 177–197.

Pickering, Michael, and Emily Keightley. 2006. "The Modalities of Nostalgia," *Current Sociology*, 54: 919–940.

Read, Jacinda. 2003. "The Cult of Masculinity: From Fan-Boys to Academic Bad-Boys". In Mark Jancovich, Antonio Lázaro-Reboll, Julian Stringer and Andy Willis, eds, *Defining Cult Movies: The Cultural Politics of Oppositional Taste*. Manchester: Manchester University Press: 54–70.

Sconce, Jeffrey. 1995. "'Trashing' the Academy: Taste, Excess, and an Emerging Politics of Cinematic Style," *Screen*, 36.4 (Winter): 371–393.

Seiden, Henry M. 2009. "On the Longing for Home," *Psychoanalytic Psychology*. 26.2 (April): 191–205.

Sprengler, Christine. 2009. *Screening Nostalgia: Populuxe Props and Technicolour Aesthetics in Contemporary American Film*. New York: Berghahn Books.

Staiger, Janet. 2000. *Perverse Spectators: The Practices of Film Reception*. New York: New York University Press.

Telotte, J.P. 1991. "Beyond All Reason: The Nature of the Cult". In Telotte, J.P., *The Cult Film Experience: Beyond all Reason*. Austin: University of Texas Press: 5–17.

Urban, Ken. 2007. "Ghosts from an Imperfect Place: Philip Ridley's Nostalgia". *Modern Drama*, 50.3 (Fall): 325–345.

17

OC/CULT FILM AND VIDEO

Anna Powell

Introduction

Saturday, November 14, 2007, Filmmuseum, Brussels: Kenneth Anger introduces a screening of *Lucifer Rising* unfamiliar to cult fans. Bobby Beausoleil's portentous chords are replaced by the earlier Jimmy Page soundtrack. This new *Lucifer* is an affective revelation, which *sounds* and *feels* very different. Yet the filmmaker's intriguing background "revelations" do not actually reveal the oc/cult film experience any further. To "occult" means to "shut off from view or exposure", so this encounter will, of its very nature, stretch analytical thought beyond its limits (Merriam-Webster 2016). An elusive element inevitably escapes the language of critical writing deployed in its pursuit.

The Occult has a special status in cult film history stretching from German Expressionism's flaming circles and grimoires to the camera's ritual participation in contemporary chaos magick. Oc/cult and esoteric films use special techniques to engineer a specific type of "buzz" for aficianados. Ernest Mathijs and Jamie Sexton's substantial study *Cult Cinema* contends that "overall, critics and scholars are vague about this component" (2011: 132). They reference the orgiastic cult of Dionysus as their own analogy for "the experience of time ungoverned and the visceral experience of sexual energy" (Mathijs and Sexton 2011: 34). They note that the special "religious cultism" surrounding certain films is apparently "not just the result of midnight screenings and devoted fandom but of their religiosity itself" (Mathijs and Sexton 2011: 137). To develop this perspective, they cite auteur theorist Andrew Sarris's "confession" of obsessive film fandom, which includes initiation into a "secret society" and "subcultural outsidership" (Mathijs and Sexton 2011: 138). Sarris engages with "the mystical/religious experience of viewing" and his direct experience of these "ritualistic encounters" produced a "powerful connection with being alive and becoming a cultist" (Mathijs and Sexton 2011: 138). Mathijs and Sexton conclude that films directly about religious cultism act to "not only channel that connection, but to enable it" (2011: 138).

My subjective history of oc/cult film fandom is extended by Gilles Deleuze's film-philosophical technique of 'schizoanalysis'. Whilst offering a conceptually rigorous typology of cinema, schizoanalysis questions whether a cohesive "I" actually exists during the viewing experience, or whether "I" become a "centre of indetermination", a cluster of fluctuating affects, percepts and concepts (Deleuze 1986: 59). Is film a 'spiritual automaton' operant on a different plane to the subjective ego; in this case, a plane of the 'spirit'? Films are affective events experienced by "my" shifting singularity in assemblage with them. For philosopher Henri Bergson, affect is a qualitative feeling, an "intensive vibration" on a 'sensible nerve' (Bergson 1991: 55–56) or, as Deleuze puts it, a "motor effort on an immobilised receptive plate" (Deleuze 1986: 66). In this case, the plane of the spirit might generate numinous or uncanny affects, none of which remain "pure" but overlap with factors from other areas.

The "Cultographies" website provides a thorough and helpful typology of cult film components (Cultographies 2016). My own work fits their category of "anatomy", the formal, thematic and generic characteristics of the film itself. Some oc/cult films evince "badness", that is, "strange topics and allegorical themes that rub against cultural sensitivities [and] transgress common notions of good and bad taste" and I also consider time-travel though this may not be literal (Cultograpies 2006). I will also find "intertextual references, gore, loose ends in storylines, or the creation of a sense of nostalgia" (www.cultographies.com). Within a broad division of mainstream/exploitation and experimental/underground films, I feature the occult subgenres of ritual magic, alchemy, voudoun, and chaos magic.

Given the longevity of the oc/cult film mode and the studies already published (on "witchcraft" for example), I focus more on "magic", this special, numinous, element of alterity. Magic is definable as "a special and exciting quality that makes something seem different from ordinary things", the numinous as "having a mysterious, holy, or spiritual quality" which might be "incapable of being expressed in words" (*Merriam-Webster* 2016). The occult's *modus operandi* involves "the action or influence of supernatural or supernormal powers or some secret knowledge of them" (*Merriam-Webster* 2016). The esoteric is "designed for or understood by the specially initiated" and "of special, rare, or unusual interest" (*Merriam-Webster* 2016).

As Tanya Krzywinska reminds us (after Kenneth Anger) "cinema is an extension of magical thinking: it has the ability temporarily to possess us through our suspension of disbelief and identification with new incarnations of old gods" (Krzywinska 2000: viii). Her insightful study of occult cinema focuses on mainstream films, some with cult status. Their ambivalent treatment of esoteric themes is typically Gothic. She highlights their "intense engagement with the sublime terrors and ecstasies of corrupting and liberating forces" (Krzywinska 2000: viii). These films present the occult as "primitive and barbaric, yet it is often couched within complex and highly refined esoteric systems of knowledge" (Krzywinska 2000: viii). By the ambivalence of occult cinema, "countercultural desires are unleashed while the conventional forces of a capitalist economy are presented" (Krzywinska 2000: ix). Central devices are "vicarious spiritual and physical danger, the acquisition of power, and the experience of powerlessness" (Krzywinska 2000: ix). These dualistic concerns are prominent even when the mainstream/experimental divide was less developed, in the earliest examples of occult film.

Early oc/cult prototypes: *The Golem, Faust, The Magician*

My initial concern is ritual magic in film. Among the sources of its representations are medieval magic, often via the Nineteenth century occult revival which included spiritualism, theosophy and the Masons. Other fields of source material are anthropology and psychology. Three early occult films are linked by the intriguing Paul Wegener, who in 1914 directed and performed the lead role in *The Golem* (sadly incomplete) and its better-known successor *The Golem and How He Came into the World* (co-directed with Carl Boese in 1920). Wegener also played the evil magician Oliver Haddo in Rex Ingram's 1926 film of Somerset Maugham's novel *The Magician* (1908), the poster for which promises "a thousand thrills and mysteries never seen on the screen". Haddo was intended as a satirical sketch of the occultist Aleister Crowley, the "pagan *agent provocateur*" and inspirer of both cult followers and cult films (Krzywinska 2000: x). The occult highlight of *The Magician* features orgiastic visions of a Pan-like demon conjured up by Haddo to impress his intended victim Margaret (Alice Terry).

Wegener's second Golem film offers cinematic templates of medieval-style magic. In the opening sequence, senior Rabbi Löw (Albert Steinruch) interprets astrological configurations through a telescope. In his chambers, with their flame-like sets marked with Kabbalistic symbols, he animates a clay Golem both to protect the ghetto against attack and to guard his wayward daughter Miriam (Lyda Salmonova). Isenberg notes the sinister presentation of Rabbi Löw's agenda, his "deep immersion in the art of necromancy – as he consults his quasi-scientific, astrological and religious treatises, examines obscure numerological charts; and works up various magical formulae and incantations" (Isenberg 2009: 37).

Using the "great spell" from the grimoire *Necromancie: The Key of Solomon*, Löw invokes Ashtaroth (a goetic demon and Duke of Hell). His props include a symbol-laden hat, a wand and a large hexagram. Surrounded by smoky darkness front-lit by a flickering fire, Löw casts a circle, dragging his assistant (Ernst Deutsch) into it for safety. As he spins and brandishes the hexagram, glittering lights appear. The demon Ashtaroth manifests as a floating, disembodied mask with empty eyes and breathing smoke. Löw conjures him "on behalf of the Law of the Spirits" to name the "terrible life-giving word" which appears on a scroll as "Aemaeth" (truth and life) and lightening enters the room. Once the smoke has cleared, Löw writes this word, "snatched from the dark powers that be" on a parchment contained in a hexagram case worn by the Golem to animate and control his power.

The uncanny otherness of Wegener's Ashtaroth contrasts with the fleshy literalism of Mephistopheles in *Faust* (F.W. Murnau, 1926). The demon's invocation by Dr Faustus the alchemist can, however, be compared to Löw's conjuration. Both magicians are venerable, if flawed, characters driven by altruistic motives to save their communities. His elixir fails to reanimate the dead, so Faustus burns all his books including the Scriptures. When a burning grimoire opens at the conjuration of a demon, Faust rescues the book to help his plague-stricken fellows. At a crossroads by moonlight, Faust casts a fiery circle, the flames encasing him in hoops of light as the wind brings a ghostly chariot. Flames rise to envelop the screen as he summons Mephistopheles. The demon appears as a malignant elderly man with glowing eyes, making servile obeisances, before tricking Faustus into signing his soul away by a one-day trial. The pact to renounce God appears in fiery letters on a parchment, which Faustus signs with his blood, being later repelled by a crucifix when healing the sick. Mirror magic reveals visions of the worldly young Faustus and a skull. As Mephistopheles expands and becomes a dandified young demon, a spout of a mysterious, glittering substance rises out of Faust's body to rejuvenate him. At the end of the film, Faustus, now an ineffectual old man, shares the punishment of his mistress Gretchen, death by fire for immorality. Both rise up to meet the angel of the film's opening. The devil is vanquished and the final shot is a flaming heart inscribed "*leibe*". As well as being of considerable political and aesthetic significance, these early films, which straddle the art-house/cult divide, offer typical models of the occult for later films.

Evil magicians and sinister covens: Mainstream oc/cult films

Most films with occult themes and a cult following are commercially led, designed for a mass audience and with more formulaic plots and characterisation. Low budget films might have high production values (like Roger Corman's Poe Cycle). Many revisit the same goetic and alchemical sources as early prototypes, via their modern popularisation by occultists like Crowley and Gurdjieff. Like *The Magician* many are set in contemporary society, combining traditional rituals with hypnotism and other contemporary psychological techniques. Emerging from the popular Gothic melodramas of the 1940s, two low budget, artistically crafted films, *Seventh Victim* (Robson, 1943) and *Night of the Demon* (Tourneur, 1957) had depicted contemporary "secret cults or magical orders" comprising urban sophisticates under the sway of a charismatic leader and posing a "conspiratorial threat to the social order" (Krzywinska 2000: 75).

The late 1960s and early 1970s saw a widespread international flowering of occult and neo-pagan films, both mainstream and experimental, which gained cult followings. Mathijs and Sexton note the esoteric appeal of "satanic film cultism" in late 1960s Hollywood. *Rosemary's Baby* (Polanski, 1968) emerged from "a sub-genre of production-line horror movies and an attempt to exploit what seemed like a niche sensibility with mileage" that increased after the Manson murders (2011: 139). One low-budget/high magical film, which mixes camp, psyche-delia and esoteric cult appeal is *Simon, King of the Witches* (1971, Bruce Kessler). A box-office failure despite sensational publicity, it is now a cult "classic" because of its combination of insider knowledge and parody of it. It charts the picaresque rise of disenfranchised ritual magician, Simon Sinestrari (Andrew Prine) and Turk (George Paulsin) his gay hooker assistant, into the nouveau-riche, demolishing a rival coven priestess (Ultra Violet) on the way. Comic highlights include unsuccessful sex magic and the conjuration of a baleful fireball which knocks a plant pot onto a victim's head.

The oc/cult mainstream films emerging from British studios specialised in rural and period paganism/Wicca (*Blood on Satan's Claw*, *The Wicker Man*). Several oc/cult films have contemporary settings, such as *The Witches* (1966, Cyril Frankel) in which the cult do their ritual cavorting to jazz. Aleister Crowley, a prototype evil occultist, was adapted in several British films. As the self-styled Great Beast, Crowley's magical Will-to Power and predatory sexuality, his "demonic" reputation and 'satanic cultural capital' are ideal attributes for a Gothic villain (Krzywinska 2000: 91). Crowley is the basis of "left-hand-path" occultists in *The Devil Rides out* (Terence Fisher, 1968) and *To the Devil a Daughter* (Peter Sykes, 1976) both adapted from novels by Dennis Wheatley who had met Crowley. Mocata (Charles Gray) is the charismatic leader of a sinister secret cult in *The Devil Rides Out*. One specifically Crowleyan element is the dramatic invocation of Baphomet, culminating in the "perverse and satanic" materialisation of a "Pan-like entity" on the altar, again recalling the Pan figure of *The Magician* (Krzywinska 2000: 90).

Mocata's adversary, The Duc de Richleau (Christopher Lee) is a right-hand path occultist who draws on Golden Dawn rituals in his postures, protective circle and the 'Susama ritual', which alters time and space and shifts the psychic battle to the astral plane. Ashtaroth, the sin-ister, smoking mask of *The Golem* is mentioned in both films: the black nuns of *To the Devil a Daughter* are the demon's devotees. Reference to the "Antichrist" indicates a stereotypical Satanism as inverted Christianity. The film was released in the year of the Manson murders, which further enhanced its cult status. My next section shifts focus to affirmative or celebra-tory films made by occultist directors, some of whom perform rituals in their own films. Their uncompromisingly experimental form as well as esoteric content alienate some generic fans but intrigue others for whom they stimulate further engagement and discovery.

Kenneth Anger's magick lantern

Anger's credentials as oc/cult auteur *par excellence* are due to his subcultural capital as well as aesthetic skill. *Inauguration of the Pleasure Dome* (1954) performs an orgiastic Crowleyan ritual. Overtly "about" delirium, the film's visual overload is deliberately used to engineer psychic receptivity (Powell 2007: 84–87). Anger's cult status was firmly established with *Scorpio Rising*

(1964) in which homoerotic and sacrilegious biker rituals are ironically mixed with pop songs and intercut with Sunday School footage to blasphemous intent.

Invocation of my Demon Brother (1969) and *Lucifer Rising* (1970–1981) rework the same original footage to fundamentally different oc/cult ends. *Demon Brother*, described by Anger as a "burn", is an eleven-minute assault on the sensorium. Though demanding to watch, it is charged with cultic significance. Rapid-fire cutting of apparently random but highly deliberate, overlaid, images, including a Vietnam helicopter, is soundtracked by Mick Jagger's repetitively abrasive Moog Synthesiser. Footage of a Rolling Stones concert, and of Anton la Vey of the Church of Satan, are intercut with cavorting naked youths. In manic, speeded-up footage Anger gyrates widdershins around a magic circle. Beausoleil, Anger's lover and later a Manson acolyte, appears in top hat and wings as Lucifer. Occult symbols (sometimes flash-frames) are designed to mainline into the unconscious. The film climaxes with a rush of light and kaleidoscope shots of ecstatic devotees.

In contrast, *Lucifer Rising* displays the spatial immensity of archaeological sites in Egypt, Avebury and Excernsteine, the invocation of ancient gods and the evocation of timeless grandeur. Natural sunlight and location shooting enhances geographical dimensions and a symbolic colour scheme enhances the magical charge of objects and costumes. Of further cult interest is the casting of Isis (Miriam Gibril) Osiris (Donald Cammell) and Lilith (Marianne Faithfull). One effective oc/cult device is vertical editing to convey interlocking planes of physical and metaphysical, so that actions by human adepts have spiritual repercussions. The breathing of a sleeping adept is made manifest as coloured streams of light. Ritual footage shows Anger spinning in a circle marked with Crowley's pantheon–Lucifer, Nuit, Ra Hoor Kuit, Chaos, Babalon and Lilith. In fast-motion shots, the magic climaxes as simultaneous planes are accessed. The frantic spin is countered by the extreme slow motion of ripples in water. Match cuts link a light cone, a pointed hat and an explosive jet of volcanic spume. Forces unleashed by the ritual create a vortex, splitting the screen inwards (a Venetian wipe). A cone of energy like a dazzling spotlight beam of light particles materialises as the Magus shifts planes outside space and time.

Anger has overt designs upon the viewer as the "Magick Lantern Cycle" casts its glamour. Classic methods of trance induction mix new stimulus and hypnotic repetition to engineer altered states of consciousness. Their ambience mixes intense engagement and camp humour. Anger's intent was to extend and modernise Crowley's system via magickal iconography of symbols from homoeroticism, youth subcultures, fashion, rock music and Hollywood movies. He deploys the cinematic arts as magickal generators to transform and accumulate psychic energy, to stimulate the imagination and bring the occult (the hidden) into visible form as the films weave between physical and metaphysical planes. In Mathijs and Sexton's view, "only a few fans or critics take Anger's ideas seriously", yet both films were "used within networks of cult reception as provocative examples of a willingness to mix popular culture and religiosity" and to "promote cultism as an exciting alternative" to established religion (Mathijs and Sexton 2011: 139). Whilst endorsing their assessment, this particular fan/critic still "takes them seriously" on the level of enduring fascination.

"Realistic magic": Jodorowsky as oc/cult maverick

Whilst Anger's films are positioned in the un-commercial underground, Alejandro Jodorowsky is a "cult maverick: a mad visionary who is able to make strange and remarkable films" only if outside the commercial mainstream (Mathijs and Sexton 2011:70). He did, however, attract substantial finance for the esoteric film *The Holy Mountain* (1973), funded by John Lennon and Yoko One with Beatles manager, Allen Klein, as producer. A follower of Gurdjieff's occult philosophy and the ritual magic of Eliphas Levi, Jodorowky's esoteric world is also shaped by alchemy, Tarot, Kabbalah and Sufism. He uses "realistic magic", a transformative relation with the real partly shaped by his Surrealist connections (Jodorowsky interview 2016). Jodorowsky and fellow-filmmaker Fernando Arrabal founded the Panic movement, a radical art collective influenced by Artaud's Theatre of Cruelty. Jodorowsky also evolved his own eclectic technique, psychomagic. *The Holy Mountain* unfolds "a bizarre concoction of occultism, surrealism, and demystification" and it attained a cult following on the midnight movie film circuit (Mathijs and Sexton 2011:70). Like Anger, Jodorowsky intends his films to offer access points into "other universes, but with different modalities" ((Jodorowsky interview 2016). Images in *The Holy Mountain* have a hyperreal colour and sharp clarity and the films is densely laden with occult symbols. Both Anger and Jodorowsky mix esoteric and popular cultural sign systems (such as kitsch) intertextually to create such an idiosyncratic system that even the oc/cultist viewer "in the know" must research more deeply to gain further insight.

Twenty minutes into *The Holy Mountain* a magical transformation occurs. The Thief (Horácio Salinas), who physically resemblances Jesus, undergoes the horror of discovering statues of himself on the cross, endlessly replicated for use by the pious. Climbing a tower to seek for gold, he finds spiritual treasure instead when he encounters the Alchemist (Jodorowsky). The Thief undergoes an alchemical ordeal and becomes a guide for others on their own spiritual quest. This journey, both physical and metaphysical, is developed from the incomplete novel *Mount Analogue* (1952) by French mystic and surrealist René Daumal, a fellow Gurdjieff seeker. Jodorowsky performs with kitsch panache, clad in white, with platform boots and wearing an enneagram (a Gurdjieff symbol), on a throne flanked by naked, shaven twins (later by twin goats). The hypnotised Thief is operated on by the Written Woman (Ramona Saunders) who pulls a blue chicken from a wen on his neck. The Alchemist proclaims to the Thief "You are excrement. You can change yourself into gold" and has him ritually bathed for his transformation. In a remarkable scene, the Thief shits into a crystal vessel then squats inside the glass dome of an alchemic alembic. A close-up of the shit cooking mixes beauty and abjection as it transforms into a block of gold. Emerging regenerate, the Thief's first act is to smash his mirror image, rejecting his former self.

The Alchemist, robed in black, prepares the acolyte for his quest. The Thief, wearing an enneagram, finds that mirrors now reflect his different facets, not a fixed identity. The Alchemist breaks a crystal from a rock which fragments as the room spins round to form a mandala. In another circular room panelled with cartoon-like Tarot, the Thief is presented with magical tools, a silver pentacle, a sword and an incense thurible. A Bull and a black vulture complete his initiation and prepare him to lead an expedition of characters who symbolise the negative aspects of seven planets. The film, not widely circulated on first appearance, attracted a small cult following, which increased thirty years later when a restored print and DVD were released. My next oc/cult director's film moves away from the "Western Mysteries" to espouse the religiosity of another culture: Haitian Voudoun.

White darkness

Like Anger and Jodorowsky, Maya Deren had Surrealist connections, working with Encharito Matta and Marcel Duchamp. The unfinished *Witches Cradle* (1943) made with Duchamp; uses occult symbols (pentagrams) and ritualised postures. Deren's rushes for *Divine Horsemen: The Living Gods of Haiti* was shot 1947–1951 but the film was only released in 1985, having being edited posthumously by her husband, Teiji Ito. The monochrome documentary footage of ceremonial dancing has a soundtrack of Voudoun drumming which, running at its correct speed, is out of synch with the slow-motion dancers. The additional use of Ito's own music, however, acts to slow the moving images further, adding an other-worldly character. The occasional (male) voice-over commentary cites from Deren's own well-researched book on Voudoun (Deren 1998). Her book ends with her own ecstatic experiences of what she calls "white darkness" when possessed by a *loa* in ritual trance. She was herself initiated as a priestess and allowed to film previously unrecorded material from the *Rada* and *Petro loa* rituals.

Deren's other films use more rigorous formal structures to present oneiric alterity. Here, though, the rituals are presented with less aesthetic intervention, through the bodily motions and facial expressions of the celebrants themselves. Slow-motion dancing and celebrants shaking the *asson* (calabash rattle) express an ecstatic trance state without climax, or, rather, with multiple, extended climaxes when particular devotees are possessed by *loas*, including facial close-ups of those overpowered by these spirits. The bright sunlight also produces a bleaching-out effect conducive to alterity. Elaborate *vévés* traced on the ground act are the symbolic 'signature' of the particular entity being summoned. One ritual element that might disturb outsiders is the sacrifice of living creatures, cocks and goats, to summon the *loas*. Here, the slow-motion serves to extend the death throes of the birds, spraying blood as they writhe and flutter.

Unlike her earlier film roles of protagonist, Deren does not appear as an actant. Partly a practical necessity whilst filming, her bodily absence enhances the impression of a closely bonded local and communal ritual. Many cinematic versions of Voudoun present it either as 'satanic', anti-Christian black magic, or as childish superstition (Krzywinska 2000: 159). The first Voodoo film, Victor Halperin's *White Zombie* (1932), deploys Bela Lugosi as the evil entrepreneur Murder Legendre, whose sugar cane mill is worked by enslaved zombies. Legendre uses hypnotism, drugs and wax dolls to manipulate and seduce his victims. Deren's film, however, is closer to Krzywinska's category of Voodoo as counter-discourse, thus "a romantic and exotic form of magic that carries with it a Western dissatisfaction with rationalism and other key values" that involves identification with Voodoo (2000: 159). In Deren's case, identification is taken beyond the merely affirmative to initiation and total possession and her film evokes some of the rapture of the faith. Having considered films by occult practitioners designed to engage viewers in their "classical" systems of belief, I will now sketch some emergent tendencies that use film in more chaotic styles of magical practice.

Cult/occult/chaos

Chaos Magick is a more postmodern form of occultism with close links to performance art and film. Mathijs and Sexton suggest that the citing of Chaos Magick by film cultists indicates a closeness with their own community (Mathijs and Sexton 2011: 114). So what is Chaos Magick? In 1981, performance artist Genesis P. Orridge, then in the industrial band Throbbing Gristle (later Psychic TV) set up an eclectic esoteric network. The Temple of Psychic Youth (TOPY) experimented with extant occult systems like Austin Osman Spare's sigils and generated new ones. The UK alternative scene saw further developments in 1987 with publication of Pete Carroll's *Liber Null and Psychonaut* and the launch of his order, the Illuminates of Thanateros (IOT). Chaos Magick is broadly characterised by playful self-reflective humour and a heterogeneous mix of traditional occultism, scientific ideas and subcultural material (such as novels by IOT initiates Robert Anton Wilson and William S. Burroughs.) Politically anarchistic, it seeks to dismantle the magician's egoic identity by such methods as Tantric sex. Many practitioners are artists and encourage the creation of new rituals, using sigils to invoke servitors and make egregores (thought forms) generated by the shared group mind.

As well as novels with occult parameters, Burroughs made anarchic films such as *Towers Open Fire* (1963) with Antony Balch, using jagged edits, repetitive looping, dream machines, sigils, masturbation and other disorientation devices. Derek Jarman, whose own films have esoteric interests, made *Psychic Rally in Heaven* for Orridge's band Throbbing Gristle in 1981, whose music is the soundtrack. This uses rapid-fire editing, retardation and a flicker effect, with semi-abstract images shot through reddish brown filters. I will briefly cite two examples of Chaos film projects that aim to subvert clock time.

Razorsmile (formerly Keyman) made *Fotamecus Film Majik* (2002) to invoke the egregore of Fotamecus, a temporal servitor (Razorsmile 2016). This ritual, with its philosophical link to Henri Bergson's concept of duration aimed to interfere with time. A substantial amount of footage was shot with a 16mm clockwork camera as the key magical tool, but a financial shortage put the project on ice. Excerpts and a trailer include nocturnal ritual footage, images of clocks and other implements (including sigil biscuits), and the Chaos Magick sigil itself, the chaosphere, a black globe emitting arrows or rays (*Fotamecus Majik* 2016). Rapid-fire intercutting of still images and touches of animation add a "black scratch of colour and movement" (Humphreys and Vayne 2004: 36). A group project, *Fotamecus Majik* was designed for a consensual audience who takes part in the invocation so that screenings would "allow the viral meme servitor to reproduce in the consciousness of the viewer" (Humphreys and Vayne 2004: 36).

The use of film as a ritual actant is echoed by Orryelle Defenestrate Bascule, an Australian artist and performer (Bascule 2016). *Chaos Clock* (2012) was based on a public performance by The Metamorphic Theatre, who aimed to engage the audience in the magic. The film features Orryelle wearing clocks as masks whilst he gyrates and plays discords on his violin. Multiple superimpositions of clock faces and sigils combine with rapid zooms and Orryelle's animated figurines (*Chaos Clock* 2016).

Oc/cult film production and circulation continues in both mainstream commercial "occultism" and material from within oc/culture itself. For Mathijs and Sexton, since the 1990s, only a few films combine "a sincere or non-antagonistic approach to religious cultism with a cult reputation of their own" (Mathijs and Sexton 2011: 140). Their example, E. Elias Merhige's experimental *Begotten* (1991) re-tells Genesis via Gnosticism and "Dionysiac orgiastic cultism" using explicit sequences of violence and sex. They note that underground bootleg exchange enhanced its cult reputation, although it is now available on YouTube. Recent feature films with occult themes, such as *Kill List* (Ben Wheatley, 2011) and *The Conspiracy* (Christopher MacBride, 2012) present a frightening and destructive image of cultism. The Crowley subgenre continues with *The Chemical Wedding* (Julian Doyle, 2008).

For Mathijs and Sexton, oc/culture's desire for "unbound, untamed and untimed life" is undesirable to mainstream society (2011: 140). They argue that cultic ritual is only "condoned without sanction" in circumscribed situations, such as the ritualised film cult experience, which offers a placebo for occult ritual participation in such elements as togetherness, shock, astonishment, and drug-like hallucinations (Mathijs and Sexton 2011: 140). This pessimistic diagnosis of mainstream culture's attempt to limit occulture to cult film viewing is valid to some degree, but I would also assert that the oc/cult film experience, whether a public or private, domestic event, can also mobilise desires that may well be used subversively outside the viewing experience.

Oc/cult films are affective events experienced by the fan's shifting singularity in affective connection with them. Affects operate in assemblage with percepts and concepts that might lead to actions. The molecular flux of affective images acts to dismantle outworn structures of feeling and thought as new formations, submerged by societal repression, emerge. Oc/cult films use particular formal affects to induce alterity. Overtly metaphysical themes are reinforced by colour, light, shape, sound and movement. These extend beyond the signifying codes of meaning to operate on the plane of mind or spirit. They might also express and mobilise anti-totalitarian forms of desire as virtual becomes actual.

References

Bergson, Henri. 1991. *Matter and Memory*, trans. Nancy Margaret Paul and W. Scott Palmer, New York: Zone Books.
Chaos Clock film, accessed 19 June, 2016, www.youtube.com/watch?v=yjkMYO95kKI.
Cobb, Ben. 2007. *Alchemy and Anarchy: The Films of Alejandro Jodorowsky*. London: Creation Press.
Cultographies editorial resource, accessed 15 March 2016, www.cultographies.com.
Deleuze, Gilles. 1986. *Cinema 1: The Movement-Image*, trans. Hugh Tomlinson and Barbara Habberjam, Minneapolis: University of Minnesota Press.
Deren, Maya. 1998. *Divine Horsemen: The Living Gods of Haiti*. New York: McPherson.
Fotamecus Majik film trailer, accessed 10 May 2016. www.youtube.com/watch?v=yjkMYO95kKI.
Humphries, Greg and Julian Vayne. 2004. *Now That's What I Call Chaos Magick*. Oxford: Mandrake.
Hunter, Jack, ed. 2002. *Moonchild: The Films of Kenneth Anger*. London: Creation Press.
Isenberg, Noah. 2009. *Weimar Cinema: An Essential Guide to Classic Films of the Era*. New York: Columbia University Press.
Jodorowsky, Alejandro interview, May 29, 2015, accessed 13 May 2016, http://lithub.com/alejandro-jodorowsky/an interview.
Jodorowsky, Alejandro. 2008. *The Spiritual Journey of Alejandro Jodorowsky*. Rochester, VT: Park St Press.
Krzywinska, Tania. 2000. *A Skin for Dancing In: Possession, Witchcraft and Voodoo in Film*. Trowbridge, UK: Flicks Books.
Mathijs, Ernest and Jamie Sexton. 2011. *Cult Cinema*. Chichester: Wiley-Blackwell.
Merriam-Webster online dictionary, accessed 30 March 2016, www.merriam-webster.com/dictionary.
Orryelle Defenestrate Bascule bio, accessed 25 June 2016, www.crossroads.wild.net.au/bio.html.
Powell, Anna. 2007. *Deleuze, Altered States and Film*. Edinburgh: Edinburgh University Press.
Razorsmile Fotamecus project, accessed 12 April 2016, http://razorsmile.org/fotamecus.

18

TRANSGRESSION IN CULT CINEMA

Thomas Joseph Watson

Transgression: Theories and concepts

Transgression involves an apparent violation of accepted or imposed boundaries, especially those of social acceptability. The concept itself has a critical history within the arts whereby orthodox cultural, moral, and artistic boundaries are challenged by the representation of unconventional behaviour and the use of experimental forms. I think it is here that we face one of the critical problems when attempting to define transgression in relation to cult cinema; namely that both the terms 'subversion' and 'transgression' have been confused in the discourse surrounding cult cinema and used interchangeably when they do not mean the same thing.

If cult cinema is something that resists a fixed definition (or rather, has attained several attempts at such a definition when the parameters of cult are indeed fluid), transgression, by extension, is also a slippery concept to define. In describing a text(s) as transgressive in the first instance, you immediately identify those elements that transgress. Such identification therefore frames transgression and normalizes it (an action I am aware that this present chapter is implicated in). The term itself is stretched to the extent that it becomes meaningless. If *everything* is defined as transgressive, either in terms of representation or form, transgression can no longer be oppositional. This can either be productive in the sense that it presents the opportunity for further transgression to occur, although it is also limiting to the extent that 'transgression' becomes normative. How oppositional can cult cinema be if transgression is applied to *all* cult films, when transgression then becomes the norm? The following unpicks the semantic nuances between these terms to explore such a question.

To transgress is to infringe or go beyond the bounds of a moral principle or other established standards of behaviour, the term itself relating to infractions, violations and law breaking. Subversion involves the *intention* to subvert an established system or institution through disruption and agitation. To subvert is to undermine the power and authority of an established system. Subversion entails a satirical impulse that seeks to expose the limit/ boundary, thereby drawing attention to its artificialness, constructed-ness and arbitrary nature. It is an inversion of perceived boundaries and limits, in a moral sense and so forth. Transgression goes further in that it seeks to bend or break the limit/ boundary that is approached, creating something new that follows an apparent infringement. Subversion touches the boundary, whereas transgression aims to do more and affect change.

In recent scholarship, Steve Jones has interrogated the implications of ubiquitous labelling in discussions of 'extreme' porn. The term 'extreme', attached to specific examples of pornography, signifies that the pornographic referent in these cases is transgressive, i.e. it is 'extreme' in a way that it pushes the boundaries of normative sexual propriety. The labelling of such representations as 'extreme' does little to interrogate the content attached to the descriptor. As such, 'labels carry a host of implicit values, and when labels are used to the point of saturation - when the label's connotations are presumed to be obvious, and so are rarely questioned - those values are obfuscated' (Jones 2016: 295–296).

The same principle befalls descriptors of transgression, or when a film is marked as transgressive. It is often unclear as to what specific aspects mark a film out as being transgressive, and if transgression is used as the criterion of cult, the term is diluted of its meaning and is therefore redundant. The term transgression, as it has been applied to cult cinema, does very little to interrogate what is 'transgressive' about different cult texts beyond issues of performance, aesthetic form and thematic tropes. Such labelling also elides the fact that elements of transgression are often context-dependent. For example, a film that was once 'transgressive' on the basis of a turbulent censorial history and apparent illicitness may not be looked upon in the same transgressive light when it is certified uncut years later or released in elaborate, deluxe home media editions (the censorial history of *The Texas Chainsaw Massacre* [1974] in the United Kingdom is an example of this shift).

Standards of taste and propriety are not fixed and are subject to change. There is therefore an inherent tension between the heterogeneity of cult films and the homogenous connotations 'transgression' implies. Jones convincingly argues that 'when using labels as explanatory frameworks, one should seek to employ labels that explicitly refer to distinct objects, rather than vague, ill-defined notions' (ibid: 303). The varied definitions of cult cinema indicate that it cannot exist as a distinct object (regardless of changing degrees of consensus). As such, transgression, when the term is used as an explanatory framework, needs to be interrogated further.

Transgression and cult cinema

Transgression in cult cinema functions as a threefold process with substantial degrees of overlap between these demarcations. Firstly, transgression functions in relation to cult films when referring to a heterogeneous group of texts or when defining cult cinema as a 'super genre' (Andrews 2013: 95). When conceptualized in this light, transgression refers to themes, images and aesthetic forms, which are placed in opposition to normative, taste cultures, boundaries of propriety and standards of traditional filmmaking (i.e. mainstream productions). Secondly, transgression is signalled at the level of censorship and formal regulation. By breaking boundaries governed by censorial/regulatory edicts, something that is inherent to audiovisual culture, certain examples of cinema are transgressive in that these boundaries can be broken and repositioned. Instances of formal regulation and censorship are not only fundamental in constructing cult texts or groupings of cult films, but such instances can also give way to a productive third level of transgression in the formation of active subcultures. Naturally occurring audiences go on to form subcultures surrounding examples of censored, and therefore 'illegitimate' cinema. Cult audiences engage in transgressive behaviour in so much as they go on to flout perceived boundaries when accessing prohibited cult cinema. The present chapter explicates these contexts when discussing an apparent *cult of the censored*.

Concepts of transgression have permeated discussions of cult cinema since it became an area of academic interest. Initially appearing in the first scholarly collection on cult cinema (*The Cult Film Experience*), Barry K. Grant's work on cult horror and science fiction suggests that a sense of unification exists between cult films that are underpinned by the 'transgressive' elements they contain. Approaching cult texts through the prism of genre criticism, Grant finds critical value in the suggestion that all cult texts in some way 'involve a form of "transgression"' and 'that this quality is central to their appeal' (1991: 122–137). For Grant, transgression covers representations of 'freakery' and the grotesque (*Freaks* [Browning, 1931]), countercultural attitudes and oppositional tastes (read as the 'trash' aesthetics of John Waters' *Pink Flamingos* [1972]), and representations of excessive violence and the macabre. In addition to such content, nonconventional formal/ visual styles of filmmaking are also considered to be transgressive (compounding the already transgressive acts and content represented in these films).

These latter accounts of transgression are linked to examples of 'bad cinema' that have gone on to attain cult status. This is due to an apparent lack of creative quality and/ or practical competency. Grant points to the status of Edward D. Wood Jr, 'the worst filmmaker of all time', as an example of transgressive form in cult cinema. *Troll 2* (1990) and Tommy Wiseau's *The Room* (2003) are recent examples of so-called 'bad-film' that have been appropriated by cultists in the ironic celebration of these concerns. As Grant continues:

> While it is true that cult films seem commonly to offer some form of transgression ... what essentially makes these movies *cultish*, is their ability to be at once transgressive *and* recuperative, in other words, to reclaim that which they seek to violate ... the viewer ultimately gains the double satisfaction of both rejecting dominant cultural values and remaining safely inscribed within them.

This recuperative aspect of cult cinema is echoed in broader theories of transgression in audio-visual culture. Jencks, for example, argues that 'transgression is a deeply reflexive act of denial and affirmation' (2003: 2) and 'is not the same as disorder' as 'it opens up chaos and reminds us of the necessity of order' (ibid: 7). To transgress is not only to oppose limits and boundaries; it is also to engage in a reciprocal relationship with these boundaries to remind us *what* they are and *why* they are in place.

Ideas of transgression are then taken beyond the confines of the cult texts themselves and are consolidated around audience engagement. Mathijs and Sexton propose the notion of 'affective receptions', whereby 'affective appreciation is a specifically crucial element in the perception and experience of transgression and freakery. In particular, cult cinema receptions negotiate *negative* forms of affect such as disgust, revulsion, and aversion' (2011: 97). These affective receptions relate to Annette Hill's earlier scholarship on audiences and violent media content. Hill is interested in the reasons why audiences are attracted to such transgressive material in the first place and the pleasures to be derived from such representations. Cult audiences that engage with transgressive content choose to watch such material they find affronting or disturbing (see Hill 1997: 51–74) and may use that material to test the boundaries and limits of their own personal thresholds (ibid).

I.Q. Hunter asserts a similar point when he argues that 'films like *Bloodsucking Freaks* enable us to rehearse in mediated safety our reactions, both fascinated and repulsed to the point of nausea, to the traumatic experience of encountering something liminal and outside the social and cultural order' (2016: 159). Linking such discussions back to cult cinema specifically, Sexton and Mathijs suggest that cult audiences are attracted to certain films and their affective charges as a result of transgressive content and form. As such, this attraction:

> Could be out of a sincere sense of rebellion against what is perceived as a suffocating pressure from dominant morality. It could be out of a performative desire to provoke

reaction. It could be out of an attitude that attempts to challenge intellectualizations of film viewing - and cultural appreciation in general. It could also be out of empathy and alignment with the margins of society.

(ibid)

Although these definitions of transgression present ideological complications in addition to the production and reception of cult cinema, they do not present a 'one size fits all' model that can be attributed to all cult films. This is complicated further in recent scholarship that aims to discursively frame cult cinema. Drawing on the work of Dan Bentley-Baker, I.Q. Hunter alludes to the following criterion that enables cult films to be defined beyond their 'textual qualities' (2016: 3):

1. Marginality	Content falls outside general cultural norms
2. Suppression	Subject to censor, ridicule, lawsuit, or exclusion
3. Economics	Box office flop upon release but eventually profitable
4. Transgression	Content breaks social, moral, or legal rules
5. Cult Following	Generates devoted minority audience
6. Community	Audiences is or becomes self-identified group
7. Quotation	Lines of dialog become common language
8. Iconography	Establishes or revives cult icon

In Bentley-Baker's original article, the case is made whereby the scat-fetish video *2 Girls 1 Cup* retains several dimensions of a cult film defined by such criterion (particularly marginality [coprophagia and emetophilia], transgression [the display of niche paraphilias], and community [coprophiliac fetishists, voyeurs]). The clip falls outside of general cultural norms, is not exactly available for wider, formally 'official' distribution, is transgressive in the acts depicted (defecation and coprophagia in a sexual context) and has also fostered a sense of community given the phenomenon of reaction videos circulating on YouTube and in wider popular culture (the adult animation series *Family Guy* uses the reaction video motif as a point of quotation).[1] Cult film credentials are therefore supplanted onto this short video extract, indicating its induction into a tentative canon, encompassing films as disparate as *Suspiria*, *Fight Club*, and *The Big Lebowski*. These films are transgressive in their own ways, but useful analysis of such transgressions needs to take place on a text-by-text basis to distinguish what is 'transgressive' about these cult texts. Again, transgression is taken as a given.

David Andrews furthers this point when arguing that 'cult theorists at times present the reality of *some* cult art as the ahistorical essence of *all* cult art' and also notes how 'this can't work' (2013: 96). Questions arise such as, 'have all cult films had "troublesome production histories"?' and 'have they all "challenged genre conventions and coherent storytelling"?' (ibid). The same question can be leveled at transgression when the term is used as a generic descriptor when referring to cult film. Can cult films be defined as transgressive beyond a base opposition to mainstream codes and conventions? I believe they can, and this is especially true when considering the role of transgression in the formation of marginalized subcultural communities and related fandom(s). It is in this respect that I ascribe to Jancovich et al.'s conception of cult cinema as an 'eclectic category...not defined according to some single, unifying feature shared by all cult movies, but rather through a "subcultural ideology" in filmmakers, films or audiences...existing in opposition to the "mainstream"' (2003: 1). Transgression therefore traverses specific films and affects the extra-textual contexts of contemporary film culture, acting as a manifestation of a 'subcultural ideology'. This idea has yet to receive sustained examination in cult film discourse.

Stephanie Watson argues that 'transgression appears to us as a 'named event' in perceiving opposition to limits, which are both informed by, and inform, transgression.' She goes on to suggest that these 'limits are called into place within the context of a particular form of socio-economic organization' and that 'these socio-economic forms are complicit with the language and knowledge systems which are never radically altered. Consequently, 'these limits are reproduced in altered, displaced and inverted forms' (1995: 75). Watson's conceptions of transgression refer to 'The Cinema of Transgression', perhaps the most cohesive manifestation of a subcultural ideology relating to film, transgression and aspects of 'cult'. The cinema of transgression refers to a group of filmmakers and performers in the mid-1980s/ early 1990s that voiced anti mainstream attitudes (directed both towards avant-garde and popular film cultures) and a scepticism concerning 'acceptable culture' more broadly. The group's manifesto, penned by filmmaker Nick Zedd, alludes to a 'new generation of filmmakers daring to rip out of the stifling straightjackets of film theory in a direct attack on every value system known to man' and suggest that 'any film which doesn't shock isn't worth looking at' (see Sargeant 1995: 7).

Jack Sargeant discusses the contemporaneous difficulty these films faced in terms of exhibition and distribution. Given their confrontational subject matter and vitriolic manifesto that underpinned their production, it is perhaps unsurprising that these films were seen very little outside of a few select subcultural circles. Later, a far wider cult audience would come to these films via a climate of burgeoning home media technology and informal networks of distribution. As Sargeant states, 'the growth of home-video technology was one method by which filmmakers associated with the Cinema of Transgression were able to distribute their work' (1995: v). However, doing so via home media technology (external to sanctioned art spaces or independent cinema clubs capable of risking the exhibition of 'transgressive' content) meant that such distribution echoed the independent, DIY sensibility that underscored the films in the first place. [2] This meant that such distribution was largely unregulated and informal. In the contexts of my own geographical confines, 'many of the available copies of Zedd's and Kern's movies circulating in England are second, and sometimes third or fourth, generation copies' (ibid). Issues of transgression and informal distribution are discussed in the following subsection.

Cult of the censored: Transgression and formal regulation

When considering transgressive imagery in marginal, Anglo-American cinema, Joel Gwynne argues that:

> examining controversial images and content within cult cinema is important in terms of understanding media production more discursively, since it exposes the mechanisms of censorship and regulation and the limits and conventions of media forms; how they are challenged and overturned.
>
> (2016: 1)

Films with established cult followings have also been implicated in moral and ethical discussions concerning both transgressive representation and the representation of transgression. It is in this sense that transgressive acts are still viewed as contentious in contemporary film culture, evidenced by regulatory and censorial decisions made in attempts to control and contain said transgressions. In terms of representation, it is the way films represent graphic, sometimes genuine, instances of transgressive behaviour onscreen that sets them aside from other, and perhaps more legitimate examples of cinema.

Transgression on a moral level is therefore a central factor in the cultivation and fostering of distinctive subcultural fan communities. This is no less evident in the subcultures associated with cult cinema and specific cult texts. Cultists and 'paracinephiles' act as custodians of cult film history and respond to the different cuts and versions of films in circulation. This occurs when films have befallen different regimes of regulation and film censorship over time and locale, effectively transgressing the boundaries and limits of censorial edicts. This leads to the formation of collector cultures and fan communities that have formed due to the transgressive and 'illegitimate' nature of certain films. Audiences can themselves be transgressive as they flout norms of propriety and choose to access films that are otherwise forbidden or have been positioned as clandestine cultural objects.

Following the implications of an inherent transgression already existing within cult cinema, films that have been codified as horror, exploitation, or indeed examples from the avant-garde that are deemed more 'extreme', have faced different regulatory pressures, which have impeded their production and distribution amongst audiences. Moreover, films that confuse and conflate limitations and boundaries in their transgression have proven an extended problem for regulatory bodies and institutions (I have examined this elsewhere in relation to the hardcore horror-porn hybrid *The Texas Vibrator Massacre* [see Watson, 2013]). Modes of censorship therefore effect the consumption of films and provoke informal ways of gaining access to otherwise prohibited material. Transgressive content and the rules and regulations that govern such content in wider film culture are never the same and tend to be culturally and temporally specific. For example, the BBFC has revised its classification guidelines several times since the Video Nasties furor of the 1980s and now holds itself accountable for a greater level of transparency with regard to the censorial decisions it makes (although this is not without contention). The BBFC is different from the Motion Pictures Association of America (MPAA), and both are different from the Australian Board of Film Classification and so forth. Content that is acknowledged as transgressive in one context will not hold the same cultural meaning in other territories.

Despite the negative connotations associated with censorship and the inability to access certain films, formal censorship and prohibition has also resulted in the formation of underground filmmaking subcultures and alternative ways of distributing those films deemed culturally transgressive. The tension existing between transgression and censorship is useful and formative in this respect. In recent years, this has taken the form of 'Hardcore Horror' films such as *August Underground's Mordum* (Vogel, 2003) and Lucifer Valentine's *Vomit Gore* films (2006–2015). Examples of hardcore horror cinema typically contain representations of genuine self-mutilation, staged violence and graphic sex coded as abuse within an over-arching aesthetic of snuff fiction. These films are situated in 'long tail' markets 'where budgets are low and audiences tiny' (Lobato and Ryan 2011: 194). These 'long tail' distribution networks provide an outlet for films that would not have otherwise received any substantial distribution. This is true of hardcore horror as an example of an 'extreme niche market' (ibid), a market likely to be accessed by those invested audiences interested in such subversive, transgressive content, i.e. cult audiences that are cine-literate and responsive to transgressive subject matter. Indeed, Fred Vogel formally distributes his films through his own Toe Tag film label in addition to other independent hardcore horror distributors such as Brain Damage Films and Unearthed Films (these labels themselves maintaining a transgressive, subcultural cachet).

The means of circumventing interventionist, regulative censorship creates a wider space to discuss the discourses surrounding the prohibition of particular films. For Ramon Lobato, 'informal circulatory networks are largely subterranean, meaning that texts move through space and time with a lower level of interference from copyright law...and state censorship' (2012: 43).[3] The formation of these networks, typically driven by fan communities and those invested in anti-censorship, has led to the promotion and unofficial distribution of uncut and unrated horror films that have since gained larger subcultural capital (see Church 2015: 13–19). Richard Burt identifies these practices as 'the fetish of censorship', whereby 'censorship may be usefully regarded as a metaphor for the fetishistic practices of cultural differentiation and legit-imation by which texts are put into circulation as desirable commodities' (1998: 19). Further to this, 'censorship involves the negotiation and construction of small differences that make the text desirable (either because it is the uncensored version or because it is the censored version)' (ibid). Regulative censorship as a response to transgression therefore leads to constitutive dis-course through the formation and preservation of subcultural capital and associated identity.

When writing about fan communities and active audiences, Matt Hills argues that 'subcul-tural investment in the "underground" and its transgressiveness can lead us to view horror's "subcultural citizenship" in a very specific way; that is, as a reflexive attempt to violate norms and regulations of the dominant, national culture' (2005: 102). As Hills states, 'the "enemy" of censorship that is so frequently railed against simultaneously allows for the validation of "true" horror fandom and its distinctiveness' (ibid: 102). Therefore, censorship that is opposed by these communities simultaneously allows for their constitution. Moreover, censorship as an inter-vention can be creative and productive and ultimately sustains these associated discourses of fandom:

> Censorship establishes that specific texts are tabooed or prohibited, and subcultural
> fan practices then seek to transgress/ violate this cultural category of 'censored' or
> restricted material. The pleasure-agency that is discursively articulated is thus one of
> boundary crossing in relation to how texts are culturally classified, rather than being a
> response to textual content *per se*.
>
> (Hills 2005: 106)

For Hills, the pleasure for the subcultural fan is not necessarily the transgressive content represented in the film but rather the fact that this content has crossed the proverbial 'line' in some way. Transgression in this instance involves the fan intentionally flouting the rules governing officially 'restricted material' and seeking to view or possess that which is deemed as transgressive or taboo via other means (informal or otherwise). Transgression in this sense is two-fold. Firstly, content demarcated as taboo transgresses sanctioned rules and guidelines and must be controlled and contained via censorship. Secondly, this process instigates further transgression, as subcultural fans are then willing to access such material because it has been sanctioned following its definition as 'transgressive'. This mentality prevailed amidst collectors of prohibited video nasties in the 1980s, whereby a banned list of films provided fans with a veritable shopping list of transgressive titles. Independently produced British magazines such as *Samhain* and *The Darkside* included classified sections detailing the sale and trade of VHS films prohibited by the BBFC that had been commercially available prior to the implementation of the Video Recordings Act legislation (using distinctive codes to occlude the fact that it was indeed illegal tapes that were being sold and traded [see Egan 2007: 114]). Additionally, mail order networks of tape trading and duplication were established that furthered the (informal) distribution of illegal material. In certain cases, this was met with punitive consequences (see Kerekes and Slater 2001: 287–313). These contexts relate back to Burt Richards' conception of a 'fetish of censorship' as these films became desirable texts precisely because they were censored.[4]

Conclusion

In their definition of cult cinema, Jancovich et al. argue that the concept of 'cult' 'is largely a matter of the ways in which films are classified through consumption, although it is certainly the case that filmmakers often share the same "subcultural ideology" as fans and have set out to make self-consciously "cult" materials' (2003: 1). This latter point problematizes concepts of transgression if the intent to transgress is obvious and intentional, an issue relating to 'programmatic cult' or 'ready-made' cult cinema. This self-reflexivity is often presented through exaggerated representations of previous transgressions that ultimately fall short of their transgressive predecessors. The desire to pay homage to a previous film, or period of film history, is symptomatic of postmodern appropriation in cinema more generally. Transgression in these later films is relatively contained as the boundaries have already been transgressed and taboos have already been broken. Therefore, homage to transgression will never be transgressive in the same way, as it is automatically rendered in a safer space as pastiche. However, as I have argued for the contextual importance of understanding transgression, I do not want to rule out the potential for a text to be viewed as transgressive in different social or political circumstances.

The appropriation of transgressive content and formal style to make transgression acceptable and palatable is problematic in the sense that, when a text is labelled as transgressive, that text has been discursively codified and even neutralized. Once this identification has taken place, the text is immediately subsumed into those discursive systems that define it as such, therefore reinstating the dominance of these systems. These claims echo the points made by Barry K. Grant outlined earlier in the chapter and consolidates the evident failures where attempted transgression is concerned. As such:

> If the transgressive act, image, or concept originates not from an organically developed testing of the edges, but from a calculated use of the *idea* of transgression to create allure or hype, the project has already failed to transgress before it has begun.
> (Foley, McRobert and Stephanou 2012: xi)

It is here that transgression, determined through the lens of intention, perhaps fails as a critical endeavour, and is effectively sidelined to describe cult films as different from the mainstream.[5] If we are positioned in a film culture where past transgressions have been appropriated to the extent of homage, pastiche and reflexivity, where can transgression go from here? Can it still exist? One way of engaging with transgression is to assert the 'affective resonances' outlined by Sexton and Mathijs, but more specifically in terms of transgressive actions and performance. As such, Clemens Marschall argues that 'transgression is not about ignoring or denying boundaries, but about deliberately exceeding and questioning them' (2016: 12). Directing such criticism at cult figures and cult films such as *Hated: GG Allin and The Murder Junkies* (Todd Phillips, 2003), Marschall writes that an audience can be punished in a transgressive act, 'because such an on-stage witness is a transgressive character', in 'trying to gain information about the other characters in illicit ways, the witness frequently becomes a victim of some form of violence' (ibid). To reinstate transgression as a valid concept, an emphasis is placed on past examples of transgressive culture and the respective cultural changes they instigated. If certain cult films are taken as examples, largely based on their respective transgressions, it no longer matters that they have been appropriated into alternative canons or re-released in lavish home media packages and so forth. What matters is the impact of their transgressions, as and when they occurred. These lasting impacts of transgression are what ultimately count and what constitute the status of films as cult.

On one hand, transgression may lead to the re-negotiation of boundaries and reconsideration as to what elements are considered taboo, and therefore transgressive. On the other, boundaries can be strengthened further to better control and contain transgressive content. This is not so much a circular movement but is suggestive of the push/ pull nature of transgression. Boundaries that are broached by examples of cult cinema are in a constant state of re-negotiation and flux. When a threshold is broached, transgression is either co-opted or that threshold is altered. As Michel Foucault argues, 'transgression incessantly crosses and re-crosses a line which closes up behind it in a wave of extremely short duration and thus is made to return once more right to the horizon of the un-crossable' (1977: 33–34). This chapter has, at least momentarily, aimed to grant some stability to the definitions of transgression within and beyond the contexts of cult cinema, pointing to the way these 'horizons of the un-crossable' can be better understood.

Notes

1 For contemporary scholarship detailing the trajectory of the 'shock video' *2Girls1Cup*, see Steve Jones (2017).
2 Films within this body of work include *The Bogus Man* (Zedd, 1980), *Stray Dogs* (Kern, 1985), *Sewing Circle* (Kern, 1992) and *War Is Menstrual Envy* (Zedd, 1992).
3 Independent British horror cinema is discussed in these terms by Walker (2014, 224–225), focusing on means of self-distribution as circumventing the monetary impact of the BBFC's classificatory procedures.
4 Notable work concerning the collectability, fandom and commodity fetishism surrounding censored/uncensored films includes discussions of VHS collecting (Egan 2007; Walker 2011), Fanzines and independent media (Szpunar 2013: 701–704; Flint 2014) the marketing of films in their 'unrated' or 'uncut' versions (Bernard 2014) and internet piracy associated with 'extreme' cinema (Kapka 2014).
5 This is not to limit other valid forms of transgression that emerge from unintended reactions or contextual outcomes afforded to certain films. These unintended (but, nevertheless, potentially desirable outcomes) can relate to certain films being caught up within significant controversies or contested debates or the focus of adverse reactions from different audiences.

References

Andrews, David. 2013. *Theorizing Art Cinemas: Foreign, Cult, Avant-garde, and Beyond.* Austin: University of Texas Press.
Bentley-Baker, Dan. 2010. "What Is Cult Cinema? A Checklist." *Bright Lights Film Journal.* brightlightsfilm.com/what-is-cult-cinema-a-checklist/#.XUhGK1Ao-8o [accessed August 2019].
Bernard, Mark. 2014. *Selling the Splat Pack: The DVD Revolution and the American Horror Film.* Edinburgh: Edinburgh University Press.
Brottman, Mikita. 2005. *Offensive Films.* Nashville, TN: Vanderbilt University Press.
Burt, Richard. 1998. "(Un) Censoring in Detail: The Fetish of Censorship in the Early Modern Past and the Postmodern Present." In *Censorship and Silencing: Practices of Cultural Regulation*, edited by Robert C. Post, 17–41. Los Angeles: The Getty Research Institute.
Church, David. 2015. *Grindhouse Nostalgia: Memory, Home Video and Exploitation Film Fandom.* Edinburgh: Edinburgh University Press.
Egan, Kate. 2007. *Trash or Treasure? Censorship and the Changing Meanings of the Video Nasties.* Manchester: Manchester University Press.
Flint, David. 2014. *Sheer Filth.* London: FAB Press.
Foley, Matt, Neil McRobert and Aspasia Stephanou, eds. 2012. *Transgression and its Limits.* Newcastle upon Tyne: Cambridge Scholars.
Foucault, Michel. 1977. "A Preface to Transgression." In *Language, Counter-Memory, Practice: Selected Essays and Interviews by Michel Foucault*, edited by Donald F. Bouchard, 29–52. New York: Cornell University.
Foust, Christina R. 2010. *Transgression as a Mode of Resistance: Rethinking Social Movement in an Era of Corporate Globalization.* Plymouth: Lexington Books.

Grant, Barry K. 1991. "Science Fiction Double Feature." In *The Cult Film Experience: Beyond all Reason*, edited by J.P. Telotte, 122–137. Austin: University of Texas Press.

Gwynne, Joel. 2016. *Transgression in Anglo-American Cinema: Gender, Sex and the Deviant Body*. New York: Columbia University Press.

Hill, Annette. 1997. *Shocking Entertainment: Viewer Response to Violent Movies*. Luton: University of Luton Press.

Hills, Matt. 2005. *The Pleasures of Horror*. London: Continuum.

Hunter, I.Q. 2016. *Cult Film as a Guide to Life*. New York: Bloomsbury.

Jancovich, Mark, Antonio Lázaro-Reboll, Julian Stringer and Andy Willis, eds. 2003. *Defining Cult Movies: The Cultural Politics of Oppositional Taste*. Manchester: Manchester University Press.

Jencks, Chris. 2003. *Transgression*. London: Routledge.

Jones, Steve. 2016. "'Extreme' Porn? The Implications of a Label." *Porn Studies* 3 (3): 295–307, DOI: 10.1080/23268743.2016.1196011.

Jones, Steve. 2017. "The Origin of the Faeces." *Porn Studies*, DOI: 10.1080/23268743.2017.1385414

Kapka, Alexandra. 2014. "Understanding *A Serbian Film*: The Effects of Censorship and File-Sharing on Critical Reception and Perceptions or Serbian National Identity in the UK." *Frames Cinema Journal* (6).

Kerekes, David, and David Slater. 2001. *See No Evil: Banned Films and Video Controversy*. Manchester: Critical Vision/Headpress.

Lobato, Ramon. 2012. *Shadow Economies of Cinema: Mapping Informal Film Distribution*. London: BFI/Palgrave Macmillan.

Lobato, Ramon, and Mark David Ryan. 2011. "Rethinking Genre Studies Through Distribution Analysis: Issues in International Horror Movie Circuits." *New Review of Film and Television Studies* 9 (2): 188–203.

Marschall, Clemens. 2016. *Avant-garde from Below: Transgressive Performance from Iggy Pop to Joe Coleman and GG. Allin*. New York: Rokko's Adventures.

Mathijs, Ernest, and Jamie Sexton. 2011. *Cult Cinema: An Introduction*. London: Wiley-Blackwell.

Sargeant, Jack. 1995. *Deathtripping: An Illustrated History of the Cinema of Transgression*. London: Creation Books.

Sheehan, Paul. 2013. *Modernism and the Aesthetics of Violence*. New York: Cambridge University Press.

Szpunar, John. 2013. *Xerox Ferox: The Wild World of the Horror Film Fanzine*. London: Headpress.

Walker, Johnny. 2011. "Nasty Visions: Violent Spectacle in Contemporary British Horror Cinema." *Horror Studies* 2 (1): 115–130.

Walker, Johnny. 2014. "Low Budgets, No Budgets and Digital Video Nasties: Recent British Horror and Informal Distribution." In *Merchants of Menace: The Business of Horror Cinema*, edited by Richard Nowell, 215–228. London: Bloomsbury.

Watson, Stephanie. 1995. "The Transgressive Aesthetic." In *Deathtripping: An Illustrated History of the Cinema of Transgression*, edited by Jack Sargeant, 34–37. London: Creation Books.

Watson, Thomas Joseph. 2013. "There's Something Rotten in the State of Texas: Genre, Adaptation and *The Texas Vibrator Massacre*." *Journal of Adaptation in Film and Performance* 6 (3): 387–400.

19

ACCESS ALL AREAS?

Anglo-American film censorship and cult cinema in the digital era

Emma Pett

Introduction

The neoliberal character of Anglo-American film regulation has, across the last two decades, oscillated between the apparently contradictory poles of liberalising and restrictive regulatory practices. Beginning within a comparative analysis of US and UK regulatory contexts, this chapter draws out some of the key differences between the practices of the Motion Picture Association of America (MPAA) and the British Board of Film Classification (BBFC); in particular, it considers the impact of their policies on the cultification of transgressive and controversial forms of cult cinema, and examines how these two institutions have responded to an increasingly complex cultural landscape by catering to both ends of the spectrum of popular opinion, albeit in very different ways. The second half of the chapter then discusses the regulation and circulation of five transgressive films that have been released and distributed, both legitimately and illegally, across the last decade: *Antichrist* (Lars von Trier, 2009) *Grotesque* (Koji Shiraishi, 2009), *A Serbian Film* (Srdjan Spasojevic, 2010), *The Human Centipede II (Full Sequence)* (Tom Six, 2011) and *Hate Crime* (James Bressack, 2012). These case studies are firstly investigated to gauge the extent to which the censorship of the films has generated the same levels of subcultural cachet amongst Anglo-American cult film audiences as they did in the pre-digital era. These shifts in regulatory processes and policies, which have played out against the rapidly evolving backdrop of digital distribution networks and the rise of streaming culture, are thus evaluated in terms of their significance in relation to the cultification of cinema in the digital era.

The rise of neoliberal film regulation

In focusing on the regulatory activity of the MPAA and BBFC, this chapter does not set out to promote the cultural hegemony of either institution. Indeed, it recognises that there is a long history and developing field of scholarship problematizing the influential power of both institutions within a broader, transcultural context (Quinn 2006; Peredo-Castro 2011; Biltereyst and Vande Winkel 2013). Whilst acknowledging the problematic significance of these historical and contemporary instances of cultural hegemony, the repercussions of the neoliberal regulatory policies pursued by these two institutions on the circulation of marginal and controversial films (which often attain cult status) within their own geographical and institutional boundaries forms the focus of this chapter. As such, the case studies selected as a means to investigate the regulation and circulation of Anglo-American cult cinema reflect a predominantly white, western and masculine taste culture.[1] In taking this taste culture as the object of study, I am not positioning it as being a normative or representative form of cult cinema; rather, it offers a pertinent focus for conducting an investigation into the relationship between Anglo-American regulatory institutions and the category of cult in this specific cultural moment.

While quite different in their origins and institutional remits, the MPAA and BBFC are both non-governmental regulatory bodies who work closely with the industry to ensure that films reach the widest audience possible.[2] American film scholars have argued that the MPAA functions primarily as the public relations arm of the US film industry (Lewis 2007: 150). To fulfil this purpose, both institutions operate a successful behind-the-scenes process of cutting films for category. This ensures that distributors get the ratings they desire to capture the largest audience possible, thus maximising their revenue for both theatrical and domestic releases. In this respect, both the MPAA and BBFC can be described as being in the pockets of the film industry, and both thus epitomise neoliberal media regulation within the aggressive marketplace of the contemporary film industry. This shared strategy, between the industry and the industry regulators, also underpins the desire of both the MPAA and BBFC to extend their regulatory remit to encompass digital film distribution and combat piracy. The illegitimate distribution industry has potentially threatened the profit margins of both legitimate distributors and their regulators, resulting in an ongoing 'international war' against digital piracy on both sides of the Atlantic (Lewis 2007: 146; Crisp 2015a: 154). This has most recently manifested in the form of the Ace Coalition (Alliance for Creativity and Entertainment), a global anti-piracy organisation founded in 2017 and heavily championed by the MPAA. For these reasons, regulatory policy over the last fifteen years has gradually been tightened in relation to digital distribution, whilst simultaneously there have been increasingly fewer films censored.

The neoliberal impulse driving the regulatory policies of the MPAA and BBFC has also affected the classification of controversial cult films. The MPAA and the BBFC have both initiated significant changes, in that they have created or revised ratings categories at the top of the classification scale in a move towards a gradual liberalisation of explicit or violent material. In the United States, the NC-17 was introduced in 1990, while in the United Kingdom changes were made to the R18 category in an attempt to liberalise the top end of the classification scale.[3] Likewise, both institutions have also engaged in a programme of public consultations in an attempt to justify their regulatory decisions, and have shared a strategy of generating public endorsements to justify the rationale for their policies (BBFC 2012; MPAA/Nielsen 2015). These consultations frame the general public as consumers, thus reinforcing the neoliberal apparatus with which they operate. In this respect, there has been a shift towards catering to a populist discourse, in a way that has mirrored developments in the cultural and political landscape more broadly.

These parallel policies of liberalisation on both sides of the Atlantic have, however, met with markedly different results. Longstanding structural similarities and differences between the MPAA and the BBFC are key to understanding these divergent outcomes. While both institutions are non-governmental regulatory bodies, the MPAA operates on a voluntary basis whereas the BBFC has statutory powers dating back to the Video Recordings Act (1984). It could be argued that this distinction between these two institutions makes little difference in practice: mainstream US cinema chains will generally only exhibit films certified by the MPAA, and likewise local councils in the United Kingdom will generally uphold the classificatory decisions made by the BBFC, rarely opting to exercise their legal right to challenge the BBFC's decisions. However, in the United States this approach has facilitated a buoyant market in 'unrated' videos and DVDs, as the introduction of the NC-17 certificate has largely been viewed as an unmitigated failure. Mark Bernard argues that this is partly due to the historical practice of framing the rating system within a family discourse. In this respect, the US regulatory apparatus appears to situate marginal or disreputable films outside of mainstream culture. Although, historically, the UK scenario has differed in that there exists a longstanding public appetite for 18-rated films, nevertheless a similar discourse promoting family values has gained momentum over the last ten to twenty years. The growing influence of Mumsnet and similar pressure groups in the United Kingdom, following the Bailey Report of 2011, has been understood as an attempt 'to reconstitute "the public" around a supposedly neutral terrain of children and families' (Bragg 2012: 412). This family discourse is evident, for example, in the BBFC's 2019 announcement to launch a pilot regulatory scheme in collaboration with Netflix, in which BBFC Chief Executive David Austin explains that 'we want to work with the industry to ensure that families are able to make the right decisions for them when watching content online' (BBFC 2019).

The expanding market for 'unrated' films within the US circuit has, paradoxically, developed a more mainstream presence. As Bernard points out, the popularity of DVDs in the US from the early 2000s meant that films designated 'unrated' became increasingly ubiquitous within the DVD market. Their presence was primarily facilitated by the Blockbuster home video chain, a key retailer within the American DVD and home video market. The North American regulatory institution, built on the premise of protecting family values, has thus been unsuccessful in its attempts to incorporate a more liberal sensibility into its mainstream regulatory framework, particularly in relation to explicit arthouse, cult and low-budget fare. The BBFC, by contrast, has negotiated a more successful pathway for certificating borderline arthouse films with explicit content. Mattias Frey argues that this was because they have 'balanced stakeholder demands and provided a cinephile, liberal bias that has allowed for and incentivized the existence of extreme cinema' (Frey 2016: 95). In particular, the BBFC's commissioning of research into sexual violence and pornography has functioned as a means to deflect attention away from the relaxed restrictions on explicit arthouse cinema. While there are parallels between the US and UK contexts, then, the ways in which their neoliberal approach to film regulation has been operationalised are markedly different.

Running parallel with these liberalising gestures at the top end of the classification system, however, has been a simultaneous tightening of regulatory policies, particularly in relation to the consumption of marginalised films and other media online. In the United Kingdom, a succession of laws including the Criminal Justice and Immigration Act (2008), the Coroners and Justice Act (2009), the Criminal Justice and Courts Act (2015), the Investigatory Powers Act (2016) and the Digital Economy Act (2017) has shifted the focus of media regulation onto the surveillance and prosecution of the individual.[4] Whilst instances involving the prosecution of individuals for the possession of marginalised or cult media are rare, they are not unknown (Pett 2016: 390). Similar legal restrictions have also been introduced in the United States and are often framed within an anti-terrorist discourse, as evidenced by the Patriot Act (2001) and the Freedom Act (2015). Matthias Frey argues that the MPAA and BBFC are 'two of the strictest [regulatory bodies] in developed Anglophone countries, and among the most conservative in the world's richest nations' (Frey 2016: 95). I argue that the regulation of marginal and cult films in the United States and United Kingdom has, in this period, developed in two distinctive ways. On one hand, there has been a broad shift towards a more transparent and liberal approach to the classification of violent and sexually explicit material. This apparent relaxation of film regulation has been facilitated, in part, by the widespread availability of banned film titles online and through illegitimate distribution networks, which have rendered acts of censorship largely inef-fective.[5] On the other hand, however, there has been a gradual tightening of the surveillance and regulation of the private consumption of such marginalised media forms online. I suggest that these developments in Anglo-American neoliberal regulatory mechanisms reflect an increas-ingly divergent liberal and conservative schism in public attitudes more broadly. Polarised pol-itical attitudes, replicated and reinforced in the media and popular press, have been catered to and courted by the neoliberal MPAA and BBFC, who are keen to secure public backing to ensure their continued mandates to regulate media consumption. This apparent paradox raises questions as to how we can understand these contradictory and yet co-existent developments in film regulation in the US and UK, and the way in which they facilitate the cultification of violent and controversial titles.

Netflix, FlixFling and Amazon: Anglo-American cult cinema in the digital age

This chapter now turns to an examination of the ways in which the culture of neoliberal film regulation has, over the last ten years, affected the cultification of films that have been censored by either the BBFC or the MPAA. Whilst notorious cases of censorship have long been instru-mental in fuelling the cult reputation of controversial films, scholars have debated the extent to which this has continued to remain the case in the twenty-first century. Alexandra Kapka observes that 'it is simpler than ever to obtain a film uncut through streaming media (via various free to access virtual private networks) and peer-to-peer file-sharing, despite attempts at gov-ernment interference' (Kapka 2014). One repercussion of such technological change is that the availability of prohibited cult texts, once difficult to source, appears to produce a markedly different effect on their subcultural status. Films that were once distinguished by their inaccess-ibility and rarity are now relatively easy to track down. The accessibility of censored titles thus potentially undercuts the subcultural cachet that once developed around illegitimate products, leading several cult film scholars to suggest that we have entered an age of 'post-cult' in which the category only exists within an historical context (Sconce 2007: 48; Smith 2007: 215). For these reasons, Barbara Klinger has argued that developments in film distribution have led to a "mainstreaming" of cult phenomena (2010: 2). This "mainstreaming" of cult cinema is evident in the creation of a 'cult films' category on Netflix, which promotes a range of historical, off-beat and controversial films under the cult banner. In this specific distribution context, the cult film category has been fully legitimated and commodified by the streaming platform, and now functions more like a genre that appeals to a specific sector of their consumer base. While some cult connoisseurs have described these processes as a co-opting of cult cinema by the industry, Klinger interprets this development as being indicative of the ways in which technological change, in combination with other factors, can influence and shape the processes by which films sustain and extend their cult reputation. Similarly, Matt Hills contests the 'mainstreaming' dis-course of technological change, arguing that it 'fails to substantively consider the "generation" of subcultural capital; new media might support new modes of subcultural distinction rather than merely challenging established taste hierarchies' (Hills 2015: 202).

However, the extent to which these changes in patterns of film distribution intersect with cult films and the ways in which they are censored is complex and somewhat uneven. Ernest Mathijs and Jamie Sexton argue that 'the growth of niche markets does not erode the bound-aries between what constitutes mainstream and cult, but it does certainly alter the way that these concepts become mobilized in relation to cultural trends' (Mathijs and Sexton 2011: 65). As has already been discussed within the US context, mainstream and marginal or unclassified films have, in recent years, co-existed alongside each other in the retail marketplace. Additionally, whilst network culture might make censored films easier to locate, it also facilitates a proliferation of different versions of censored films, thus enabling the cult collector to engage in completist cultural practices. The mobilization of the cult category is often associated with (but not always synonymous with) the designation of films as disreputable or 'other' by mainstream tastemakers. Regulatory bodies such as the BBFC and MPAA therefore play an important role in their attempts to designate films as either acceptable or unacceptable to mainstream cinema audiences.

This discussion begins with the uncut release of Lars von Trier's *Antichrist* (2009) in both the United States and the United Kingdom. Whilst *Antichrist* was never submitted to the MPAA and circulated as an unrated film in the United States, in Britain the BBFC made the controversial decision to release it with an 18 certificate. Although the Board made a significant effort to pre-empt a critical response from the mainstream British media by releasing a statement to explain their decision (an unusual step to take in relation to a film that had *not* been censored in any way), they were still subject to harsh criticism. This came not just from the usual sources, such as a call for tighter censorship laws from Christopher Hart in the *Daily Mail*, but also in the form of an article by Bryan Appleyard in the *Sunday Times* which described the BBFC as being "unnecessary" in the digital age. The British media's response to the BBFC's decision not to cut *Antichrist* clearly bothered the regulators enough for them to publish two separate responses to the situation, firstly in their 2009 Annual Report, and secondly in a reflective assessment of the case on a BBFC webpage (BBFC 2011). In sum, both before and after the release of *Antichrist*, the BBFC attempted to negotiate popular opinion through a series of public statements. The case illustrates not only how keenly attuned the BBFC were to public opinion, but also how their sense of what would be unacceptable to British mainstream tastes was shaped by such negative responses from the press, as less than a month later they rejected the Japanese horror film *Grotesque*.

On August 19, 2009, the BBFC released a press statement announcing their decision to reject *Grotesque* (BBFC 2009). This meant it was not issued with a certificate and, under British law, it became illegal to distribute it either online or via conventional retail outlets; in effect, *Grotesque* was banned in the United Kingdom.[6] Reports in the British media on the banning of *Grotesque* invariably mention the criticism the BBFC had fielded over its decision to pass *Antichrist* uncut. In one BBC report it was noted that 'the BBFC drew criticism earlier this year for passing Danish horror *Antichrist* uncut, despite its graphic scenes of sex, violence and mutilation' (BBC 2009). However, unlike many previously banned titles, *Grotesque* was available to buy from mainstream online retailers, such as Amazon UK. The case of *Grotesque* is further complicated by the marketing materials used to promote it. The DVD cover of the unauthorized 4Digital Asia release, available on Amazon UK in 2009, used the tagline '*Saw* and *Hostel* were just appetisers'. This association was interesting in that neither of these two 'torture porn' films were subject to censorship in the United Kingdom, and both received relatively mainstream releases (and both are available on Netflix at the time of writing). The inclusion of a counterfeit BBFC 18 logo on the cover further reinforced their marketing strategy. On the UK-based *Snowblood Apple* forum, an online community set up by fans of Asian Extreme cinema, the news that the BBFC had rejected *Grotesque* only generated thirteen responses on a thread dedicated to it – this compared with over one hundred comments posted on a thread devoted to discussion of the cuts made by the BBFC to *Ichi the Killer*. However, while *Grotesque* did not develop any discernible cult status as a result of censorial activity on the part of the BBFC, Mike Dillon has argued that the marketing of the film nevertheless appealed to 'cult cinema registers by presenting Shiraishi as a Japanese auteur as well as an unrestrained button-pusher' (Dillon

2016: 29). In the case of *Grotesque*, then, the decision to reject the film in the United Kingdom did not have a significant effect on the availability or cultification of the title but did inform the way it continued to circulate.

Another contentious title that was the subject of regulatory action during this period was *A Serbian Film*. Released on a number of formats and as different and distinctive versions, the film established both a highly controversial reputation and a discernible online following in both the United States and the United Kingdom. In the United Kingdom, the BBFC made a series of cuts to *A Serbian Film* before its release in December 2010. The critical response and public discourse generated by this instance of censorship was reflected in the British media's reaction to the BBFC's decision. While the tabloid press generally registered a tone of disgust in relation to the content of the film, specialist film publications considered the decision specifically in the light of distribution cultures and the availability of the film online. *Total Film*, for example, asked readers whether they would look for an uncut copy online; the significance of this question was not whether or not the film was available, but whether they were interested in accessing it. The more cerebral *Sight and Sound* suggested that the BBFC's censorship *of A Serbian Film* would 'boost the film's notoriety but wreak havoc on its chances of making money in regions where it is cut: no transgressive film fiend wants to see a neutered film, and everyone knows where they can find intact copies'.[5] Both publications thus made explicit references to cultural practices around film piracy and cult connoisseurship. As with the video nasties and other censored horror films of previous eras, changes in the distribution and availability of marginalised or once-prohibited cultural products functioned to heighten their cult reputation.

In the United States, specialist interest groups developed in relation to a number of different versions of *A Serbian Film*, both online and via streaming services. A cut for category version of *A Serbian Film* was briefly released in US theatres in May 2011 with an NC-17 rating, followed by a slightly less heavily edited version distributed via Flixfling, a US-based streaming service, at around the same time. However, due to popular demand, Flixfling then made an uncut version of *A Serbian Film* available in 2012, prompting one online film reviewer to write 'at long last, an official UNCUT version of the controversial film will be released. It may be hard to believe given the subject matter, but *A Serbian Film* was one of my favorite horror films a couple of years ago' (Haffner 2012). In this case, the existence of different versions of the film within the US market clearly functioned to enhance specialist interest amongst audiences of illegitimate horror and arthouse cinema. What was significant in the case of *A Serbian Film* was that the liberalising activity of regulatory bodies such as the BBFC and MPAA was instrumental in generating the attention of specialist audiences interested in accessing a different, uncut version of the film.

Perhaps the most tangible instance of regulatory backtracking in response to public opinion was the BBFC's censorship of *The Human Centipede II (Full Sequence)* in 2011. In June 2011, the BBFC rejected the film on the grounds that it would 'risk potential harm within the terms of the VRA, and would be unacceptable to the public' (BBFC 2011). However, their decision prompted widespread attention and debate in the British press, including a statement from director Tom Six published in *Empire* magazine which questioned the BBFC's rationale. More notably, *Guardian* journalist David Cox weighed in against the censors, questioning the likelihood that watching such a film would 'turn us into kinky torturers' (Cox, 2011). The avalanche of ensuing discussion around the role of the BBFC that followed in the *Guardian* comment section revealed that the issue of film censorship continued to divide the British public. Once again, the BBFC found themselves on the wrong side of the liberal press and started oscillating in their approach to the film. After further negotiations with the director, a heavily censored version of the film was released in October of the same year, with an 18 certificate. The case of

The Human Centipede II (Full Sequence) vividly illustrates the role of the regulatory institution as one of an appeaser of popular opinion, flip-flopping between the apparently contradictory poles of liberalising and restrictive practices in order to maintain public approval. It is perhaps no small coincidence that there were no further instances of controversial horror or arthouse films being rejected by the British censors for another five years.

As Kapka and others have noted, the rapid development of the digital download and streaming market increasingly enabled cult film fans to entirely bypass UK and US censorship laws altogether during this period. Extreme horror titles such as *Grotesque* and *The Bunny Game* were both rejected in the United Kingdom by the BBFC, and yet both were easily available through online retailers. As with the situation in the US regarding "uncut" films being distributed via mainstream retail outlets, films like *Grotesque* have long been available via mainstream online retailers. Within this climate of readily accessible censored titles, in March 2015 the BBFC prohibited the UK VOD release of the American horror film *Hate Crime* (Bressack, 2012). *Hate Crime* was a horror film released in the United States in 2012, and made available to the American public via mainstream distribution platforms such as Amazon. Following the BBFC's controversial decision, film producer and distributor Phil Wheat commented:

> Now we all know that, thanks to the internet, censorship is a dying beast. Hell, if you're interested in seeing *Hate Crime* it's only a couple of clicks away; and no I'm not talking torrents. The film is readily available on VOD and DVD across the United States and if, like me, you know how to access them, you can stream the film legally from the likes of Amazon.
>
> (Wheat 2015)

Wheat thus highlighted the broad accessibility of the film to those interested in watching it, without even mentioning that, like *Grotesque* and other films banned in the UK, it is available to order as a DVD from Amazon UK. The BBFC's decision to reject *Hate Crime* was unusual and predicated on the film's representation of race. An empirical study of 201 British horror fans carried out not long after the ban revealed that the BBFC's decision functioned to generate interest in the title amongst cult horror fans, and that 'thanks to new forms of distribution, the BBFC cannot prevent those that want to see a film from doing so. Instead, a BBFC ban serves as a marketing tool: a badge of honour' (Kapka 2017: 92). As a regulatory body with statutory powers, the BBFC has exercised a more notable degree of hegemonic influence in this respect, with film distributors in other territories often picking up on the subcultural cachet produced by their censorial actions.

Conclusion: Shifting discourses in Anglo-American media regulation

The twenty-first century has witnessed the institutional mechanisms of US and UK film censorship operating within an increasingly polarised and complex cultural landscape. The regulation of the media industries continues to evolve at a brisk pace, and 2019 has seen some indication of a potential shift in emphasis away from surveillance of the individual and towards a renewed focus on the accountability of larger media corporations. In the United Kingdom, for example, the Digital Economy Act (2017) has empowered the BBFC to police and block websites that are non-compliant with new regulations on pornographic content. Similarly, the Online Harms White Paper (2019) advocates the necessity of empowering an independent online regulator with a range of new enforcement sanctions; these new powers would potentially hold media companies accountable in relation to the 'need to fulfil their duty of care, particularly to counter illegal content and activity' (DCMS 2019). The extent to which these proposals become legally enforced is yet to be established. However, the provisional nature of the white paper has not deterred the UK Culture Secretary, Jeremy Wright, from proclaiming that 'the era of self-regulation for online companies is over' (BBC 2019), and the speaker of the US House of Representatives, Nancy Pelosi, has been quick to echo these sentiments (Ruiz-Grossman 2019). It is possible, then, that the neoliberal Anglo-American regulatory practices and mechanisms discussed in this chapter might be superseded by a new era of stricter media regulation and control. Should this transpire, then it will no doubt be mirrored by a corresponding nonconformist movement of anti-censorship resistance.

The period leading up to this moment has been characterised by the apparently contradictory poles of liberalising and restrictive Anglo-American regulatory practices. This chapter has argued that the regulation of transgressive cult films in the United States and United Kingdom in the early twenty-first century has, in developing both liberalising and restrictive policies, revealed the inherently contradictory and incoherent nature of neoliberal Anglo-American culture. The marketisation of the regulatory system, and the framing of media audiences as 'consumers', has facilitated an inconsistent classification system that has flip-flopped in its approach to the regulation of films intended for adult audiences. The extent to which regulatory activity on the part of the MPAA and BBFC has contributed to the cultification of censored titles during this period is a contentious one. While Smith and others argue that the widespread availability of marginalised films online diminishes their cult status, Hills suggests they are reconfigured through this process and acquire new forms of subcultural capital. The brief discussion offered here offers a slightly different perspective. Rather than diminishing or reconfiguring their cult status, the uneven outcome of censorial activity on the circulation and cult status of the films considered here instead reflects the nebulous and unpredictable character of cult cinema itself within this specific Anglo-American taste culture.

Notes

1 Whilst this is a fairly broad characterisation of cult audiences for transgressive films of this type, a snapshot illustration of this demographic is provided by Martin Smith (2018) in his audience study of *A Serbian Film*, which reveals a heavily skewed male-to-female ratio, and more responses from the United States and the United Kingdom than elsewhere. The recognition of these audiences as being primarily white is drawn from personal observation at UK screenings. The purpose of identifying the predominant characteristics of audiences for these films is simply to make them visible; this acknowledgment is not intended to diminish the significance of minority audiences for these films who do not fall into the category of white, Anglo-American males.
2 Although the Home Office is involved in the appointment of key personnel at the BBFC, as an institution it positions itself as being largely independent of government interference – though this is a contested view (see, for example, Petley [2011] on Jack Straw and the R18.) There are also many instances, such as those documented by Kate Egan (2015) and Sian Barber (2016), in which local authorities override the decisions made by the BBFC; however, these are predominantly historical and there are no recent examples of this practice.
3 For a full account of this protracted process, see Petley (2011, 127–157)
4 The Digital Economy Act (2017) introduced measures to regulate online pornography that require all commercial porn websites to introduce mandatory age verification controls; the introduction of these new regulations have raised concerns around privacy and data protection. The law also introduced new measures to police websites, which might suggest a shift towards the regulation of media companies rather than individuals.
5 To the extent that the BBFC themselves have noted that trying to main regulation in this context is 'like trying to shut the stable door when the horse has bolted' (BBFC 2006: 3).
6 Between August 2009 and January 2010 there was a brief period during which the Video Recordings Act (VRA) was not enforceable due to the discovery of a legal loophole; this situation was rectified by

the Digital Economy Act (2010). The BBFC states in their annual report of 2009 that during this period the majority of film distribution companies continued, on a voluntary basis, to submit works to the BBFC for classification prior to their release in the United Kingdom.

References

Appleyard, Bryan. 2009. 'Should Lars von Trier's *Antichrist* Be Banned? *The Sunday Times*, July 12, 2009.

Barber, Sian. 2016. 'Exploiting Local Controversy: Regional British Censorship of *Last Tango in Paris* (1972). *Historical Journal of Film, Television and Radio* 36 (4): 587–603, doi: 10.1080/01439685.2015.1119360.

Bernard, Mark. 2014. *Selling the Splat Pack: The DVD Revolution and the American Horror Film.* Edinburgh: Edinburgh University Press.

Biltereyst, Daniel, and Roel Vande Winkel (eds). 2013. *Silencing Cinema: Film Censorship around the World.* Basingstoke: Palgrave Macmillan.

Bragg, Sara. 2012. 'Dockside Tarts and Modesty Boards: A Review of Recent Policy on Sexualisation.' *Children and Society* 26: 406–414.

BBC. 2009. Censors Reject Sadistic Horror. London: BBC.

BBC. 2019. Websites To Be Fined over 'Online Harms' under New Proposals. London: BBC. Accessed on April 15, 2019. www.bbc.co.uk/news/technology-47826946

BBFC. 2006. Annual Report 2005. London: BBFC. Accessed on July 18, 2016. www.bbfc.co.uk/downloads/pub/BBFC%20Annual%20Reports/BBFC_AnnualReport_2005.pdf.

BBFC. 2009. 'BBFC rejects sexually violent Japanese horror DVD', found online at: www.bbfc.co.uk/about-bbfc/media-centre/bbfc-rejects-sexually-violent-japanese-horror-dvd. Accessed on 1 August 2013.

BBFC. 2010. 'Case Study: Antichrist' found online: www.sbbfc.co.uk/CaseStudies/Antichrist [accessed 13 June 13 2011]. Internet archive address created using Wayback Machine: http://web.archive.org/web/20121106013133/http://www.sbbfc.co.uk/CaseStudies/Antichrist

BBFC. 2011, 'BBFC reject The Human Centipede II (Full Sequence),' [accessed February 12, 2017]. www.bbfc.co.uk/about-bbfc/media-centre/bbfc-rejects-human-centipede-ii-full-sequence

BBFC. 2012. *Sexual and Sadistic Violence: Response of the BBFC to Public Attitudes and Concerns*, London: BBFC. [accessed May 21st 2017] www.bbfc.co.uk/sites/default/files/attachments/BBFC%20sexual%20and%20sadistic%20violence%20policy%20response%20December%202012.pdf

BBFC. 2019. 'BBFC and Netflix Announce New Age Ratings Partnership as Parents Demand Greater Consistency Across Video on Demand and Online Games Platforms'. London, BBFC. Accessed on April 15, 2019. www.bbfc.co.uk/about-bbfc/media-centre/bbfc-and-netflix-announce-new-age-ratings-partnership-parents-demand-greater

Cox, David, 2011. 'The Human Centipede II: No Sexual Sadism Please, We're British.' Accessed on February 12, 2017. www.theguardian.com/film/filmblog/2011/jun/07/human-centipede-sequel-ban-sexual-sadism.

Crisp, Virginia. 2014. 'To Name a Thief: Constructing the Deviant Pirate.' Accessed on March 30, 2017. https://curve.coventry.ac.uk/open/file/c2df63fc-409e-4767-be8c-7fe3d3ed1eb8/1/To%20name%20a%20thief.pdf.

Crisp, Virginia. 2015. *Film Distribution in the Digital Age: Pirates and Professionals.* London: Palgrave Macmillan.

DCMS. 2019. 'Online Harms White Paper – Executive Summary'. Accessed on April 18th, 2019. www.gov.uk/government/consultations/online-harms-white-paper/online-harms-white-paper-executive-summary--2.

Dillon, Mike. 2016. 'Butchered in Translation: A Transnational "Grotesuqe."' *Transnational Horror Cinema: Bodies of Excess and the Global Grotesque.* Siddique, Sophia, and Raphael Raphael (eds). London: Palgrave Macmillan.

Egan, Kate. 2015. '*Monty's Python's Life of Brian*, British Local Censorship and the "Pythonesque"'. *Antenna*. Accessed on July 27, 2016. http://blog.commarts.wisc.edu/2015/05/07/monty-pythons-life-of-brian-british-local-censorship-and-the-pythonesque/.

Frey, Mattias. 2016. *Extreme Cinema: The Transgressive Rhetoric of Today's Art Film Culture.* New Brunswick, NJ: Rutgers University Press.

Haffner, Michael. 2012. 'The US Will Finally Be Getting 'A Serbian Film' Completely Uncut and on DVD.' Accessed July 28, 2016. www.destroythebrain.com/movies/home-invasion/the-us-will-finally-be-getting-a-serbian-film-completely-uncut-on-dvd

Hart, Christopher. 2009. 'What Does It Take for a Film to Get Banned These Days?', *The Daily Mail*, July 20, 2009.

Hills, Matt. 2015. 'Cult Cinema and the 'Mainstreaming' Discourse of Technological Change: Revisiting Subcultural Capital in Liquid Modernity.' *New Review of Film and Television*, 13 (1): 100–121.

Kapka, Alexandra. 2014. 'Understanding *A Serbian Film*: The Effects of Censorship and File-Sharing on Critical Reception and Perceptions of Serbian National Identity in the UK.' *Frames Cinema Journal*. Accessed July 27, 2016. http://framescinemajournal.com/article/understanding-a-serbian-film-the-effects-of-censorship-and-file-sharing-on-critical-reception-and-perceptions-of-serbian-national-identity-in-the-uk/.

Kapka, Alexandra. 2017. "'Cuts Are Not a Viable Option': The British Board of Film Classification, *Hate Crime*, and Censorship for Adults in the Digital Age.' *Journal of British Cinema and Television*. 14 (1): 77–97.

Kimber, Shaun. 2014. 'Transgressive Edge Play and *Srpski Film/A Serbian Film*'. *Horror Studies*. (5) 1: 107–125.

Klinger, Barbara. 2010. 'Becoming Cult: *The Big Lebowski*, Replay Culture and Male Fans.' *Screen*. 51 (1): 1–20.

Lewis, Jon. 2000. *Hollywood v. Hardcore: How the Struggle over Censorship Created the Modern Film Industry*. New York: New York State University Press.

Lewis, Jon. 2007. "'If You Can't Protect What You Own, You Don't Own Anything'": Piracy, Privacy, and Public Relations in 21st Century Hollywood.' *Cinema Journal*, 46:2, 145–150.

Lobato, Ramon. 2012. *Shadow Economies of Cinema: Mapping Informal Film Distribution*. London: Palgrave Macmillan/BFI.

Mathijs, Ernest, and Jamie Sexton. 2011 *Cult Cinema: An Introduction*. Chichester: Wiley-Blackwell.

MPAA/Nielsen. 2015. *Parents Ratings Advisory Study – 2015*. Assessed May 21, 2017. www.mpaa.org/wp-content/uploads/2015/11/Parents-Rating-Advisory-Study-2015.pdf.

Newman, David. 2013. 'British Colonial Censorship Regimes: Hong Kong, Straits Settlements, and Shanghai International Settlement, 1916–1941.' In Biltereyst, Daniel, and Roel Vande Winkel (eds). *Silencing Cinema: Film Censorship around the World*. Basingstoke: Palgrave Macmillan, 167–190.

Noto la Diego, Guido. 2015. 'On Porn Censorship and Liberal Ethics in the UK: Brief Notes of the Audio-Visual Media Services Regulations 2014.' Accessed on July 26, 2016. http://papers.ssrn.com/sol3/Papers.cfm?abstract_id=2550269

Peredo-Castro, Francisco. 2013. 'Inquisition Shadows: Politics, Religion, Diplomacy and Ideology in Mexican Film Censorship'. In Biltereyst, Daniel, and Roel Vande Winkel (eds). *Silencing Cinema: Film Censorship around the World*. Basingstoke: Palgrave Macmillan, 63–78.

Petley, Julian. 2011. *Film and Video Censorship in Modern Britain*. Edinburgh: Edinburgh University Press.

Pett, Emma. 2015. 'A New Media Landscape? The BBFC, Extreme Cinema as Cult and Technological Change.' *New Review of Film and Television*, 13 (1): 83–99.

Pett, Emma. 2016. 'Blood, Guts and Bambi Eyes: *Urotsukidoji* and the Transcultural Reception and Regulation of Anime,' *British Journal of Cinema and Television*, 13: 3, pp. 390–408.

Quinn, Siobhan. 2006. 'Censorship, Classification and Economic Control: Systems of regulating film in Canada.' Accessed on 27 July 2016.

Ruiz-Grossman, Sarah. 2019. Nancy Pelosi Says Tech's 'Era of Self-Regulation' Should 'Probably' Be Over. *Huffington Post*. Accessed on April 15, 2019. www.huffingtonpost.co.uk/entry/nancy-pelosi-big-tech-regulation_n_5cb0d027e4b0ffefe3b01cc0.

Sandler, Kevin S. 2001. 'The Naked Truth: *Showgirls* and the Fate of the X/NC-17 Rating.' *Cinema Journal*, 40:3, 69–93.

Sconce, Jeffrey. 2008. 'Cult Cinema: A Critical Symposium – Jeffrey Sconce.' *Cineaste* XXXIV (1): 48–49.

Smith, Justin. 2010. *Withnail and Us: Cult Films and Film Cults in British Cinema*. London: I.B. Tauris.

Smith, Martin. 2018. 'Serb Your Enthusiasm: Anti-Fandom and *A Serbian Film*. *Participations: Journal of Audience and Reception Studies*, 15:2, 115–134.

Wheat, Phil. 2015. 'James Cullen Bressack's Hate Crime banned by the BBFC.' Accessed on July 27, 2016. www.nerdly.co.uk/2015/03/02/james-cullen-bressacks-hate-crime-banned-by-the-bbfc/.

20

CULT CINEMA AND CAMP

Julia Mendenhall

In his 1909 slang dictionary, *Passing English of the Victorian Era. A Dictionary of Heterodox English Slang and Phrase,* James Redding Ware defines the noun "camp" as those various human "actions and gestures of exaggerated emphasis" (Cleto 1999:10). The *Oxford English Dictionary* (*OED*) cites more of Ware's camp definition under its definition of camp as an adjective: "Probably from the French. Used chiefly by persons of exceptional want of character. 'How very camp he is'" (J.R. Ware quoted in the *OED* 1993: 9). From this modest beginning, the obscure slang word "camp" has been defined and redefined over its long history, and it has lately become a key concept of cultural theory, eventually being referenced in Judith Butler's renowned gender theorizing through camp's association with drag. Not surprisingly, camp is also an integral component of cult films, and some well-loved cult film favorites contain campy character behaviors and camp imagery, including *King Kong* (1933), John Waters' *Pink Flamingos* (1972), *The Rocky Horror Picture Show* (1975), *The Big Lebowski* (1998), and *Black Swan* (2010). Cult movie fans often have a taste for camp, and they are the tastemakers who make camp films into cult favorites. Although campy cult films will likely never be seen as "high art," they do provide meaning and self-determination to the specialized camp cult film viewer.

Despite prominent intellectual Susan Sontag referring to camp as "one of the hardest things to talk about," her 1964 essay "Notes on 'Camp'" remains the definitive explanation of this difficult concept. As a nod to Oscar Wilde's campy epigrams, Sontag writes her "notes" in the form of 58 numbered aphorisms. According to Sontag, camp can be defined in two major ways; one definition is a "quality discoverable in objects and the behavior of persons" and the other is a kind of taste or sensibility that a viewer can cultivate (Sontag 1964: 277). In the former sense of camp, Sontag points out that "there are 'campy' movies, clothes, furniture, popular songs, novels, people, buildings" – they qualify as camp because they are exaggerated, artificial, garish, comical, flirtatious, and stylized (277). For example, a campy movie is *Whatever Happened to Baby Jane* (LaBruce)*;* campy clothes could be outrageous feathered or sequined gowns worn by Cher and Lady Gaga; campy furniture would be Tiffany Lamps (Sontag); a campy popular song might be Mae West singing "Love Will Keep Us Together" in [the film] *Sextet* (LaBruce); a campy novel is *Valley of the Dolls* (LaBruce)*;* campy persons are Liberace or Adam Lambert (LaBruce); and campy buildings would be those of the architect Antoni Gaudí (Sontag). As Mark Booth states "Troglodytes sometimes confuse camp with homosexual" (1983: 70). However, with these examples, we see that camp is not synonymous with "homosexual," although it may have started as such and camp is often seen as a "gay white male practice" even today. (Muñoz 1999: 130). The campy objects above exemplify the *Oxford English Dictionary*'s definition of camp, as an adjective, as that which is "ostentatious, exaggerated, affected, theatrical" (*OED* 1993:).

In terms of film, and according to Sontag, a camp film would usually be a comedy, not a drama. As Sontag pronounces in aphorism 44: "Camp proposes a comic vision of the world. But not a bitter or polemical comedy" (288). She goes on to argue, in a much-cited passage, that "The whole point of Camp is to dethrone the serious. Camp is playful, anti-serious. More precisely, Camp involves a new, more complex relation to 'the serious.' One can be serious about the frivolous, frivolous about the serious" (288). The musical *The Rocky Horror Picture Show* is the quintessential comedic camp cult film. Firstly, musicals themselves are usually camp because they are artificial and "over-the-top." In other words, when the characters break into song, the realism is broken, thus calling attention to the artificial, constructed nature of the film, which results in a camp moment. Additionally, when Sontag asserts that "46. The connoisseur of Camp has found more ingenious pleasures. Not in Latin poetry and rare wines and velvet jackets, but in the coarsest, commonest pleasures, in the art of the masses" (289). *The Rocky Horror Picture Show* comes immediately to mind as one of those "ingenious pleasures" that intends itself to be, and has become, "the art of the masses." Over forty years after its first release, crowds of fans still show up for midnight screenings of the classic horror film spoof, many dressed as the characters (see Midnight Movie in this volume). *The Rocky Horror Picture Show* tells the story of Dr. Frank-n-Furter (Tim Curry) the bisexual, "sweet transvestite" from Transsexual, Transylvania. He definitely "camps it up" – he uses exaggerated movements with his flaring nostrils, garish lipstick, mascara, and eye shadow, along with high heels, black hose, garter belt, and bikini bottom topped off with a black sequined bustier, long black gloves, and big white pearl necklace. Furthermore, Dr. Frank-n-Furter's "affected flamboyance in speech and mannerisms" lend support to the notion that the word camp came from the French, *se camper*, meaning "to pose or to flaunt." To camp it up, or to camp, seems almost synonymous with "to flaunt," especially if "to flaunt" means, as the *OED* states, "to obtrude oneself boastfully, impudently, or defiantly on public view" or "to be extravagantly gaudy or glaringly conspicuous in appearance" (*OED* 1993: 602). In particular, Dr. Frank-n-Furter "flaunts" or "camps it up" as a man "in drag" – as a man who wears women's clothes throughout the film – and subsequently "to camp" comes to be closely related with "to do drag," as I will discuss below with Judith Butler's notion of drag as gender parody.

By contrast, there can also be camp elements in otherwise serious, dramatic films; for example, Marlene Dietrich's films made with Josef von Sternberg are actually serious dramatic romances that cleverly incorporate camp scenes. In these films, Dietrich usually plays a nightclub singer who flaunts her femininity and her sexual agency in a glamorous yet comedic way while dressed in campy gowns complete with feathers and sequins. At the same time, she moves with sexual suggestiveness. For instance, in a famous scene in the film *Morocco* (1930), her nightclub performer character Amy Jolly dons a black tuxedo, white tuxedo shirt, vest, bowtie, pocket square, and black top hat, worn askew. As she sings, smokes, and roams through the nightclub's patrons, she hikes up her leg onto a chair, and then her pants' leg in a manly way. She's effectively doing drag here, but she is not a "drag queen" – a man who dresses as a woman – here she is what has come to be called a "drag king" – a woman dressed as a man. Continuing her drag king act, Amy Jolly suddenly stoops to kiss a woman in a jolly, playful moment of lesbian camp display, in this otherwise serious heterosexual romantic drama. *Morocco* is a serious dramatic film with campy moments, like the recent film *Black Swan* (2010), which I will discuss further below.

In Sontag's second sense of camp, she explains that camp is a kind of taste that one may possess, a kind of individual preference that Sontag refers to as a "camp taste." Sontag implies that, if a film is deemed to be "bad" by mainstream critics, it may be redeemed as "good" camp by camp connoisseurs who possess a camp taste. (282). In the following, Sontag attempts to explain the difference between a bad film (to her mind), the film *On the Beach*, and "bad movies" which she redeems as camp, with her camp taste, such as *The Prodigal* (1955) and *Samson and Delilah* (1949):

> [Aphorism] 29. The reason a movie like *On The Beach* ... [is] bad to the point of being laughable, but not bad to the point of being enjoyable [i.e. camp], is that they are too dogged and pretentious. They lack fantasy. There is Camp in such bad movies as *The Prodigal* and *Samson and Delilah* ... because, in their relative unpretentiousness and vulgarity, they are more extreme and irresponsible in their fantasy – and therefore touching and quite enjoyable.
>
> (285)

In Sontag's opinion, *On the Beach* is just a bad film; it is not "touching" and not "enjoyable," and therefore it cannot be redeemed, via her camp taste, as a camp film. I would also note that *On the Beach* is a serious drama, not a comedy, and it contains no campy character behaviors or camp iconography. By contrast, *The Prodigal* and *Samson and Delilah* contain camp elements and indeed are "touching" and "enjoyable" and are redeemed by Sontag, the one with a camp taste, as camp. While *On the Beach* contains no camp elements, *Samson and Delilah* embodies camp elements galore, including the male Philistines' garish costumes and effeminate, artificial accents; the "exaggerated he-man-ness of" hypermasculine Victor Mature's Samson (a camp analogue to hyperfeminine Mae West), and the over-the-top Feather Dance, at the wedding feast of Samson and Semadar, which is performed by two effete men in short skirts, who frolic and fake fight, one with a sword and the other with a large red feather that is reminiscent of a feather boa (Sontag 1964: 279).

Although a recent midnight cult film, Tommy Wiseau's *The Room* (2003), has been called camp, one could argue, using Sontag's criteria, that it is not camp. It is, like *On the Beach*, a serious, realist film, but it is not "enjoyable" and not "touching" – it is quite painful to watch because its production values are so low. Furthermore, the film contains no camp character behaviors, costumes, or dialogue – though it has one self-ironizing line, when someone asks, "how many people come in and out of here?" referring to the room and its heavy traffic of weird characters showing up unexpectedly. Importantly, Sontag states that "34. Camp doesn't argue that the good is bad, or the bad is good" (286). Although the *Historical Dictionary of American Slang* includes a definition of camp as: "4c. something that is so affected, outdated, contrived, tasteless, etc. as to be amusing," *The Room* is certainly tasteless, but it is not "amusing," and it is therefore not camp (Lighter 1994: 351). Paul Roen asserts that "by definition a camp film must contain camp elements" (1994: 10). Following Sontag and Roen, I argue that a film cannot be redeemed as camp without camp elements. In short, just because a film is bad does not automatically qualify it as camp – it is still bad, which is a separate category distinct from camp.

Sontag also has two other categories of camp, naïve camp and deliberate camp. In deliberate camp, films are consciously, intentionally made in the camp style – a "camp which knows itself to be camp" (1964: 280). Sontag's examples of deliberate camp include *Trouble in Paradise* (1932), *The Maltese Falcon* (1941), along with the film performances of Mae West and Edward Everett Horton. More contemporary examples would include John Waters' films *Pink Flamingos* (1972) and *Female Trouble* (1974), and the Coen Brothers' *Hail Caesar!* (2016). In naïve camp, films are presented "straight" and without intentional camp ingredients. Sontag asserts that

23. In naïve, or pure, Camp, the essential element is seriousness, a seriousness that fails. Of course, not all seriousness that fails can be redeemed as Camp. Only that which has the proper mixture of the exaggerated, the fantastic, the passionate, and the naïve.

(283)

Examples, for Sontag, of naïve camp include, *42nd Street* (1933), *The Gold Diggers of 1933* (1933), and Marlene Dietrich's films with Josef von Sternberg, especially *The Devil is a Woman* (1935). Acclaimed pop intellectual Andrew Ross notes that "Sontag…reserve[s] her purist praise for the category of *naïve* camp, presumably because…it is the critic and not the producer who takes full cultural credit for discerning the camp 'value' of a text" (1989: 145). Extending Sontag's theorization of camp, one can suggest that camp is "a quality discoverable" by those with a "camp vision," or camp taste. However, as Sontag sums up: "not everything can be seen as Camp. It's not *all* in the eye of the beholder" (277).

One of the main critiques of Sontag's article is that she changed camp, a "basically homosexual mode of self-performance into a de-gayified taste" (DA Miller quoted in Cleto 1999: 10). But as we have seen above, many different kinds of objects and human performances may qualify as camp. When she implies that anyone can perform camp, that anyone can camp it up, and that anyone can cultivate a "camp taste" or "camp vision," Sontag merely opens the definition of camp up to all genders and sexual varieties. Her expanded definition of camp is in contrast to the ways in which the *Historical Dictionary of American Slang* defines camp as something that only homosexual men do. For example, its definition of camp as a noun comes in three senses. A camp can be: "2a. a homosexual man who behaves in an exaggeratedly effeminate manner" (1994: 351). Or a camp can be "3. a gathering place for homosexual men…Camp, a meeting place of male sexual perverts where they dress as females" (1994: 351). Or, lastly, camp is "4a. affected flamboyance in speech or mannerisms displayed by a homosexual man; ironic or exaggerated verbal posturing." Perhaps camp as "a quality discoverable in objects and in persons" and as a taste, a vision, originated in the white male homosexual underworld in the early twentieth century, but by the late twentieth century, it had been borrowed, for better or worse, by straight mass culture.

Additionally, Sontag has been lambasted by subsequent critics when she asserts that "it goes without saying that the camp sensibility is disengaged, depoliticized – or at least apolitical" (1964: 277). However, and very importantly, at the end of her "jottings," she contradicts herself, as she claims: "52. Camp is a solvent of morality. It neutralizes moral indignation, sponsors playfulness" (1964: 290). Thus, according to Sontag, camp can be political and it condemns conventional morality via its playful vulgarity. Bruce LaBruce elaborates camp's political cultural work:

The camp sensibility [has] the qualities of sophistication and secret signification that were developed out of necessity by the underground or outsider gay world, which originally created camp as a kind of gay signifying practice not unrelated to black signifying. … It was developed as a secret language in order to identify oneself to likeminded or similarly closeted homosexuals, a shorthand of arcane and coded, almost kabbalistic references and practices developed in order to operate safely apart and without fear of detection from a conservative and conventional world that could be aggressively hostile towards homosexuals, particularly effeminate males and masculine females.

(2013)

But eventually straight mass culture could decode these references and sought to use the power of camp for more than just representations of effeminate males and masculine females. A camp film harnesses the political, subversive power of camp for a project of self-affirmation and self-determination. As Ann Pellegrini reminds us, "the political meaning of camp depends not on some ontology of camp, what it inherently is, but on *who* is using it, *how* it is done, and *where* its effects are concentrated" (2007: 170).

Many "camp cult films" are indeed politically subversive. These films often use their camp characters and iconography tacitly or overtly to endorse gender and sexual minorities and to oppose compulsory heterosexuality. For example, *The Rocky Horror Picture Show* uses its campy representation of Dr. Frank-n-furter's bisexuality comically, in order to satirize and critique the sexual repression of its heterosexual characters, Brad Majors (Barry Bostwick) and Janet Weiss (Susan Sarandon). The good doctor urges Brad and Janet to explore new sexual pleasures and identities with the line of dialogue: "don't dream it, be it."

After Sontag, other critics tended to expand the definition of camp. For instance, in 1983, Mark Booth suggests that "To be camp is to present oneself as being committed to the marginal with a commitment greater than the marginal merits" (69). Other subsequent commentators on camp focus in on camp as drag, or as Sontag points out that "11. Camp is the triumph of the epicene style." Here epicene refers to "having characteristics typical of the other sex," and comes to be, for Sontag, synonymous with drag, or cross-dressing, especially when she states that "10. To perceive Camp in objects and persons is to understand Being-as-Playing-a-Role" (1964: 280). Esther Newton writes about female impersonators – drag queens – and gender theorist Judith Butler draws on Newton to formulate her theory on gender parody. For Butler, gender is akin to a drag performance, a parodic repetition of gender identity that works to constitute gender identity and that calls attention to gender (and sexuality) as a construct, naturalized through repetition. But as Butler asks famously: what if the gender parody fails to repeat and there is a break in the gender identity? If camp is "Being-as-Playing-a-Role," or doing gender parody (drag), what if one, through agency and self-determination, chooses to play a new role? What if metamorphosis is possible? This change in role via campy gender parody is central to the meaning of the recent film, *Black Swan*.

Black Swan tells the story of Nina Sayers (Natalie Portman), an ambitious soloist in a New York City ballet company who is trying out for the prestigious dual role of the White Swan and the Black Swan in the classical ballet *Swan Lake*. Nina gets the role, and the artistic director Thomas Leroy (Vincent Cassel) tells her to "lose yourself" in the role. He sees her as the perfect White Swan – childlike, virginal, pure, frigid – but she needs to transform herself into the Black Swan – the figure of sexual freedom, dominance, and agency. And that is what she does; she loses her "self," her identity, as the White Swan, and becomes the sexually freer Black Swan. That is the overt story line. I argue that Nina concomitantly, through her metamorphosis, becomes a more independent, more mature adult, by means of a lesbian "wet dream" that she has after taking the drug ecstasy. In sum, the film works to endorse lesbian sexuality as a means to sexual awakening and agency and works to effect a critique of heterosexuality. Although Freud famously saw lesbianism and homosexuality as the "arrested development" of the sexual maturation process, here Nina's dream of lesbian sexuality in fact propels her maturation process and agency.

Interestingly, Sontag categorizes the ballet *Swan Lake* as camp, as she notes that "33. opera and ballet are experienced as such rich treasures of Camp, for neither of these forms can easily do justice to the complexity of human nature" (1964: 286). But is this film camp? At least one critic, Stuart Klawans of *The Nation* opines rhapsodically: "How they would have reveled in it, the camp followers of my '60s youth, delighting to see a movie claw its way up the gilded peaks of sublimity, only to display, for all eyes, the idiot underpants of bathos!" Clearly, Klawans thinks the whole film is camp and he subsequently gives it a bad review (2010). I conclude that *Black Swan* is a serious psychological thriller with some key camp moments. *Black Swan* is also an example of Sontag's naïve, unintentional camp, as its "[camp] humor derives from a certain ironic discrepancy between [laughable] results and [serious] intentions" that occur at key moments of transformation in the film (1994: 9). It is a good film and a camp cult film. As Sontag concludes about camp

> 24. When something is just bad (rather than Camp), it's often because it is too medi-ocre in its ambition. The artist hasn't attempted to do anything really outlandish. ('It's too much,' 'It's too fantastic,' 'It's not to be believed, are standard phrases of Camp enthusiasm).
>
> (283)

Black Swan is certainly ambitious and fantastic.

The film *Black Swan* also deftly illustrates Butler's idea that

> the failure of naturalized heterosexuality … can become an occasion for a subversive and proliferating parody of gender norms in which the very claim to originality and to the real is shown to be the effect of a certain kind of naturalized gender mime.
>
> ("Imitation and Gender Insubordination" [1991: 23])

The film must initially – and realistically – establish and naturalize Nina's appearance and behaviors as "heterosexual" in order to demonstrate Nina's later failure to reinstitute her "het-erosexuality." The film is not camp until the end; it contains no overt camp elements until Nina's transformation into the Black Swan at the end of the film. Initially, however, we see Nina as a feminine woman, but with her pulled back hair, her thinness, and her small breasts, she projects the image of the "androgyne" – one who comprises both male and female characteristics and features. As Sontag suggests:

> 9. The androgyne is certainly one of the great images of Camp sensibility. Examples: the swooning, slim, sinuous figures of pre-Raphaelite painting … the thin, flowing, sexless bodies in Art Nouveau prints and posters … [and] the haunting androgynous vacancy behind the perfect beauty of Great Garbo.
>
> (1964: 279)

Nina is "slim" and "sinuous" and "sexless" as she seems to be frozen in time at age eleven. She still lives with her suffocating, overprotective mother, her room filled with the furniture, sheets, and stuffed animals of a pre-pubescent. To further establish Nina as the White Swan of virginal heterosexuality, she wears a white scarf around her long, swanlike neck, and wears mostly white clothes throughout these initial scenes.

Out of nowhere, a new ballerina joins the company, as Lily (Mila Kunis) arrives from hedon-istic San Francisco. Lily, dressed in black, becomes Nina's alternate and on the subtextual level, she acts also as Nina's sexual liberator, as a Black Swan figure. Against her mother's orders, Nina runs out for a night on the town with the adventurous Lily. Lily offers Nina ecstasy, which Nina refuses at first; but then she consciously changes her mind, seemingly wanting to be like Lily, to experience as Lily does. They drink, go to bars, and Nina runs out on a male partner before intercourse commences. In what later turns out to be a dream sequence, Nina brings Lily home, bars her bedroom door against her mother, and approaches Lily to kiss her hungrily. The lesbian sex scene is filmed realistically, not campily. While Lily performs cunnilingus on Nina,

Nina sees a black swan tattoo on Lily's back. Then Lily raises her head and looks at Nina, and Nina's own face appears, flashing over Lily's to signify that this is both a fantasy, and a fantasy of transformation of sexual self, via the sexual agency of the dream. The film also makes it clear that her sexual maturation and liberation occur via this lesbian dream, because Nina refuses to have sex with Thomas.

After this dream, we see Nina continue to evolve as the black swan, the mature sexual being. She no longer wears the white scarf, she puts on Lily's black clothes, and she wears gray dance gear. The camp moments occur when Nina is seen to be (literally) transforming into the black swan – when we hear cracking sounds as the black swan legs appear and when the black feathers sprout on her scapula. It is laughably camp when Nina's toes become glued together like webbed feet. The highest camp moment happens when Nina transforms fully into the black swan on the stage during the premiere of the ballet. While performing a pirouette, Nina's body transforms from bare skin to being covered with jet black swan feathers; as she whirls, more and more feathers appear. It is an artificial, stylized moment, and it is the failed serious-ness of naïve camp that elicits laughter and enjoyment. Nina has outrageously transformed into the Black Swan role at last. If, as Sontag informs us, "25. The hallmark of Camp is the spirit of extravagance. Camp is a woman walking around in a dress made of three million feathers" (1964: 283), then *Black Swan* is definitely camp here. She imagines her transformation, but we really see it, and it is preposterous, over-the-top, artificial, and unreal. As Butler states "[het-erosexuality] requires to be instituted again and again," and thus "runs the risk of becoming de-instituted at every interval" (24). In *Black Swan*, Nina fails to reinstitute her former "het-erosexuality," she instead consciously institutes her own maturation and lesbian sexual agency. When she is lying on a mattress bleeding from her own self-inflicted wound, Nina has killed off her white swan self and births her new black swan self. And at the very end of the film, we and Nina can hear the audience cheering "Nina! Nina! Nina!" and with this camp fantasy, the film endorses Nina's sexual maturation, via lesbian dream, and liberated sexual agency. If, as Judith Butler theorizes: "Only from a self-consciously denaturalized position can we see how the appearance of naturalness is itself constituted" then camp cult films offer to their viewers that "self-consciously denaturalized position" from which to prise open the naturalized sexual constructs of "heterosexuality" and "homosexuality" (Butler 1999: 140).

References

Booth, Mark. 1983. "*Campe-Toi!* On the Origins and Definitions of Camp" in Cleto, Fabio (ed) *Camp: Queer Aesthetics and the Performing Subject*. Ann Arbor: University of Michigan Press.

Butler, Judith. 1999. *Gender Trouble: Feminism and the Subversion of Identity*. 2nd ed. New York: Routledge.

Butler, Judith. 1991. "Imitation and Gender Insubordination" in Kearney, Mary Celeste (ed) *The Gender and Media Reader*. New York: Routledge.

"Camp." 1993. *Entry on, in the Compact Oxford English Dictionary*. 2nd ed. Oxford: Clarendon Press.

Cleto, Fabio. 1999. *Camp: Queer Aesthetics and the Performing Subject*. Ann Arbor: University of Michigan Press.

"Flaunt". 1993. *Entry on, in the Compact Oxford English Dictionary*. 2nd ed. Oxford: Clarendon Press.

Klawans, Stuart. 2010. "Worlds of Wonder: *The King's Speech, The Illusionist, Black Swan. The Nation*. 2 December.

LaBruce, Bruce. 2012. "Notes on Camp/Anti-Camp." *Nat. Brut.: The Responsible Future of Art and Literature.* Online. Issue 3: April 2013.

Lighter, J.E. 1994. *Random House Historical Dictionary of American Slang*. Volume 1, A–G. New York: Random House.

Meyer, Moe. 1994. *The Politics and Poetics of Camp*, London: Routledge.

Muñoz, José. 1999. *Disidentifications: Queers of Color and the Performance of Politics*. Minneapolis: University of Minnesota Press.

Pellegrini, Ann. 2007. "After Sontag: Future Notes on Camp." in Haggerty, George E., and Molly McGarry (eds) *A Companion to Lesbian, Gay, Bisexual, Transgender and Queer Studies.* Malden, MA: Blackwell Reference Online: 168–193.

Robertson, Pamela. 1996. *Guilty Pleasures: Feminist Camp from Mae West to Madonna.* Durham, NC: Duke University Press.

Roen, Paul. 1994. *High Camp: A Gay Guide to Camp and Cult Films.* Vol. 1. San Francisco: Leyland Publications.

———. 1997. *High Camp: A Gay Guide to Camp and Cult Films.* Vol. 2. San Francisco: Leyland Publications.

Ross, Andrew. 1989. *No Respect: Intellectuals and Pop Culture.* New York: Routledge.

Sontag, Susan. 1964. "Notes on 'Camp,'" in S. Sontag (ed) *Against Interpretation and Other Essays.* New York: Picador USA, Farrar, Straus, and Giroux: 275–292.

Warner, Sara. 2013. *Acts of Gaiety: LGBT Performance and the Politics of Pleasure.* Ann Arbor: University of Michigan Press.

PART IV

Exhibition, distribution

Cult film distribution and exhibition

Distribution and exhibition have played a crucial role within the history of cult cinema and have, in line with broader shifts in film culture, altered significantly over time. The frequent use of the term 'cult film' emerged alongside the development of the midnight movie circuit, a mode of programming films after normal hours that was particularly widespread in the 1970s and early 1980s in the United States. The late screening hours of non-mainstream films attended by audiences who were often considered subcultural imbued the cult film with a subversive edge. In the age of cinema as a primarily public event, the midnight movie circuit offered an alternative to more mainstream, daytime programming, through which low-budget independents, foreign films, and older releases could be seen. The circuit also provided opportunities for people on the margins of society to gather in spaces where they often felt comfortable with like-minded others. This led to a communal atmosphere at many midnight screenings, particularly for specific films such as *The Rocky Horror Picture Show* (Sharman, 1975), which often drew together a sizeable crowd of cross-dressers and queer audiences. During this era, films mostly gained cult status through long runs on the midnight circuit, which indicated their appeal amongst subcultural audiences, many of whom would return to watch a particular film repeatedly.

Midnight movies screened in a range of theatrical venues, though most commonly – as mentioned by David Church in his chapter – in urban repertory theatres and university film societies. Beyond these types of venues, the drive-in and the grindhouse also occupy privileged places within cult film history. Both pre-date the emergence of cult film as a discursive concept but have, historically, screened a number of exploitation films, a category of filmmaking which has increasingly gained cult attention since the 1970s. As Church argues, however, the cult reputations of such venues largely accrued at the point when they were disappearing from the cultural landscape. Consequently, the cultification of such venues is partly fuelled by a nostalgic 'mis-remembering' of a bygone period. During the 1980s they were superseded by the increased popularity of video, which also led to the gradual diminution of the midnight movie circuit.

Video cassettes led to films being watched more in the home than in public theatres and provided new routes by which a film could gain cult status. In one sense, video shifted cultism away from a characteristic that had hitherto contributed to its definition: a communal, public, ritualistic space in which a film screening could cement shared values. Video did not, however, destroy such communality as people still organised special screenings of favourite films for friends. In other ways, video would introduce new dimensions to cultism and/or exacerbate previously noted attributes. Firstly, the notion of repeat viewing took on new importance: if a person owned a film on video cassette (whether an officially released tape or a bootleg recording) then they could theoretically watch the film numerous times, without the restrictions of being in a certain space at a certain time and having to pay for each viewing. Bootlegging itself started to become not just a concern for the film industry but also a process that could either aid access to cult films or provide new ways by which films could become cult. Video also provided filmmakers and distributors with opportunities to make money from films that had never been released at the cinema, providing them with an opportunity to gain cult status. As Johnny Walker argues in his chapter on straight-to-video horror, many of these low budget films were positioned as possible cult titles through being promoted in cultist publications such as *Fangoria*.

Following on from analogue video, digital technologies would extend access to a range of films from one's own home via playback technologies such as DVD and then Blu-ray, and through downloading or streaming films over networked technologies. Digital technologies have also expanded the home, and other viewing sites, by enabling audiences to watch films on mobile platforms. In the current era it is possible to own and access a huge range of films and to watch them across numerous platforms. Barbara Klinger (2010: 2) has noted how the digital media environment provides more opportunities for films to gain cult status, challenging the more exclusive nature that such fandoms previously enjoyed. A number of scholars and critics have lamented this mainstreaming of cult cinema and subsequently dismissed the concept of cult as now being thoroughly cop-opted and commodified. While cult cinema has become enmeshed within industry discourse, it would nevertheless be false to conclude that greater accessibility expunges the exclusivity previously connected with cult status. In an age where so much content is available, it is actually difficult to gain awareness for products. James G. Webster (2014: 4) has contended that the 'widening gap between limitless media and limited attention makes it a challenge for anything to attract an audience.' In this sense, exclusivity within cultism still continues through awareness of (and fondness for) particular films that might not be very well known outside certain taste communities. In his chapter in this section, Iain Robert Smith examines the more exclusive, marginal sense of cultism in the digital age through the private torrent site Cinemageddon.

While the proliferation of platforms by which films can be accessed has led to the reduced centrality of cinema theatres, such spaces do still continue to foster cult appreciation. Two important ways that they do so, as covered in Carter Moulton's and Russ Hunter's chapters, are through midnight screenings and film festivals. While the midnight movie circuit will never again reach its peak of the 1970s, midnight screenings do still occur and continue to be linked to cultism, as detailed in Moulton's chapter. Certain film festivals, particularly the more genre-based festivals, also incorporate events that link to cult practices including special midnight screenings, cosplay events, and special guest appearances. These more public film events also link to exclusivity; if watching a particular title is now easier than it once was, the contexts in which films are viewed assumes greater significance. Attending a preview midnight screening of a new film or a film festival, for example, may bestow such exclusivity and allow cult fans to experience a special event that is separated from more common viewing experiences. Types of 'experiential cinema', also noted by Moulton, are a particularly striking form of such exclusive modes of cinema viewing. These are usually special events that attempt to produce a particularly distinctive viewing experience linked to the content of the screened film (such as Secret Cinema), or they might be specifically marked as events which encourage forms of audience participation. A number of these are organised around films that have already gained cult status. So, while films are now mostly watched in private spaces, the cinema theatre and other public spaces continue to act as important sites through which cult films might be viewed in more distinctive ways.

References

Klinger, Barbara. 2010. 'Becoming Cult: *The Big Lebowski*, Replay Culture and Male Fans.' *Screen*, 5.1 (Spring), pp. 1–20.

Webster, James G. 2014. *The Marketplace of Attention: How Audiences Take Shape in a Digital Age*. Cambridge, MA: MIT Press.

21

MIDNIGHT MOVIES

Carter Moulton

Midnight *movies*

Though the term "midnight movies" appears in trade journals as early as the 1920s to describe the methods by which a filmmaker might construct an "'apparent' night scene" while shooting in daylight (Richardson 1927), its relationship to "cult" or "underground" film begins in the 1950s and early 1960s. As local television stations began dumping low-budget films into their late-night time slots, outside the home, midnight screenings of "obscene" films like Jack Smith's *Flaming Creatures* and Kenneth Anger's *Scorpio Rising* were being cancelled by city officials and theater managers who were concerned that the "low quality of the underground" might damage their theater's reputation (Hoberman & Rosenbaum 1983: 51). Over the course of the 1960s, though, a number of moviehouse owners in New York and Los Angeles began to recognize the potential of the underground market as a means of drawing in a younger generation of "countercultural" filmgoers, many of whom were marginalized by mainstream culture along the lines of class, sexuality, and politics. Ben Barenholtz of the Elgin Theater in New York opened his doors to the idea of midnight screenings in 1970, hoping they "would attract hipsters, encourage a sense of 'personal discovery,' and stimulate word of mouth" (Hoberman & Rosenbaum 1983: 93).

The first film to find lasting success at the Elgin was Alejandro Jodorowsky's *El Topo* (1970), an apocalyptic Mexican western with bizarre religious symbolism, explicit gore and sexuality, and "freakshow" characters who rebel against their oppressors. The film received next-to-no advertising, but word-of-mouth buzz helped *El Topo* sell out the Elgin for six straight months. This word-of-mouth snowballed into public discourses with help from celebrity endorsements (John Lennon championed the film) and mainstream media coverage (the *Village Voice* referred to *El Topo* at the Elgin as a ritualistic experience akin to "midnight mass") (O'Brien 1971).

Following the success of *El Topo*, the midnight movie circuit exploded into a vibrant and lucrative model of alternate cinema exhibition. Scholar and filmmaker Stuart Samuels (2005) canonizes *El Topo* and five other films – *Night of the Living Dead* (1968), *Pink Flamingos* (1972), *The Harder They Come* (1972), *The Rocky Horror Picture Show* (1975), and *Eraserhead* (1977) – as the definitive midnight movies "hits," although many more films gained traction on the midnight circuit. Older exploitation movies and "forgotten crap" (Patterson 2007) like *Reefer Madness* (a 1936 film about the life-threatening dangers of marijuana) and *Freaks* (a 1932 film about circus "freaks" which was banned for 30 years in the United Kingdom), also held regular midnight slots throughout the 1970s.

Scholars have taken two major approaches when researching the midnight movie phenomenon. The first, "midnight *movies*," approaches midnight movies as a set of cult films and emphasizes the aesthetics, narratives, themes, genres, and production and distribution histories of these "successful" midnight texts. And because the phenomenon emerged in a time of (counter) cultural anxiety and precariousness, midnight movies have been conceptualized as a group of transgressive movies with "radical aesthetics," camp, taboo or exploitative content, "graphic depictions of sex and violence," "explorations of immorality," and an "anti-establishment stance" (Mathijs & Sexton 2011: 14). A few highlights include zombie cannibalism in *Night of the Living Dead*, incest and coprophagia in *Pink Flamingos*, transvestism in *Rocky Horror*, drug use in *The Harder They Come*, and the infamous freak "baby" in *Eraserhead*. This has led to the proposition that aesthetic and stylistic transgression (Grant 1991), sexual excess (Studlar 1991), or subversive racial politics (Kinkade & Katovich 1992) are core characteristics of the midnight movie. Others such as Gregory Waller (1991) examine the genres of midnight movies, noting that oppositional or lowbrow faire was the most fertile for cultivation on the 1980s midnight circuit, in the form of comedies which challenged "good" taste (*Monty Python and the Holy Grail*), heavy-metal movies (*Pink Floyd: The Wall*), and campy horror films (*An American Werewolf in London*).

In addition to their transgressive images and themes, midnight movies have also been categorized by their failures. The backstories of Ed Wood's "failure" as an auteur and Bela Lugosi's "failed" comeback inject so-bad-they're-good movies like *Plan 9 From Outer Space* and *Glen or Glenda?* with a cultish aura. Similarly, films which flopped during their original release were picked up and embraced by the midnight circuit. *The Harder They Come*, *Rocky Horror*, and *Night of the Living Dead* all constituted critical and commercial failures when they were first released in the United States – the latter even failed elementary distribution procedure when it entered the public domain by way of a forgotten copyright notice.

While these insights are invaluable, one problem with "midnight *movie*" approaches when taken alone is that they often use the terms "midnight movie" and "cult film" synonymously, at times even interchanging one for the other within the same sentence. The conflation of these two terms not only diminishes the intricacies and relevance of "midnight movies" as both a concept and an experience, but it also leads scholars to either privilege a select grouping of films or to paint an unnecessarily-nostalgic "golden age" in film history rather than to examine a cultural practice which continues to evolve today. As a result, scholars sometimes engage in what Matt Hills (2015: 104) calls a "mainstreaming discourse" which frames technological advancements that offer ever more accessible and "easy" forms of consumption – the VCR, Netflix, and YouTube – as detrimental to the subcultural capital of cult fandom. Hoberman, for instance (1983: 328), suggests that by the end of the 1980s "serious" midnight movies were fading and that "students no longer head to cinemas at midnight looking for a participatory and collective experience that might change their lives." Indeed, the arrival of the VCR prompted many of the original midnight theaters to close their doors by the end of the 1980s (Mathijs & Sexton 2011: 14) and only a handful of "midnight *movies*" would gain traction over the next three decades, among them *Liquid Sky*, *The Adventures of Priscilla, Queen of the Desert*, *Donnie Darko*, and *The Room*.

Yet, while the 1980s and 1990s lacked new midnight-movie "originals," they gave rise to important trends which wholly contradict the "midnight *movies*" approach: most notably a co-option of midnight exhibition practices by mainstream multiplex cinemas and Hollywood distributors. In 1980, for instance, a number of theaters held midnight premiere screenings of *Star Wars Episode V: The Empire Strikes Back*. Echoing the media coverage of *El Topo* ten years earlier, The Seattle-Post Intelligencer (Egan 1980) described these screenings as religious, ritual-istic experiences: "The midnight show was for the most religious of followers, and that showed in the instant recognition every nuance and slice of trivia evoked." Franchise and tentpole releases like *Star Wars Episode VI: The Return of the Jedi* (1983), *Batman* (1989) and *Batman Returns* (1992), *Jurassic Park* (1993), and *Titanic* (1997) also received limited midnight premieres throughout this period.

The monumental midnight release of *Star Wars Episode I: The Phantom Menace* (1999) precipitated a model in which midnight premieres became not only normalized as an exhib-ition practice but also packaged and sold as exclusive "events." This co-option of midnight con-sumption culture emerged as a mode of harnessing the fleeting nature of time to construct more exclusive, inaccessible spaces within a mainstream market of accessibility and social acceleration (Hills 2015). Other factors that propelled the co-option process include an increasing cultural fascination with box-office numbers and records, the instantaneity of social media and digital word-of-mouth, a sharp collapsing of a film's average theatrical run and theatrical window, and a heightened debate over public and private modes of consumption (Moulton 2014: 361).

Since 2000, multi-film franchises like *Harry Potter*, *The Pirates of the Caribbean*, *The Lord of the Rings*, *Transformers,* and Marvel's "Cinematic Universe" continue to break midnight box-office records. In 2015, *Harry Potter and the Deathly Hallows: Part 2's* midnight record of $43.5 million – which constitutes an incredible 11% of its domestic revenue – was shattered by *Star Wars: The Force Awakens* ($57 million).[1] Midnight premieres are now often pushed to earlier, Thursday-evening time slots – a move that began with *The Matrix Reloaded* in 2003 (10 P.M. showing) and intensified in 2012 after the shooting in Aurora, Colorado at a midnight screening of *The Dark Knight Rises.*

In addition to midnight blockbuster premieres, midnight cinemagoing continues today pri-marily in two other forms: a "meta-midnight" circuit and "experiential cinema" (Atkinson & Kennedy 2016a). The first, a "meta-midnight" circuit, which flows through college towns and independent cinemas around the world, continues the regular screening of cult films at midnight. Film festival programming like the Toronto International Film Festival's "Midnight Madness" and South-By-Southwest's "Midnighters" also fit into this meta-midnight model, wherein audiences are "aware of the legacy of the midnight movie phenomenon" and con-tribute to the "heritage of the phenomenon by keeping it alive" (Mathijs & Sexton 2011: 15). The notion that meta-midnight audiences are cognizant of a cinemagoing tradition larger than themselves makes sense given the "just-before-my-childhood" nostalgia – films like *Back to the Future*, *The Goonies*, *Ghost World*, *Ferris Bueller's Day Off*, *Labyrinth*, and *Blue Velvet* – that pervades the meta-midnight circuit today. Additionally, these films allow a slightly older group of filmgoers to revisit their childhood favorites while displaying a "badge of honor" – a retro-active, pre-subcultural capital in the form of memories and lived experience (Hills 2015: 108).

Second, "experiential cinema," or what Donna de Ville (2011: 1) calls "full immersion film events," constitute more explicitly-thematized and social exhibition contexts which are usually offered as one-off or semi-annual special events. Experiential cinema programming enhances and augments film screenings through "synchronous live performance, site-specific locations, technological intervention, social media engagement, and all manner of simultaneous interactive moments including singing, dancing, eating, drinking, and smelling" (Atkinson & Kennedy 2016a: 139). In this market, specialty exhibitors – including the Alamo Drafthouse, Rooftop Cinema Club, Secret Cinema, and the El Capitan Theatre – often become the subject of cult followings themselves (de Ville 2011: 14). Special-event offerings such as quote-a-longs (*Ferris Bueller's Day Off, The Princess Bride*) and sing-a-longs (*Frozen, The Sound of Music*) also belong in this category.

Fitting the widespread incorporation of midnight exhibition into textual or aesthetic approaches to midnight movies presents a challenge, since many mainstream films – especially blockbusters – simply cannot be explained using a model which emphasizes oppositional aesthetics, transgressive textuality, or commercial failure. Mathijs and Sexton (2011: 215) make an attempt by proposing that these newer midnight blockbusters might also be explained through excess, as being "too big," "supersized" texts which cram every nook of public culture with their special effects and "illogical, unhinged stories." They (2011: 217) and other scholars have also cited the pre-sold, intertextual nature of blockbusters to suggest that such films often contain "built-in cult potential" found either in related materials that already have cult followings (books, video games, theme park rides, board games, previous films) or in "pre-existing worlds" in which fans can easily enter ("The Wizarding World," Middle-Earth, or Gotham City).

A second approach to midnight movies, which examines the social, participatory, collective practices involved in midnight exhibition and filmgoing, provides a broader conceptual framework for understanding the connections between films as diverse as *Freaks, Harold and Maude,* and *Iron Man.* Shifting the emphasis to "*midnight* movies," this approach treats midnight movies as "the most social form of cinemagoing" (Hoberman & Rosenbaum 1983: 301) and refuses to strip films from their indispensable reception contexts. Here, midnight movies are defined not as a group of films or aesthetics but as distinct phenomenological events in the spaces where films, screens, and cult audiences meet. Throughout the remainder of this chapter, I build on this work by conceptualizing "*midnight* movies" through four specific phenomenological sensations: *exclusivity, liveness, collectivity,* and *thematic immersion* – or, an intense closeness with the themes of the film text. Recent trends in blockbuster exhibition emphasize that the employment of "midnight" here is not necessarily literal but evokes cultified cinemagoing practices – such as long lines, sing-a-long participation, costuming, trivia, fan performance, prop-use, etc. – set apart from everyday, conventional modes of filmgoing.

Midnight movies

Exclusivity

Midnight movies bring with them a "sense of a truly unique, forbidden experience" set apart from the rest of the world (Mathijs & Sexton 2011: 160). Writing on *The Rocky Horror Picture Show,* J.P. Telotte (1991: 103) also observes this "magical change or transformation" of the cinema auditorium at midnight, as onscreen media and offscreen activities construct an energy and aura unbeknownst to and set apart from "ordinary" cultural rhythms. This phenomenological exclusivity, or the notion that audiences feel as if they are taking part in a more "eventful," "special" form of cinemagoing, is *constructed* and *experienced* by both fan and industry practice, namely through modulations in *temporality* (the amount of time spent at the theater, the late-night showtime), *sociality* (the intensification of audience participation and interaction), and *materiality* (the construction of a themed environment which surrounds the film screening). Most obviously, the hour of midnight itself brings with it a certain built-in exclusivity since, by attending a movie in the late hours of the night – when much of the outside world is fast asleep – audiences distinguish themselves from more accessible, "mainstream" modes of cinema consumption.

Undoubtedly the most-studied midnight movie, *Rocky Horror* points to another form of exclusivity which emerges through social and participatory activity. In the autumn of 1976, a group of cinemagoers began "talking back" to characters, providing "counterpoint dialogue" in the form of "wisecrack retorts" such as answering rhetorical questions or mocking and scolding onscreen characters – "Buy an umbrella, you cheap bitch!" was yelled when Janet uses a newspaper to shield herself from the rain (Hoberman & Rosenbaum 1983: 176). A few weeks later, coinciding with Halloween, fans began dressing up as *Rocky Horror* characters. Prop-aided activities were soon worked into the script: bells were rung; rice, hot dogs, toast, playing cards, and toilet paper were tossed around; water guns were fired, umbrellas were opened – activities which, importantly, coincided with specific scenes of the film. Costumed characters began running to the front of the auditorium to perform mid-screening "floor shows" – the most notable being "The Time Warp" – ranging from improvisational lip-synching to highly-choreographed dance sequences.

Because the social and participatory experience of *Rocky Horror* is so potent and phenomenal, it sometimes obscures the larger system of midnight filmgoing in which it is situated. The link between "midnight movies" and participatory cinemagoing can be found as early as the 1930s, when films were screened at midnight as part of "formal affairs" such as fundraisers and political conventions. These upper-class functions – which brought with them an additional class-based form of exclusivity – enveloped film screenings in social activities such as "patriotic dances," banquet dinners, and as one journalist observed at the midnight gala of *Broadway To Hollywood*, "general hoop-la outside the theater while the invited audience was gathering" (Mantle 1933).[2] Some of the earliest midnight exhibitions in 1960s New York also constituted "social events" where drugs, live music, and conversation all figured into the experience – they were "a lot like a party," as Andy Warhol remembered them (Hoberman & Rosenbaum 1983: 177). The most widely-used prop in midnight movie history, marijuana, perfumed the screenings of *El Topo*, *Reefer Madness*, *The Harder They Come,* and *Eraserhead*; at revival screenings of *Night of the Living Dead*, sections of campy dialogue were spoken in unison (Hoberman & Rosenbaum 1983: 126); live performance, scratch-n-sniff "Smell-O-Vision" cards, and complimentary "Pink Phlegmingo" vomit bags accompanied screenings of John Waters' *Multiple Maniacs*, *Polyester*, and *Pink Flamingos*, respectively*;* theaters in Australia screened *The Adventures of Priscilla, Queen of the Desert* in "Dragarama" by installing disco balls and colored lights which were activated during the film's final party scene (Cettl 2010: 8).

Today's midnight exclusivity builds on earlier exhibition traditions. Whereas *Rocky Horror* exhibitors circulated pre-printed tickets and allowed advanced-booking, today's promotional campaigns for cult blockbusters liken the ticket-purchasing process to a Broadway show, calling on audiences to "Pre-book your tickets to the 3D event of the year" (Moulton 2014: 363); 1970s New York theaters permitted marijuana use in the auditorium, while contemporary exhibitors favor on-tap alcohol at their midnight programs; variations of the disco-induced "Dragaramas" of *Priscilla* continue at Secret Cinema's dance-party productions of *Grease* and *Dirty Dancing*; and, like the distribution of vomit bags at screenings of *Pink Flamingos*, exhibitors today provide free whoopee cushions (*Labyrinth*), inflatable "Inigo Montoya" swords (*The Princess Bride*), and franchise-specific "giveaways."

A few examples of these midnight giveaways include IMAX's "12:01" poster series for blockbusters such as *Cinderella, The Avengers* and *Skyfall*; collectible figurines at *The Amazing Spider-Man*; temporary tattoos at *Divergent*; and Harry Potter-inspired 3D glasses at *Harry Potter and the Deathly Hallows Part 2.* For premiere screenings of *Star Wars: The Force Awakens*, theater lobbies were transformed into storefronts for "Galaxy Premiere" merchandise, including individually numbered collectable tickets (30,000 were printed) inlaid with gold foil and tucked between sheets of acrylic. These "exclusive" giveaways in particular incentivize midnight screenings and make holdable an otherwise-immaterial experience of cinemagoing.

These examples may at first appear to contradict the grassroots, word-of-mouth spirit of midnight cinemagoing since, as properties of conglomerate Hollywood, their screenings are highly constructed, controlled, and commercial. Yet, as Mathijs and Sexton remind us (2011: 242), even the midnight movies of the '60s and '70s did not emerge through a purely "'bottom-up' process." The implications here are threefold. First, it illustrates that pre-co-opted midnight movies were always in a sense co-opted, made possible and *constructed* by exhibitors and distributors. Consequently, "events that are 'manufactured, packaged, and controlled' should not necessarily be regarded as negating cult value" (Mathijs & Sexton 2011: 242).³ Second, it means acknowledging the existence of power hierarchies among and within midnight communities. McCulloch (2011: 200–201), Mathijs and Sexton (2011: 176), and Grant (1991: 130) note that midnight participation is often accompanied by an "implicit pressure" to follow and conform to those with more knowledge, experience, and in turn, control in shaping midnight practices. Third, as Mark Jancovich (2002: 314) points out, although midnight movies first emerged and continue to be embraced as liberatory spaces for marginalized and underrepresented communities, midnight audiences "do not share a single, and certainly not a uniformly oppositional, attitude" toward mainstream society. They function not through a mechanism of opposition to mainstream but through a subcultural identity predicated on distinctiveness, "rarity," and "exclusivity" (Jancovich 2002: 309). Seen in this light, the cult value of blockbuster premieres and experiential cinemas resides in their ability to construct phenomenologically exclusive reception spaces – spaces which are felt as distinct from but in reality are shaped through commercial media industries.

Secret Cinema, a London-based experiential cinema company, offers highly-thematized screening events in which fans, explorable film-specific sets, and hired actors coalesce in ways that both intensify the film's reception and craft phenomenologically new, alternate narratives within the film's thematic framework. They promote their experiential screenings through a motto of "Tell No One," a model which invites fans to purchase expensive tickets without knowing which film will be screened – or even where it will be screened. Through an "aesthetic of secrecy" (Kennedy & Atkinson 2016b: 254), Secret Cinema's promotional campaigns drop thematic clues in social media spaces in the form of atmospheric trailers, carefully-worded riddles, and half-obscured photographs. Nick Curtis of *The Evening Standard* (2012) describes his ticket-purchasing experience as such:

> In November I attended Secret Cinema's screening of Frank Darabont's *The Shawshank Redemption*. After signing up online, I was issued with a new identity, Hal Wood, by the 'State of Oak Hampton' and told to report to Bethnal Green Library one Sunday evening. There were obscure clues to the film's identity (I thought it was *12 Angry Men*), hints that 1940s-style men's suits would be suitable apparel, under which guests should wear long johns and a T-shirt, for reasons that later became apparent.

Here, exclusivity is constructed by purposely concealing information in a medium and a market which typically provide instant gratification and open access.

Crucially, once midnight fans step into these reception spaces, they construct their own iterations of exclusivity and eventfulness through a process of "cultification" (Hills 2006: 162) in which typical, everyday cinemagoing practices are "cultified" through *elongated, immediate,* and *intense* fan engagement. Just as cult fans engage with movie texts over a long period of time by quoting, re-watching, and discussing, midnight fans also *elongate* the "ordinary" practice of going to the cinema. They purchase tickets days or weeks in advance; they anticipate, consume, and theorize pre-textual material – sometimes attending other film screenings just to catch the premiere of a teaser trailer; they re-watch the film to rehearse their cues; they buy props or stitch costumes; they plan pre-screening meet ups and contests; and they arrive to the theater hours or days early for a spot in line; and they socialize before, [sometimes] during, and after a film's screening. Hoberman & Rosenbaum (1983: 181) note that *Rocky Horror* queues became social events in and of themselves, spaces where fans would "swap information, sing and dance on the sidewalk, compare their costumes," and discuss potential mid-screening cues. *Star Wars: Episode I* fans displayed this social elongation on national TV during CNN's "live, exclusive" interviews of fan queues. More recently, Hogwarts "house parties," official *Hobbit* "line parties," and more casual tailgating continue to cultify cinemagoing by expanding and stretching the spatiotemporal practice of moviegoing in outward directions.

Liveness and collectivity

Midnight fans also cultify and experience a mode of cinemagoing that is distinct from main-stream cinema receptions because of its heightened sense of "liveness." Martin Barker's work (2013: 57) compares various fields – sports studies, television studies, film studies, music studies, among others – to conclude that most scholars conceptualize liveness as a phenomenon which arises through a *simultaneity* of production and reception, a *bodily co-presence* between performers and viewers, and an *experienced risk* wherein "the performance is not 'locked,' and might be shaped by the audience's responses." This would seem to disqualify the pre-recorded, non-present, packaged experiences cinema offers its viewers; but at midnight, fans themselves become producers, performers, and shapers of textual and discursive meaning – as illustrated by Nick Curtis' aforementioned transformation into "Hal Wood." John Fiske (1992: 37) refers to these fan contributions as "enunciative productivities."

During midnight screenings of *The Room,* for instance, "fans" refashion themselves into improvisers, impersonators, cultural critics, and Tommy-tormentors as they dress up in tuxedos, throw footballs around the auditorium, toss spoons at the sight of the stock photo artwork in Tommy's Apartment, and cheer on the camera – "Go! Go! Go!" – as it yet again transitions between scenes by tracking across the Golden Gate Bridge. At other midnight events, franchise-specific information is shared and debated during trivia, costume, and impersonation contests; fan performances of original songs and poems pepper familiar worlds with new stories and emo-tional associations; costumed fans actively "try on" different identities, negotiating and articu-lating the (often hilarious) differences between superheroes and themselves. These live-action role plays may become quite intense – lightsaber or spell-casting duels in the cinema lobby, for instance – and serve as pre-textual entertainment for all midnight attendees. Borrowing from other "live" formats such as theater (role-playing), concerts (performance), sporting events (tail-gating), and game shows (trivia), these enunciations transform cinemas into themed, electrically live spaces of participation distinct from the pre-programmed, prizeless, and unspecific nature of conventional pre-screening entertainment.

Experiential cinema, the most phenomenologically "live" of the midnight categories, may utilize outdoor or open-air screening spaces (Street Food Cinema and Rooftop Cinema Club), themed menus ("Tattoine Sunset" cocktails served at *Star Wars: The Force Awakens*) or live scoring (performances of John Williams' score alongside *Home Alone*) to infuse screenings with new, unorthodox sensory experiences (Atkinson & Kennedy 2016a). Fans who attend Alamo Drafthouse: Rolling Roadshow's annual "*Jaws* On The Water" view *Jaws* atop floating inner-tubes while scuba divers swim underneath and grab at their legs (de Ville 2011: 3). Secret Cinema plants performers – whose job often concerns pushing an event narrative forward – among the also-costumed audience, making attendees and actresses indistinguishable from one another. At productions of *Casablanca*, audiences might be invited to dance by a charming stranger, questioned by immigration officers, or approached by a "Hungarian wife who needs money to fly to the sanctuary of America" (Kingsford-Smith 2013) – or, at Secret Cinema's *28*

Days Later, they might find themselves covered in fake blood, strapped into laboratory beds, and "forced" to watch the film. It should be noted that even in these industry-constructed spaces of extreme phenomenological immediacy, fans play an active role in contributing to and reshaping them.

Regardless of the degree to which "liveness" imbues a midnight movie experience, midnight fans feel a sense of "alive-ness," what Barker calls "eventness," or "the creation of and participation in senses of heightened cultural togetherness" in the contexts of what fans perceive to be a once-in-a-lifetime gathering (2013: 57). This construction of subcultural togetherness begins merely by showing up to the "once-in-a-lifetime" event. Here the act of "having been there" is an "authenticating experience" which acts as a form of subcultural capital (Hills 2015: 105). The prestige and self-love that accompanies "having been there" denotes a level of commitment; it may indeed involve the hour of midnight (a commitment to stay awake), the price (a commitment to pay), the duration (a commitment to endure), the logistics (a commitment to research and plan ahead), or the location (a commitment to travel). Midnight fans actively choose to take part in a more inaccessible, taxing form of cinemagoing. They therefore tend to make assumptions about and project themselves onto other attendees, positing them as more committed, knowledgeable, and like-minded than typical cinemagoers (Moulton 2014: 371; de Ville 2011: 12).

Driven by this "impression of a collective effort," (Mathijs & Sexton 2011: 19) midnight crowds emerge as partly-imagined communities built on respect, affection, collectivity, homage, and camaraderie (Kawin 1991: 24; Mathijs & Mendik 2007: 4–8). Non-communal or negative behavior which might rupture this communalistic energy is regarded as violative (Moulton 2014: 372), and, while midnight fans can acquire subcultural capital through the "to-be-looked-at-ness" of a costume (Hills 2002: 133), the prestige that accompanies a trivia prize, or the laughter that follows a funny comment, fans who flaunt or try too hard to earn subcultural capital are often met with rejection (McCollugh 2011: 211).

Thematic immersion

In this final section, I want to suggest that cultified sensations of exclusivity, liveness, and (sub) cultural togetherness – when experienced in thematically-continuous screening spaces – can propel a process of *thematic immersion* in which fan phenomenologies move inward through the screen from the cinema auditorium into the thematic world of the text – *and that they do so collectively*. This notion of perceptual inward movement into the thematic world of the film is not a radically new idea. Hoberman and Rosenbaum (1983: 16) hint at it when they liken midnight movie viewing to Catholic transubstantiation, as "a spiritual passage from the physicality of a seat in a darkened theater to the physicality of an imaginary time-space continuum." Kinkade and Katovich (1992: 196) also write of an escapist "merging with the film." Mathijs and Sexton (2011: 18) emphasize the closeness "to the screen (enthrallment with the giant canvas), to fellow viewers (huddled together in communion), and to the subject matter (overly close-reading of themes and motives)."

Elsewhere (Moulton 2014: 374), I have mobilized Charles Acland's work on themed spaces (2003: 95) to argue that the intensified, continuous theming of reception spaces – either through industry constructions (franchise-specific decorations, hired performers, and giveaways) or fan constructions (costuming, prop-use, role-playing, and conversations) – can play a meaningful pre-textual role in the cultivation of phenomenological immersion and serve "as an entryway paratext for the movie to come." Literal examples of themed entryways are often observed in experiential cinema. For instance, The Alamo Drafthouse "erected a wooden house filled with

25,000 flies through which patrons could pass to attend" *The Amityville Horror* (2005) (de Ville 2011: 10); or take their presentation of *The Texas Chainsaw Massacre* (1974), which was held at Leatherface's house – complete with "skin lamps and rotting bones" – and accompanied with headcheese hors d'oeuvres. De Ville (2011: 10) shows how these pre-textual, themed exhibition practices actually date back to the traveling roadshow exhibitions of the 1920s and William Castle's horror-movie gimmickry of the 1950s. Castle would not only thematize lobby displays but also stage pre-screening activities which tapped into the thematics (often anxiety and dread) of the upcoming film – such as signing waivers and life insurance policies or, at screenings of *Les Diaboliques* (1955), situating ambulances outside and nurses inside cinema auditoriums (Clepper 2016).

In spaces where such intense thematic immersions are not offered by the industry, the many cultified cinemagoing practices discussed in this chapter offer a way of filling cultural lack (Fiske 1992: 33). As a diverse variety of film-specific enunciations coalesce, fans find themselves in an environment in which onscreen characters, songs, and objects obtain tangible presence off-the-screen. Fans thusly move closer to the fictional world, "a little way out of normal structures and arguably into a liminal border zone between the real world and the diegesis, where the viewer eats the same snacks or wears the same outfits as the characters on screen" (Brooker 2007: 155). Will Brooker, who focuses primarily on television viewing, writes that pre-viewing and viewing rituals allow fans to access and experience "flow," a term borrowed from psychologist Mihaly Csikszentmihalyi to describe the total "sense of immersion, where the everyday is transcended and the participant enters a different state of being, a form of communion with a text, with a process, and sometimes with other participants" (2007: 152). Pre-viewing and viewing rituals, Brooker writes, include both simple practices such as providing commentary, turning off lights, and silencing phones and more extensive practices such as "dressing up for a *Star Wars* home screening in Queen Amidala lipstick with Leia hair-buns while feasting on 'Wookie Cookies' and 'Yoda Soda'" (2007: 155).

Brooker's framing of thematic ritual as a gateway to immersion allows room for both the midnight viewing performances (*Rocky Horror, The Room*) and outbursts (*Troll 2, Freaks, Pink Flamingos*) during repeated immersion experiences and the intensification of everyday cinematic viewing etiquette – such as "don't talk," and "don't text" – during first-time immersions (blockbuster premieres, in particular). However, Brooker's argument (2007: 159) puts forth the notion that this phenomenological immersion into the diegesis "does not seem dependent on the company of others." This hiccup contradicts scholarship on both classic midnight movies (Wood 1991: 160; Austin 1981) and newer midnight experiences (Moulton 2014; Klinger 2007) which observes that fans experience inward sensations of immersion while also retaining an appreciation and a sense of belonging with each other even after "flow" begins.

Midnight blockbuster attendees, for instance, describe midnight audiences as more "quiet," "respectful," and "appropriate" than "everyday" audiences (Moulton 2014: 374–375). That is, midnight audiences laugh, cheer, and cry at the "right" times. Take this fascinating account from a fan as he recalls his first midnight screening of *Batman* (1989):

> The movie kicked off at midnight and ... *those loud fuckers made this one of the best moviegoing experiences of my life.* As the opening credits rolled, *the theater roared with applause.* With each name that appeared, *the crowd got louder.* Somewhere around Bob Ringwood and Danny Elfman, *the place was going bananas.* And then this popped up on the screen: "Songs Written and Performed By Prince." *The crowd booed like mad.* And then, just as quickly it started recognizing *how hilarious it was that they cheered every-*thing except Prince and then *they started laughing.* I mean ... wow, this was already an

awesome time! *The crowd achieved self-awareness and a singular mind* at this moment. And throughout the rest of the movie, *it carried us through* the soon-to-be classic one-liners, action sequences and reveals.

("FlashBack 66: *Batman* (1989)," emphasis added)

These observations speak to Julian Hanich's (2014: 339) work on collective viewing, where he argues that a "higher level" of continuous – what he calls "thematic" – recognition and appreciation of other fans can occur in "specific moments of high emotionality and collectivity." In this instance, immersion and enjoyment are increased as moviegoers perceive each other to be "acting jointly" and "feeling jointly" as they watch the film together. Put another way, midnight fans in particular remain aware of the synchronicity and harmony with which the community *jointly acts*, whether in the form of unified participation cues during *Rocky Horror* (Mathijs & Sexton 2011: 176; Wood 1991: 157; Grant 1991: 130) or the "appropriate," well-timed emotional responses at midnight blockbuster premieres.

The phenomenological sensation of "homecoming" (Brooker 2007: 163) in a thematically-continuous space with assumedly like-minded people strengthens the sensations of what Hanich (2014: 344) calls "we-intention": *practical collective intentionality* (as midnight fans we have a common goal to enjoy the midnight experience together), *cognitive collective intentionality* (we share a common knowledge, opinion, or taste), and *affective collective intentionality* (we have a common mood, emotional response or energy). This suggests that fans would rather enter into an immersive experience of "flow" with others rather than journey there alone. Viewed in this context, we might rethink cultified cinemagoing not as a practice set apart from or in resistance to conventional consumption but as a blueprint of moving beyond it, of setting the terms for fans to become immersed in a themed world made up of both physical and filmic elements – an immersion, as Andrew Sarris once wrote, "beyond all reason" (Telotte 1991: 5).

As this chapter has shown, we need to undertake a holistic approach to *midnight movies,* one which both digs deeper into the forms of immersion at midnight movie events and re-examines specific *midnight* cinemagoing practices in relation their *movies'* thematic framework or diegetic world. How might watching *Eraserhead* or *Donnie Darko* in a sparsely attended theater while the outside world is fast asleep funnel phenomenologies into textual themes of isolation, death, and dreams? How does thematic immersion function when pre-or-mid-viewing enunciations are shifted to post-viewing environments, like the two-day "Lebowskifest" in which fans screen *The Big Lebowski* and head to bowling alleys the following night? Might there be a thematic connection between so-bad-they're-good films and the collective heckling that occurs at their viewings, in which socially "bad" behavior is used to construct "good" sensations of community? How might midnight blockbusters' recent shift toward a decentralized "first" through earlier time slots affect sensations of exclusivity and participatory culture? There are many questions to answer – and the clock is ticking.

Notes

1 It should be noted that *The Harry Potter and the Deathly Hallows: Part 2* record included only midnight screenings while *The Force Awakens* screenings began at 7 P.M. (through midnight) on Thursday and included marathon ticket sales, which were sold for as much as $59.99 each.

2 For additional examples see "City to welcome FIDAC Tomorrow," in *The New York Times*, September 14, 1930, pp. 33; "Midnight Movie Stars Kay Kyser: 'That's Right, You're Wrong'" in *The Atlanta Constitution*, December 14, 1939, p. 8; and "ODD Fraternity To Entertain At Swimming Party This Evening," in *The Atlanta Constitution*, February 19, 1938, pp. 11.

3 I am by no means negating or calling into question the role of fans in the creation of midnight cinema-going experiences, and indeed, the commercial failures of overly-designed midnight faire such as the *Rocky Horror* sequel *Shock Treatment* or the more recent *Snakes On A Plane* speak to that power.

References

Acland, Charles. 2003. *Screen Traffic: Movies, Multiplexes, and Global Culture.* Durham, NC: Duke University Press.

Atkinson, Sarah and Helen W. Kennedy. 2016a. "Introduction: Inside-the-Scenes: The Rise of Experiential Cinema," *Participations: Journal of Audience and Reception Studies.* 13.1: 139–151.

Atkinson, Sarah and Helen W. Kennedy. 2016b. "From Conflict to Revolution: The Secret Aesthetic, Narrative Spatialization and Audience Experience in Immersive Cinema Design," *Participations: Journal of Audience and Reception Studies,* 13.1: 252–278.

Austin, Bruce. 1981. "Portrait of a Cult Film Audience: *The Rocky Horror Picture Show*," *Journal of Communication,* 31.2: 43–54.

Barker, Martin. 2013. *Live to Your Local Cinema: The Remarkable Rise of Livecasting.* London: Palgrave.

Brooker, Will. 2007. "A Sort of Homecoming: Fan Viewing and Symbolic Pilgrimage" in Jonathan Gray, Cornel Sandvoss, and C. Lee Harrington, eds, *Fandom: Identities and Communities in a Mediated World.* New York: NYU Press: 149–164.

Cettl, Robert. 2010. *Australian Film Tales.* Adelaide, South Australia: Wider Screenings.

Clepper, Catherine. 2016. "'Death by Fright': Risk, Consent, and Evidentiary Objects in William Castle's Rigged Houses," *Film History,* 28.3: 54–84.

Curtis, Nick. 2012. "Secret Cinema: How to Get 25,000 People to Pay £50 for a Film Ticket, Without Knowing What the Film Is," *The Evening Standard.* https://tinyurl.com/yau9azff (accessed June 1, 2016).

de Ville, Donna. 2011. "Cultivating the Cult Experience at the Alamo Drafthouse Cinema," *Scope* 20: 1–23.

Egan, Timothy. 1980. "It's Star Wars Madness All Over Again," *The Seattle Post-Intelligencer.* http://blog.seattlepi.com/spi/2008/07/15/could-midnight-premieres-owe-their-existence-to-the-star-wars-franchise (accessed May 20, 2016).

Fiske, John. 1992. "The Cultural Economy of Fandom" in L. Lewis, ed., *The Adoring Audience: Fan Culture and Popular Media.* New York: Routledge: 30–49.

"FlashBack 66: *Batman* (1989)". 2014. PreOrder66.com, http://preorder66.com/2014/06/flashback66-batman-1989.html (accessed June 26, 2016).

Grant, Barry Keith. 1991. "Science Fiction Double Feature: Ideology in the Cult Film" in J.P. Telotte, ed., *The Cult Film Experience: Beyond All Reason.* Austin: University of Texas Press: 122–137.

Hills, Matt. 2002. *Fan Cultures.* London: Routledge.

Hills, Matt. 2006. "Realising the Cult Blockbuster: *The Lord of the Rings* Fandom and Residual/Emergent Cult Status in 'the Mainstream'" in Ernest Mathijs, ed, *The Lord of the Rings: Popular Culture in Global Context.* London: Wallflower Press: 160–171.

Hills, Matt. 2015. "Cult Cinema and the 'Mainstreaming' Discourse of Technological Change: Revisiting Subcultural Capital in Liquid Modernity," *The New Review of Film and Television Studies.* 13.1: 100–121.

Hanich, Julian. 2014. "Watching a Film with Others: Towards A Theory of Collective Spectatorship," *Screen,* 55.3: 338–359.

Hoberman, J., and Rosenbaum, Jonathan. 1983. *Midnight Movies.* New York: Da Capo Press.

Jancovich, Mark. 2002. "Cult Fictions: Cult Movies, Subcultural Capital and the Production of Cultural Distinctions," *Cultural Studies,* 16: 306–322.

Kawin, Bruce. 1991. "After Midnight," in J.P. Telotte, ed., *The Cult Film Experience: Beyond All Reason.* Austin: University of Texas Press: 18–25.

Kingsford-Smith, Andrew. 2013. "Bringing Casablanca Back To Life: Future Cinema's Immersive Experience," *The Culture Trip.* http://theculturetrip.com/europe/united-kingdom/england/london/articles/bringing-casablanca-back-to-life-future-cinemas-immersive-experience (accessed June 30, 2016).

Kinkade, Patrick and Michael Katovich. 1992. "Toward a Sociology of Cult Films: Reading *Rocky Horror*," *Sociological Quarterly* 33.2: 191–209.

Klinger, Barbara. 2007. "What Do Female Fans Want? Blockbusters, *The Return of the King*, and U.S. Audiences" in Martin Barker and Ernest Mathijs, eds, *Watching the Lord of the Rings: Tolkien's World Audiences.* London: Peter Lang: 69–82.

Mantle, B. 1933. "Drama Critic goes To A Midnight Movie," *The Chicago Daily Tribune*, September 30: E1.

Mathijs Ernest and Xavier Mendik. 2007. "Editorial Introduction: What Is Cult Film?" in Ernest Mathijs & Xavier Mendik, eds, *The Cult Film Reader*. Berkshire: Open University Press: 1–12.

Mathijs, Ernest and Jamie Sexton. 2011. *Cult Cinema: An Introduction*. Chichester: Wiley-Blackwell.

McCulloch, Richard. 2011. "'Most People Bring Their Own Spoons': *The Room's* Participatory Audiences as Comedy Mediators," *Participations Journal of Audience and Reception Studies*, 8.2: 189–218.

Moulton, Carter. 2014. "Midnight in Middle Earth: Blockbusters and Opening-Night Culture," *The New Review of Film and Television Studies*, 12.4: 357–379.

O'Brien, Glenn. 1971. "Midnight Mass at the Elgin," *Village Voice*, March 25.

Patterson, John. 2007. "The Weirdo Element," *The Guardian*. http://theguardian.com/film/2007/mar/02 (accessed May 11, 2016).

Richardson, H. 1927. "Midnight Movies," *Amateur Movie Makers* 2.12: 13–14, 63.

Studlar, Gaylin. 1991. "Midnight S/Excess: Cult Configurations of 'Femininity' and the Perverse," in J.P. Telotte, ed., *The Cult Film Experience: Beyond All Reason*. Austin: University of Texas Press: 138–155.

Telotte, J.P. 1991. "Beyond All Reason: The Nature of the Cult," in J.P. Telotte, ed., *The Cult Film Experience: Beyond All Reason*. Austin: University of Texas Press: 5–17.

Telotte, J.P. 1991. "The Midnight Movie," in J.P. Telotte, ed., *The Cult Film Experience: Beyond All Reason*. Austin: University of Texas Press: 103–106.

Waller, Gregory. 1991. "Midnight Movies, 1080–1985: A Market Study," in J.P. Telotte, ed., *The Cult Film Experience: Beyond All Reason*. Austin: University of Texas Press: 187–200.

Wood, Robert E. 1991. "Don't Dream It: Performance and *The Rocky Horror Picture Show*," in J.P. Telotte, ed., *The Cult Film Experience: Beyond All Reason*. Austin: University of Texas Press: 156–166.

22

DRIVE-IN AND GRINDHOUSE THEATRES

David Church

The antecedents of cult film consumption are to be found as far back as the birth of movie fandom itself, but audience predilections for niche tastes in certain stars, genres, or cinematic variants have long been tied to specific theatrical exhibition spaces as well. From the lavish picture palaces whose opulent environs allegedly fostered a "cult of distraction" by mirroring dominant cinema's own luxurious illusionism (Kracauer [1926] 2008), to the lowly storefront nickelodeons whose unruly urban spaces proffered immigrants, women, and other marginalized patrons an alternative public sphere (Hansen 1991), specialized theatres have long connoted specialized experiences for viewers variously perceived as distinctive, distracted, or subaltern. The 1970s-era exhibition of midnight movies, commonly associated with urban repertory theatres and university film societies, may hold an especially privileged place in cult film history for segregating esoteric films into less accessible viewing contexts, but drive-in and grindhouse theatres also occupy a significant place in the annals of cult spectatorship. Moreover, these alternative theatrical markets, primarily remembered today for their undisciplined audiences and exploitation film programming, continue to serve as (sub)cultural touchstones for the recirculation of cult cinema on home video and beyond.

The origins of grind houses and drive-in theatres, however, predate their respective associations with exploitation and cult films. Contrary to the oft-repeated belief that grind houses owe their name to the "bump-and-grind" of burlesque dancing, the term actually originated in the early-twentieth-century industry slang "grind policy," referring to the continuous all-day exhibition of films for a low admission price (a "grind scale") that increased incrementally over the course of the day. Unlike the then-standard industry practice of offering a handful of daily shows at graduated seating prices (akin to attending the legitimate theatre), grind policies delivered discounted, undifferentiated seating to capitalize on the sheer quantity of daily audience turnover instead of the socioeconomic "quality" of potential patrons (Church 2015). Much as representatives of the mainstream film industry similarly denigrated "serial houses" for indiscriminately "grinding" through both films and viewers (Smith 2016), grind houses soon became associated in both the trade and popular press with unruly, undiscerning moviegoers who supposedly cared little for which films were screened. These anxieties about independent theatres deliberately catering to the déclassé viewer only became more pronounced during the Great Depression, when many former first-run theatres were forced to adopt grind policies to survive.

As an exhibition policy that did little to combat cinema's generalized disrepute as a populist entertainment above all else, it is little surprise that independently owned theatres operating on grind policies earned special scorn as potential economic threats to studio-established exhibition practices. The film establishment's denigration of grindhouse patrons' supposed tastes (or lack thereof) was, however, rooted in the very restrictions imposed upon such theatres by the studio-era monopoly on film distribution. The major Hollywood studios were generally reluctant to release their films to such houses (except as a final stop for subsequent-run films already on their way out of circulation), for fear that exhibiting their films at discount theatres would lower the cultural standing of the films themselves. Hence, apart from scraping up Hollywood's sub-run offerings, grind houses generally had to make do with an eclectic mix of films distributed via the states' rights market, including the exploitation films that would later proliferate in the more open and independent post-studio era.

Although Hollywood-made films dominated grindhouse screens until at least the 1950s–1960s, these theatres' willingness to luridly advertise a variety of violent genre films and adults-only exploitation fare in dilapidated, male-dominated environs made them targets for urban renewal from the 1930s onward. Unlike more conventional theatres, they were reputed to attract a variety of male "undesirables," including criminals, perverts, drunks, and the homeless. Furthermore, the gradual transition of the term "grindhouse" from a specialized theatre type to generic shorthand for exploitation cinema did not predate the 1950s–1960s, when grind houses, art houses, and drive-in theatres all became profitable alternatives to more traditional exhibition venues. During the 1960s, for example, European art films and American sexploitation fare shared space in both grind houses and art houses because readily exploitable for their sexual content (though less commonly programmed at drive-ins, due to concerns about underage viewers and distracted drivers on nearby roads). Once hard-core pornography profitably exploded on their dilapidated screens in the 1970s, grind houses became all the more emblematic of both physical and social decay, a perversely attractive and repulsive blight screaming for urban renewal (Gorfinkel 2011: 60). It was therefore no coincidence that the names of all three exhibition contexts became transmuted into reductive generic terms ("grindhouse movies," "arthouse films," "drive-in movies"), naming these theatres and their purported fare as somehow different from the mainstream industry's unmarked norm (Church 2015).

If grind houses generally flourished in downtown urban areas where constant foot traffic brought high volumes of transient viewers, such as New York City's 42nd Street at Times Square, drive-in theatres once thrived in open, rural spaces. Although experiments with outdoor film projection for car-bound viewers had existed since the 1910s, Richard M. Hollingshead Jr. first patented the drive-in theatre (his innovations included the rows of earthen humps for cars to park at a vertical incline for less obstructed screen views) in Camden, New Jersey, in 1933. Further experiments with drive-ins continued over the next two decades, but drive-in theatres did not become a major part of the cultural landscape until the post-World War II boom in American car culture (Segrave 1992). Often located on the outskirts of towns and cities, where land prices and property taxes were generally lower, these theatres quickly populated roadside America, peaking at over 4500 screens nationwide by the late 1950s (Austin 1985: 64). These boom years also saw drive-in theatres spreading to Canada, Australia, and other nations with high rates of car ownership relative to the low population density necessary for cheap acquisition of undeveloped land (e.g., Goldsmith 1999).

Driven by a combination of postwar prosperity, infrastructural investments (such as the Eisenhower-era interstate highway system), and "white flight" to the suburbs (which meanwhile ghettoized the inner-city areas that grind houses called home), drive-in theatres joined drive-in diners and other auto-friendly businesses catering to the mid-century explosion of car ownership. The total number of US drive-in screens and attendance fluctuated over the decades, dipping over the 1960s and recovering in the 1970s, until a long industry collapse over the 1980s (Horton 1976: 236; Austin 1985: 64).

Indeed, drive-ins' fluctuating fortunes partly reflected consecutive trends in the youth-driven car cultures that ended up parked before their screens – as further reflected in the films they screened. Drive-in theatres' late-1950s peak coincided with a rash of American International Pictures exploitation films about hot-rod culture (Stanfield 2015: 113–114), for example, while drive-ins' brief 1970s resurgence accompanied Crown International Pictures' exploitation cycle about teenage van culture and a generalized trend toward rural-set car-crash movies and soft-core comedies (Waller 1983; Nowell 2016). Much as the sex-and-violence-heavy films increasingly shown at grind houses during these same years seemed to eliminate the boundaries between onscreen thrills and off-screen misbehavior, the automotively inclined audiences at drive-ins appeared to similarly blur the boundaries between cinematic and lived spaces in potentially disreputable ways.

Dubbed "ozoners" by the trade press, drive-ins were first promoted for their novelty, convenience, and family-friendly ambiance, especially appealing to viewers who might otherwise feel marginalized in "hardtop" (indoor) theatres – such as the young, disabled, non-white, female, obese, or parents with young children. Although drive-ins largely catered to families at first, then, the actual commingling of much more diverse and even unconventional audiences earned these spaces a continuing notoriety as "passion pits" for amorous teenagers, not unlike how urban grind houses were similarly denigrated for their supposedly class-less and degenerate viewers (Morley Cohen 1994: 478–479). Moreover, the largely rural settings and low admission costs (e.g., a double or triple bill for the price of one indoor film) of so many drive-in theatres enhanced their popularity with country-dwelling working-class viewers – a demographic that increasingly attended drive-ins from the 1960s onward, and thereby helped cement popular associations between these theatres and blue-collar audiences. Compared to indoor theatres, drive-ins generally earned a larger percentage of their revenues from concession sales, since a full evening's entertainment might include dinner and snacks for the whole family; and it was common for drive-ins to build playgrounds and other attractions for children to enjoy while under their nearby parents' gaze. But as industry-wide censorship restrictions fell throughout the 1960s, exploitation films increasingly pushed out drive-ins' family-friendly and general-release fare, with more sensationally "adult" content more likely to draw crowds.

The novelty of engaging in less disciplined behavior (e.g., eating, talking, playing, smoking, making out, etc.) in the semi-privacy of one's own vehicle was especially compensatory, because drive-in theatres faced many of the same programming restrictions that were imposed on grind houses during the studio era. The vast majority of drive-ins were independently operated, and therefore had little access to first-run Hollywood features until after the 1950s, instead making do with a mix of sub-run studio films, B movies, and exploitation product. Owners of indoor theatres often accused drive-ins of siphoning away their viewers, and the major studios generally sided with the former, not least because drive-ins' seasonal operating schedules gave them less leverage in negotiating for newer or bigger films. Much as the major studios did not want their films tainted by associations with drive-ins' less conventional audiences, they also resented the technological limitations of drive-in exhibition, including the substandard picture and sound quality created by outdoor spaces (Church 2015: 34–37). Ambient light pollution and the unconventionally long distance between projector and screen created dim, washed-out images, while improvements in sound quality only came with the gradual shift from loudspeaker towers to detachable in-car speakers to short-wave AM/FM radio transmission. Drive-in theatres' design flaws thus inspired complaints similar to grind houses' associations with a creeping decrepitude that might detract from the films themselves, even as these same déclassé traits have inspired fond remembrance among future generations of cult film fans.

Despite their year-round exposure to the elements, the small profit margins gained from seasonal operation meant that many drive-in owners were hesitant to invest large sums in regular maintenance. Because the number of newly opened drive-in screens peaked in the late 1950s, these venues thus found themselves falling into disrepair by the 1970s–1980s. The outward spread of nearby suburbs had also increased land values by this period, so many drive-in owners opted to sell their once-cheap tracts – many of which were subsequently developed into shopping malls with multiplex theatres – instead of investing in overdue refurbishment. Small wonder that an Australian film like *Dead End Drive-In* (Brian Trenchard-Smith, 1986) would depict a decrepit drive-in as a post-apocalyptic concentration camp, trapping unemployed youth, forcing them to live in their cars, and keeping them docile on a steady diet of junk food, drugs, and exploitation movies (Johinke 1999). If drive-ins increasingly looked like post-apocalyptic relics of an earlier time, it is not difficult to see why the more fantastic representations of these largely bygone venues as a teenage wonderland/wasteland would be so nostalgically appealing to today's cult cinema fans.

Meanwhile, back in the major cities, the gradual gentrification of downtown areas closed many grind houses – many of which had switched to exclusively hard-core porn programming with the 1980s advent of video projection – and these urban spaces were similarly refashioned by a shopping-mall aesthetic. In the Times Square area, for example, moral panics over the AIDS and crack cocaine epidemics shuttered many grind houses, while zoning regulations against adults-only businesses combined with eminent domain seizures to force out many theatre owners, enabling the urban renewal efforts funded by major corporate interests like the Walt Disney Company. Overall, though, audiences for both drive-ins and grind houses fell away with the rise of a 1980s video rental market in which exploitation films were some of the most populous early titles, filling shelves during the major studios' reticence to release their movies to the growing non-theatrical market.

Moreover, drive-in and grindhouse spectatorship each foreshadowed the very modes of domestic film consumption that would eventually decimate these specialized exhibition venues upon the rise of home video. Both venues fostered distraction-prone viewing over rapt attention, with unruly neighboring viewers liable to become an added part of the show. The all-hours programming and generic diversity found at grind houses modeled home video's time-shifting capabilities and flexible viewing options, while the audiovisual inferiority and semi-privacy of in-car spectatorship at drive-ins permitted a combination of active sociality and more isolated "mobile privatization" (Morley Cohen 1994: 479; Church 2015: 46). These television-like dynamics were literalized by the "Autoscope," a short-lived variety of drive-in theatre in which each car had its own small, individual screen; parked in a circular formation around a central projector booth, the film would be beamed through a refracting lens and mirror array, bouncing the image onto each screen via rear projection. Indeed, much as certain aspects of the drive-in experience, such as individual control over sound levels, more closely resembled television spectatorship than traditional moviegoing, the 1950s boom in drive-in attendance may have helped offset the sheer number of postwar ticket receipts lost to television (Austin 1985: 67).

Overall, then, both grind houses and drive-ins encouraged a curious admixture of pleasurable distraction and rapt attention, providing spaces of physical immersion where generic thrills could seemingly bleed outward from the movie itself into the audience. Memoirs of attending such theatres (McDonough 2001; Landis and Clifford 2002; Stevenson 2010) have been especially influential here, though these remembrances are infused with confirmation bias, whether by vastly overstating the proportion of exploitation films to sub-run Hollywood films shown in such theatres or disproportionately focusing on audience misbehavior over more anodyne viewing experiences. The blend of ironic distance (e.g., heckling and shouting at the screen) and sincere appreciation (e.g., the epiphanic experience) associated with such theatres has since become reproduced in the very contours of cult film reception, from the ironic mockery-cum-celebration of "paracinema" (Sconce 1995) to the non-ironic enjoyment of exploitation films whose original appeals transcend their historical datedness. These sometimes-contradictory tendencies in cult film reception find a spatial home in memories of the drive-in as a site where rural "redneck" patrons eagerly consumed the populist genre thrills of exploitation movies, even as latter-day subcultural elitisms require cult film fans to somehow distinguish their own enjoyment of those same thrills from the taint of populist unsophistication. In other words, the latter-day nostalgia for drive-ins and grind houses among cult film fandom may provide certain pleasures as culturally bygone exhibition sites, but their remembrance remains riven by anxieties over how closely to imaginatively identify with such venues' historical patrons without compromising one's own subcultural capital (Church 2015: 52–53).

As these venues gradually became endangered species, period-era films depicting grindhouse and drive-in theatres have increasingly informed their selective remembrance by cult cinema aficionados, from the urban anomie vividly captured in Martin Scorsese's now-canonical *Taxi Driver* (1976) to a slew of minor titles figuring them as spaces of cinephiliac fantasies for today's retrospective viewers. Whereas *Taxi Driver*'s portrait of 42nd Street in decline visually echoes Travis Bickle's degenerating psychology, affording cult film fans a vicarious experience of cultural slumming, the teenpic *Times Square* (Allan Moyle, 1980) paints 42nd Street as a lawless realm of anarchic possibility for two runaway teenage girls. Having escaped together from a mental hospital, Nicky and Pamela make Times Square their home, eventually forming an underground punk band called the Sleez Sisters, which performs atop the marquee for the eponymous Times Square grind house in the film's closing scene. Mental illness tropes abound here as well – they stop to mock a marquee advertising *House of Psychotic Women* (Carlos Aured, 1974) at one point – but their parents (one of whom is a Times Square redeveloper) had unjustly committed the girls for average teenage behavior. Unlike the psychopathic Bickle, then, the girls find well-deserved freedom within the déclassé grindhouse milieu, their adventures propelled by a similar punk/new-wave aesthetic seen in *Dead End Drive-In*'s youth subcultures. It is not difficult to see how latter-day cult fans would invest grindhouse nostalgia with related fantasies about rebellion and subcultural distinction.

In contrast, however, Bette Gordon's film *Variety* (1983) depicts grind houses as much more ambivalent, and even potentially dangerous, spaces for women. When Christine takes a job in the ticket booth of Variety Photoplays, a real-life porn-driven grind house, she begins hesitantly imagining herself up on the pornographic screen, and begins entering adults-only theatres and bookstores where male patrons give her a wide berth, as if the presence of women disrupts these privileged spaces of masculine fantasy. Unlike *Times Square*'s teen-friendly vision of Nicky and Pamela as urban rebels, *Variety* thus presents a more mature, circumspect analysis of gendered tensions within and around grind houses. Today, the overwhelmingly male demographic of cult film fans tends to uphold masculinist fantasies about drive-ins and grind houses as gender-limited territory, imagining these venues as distanced from the "feminizing" taint of domesticity and easy accessibility associated with more mainstream cinema. A female viewer must effectively become "one of the boys" to avoid seeming out of place within the latter-day fandom of exploitation films associated with screening at such exhibition spaces (Church 2015: 88–91). Also complicating such masculinist nostalgia is the prevalence of homosexual cruising associated with grind houses. Unlike the lesbian romance between *Times Square*'s protagonists that was left on the cutting-room floor, some films depicting grind houses, such as *The Back Row* (Jerry

Douglas, 1972) and *A Night at the Adonis* (Jack Deveau, 1977), directly (and pornographically) documented the importance of such spaces for fostering post-Stonewall queer communities (Cante and Restivo 2004; Capino 2005). Present-day cult fans may cathect around the perpetually unfulfilled promises offered by lurid grindhouse advertising, but for queer patrons, these spaces could offer an almost utopian (sexual) fulfillment rooted in cross-racial and cross-class intimacies later destroyed by the heterosexist/capitalist forces of gentrification (Delaney 1999).

It is precisely the disappearance of actual drive-ins and grind houses from the physical landscape that has paradoxically fueled their selective remembrance, allowing these venues to gain subculturally heralded meanings that may be largely unfettered from reality. Although some repertory theatres may host "grindhouse"-themed nights, few (if any) former grind houses operate today as they once did. Drive-ins have been somewhat more fortunate, though the relatively few remaining US theatres have typically sanitized their environs through associations with 1950s-era Americana (a differently tinged nostalgia than exploitation film buffs tend to hold) – their rarity marking a return to their original novelty value and family-friendly ambience – even as they primarily play double features of first- and second-run Hollywood movies today. Some have survived as multi-purpose spaces – home to flea markets by day and movies by night – though their latter-day dependence on Hollywood films has proven a mixed blessing, since the mid-2000s Digital Cinema Initiative forced many drive-ins to close if unable to invest in new industry-standard digital projection.

With grind houses vanished and drive-ins now aligned with multiplex programming, these sites have become especially vital for cult film fans to nostalgically recall in a post-theatrical age in which home video consumption predominates. Imagining oneself in the shoes of the urban *flâneur* or cruising drive-in patron – an experience now recalled by playing through "grindhouse"-themed trailer compilations like the *42nd Street Forever* DVD series – has become a mnemonic realm of subcultural refuge, particularly now that so many exploitation films are readily available on DVD and Blu-ray (often in restored versions), more easily accessible now than ever before. In effect, the exploitation films so often associated with drive-in and grindhouse exhibition have themselves become "cleaned up" and "renewed" for officially sanctioned economic purposes, not unlike the lived spaces these theatres once inhabited. Nostalgia for bygone theatrical spaces like drive-ins and grind houses has thus become more important since the 2000s as a reaction against anxieties about exploitation film fandom's own obsolescence when the once-obscure films that one previously had to be subculturally "in the know" to obtain (via VHS-era fanzine and bootleg markets) can now be easily purchased online and in pristine condition on mass-produced DVDs/Blu-rays. "Grindhouse-quality" artifacting (e.g., scratches, discoloration, jump cuts from missing frames, etc.) – those signs of wear and tear created by all-day "grinding" through the projector – has become a subcultural signifier of value at a cultural moment when shooting and screening on celluloid has itself become increasingly obsolete. Indeed, these "authentic" signs of celluloid decay can also be digitally simulated as ersatz dilapidation, as seen in Robert Rodriguez and Quentin Tarantino's 2007 omnibus film *Grindhouse*, released in the United States as a theatrical double-feature event. This film and its many "retrosploitation" imitators popularized the idea of "grindhouse" less as a historically distinct exhibition context than as a transmedia concept subsequently applied to a wide variety of DVDs, short films, commercials, video games, and other media texts exhibiting a retro-styled pastiche aesthetic. To capitalize on this late-2000s trend, independent distributors increasingly re-released exploitation films on "grindhouse"- and "drive-in"-themed DVDs: often double features of public-domain films, intermingled with trailers and other theatrical paratexts meant to collectively evoke the grindhouse/drive-in experience. Overall, then, the actual erasure of these venues has allowed their symbolic import to more easily circulate as a marketing label – a pop-culture mythology drifting free from historical specificity – much to the chagrin of some exploitation film fans (Church 2015).

Although recent research in exhibition studies has focused on separating the historical facts from the mythological import of such theatres, directions for future research would include fine-grained empirical analysis of exhibition contexts beyond New York's iconic 42nd Street. Detailed studies of the grind houses that proliferated in Los Angeles (Broadway), Chicago ("the Loop"), San Francisco (Market Street), Seattle (First Avenue), Boston (the "Combat Zone"), New Orleans (Canal Street), and elsewhere are largely yet to be written. Moreover, drive-in theatres continue to occupy underexplored territory, whether due to their working-class audiences' presumed political conservatism (Herring 2014) or film studies' overwhelming bias toward studying urban exhibition contexts over rural or small-town ones. Because drive-ins and grind houses originated in the United States, international variations or equivalents that specialized in exploitation cinema are also sorely understudied – including British "fleapit" cinemas (and their intersection with private cinema clubs like London's Scala), Japanese "pink film" theatres (some of which are still operating to this day), and European movie theatres located in transient areas near major railway stations. As the post-Tarantino popularization of one selective vision of "grindhouse" history recedes into the past, space will emerge for more nuanced histories of specialized exhibition venues and the equally specialized subsets of cult film fandom that keep their memory alive.

References

Austin, Bruce A. 1985. "The Development and Decline of the Drive-In Movie Theater," in Bruce A. Austin, ed., *Current Research in Film: Audiences, Economics, and Law*, vol. 1. Norwood, NJ: Ablex: 59–91.

Cante, Rich and Angelo Restivo. 2004. "The Cultural-Aesthetic Specificities of All-Male Moving-Image Pornography," in Linda Williams, ed., *Porn Studies*. Durham, NC: Duke University Press: 142–166.

Capino, José B. 2005. "Homologies of Space: Text and Spectatorship in All-Male Adult Theaters," *Cinema Journal* 45(1): 50–65.

Church, David. 2015. *Grindhouse Nostalgia: Memory, Home Video, and Exploitation Film Fandom*. Edinburgh: Edinburgh University Press.

Delaney, Samuel R. 1999. *Times Square Red, Times Square Blue*. New York: New York University Press.

Goldsmith, Ben. 1999. "'The Comfort Lies in All the Things You Can Do': The Australian Drive-in – Cinema of Distraction," *Journal of Popular Culture*, 33(1): 153–164.

Gorfinkel, Elena. 2011. "Tales of Times Square: Sexploitation's Secret History of Place," in John David Rhodes and Elena Gorfinkel, eds, *Taking Place: Location and the Moving Image*, Minneapolis: University of Minnesota Press: 55–76.

Hansen, Miriam. 1991. *Babel and Babylon: Spectatorship in American Silent Film*. Cambridge, MA: Harvard University Press.

Herring, Scott. 2014. "'Hixploitation' Cinema, Regional Drive-Ins, and the Cultural Emergence of a New Queer Right," *GLQ* 20(1–2): 95–113.

Horton, Andrew. 1976. "Turning On and Tuning Out at the Drive-In: An American Phenomenon Survives and Thrives," *Journal of Popular Film*, 5(3/4): 233–244.

Johinke, Rebecca. 2009. "Not Quite *Mad Max*: Brian Trenchard-Smith's *Dead End Drive-In*," *Studies in Australasian Cinema* 3(3): 309–320.

Kracauer, Siegfried. [1926] 2008. "Cult of Distraction: On Berlin's Picture Palaces," in Ernest Mathijs and Xavier Mendik, eds, *The Cult Film Reader*, Maidenhead, UK: Open University Press/McGraw-Hill Education: 381–385.

Landis, Bill and Michelle Clifford. 2002. *Sleazoid Express: A Mind-Twisting Tour through the Grindhouse Cinema of Times Square*. New York: Fireside Books.

McDonough, Jimmy. 2001. *The Ghastly One: The Sex-Gore Netherworld of Filmmaker Andy Milligan*. Chicago: A Cappella Books.

Morley Cohen, Mary. 1994. "Forgotten Audiences in the Passion Pits: Drive-In Theatres and Changing Spectator Practices in Post-war America," *Film History*, 6(4): 470–486.

Nowell, Richard. (2016) "Cars and Girls (and Burgers and Weed): Branding, Mainstreaming, and Crown International Pictures' SoCal Drive-In Movies," in Austin Fisher and Johnny Walker, eds, *Grindhouse: Cultural Exchange on 42nd Street, and Beyond*. New York: Bloomsbury Academic: 107–128.

Sconce, Jeffrey. 1995. "'Trashing' the Academy: Taste, Excess, and an Emerging Politics of Cinematic Style," *Screen*, 36(4): 371–393.

Segrave, Kerry. 1992. *Drive-in Theaters: A History from their Inception in 1933*. Jefferson, NC: McFarland.

Smith, Phyll. 2016. "'This Is Where We Came In': The Economics of Unruly Audiences, their Cinemas and Tastes, from Serial Houses to Grind Houses," in Austin Fisher and Johnny Walker, eds, *Grindhouse: Cultural Exchange on 42nd Street, and Beyond*. New York: Bloomsbury Academic: 31–51.

Stanfield, Peter. 2015. *The Cool and the Crazy: Pop Fifties Cinema*. New Brunswick, NJ: Rutgers University Press.

Stevenson, Jack J. 2010. "Grindhouse and Beyond," in John. Cline and Robert. G. Weiner, eds, *From the Arthouse to the Grindhouse: Highbrow and Lowbrow Transgression in Cinema's First Century*. Lanham, MD: Scarecrow Press: 129–152.

Waller, Gregory A. 1983. "Auto-Erotica: Some Notes on Comic Softcore Films for the Drive-In Circuit," *Journal of Popular Culture* 17(2): 135–141.

23

BLOOD CULTS

Historicising the North American "shot on video" horror movie

Johnny Walker

Introduction

In an article recently published in the *Journal of Film and Video*, Daniel Herbert (2017) examines the curious phenomenon of "VHS distribution in the age of digital delivery", surveying a range of independent companies which, over the last five years or so, have issued several horror films on videocassette for contemporary fans of cult film. Herbert, chiming with other scholarly interventions into the relationship between video technology and cult cinema (Hawkins 2000; Egan 2007; Church 2014a; Walker 2014), argues that independent North American distributors such as Intervision, Massacre Video and MPI, and the customers they serve, "appear to long for an imagined 'golden age' of VHS". Through exclusively releasing obscure horror and exploitation films, such companies, Herbert maintains, "reformulate the cultural meaning of VHS technology by yoking it solely to cult movie texts" (2017: 8). In many instances, such "cult" movies also happen to be horror movies and include such no-budget titles as *Sledgehammer* (1983), *Black Devil Doll from Hell* (1984), *Tales from the QuadeaD Zone* (1987) and *Things* (1989).

Herbert's analysis resonates with two recent documentaries about video collecting, *Adjust Your Tracking: The Untold Story of the VHS Collector* (2013) and *Rewind This!* (2013), both of which profile practices within contemporary American video collecting communities and which almost exclusively align these "cult" practices to marginal horror product. Central to these documentaries are the video collectors themselves. The documentaries show how these collectors – affectionately referred to in the fan community as "Videovores" (Schafer 2013) – seek to keep the memory of obsolete VHS and associated exploitation films alive in the twenty-first century by collecting tapes (and associated ephemera such as posters and cardboard standees) and, in some cases, displaying their wares on shelving units in their homes to recreate the "material character" of small-town video rental stores (Herbert 2014: 123). Particularly desirable among these communities are horror movies which in all instances bypassed theatrical distribution, going *direct to* video (DTV) and, in other instances, were *shot on* video (SOV) as opposed to celluloid film.

While Herbert's article and the aforementioned documentaries succeed in offering a fairly well-rounded picture of US video collectors and the legacy of SOV horror films in the twenty-first century, they are less concerned with the industrial contexts that birthed the SOV horror phenomenon in the 1980s. The present chapter seeks to shed some light on these overlooked areas and show how pioneering video distributors exploited home video technology to produce new horror films, using marketing materials that chimed with the interests of cult horror audiences at the time. Central to this was a drive to appeal to the readership of the popular magazine *Fangoria* by foregrounding gory images in advertising akin to those usually found in the magazine's colour sections. This chapter also examines how distributors looked to appeal to cult audiences by directly addressing broader issues that directly affected their interests: namely the moral outrage being directed towards gory horror videos and their audiences by eminent film journalists. If, as Herbert recognises, the attraction of purchasing VHS copies of SOV horror films in the digital age is driven by a sense of *nostalgia* bound to the cult status of specific films, this chapter shows how contemporaneous video distributors working in the 1980s were also interested in "yoking" VHS to "cult" movies, albeit by capitalising on the potential of video to offer horror fans *new* filmic experiences.

Splatter in the living room

In 1977, only fifty feature films were commercially available on home video in the United States. This would change drastically over the next few years as more began warming to pre-recorded video's potential as, an access point for consumer entertainment and, in the respect of film and media companies, an opportunity to generate profits (Greenberg 2007: 52–62). By the mid-1980s, the videocassette was a staple of North American households and, consequently, was rapidly becoming a primary distribution platform for film production companies. Horror was a particularly popular genre as the "second wave" of slasher movies – ushered in by such films as *A Nightmare on Elm Street* (1984) and the popular sequels to *Halloween* (1978) and *Friday the 13th* (1980) – translated well into video rentals. The success of horror movies on video was abetted by the growing popularity of the mainstream horror-themed magazine *Fangoria*, which, having launched in the late 1970s as a science fiction/fantasy publication, had by the mid-1980s almost exclusively switched its focus to horror.

As with subsequent fanzines of the video era such as *The Splatter Times* (est. 1983), *Deep Red* (est. 1987) and *Videooze* (est. 1990), *Fangoria* regularly dedicated pages to the growing popularity of gory so-called "splatter" movies that were emerging from the United States and Europe, and which were proving to be particularly popular on video (see, e.g., Anon 1982; Anon 1983; Schlockoff with Everitt 1983). In addition to offering production information and features on the special effects artists behind these films – such as Tom Savini and John Carl Beuchler (Jancovich 2002; Skal 2001: 328; Mathijs 2009) – the magazine also published retrospectives on those older filmmakers enjoying somewhat of a second wave on video, such as Herschell Gordon Lewis, as well as directors who, by making gory films on shoestring budget, were thought to be continuing a grand tradition of exploitation filmmaking. By dedicating considerable space to the promotion of low-cost movies made by so-called mavericks, these zines fostered a culture whereby a film's cheapness was framed as admirable resourcefulness and that true talent could shine in spite of the most severe limitations (see, e.g., Martin 1981; Carlomagno 1982; Carlomagno and Martin 1982; Landis 1982). Seemingly, gory, rough and ready horror films released on video thus became part of the magazine's appeal among a section of its cult readership (see, e.g., "The Readers on Gore" 1981).

A significant turning point came in 1982, with the publication of an article entitled "Splatter in the Living Room", in which *Fangoria*'s then-Manager Editor David Everitt reported on the levels of success that video companies working "in the gore field" were enjoying (Everitt 1982: 24). The article's focus is on LA-based Wizard Video, a company owned by the soon-to-be movie mogul Charles Band, whose future credits would include notable cult films such as *Re-Animator* (1985) and the *Puppet Master* series (1989–present). Everitt provides numerous examples of Wizard's spatter video successes. These include the company's release of Lucio Fulci's *Zombie* (1980), reported as one major video dealer's "greatest seller of all time", and the now infamous "rape/revenge" film *I Spit on Your Grave* (1978) that, for one dealer, reportedly outsold copies of 1980's Academy Award-winner *Ordinary People* "20 to one" (Marshall quoted in Everitt 1982: 24). The historical significance of this article – as far as the present chapter is concerned at least – is twofold. First, it identifies, through positioning gory horror films against mainstream hits and then championing the former's success over the latter, the privileging of "trash" over mainstream filmic orthodoxies said to permeate horror fan subcultures in the video age (Sconce 1995; Jancovich 2000; Herbert 2017). In another respect, the article points to the economic potential of such films as widely popular commodities that owed little-to-nothing to the informal distribution contexts often identified in such discussions (Sconce 1995; Hawkins 2000), but more to the broad market channels video opened up for film producers and distributors in the early 1980s. The success of films such as those released by Wizard showed other distributors that the "gore field" was worth investing in. It was, therefore, only a matter of time before film producers saw the potential of video as a primary outlet for the sorts of cheaply made horror films covered so favourably within the pages of the fan press.

Pandora's (video) box

The first SOV horror film, *Boardinghouse* (1982), had a limited theatrical release in October 1983, and found its way onto video the following year (Anon 1985a: 28; http://vhscollector. com). As a chance-act of derring-do by amateur filmmakers, the film did not represent a concerted industry effort to exploit video as a means of targeting audiences. Rather, the choice to shoot on video was, in this instance, dictated by the director's determination to make a movie despite lacking access to "professional" resources (*Boardinghouse* DVD 2015). While the film failed to generate little in the way of critical or commercial recognition either in cinemas or on video, it was a pioneering film nonetheless and consequently, as one reviewer writing for *Variety* predicted, "open[ed] a Pandora's box for future no-budget … taped horror films" (Lor 1984: 26). Indeed, it was from said box that the likes of *Sledgehammer* and *Black Devil Doll from Hell* emerged. Yet, like *Boardinghouse* before it, and in contrast to their visibility in cult communities today, these films failed to have any real impact on the horror fan culture of the period.

A company arguably more attuned to the video market than the makers of *Boardinghouse*, *Sledgehammer* and *Black Devil Doll*, was United Entertainment International. UEI was a subsidiary of VCI Video – an independent home entertainment distributor with interests in film and TV production – established to extend VCI's business interests as a producer and distributor of new low budget films. Prior to establishing UEI, VCI's operation was typical of an independent video distributor: most of its catalogue constituted films that had at some point, and in one context or another, been shown theatrically. The crucial differentiating factor of UEI was that it was, first and foremost, a production house, and its films were intended to elude theatres and go straight to video (Bierbaum 1985a: 1, 27).

A couple of reasons underpinned the establishment of VCI's new venture. The first, simply, was the aforementioned popularity of low-budget horror movies in the video market. VCI already had some experience in this area, having enjoyed modest success with a range of genre films including those in its self-knowing "Le Bad Cinema" series, which featured various scifi and horror films from the 1950s onwards (Wooley 1985: 41). The catalogue, however, was comparatively lacking in the sorts of new, bloodier, horror films regularly released by company rivals. Indeed, when compared to the range of modern horror hits available from one of the market's biggest indie distributors, Media Home Entertainment, such as *Halloween* (1978), *Hell Night* (1981), *Basket Case* (1982) and *The Dorm that Dripped Blood* (1982), VCI's range of old (and self-knowingly "bad") B-movies looked tame and outdated. The establishment of UEI afforded VCI a fresh start to venture into pastures new, producing SOV movies that riffed on the success experienced by theatrical and video distributors of widely popular independent horror films but at a fraction of the cost. As one independent filmmaker explained to the fan press in 1985:

> To really compete with the *Nightmare on Elm Streets* out there, [a] $350,000 [produc-
> tion budget] is about as cheap as you can go. But you can make a quality video for
> about $30,000. […] [I]t's the smartest way for an independent producer to go.
>   (Hogue quoted in Wooley 1985: 43)

Aware of trends in contemporary horror cinema, and abreast in the popularity of horror as video commodity, UEI produced a film firmly positioned to respond to these market demands. As the company's CEO, Bill Blair, explained to *Daily Variety* in November 1985: "Slasher-type movies are in demand. […] [Y]ou can't argue with success" (Blair quoted in Bierbaum 1985b: 14).

Blood Cult (1985), UEI's first venture, was shot by a professional television crew in and around the headquarters of UEI in Tulsa, Oklahoma, with a micro-budget of $125,000 (Bierbaum 1985a: 27). As a film made for video, it made many allusions to the sorts of horror film it was destined to share shelf space within rental stores. Above anything, it was a contrived "slasher-type" movie of the sort identified by Blair, balancing a murder mystery element and frequent on-screen murders by an unseen, meat-cleaver-wielding, assailant. Its gory special effects, scenes of people being chased and then killed in a woodland setting, and the inclusion of a surprise twist ending, all helped position *Blood Cult* amid this popular trend. In fact, one of the adverts used to promote *Blood Cult* partly anchored it in relation to popular theatrical hits of the period, as a film "that has been compared with *Friday the 13th*": a film which by the time of *Blood Cult*'s release, had five sequels in addition to a presence at the box office and on video shelves throughout the world, and, thus, more visibility than UEI could ever hope for but which they could still acknowledge in their marketing.

However, there were other factors UEI was able to draw on when promoting *Blood Cult*. As we have seen, the film's adherence to the slasher template in many ways made it a typical 1980s horror film: it brought with it a sense of familiarity that its producers hoped would chime with an extant audience. On the other hand, however, as a film intentionally foregoing cinema release, it was also atypical: the "made for video" angle was pioneering and thus a wholly exploitable gimmick. Indeed, while Herbert notes that VHS distributors of the twenty-first century "sell a rejection of the corporate logic of 'newer is better'" (2017: 17), the "newness" of video was regarded as being central to VHS distributors' appeal to, and subsequent success in, the horror movie market. Moreover, as far as horror fans were concerned "video" often meant "uncensored". Horror films released theatrically would most always carry a rating from the Motion Picture Association of America: most usually the "R" rating, meaning that people aged under 17 will only be admitted providing an adult accompanies them. To release a film "unrated" would often inhibit one's chances of being able to exhibit your film at a mainstream theatre and, consequently, drastically limit your market. Distribution companies would there-fore edit down gory sequences from splatter movies for this reason (Bernard 2014: 76–81). One of the advantages of video, as Wizard and others had recognised, was that – in the days prior to Blockbuster Video's stranglehold of the rental market with its "clean and bright" family image (Greenberg 2007: 127; see also Guins 2009: 98–99) – video stores would show little to no reluctance in stocking graphically illustrated unrated horror videocassettes. Therefore, with *Blood Cult*, UEI could tap into the so-called "gorehound" market as catered to by Wizard and its contemporaries, in positioning the film as one indebted to trends in niche horror-viewing subcultures. UEI partly achieved this by publishing a gruesome ad within the pages of *Fangoria* (November 1985, p. 70), to which I now turn.

The design of the ad in question directly mirrors the promotional strategies adopted by Wizard when promoting its range of "VIOLENT VIDEOCASSETTES" in August 1982 (*Fangoria* #21, p. 68; see Figure 23.1). The colour palettes are near identical. In both cases, grisly images depicting the victims of violent and bloody attacks are offset against a black background and copy that is rendered red and white. Wizard's showcases two films that are new to video, *The Diller Killer* (1979) and *Drive In Massacre* (1976) – "JUST RELEASED!" the strapline declares – with *Blood Feast* (1963) and *Snuff* (1976), two controversial movies with long-standing reputations that Wizard had been handling for a year or so (see McKenna 2016: 125–126). Bringing together these old and "new" films under the connotative legend "4 SPLATTER MOVIES", instils in the newer films the same level of iconicity as the classics. UEI's ad is similar in that it advertises its new release *Blood Cult* alongside "a lost classic" from 1968, *Doctor Gore*, in the process equating two different films from different eras (*Fangoria* #49, p. 70; see Figure 23.1). What appears most important for UEI, similar to Wizard, is that both *Blood Cult* and *Doctor Gore*, in spite of their different ages, are both gory horror movies and thus will appeal, as the UEI ad has it, to "'Fango' readers". UEI therefore appears to align itself with Wizard, underscoring *Blood Cult*'s status as a pathbreaking made-for-video film comparable in quality and "gore" to revered horror films of yesteryear, positioning the film as one that will satisfy the niche tastes of video's new audiences. By aping Wizard's marketing strategies UEI spoke outwardly to the readership of *Fangoria*, presenting *Blood Cult* as violent and special-effects heavy and thus worthy of the gorehounds' attention.

Figure 23.1   Advertising for Wizard Video's range of "violent videocassettes" (L) and UEI's first print ad for *Blood Cult* (R). Images courtesy of the Popular Film and Television Collection. Ads from *Fangoria* magazine (issue 49, 1985)

Blood Cult surpassed all expectations on video, having sold a reported 25,000 units to wholesalers and individual buyers in its first year, bringing in $800k of revenue for UEI, around $600k of which was profit (Bierbaum 1985b: 14). Following this level of success, UEI would soon cease shooting on video, opting to shoot its future productions, which included a sequel to *Blood Cult*, *Revenge* (1986), on celluloid (Anon 1986: 4). Prior to this, UEI remained determined to maintain its focus on niche horror audiences with its second SOV film, *The Ripper* (1985): a film based on the Jack the Ripper legend, and which stars horror make-up artist Tom Savini as the titular character. Mark Jancovich has remarked that while SFX artists such as Savini and his contemporaries "are themselves, amongst sections of horror fandom, the subject of great adoration" they are "hardly figures who would be familiar to the majority of moviegoers" (Janovich 2002: 313). The choice of Savini for the role of Jack was therefore made due to him being a well-known figure among UEI's "target audience – the horror homevideo [sic.] fans" (Wooley 1986: 53), and it was clearly hoped that his name and reputation for gory special effects would help sell the film to a clearly demarcated audience of horror fans, offering them a curious glimpse of a talent whose work was usually appreciated when he was behind the camera. Indeed, the video box art exhibits UEI's desire to draw on his fanbase. The front cover features an illustration of Savini's face above the legend "TOM SAVINI AS THE RIPPER", while the back cover identifies Savini and "the master of film gore", before going on to list several of his most popular films: *Friday the 13th*, *Day of the Dead* (1985) and *Creepshow* (1982). That Savini is used here as a *star* clearly speaks to his cult status and thus, by association, the draw UEI would hope his being in the movie would have on sales. As with *Blood Cult*, *The Ripper* was aimed at a niche horror audience, its makers using video to capitalise on the contemporary cult status of some of the most recognisable films and their creators.

"The saviour of schlock"

The release of *Blood Cult*, *The Ripper*, and the continued popularity of violent slasher movies in theatres and on video across North America, encouraged the development of more SOV films by independent producers and distributors. Most companies had even fewer resources than UEI but were still determined to target the cult video market. In 1988 *Variety* reported, "Of 1986's [horror] output … one-third of the 89 titles already have been released directly to home video with no domestic theatrical exposure" (Cohn 1988: 1). By 1989, according to *Fangoria*, DTV had become "the rule rather than the exception in the horror genre" (Dr Cyclops 1989: 40); a statement evidenced by a plethora of campy low-budget movies such as *Zombie Nightmare* (1986), *Rock 'n' Roll Nightmare* (1987), *Killing Spree* (1987) and *Lunch Meat* (1987).

Horror movie critics, while still willing to commend the efforts of indie filmmakers operating at the fringes of the film industry, began tiring of the inevitable low production values of such films: the aforementioned *Lunch Meat*, for example, was reviewed unfavourably in *Fangoria* as "a grainy, homemade no-budgeter that is literally torture to sit through" (Dr Cyclops 1988: 25). Nevertheless, newer DTV films remained popular with cult audiences who would often embrace aesthetic "flaws" as markers of "quality" of a type not found in mainstream cinema. Thus, *Lunch Meat*'s box art proudly identified the film as the "#1 'B' HORROR MOVIE!", while the independent production house and film distributor Troma Entertainment began steadily catering to this market with a string of hurriedly produced micro-budget features subsequently celebrated in cult communities for their "trash aesthetic" (Conrich 2005: 109; see also Church 2014a: 141). An exemplar of the appeal of such films is Troma's first SOV release, *Redneck Zombies* (1989), which confirmed for one journalist that "shot-on-video product is a natural in this fan-dominated demimonde" (Dr Cyclops 1989: 40).

Other video distributors emerged, embracing rather than challenging what some working in the industry described as the "made-for-video stigma" (Warren 1989: 17). One such company, the appositely named Camp Films and Video, released numerous ultra-low-budget, yet highly introspective, SOV horror films. Perhaps the most notable of all Camp's releases is *Video Violence … When Renting is Not Enough* (1988), the action of which takes place in and around a video store in small town America where the locals have a lust for violent horror movies and pornography but are bored by titles formally released by legitimate companies. Consequently, they videotape themselves murdering tourists and newcomers to the town, building up a library of rentable snuff movies in the process.

The film directly alludes to contemporary horror video culture throughout, echoing the many criticisms often levelled at horror film audiences. The manager of the video store is a former theatre owner who is happy that "business is brisk", but despairs at the poor taste of his clientele, exclaiming to his colleague early in the movie that, "all these people want are horror movies and slasher movies, and occasionally a 'triple-X-er' from the back!" Clearly, this is a gag at the expense of those vocal opponents of horror (and pornography) in the 1980s. Indeed, horror was widely unfavourable with many mainstream film critics, including, most notably, Gene Siskel and Roger Ebert, who routinely condemned routine depictions of onscreen violence (Bernard 2014: 78; see also Reboy 1981). In 1987, two years prior to the release of *Video Violence*, Siskel and Ebert dedicated a segment of their film review show *At the Movies* to warning parents about so-called "gross out" videos, which, allegedly comprised solely of "blood and guts", were, they claimed, widely popular among young children and teenagers (*At the Movies* 1987). The films targeted in this instance were "shockumentaries" purporting to feature real human tragedy, such as *Faces of Death* (1978) that was released by Gorgon Video in the late 1986. *Video Violence*, a film which features many gory special effects, appears to insincerely lament not only an alleged lost era of cinema that is now being steadily replaced with gory horror videos, but also the avaricious appetite for such material in American suburbia. That the townsfolk have a penchant for footage of genuine human atrocity and gore is particularly notable in this regard, given Siskel and Ebert's attitudes towards *Faces of Death* and other lower-end exploitation films, such as *Bloodsucking Freaks* (1976), which were widely popular within some sections of the horror fan community. By setting the action in a video store where such films were readily available, *Video Violence* identifies its close proximity to them and the cult communities to whom they appeal.

A stream of self-aware SOV releases followed the release of *Video Violence*, which all, in various ways, showed a knowingness of horror video culture and cult viewing practices, including *Video Violence 2* (1987), *Cannibal Campout* (1988) and *Woodchipper Massacre* (1988). While none of these films reached the profitable heights of a film like *Blood Cult*, the late 1980s and early 1990s did see some commercial longevity for trashy SOV horror films for a cult viewership. For example, speaking to the trade press in 1990, Max Lieberman, head of Triworld Films, boasted about having sold 15,000 copies of the "total piece of garbage" that was *Cannibal Hookers* (1987), which he released to video in 1988. As with *Blood Cult*, the "offbeat title and titillating cover art" of *Cannibal Hookers* – and, frankly, the majority of the SOV movies discussed in this chapter – "gave vidstores something to chew on" in the absence of any theatrical potential, and helped squarely position them in the eye-line of gorehounds across North America (Stewart 1990: 39).

Conclusion

In *Shadow Economies of Cinema*, Ramon Lobato argues that:

> Every year, thousands of movies are released into nontheatrical markets, and most disappear of the radar without having made any kind of mark. Some are watched by only a handful of people.
>
> (2012: 21)

This description could apply to any number of SOV horror movies produced since the release of *Blood Cult*, which, while popular among certain factions of horror's video audiences on their original release, remain absent from all academic histories of the modern American horror film (Hutchings 2004; Worland 2007; Dixon 2010). However, SOV horror has been – and, for that matter, continues to be – very much part of horror movie culture.

In recent years, such films have received an unprecedented level of cultural visibility. This is partly due to the reissue of numerous titles on VHS and DVD in deluxe special editions (Herbert 2017). However, it is also due to a broader interest in VHS as an historical arte-fact, and horror cinema's centrality to this history. Indeed, analogue video technologies, along with vinyl records, have now become of interest to hipsters and cult film enthusiasts (Church 2014b; Sexton 2015). Meanwhile, the academy is starting to wake up to the historical value of such movies, evinced by Yale University's recent acquiring of over 3,000 horror movies on video, including original copies of *Boardinghouse*, *Sledgehammer*, *Black Devil Doll from Hell* and *Blood Cult* (Piepenburg 2013; Gary 2015). This newfound visibility on the one hand attests to the rose-tinted nostalgic appeal of VHS that Herbert writes about: Yale's VHS collection was bought from a long-time collector that "loved and enjoyed these movies" and, a la practices of VHS collectors, preserved them to a library-standard in their "original boxes" (Gary quoted in Gonzalez 2015). But it also speaks to the (belated) realisation by the academy that such movies – pieces of garbage or otherwise – are *worth* preserving after all and that they deserve a place in the history of horror and cult cinema.

Acknowledgements

Thanks are due to Michael Guarneri for providing me access to a number of fanzine articles I initially had trouble getting my hands on, and to Dan Herbert for sharing with me an early draft of his "Nostalgia Merchants" article.

References

Anon. 1981. "The Readers on Gore", *Fangoria* (12): 8.
Anon. 1982. "More Home Splatter", *Fangoria* (24): 58.
Anon. 1983. "Video Vomitorium", *The Splatter Times* (1): 10–11.
Anon. 1985a. "1984 Films Released in U.S. By Company", *Variety* 317 (13): 28.
Anon. 1986. "3d UEI Made-For Vid To Debut", *Daily Variety* 212 (60): p. 4.
At the Movies. 1987. [TX], date of broadcast unknown, available at: www.youtube.com/watch?v=M7fINHOibX0&t=80s (accessed 24 May 2017).
Bernard, Mark. 2014. *Selling the Splat Pack: The DVD Revolution and the American Horror Film*. Edinburgh: Edinburgh University Press.
Bierbaum, T. 1985a. "United Planning Homevid Prod'n Syndication Entry", *Daily Variety* 207 (43): 1, 27.
Bierbaum, T. 1985b. "UEI Finds Market for Blood and Guts", *Daily Variety* 209 (45): 14.
Carlomagno, Ellen. 1982. "Rest in Peace", *Fangoria* (18): 52–54.

Carlomagno, Ellen and Bob Martin 1982. "Young & Independent: Coming Attractions from a New Breed of Filmmakers!", *Fangoria* (17): 21–22, 46–47.

Church, David. 2014a. *Grindhouse Nostalgia: Memory, Home Video and Exploitation Film Fandom*. Edinburgh: Edinburgh University Press.

Church, David. 2014b. "The Untold Story of the Original, Factory-produced, Horror/Exploitation VHS Collector", *Flow Journal* 26 November. www.flowjournal.org/2014/11/the-untold-story-of-the-vhs-collecto (accessed June 2019).

Cohn, L. 1988. "Filmers Resort to Old Scare Tactics", *Variety* 331 (7): 1, 24.

Conrich, Ian. 2005. "Communitarianism, Film Entrepreneurism, and the Crusade of Troma Entertainment", in Chris Holmlund and Justin Wyatt, eds, *Contemporary American Independent Film: From the Margins to the Mainstream*. Edinburgh: Edinburgh University Press: 107–122.

Dixon, Wheeler Winston. 2010. *A History of Horror*. New Brunswick, NJ: Rutgers University Press.

Dr. Cyclops. 1988. "Lunchmeat" (review), *Fangoria* (78): 25.

Dr. Cyclops. 1989. "Redneck Zombies" (review), *Fangoria* (84): 40.

Egan, Kate. 2007. *Trash or Treasure? Censorship and the Changing Meanings of the Video Nasties*. Manchester: Manchester University Press.

Everitt, David. 1982. "Splatter in the Living Room: The Booming Business of Video Violence", *Fangoria* (18): 24–27.

Gary, David. 2015. "Saving the Scream Queens: Why Yale University Library Decided to Preserve Nearly 3,000 Horror and Exploitation Movies on VHS", *The Atlantic*, 21 August. www.theatlantic.com/entertainment/archive/2015/08/saving-the-scream-queens/401141 (accessed June 2019).

Gonzalez, Susan. 2015. "Zombies and Monsters in the Basement of Sterling Library", *Yale News* 28 October. http://news.yale.edu/2015/10/28/zombies-and-monsters-basement-sterling-library (accessed June 2019).

Greenberg, Joshua. 2007. *From Betamax to Blockbuster: Video Stores and the Invention of Movies on Video*. Cambridge, MA: MIT Press.

Guins, Raiford. 2009. *Clean Edited Version: Technology and the Culture of Control*. Minneapolis: Minnesota.

Hawkins, Joan. 2000. *Cutting Edge: Art-Horror and the Horrific Avant-Garde*. Minneapolis: Minnesota.

Herbert, Daniel. 2014. *Videoland: Movie Culture at the American Video Store*. Berkeley: University of California Press.

Herbert, Daniel. 2017. "Nostalgia Merchants: VHS Distribution in the Era of Digital Delivery", *Journal of Film and Video* 69 (2): 19.

Hutchings, Peter. 2004. *The Horror Film*. Harlow: Pearson Longman.

Jancovich, Mark. 2000. "'A Real Shocker': Authenticity, Genre and the Struggle for Distinction", *Continuum: Journal of Media and Cultural Studies* 14 (1): 23–35.

Jancovich, Mark. 2002. "Cult Fictions: Cult Movies, Subcultural Capital and the Production of Cultural Distinctions", *Cultural Studies* 16 (2): 306–322.

Landis, Bill. 1982. "Herschell Gordon Lewis Today: The Original Godfather of Gore!", *Fangoria* (17): 23–27.

Lobato, Ramon. 2012. *Shadow Economies of Cinema: Mapping Informal Film Distribution*. London: BFI.

Lor. 1984. *Boardinghouse* [review], *Variety* 314 (7): 26.

Martin, B. 1981. "Basket Case: Writer-Director Frank Henenlotter and Producer Edgar Ievins Tell Us Just How Easy It Is to Make an Independent Horror Film", *Fangoria* (16): 54–57, 65.

Mathijs, Ernest. 2009. "They're Here! Special Effects in Horror Cinema of the 1970s and 1980s", in Ian Conrich, ed., *Horror Zone: The Cultural Experience of Contemporary Horror Cinema*. London: I. B. Tauris: 153–172.

McKenna, Mark. 2016. "A Murder Mystery in Black and Blue: The Marking, Distribution and Cult Mythology of *Snuff* in the UK" in Neil Jackson, Shaun Kimber, Johnny Walker and Thomas Joseph Watson, eds, *Snuff: Real Death and Screen Media*. London and New York: Bloomsbury Academic: 121–136.

Piepenburg, Erik. 2013. "Fairy Tale Ending in the Horror Realm: Chester Novell Turner and 'Black Devil Doll' Are Back", *New York Times*, 14 November. www.nytimes.com/2013/11/17/movies/chester-novell-turner-and-black-devil-doll-are-back.html (accessed June 2019).

Reboy, J. 1981. "Taste Will Tell", *Fangoria* (15): 37–43.

Schafer, Josh. 2013. "Greetings, Videovores!" *Lunchmeat's Midnight Snack* (Halloween), second pressing, n.p.

Schlockoff, R., and Everitt, David. 1983. "Attention Gorehounds! The Gates of Hell Are Open!" *Fangoria* (29): 9–12.

Sconce, Jeffrey. 1995. 'Trashing the Academy: Taste, Excess and an Emerging Politics of Cinematic Style,' *Screen* 36(4): 371–393

Sexton, Jamie. 2015. "Creeping Decay: Cult Soundtracks, Residual Media, and Digital Technologies", *New Review of Film and Television Studies* 13 (1): 12–30.

Skal, David J. 2001. *The Monster Show: A Cultural History of Horror Movies*. New York: Faber and Faber.

Stewart, A. 1990. "Direct-to-Video: The Saviour of Schlock", *Variety*, 11 April: 39–40.

Walker, Johnny. 2014. "Low Budgets, No Budgets and Digital Video Nasties: Recent British Horror and Informal Distribution", in Richard Nowell, ed., *Merchants of Menace: The Business of Horror Cinema*. London: Bloomsbury Academic: 215–228.

Walker, Johnny. 2016. "Traces of Snuff: Black Markets, Fan Subcultures, and Underground Horror in the 1990s", in Neil Jackson, Shaun Kimber, Johnny Walker and Thomas Joseph Watson, eds, *Snuff: Real Death and Screen Media*. London and New York: Bloomsbury Academic: 137–152.

Warren, B. 1989. "Charles Band: Full Moon Rising", *Gorezone* (8): 17–21, 55.

Wooley, John. 1985. "Blood Video", *Fangoria* (48): 40–43.

Wooley, John. 1986. "SAVINI the Ripper", *Fangoria* (50): 53.

Worland, Rick. 2007. *The Horror Film: An Introduction*. Oxford: Wiley Blackwell.

24

CULT CINEMA IN THE DIGITAL AGE

Iain Robert Smith

In his 2010 article 'Wake Up, Geek Culture: Time to Die', stand-up comedian and author Patton Oswalt complains about the mainstreaming of geek culture within contemporary society, illustrating his argument with a series of provocative examples such as 'Boba Fett's helmet emblazoned on sleeveless T-shirts worn by gym douches' and 'The *Glee* kids performing the songs from *The Rocky Horror Picture Show*' (Oswalt 2010). With a semi-ironic tone mixing sarcasm with unabashed nostalgia, Oswalt reflects that he used to be a nerd 'back 30 years ago when nerd meant something' but that today the 'hidden thought-palaces' that defined fandom when he was a teenager have instead been replaced by 'easily accessed websites, or Facebook pages with thousands of fans' (2010). Central to his critique of contemporary fandom is the notion that the Internet has made geek culture too accessible to a mainstream audience and that it therefore 'lets anyone become otaku[1] about anything instantly' (2010). For critics such as Oswalt, the exclusivity of geek culture is under threat within a digital environment that makes previously inaccessible materials available to a wider audience through streaming services such as YouTube, and it is this broadening of access to the 'mainstream' that is seen to threaten the demise of geek culture.

As should be evident to anyone who has followed recent debates within cult cinema scholarship, these comments are remarkably similar to the prevalent discourses surrounding cult cinema in the digital age. From Jeffrey Sconce's observation that cult cinema 'was very specific to a finite window in the history of cinephilia and exhibition ... when film culture itself was growing in the 1970s/1980s and yet access to certain films remained somewhat limited' (2008: 48) through to I.Q. Hunter's claim that it is 'much easier to be a cultist now, but it is also rather more inconsequential' (2008), there is a repeated emphasis within critical writings upon the threat posed by digital technologies that have made cult films more widely accessible and therefore no longer exclusive to a specific subcultural community. This issue is raised by Sconce himself when he claims that the original form of cultism 'evoked an esoteric sense of social, cultural, and esthetic exile', whereas in the contemporary era this kind of distinction is 'difficult to maintain once every film became available to every viewer' (2008: 48). The perceived threat of accessibility tends to be framed through a discourse of historical decline in which the adoption of digital technology marks the eventual death of the cult cinema phenomenon. Peter Stanfield, for example, argues that by the time a film cult comes into general view it is already dead, wrapped in a clean shroud, and being sold in the cult film section of the shopping mall's DVD store or the Internet's virtual simulacra of a downtown alternative store.

(2008: 50).

Even the most canonical cult films are seen to be under threat of losing their cult status within this context, with Mikel Koven claiming that the 'ease at which one can obtain a copy of *The Rocky Horror Picture Show* … removes the film's cult status' (2008). Underpinning these discourses of cult's transformation in the digital age, therefore, are a set of discourses that tend to reproduce the following set of oppositions:

PRE-DIGITAL	DIGITAL
Physical/Material	Virtual/Immaterial
Authentic/Real	Inauthentic/Simulacra
Difficult to access	Easy to access
Delayed gratification	Instantaneous
Non-commercial	Commercial
Anti-market	Consumerist
Radical	Apolitical
Subculture	Pop culture
Midnight screenings	Available anytime
Limited audience/Exclusive	Available to all
Marginal	Mainstream[2]

In many ways, this discourse is nothing new. There is an extensive history of criticism on cult cinema that highlights the perceived threat posed by films becoming accessible to a wider audience (see Jancovich et al. 2003; Martin 2008; Newman 2008). As I've discussed elsewhere, the transition of cult cinema into the domestic environment with VHS spurred many similar discourses of inauthenticity (Smith 2019), although it is clear that this discourse has become amplified within the digital context. Moreover, as Jamie Sexton has observed, these kinds of discourses surrounding cult's perceived decline reflect a 'nostalgic harking back to a bygone era' suggesting a 'yearning for a time when cult was more rarefied, when cult was less commercial, when cult *meant something*' (2014: 142). These attempts to contrast a contemporary era of accessibility with an earlier more exclusive age of cult cinema are therefore imbued with what Matt Hills has termed a 'mainstreaming discourse' through which 'technological developments are presumed to dilute cult's subcultural capital' (2015: 104). This notion of cult cinema being diluted and losing its sense of alterity within the digital context are therefore tied to a retro-nostalgia that contrasts a constructed notion of cult's past against a contemporary context in which cult cinema is presumed to have lost its subcultural value.[3]

In this chapter, I want to go beyond mapping out these discursive battles to explore more precisely how digital culture has impacted cult cinema. It is evident that digital technologies have had a significant impact on cult – from the increased availability of cult texts via downloading and streaming through to the emergence of digital communities of cult cinema fans online – yet there is a need to interrogate exactly how cult has evolved within this new digital context. Building on Matt Hills' work in this area, I will explore to what extent digital media 'might support new modes of subcultural distinction' (2015: 103), charting the myriad ways in which subcultural capital is being generated and fought over within digital spaces. Whereas Hills focused most of his attention upon retrospective processes whereby associations with earlier inaccessible cult forms such as midnight movies imbue older cult fans with 'retro-active subcultural capital' (2015: 118), I am instead focused here upon the ways in which digital cult cinema communities are themselves new sites for battles over cultural distinction and the emerging locations of subcultural capital. In order to establish how these digital shifts relate to a broader history of technological changes within cult cinema, I will begin by charting the prevailing discourses surrounding the introduction of digital technologies such as DVD, Blu-ray and online streaming before then discussing the specific subcultural politics under-pinning digital filesharing communities. Central to this account will be the private BitTorrent community Cinemageddon which has positioned itself as a leading hub for the circulation, res-toration and archiving of cult film materials. While cult cinema is often presumed to be a histor-ical phenomenon associated with 1970s–1980s screenings of midnight movies in mythologised cinemas such as the Elgin in New York and the Scala in London, I intend to demonstrate how cult cinema and its associated subcultural politics have adapted and flourished within the digital context. Bringing into play the power structures inherent within discourses on cult cinema and technological change, this chapter will therefore investigate the evolving meaning of cult cinema in the digital age.

Cult cinema and technology: Repetition, availability and access

In a 2008 blog discussing the relationship between cult cinema and new media technologies, Michael Z. Newman argues that 'cult media used to be pretty marginal, and it prided itself on its marginality' whereas, he reflects, in the contemporary age, 'I think it is much less so' (2008). Newman attributes this change to the rise of technologies such as DVD and online streaming since this digital technology 'makes the repetition of movies so much more available and accessible and makes the ordinary viewer more likely to engage with their favorite movies as cultists do' (2008). Repeat viewing has long been seen as a key marker of cult cinema, and this process has evolved alongside technological developments such as VHS, Laserdisc, DVD, Blu-ray and, most significantly, the Internet. As Elena Gorfinkel observes, 'Today, what video started – in its reconfiguration of conditions of films' access, scarcity and its experience of evan-escence – digital formats, DVD, Blu-ray, Netflix, YouTube, and the iPhone have considerably magnified' (2008: 37). The broadening of access to cult film materials and linking up of cult cinema fans through digital networks has offered many opportunities for cult communities to develop online, but that broadening of access has also functioned to threaten the subcul-tural politics underpinning the cult cinema phenomenon. As editors Mark Jancovich, Antonio Lázaro-Reboll, Julian Stringer and Andy Willis observe in the introduction to their *Defining Cult Movies* collection:

> On the one hand, these technologies have made cult movie fandom much less dependent on place, and have allowed the distribution and diffusion of cult materials across space. This has made possible the creation of large niche audiences that may be spatially diffuse but can constitute a powerful market force. On the other hand, this also threatens the sense of distinction and exclusivity on which cult movie fandom depends, and threatens to blur the very distinctions that organise it.

> (2003: 4)

There is a clear tension underpinning this shift from cult being conceived primarily as a public, social practice located at repertory cinemas to a more private, individualised practice within the home. On the one hand, there is a presumed loss of the post-countercultural communitarian ethos of collective film screenings since audiences more often watch cult films at home on their own, but, on the other hand, the networked nature of digital technologies provides opportunities for those same audiences to share material and interact with each other as part of a larger global cult community. Rather than disparate isolated individuals cut off from the collective experience, therefore, we see the emergence of thriving communities on social networks such as Facebook and Reddit devoted to particular strands of cult cinema and this digital infrastructure functions to support and sustain the development of numerous cult communities online. This process also means that information on cult cinema is more widely shared with detailed accounts of cult film traditions no longer restricted to print publications such as fanzines and movie guides but made freely available on online blogs and on user-generated sites such as Wikipedia. Digital technology therefore both facilitates these fan practices by allowing these cult communities to develop and flourish, but also functions to diminish the associated subcultural capital since knowledge about these films is no longer restricted in the way it was in the pre-digital era.

One of the responses to the increased digital availability of cult cinema online is an embrace of analogue technologies that are associated with earlier periods within the history of cult cinema. As Jamie Sexton has observed, 'Although many cultists have embraced new technologies, there exists a marked enthusiasm for older technologies and practices within sectors of cult fandom' (2015: 15). From the resurgence of interest in vinyl film soundtracks through to the rise of collectors of VHS cassettes, there is a prevailing emphasis on the materiality of the cult object and this should be understood partly as a response to the threat posed by digital technologies which, as J. Hoberman argues, have 'deprived the cult object of its aura' (2008: 45). This romanticised nostalgia for residual technologies is reflected in the decision by the renowned cult cinema exhibitor Alamo Drafthouse to open a 'Video Vortex' store in their North Carolina cinema that is devoted to VHS rentals at a time when the film rental market is now almost entirely online (McNary 2017). Comparable to the wider resurgence of interest in vinyl records at a time when music streaming services such as Spotify and Apple Music are dominating the music industry, there is a concomitant emphasis upon the physical, material pleasures of home video packaging and an attempt to embrace pre-digital technologies such as VHS that are nostalgically tied to an earlier supposedly more 'authentic' cult moment. Alongside this phenomenon, we also have the release of cult films in 4k digital restorations and limited-edition Blu-ray box sets through labels such as Arrow, Severin, 88 Films, Mondo Macabro and Shameless, reflecting a continued interest in physical formats such as DVD and Blu-ray amongst significant sectors of the cult audience.

Nevertheless, it is clear that the sphere of cult cinema fandom that has been most heavily impacted by digital technologies are the 'informal' (Lobato 2012) distribution channels through which fans share rare or inaccessible films with each other. Following the introduction of VHS, there has been a long history of 'grey-market' trading of these kinds of titles amongst cult cinema fans – from films that were outright banned such as the 'video nasties' in the United Kingdom through to titles that have been withdrawn from circulation such as *Superstar: The Karen Carpenter Story* (1987) – but this is a practice that has expanded considerably with the introduction of digital filesharing and streaming. Through private BitTorrent communities such as Cinemageddon and Karagarga, there are now thousands of previously rare and obscure films that are being made available and circulated through networked communities of cult cinema fans. Digital filesharing and streaming has therefore meant that these kinds of films are no longer exclusive to a small number of VHS or DVD-R collectors but are instead being shared widely through communities such as Cinemageddon to all who have registered with that particular tracker. In doing so, these communities have developed what I have elsewhere termed 'bootleg archives' (Smith 2011) in that they are building an extensive collection of films that were previously relatively inaccessible, and are thereby helping to make available entire strands of cult film history that have been hitherto neglected. For Jeffrey Sconce, this trend towards amassing extensive collections of numerous cult film traditions 'suggests that today's cultism is less about the intense fetishization of a single film than an obsessive mastery over an entire genre or subgenre' and he argues that within the digital sphere, 'everyone can serve as an archivist of his or her own obscure pocket of film history' (2008: 48–49). What this perspective ignores, however, is the collaborative nature of this phenomenon. Within communities such as Cinemageddon, these are not individual archivists tending to their own personal collections but rather a collective of archivists working together through digital platforms to restore and preserve areas of film history that have been largely forgotten elsewhere. It is important therefore that we address how these communities function in relation to prevailing discourses on cult cinema, especially in relation to the generation of subcultural capital, and investigate what they can tell us about the evolution of cult practices in the digital age.

Cinemageddon: Bootleg archives, collaboration and community

Launched on 17 April 2007, the private BitTorrent tracker Cinemageddon functions as an informal digital archive of cult cinema traditions worldwide with a community of 24,296 registered users sharing a total of 162,128 active torrents.[4] Uploads are organised into generic categories, such as Action, Exploitation, Gore, Hidden Gems, Martial Arts, Sci-Fi, Tinfoil Hat and XXX, and while films are the primary focus of the collection the site also collects eBooks, soundtracks, posters and other cult paraphernalia. As with other private trackers, Cinemageddon functions on an 'invite-only' system where users can only join the community if they have been sent an invite from an existing member. This process encourages a sense of exclusivity that contrasts with public BitTorrent trackers such as The Pirate Bay and freely available streaming services such as YouTube. The Cinemageddon community is particularly encouraged to upload materials that pertain to one of the site's forty-one ongoing 'Projects' which are designed to help compile exhaustive archives of films from specific cult directors such as Godfrey Ho, Joe D'Amato or Jess Franco and cult genres such as Eurospy, Pinky Violence or Clones of Bruce Lee. The broad success of this strategy is reflected in the site's Eurocrime project which has 1,287 titles in its archive, comprising arguably the most comprehensive collection of Italian 'Poliziotteschi' films in existence alongside various other European crime film traditions.

These projects generally conform to pre-digital cult categories with a particular focus on cinema traditions from the 1960s–1980s featuring directors and stars whose cult reputations were established well before the advent of digital streaming and filesharing. The emphasis is less on the discovery of 'new' cult cinemas, therefore, than it is on the preservation and maintenance of pre-established and pre-digital cult film traditions. However, what sites like Cinemageddon have facilitated is the exhaustive attempt to track down and share every example of these particular cult traditions with the rest of the community, shifting the emphasis away from individual cult films towards the collecting and archiving of entire bodies of work. Moreover, the administrators at Cinemageddon impose a number of rules on uploads designed to support the sharing of particular kinds of cult films, and to exclude films which are perceived to be too popular or otherwise inappropriate for the site. For example, it is advised that any film that has more than 3,000 votes on IMDB is probably too popular for Cinemageddon while films such as *This Is Spinal Tap* (1984) and *The Wicker Man* (1973) and franchises such as *Friday the 13th* (1980–) and *The Evil Dead* (1981–) are all specifically named as titles that are excluded. The site therefore functions under a particular understanding of cult cinema that privileges the rare and the marginal at the expense of anything that might be perceived as popular or 'mainstream' cult. This privileging of specifically marginal forms of cult cinema within the Cinemageddon community functions both to diminish the threat of copyright claims being made against the community from major film studios, and also to reassert a sense of subcultural distinction from the mainstream within a digital context where subcultural capital is perceived to be under threat.

What particularly marks this community out from pre-digital collections of cult cinema are the increased opportunities for collaboration between fans in building this archive, and one of the ways in which the community collaborates and adds value through their labour is via fansubbing. While limited processes of fan translation and subtitle production have been undertaken since the early days of VHS, this practice has flourished in the digital era and while it is particularly associated with anime fan communities (Denison 2011), the practice has spread to encompass numerous other film traditions. Whereas anime fansubbing communities tend to be focused on making the latest releases available to non-Japanese speaking audiences, the Cinemageddon community primarily focuses on broadening access to titles from 1960s–1980s cult film traditions that have never been subtitled before, and they do this by incentivising contributors to work together to translate and subtitle films from particular directors and generic cycles. Given that cult discourse is still primarily an Anglophone phenomenon and that non-US/UK titles within the cult canon tend to be those that have previously picked up international distribution in the West through a dubbed or subtitled release, these communities are therefore working together to widen access to areas of global cult cinema that have not hitherto been available through formal circuits of distribution.

Furthermore, these collaborative processes also help build a sense of community and collective participation amongst the membership. There are parallels here with Virginia Crisp's research into the online dissemination of East Asian cinemas through English-language filesharing communities. What she found in these groups is that 'there is an important collaborative and community aspect to online distribution. It shows that the films themselves are not the primary focus, but act as the facilitator to community participation' (Crisp 2015: 153). As I discussed earlier, digital technology is often framed in terms of broadening access to cult cinema and its practices – and the attendant risk that this poses to processes of subcultural distinction – but it is important to recognise that a site like Cinemageddon also facilitates the collaboration of fans who work together to restore, preserve and archive cult film materials. The site would therefore qualify as a 'rogue archive', which Abigail De Kosnik defines as follows:

> Internet sites that can be accessed by all online users[5], with no paywalls or institutional barriers; that allow all content to be streamed or downloaded in full; that do not delete, hide, or edit content based on copyright holders' allegations of legal infringement or for any other reason; that are committed to the persistent publication and long-term preservation of all content that they store; that have search-and-retrieval features so that users can locate specific texts; and that have either weak ties or no affiliations with traditional memory institutions such as government archives, university libraries, and brick-and-mortar museums.
>
> (2016: 18)

As De Kosnik notes, these kinds of archives are 'not restricted by copyright laws… and some simply contravene copyright laws that they feel hinder, rather than help, cultural preservation' (2016: 77). Unlike public trackers such as The Pirate Bay which are primarily designed for the free sharing of all kinds of content, private trackers such as Cinemageddon incentivise their members to contribute to building a stable archive that can preserve a particular kind of content – through rewards for contributing titles that are not already part of the collection, and for maintaining a seeding ratio so that these titles continue to be available for other members to download. To some extent, therefore, the members of Cinemageddon share the attitude that De Kosnik has identified amongst other filesharing communities who tend to think of 'media piracy as a form of collecting' (2012: 524) and frame themselves as 'media archivists' who are preserving 'films and television shows that official institutions might ignore, allow to be lost, or keep out of circulation for a prolonged period of time or indefinitely' (2012: 529).

It is clear then that there is a significant amount of fan labour involved in these processes, including the time taken to track down the films, to translate and subtitle them, and to then carefully catalogue and organise them into an archive. As Oliver Carter has observed in his ethnography of a file-sharing community he refers to as CineTorrent, these communities function as an 'alternative economy of fan enterprise where fans are responding to the current limitations of commercially released … cinema on DVD by taking it upon themselves to make unreleased titles available for distribution within the alternative economy' (2018: 33). This informal 'alternative economy' therefore functions in a symbiotic relationship with the formal distribution companies, often making films available that are perceived to have relatively little commercial value. Indeed, Carter observes that 'though legally uncertain, the activities of CineTorrent and its membership are expressed as a moral act, providing a service that is not economically viable outside of this alternative economy' (2018: 139). What is interesting is that even established critics such as Tim Lucas, who discussed Cinemageddon in his long-running magazine *Video Watchdog* (1990–2017), have praised the site for making films available with fansubs or dual audio tracks, given that these are 'unlikely to surface commercially' (2009: 5). According to Lucas,

> If you go to the movie file-sharing site Cinemageddon … and are lucky enough to find a window into their limited membership, awaiting you there is a wonderland of opportunities under the searchable terms 'fansubbed' or 'fansubs.' By typing these words into the CG search engine, you can access dozens, even hundreds of downloadable files wherein the uploader has wedded home-made English subtitles to an official or televised film source from another country.
>
> (2009: 4)

It is important to note, however, that Lucas is highly critical of the fact that members sometimes upload commercially available titles, which he feels is

> ripping off the companies who are investing in the restoration of the films its members hold dear, rather than merely focusing on the homegrown archaeology that makes them a truly vital source for anyone interested in arcane avenues of film.
>
> (2009: 5)

What we see here are the tensions between these BitTorrent groups and other valued members of the cult community such as the commercial companies that restore and release films for formal distribution on DVD and Blu-ray. While the administrators at Cinemageddon have introduced a '12-month rule' that means that community members cannot share any new DVD or Blu-ray rips for a period of a year from release, there has nevertheless been a heated debate within the cult fandom surrounding the ethics of Cinemageddon and especially its impact on the wider cult eco-system.

To explore these debates within the cult community and their relation to broader battles over subcultural distinction within the digital context, it is worth focusing briefly here on a representative discussion that took place on the message board 'The Latarnia Forums' in 2009. On a thread titled 'Rethinking "That" Site', author Mirek Lipinski starts by making clear his own ambivalence about the piracy taking place on the site, but he then admits that 'whenever I check out Cinemageddon, I'm instantly enticed by the care and dedication over its "projects," which seem valuable to me as a library of rare or hard to get films – an archive of film history, if you will' and he notes that 'there is wonderful work being done in making rare foreign films available – and with English subtitles' (Lipinski 2009). Similarly, templar71 declares that they are 'astounded at the work that some enthusiasts have put into their uploads, whether it be adding subtitles or making composite prints to come up with the closest thing possible to an uncut version of a film' but, on the other hand, they are 'dismayed by those who choose to upload readily-available films that you can rent in any Blockbuster or buy in any chain store' (templar71 2009).

For these members, the primary ethical problem with Cinemageddon is the sharing of films that are already available to buy, and while this is partly related to the relative subcultural value of marginal as opposed to popular cult films (as indicated by the specific choice of 'Blockbuster' and 'any chain store' as locations for signalling their wide availability), the opposition to this practice is more often framed in relation to the threat to the formal distribution companies that produce DVDs and Blu-rays of cult films. As Lapinski explains, 'If such sites become the norm, particularly with cult stuff, for which there is a limited audience, why would DVD companies want to put out official releases of these films, when they know that much of the audience already has these as [sic] films as downloads?' (Lapinski 2009) The risk posed to formal distributors is therefore not only that their DVDs and Blu-rays will be ripped and uploaded to the community, but that the availability of so many rare cult films on Cinemageddon will reduce the potential market for these titles if they were to be given a formal release. Nevertheless, despite this threat to the economic viability of formal distributors, the contributors to the Latarnia thread still express some level of admiration for what the community on Cinemageddon has produced, with 'Howling Beast' admitting that

> I'd probably be pretty angry if I was a company like Code Red and found my stuff up on there. But when you look at all the fansubbed Naschy films, Santo films, Italian western and horror films, it just really makes you understand how important the site is.
> (Howling Beast 2009)

The value of a site such as Cinemageddon is therefore related to the notion that it is providing a resource that isn't available elsewhere, and that through restoring, fansubbing and circulating these films they are building an archive that wouldn't otherwise exist.

This debate is therefore tied to a broader discussion of the ethics of piracy, and I think it is important that, as Ramon Lobato has argued, we avoid thinking about piracy as a 'singular practice' and instead think about numerous 'piracies' that can encompass a variety of ethical positions (2012: 70). For example, in his study of a pirate DVD vendor named 'Juan' in Mexico City, Lobato foregrounds how 'pirate circuits can also be networks for film preservation and archiving' (2012: 70) and he traces the processes through which Juan makes Mexican films available that have no formal distributor in place. Lobato argues that what is 'distinctive about Juan's form of piracy' is that this is often 'the only distribution these films receive' (2012: 89), and he contends that this complicates the ethical position of this form of piracy given that it preserves and makes available these films in economic circumstances where the 'profit potential for many of these titles is slim to non-existent, and few legitimate distributors would bother with them' (2012: 90). As should be evident, BitTorrent sites such as Cinemageddon function in a similar manner – preserving and archiving titles that have no formal distribution and making them available to anyone who signs up to the private community. Such sites therefore provide a valued function within the wider cult eco-system, and while their reliance on acts of piracy creates evident tensions within the cult community, the illicit nature of such acts clearly plays into the transgressive subcultural politics of cult fandom and its broader association with non-conformist politics.

Conclusion

In his deliberately provocative critique of the concept of cult cinema within the contemporary era, Adrian Martin argues that 'there is a difference between the pleasure of discovery [as] a solitary pursuit and the instant ecstasy of an on-line community' (2008: 41), and he concludes his account by posing the following question:

> Honestly, what would you prefer: a film that you discover for yourself, via some obscure distribution or exhibition byway, before uncovering the existence of a few scattered soul brothers or sisters around the world, alike only in their love for this Unidentified Filmic Object – or a film that is smoothly conveyed to you, signed, sealed and delivered as a certified cult item?
>
> (2008: 42)

For Martin, the ways in which the concept of 'cult cinema' has become used as a marketing tool adopted by the industry, rather than emerging through happenstance and word-of-mouth, means that cult in the digital era has become tainted by commercialism and ultimately has been co-opted by the mainstream. What this kind of account neglects, however, is that the digital era of cult cinema also comprises private BitTorrent communities such as Cinemageddon which are precisely based around bringing together scattered communities of fans from around the world who are invested in sharing an explicitly marginal form of cult cinema through a relatively obscure distribution byway. Indeed, the Cinemageddon community complicates many of the oppositions between digital and pre-digital cult culture that underpin Martin's argument, and that I set out in my introduction. While cult cinema in the digital age is often presented as being 'easy to access' and 'available to all', we find in these BitTorrent communities a continued emphasis upon a limited, relatively exclusive group of users who have access to the cult materials and that control who is invited to be part of the community. Moreover, the nature of their non-commercial (and to some extent anti-market) practices and their sustained emphasis on explicitly non-popular forms of cult cinema, means that they clearly function as locations for the production of subcultural capital in distinction to an imagined notion of the 'mainstream'.

The technological developments underpinning cult cinema in the digital age, therefore, may technically make the films more widely available, but that doesn't necessarily lead to the inevitable commercialisation or co-option of cult practices. As Jamie Sexton observes, access is not the only factor that influences cult cinema and 'equally important are issues such as knowledge, awareness, and expertise' (2014: 142). In other words, cult materials may be more easily available within a digital context where audiences can easily seek out films on YouTube and information on Wikipedia, but that doesn't necessarily mean that these practices will be adopted more broadly. Cult communities are continuing to emerge that rely explicitly on processes of subcultural distinction from the mainstream, and BitTorrent communities such as Cinemageddon demonstrate that digital technologies are actually contributing to and facilitating that process.

Digital technology has not led to the death of cult, therefore, but has instead been the stimulus for another stage in the evolution of cult cinema practices.

Notes

1 Otaku is a Japanese term for an obsessive fan. Initially pejorative, the term has since been taken up as a self-description by fans both within Japan and internationally.
2 These are similar to the oppositions between subcultures and the mainstream set out by Sarah Thornton in her 1995 study *Club Cultures: Music, Media, and Subcultural Capital* so it is clear that this discourse surrounding the threat of digital technology is tied up with a broader oppositional politics in relation to conceptions of the 'mainstream'.
3 Declarations of the death of cult cinema are reminiscent of the claims of the end of youth culture identified by Rupa Huq who has observed that 'journalists who had long left behind their own gilded youth declared that modern music was bankrupt of pop's resistive role of earlier generations' (Huq 2006: 4). Given that cult cinema is so intimately tied up with youth culture, it is perhaps inevitable that this nostalgic longing for a more 'authentic' earlier period of cult cinema is often tied up in a nostalgia for the author's own youth.
4 These details are correct as of 22 February 2019.
5 Private BitTorrent trackers such as Cinemageddon and Karagarga do require users to register via an invitation from an existing member, so while theoretically 'all online users' could access the site, in practice the membership is more restricted – nevertheless, there is no paywall or institutional barrier in place.

References

Carter, Oliver. 2018. *Making European Cult Cinema: Fan Enterprise in an Alternative Economy.* Amsterdam: Amsterdam University Press.

Crisp, Virginia. 2015. *Film Distribution in the Digital Age: Pirates and Professionals.* Basingstoke: Palgrave Macmillan.

De Kosnik, Abigail. 2012. 'The Collector Is the Pirate', *International Journal of Communication*, 6: 529–541.

De Kosnik, Abigail. 2016. *Rogue Archives: Digital Cultural Memory and Media Fandom.* Cambridge, MA: MIT Press.

Denison, Rayna. 2011. 'Anime Fandom and the Liminal Spaces between Fan Creativity and Piracy', *International Journal of Cultural Studies*, 14 5: 449–466.

Gorfinkel, Elena. 2008. 'Cult Film or Cinephilia by Any Other Name', *Cineaste*, 34.1: 33–38.

Hills, Matt. 2015. 'Cult Cinema and the 'Mainstreaming' Discourse of Technological Change: Revisiting Subcultural Capital in Liquid Modernity', *New Review of Film and Television Studies*, 13. 1: 100–121.

Hoberman, J. 2008. 'Cult Cinema: A Critical Symposium', *Cineaste*, 34.1: 44–45.

Howling Beast. 2009. 'Rethinking "That" Site' [Online forum comment]. Message posted to www.tapatalk.com/groups/thelatarniaforums/rethinking-that-site-t8372.html

Hunter, I.Q. 2008. 'Cult Cinema: A Critical Symposium (Web Edition)', *Cineaste*, 34.1. www.cineaste.com/winter2008/cult-film-a-critical-symposium [accessed 29 July 2019].

Huq, Rupa. 2006. *Beyond Subculture: Pop, Youth and Identity in a Postcolonial World.* London: Routledge.

Jancovich, Mark, Antonio Lázaro-Reboll, Julian Stringer and Andy Willis. 2003. 'Introduction', in Jancovich, Lázaro-Reboll, Stringer and Willis, eds, *Defining Cult Movies: The Cultural Politics of Oppositional Taste.* Manchester: Manchester University Press: 1–13.

Koven, Mikel. 2008. 'Cult Cinema: A Critical Symposium (Web Edition)', *Cineaste*, 34.1. www.cineaste.com/winter2008/cult-film-a-critical-symposium [accessed 29 July 2019].

Lapinski, Mirek. 2009. 'Rethinking "That" Site' [Online forum comment]. Message posted to www.tapatalk.com/groups/thelatarniaforums/rethinking-that-site-t8372.html

Lobato, Ramon. 2012. *Shadow Economies of Cinema: Mapping Informal Film Distribution.* London: BFI.

Lucas, Tim. 2009. 'AVI Watchdog', *Video Watchdog*, 153: 4–5.

Martin, Adrian. 2008. 'What's Cult Got to Do with It? In Defense of Cinephile Elitism', *Cineaste*, 34. 1: 39–42.

McNary, Dave. 2017. 'Alamo Drafthouse Launching Video Rental Store in 2018', *Variety* (18 December). https://variety.com/2017/film/news/alamo-drafthouse-video-rental-store-1202643737 [accessed 29 July 2019].

Newman, Michael Z. 2008. 'Notes on Cult Films and New Media Technology', *zigzagger* (02 August). http://zigzigger.blogspot.com/2008/08/notes-on-cult-films-and-new-media.html [accessed 29 July 2019].

Oswalt, Patton. 2010. 'Wake Up, Geek Culture. Time to Die', *Wired* (27 December). www.wired.com/2010/12/ff-angrynerd-geekculture [accessed 29 July 2019].

Sconce, Jeffrey. 2008. 'Cult Cinema: A Critical Symposium', *Cineaste*, 34.1: 48–49.

Sexton, Jamie. 2014. 'From Bad to Good and Back to Bad Again? Cult Cinema and Its Unstable Trajectory', in Perkins and Verevis, eds, *B is for Bad Cinema: Aesthetics, Politics, and Cultural Value*. Albany: State University of New York Press: 129–145.

Sexton, Jamie. 2015. 'Creeping Decay: Cult Soundtracks, Residual Media, and Digital Technology', *New Review of Film and Television Studies*, 13.1: 12–30.

Smith, Iain R. 2011. 'Bootleg Archives: Notes on BitTorrent Communities and Issues of Access', *FLOW*, 14: 02 (23 June). www.flowjournal.org/2011/06/bootleg-archives [accessed 29 July 2019].

Smith, Iain R. 2019. 'What Is Cult When It's At Home?: Reframing Cult Cinema in Relation to Domestic Space', in Baschiera and De Rosa, eds, *Film and Domestic Space*, Edinburgh: Edinburgh University Press.

Stanfield, Peter. 2008. 'Cult Cinema: A Critical Symposium', *Cineaste*, 34.1: 49–50.

templar71. 2009. 'Rethinking "That" Site' [Online forum comment]. Message posted to www.tapatalk.com/groups/thelatarniaforums/rethinking-that-site-t8372.html [accessed 29 July 2019].

25

CULT CINEMA AND FILM FESTIVALS

Russ Hunter

It is easy to ignore the impact that film festivals can have upon cult cinema. Whilst the phenomenon of midnight movies demonstrated that cult film viewing could be a very public and often participatory spectacle based around specific exhibition circumstances, more recent ideas within fan studies have tended to stress the rather more individualistic nature of fandom and cult film consumption. With very few exceptions (see Mathijs and Sexton, 2011), cult cinemas role and presence at film festivals has largely remained unexplored. In part the problem resides in the specific aspects of festivals scholars have tended to focus on to date and, in particular, the kinds of festivals deemed worthy of wider critical attention. The publicly popular idea that film festivals are always large-scale, glitzy affairs with prestigious red-carpet events, a host of international movie stars and glamorous parties has been reflected in literature on the subject. In line with this, historically, both popular and academic writing has focused upon a very narrow range of festivals and festival types. Thus, as Richard Porton has astutely noted, for most 'critics, programmers and the public, Cannes, for better or worse, has come to exemplify the quintessential film festival' (Porton, 2009: 5). As de Valck (2012) has observed, in reality larger 'A list' festivals such as Berlin, Cannes or Venice represent only a small proportion of active festivals worldwide. But the field of festival studies has developed at a rapid pace in the last decade and more recently writers have begun to unpack the diversity and breadth of the festival circuit, noting the range and of festival types, sizes and audiences. The work of a variety of scholars, such as Dina Iordanova, Marijke de Valck and Skadi Loist, has therefore elaborated upon the protean nature of film festivals and is so doing has advanced the field of festival studies immeasurably. Cult cinema has, however, remained largely overlooked within such studies.

Whilst it can appear across a number of festival types, cult cinema has typically found its expression at genre film festivals. Although an amorphous category that loosely refers to festivals that focus upon a number of genres, predominant amongst these are fantasy, horror and science fiction. As I have noted elsewhere (see Hunter, 2018), genre festivals are not homogeneous and vary greatly in terms of their size, budget, reach, function and geographical location. The Montreal based Fantasia or the Sitges Film Festival, for instance, are firmly industry-facing events with large audiences and (relatively) large budgets, whilst others such as the Sheffield's Celluloid Screams or the Ljubljana based Kurja Polt have tighter budgetary constraints and are more straightforwardly audience oriented. In any case, as Mark Peranson (2009) has noted in relation to film festival structures more generally, most fall somewhere on a continuum between 'business' and 'audience' festivals. Regardless, the nature of such events as not just showcases for new talent, but as celebrations of both genre canons and genre stars, means that they are often programmed in a way that means they include a sizeable number of cult films. As such, genre film festivals are fan-focused events that feature a mixture of new, classic and rare screenings, as well as the appearance of special guests and a number genre-themed side events. This multifaceted programming strategy has been stressed by Mathijs and Sexton (2011), who have noted that cult film festivals celebrate the canonical as well as embracing the new. In this way, they argue, they can often be the first to screen new or challenging genre material, such as the Brussels International Fantastic Film Festival championing of J-horror in the early 2000s. As such, they tend be at the forefront of promoting new genre trends and – at the same time – screen what might later may become cult properties.

The precise number of active film festivals worldwide is necessarily hard to assess, a task complicated by the lack of an all-encompassing festival association. Writing in 2013 Stephen Follows observed that nearly 10,000 film festivals had run at least once in the preceding fifteen years, with there being approximately 3,000 still active. Regardless, few are specifically and explicitly dedicated to cult cinema. Rather, the concentration of cult cinema within the broad bounds of genre cinema has often meant that its exhibition has tended to be, for the most part, at genre film festivals. Although genre-focused festivals have existed as far back as the establishment of Sitges in 1968, there has been a mushrooming of them since the turn of the millennium (in line with developments within film festivals more generally). Although they exist worldwide, Mathijs and Sexton (2011) have identified Europe as a particular nodal point for the development of genre film festivals and, as Hunter (2018) has noted, there are more than 120 festivals that could be identified as genre film festivals currently active in Europe. Whilst the majority of these festivals focus in some ways upon fantasy, horror and sci-fi genres, they often feature a variety of other popular genres and tend to accommodate a broad series of taste cultures. Thus, whilst attending a genre film festival audience are likely to see the contemporary genre releases as well as, for instance, Japanese cult films as diverse as *Matango: Attack of the Mushroom People* (Ishiro Honda, 1963) or the nunsploitation *Wet Rope Confession* (Koyu Ohara, 1979), or American cult properties as varied as the Chuck Norris vehicle *The Delta Force* (Menahem Golan, 1986) or the iconic *The Texas Chainsaw Massacre* (Tobe Hooper, 1974). Thus, the new sits cheek-by-jowl with the canonical.

Identifying cult cinema with film festivals is, in one sense, a rather problematic exercise. It should be noted that with regard to the exhibition of cult cinema there is not necessarily a straightforward split between festivals catering for art-house fare on the one hand and genre cinema on the other. So, whilst cult cinema *tends* to be programmed most predominantly at genre film festivals, this is not exclusively so. A number of examples of cult cinema are also art films and so are often subject to very different reading protocols and are subsequently valorised in an entirely different way at more prestigious, larger A list festivals. Neither are they always exhibited in ways that celebrates their cult qualities. Some films and filmmakers have two, simultaneous addresses, having largely separate screening lives at radically different kinds of festivals. Symptomatic of this are the works of Alejandro Jodorowsky, which appeal to both cult and arthouse audiences. In 2017, for instance, Jodorowsky appeared as guest of honour at the Lisbon-based MotelX horror film festival, having previously had his work explored at the Mexican Mórbido Film Fest. But as Cerdán and Fernández Labayen point out, when digitally remastered version of *El Topo*, *The Holy Mountain* and *Fando Y Lis* were screened at the 2006 Cannes Film Festival, they were 'once again situated within the viewing category of French cinephilia' (2009: 113). Indeed, as they note, in the same year Jodorowsky was awarded Sitges's

Premi Máquina del Temps – a lifetime achievement award normally given to those whose career has been spent working in genre cinema.

Given that cult is not a distinctive production genre (although, at times, some have attempted to make it so), the question remains as to whether or not festivals show films that *are* cult or have a role in *making* films cult. Undoubtedly there are contemporary genre films that are designed specifically to play well at festivals, in the same way that the idea of 'the festival film' operates in relation to art cinema. The concept of the festival film is well established, but it has not typically been mobilised in relation to cult cinema. In part this is because cult cinema is ordinarily not seen to be something that can be pre-ordained and so the idea of *creating* films that would play well to cultists has tended to have little traction. However, it is clear that a number of recent works, such as *Brawl in Cell Block 99* (S. Craig Zahler, 2017) or *The Greasy Strangler* (2016) have been both designed with the festival circuit in mind (both genre-specific and more broadly) and found considerable success there.

In general terms, regardless of their size or audience address, festivals have been viewed as existing in order to 'nurture independent films, showcase national cinemas, and bring international films to ever-increasing audiences' (Ruoff, 2012: 1). Whilst this is generally true, it tends to ignore the role festivals play in both celebrating and canonising older films. For the most part this take place via retrospective screenings that are either one-off celebrations of a particular film (or director) or as part of a more extended programming strand. Ordinarily, however, cult films at festivals tend, by their very nature, to already be well established as cult properties and hence feature as retrospectives. In this regard festivals can be seen to be reinforcing, reigniting or providing an alternative reception trajectory for films that already have some form of cult reputation. Although there has long been an association between film festivals and the exhibition of new, hard-to-access cinema (de Valck, 2012), for cultists festival programmes need to provide access to new genre films (some of which might later become cult films) whilst also allowing for the celebration of the wider canon of cult cinema. In the case of genre film festivals these form a crucial part of the overall programme, with the valorisation of older work forming a key structuring element to the overall festival experience. Typically, the programming of a particular retrospective strand might be accompanied by the attendance of an industry guest that compliments the liveness of the festival attending experience – ordinarily such guests are an actor or director, but increasingly encompassing composers, make-up artists, SFX specialists or poster and video/DVD artists.

As Dina Iordanova (2016: xiii) has observed, it is increasingly the case that films are just 'one of many elements that make up a festival'. This is particularly true for genre festivals, where the concentrated presence of fans means that both the appearance and availability of guests, as well as events that engage with their object of fandom more generally, are highly desired. As such, festival programmes are often centred, at least in part, around the presence of a guest (or a number of guests) who partake in a variety of extra-filmic activities. These can range from providing introductions to films with which they were involved, taking part of in onstage interviews and Q&As or offering a workshop that relates to their own particular expertise. Most frequently guests are directors or actors, but a range of other creative influences on a film, such as composers, writers and SFX specialists, are increasingly sought after, meaning that the precise nature of their participation can vary. In this way an actor such as Christina Lindberg might recount tales of her time working on *Thriller: A Cruel Picture* (Bo Arne Vibenius, 1973) as she did at the Ljubljana based Kurja Polt Genre Film Festival in 2017; Rick Baker might provide a demonstration on special makeup effects as he did at Sitges in 2015; or John Waters might offer a directing masterclass as he did at the Brussels-based Offscreen Film Festival in 2013. Marijke de Valck has noted that in the 1980s film directors realised that a form of 'alternative' career could be found on the film festival circuit, which could be enhanced by making films specifically aimed at and for it (2012: 33). But for genre festivals the idea of an alternative career has taken on an added element that goes beyond attempting to create festival films. The sheer quantity of genre festivals has meant that it is possible for guests to develop an alternate career by travelling from festival to festival in any given calendar year. As festivals budgets are, for the majority of festivals, limited, fees are rarely high (and sometimes non-existent) and motivations vary from guest to guest. For some it provides an opportunity to see new cities, meet fans and explore the significance of their earlier works (particularly for those who are no longer working regularly or who have retired), for others it is a way to promote new material, remain visible or earn extra income. Either way, the presence and accessibility of cult actors, directors and other involved with particular cult films at festivals has increasingly proved appealing to DVD/Blu Ray labels and it is now the commonplace for DVD extras to be filmed at festivals.

It is increasingly possible to view film festivals as alternative distribution circuits (de Valck, 2007). This idea has generally been conceived of in relation to art cinema, where a shrinking number of independent cinemas and their lack of distribution in mainstream cinemas has meant that festivals often represent the only public exhibition art films are likely to receive. Moreover, they offer a platform for filmmakers to showcase work, providing a crucial marketing function for films that, for the most part, lack substantial promotional budgets. As Cindy Hing-Yuk Wong notes 'while film festivals play pivotal roles both in defining a shared canon of "great" cinema and in adding cultural value to films, they are also significant because they create nodes of global business in which films circulate as commodities' (2011: 129). For cult films, which may not have been exhibited for many decades (if they ever received significant and sustained theatrical distribution), this dynamic is rather complicated. Many will have circulated, in various media forms since their release, but their lack of recent cinematic exhibition means that distributors increasingly view festivals as micro distribution circuits. The lack of precedent for print prices for a film that has not screened in many years, such as *Nightmare City* (Umberto Lenzi, 1981), for instance, means a premium can be charged, which can place increasing financial pressure on festival budgets.

The nature of genre festivals as fan-oriented, but curated, events, has several implications. For older cult properties, that might previously have received either cinematic or video distribution (on whatever scale), the event is an opportunity for viewers and fans to reengage with the film anew in the presence of an audience. Typically, discussions will follow, perhaps in the bar or outside the screening room, about the relative state of the print, the merits of seeing the film on 'the big screen' or pieces of trivia about it will be argued over. For others the festival and its carefully curated nature means discovering for the first time a whole new raft of cult films. Either way, the rather unpredictable, variable and sometimes esoteric nature of cult cinema means that distributors frequently charge a premium for festival prints. Regardless of its quality, the desire for festival audiences at genre festivals to view 35mm print versions of films has means that there is pressure on festival organisers to show any given film in the 'right' format. For cult cinema audiences, attention to detail is a key part of the festival experience.

Bosma observed that a 'film festival is simultaneously an individualistic search for satisfaction and a social gathering' (2015: 70) and for cult film fans this is particularly pertinent as festivals offer a communal space within which to explore, express and share aspects of their fandom. In drawing upon Sarah Thornton's readings of Pierre Bordeau and applying it to horror fandom, Matt Hills has explored the dynamics and function of subcultural capital amongst fan groups. For Hills, subcultural capital amongst fans remains 'potential' or 'fixed' if they are not in a position to *demonstrate* and interpolate it. In this way he argues that subcultural capital only becomes 'actual' or 'circulating' in shared experiences where fans can effectively 'convert' it by meeting other fans and interacting with them. Genre festivals, which typically feature an area that audiences can congregate in between screenings (be it a bar, café or other space), are ideal events for this circulation of subcultural capital.

In line with Henri Langlois' notion that 'a film is only alive when screened' and stressing the influence of the Pesaro model, de Valck (2012: 31) suggests that festivals offer a number of ways in which audiences can engage with films that goes beyond their exhibition. Whilst the Pesaro model has tended to suggest festivals can offer discursive engagement with films via a variety of public lectures, interviews and even conferences, genre festivals offer the opportunity for films that are established cult properties to be explored anew. So, although this might be via introductions or talks that help to contextualise a film by experts, or a Q&A with someone involved with the film (be that an actor, director or otherwise), it can also mean participating in other ways. Genre film festivals are not just about the exhibition of films, offering fans opportunities beyond collectively watching and celebrating cult films. Participatory patterns that developed for cult films during their theatrical exhibition, at film clubs or even during home viewing, can often carry over into festival screenings. As such, they offer audience members the opportunity to participate in cult film practices they might otherwise never encounter. This can happen in a number of ways. In general terms this means festivals offering events that stray outside of the bounds of straightforward screenings. Lucio Fulci's *The Beyond* provides a good example of how offering events beyond straightforward exhibition offers cult fans the opportunity to re-engage with films in new and unusual ways. As Jeffrey Ruoff has noted, a 'film is a live event. Successful festivals maximise this live dimension' (2012: 3). In 2016 Italian composer Fabio Frizzi, along with his Frizzi 2 Fulci band, performed a live accompaniment to his score for *The Beyond* at Abertoir Horror Festival (based in the small Welsh coastal town of Aberystwyth and named to reference the town). For most attendees of the festival this represented way of revisiting the film via live performance of the soundtrack. More than that, it also meant that they could do it whilst in the same physical space as the original composer, an element of liveness that was particularly important for fans of the film.

Another example from the same festival helps to reinforce this point. At the 2011 edition of Abertoir Horror Festival William Castle's *The Tingler* (1959) was programmed as part of an annual homage to the festivals 'patron saint' (and the film's star), Vincent Price. Unbeknownst to the audience buzzers had been attached under selected seats in the cinema, which were activated at a key moment in the film. At the climax of Castle's film the screen momentarily goes black and Price cries "*Scream! Scream for your lives! The Tingler is loose in the theater!*", breaking the fourth wall and directly addressing the audience. In line with his usual fits of showmanship, Castle had ensured that theatres had rigged their seats up so that buzzers would go off just at this moment, suggesting that the titular Tingler had escaped into the auditorium and that the audience were in danger. Screening the film and fitting buzzers to seats offered opportunities to revisit what has long been considered a cultish moment within the film, but one that most festival goers would not have experienced given the film's release date. Similarly, for its 2012 Screening of Tommy Wiseau's *The Room*, a film regularly categorised as amongst the worst of all time, the Brussels-based Offscreen Film Festival provided audience members with wooden teaspoons prior to entering the cinema. This was to facilitate what had become an established fan practice of throwing spoons at the screen during public screenings of the film, something that had developed in response to notorious shots in *The Room* where a picture frame containing – absurdly – a photograph of a spoon in it can be seen in the background. But the film has, in line with the likes of *The Rocky Horror Picture Show* (Jim Sharman, 1975), developed an audience 'script' whereby certain lines in the film are either pre-empted by audiences or repeated along with the actors. Thus, for *The Room* cult fans present at the Offscreen showing merrily called out 'I did not hit her ... I did not ... Oh, hi Mark' and 'you're tearing me apart, Lisa!', along with other improvised shout-outs. All of which played into an already established pattern of watching the film ironically and in a raucously celebratory manner.

Mathijs and Sexton have noted that audience-led rituals can actually become ingrained, especially where audience members return year after year and can hence fall into repeated patterns of behaviour. They cite audiences at the Brussels International Fantastic Film Festival (BIFFF,) who have developed a set routine of shouting out 'pigs in space' – as well as a number of other regular performative interventions – at the beginning of each screening. Such audience interventions can often develop along strictly formalised, hierarchical lines and anyone shouting out the wrong line – going off script, as it were – or saying it in the wrong place can find their remark met with stony silence. There are also incidents within events themselves that generate what we might term 'cult moments'. Prior to the 2012 edition of Abertoir Horror Film Festival, co-festival directors Gaz Bailey and Nia Edwards-Behi received a letter from the local council threatening to close down what they had identified as an illegal abattoir! Although the incident was a misunderstanding based upon the festival name punning the location of the event, the festival director, read the letter out to attendees before a screening of the *Rocky Horror Picture Show* to riotous laughter and applause (live exhibition can add these surreal tinges). For those present this merely reinforced the feeling that participation in the festival had a vaguely transgressive quality, as well as providing the kind of light relief that acted as an important bonding experience for the audience.

Given that such events 'filter the plenitude of film productions and take well-grounded personal taste as the starting point to do so' (Bosma, 2015: 69), the figure of the festival director often becomes a central node around which the entire event is experienced. Although they are predominantly about the exhibition and discovery of both new and old cinema, festivals can, significantly, 'involve showmanship' (Ruoff, 2012: 3). Jeffrey Ruoff compares programmers to circus ringmasters, a call back that in some ways links them back to the origins in fairgrounds, music halls and other public 'performance' venues. Both festival directors and programmers effectively act as (sub)cultural gatekeepers, in that the notion of what counts as 'good' genre cinema, what might form part of the canon and what might been seen as 'cultish' are filtered through their screening decisions. By their nature genre film festivals tend to highly curated events and, as such, the programme director and programming team are key in shaping the entire festival experience for audiences. The reasons for this are varied. Firstly, festival directors are ordinarily fans of genre cinema who run and programme the event from a fan perspective. In reality this means a keen awareness of fan canons and a keen awareness of appealing genre guests, which translates directly into programmes designed with this in mind. For more intimate festivals, in particular, audiences directly associate the festival with the figure of the festival director as they ordinarily front the festival's opening and closing ceremonies, introduce each film, interview guests and provide a 'recognisable face' for the festival experience as a whole. The festival director therefore becomes a recognisable – and frequently beloved, even cultish – figure during the event. In this way the organisation, programming and running of the event 'seeks to highlight the event status, the sense of community, face-to-face contact with audience members, programmers and filmmakers' (Ruoff, 2012: 3).

A recent development has seen festivals make use of their geographical specificity to offer site-specific screenings. Although this is a relatively new phenomenon, a number of festivals have begun to look at ways they can offer audience members a new experience of well-known and (usually) canonical genre cinema. Whilst festivals take place in a number local and regional locations, the rise of site-specific screenings has meant that local landmarks, filming locations or points of interest can themselves become exhibition spaces. This can take a number of forms.

For instance, in 2015 the Montenegro International Fantastic Film Festival, which takes place in the coastal town of Tivat, screened *Das Boot* (Wolfgang Peterson, 1981) all day on a Hero p-821 submarine moored at the harbour at the Porto Montenegro Museum. Likewise, Abertoir Horror Festival has programmed a number of site specific screenings since its inception in 2006. In 2014, audiences were treated to a trip from Aberystwyth on the Vale of Rheidol steam train, before an on-platform screening of Eugenio Martin's *Horror Express* (1972); in 2015 they attempted to screen Neil Marshall's *The Descent* (2005) in a local cave system (an attempt that was abandoned due to health and safety concerns); and in 2016 they planned to screen *The Fog* (John Carpenter, 1980) on top of a hill overlooking the bay of Aberystwyth, a picturesque spot that would also act as a jocular nod to the film's iconic Antonio Bay location. However, the appearance of a freak mini-tornado (that peaked with winds up to ninety-four miles hour) meant that the screening had to take place in the safer surrounds of its normal exhibition space in Aberystwyth Arts Centre. Such problems rather than being a logistical problem for the festival organisers instead merely enshrined the absurdity as a cult moment within the festival itself. In a sense the failure to screen the films (and the reasons for those failures) merely reinforced the already strong cult status of the films concerned and, more broadly, of the festival itself.

Sometimes festivals themselves are structured and organised in a way that lends them an inherently cultish quality that supersedes the cult status of the films they programme. The Grossman Fantastic Film & Wine Festival, which takes place annually in the small Slovenian town of Ljutomer (in the Prlekija wine region of the country), is a case in point. Held on an annual basis, the festival broadly aims to promote fantastic cinema within Slovenia. But it is unique amongst genre film festivals in that a parallel wine competition takes place, with the best wines voted upon the festival guests. The idea here is to simultaneously promote and celebrate Slovenian wine industry alongside genre cinema. Given that the screenings also largely take place outside on large public screens in the town centre, the festival has a curiously bacchanalian cult quality. Whilst this suggests that festivals can themselves become cultish events, identity-based festivals (of which we might see genre festivals as a part) generally offer a very specifically communal experience, which Ruoff argues is typically based around cultural politics (Ruoff, 2012). Genre festivals are a heady mix of long days, late nights and chance meetings – places where the cultural politics of fandom circulates and is celebrated.

References

Bosma, Peter. 2015. *Film Programming: Curating for Cinemas, Festivals, Archives*. London: Wallflower Press.

Cerdán, Josetxo, and Miguel Fernández Labayen. 2009. 'Arty Exploitation, Cool Cult, and the Cinema of Alejandro Jodorowsky,' in Victoria Ruétalo and Dolores Tierney, eds, *Latsploitation Exploitation Cinema, and Latin America*. Abingdon: Routledge: 102–114.

de Valck, Marijke. 2007. *Film Festivals: From European Geopolitics To Global Cinephilia*. Amsterdam: Amsterdam University Press.

de Valck, Marijke. 2012. 'Finding Audiences for Films: Festival Programming in Historical Perspective,' in Jeffrey Ruoff, ed., *Coming Soon to a Festival Near You: Programming Film Festivals*. St Andrews: St Andrews Film Studies: 25–40.

Hills, Matt. 2005. *The Pleasures of Horror*. London: Continuum.

Hills, Matt. 2010. "Attending Horror Film Festivals and Conventions: Liveness, Subcultural Capital 'Flesh and Blood Genre Communities,'" in Ian Conrich, ed., *Horror Zone*. London: I.B. Tauris: 87–102.

Hunter, Russ. 2018. 'Genre Film Festivals and Rethinking the Definition of "The Festival Film,' in Tricia Jenkins, ed., *International Film Festivals: Contemporary Cultures and History Beyond Venice and Cannes*. London: I.B. Tauris: 98–108.

Iordanova, Dina. 2010. "Foreword: The film festival and film culture's transnational essence" in de Valck, Marijke, Brendan Kredell and Skadi Loist, ed., *Film Festivals: History, Theory, Method, Practice*. Oxford: Routledge, pp.xi-xvi.

Mathijs, Ernest, and Jamie Sexton. 2011. *Cult Cinema*. Oxford: Wiley-Blackwell.

Peranson, Mark. 2009. 'First You Get the Power, Then You Get the Money: Two Models of Film Festivals,' in Richard Porton, ed., *dekalog: On Film Festivals*. London: Wallflower Press: 23–37.

Porton, Richard. 2009. 'Introduction,' in Richard Porton, ed., *dekalog: On Film Festivals*. London: Wallflower Press: 1–9.

Ruoff, Jeffrey. 2012. 'Introduction: Programming Film Festivals,' In Jeffrey Ruoff, ed., *Coming Soon to a Festival Near You: Programming Film Festivals*. St Andrews: St Andrews Film Studies: 1–21.

Wong, Cindy Hing-Yuk. 2011. *Film Festivals: Culture, People, and Power on the Global Screen*. London: Rutgers University Press.

PART V

Fandom

Cult fandom

Fandom is a sprawling subject area in the study of popular culture, psychology, sociology, and cultural studies. It has also become a recurrent and stable feature in the study of film and media texts – films, television series, video games, internet platforms, and popular music. The field of fan studies is so spread out, in fact, that this introduction is unable to chart even in a skeleton cursory way the variety of sub-subject areas of interest, other than to notice their prominence.

This prominence has led to comments that since the beginning of the twenty-first century most studies of popular culture consumption are, in one way or another, fan studies, because there has been an intensification of how viewers and audiences attach to popular media; when one discusses viewing films one has to tackle the assumption that one is dealing with fans. Some of the largest efforts of studying film audiences, such as the two-pronged multidimensional and international study of audiences of *The Lord of the Rings* (Jackson, 2001–2003) and *The Hobbit* (Jackson, 2012–2014), or a similarly large study of *Game of Thrones* (2011–2019) viewers, have had to come to terms with and on occasion accept that their respondents would be, by default, fans, or viewers likely to describe themselves as such.[1]

The prominence of the study of fans is in no small way fuelled by mass media's eagerness to report on fans. From sports fans, fans of events (often emotionally charged events, such as the funerals of Rudolph Valentino or Judy Garland), to enthusiastic audiences at political rallies, fandom has piqued the interest of those concerned with displays of crowd behavior, public displays of affection that go beyond the boundaries of moderation, and deep-felt allegiances declared and defended as a life choice. One can hear the whisper of the word 'cult' in this eagerness, and in the desire, or concern, to 'place' fans outside the realm of 'proper' behavior. Even when fandom is considered a 'normalized' form of consumption, inclusive of responsive acts (from writing letters to cheering and swooning to forming a fan community in liaison with the subject of fandom, up to a form of activism on behalf of stars and films), collecting, mimicking (from karaoke to cosplay), fan production (fan fiction literature or imagery, collages and montages, supercuts, remixes, and mash-ups – many connected to the art of copying and pasting creatively) to performances and attitudes of anti-fandom (snarky-ness, irony, sarcasm, …), are still placed outside the 'standard' of moderate and civil living. Fandom may have made its way into the living room, but there is still a feeling it needs policing at the family dinner table.

In terms of heritage, the study of fandom took off, as Lynn Zubernis notes in her chapter, in the late 1980s and early 1990s, and drew a lot of its inspiration from accelerations in cultural studies and communication studies. The work of Lawrence Grossberg et al. (1992) and Camille Bacon-Smith (1992), and an edited collection by Lisa Lewis (1992) are amongst the pioneering materials. These and other works draw an important distinction between types of viewers, in order to carve out space for 'the fan', who is identified as (1) a consumer (someone who pays their way into access to a product), (2) a spectator (a viewer with a sense of self – i.e. a conscious person), and (3) an audience member (a viewer who is part of a group or cohort of people who congregate and communicate around a shared interest or event, up to the building of a 'fan world'), who on top of that (4) separates themselves from other audiences through their affection. Affective labour, or the work that goes into being a fan, has therefore become a prime focal point for fan studies. It has also become pivotal in the study of cult fans.

To a large extent, the methods used to study cult fans are the same as those used to study fans at large. Empirical methods come in three kinds, each of them with a lineage in communication and cultural studies: effects studies, uses and gratifications studies, and encoding-decoding studies. Media effects studies stresses how audiences are impacted by media texts: how they are prompted, cajoled, lured, and seduced into states of desensitization, acceptance, agitation, euphoria, or depression (and many others, but these terms give an idea of the kind of affects often selected by viewers who identify as cult fans – see Mathijs and Sexton 2011). A recurrent concern of media effects studies is their 'worry' about the wellbeing of those engaging with films. Should they be protected? That question, while it prevails in many studies of religious and spiritual cults, is largely absent from the study of cult fandom. Uses- and gratifications studies too assume that media texts have an impact, but they acknowledge that 'users' seek out these texts to satisfy (pre-existing) needs, and therefore have agency over their actions. The encoding-decoding model, popularized by Stuart Hall, but embryonically present in, for instance, the writings of Roland Barthes and Walter Benjamin (who commented on how popular culture texts created and were simultaneously endorsed with narratives, signage, and myths and auras that audiences use to affectively navigate their everyday lives), holds that fandom is the result of affective negotiation by audiences who are addressed by the media texts they encounter and who evaluate these in the light of their situations and lives. A good sense of the contexts within which fandom occurs is therefore necessary. The encoding-decoding model has been of high influence in the study of subcultures (see, for instance, Martin Barker on fans of comic books and science fiction films; Barker 1998). There are many textbooks in audience studies that cover this ground and offer summaries of fan studies' inspirations and methods (Brooker and Jermyn 2003; Sandvoss 2005; Croteau and Hoynes 2013).

Cult fandom can be said to inhabit fandom at large, and as such it is difficult to make a distinction. Yet there are three ways in which cult fandom separates itself from regular fandom (if those terms can be used in a relativist sense). The first is that cult fandom is a particularly intense and loyal type of fandom. Matt Hills (2011) has made this case for blockbuster fandom. And Barker and Mathijs (2006) also see it as part of the massive reception of *The Lord of the Rings*. It is a niche within a niche, if you want. The second way in which cult fandom is separate is through its actions: as pilgrimages, vocalizations, dressing up, collecting, and other activities that 'show' to oneself and to the world one's fandom in a way that is separate from other forms of fandom. Exuberance, volume, and excess and hyperbole are characteristics of this expression of cult fandom, and one can easily make the connective assumption that this type of fandom emphasizes the 'experiential' component of cultism – the being there and acting out. The speaking back to the screen noted by so many scholars of *Casablanca* and *The Rocky Horror Picture Show*, or totalistic immersion and performance of movements from the films, are exemplars. The third way in which cult fandom is different is one that was noticed by Mathijs and Sexton (2011) in their discussion of DIY fandom. It involves a degree of fandom that relies heavily on elevated levels of knowledge (often of 'being in the know'), of sophistication and aesthetic expertise (or performances thereof), and on fandom that is articulated through professionalism. This is close to the kind of insider tribalism that Leon Gurevitch describes in his chapter in the section on aesthetics, and similar to what John Thornton Caldwell (2008) sees as a characteristic of media professionals who publicly declare (as many do) their admiration for certain films, from "street credibility" alliances to "guilty pleasures." (A term pioneered by magazine *Film Comment* – whose affiliation with cult cinema has already been mentioned in the chapter on exploitation). John Waters' highly ironic run-on rant in one of *Film Comment*'s "guilty pleasures" series of articles states that "deep down", amidst all his posturing as an aficionado of revulsive films, he is also a fan of "arthouse cinema." He then proceeds to list all of the intellectual determination it requires (including foreign languages, scheduling visits to theatres and sites of interest, pilgrimages, keeping up to date, ...). Add activities such as list-making, planning festival 'binges', selecting special screenings and retrospectives, panel participations, curatorial activities, ... and it is not difficult to see this is an effort that relies heavily on notions of talent, effort, skill, craftsmanship, connoisseurship, and other means through which the cult fan demonstrates (or at least performs) a degree of superiority over other fans – again, this is not unlike the feeling of 'purity' religious cults put on display in their worship, as if it is not only something that is an achievement or accomplishment, but also an innate suitability not given to everyone. Two works that have come to define this approach are Henry Jenkins' *Textual Poachers* (1992) and Matt Hills' *Fan Cultures* (2002). Both use cult examples as their starting points for discussing degrees of fandom that have become foundational for the study of cult cinema receptions. When Zygmunt Bauman (1996) describes instances of fluid cultural identity in the postmodern age, the types of activities he lists (tourism, strolling, thrill-seeking, ...) come very close to the DIY exercises of cult fandom.

The four chapters in this section are queries into the cult fandoms at play, and each of them updates and pushes forward the notions of cult fandom as sketched above. Lynn Zubernis focuses on conventions, cosplay and pilgrimages as outside-looking activities. Her and Katherine Larsen's groundbreaking *Fandom at the Crossroads* (2012) put elements of collective affection such as shame into perspective (with regard to the television show *Supernatural*; 2006–2020), and this chapter builds on that knowledge, by stressing the 'fierce loyalty' of cult fans. She also acknowledges the element of world-building that science fiction and fantasy cult fandom has been organized around. Amanda Ann Klein explores cult fandom's relationship to gender. When it emerged as a discipline, the study of fandom was on occasion seen as a way of 'validating' female media pleasure (please note how Bacon-Smith's book carries its title, *Enterprising Women*). Looking at the cult fandom around the film *Magic Mike XXL* (Jacobs, 2015), in itself a re-examination of *Magic Mike* (Soderbergh, 2012), which already centers on performances of affective pleasure – albeit through the lens of a strip club, not a fandom behind screens – Klein studies the demonstrations of sexuality and appeal. Her analysis extends to other films whose female cult fandom received unfavorable criticism (*Twilight* and *Fifty Shades of Grey* amongst them). Klein's analysis calls into focus how cult fandom relies heavily on constructing and then breaking down codes for gendered representations of desire, playful and radical, and potentially transgressive. The chapters by Jenna Ng and Matt Hills take cult fandom to the level of semi-professionalism in their examinations of *machinima* and fan remixes, and aca-fandom, respectively. Ng describes how the use of glitches in (for instance) video games is an opportunity for committed fans to make their own interventions, and 'work' almost on behalf of the industry's failed accomplishment, playing in the margins of codes and hypertexts alongside professionals (and often with the same gear), perhaps even posing as their 'honest' counterparts as they express the flaws and opportunities of 'remixed' labour. *Machinima*, as the activity is known, blurs the boundaries between DIY, super-fandom and professionalism. It also skirts new territories aesthetically. Finally, Hills links the semi-professionalism of, amongst others, scholars of cult films who turn their fandom into a career, to a moment in the development of neo-liberalism that is testament to the increased ways in which one's personal tastes become part and parcel of a competitive rat race-like contest towards hyper-fandom – or, one could argue, a degree of super-specialization similar to the one that academic scholarship and science careers aim for, and claim. Does this mean that to re-claim this labour of 'self-realization' through professionalized cult fandom is to re-claim the human factor (in entrepreneurship or in other 'worthy' pursuits trumped by neo-liberal economies)? And does linking affect and labour, against alienation, in order to dissolve the detachment of what we do to how we (want to) live, and, thereby, become *whole* again in our pursuits, expose the rhetoric of the neo-liberal market place? It may well, Hills concludes. At the very least it restores hope in the notion of authentic living. *Dr. Who*'s fan is as much a specialist of life as your house doctor, or your pallet cleanser, or your yoga teacher, in other words – the cultist supreme as your personal guide to a better life.

In sum, the chapters in this section exemplify how cult fandom is different from regular fandom in its loyalty, exuberance, layered-ness, and its semi-professionalism. If anything, it is a serious business. In its overlap with fully-fledged professionalism in the media industries it also shows such a dedication that it becomes virtually impossible to tell the freewheeling, *played* amateur from the fanatic whose act *is* their life.

Note

1 See, for instance, Barker Martin and Ernest Mathijs (eds). 2006. *Watching* The Lord of the Rings. New York: Peter Lang; Martin Barker and Ernest Mathijs (eds). 'The Hobbit Project', book-length issue of *Participations: Journal of Audience and Reception Studies*, 13.2 (November 2016), online at: www.participations.org. For the Game of Thrones project, see https://fanlore.org/wiki/Game_of_Thrones_Research_Project.

References

Bacon-Smith, Camille. 1992. *Enterprising Women: Television Fandom and the Creation of Popular Myth.* Philadelphia: University of Pennsylvania Press.

Barker, Martin, and Kate Brooks. 1998. *Knowing Audiences: Judge Dredd, Its Fans, Friends and Foes.* Luton: University of Luton Press.

Barker Martin, and Ernest Mathijs (eds). 2006. *Watching* The Lord of the Rings. New York: Peter Lang.

Bauman, Zygmunt. 1996. "From Pilgrim to Tourist, or, A Short History of Identity," in Stuart Hall and Paul Du Gay (eds). *Questions of Cultural Identity*. London: Sage Publications: 18–36.

Brooker, Will and Deborah Jermyn (eds). 2003. *The Audience Studies Reader*. London: Routledge.

Caldwell, John Thornton. 2008. *Production Culture*. Durham, NC: Duke University Press.

Croteau, David, and William Hoynes. 2013. *Media/Society: Industries, Images and Audiences (5th edition).* Thousand Oaks, CA: Sage Publications.

Grossberg, Lawrence, Cary Nelson and Paula Treichler (eds). 1992. *Cultural Studies*. New York: Routledge.

Hills, Matt. 2002. *Fan Cultures*. London: Routledge.

Jenkins, Henry. 1992. *Textual Poachers: Television Fans and Participatory Culture*. New York: Routledge.

Lewis, Lisa A. (ed.). 1992. *The Adoring Audience: Fan Culture and Popular Media*. London: Routledge.

Mathijs, Ernest and Jamie Sexton. 2011. *Cult Cinema*. New York: Wiley.

Sandvoss, Cornell. 2005. *Fans: The Mirror of Consumption*. Cambridge, UK: Polity Press.

Waters, John. 1983. "John Waters' Guilty Pleasures." *Film Comment* 4 (July/August). 20–23.

Zubernis, Lynn, and Katherine Larsen. 2012. *Fandom at the Crossroads: Celebration, Shame and Fan-Producer Relationships*. Cambridge, UK: Cambridge Scholars.

26

CONVENTIONS AND COSPLAY

Lynn Zubernis

Cult media, including films, television, books, comics and anime, have always inspired a high level of affective engagement amongst fans. Cult programs often have what Fiske (1987) called "producerly stories", which inspire a passionate response from fans and a high level of fan loyalty and involvement. The high level of emotional attachment to the text, as well as to the fictional characters and the actors who portray them, contribute to the designation of a media product as "cult". Not everyone who views a film, even one which will become a cult film, will experience this high level of emotional investment; some audience members will remain viewers and not become fans. Those films which eventually become categorized as cult films, however, will amass a group of people who go beyond the level of viewer/spectator and become fans.

Pooley (1978) distinguished between fans and spectators by the degree of engrossment and passion. He was researching sports fans, but the distinction can also be applied to media. Fans, and the community of fans (known as fandom) tend to become emotionally attached to whatever it is they love, and fandom often becomes an important part of everyday life and a component of identity. Similarly, Grossberg (1992) drew a distinction between the fan and the consumer based on affect, and Abercrombie and Longhurst (1998) described media fans as those who become particularly attached to certain programs or their stars.

The films and other media that capture the fascination and loyalty of fans are usually ones that generate a strong affective attachment. In fact, some researchers contend that cult favorites deliberately stimulate strong affect to encourage more consumption, with fans taking in those largely subliminal messages and deriving pleasure from their consumption (Clarke 2003; Grossberg 1992). Specifically, Clarke believes that certain fannish behaviors are activated by this strong affect, especially libidinal attachments to some of the fictional characters. In addition, the global culture of celebrity that currently exists also depends on fans' affective attachments – in this case, to the actors who portray cult film characters. Whether an increased fascination with celebrities is related to inherent narcissism in the age of social media, or whether fans merely seek heroes with whom they can identify, celebrities can serve as role models and sources of identification and become a source of affective attachment for fans. Fans who are very committed perceive whatever they fan as part of their extended self, suggesting that cult films are closely tied to identity for fans.

Whether deliberately generated or not, fans' passion for the films and other media that they love finds expression in fan works such as fanfiction, fan art and vidding, as well as in certain behaviors, such as collecting, fan tourism, and coming together to celebrate their love with other fans at fan conventions. These activities are illustrative of the passion fans have for their favorite media texts. Researchers like Matt Hills (2000) compare the cult fan's emotional response to a text with a sort of "neoreligiosity" – the adoption of sacred themes and ideas. Both fandom and religion revolve around similar experiences, including interpretive communities which form around texts and social communities that allow individuals to come together around a common interest. The film itself becomes a "shared property" that fans enjoy together, which intensifies the bond to both the film and the fan community (Ross 2008).

In one of the earliest studies on fans, Henry Jenkins (1992b) described fandom as an alternative social community, one not defined by traditional terms such as race, religion, gender, political view, or profession. Such an alternative community is particularly attractive to anyone who has ever felt stereotyped, marginalized, or simply outside the mainstream; Jenkins felt that fans viewed fandom as a conscious opposition to the "mundane world" or mainstream culture (Jenkins 1992a: 213). Similarly, Sconce (1995) described fan cultures as providing a sense of identity for fans by setting them apart from the mainstream. The fan communities that form around cult films and other cult media are therefore very important to their members as a source of self-definition and a source of found community.

When individuals become fans, they develop feelings of comradeship with others who are also fans of the same thing (the equivalent of sports fans who all root for the same team). Online communities form for cult films and media and are a forum for fans to discuss intricacies of the film as well as to get to know other aficionados. A communal experience of shared space, rituals of shared practices, and an exchange of social support characterize a community; thus, the online platforms on which fans gather qualify as communities (Baym 2010). Many fans find that sense of community particularly compelling, since fandom itself is a collective subculture composed of individuals whose shared interests are the basis of their communal identity, which is set apart from the "mainstream" (Kington 2015).

Conventions

Before the advent of the internet, that communal identity amongst cult film and sci fans was enacted in various ways. The earliest cult fans were the enthusiastic readers of sci fi print magazines, which developed small but passionate followings. By the 1920s and 30s, sci fi fans had formed communities around a common interest. These communities had specific cultural identities and began to develop their own traditions, rituals and communication networks, even though they were geographically dispersed. There were letter columns and discussion sections, for example, in pulp magazines such as "Amazing Stories", which began production in 1926. Fans struck up conversations in these letter columns, eager to find like-minded people and share their passions, and developed loosely organized groups. Cult fans soon organized into amateur press associations (APAs) to print and distribute by mail their own amateur publications. These publications were eventually known as "fanzines" or simply "zines", printed compilations of news and fanfiction about a particular media text. Early cult fan communities developed their own language and shorthands for communicating, as well as in-jokes that marked community members as insiders. Some of the acronyms used in fans' online communication today originated with zines, including IMO and IMHO, as did the graphic expression of emotions now known as emoticons or emojis (Merrick 2004).

Sci fi and cult media fans also came together in person when they were able. Fans began coming together locally with the organization of fan clubs, which were often referred to as Science Fiction Societies or Fantasy Clubs. In the United States, one of the first was the Scienceers, formed in New York City in 1929. In 1934, an international science fiction club, The Science Fiction League, was coordinated through the magazine Wonder Stories, and local clubs were established. The Los Angeles-based Science Fiction League (now the Los Angeles Science Fantasy Society) was established in 1934 and is still active today. In 1939, the World Science Fiction Society held its first convention, the World Science Fiction Convention (Worldcon) on the East Coast of the United States. This con was the first to bring large groups of cult fans together, followed by the American west coast version in the 1940s, West Coast Science Fantasy Convention (Westercon). In 1975, the Los Angeles Science Fantasy Society started its Los Angeles Regional Science Fiction and Fantasy Convention (Loscon). These conventions continue to run today. The largest multi-media fan convention in the United States is San Diego's Comic Con, which began in 1970 as a comic book convention for comics, film and science fiction fans (one of the founders of the Los Angeles Science Fantasy Society, Forrest J. Ackerman, was a special guest). Comic Con is now an international celebration of the popular arts attracting over 130,000 fans each year, and there are similar conventions worldwide, including Comiket (Comic Market) in Japan, which began in 1975 and now attracts nearly half a million fans, Supacon and Oz Comic Con in Australia, Fan Expo in Canada and many more.

From the beginning of conventions, there have been certain common elements including panels of guest experts and other programming, merchandise rooms, art shows and artist exhibitions, and a costume contest traditionally referred to as a "masquerade". Some conventions have also included dances and other social events, gaming rooms, or organized contests. Fan conventions have had a global flavor from the start. By the 1980s, globalization was reflected in the films which fans viewed at these conventions. For example, the 1983 World Science Fiction Convention in Baltimore held a screening of a Japanese animation film from the Space Battleship Yamato series which was wildly popular. Cult films have reflected globalization with films from around the world becoming cult favorites, including many American films and Japanese films such as 1995's *Ghost In The Shell* (Rahman, Wing-Sun & Cheung 2012).

Fandom is no longer small, but cult media fans are as fiercely loyal as those early science fiction fans, and fan communities are no less important today. Both early fans and present-day fans have described feeling set apart from the rest of the culture, with interests and outlooks that the rest of the world didn't quite understand – or outright disdained. The outside criticism has, from the beginning, drawn fans together into tight knit communities of like-minded people who felt like outsiders. Some cult fans are content to participate in online communities, but many fans want a sense of belonging and validation that can only come from meeting fellow fans face to face – this was the impetus behind fan conventions.

In one of the earlier studies of fandom, Harris (1998) provided a definition of fan conventions as "often hotel-weekend affairs involving parties, panels, guest speakers and appearances by celebrities" (Harris 1998: 8). In her 2015 study of convention culture, Candie Syphrit Kington defined fandom as "a collective subculture composed of fans of wide range of media whose shared interests serve as the basis for their communal identity" and fan conventions as "the loci of fan activity uniting fans from multiple fandoms". She describes certain essential elements of conventions that are part of the prototypical con; that is, the convention will feature guests of interest to the attendees, provide entertaining content in the form of panels and events, and will have a commerce space.

Some of the most well-known conventions in terms of mainstream awareness are for *Star Trek*, which began as an American television show and later produced multiple cult films. The first *Star Trek* convention was held in 1972 in New York City, organized by three female fans,

Joan Winston, Devra Langsham and Elyse Pines. Series creator Gene Roddenberry himself attended. They expected about 300 people; 3,000 showed up (Grimes 2008).

Although fan communities now thrive online, conventions remain a powerful experience for fans. While a common assumption is that fans attend conventions to be close to celebrities, that is not necessarily the case. The collective experience of meeting fellow fans is often more powerful than meeting any celebrities in attendance. Fans come to conventions to meet others who share their passion for a particular film or media text. Conventions have been described as like stepping through an enchanted doorway to another world, with fellow fans feeling more like family (Oler 2008). The experience of "finding" fandom is a universal one – almost every fan can describe the intense experience of being amongst like-minded people for the first time, of feeling a sense of belonging and fitting in, perhaps for the first time.

In a study of Kevin Smith cult film fandom, many of the fans who were interviewed said they probably would have come to the convention even if Smith hadn't attended. Fans referred to their fellow fans as "family", coming together at conventions for "family reunions" (Phillips 2011). Cultural capital that came from having deep knowledge of Smith's films was not necessary; the fandom and the films became secondary to the value of the community itself. Other studies which included interviews with fans also have found that fans spoke of each other as family, including the convention they were attending, their friends and even the media text itself. Fans talked about fellow fans at a convention being the people who "get me" and who understand and accept each other's quirks. (Booth & Kelly 2013). Conventions, in this sense, serve more as family reunions, a place for renewing relationships and socializing with other cult film fans.

While it is not the primary reason for many fans, some cult fans do attend conventions out of the desire to interact with and get closer to the celebrities who bring cult media to life – often the actors who portray the fictional characters in a film or television show. Whether attraction to celebrities is driven by the narcissism inherent in our current culture (Lasch 1979) or the fact that people look to others (sometimes in the media) when deciding who and how they should be (Riesman, Glazer & Denney, 1950), celebrities are a part of modern culture. Fans' attachment to celebrities and the desire to be close to them are another motivation for fan conventions, as the actors who portray the fictional characters make panel appearances, pose for photo ops and sign autographs. At conventions, fans view themselves as moving (at least temporarily) from the mediated world of audience member to a more intimate and personal relationship with the cult film actors (Zubernis & Larsen 2012). While the intimacy is more perception than reality, nevertheless conventions do offer at least a moment of face to face contact and a few words of personal conversation.

Convention attendance can also be considered a type of what is known as serious leisure, based on the idea of involvement. Involvement is a psychological drive which is an "unobservable state of motivation, arousal or interest toward a recreational activity or associated product" (Havitz & Dimanche 1997: 256). The "product" could be a film, television show or celebrity; the level of involvement influences how often and how long the individual spends participating in an associated activity, such as a convention, as well as how much money they spend on the activity (Lee 2007). Involvement has been applied to fandom, including the pleasure derived from fan participation, the importance of both the film and the fandom to the individual, how central these are to the fan's lifestyle, and whether their fan participation offers an opportunity for self-expression (McIntyre & Pigram 1992). Convention attendance can be seen as a type of serious leisure involvement because fans spend a great deal of time and money and also become emotionally attached to the film and to the actors who bring it to life. A serious leisure experience also involves negotiation of constraints that interfere with participation (time, money or the complaints of a significant other). From a serious leisure perspective, participation in a cult fandom is a means of attaining pleasure, expressing self-identity, and developing social networks (Lee 2007).

Earlier studies of fandom in the 1990s have been critiqued for being overly positive or utopian in their view of fandom as a site of cultural resistance, without acknowledging that fans are also avid consumers (Hills 2002: 29). Jenkins' pivotal work on fandom stressed its importance as providing a community and a way in which marginalized groups of people could express themselves by transforming the media that they loved (Jenkins 2006). While more recent scholars have acknowledged the utopian perspective of early work in fan studies, nevertheless they also emphasize that in the face of increasing commodification of fandom, it's important to remember that fandom is more than just its economic potential (Coppa 2014). Coppa refers to the multi fandom convention Comic Con as an industry convention disguised as a fan convention, with large film and television studios taking over much of its space and offerings. There has been increasing recognition of the buying power of cult fans, with consequent attempts to harness their passion for economic gain as producers attempt to monetize what fans love. At the same time, there is push back from fans who want to consume and transform their favorite cult films and media. Conventions have traditionally included merchandise rooms where fans can purchase items related to the films and media they love; conventions themselves have become more and more expensive, as fans also pay for the opportunity to have some proximity with actors from their favorite films.

Cosplay

When a fan loves a film or other media text, they want to take an active role in imagining and connecting with that world. Writing fanfiction to explore and expand the fictional world can be a way of doing that, but fans can also do this by entering into that world physically in some way. Conventions have traditionally offered fans the opportunity to dress up in costume at a "masquerade". Cosplay (short for costume play) is another way of immersing oneself into the fictional universe of the cult film. Cosplay is the practice of constructing costumes and props inspired by fictional characters and embodying those characters in real-world spaces such as fan conventions. It involves constructing often elaborate costumes and props inspired by fictional characters and portraying those characters. Often cosplay is enacted at conventions, but there are also arranged meet ups for cosplayers in public spaces where they pose for photos and socialize with others in the cosplay community (Peirson-Smith 2013).

The practice of wearing costumes to conventions was first noticed (and often ridiculed) by mainstream media in the early Star Trek conventions in the 1970s, but genre fans have been dressing in costume at fan gatherings from as early as the first World Science Fiction Convention held in New York City in 1939. Japanese anime director Takahashi Nobuyuki coined the term "cosplaying" after witnessing fans dressing up as their favorite characters at Worldcon in Los Angeles in 1984 on a trip to the United States (Leng 2013; Lunning 2006; Winge 2006). Japanese manga fans were also dressing in costume as a way of promoting the characters from the manga in the 1970s and 1980s, and also adopted the term.

Cosplay is a staple at large multi-fandom conventions worldwide, although the practice varies in different countries. For example, cosplay tends to be more structured in countries like Japan and less structured in the United States (Lamerichs 2013), and subject to social pressures in regard to overt displays of sexuality in countries such as Malaysia (Yamato 2016). In the United States, events like San Diego Comic Con draw gigantic crowds, with part of the draw being cosplayers, and in Japan the Comiket convention and its contingent of cosplayers is even larger. Cosplay has become more common and more visible recently, resulting in a reality TV show (Heroes of Cosplay, on SyFy), international competitions, fashion shows, staged photo shoots, and vibrant online communities.

Cosplay is a way of expressing a fan's passion for a film or a fictional character, and also a form of self-expression (Winge 2006). The practice of cosplay is in part imitation of a favorite character and in part a way of re-creating that character in the "real world". Cosplay can be seen as a theatrical performance, a playful act, or a form of self-objectification (Rahman, Wing-sun & Cheung 2012). Some cosplayers choose to portray a character whose personality traits or circumstances they admire, while others choose a character with physical traits similar to their own. Cosplay is not only a mode of self-expression, but a method of escapist fantasy which can offer a form of temporary escape from the stresses or monotony of everyday life with immersion into the fictional world of a cult film or other media text (Napier 2007).

The developmental task of identity development can be carried out through cosplay for some fans. Part of identity development is trying on identities as we construct our own, and cosplay provides a way for fans of cult films and other media to try on the identity of the characters they most admire. Some fans try on identities of powerful villains as well as super-heroes, a safe way to experiment with expression of feelings of powerlessness and frustration. Cosplayers negotiate the boundary between "real" and "fantasy", merging their real selves with an imagined self, their identity shifting back and forth over time and "real life" identity being impacted (Grossberg 1992).

Cosplay has been seen as a mimetic fan practice, motivated by a desire to replicate what has been seen onscreen, as opposed to a transformative fan practice such as fanfiction or fanvidding. Cosplayers attempt to replicate not only the appearance of the character, but mannerisms, ways of moving and walking, posture, signature poses and even dialogue. However, there is tremendous creativity involved and some cosplayers seek not so much to replicate as to interpret, making the practice more transformative than mimetic in some cases (Hills 2002). Cosplay costumes are often simultaneously derivative and unique to the individual (Oler 2014). For example, some cosplayers value getting the costume exactly as it was in the film, but others transform the cosplay, perhaps portraying a Steampunk version of Captain America or engaging in "crossplay", which gender bends the character being cosplayed. Fans who crossplay are illustrating the fact that gender is a social construction as well engaging in a transformative reworking of their favorite character and exploring aspects of their own identity; they are both subverting the cult text itself and engaging in a pleasurable embodied experience (Gn 2011).

Not all cosplayers portray characters who are similar to themselves, instead performing a character who is different in some way as a form of experimenting, or as an aspect of play (Gunnels & Cole 2011). Convention space itself can be seen as play space, relaxing the rules for how fans must behave in their "real lives" and allowing experimentation with alternative identities and ways of being, similar to Bakhtin's (1965/2009) idea of the carnivalesque. The carnivalesque exhibition of cosplay combines reality with fantasy in an environment which allows and encourages the evolution of fans' performance of identity and the transformation of the cult film narrative. Cosplay is sometimes a form of resistance to dominant ideas of race and gender which impacts not only the cosplayers themselves but other convention attendees who witness the cosplay; such resistance is possible in play space, which has different norms and rules for behavior.

The convention space in which cosplay often takes place has been categorized as a site of performance, in accordance with Erving Goffman's ideas about performance of the self, which we all do whenever we are being observed and which impacts those observing (Goffman 1956). Conventions are a site in which fans perform their identity as fans, sometimes with cosplay and sometimes simply by wearing a tee shirt of their favorite cult film character. Conventions are places for performance, where fans can take on and perform another identity, not as a substitute for their own but as an augmentation. Dressing as a favorite character is not only a celebration of that character, but a way for the fan to explore aspects of their own mediated identity. In other words, fans use augmented ideas of the self to explore and consolidate identity (Duchesne 2010). The aspect of performance which Goffman emphasizes as impacting the "other" is also relevant in cosplay – an integral part of many convention experiences is the audience's ability to interact with their favorite fictional characters face to face, with the cosplayer serving as a sort of stand in for that character in the real world. The increased popularity of cosplay may be a result of the constant feeling of being "seen" which is part of modern culture. People are accustomed to seeing and being seen on smartphones and on various social media platforms; there is a sense of performance to those ways of being seen. Cosplay is another way of being seen and another type of performed identity.

The issue of materiality in fan practices is relevant for both conventions and for cosplay. Some cosplayers professionalize their fan practices successfully, while most engage in cosplay as a fan practice and do not receive compensation other than the admiration of their fellow fans (Scott 2015). When it comes to the ways in which cult fans enact their love of a particular film or media text, certain practices necessarily require more expenditure than others. Online fanfiction can be posted and shared without expense to either the writer or the reader in most cases, but attending conventions and constructing cosplays require a material outlay. Fans must buy materials, props and makeup if they create their own costumes, or purchase ready-made costumes. Costumes must be sufficiently detailed to be identifiable as the character being cosplayed; thus finances in part determine the success of a performance. Cosplay has been criticized as frivolous and overly expensive (Rahman, Wing-sun & Cheung 2012) and materiality is recognized as a constraint in fan practices such as cosplay, fan tourism, conventions, and collecting. Some researchers have questioned whether the costs of cosplay, in terms of time, materials and emotional investment, can interfere with the benefit of a communal play experience (Seregina & Weijo 2017). Cosplayers are not solitary performers, however; they value the support, interaction and community they find with other cosplayers (Rahman, Wing-sun & Cheung 2012). Within these recognized constraints, fans continue to express their love of cult media and characters through gathering with other fans at conventions and paying homage to those characters, while simultaneously exploring their own identities and enjoying the sense of belonging that comes from sharing their passions with like-minded others.

References

Abercrombie, Nicholas and Brian Longhurst J. 1998. *Audiences: A Sociological Theory of Performance.* Thousand Oaks, CA: SAGE Publications.

Bakhtin, Mikhail. 1965/2009. *Rabelais and His World.* Translated by Helene Iswolsky. Bloomington: Indiana University Press.

Baym, Nancy. 2010. *Personal Connections in the Digital Age.* Cambridge: Polity Press.

Booth, Paul and Peter Kelly. 2013. "The Changing Faces of Fandom: New Fans, Old Practices," *Participations: Special Issue on Fandom,* 10.1 (May): 56–72.

Clarke, Jamie. 2003. "Affective Entertainment in 'Once More with Feeling': A Manifesto for Fandom," *Refractory,* 2. http://refractory.unimelb.edu.au/2003/03/18/affective-entertainment-in-once-more-with-feeling-a-manifesto-for-fandom-jamie-clarke [accessed 2/1/18].

Coppa, Francesca. 2006. "A Brief History of Media Fandom," in Karen Hellekson and Kristina Busse, eds, *Fan Fiction and Fan Communities in the Age of the Internet.* Jefferson, NC: McFarland: 41–59.

Coppa, Francesca. 2014. "Fuck Yeah, Fandom Is Beautiful," *Journal of Fandom Studies,* 2.1: 73–82.

Duchesne, Scott. 2010. "Stardom/Fandom: Celebrity and Fan Tribute Performance," *Canadian Theatre Review*, 141: 21–27.

Fiske, John. 1987. *Television Culture*. London: Methuen.

Gn, Joel. 2011. "Queer Simulation: The Practice, Performance and Pleasure of Cosplay," *Continuum: Journal of Media & Cultural Studies*, 25.4: 583–593.

Goffman, Erving. 1956. *The Presentation of Self in Everyday Life*. New York: Anchor.

Grimes, William. 2008. "Joan Winston, 'Trek' Superfan, Dies at 77," *The New York Times*, September 20. www.nytimes.com/2008/09/21/nyregion/21winston.html [accessed 1/5/18].

Grossberg, Laurence. 1992. "Is There a Fan in the House? The Affective Sensibility of Fandom," in Lisa A. Lweis, ed., *The Adoring Audience: Fan Culture and Popular Media*. London: Routledge: 51–65.

Gunnels, Jen and Carrie J. Cole. 2011. "Culturally Mapping Universes: Fan Production as Ethnographic Fragments," *Transformative Works and Cultures*, 7: https://doi.org/10.3983/twc.2011.0241 [accessed 1/6/16].

Harris, Cheryl. 1998. "Introduction," in Cheryl Harris and Alison Alexander, eds., *Theorizing Fans; Fans, Subculture and Identity*. Cresskill, NJ: Hampton Press.

Havitz, Mark E. & Frederic Dimanche. 1997. "Leisure Involvement Revisited: Conceptual Conundrums," *Journal of Leisure Research*, 29(3), 245–278.

Hills, Matt. 2000. "Media Fandom, Neoreligiosity, and Cult(ural) Studies," *Velvet Light Trap*, 46: 73–84.

Hills, Matt. 2002. *Fan Cultures*. New York: Routledge.

Jenkins, Henry. 1992a. "Strangers No More, We Sing': Filking and the Social Construction of the Science Fiction Fan Community," in Lisa A. Lewis, ed., *The Adoring Audience: Fan Culture and Popular Media*. London: Routledge: 208–236.

Jenkins, Henry. 1992b. *Textual Poachers: Television Fans and Participatory Culture*. New York: Routledge.

Jenkins, Henry. 2006. *Convergence Culture*. New York: New York University Press.

Kington, Candie Syphrit. 2015. "Con Culture: A Survey of Fans and Fandom," *Journal of Fandom Studies*, 3.2: 211–228.

Lamerichs, Nicolle. 2013. "The Cultural Dynamic of Doujinshi and Cosplay: Local Anime Fandom in Japan, USA and Europe," *Participations*, 10.1: 154–176.

Lasch, Chistopher. 1979. *The Culture of Narcissism: American Life in an Age of Diminishing Expectations*. New York: W.W. Norton.

Lee, Soojin J. 2007. Celebrity Fandom and Its Relationship to Tourism and Leisure Behaviors: The Case of Korean Wave. Doctoral diss., Texas A & M University.

Leng, Rachel. 2013. "Gender, Sexuality and Cosplay: A Case Study of Male-to-Female Crossplay," *Fandom and Neomedia Studies Association*, 1.1: 89–110.

Lunning, Frenchy. 2006. *Mechademia 1: Emerging Worlds of Anime and Manga*. Minneapolis: University of Minnesota Press.

McIntyre, Norman and J.J. Pigram. 1992. "Recreation Specialization Reexamined," *Leisure Research*, 14, 3–15.

Merrick, Helen. 2004. "We Was Cross-Dressing 'Afore You Were Born!' or, How SF Fans Invented Virtual Community," *Refractory*, 6. http://refractory.unimelb.edu.au/2004/06/17/%e2%80%98we-was-cross-dressing-%e2%80%98afore-you-were-born%e2%80%99-or-how-sf-fans-invented-virtual-community-helen-merrick [accessed 2/6/18].

Napier, Susan. 2007. *From Impression to Anime: Japan as Fantasy and Fan Cult in the Mind of the West*. New York: Palgrave Macmillan.

Oler, Tammy. 2008. "Keep on Trekkin': Star Trek and the Legacy of Female Fandom," *Bitch*, no. 40: 64–69.

Oler, Tammy. 2014. "The Power of the Pose: Why the Rise of Cosplay Matters," *The Daily Dose*, November 1, 2014. www.ozy.com/pov/the-power-of-the-pose-why-the-rise-of-cosplay-matters/36554 [accessed 2/6/18].

Peirson-Smith, Anne. 2013. "Fashioning the Fantastical Self: An Examination of the Cosplay Dress-Up Phenomenon in Southeast Asia," *Fashion Theory: The Journal of Dress, Body & Culture*, 17.1: 77–111.

Phillips, Tom. 2011. "When Film Fans Become Fan Family: Kevin Smith Fandom and Communal Experience," *Participations*, 8.2: 478–496.

Pooley, John. C. 1978. *The Sports Fan: A Psychology of Misbehavior*. Calgary, AL: CAPHER Sociology of Sports Monograph Series.

Rahman, Osmud, Liu Wing-sun and Brittany Hei-man Cheung. 2012. "'Cosplay': Imaginative Self and Performing Identity," *Fashion Theory*, 16.3: 317–342.

Riesman, David, Nathan Glazer and Reuel Denney. 1950. *The Lonely Crowd*. New Haven: Yale University Press.

Ross, Sharon Marie. 2008. *Beyond the Box: Television and the Internet*. Malden, MA: Blackwell.

Sconce, Jeffrey. 1995. "'Trashing' the Academy: Taste, Excess, and an Emerging Politics of Cinematic Style," *Screen*, 36.4: 371–393.

Scott, Suzanne. 2015. "Cosplay Is Serious Business: Gendering Material Fan Labor on Heroes of Cosplay," *Cinema Journal*, 54.3: 146–154.

Seregina, Anastasia and Henry A. Weijo. 2016. "Play at Any Cost: How Cosplayers Produce and Sustain Their Ludic Communal Consumption Experience," *Journal of Consumer Research*, 44: 139–159.

Tulloch, John and Henry Jenkins. 1995. *Science Fiction Audiences: Watching "Doctor Who" and "Star Trek."* New York: Routledge.

Winge, Theresa. 2006. "Costuming the Imagination: Origins of Anime and Manga Cosplay," in Frenchy Lunning, ed., *Mechademia 1: Emerging Worlds of Anime and Manga*. Minneapolis: University of Minnesota Press: 65–76.

Yamato, Eriko. 2016. "'Growing as a Person': Experiences at Anime, Comics and Games Fan Events in Malaysia," *Journal of Youth Studies*, 19.6: 743–759.

Zubernis, Lynn and Katherine Larsen. 2012. *Fandom at the Crossroads: Celebration, Shame and Fan/Producer Relationship*. Newcastle: Cambridge Scholars.

27

GROWN WOMAN SHIT

A case for *Magic Mike XXL* as cult text

Amanda Ann Klein

The plot of *Magic Mike XXL* (2015, Gregory Jacobs) ostensibly centers around the cast of *Magic Mike* (2012, Steven Soderbergh) travelling to a stripper convention in Myrtle Beach, road trip-style, for "one last" performance. Richie (Joe Manganiello) explains, "If I'm going down, I'm going down in a fucking tsunami of dollar bills." The guys call Mike (Channing Tatum), now retired from stripping, and lie and say that their old emcee, Dallas (Matthew McConaughey), has died (spoiler: Dallas is not dead, he just had a better gig). When Mike arrives at the seedy Dunes Inn & Suites for what he thinks is Dallas' wake, he is instead tackled by a naked Richie, who tosses him, fully clothed (his muscular dancer's body covered up in a drab suit), into the pool. Mike appears almost unnatural in comparison to the shirtless and carefree stripper bodies surrounding him; thus getting tossed into the pool by a naked Richie is like a baptism, sending him back on the righteous path to shirtlessness and male entertainment. The stripper convention is hosted by Rome (Jada Pinkett-Smith), who is the new Dallas of *MMXXL*. Dallas often appeared shirtless with black leather pants and an oiled chest, greeting the female audience with "All right, all right, all right." Here McConaughey was retreading the lazily sexual chant of David Wooderson, from his role in the cult nostalgic teenpic, *Dazed and Confused* (Linklater, 1993). Thus the character of Rome hails two different cult characters (Dallas as well as Wooderson), making Pinkett-Smith's performance an especially rich text for an analysis of the intersection of race, gender and cult cinema. Rome is first introduced to the audience as a former employer (and lover) of Mike, then as an emcee who sells sex, but also clearly still enjoys it. She seduces the crowd, readying their bodies for what their eyes are about to see. At the convention she riles the women up by asking: "Is there anybody up in here that ain't on birth control?" The crowd screams in assent, but she interrupts them, "Oh no! I'm keepin' it real with you ladies, because there's about to be some *grown woman shit up in here to-night.*" She punctuates each of these last six syllables with a bounce of her hips and shoulders. Rome knows her product is good because she, too, is a woman. The crowd goes wild.

In their analysis of *MMXXL's* unique female address, Kristen Warner and Chelsea Bullock note how rarely

> women's pleasure is instigated, indulged, or permitted in film or television. That women in *XXL* have the (welcomed) opportunity to stare – to gaze – at these men's bodies

without shame, mockery, or judgment is not something often seen or considered in mediated texts.

I am arguing that *MMXXL*, as well as other texts that are made specifically to objectify male bodies and entice a female fandom, including the original *Magic Mike* (2012, Steven Soderbergh), the *Twilight* franchise (2008, Catherine Hardwicke) and *Fifty Shades of Grey* (2015, Sam Taylor-Johnson), are the basis for another kind of cult film fandom, one which includes the fandom of women. If part of the appeal of cult films is their ability to offer what is often suppressed in mainstream films, then *MMXXL* is notable in its courting of a (diverse) female audience and its desire to fetishize their gaze. This matters because cult fandom is understood – by critics, scholars and even the fans themselves – as a primarily masculine pursuit. Cult films are made by and for and discussed by and for men. *Magic Mike XXL*, unlike the majority of canonized[1] cult films, specifically caters to a (heterosexual) female gaze.[2] While the first film drew a 73% female audience, the sequel drew in a 96% female audience in its opening weekend (Smith). In the world of *MMXXL* the gazers become the gazed upon, former sexual objects are transformed into subjects with agency, and the frame becomes a space for the cultivation and indulgence of female desire.

Masculinity and cult fandom

The term "cult" is notoriously difficult to pin down and define; some scholars define cult films by their aesthetics, their audiences, their budgets, their critical reception or their production histories. But one factor that links together such disparate definitions of cult film is what Joanne Hollows (2003) has usefully termed "the masculinity of cult." She writes "cult, although it is usually associated with a challenge to cultural hierarchies and with resistance, transgression and radicalism, serves also to reproduce cultural distinctions and cultural hierarchies along lines of gender" (49). Prior to the commercialization of home video, cult films were often screened in what came to be known as grindhouse theaters, typically located in "disreputable" urban neighborhoods. These theaters were some of the last vestiges of the city-based movie theater, before theater chains followed the white flight of patrons out to the suburbs and began building movieplexes in shopping malls to cater to this population shift. The true test of a cult film fan was a willingness to sit in these seedy, "unsafe" theaters, usually alone, and possibly next to a masturbating patron, all in order to see a cult gem. Thus, Hollows argues, the trope of the "manly adventurer," who would brave the dirtiest, most ramshackle theater to see the scared cult object, was born (43). But because women have historically been trained to avoid navigating the city alone,[3] especially "unsafe" spaces populated primarily by men, cult film exhibition sites in the 1970s represented material barriers for female fans. However, the development of VHS players in the 1970s and their popularization in the 1980s, along with video rental clubs and stores, shifted the character of American film exhibition practices. After this shift in exhibition practices, seeing a cult film meant knowing where to buy it, rather than physically going to a theater. By the 1980s, the cult film fan was less of a "manly adventurer" and more of a shopper.

Because cult identities are rooted in the practices of collecting and consuming popular culture, Jacinda Read (2003) argues that cult film fans are plagued by "anxieties of consumption." Historically, shopping and conspicuous consumption are deeply feminized, and therefore, denigrated practices in Western culture; to be a consumer is to be feminized. Cult fandom has a vested interest in promoting and upholding the masculinity of cult and therefore, it has a vested interest in disassociating fandom from women and feminized consumption (58). Shopping for rare cult film titles had to be understood as "curating" a collection. Niche pleasures, such as shopping for rare cult film titles, are elevated by their focus on the "acquisition, sharing, and distribution of this knowledge with others" (Massanari 2017: 4). The shopper becomes the "collector" or the "connoisseur." Femininity is seen as contaminant that must be exorcised.

Another roadblock to the canonization of a uniquely female cult fandom is the self-consciously or unconsciously misogynistic subject matter of many cult films embraced and adored by cult fandom. Cult favorites like *El Topo* (1970, Alejandro Jodorowsky), *Blood Feast* (1963, Hershell Gordon Lewis), *Barbarella* (1968, Roger Vadim), and *Easy Rider* (1963, Dennis Hopper) position women as absent, as the objects of male violence, or as purely sexual objects. Women are unwelcome both inside and outside the cult text. In fact, there is the sense that the presence of women somehow "ruins" the experience for male fans. For example, attendance at the San Diego Comic-Con, a convention which began in 1970 as a relatively small gathering of (mostly male) fans of comics and science fiction popular culture, has grown in recent years to the point where it is now the largest convention of its kind in the world. But not everyone is happy about that. In 2009, Summit Entertainment hosted a screening of material from the latest *Twilight* film, *New Moon* (2009, Chris Weitz) at that year's Comic-con. But this female fandom is an unwelcome presence at the traditionally male convention (Doyle). Likewise, fans of the franchise, who had never before attended Comic-con, were surprised to find that their presence was being protested by regulars. Cult fandom not only structures itself to be unwelcome to female fans, it actively works to remove them once they continue to assert a stake in the fandom.[4]

Women aren't welcome in cult exhibition sites (theaters, conventions) originated by male fans, but they are also criticized when they develop unique, female-centered fandoms of their own. Melissa Click has studied the media coverage of *Twilight*'s predominantly young, female fandom and found that overall they were described in Victorian-era terms signaling out-of-control female bodes: rabid, hysterical, obsessed: "These reports of girls and women seemingly out of their minds and out of control disparage female fans' pleasures and curtail serious explorations of the strong appeal of the series." In Western societies, cultural products associated with girls or women, either as the creator or the main audience, have often been positioned at or near the bottom of the cultural hierarchy; texts embraced and adored by women are generally denigrated as unworthy of study: "Despite three decades of influential feminist research, scholars continue to fight the persistent cultural assumption that male-targeted texts are authentic and interesting, while female-targeted texts are schlocky and mindless ..." (Click 2010). Therefore, it should not be surprising that films which cater to an almost exclusively female audience – the *Magic Mike, Twilight,* and *Fifty Shades of Grey* franchises – have become cultural punching bags.[5] It is no coincidence that all of these maligned texts appeal to women and appeal to them *sexually*. In their study of Beatlemania amongst American teens in 1964/65, Ehrenreich, Hess and Jacobs note that the moral hand-wringing over the phenomenon was at least partially rooted in its overt expression of female sexuality:

> It was ... rebellious to lay claim to the *active*, desiring side of a sexual attraction: The Beatles were the objects; the girls were their pursuers. The Beatles were *sexy*; the girls were the ones who perceived them as sexy.
>
> (1986: 18–19)

The female fan is doubly chastised when her fandom involves the implicit threat of active female sexual desire.

Naturalizing male objects and female gazers

In her interviews with and analysis of *Twilight* fans, Ananya Mukherjea notes that the franchise's appeal was largely tied to the way both the books and the films center the bodies of men as objects of the audience's gaze: "The joy of scopophilia, the love of looking, have historically been the privilege of men" (2011: 76). Historically non-white, non-male, non-heterosexual audiences have been forced to take up the point of view of a white, male, heterosexual protagonist. As Laura Mulvey notes (1999), women are the "bearers of meaning, not the makers of meaning" in Hollywood cinema. But in *MMXXL* this to-be-looked-at-ness becomes the domain of *only* male bodies. Every naked body we see is male. Women remain, for the most part, covered, and always placed in the role of the active bearer of the look. And even when female bodies vie for objectification, they are denied.[6] Likewise, *MMXXL* encourages an active spectator, a spectator whose activity is purposefully coded as both (hetero)sexual and female.

The specificity of *MMXXL*'s gendered audience address and its engagement of the female gaze is best exemplified in the film's first dance scene. Mike, who has just returned from Dallas' "wake," heads to his furniture workshop, puts on his metal welding helmet and begins working. A Spotify channel is on in the background, and when, at random, Ginuwine's "Pony" comes on, Mike slowly looks up, faces the camera, and shakes his head "no." "Pony" is the music that sound tracked Mike's most famous dance number from the first film, and this rare moment of direct address acknowledges that Mike knows that *we* (the audience) know that this is *his* song. Although the cult object initially refuses the audience's implicit request to dance, the film makes it clear that Mike cannot help but dance, as if his body were programmed by the millions of extradiegetic eyes, in hundreds of darkened movie theaters across the country. He finds his body moving to the beat as he works the blowtorch. Sparks fly out from his crotch area in time with the song's bass line. Moments later, he slithers across the table, swings from the rafters of his studio, and thrusts his drill, at crotch-level, into the worktable's surface.

When this scene played during the screening I attended, the women in the theater howled with delight. In his analysis of *The Rocky Horror Picture Show* (1975, Jim Sharman), Robert E. Wood notes that the success of a cult film is marked by "its ritualistic underpinning that responds to a deep-seated need felt by its audience" (1991: 157). The squeals in the theater are thus a reaction to the very novelty of the situation – a filmic space in which male bodies are the willing objects of the female gaze. Indeed, we can argue that Mike enjoyed himself, in spite, or perhaps, because he knows he is being watched: by the women on set, but also the women in the editing booth, and of course, the movie theaters filled with women. Through its clever use of bricolage[7] and non-choreography,[8] Mike's "Pony" reprise also demonstrates that the best (stripper) performance is one that is natural, spontaneous and real, rather than calculated. We need to believe that Mike simulates sex with a drill and a wooden table because music fills his body with sexual energy that can only be exorcised through dance, specifically, dance performed before the female gaze. The structure of the musical works in this case to naturalize male performativity and the male as object. In this context, stripping is not a vocation but a calling.[9]

The unique appeal of *MMXXL,* what makes it a uniquely feminized form of cult, is in the objectifying of maleness and in the male acceptance, even encouragement, of this to-be-looked-at-ness. For example, just after the men get on the road they pop some mollys and decide that the routines they had been rehearsing and performing in advance of the stripper convention in Myrtle Beach are no longer acceptable. Richie, in particular, clings his classic Fireman routine, which is calculated to excite women, but does nothing for the dancer (Richie admits that he has a phobia of fire). In other words, the dance is inauthentic because the dancer does not love what he is performing. When the men stop for gas at a mini mart, they goad Richie with a dare: make the sullen cashier (Lindsey Moser) smile. The idea here is that by trying to connect sexually and emotionally with a resistant stranger will help Richie choreograph his new and improved "authentic" routine.

This cashier, in comparison with the men, is utterly plain. She could be anyone and no one. Armed with a mission to please a woman, the mission that most motivates these men, Richie enters the store self-consciously. Despite the fact that Richie is big, muscular and uncommonly handsome, the clerk ignores him. The Backstreet Boys' "I Want It That Way" begins to play in the store, a nostalgic nod to another mode of male-generated pop culture crafted for a female audience. Rather than shy away from the song, a "bad" text made for women, Richie embraces it: slinking along the linoleum floors of the store, pouring bottled water over his bared, muscular chest, and simulating intercourse on the floor. Throughout the performance his buddies watch from the parking lot, performing far more enthusiasm for his expertise than the bored cashier, who only begins to study Richie with an impassive gaze halfway through his routine. Here we see a man expose his body and perform sexuality expressly for the purposes of the female gaze, a gaze that is coded as bored and even hostile to the solicitation. Her eventual smile is Richie's reward for a job well done. Thus, in a reversal of so many romantic comedies in which a man is dared by a pack of friends to get a girl's phone number or, more insidiously, steal a kiss or cop a feel, here the prize is female pleasure itself.

MMXXL converts muscular male torsos from active subjects to passive objects. These rippled physiques exist, not to take command of the narrative, like when Rambo (Sylvester Stallone) saves the day, but rather, to please women.[10] The men dance because they love dancing and they love dancing because it makes women so happy. Mike's only romantic pursuit in the film is of Zoe (Amber Heard), and his primary goal is not to bed her or even kiss her, but to make her smile (Jones). In the film's final orgiastic number, Zoe is lifted, tossed, dragged and pawed across the convention's ballroom stage by a zealous Mike. Mike (gently) pulls her hair and simulates sex with Zoe in a number potential orifices, all while R Kelly's "Cookie" blasts from the speakers (sample lyrics "Bout to bang on a pussy like I'm throwing up Crip..."). Throughout the performance, Zoe is unable suppress her smile. Thus, rather than the capturing the moment of unrestrained physical pleasure, the orgasm, we see a moment of unrestrained emotional pleasure, the smile. The woman's smile – that is, her pleasure – becomes the marker of job well-done. The final scene of the film is a wordless montage of Mike and his crew on the board walk, laughing and smiling. There is no embrace or kiss between Mike and Zoe (or any other couple for that matter). Instead the final image is medium shot of Mike watching fireworks with his crew, smiling. Then the credits roll.

Visualizing female desire and pleasure in the cult film

MMXXL generates a palpable way to express female sexual desire on screen, not simply by refocusing the object of the gaze from the female to the male form, but also by making female pleasure legible. In her canonical study of pornography, Linda Williams (1989) defines the "money shot," the moment of genital climax, "as a substitute for what cannot be seen" (95). For male performers, the money shot is the moment in which we see a close up of his ejaculation, "the quantifiable, material 'truth' of his pleasure" (101). The moment is substitutive, of course, but it is concrete in a way female ejaculation is not: "While undeniably spectacular, the money shot is also hopelessly specular; it can only reflect back to the male gaze that purports to want knowledge of the woman's pleasure in the man's own climax" (94). On screen a woman's orgasm can only be pictorialized by proxy, through the image of male ejaculation, or, less frequently, through a close up on the woman's face performing pleasure of her unseen orgasm.[11]

But *MMXXL* has clever a way around this visual problem: the aforementioned "tsunami of dollar bills." In the world of strip clubs, dollar bills function as a lure. When a patron waves around a dollar bill, it serves as an enticement to the dancer to get close enough to receive the money and gives the patron an opportunity to touch the dancer's body, if only for a second. The dancers with the most money shoved into their pants are the most successful dancers; they are the ones who have enticed and pleased (and been touched) by the most patrons. But in *MMXXL*, dollar bills carry a slightly different semantic function; they serve as a visual record of female desire, satisfied, a visualization of female climax. The dollar bill tsunami in *MMXXL* is not about touching bodies. In fact, in most cases the dancer doesn't know who has thrown the money. Instead, the dollar bill tsunami that erupts at the end of each performance (and sometimes even for the duration of a performance) becomes instead a visualization of female climax. In the film's final set piece, back-to-back performances by each of the film's dancer-protagonists, the dollar bill tsunamis become increasingly larger, signaling how each performance is better than the last. Many Hollywood musicals include a diegetic audience that cues the non-diegetic audience in about how to feel about a performance – if they clap and cheer, the performance was successful, if they sit silently in their seats, the performance was a bust. As Feuer notes, film musicals often offer up images of the diegetic audience to compensate for the "lost liveness" of the stage, serving as a stand in for the film audience's subjectivity (1993: 27). A similar effect is created in *MMXXL* by offering up, not just the woman selected from the crowd, our pleasure proxy, but by the "tsunami of dollar bills" generated by the crowd of satisfied female gazers.

A great example of the film's fetishization of the "tsunami of dollar bills" first occurs after the men crash their van near Savannah and gravely injure their emcee, Tobias (Gabrielle Iglesias). Finding their road trip narrative paused as they wait for van repairs and Tobias' recuperation, Mike suggests the men seek out Club Domina, a ladies' club run by Mike's old flame/boss, Rome and catering almost exclusively to black women. The rooms of Domina are dimly lit and crowded with women's bodies in a variety of sizes, making it difficult to distinguish identifying features of any of the female patrons. Some stand against walls, others sit on the few couches and chairs provided, but none but the camera never lingers long enough on any one woman to make her the clear object of the gaze. The camera only rests when it locks onto the gyrating torsos of Club Domina's male dancers, tracking their bodies as they slide, flip and undulate across the floor. The men's performances are only recognizable as successful by the size of the crowd and squeals of their delight, and of course, the "tsunami of dollar bills" that follows each performance. The longer and more heated the dance becomes, the more bills appear, swirling in the air around the dancers. The women, quite literally, make it rain, rewarding the dancers for pleasing them by paying (all over) them.

When the men perform at Club Domina or at the Stripper Convention, it is impossible to touch or connect with everybody in the room. Therefore, select women are drawn out of the crowd to serve as a sexual proxy. As Rome later says as seeks out two volunteers for the final performance "Let's not hate. I know we wish it was us tonight, but it's her. She's the lucky one." This message is as much to the non-diegetic audience as it is to the diegetic one; these pleasures do not need to be felt to be enjoyed. Here the eye becomes the erogenous zone. Indeed, the facial expressions of these sexual proxies – pleasure, surprise, embarrassment, then more pleasure – are backed up by the squeals and hoots of the rest of the women who are watching. The "tsunami of dollar bills," when the internal audience throws money at the men, offers a symbolic orgasm for extradiegetic female audience. *MMXXL*, much like the film musical, conditions the extradiegetic audience to view some performances as more or less sexually satisfying. Just as male viewers of pornography use the close-up male ejaculation as a signal that a climax has been achieved, the tsunami of dollar bills in *MMXXL* becomes a visual register of female pleasure.

It is significant that the men go to Club Domina after Mike's crew has spent an evening drinking and flirting with several middle-aged, wealthy, white women in what appears to be a plantation home. In other words, the men navigate one kind of female desire (white, wealthy, sitting) to another (younger, African American, dancing), shifting from demographic to demographic. In this way, *MMXXL* opens the doors to cult film viewership to all kinds of women; it is exclusively inclusive. This aspect of the film is significant since, as Rebecca Wanzo notes, gender is not the only identity which is routinely marginalized by cult fandom and fan studies scholarship; the experiences of non-white fans is noticeably absent from scholarship surrounding fandom in general and cult film in particular. As with masculinity, Wanzo notes that "an investment in whiteness may be foundational to some groups of fans" (2014: 1.4). That is, genealogies of fandom and fan studies tend to operate on their resistance to normative identities and ideologies; cult films and the fans who love them see themselves as questioning or even rejecting the status quo and embracing an outsider identity, a practice which "valorizes people who have claimed otherness for themselves, as opposed to having otherness thrust upon them" (2.3). African American fans, who are always already "outsiders," complicates these fan narratives. Thus, *MMXXL* serves as a counter narrative to cult film scholarship and fandom that excludes white women and women of color.

Conclusion

Jeffrey Sconce (2008) has argued that fans of paracinema (aka, exploitation films, cult films, and other "cinematic detritus" [101]) often define their own tastes as superior to those who enjoy mainstream cinema. He even quotes one fan who proclaims "Badness appreciation is the most acquired taste, the most refined" (109). This kind of rhetoric allows cult fans to carve a space of legitimacy for their fandom, a validation of their own specialized subset of cultural capital. Nevertheless, these discourses can also distract from the fact that paracinema fans are generally a homogenous group – educated, white, middle-class men (Sconce 104) – and without realizing it, much of their fan discourses exclude the kinds of cult texts that appealed to specifically women. For example, as *Twilight* so aptly demonstrates, female cult fandom is often marginalized because of its links to female desire and sexuality. Women expressing desire, rather than being the object of desire, is a radical, even transgressive state. By taking stock of what a uniquely female fandom looks like, we can make sense of the historical erasure of female pleasure.[12] In a true reversal of Hollywood's conventional gender roles, female *MMXXL* viewers *play* at being active lookers/spectators/gazers while male *MMXXL* viewers are offered two choices: identify with the objectified male bodies who preen and dance for female approval, or, become the active, female, bearer of the gaze. Thus, while on the surface *MMXXL* appears rather conventional – its stars are (primarily) white, straight, cis-gendered, able-bodied, handsome men – its spectatorship queers the conventional Hollywood relationship between viewer and text, constituting a cult viewing experience that revels in the rare pleasure of the female gaze.

Notes

1 See Sconce's "'Trashing' the academy: Taste, excess and an emerging politics of cinematic style."
2 When speaking of gender and sexual identification and attraction in American cinema, the primary viewing position is overwhelming coded as male and heterosexual. Thus, while gay, lesbian, trans and genderqueer viewers this equation becomes even more complex. Thus, this essay takes for granted that a film which courts a heterosexual female gaze is more appealing to women overall than one which appeals to a heterosexual male gaze.

3 See Helly and Reverby (1992) for historical analysis of women in the city.
4 This backlash against female fandom was also at the root of what Adrienne Massanari has called "toxic technocultures" of #GamerGate[4] and /r/TheFappening, both in 2014. In /r/TheFappening, users took advantage of an ICloud hack to leak private nude photos recovered from the phones of women, and a few celebrities, including Jennifer Lawrence. #GamerGate, a scandal with a longer tail and wider reach, was precipitated by what many straight, white, male gamers felt was a breach of "ethics in videogame journalism[4]." Both of these toxic technocultures highlight what Massanari sees as the ways that "certain design decisions and assumptions of use unintentionally may enable and/or implicitly encourage these spaces to become hotbeds of misogynistic activism" (2).
5 See, for example, headlines like "Fifty Shades of Grey receives SIX nominations in 'worst in film awards' The Razzies," "'Twilight' named worst movie of all time," and "Magic Mike XXL review: like watching pained strippers dry hump."
6 For example, early in the film, when the men are still at the Dunes Inn & Suites, a young, bikini-clad woman, high on acid and wearing a protective helmet, races into the hotel room and begins bouncing on the bed. Typically, a girl in a bikini would be the object of the gaze in such a scene, with repeated lingering shots of her body used as a backdrop while the men talk plot. But the camera barely notices her, focusing instead on the men's faces and bodies.
7 Feuer (1993) defines "bricolage" as using the props at hand to create imaginary world of musical performance.
8 Feuer (1993: 13) defines "non-choreography" as a strategy aimed at naturalizing effort that goes into dance so that it appears easy and ordinary: "We are never allowed to realize that musical entertainment is an industrial product and that putting on a show … is a matter of a labor force producing a product for consumption."
9 In an interview with male strippers in *People* magazine, Rudy Bundini, a dancer at the club, Hunk-O-Mania explains, "I have the same passion whether or not I make money. … It's more about our interest that we can't wait for tomorrow night to come back again and the show starts."
10 Susan Jeffords (1994) explains that hard bodies in 1980s Hollywood films were collective symbols of "the Reagan imaginary," and "national identities." These bodies were evidence of America's perceived dominance in the world (25–26).
11 Of course, since Williams' first published her book on pornography, the volume and diversity of pornographic content has skyrocketed and now there is a plethora videos featuring female ejaculation.
12 The erasure of cult fans of color, particularly African American fans, is not simply inaccurate, it also erases important insights we might gain from accounting for the non-white, non-male fan. Wanzo (2015) writes "people of color often make the erasures, complexities, and challenges of thinking about the relationship between normativity and otherness in fan communities most visible" (2.7).

References

Anon. 2012. "'Twilight' Named Worst Movie of All Time." *NBC News*. 28 December. http://entertainment.nbcnews.com/_news/2012/12/28/16197339-twilight-named-worst-movie-of-all-time?lite. Accessed 6 July 2016.

Bradshaw, Peter. 2015. "Magic Mike XXL Review: Like Watching Pained Strippers Dry Hump." *The Guardian*, 29 June 2015. www.theguardian.com/film/2015/jun/29/magic-mike-xxl-review-strippers-channing-tatum. Accessed 6 July 2016.

Chess, Shira, and Adrienne Shaw. 2015. "A Conspiracy of Fishes, or, How We Learned to Stop Worrying About #GamerGate and Embrace Hegemonic Masculinity." *Journal of Broadcasting & Electronic Media* 59.1: 208–220.

Click, Melissa. 2010 "'Rabid,' 'Obsessed,' and 'Frenzied': Understanding *Twilight* Fangirls and the Gendered Politics of Fandom." *Flow TV* 11.4. www.flowjournal.org/2009/12/rabid-obsessed-and-frenzied-understanding-twilight-fangirls-and-the-gendered-politics-of-fandom-melissa-click-university-of-missouri. Accessed 24 May 2016.

Corrigan, Timothy. 1991. "Film and the Culture of Cult," in J.P. Telotte, ed., *The Cult Film Experience: Beyond All Reason*. Austin: University of Texas Press: 26–38.

Doyle, Sady. 2016. "Girls Just Wanna Have Fangs." *The American Prospect*, 26 October. http://prospect.org/article/girls-just-wanna-have-fangs-0. Accessed 6 July 2016.

Eco, Umberto. 2008. "*Casablanca*: Cult Movies and Intertexual Collage," in E. Mathijs and X. Mendik, eds, *The Cult Film Reader*. New York: Open University Press: 67–75.

Ehrenreich, Barbara, Elizabeth Hess and Gloria Jacobs. 1986. *Re-Making Love: The Feminization of Sex*. Garden City, NY: Anchor Press.

Fecteau, Jessica. 2015. "We Watched *Magic Mike XXL* and Now We Have Questions – Real Strippers Gave Us Answers." *People*, 30 June. www.people.com/article/male-strippers-answer-magic-mike-xxl-questions. Accessed 6 July 2016.

Feuer, Jane. 1993. *The Hollywood Musical*. 2nd ed. Bloomington: Indiana University Press.

Forrester, Katy. 2016. "Fifty Shades of Gray Receives SIX Nominations in 'Worst in Film Awards' The Razzies." *The Mirror*, 13 January. www.mirror.co.uk/tv/tv-news/fifty-shades-grey-receives-six-7171377. Accessed 6 July 2016.

Grant, Barry K. 1991. "Science Fiction Double Feature: Ideology in the Cult Film," in J.P. Telotte, ed., *The Cult Film Experience: Beyond All Reason*: Austin: University of Texas Press: 122–137.

Helly, Dorothy O., and Susan M. Reverby. 1992. *Gendered Domains: Rethinking Public and Private in Women's History*. Ithaca, NY: Cornell University Press.

Hollows, Joanne. 2003. "The Masculinity of Cult," in M. Jancovich, A.L. Reboll, J. Stringer and A. Willis, eds, *Defining Cult Movies: The Cultural Politics of Oppositional Taste*. Manchester: Manchester University Press: 35–53.

Jeffords, Susan. 1994. *Hard Bodies: Hollywood Masculinity in the Reagan Era*. New Brunswick: Rutgers University Press.

Jones, Chloe Cooper. 2015. "'Magic Mike XXL' Was the Most Important Feminist Movie of 2015." *Vice*, 30 December. www.vice.com/read/surprise-magic-mike-xxl-was-the-most-important-feminist-movie-of-2015. Accessed 6 July 2016.

Margolis, Maxine L., and Marigene Arnold. 1993. "Turning the Tables? Male Strippers and The Gender Hierarchy," in B.D. Miller, ed., *Sex and Gender Hierarchies*. Cambridge: Cambridge University Press: 334–351.

Massanari, Adrienne. 2017. "#Gamergate and The Fappening: How Reddit's Algorithim, Governance, and Culture Support Toxic Technocultures." *New Media & Society* 19.3: 329–346.

Mathijs, Ernest, and Jamie Sexton. 2011. *Cult Cinema: An Introduction*. Oxford: Blackwell.

Mukherjea, Ananya. 2011. "Team Bella: Fans Navigating Desire, Security, and Feminism," in M. Parke and N. Wilson, eds, *Theorizing Twilight: Critical Essays on What's at Stake in a Post-Vampire World*. Jefferson, MD: McFarland: 70–86.

Mullin, Frankie. 2014. "A Short History of Female Ejaculation." *Vice*, 4 December. www.vice.com/read/a-short-history-of-female-ejaculation-290. Accessed 6 July 2016.

Mulvey, Laura. 1999. "Visual Pleasure and Narrative Cinema," in L. Braudy and M. Cohen, eds, *Film Theory and Criticism: Introductory Readings*. 5th ed. New York: Oxford University Press: 833–844.

Read, Jacinda. 2003. "The Cult of Masculinity: From Fan-Boys to Academic Bad-boys," in M. Jancovich, A.L. Reboll, J. Stringer and A. Willis, eds, *Defining Cult Movies: The Cultural Politics of Oppositional Taste*. Manchester: Manchester University Press: 54–70.

Sconce, Jeffrey. 2008. "'Trashing' the Academy: Taste, Excess and an Emerging Politics of Cinematic Style," in E. Mathijs and X. Mendik, eds, *The Cult Film Reader*. New York: Open University Press: 100–118.

Smith, Nigel M. 2015. "Magic Mike Is an XXL Hit with Women But Why Did It Turn Men Off?" *The Guardian*, 6 July. www.theguardian.com/film/2015/jul/06/magic-mike-xxl-attracts-women-scares-men-box-office. Accessed 6 July 2016.

Telotte, J.P. "Beyond All Reason: The Nature of the Cult," in J.P. Telotte, ed., *The Cult Film Experience: Beyond All Reason*. Austin: University of Texas Press: 5–17.

Wanzo, Rebecca. 2015. "African American Acafandom and Other Strangers: New Genealogies of Fan Studies." *Journal of Transformative Works and Cultures* no. 20. http://journal.transformativeworks.org/index.php/twc/article/view/699/538. Accessed 6 July 2016.

Warner, Kristen, and Chelsea Bullock. 2015. "'Any God Worth Believing in Sends You Dudes in Thongs When in Need': Exploring Women's Pleasure in *Magic Mike XXL*." *Antenna*, 17 July. http://blog.commarts.wisc.edu/2015/07/17/womens-pleasure-magic-mike-xxl. Accessed 6 July 2016.

Williams, Linda. 1989. *Hard Core: Power, Pleasure, and the "Frenzy of the Visible."* Berkeley: University of California Press.

Wood, Robert E. 1991. "Don't Dream It: Performance and *The Rocky Horror Picture Show*," in J.P. Telotte, ed., *The Cult Film Experience: Beyond All Reason*. Austin: University of Texas Press: 156–166.

28

THE CUT BETWEEN US

Digital remix and the expression of self

Jenna Ng

"WHAT AM I," then? Since childhood, I've passed through a flow of milk, smells, stories, sounds, emotions, nursery rhymes, substances, gestures, ideas, impressions, gazes, songs, and foods. What am I? Tied in every way to places, sufferings, ancestors, friends, loves, events, languages, memories, to all kinds of things that obviously *are not me*. Everything that attaches me to the world, all the links that constitute me, all the forces that compose me don't form an identity, a thing displayable on cue, but a singular, shared, living *existence*, from which emerges – at certain times and places – that being which says "I."

– Invisible Committee (2011, emphasis in original)

Provided that we take a text's existence in an objective sense as an independent and culturally produced artifact (Blanchot 1995), we may acquire its meaning in any of three ways. The first is through a conventional reading of the text, whereby the reader uses various methods, interpretations, histories, politics, and social contexts as lenses through which the text is understood to contain meaning. The second way is to transpose the text into a different contextual matrix (e.g., space, time, media, and culture) so that it can be read anew and thereby take on new meaning. A dominant illustration of this is found in art: Duchamp (1951), as one example out of many, transforms a bicycle wheel from an ordinary object out of ordinary life into an art object by upending it on a stool and exhibiting it in a gallery. (Dis)placed thus, the wheel acquires new meaning not because its fundamental objective existence – as a wheel – has been changed in any material way, but because it has been shifted from one cultural understanding to another: "it [is] transferred from the sphere of tools or use objects to that of aesthetic contemplation" (Sonesson 1998: 85). Another example is found in cinema, or what Eli Horwatt (2009) defines as found footage filmmaking: "the practice of appropriating pre-existing film footage in order to denature, detour or recontextualize images by inscribing new meanings onto materials through creative montage" (76). Used in different spaces and times, found images become an alternative media text that is conceptually, if not visually and aurally, different as previously understood in the images' prior space and time. A text may also acquire new meaning by being turned from one media form to another, such as cinema becoming performance when "film jockeys" show, loop, edit, re-work, perform live soundtracks to, and otherwise manipulate images in real time, with their modulations of media creating new meanings, as suggested by one group's tagline: "expect cinema but don't think you will see a film" (Mindpirates 2012). Machinima, or real-time films made in virtual worlds, likewise recontextualize the video game into other media forms (e.g., cinema, performance, and television), which Henry Lowood (2008) identifies as "found technology" (169). Using video games or virtual worlds in new communicative ways subverts their original purpose and content, thereby creating new meanings and ways of understanding the text.

The third way – and the focus of this chapter – is through the text's *interstices*. Here I want to think about how a text changes when put into a state of *between-ness* – between lines, between words, between letters, between edges, between pages, between frames, between sounds, between marks, between binaries (light/darkness; sound/silence; line/space). How may between-ness be a useful concept to think about the act of authoring or creating, specifically in the digital age, with its profound imbrications of (im)materiality, reception, referencing and inspiration? In particular, I want to think about *the cut* as the operative tool for understanding between-ness, as the act which crystallizes the fissure represented by that space of the in-between (the cleaving of two positive spaces literally delivers a space betwixt – a fissure, a breach, a cleft). As a central issue, I want to think about the cut, not in terms of production, but destruction, or, more specifically, *creation in destruction*. A cut is ordinarily destructive: it carves up rather than constructs; it dissects rather than constitutes. It is the converse of more conventional production tools which put things together – the pen which assembles words and paper to create a text, the brush paint and canvas to create a painting, the camera light and film a photograph, and so on. Cutting, instead, renders asunder.

In this chapter I want to argue the cut as a productive method, one that can create an active space of between-ness, enabling new meanings to be formed, new juxtapositions to be made, new ways of seeing and new content to be created. I will use as my primary example the digital remix, a media form created precisely by shredding up its original contents and re-organizing them to bring about new meaning. As I explore the digital remix, I am also mindful of how it is an integral part of the larger creative wave of grassroots activity that informs contemporary digital culture, one which addresses fan production and criticism, cult objects, YouTube homages and other amateur work in what Mathijs and Sexton (2011) call the "sphere in which the experience of subjectivity is essential" (53). At the heart of this sphere is an almost palpable sense of love – contested as they are between cultism and cinephilia (Gorfinkel 2008: 33; Martin 2008) – but in whichever form is ultimately of a regard so intense it has to find itself in outward expression and, more importantly, so strong that it forms a part of one's core. To that extent, I also want to consider remix specifically in its digitality as an agent of such subjectivity, and in the process think through how remix may shed light on cultural transformations that navigate identity, experience, selfhood and individual expression.

The cut: Between violence and creativity

In thinking about the cut, I look to two ideas in particular as a backdrop: the first is Sergei Eisenstein's essays on montage, and the power of collision between images which he advocates as montage's main characteristic: "What then characterizes montage and, consequently, its embryo, the shot? Collision. Conflict between two neighboring fragments" (Eisenstein [1929] 1988: 144). For Eisenstein, the key to montage is the interaction – more specifically "collision" – in that space of between-ness amid "two neighboring fragments." This perspective effectively shifts the locus of meaning from the images to their interstices, whereby our understanding is derived not from what is shown but from what is *not* shown. To Eisenstein, that negation is a potent one as it gives rise to montage. Between-ness here is thus more than just a defined absence – what is not in the boundaries – but an active and significant place of encounter from which meaning arises. The second idea is the material ontology of film-based cinema, namely, a reel of individual still frames segmented by strips of black that, when run through a projector along with persistence of vision, creates the illusion of moving images we are now familiar with as cinema. Again, the interstices of black here are not just divisions but creative loci that re-contextualize photography into cinema, concocting new meanings through the playing of between-ness in stasis and movement, light and darkness, images of color and narrow slivers of black.

In both cases the key lies in conceptualizing between-ness as spaces that actively open up new meanings, rather than being mere conduits or boundary markers. In a sense, this positivity of between-ness runs counter to its nature, which is to exist not as a discrete space but one that relies on other entities for its existence; it must be defined *relationally*. As Elizabeth Grosz (2001) observes, between-ness, or what she terms "the in-between," is a space

> whose form is the outside of the identity, not just of an other (for that would reduce the in-between to the role of object, not of space) but of others, whose relations of positivity define, by default, the space that is constituted as in-between.

> (90)

Grosz's observation is significant as it renders the relational feature of between-ness a specific place for action and potential: it "is the only place – the place around identities, between identities – where becoming, openness to futurity, outstrips the conservational impetus to retain cohesion and unity" (91). To that end, the in-between is bound up with movement and realignment precisely because it is defined only in the flux of boundaries, intentions, and identities. It is in this potentiality that I want to explore the making of meaning not just in the space of between-ness, but also in the cut which, as explained, formalizes that space. Moreover, to Grosz's characterization of the in-between (as the place for becoming), I wish to add the idea of violence. Like the Higgs-Boson particle,[1] between-ness can only be conceived as a flash point; it is extant only by a collision against others. Because it is such a flash point, it is also a violent space; indeed, Eisenstein identifies it primarily with collision and conflict. The destructive force of the cut thus also converges with this violence, for the cut as both act and metaphor ("I feel cut up"; "your words are cutting"; "to cut one out"; "to cut one off") connotes hurt, pain, and injury. Violence can also be conceived in terms of friction and resistance, insofar as between-ness is a space for movement ("one could say that the in-between is the locus of futurity, movement, speed" [Grosz 2001: 93]). Without qualifying Grosz's characterization, I argue that movement can evoke not just speed but also resistance in terms of confronting friction, chafing and traction. Movement (and, for that matter, transformation) is not just blitzing down a smooth highway, but also an overcoming of innumerable points of contact, each one requiring effort and energy.

The in-between is thus a space of two possibly conflicting elements – the potential transformations in its openness and futurity, and the violence it entails in achieving that potentiality. In that sense, between-ness is also a delicate space: it can only exist relationally, so it cannot be taken too far from the objects between which it exists. The violence of the space thus also threatens its existence – taken too far, the in-between becomes instead an unbridgeable chasm. Thus, we may understand and create texts not just in themselves, but also in the between-ness of spaces they occupy with other texts as well as *with themselves*. When cut and dis/reassembled, a text may be seen anew in more than just its positive and in-between spaces, but also in the fundamental creative frictions it engages in collision with others. Thinking about the cut and its complex destruction/construction binary may thus also change our perspectives of authorship and readership, paving the way for more merged creative roles in digital media between "making" and "cutting," to occupy the paradoxical binaries of constructive destruction/destructive construction. The primary task in the rest of this chapter, then, is to think about ways in which that destructive mode can, without implosion, be made into a creative and constructive force. This I will aim to do here using illustrative cases of digital remixes and, in particular, video remixes.

The digital remix

The remix can be better understood today as a discourse rather than any particular set of cultural practices or techniques. The remix has its roots as a musical practice starting from the late 1960s in Jamaican music (Brewster and Broughton 2000; Poschardt 1998) and developed in the 1970s with the growing practices of sampling in disco and hip hop culture. Since then, however, and particularly so in the twenty-first century, it has been appropriated for various contexts and applications, ranging from literature to architecture to pedagogy to Web 2.0 technologies (Navas 2010; Sonvilla-Weiss 2010) so that it is now almost a language, connecting and pointing with its own semiotics at its original texts (or allegorizing them, as Navas puts it).

Due to the wide range of applications, the exact parameters of practices constituting remix have become a little muddy. In its most basic form, "remix means to take cultural artifacts and combine and manipulate them into new kinds of creative blends" (Knobel and Lankshear 2008). Navas divides the remix into four categories. The first two categories are the extended remix (where long instrumental sections are simply added to the original composition "to make it more mixable for the club DJ" [159]); and the selective remix (a more complex version of the extended remix, where new material, sections or sounds are not only added to but also subtracted from the original composition, resulting in a more elaborate derivative work but whose original composition is still recognizable). Significantly, these two types of remixes, despite the changes they make, retain the essence and identity of the original composition, or what Navas calls its "spectacular aura." The third category of remix – the reflexive remix – does not. The reflexive remix "allegorizes and extends the aesthetic of sampling," typically from numerous sources. Its root in material practice here is the collage, where different materials are used to invoke a uniting groove or idea or emotion, rather than to point to any one original composition. Navas's main example of the reflexive remix is the music megamix – a medley of sampled brief sections of preexisting songs ("often just a few bars, enough for the song to be recognized") to basically form a musical collage that does "not allegorize one particular song but many," recalling not necessarily a single artist or composition but "a whole time period." The fourth category is the regenerative remix, something Navas identifies specifically to new media and networked culture, whereby "remix as discourse becomes embedded materially in culture in nonlinear and ahistorical fashion":

> Like the other remixes [the regenerative remix] makes evident the originating sources
> of material, but unlike them it does not necessarily use references or samplings to val-
> idate itself as a cultural form. Instead, the cultural recognition of the material source
> is subverted in the name of practicality – the validation of the Regenerative Remix
> lies in its functionality.
>
> (162)

Here the allegorical ethos of remix is subverted "not to recognize but to be of practical use," and its operative principle is of periodic change and updates, an issue that is particularly in keeping with the fluidity of digital media.

What I am interested in here are the critical implications of between-ness in the third category of the reflexive remix, where new texts are made with their own creative charge without allegorizing the original composition. I see the reflexive remix co-opting the space of between-ness by operating across boundaries in two ways. The first is in the between-ness of *texts*, or their sampled materials. As explained, the general principle of allegory in remix specifically points to its original text in various ways – by extending it, by adding to or subtracting from it, by sampling and so on. Film scholars tend to emphasize the connections or commonalities presented by remix, particularly in terms of intertextuality and community: for example, Chuck Tryon (2009) discusses how remixes can be (to take Matt Hills's term) of "semiotic solidarity" with other fans, and used to express their affection, fandom, or even geekdom for the original texts; Henry Jenkins (2003) writes of remix as a practice that forms part of a participatory culture, tying the remix to a larger culture or community.

Without qualifying their arguments, I argue that the semiotic of remix also, as with Eisensteinian montage, relies on a certain friction in the space between texts for their creative energy. Remix is a unique combination of simultaneously stitching together commonalities and ripping them apart with collisions, contrasts and conflicts, so that meaning arises precisely from that complex negotiation between conflict and alignment. For instance, in "Buffy vs Edward: Twilight Remixed" (2009), Jonathan McIntosh remixes the *Buffy the Vampire Slayer* TV series with the first *Twilight* movie, specifically editing together scenes featuring Buffy with Edward Cullen from *Twilight* so that they look like they are talking to and interacting with each other. The editing is, not surprisingly, highly flawed – the eyelines do not match, let alone the backgrounds – but these discontinuities are smoothened out by their commonalities: both deal with vampires and the remix makes good use of voice cuts and shared situations such as telephone calls, school cafeteria lunches, and to-the-death fights. However, the success of the video stems primarily from the friction created by pitting the respective texts against each other, specifically their gendered politics: *Buffy's* strong, independent, take-no-nonsense female protagonist against the brooding romantic hero represented by Edward and the general sexist gender roles in *Twilight* (male = strong protective hero; female = helpless and in constant need of being rescued). As the write-up on its YouTube video site judicially states: "Ultimately this remix is about more than a decisive showdown between the slayer and the sparkly vampire. It also doubles as a metaphor for the ongoing battle between two opposing visions of gender roles in the 21st century." The two texts as spliced together are more than an alignment of two popular texts about vampires, but about a clashing dialogue (above the literal one created in illusion between Buffy and Edward) of their conflicting politics. Meaning thus arises not out of the connections or allegories to the original texts, but out of the violence of how they conflict, contrast and collide with each other.

The second mode of between-ness in the remix lies in the information surrounding the materials. The meanings that can be created out of the violence of the cut and its ensuing friction and collision does not only apply to inter-textual cuts, but also those that are intra-textual, where a single text may be cut not to connect with other texts but with different parts of itself as *imbued with additional information*. This may be anything from genre knowledge to additional music and sound, with the result being to present the original text with a new creative energy. While there are many examples of such creative remixing, two stand out for their extremity (and hilarity). The first is the "5 second movies" genre, where micro-second fragments of feature-length films are cut and remixed into 5-second long videos "that can be seen as the essence of the said films" (Jedi & YF 2011). There is violence in the practice: assuming the average length of a feature film to be 2 hours long, editing out a 5-second movie represents snipping 99.03% of its original text.

However, what is most interesting about this genre is how the interpretation of "the essence of the said films" becomes (dis/mis)-placed in these violent edits. For example, one "*Pulp Fiction* in 5 Seconds" movie spliced together split seconds of the word "motherfucker" uttered from the movie; considering the profanity of *Pulp Fiction* (which, among other aspects, forms a large part of the ebullient dialogue that made the film famous), this video certainly points to a valid "essence" of the film. As a contrast, though, another placed together snippets in the film referencing food – "burger," "Sprite," "milkshake," "red apples," "blueberry pancakes": this is as innocuous as they come. Yet there is a logic to the video – *Pulp Fiction*, while unabashedly profane and violent, carries an undertone of being child-like, even tenderness – and the food references convey that. The video is ironic, witty, smart … and not completely incorrect.

The second example is what Chuck Tryon (2009: 161) calls the "genre remix," where scenes from a film are remixed and recombined to convert it from one genre to a significantly different genre. The most common illustration, also cited by Tryon, is the remix in 2005 by Robert Ryang of Stanley Kubrick's horror film, *The Shining*, to create a fake trailer portraying it as a family drama-comedy. In this case the remix allegorizes only one text, so it does not operate in the between-ness with another text. Instead, it engages with additional data about the film, creating meaning in the between-ness of the information we have about it (a classic horror) and the genre-establishing data we receive from its "trailer," and deliberately creating friction in that space. Tryon points out how scenes have been edited "to suggest bonding moments between father and son, while Jack Nicholson's feverish dancing is recast as cheerful exuberance, in large part through careful visual and sound editing" (161). Music is also a part of the data: the song in the fake trailer, Peter Gabriel's "Solsbury Hill," evokes romantic drama, used "most memorably in ads for the Topher Grace–Scarlett Johansson romantic drama *In Good Company* and the Tom Cruise–Penelope Cruz romantic thriller *Vanilla Sky*" (161). Other elements include the deep and chipper voice-over of the unseen narrator ("Meet Jack Torrance … he's a writer looking for inspiration!") and the use of "a quiet moment" (shots fading into each other, accompanied by soft keyboard notes played slowly in the background) to present an emotional hook, here presented as a father-united-with-son drama. As the narrator intones, "but now … sometimes … what we need the most … is just around the corner," his statement finishes with an eyeline shot from Danny to Jack, suggesting that what Danny needs most, earlier shown complaining that he has no one to play with, is his father, Jack. It is precisely in the collision, rather than in the solidarity, with the original text (in which a crazed Jack ends up trying to murder Danny) that the shot is now imbued with new meaning. The creative force of the remix's irony, humor and subversion come through in contrasts and juxtapositions such as shown in that eyeline shot: Danny really needs Jack as he needs the proverbial hole in the head, or, more accurately in this case, an axe in the skull. This conflict deliberately invoked in the between-ness of meta-data is not limited to Ryang's remix; virtually all genre remixes use this mode of conflict and collision (*Mary Poppins, Sleepless in Seattle,* and *Ferris Bueller's Day Off* as horror films, *Back to the Future* as a Brokeback-style gay romance film, etc.).

In both cases, a new work, charged with creative energy, presents meaning out of the violence of the cut and the interstices between itself and the original text. Cutting thus becomes not only creative practice in the way of bricolage or collage, but also a practice out of "love of the movies," merged between film-viewing, filmmaking, cinephilia, cultism, and an undoubted wielding of specialist film knowledge evident in what Mathijs and Sexton (2011) call "DIY criticism" (55) as associated with cult connoisseurship.

Remix thus operates effectively in the friction created in this space of the in-between. Yet between-ness is also a paradoxical space, for one of the main operative tools (on top of the effective use of music, well-written narration, etc.) for bringing about this creative space in the digital remix is the somewhat destructive operation of cut and paste. This would be so in its literal sense if the remix had been spliced from an analogue reel, as the frames would have to be first snipped from the reel and then subsequently glued or placed together to form a separate continuous reel. In the context of the analogue, the cut is also of particular violence and finitude. For instance, these descriptions of Godard's jump cuts, and probably one of the most dramatic uses of the cut, as featured in his classic representation of the French *nouvelle vague, A Bout de souffle*, feature strong language: "Godard *chopped* it up any which way …"; a "disconnected cutting" as "pictorial *cacophony*"; "[Godard] chopped it about as a manifestation of *filmic anarchy, technical iconoclasm*" (Raskin 1998, emphasis added). While these comments are obviously directed toward the anarchistic aesthetic of the jump shots so in contradiction to the smoothness of continuity editing then in conventional film language, the violence and finality underpinning those descriptions and the fundamental nature of the cut – as the chop, no less – is clear.

However, in the digital sense, cut and paste takes on new meanings. It obviously ramps up the ease and convenience of the edit, underscoring the fluidity of the digital text and the unprecedented ways in which we may navigate its new spaces. With digital technology, we can now find, manipulate, and put together films more easily than ever. However, scale here is a minor issue. Rather, I argue that the digital cut, in enabling frames to be effortlessly found, re-worked, and pasted together, transforms the violent undertones of the cut and the finality of the act it implies: in its digital form, the cut is no longer about finitude but about endless possibilities. In that sense the continued icon of the scissors for the "cut" function in common digital video editing interfaces such as Windows Movie Maker and Final Cut Pro is anachronistic: the cut is no longer annihilative but the conduit for continuous transformation. More than that, the cut in relation to the immateriality of the digital text signifies a fundamental change to the nature of text and authorship. A film strip can only be literally cut once, but a digital text can be "cut" endlessly. No longer destructive or terminal, the digital cut is instead an act signifying innumerable second chances, creative acts that can take into account all kinds of mutability and change, resulting in a final product that need never be final but be instead a constantly resurrecting entity. With digital editing, the text is stripped of both finality and finitude. Making is now in the flow of these changes, struck up by a destructive force that is paradoxically also its very agent of creativity and transformation.

The example that I think takes this paradoxical creative energy to its highest limits so far is Kevin Macdonald's documentary film, *Life in a Day* (2011) On July 1, 2010, Macdonald launched an open call on YouTube for contributors – "thousands of people, everywhere in the world" – to upload onto the video sharing site a recording that they were to make of one day in their lives, the day of July 24, 2010. Macdonald and his team would then use the material "to make a film that is a record of what it's like to be alive on that one day"; it is to be "kind of like a time capsule … a portrait of the world in a day" (Macdonald, 2011). The result presents some astonishing numbers: over 80,000 videos were submitted from 190 countries, amounting to over 4,500 hours of footage, out of which the 95-minute film was ultimately "made," apparently featuring more than 1,000 clips from YouTube contributors (Moner 2011). Its premiere was eventually screened at Sundance in January 2011, before being generally released in June 2011.

Life in a Day is an innovative project in a number of ways. For one, it is unprecedented in the scale it calls for and implements user-generated content.[2] William Moner, distinguishing *Life* from other amateur and small-scale productions proliferating online, calls it "the first major United States motion picture to engage crowdsourced labor for content." In the same vein, it is also one of the most collaborative creative film projects to date, technically involving more than 80,000 parties who submitted footage for the film (albeit a collaboration of which Moner is also highly critical, arguing that the contributors were effectively undercompensated labor, having signed away all rights and receiving no monetary payment for their work).

For the purposes of this chapter, I note that the film is also innovative as an example *par excellence* of the cut as its primary operating tool. Like the 5-second movie, *Life* must have involved extensive editing in order to cut and put together a coherent 95 minutes out of 1,000 clips. Yet the average Hollywood blockbuster, with its hyperkinetic action, probably contains more or at least as many cuts: a standard movie today, after all, has about 5,000 cuts (Murch 2004). In any case, what I am interested in is not the scale, but the role of the cut. Here the overwhelming operative mode of making the film, as created by Macdonald, is by cutting and pasting together submitted clips. It does not matter so much *what* was being filmed as opposed to *how* it was being put together.[3] The job of the director effectively converges with editor as he "directs" a film with footage he had *not* directed, nor indeed ever seen before. Yet for *Life* this is all a matter of semantics now as it is all in the editing. *Making is now in the cutting.*

Self-reflexively or otherwise, this mode of cutting resonates with the themes of the film. Taking Robert Plant Armstrong's (1975) ideas of synthesis and syndesis (the former an accumulative linear progression; the latter an accretion of repeated units), the digital cut and paste of *Life in a Day* seems to be simultaneously both. All films are edited to be synthetic: one frame is pasted to the next so that they all follow each other linearly. Yet for *Life*, there is also a sense of inevitability that marks the repetitive nature of syndesis: the film progresses linearly, starting from the break of dawn to midnight. While we only see a small fraction of all the videos submitted, we cannot help but realize the existential repetitions with which this day is composed: fleeting (and fleeing) seconds to minutes piling upon each other to hours turning on slow axles to dawn lightening into day before darkening into night, only for it all to be repeated the next day, and the next, and the next. The endlessness of cutting and pasting in this case becomes Sisyphean, mirroring the temporal labor that is the making not only of the film but indeed life itself: frame upon frame, clip upon clip, time upon time, age upon age. It is not only the central creative act of the film's making but also a self-reflexive statement of its truth: a slow march to a relentless rhythm of sunrises and sunsets, toward an end that we only faintly comprehend in the stillness of others' passings and the chilling glimpses of our mortality.

Conclusion: Remix and the expression of self

I have argued here for how between-ness, in particular as exposed by the cut, may be creative and meaningful spaces, and uses the digital remix to illustrate this. In that sense, the cut echoes Pier Paolo Pasolini's (1967: 6) poignant account of the edit as *precisely* that which renders meaning, because the cut passes the present into the past. It completes action – the practical equivalence of death, which makes our lives meaningful by converting a chaotic, infinite, and unstable present into a clear, certain, and stable past: "It is thanks to death that our lives become expressive." The cut exposes not only the space of the in-between but, more important, the constitution of being in that between-ness, spaces that form being in their complex and fluid combinations of connections, dialogue, confluence, and relations.

This understanding of cutting and being may thus also relate to our understanding of "movie love" – cinephilia, filmic cultism, filmic practices, amateur making, creative expression – in a number of ways: first, in understanding digital materiality itself, of both its fluidities and fluencies in changing our thoughts on the discreteness of things and the connections between and betwixt; and second, in opening up spaces for digital "making," so that fandom, connoisseurship, criticism and, ultimately, the demonstration of devotion lies not only reception but also in creativity, and specifically in the in-between spaces of cutting, collision and violence. The third way, then, may be in thinking through the expression of subjectivity, so much a driving force for love, and how we are not as separate(d) as we might think. In that sense, the exploration of the limbo of between-ness is not only creative and constructive, but also productive. Might there not be greater potential by making use of the destructive force of the cut, drawing on violence and acting on conflict in precisely those spaces of the in-between? Might not more (in ideas, understanding, and knowledge production) be achieved via collisions rather than ruptures? Recent research revealed a new scientific understanding of what the human being is in biological terms: the conventional view is that a human body is a collection of cells – ten trillion strong, to be precise, produced from 23,000 genes. However, scientists have now discovered the microbiome, which is bacteria of "several hundred species bearing 3 million non-human genes," in the numbers of hundreds of trillions. In other words, by counting the microbiomes too, "humans are not single organisms, but superorganisms made up of lots of smaller organisms working together" ("Microbes maketh man" 2012; "The human microbiome" 2012). On this account, the space of between-ness intrudes on our fundamental ideas of identity and thoughts about who we are: the expression of the self being not in who I am but in all the ties from myself to everything else, "to places, sufferings, ancestors, friends, loves, events, languages, memories, to all kinds of things that obviously *are not me.*" Like the remix, what is significantly meaningful is not the entity in itself but the friction, the collisions, the contact with all others. I am not in the entity of the human being; I am in the microbes that make up literally the biological ecology in which I exist. I am not in "I"; I am in everything that flows from, into and out of me.

Notes

1 Discovered as a breakthrough in July 2012, the discovery of the Higgs-Boson particle could only be achieved by smashing subatomic particles together at high energy levels in the Large Hadron Collider, based at CERN in Geneva, Switzerland, and observing their crash to see if a Higgs particle "would momentarily pop out in view of the detectors" (Connor 2012).

2 Notably in the sense of requesting for and using moving images. Note that there have been previous photographic projects in the same style, albeit via the use of still images rather than videos (see Schiller 2012).

3 Note earlier examples, such as those by William Burroughs, Brion Gysin, and Antony Blanch (who worked in advertising): see The Cut Ups www.youtube.com/watch?v=MMQSDwQUwWM&feature =youtu.be (1966).

References

Armstrong, Robert Plant. 1975. *Wellspring*. Berkeley: University of California Press.

Blanchot, M. 1995. *The Work of Fire*. Translated by C. Mandell. Stanford: Stanford University Press.

Brewster, Bill, and Frank Broughton. 2000. *Last Night a DJ Saved My Life*. New York: Grover Press.

Connor, Steve. 2012. 'Eureka! Cern announces discovery of Higgs boson "God particle"'. *The Independent*, Thursday, 5 July. www.independent.co.uk/news/science/eureka-cern-announces-discovery-of-higgs-boson-god-particle-7907677.html [accessed 12 September 2012].

Duchamp, Marcel. 1951. 'Bicycle Wheel'. www.moma.org/collection/object.php?object_id=81631 [accessed 12 September 2013].

Eisenstein, Sergei M. 1929 (1988). 'Beyond the Shot,' in *Selected Works, Vol. 1, Writings, 1922–34*, edited and translated by Richard Taylor. London: BFI Publishing.

Gorfinkel, Elena. 2008. 'Cult Film, or Cinephilia by Any Other Name,' *Cineaste*, 34.1: 33–38.

Grosz, Elizabeth. 2001. *Architecture from the Outside: Essays on Virtual and Real Space*. Cambridge, MA: MIT Press.

Horwatt, Eli. 2009. 'A Taxonomy of Digital Video Remixing: Contemporary Found Footage Practice on the Internet.' in Iain Robert Smith, ed., *Cultural Borrowings: Appropriation, Reworking, Transformation*.

Scope: An Online Journal of Film and Television Studies: 76–91. https://www.nottingham.ac.uk/scope/documents/2009/culturalborrowingsebook.pdf [accessed 6 August 2019].

The Human Microbiome: Me, Myself, Us. 2012. 18 August 2012. www.economist.com/node/21560523 [accessed 20 December 2013].

Invisible Committee, The. 2011. *The Coming Insurrection*. No place of publication: self-published.

Jedi, George THE AWESOME & Y.F. 2011. 5 Second Movies. https://knowyourmeme.com/memes/subcultures/5-second-movies [accessed 30 April 2019.]

Jenkins, Henry. 2003. 'Quentin Tarantino's Star Wars? Digital Cinema, Media Convergence, and Participatory Culture,' in David Thorburn and Henry Jenkins, eds, *Rethinking Media Change: The Aesthetics of Transition*. Cambridge, MA: MIT Press: 281–314.

Knobel, Michele, and Colin Lankshear. 2008. 'Remix: The Art and Craft of Endless Hybridization,' *Journal of Adolescent & Adult Literacy* 52.1: 22–33.

Lowood, Henry. 2008. 'Found Technology: Players as Innovators in the Making of Machinima,' in Tara McPherson, ed., *Digital Youth, Innovation, and the Unexpected*. Cambridge, MA: MIT Press: 165–196.

Martin, Adrian. 2008. 'What's Cult Got to Do With It? In Defense of Cinephile Elitism,' *Cineaste*, 34.1: 39–42.

Mathijs, Ernest, and Jamie Sexton. 2011. *Cult Cinema: An Introduction*. Walden, MA: Wiley-Blackwell.

Microbes maketh man. 2012. 18 August. www.economist.com/node/21560559 [accessed 20 December 2013].

Mindpirates. 2012. 'Mindpirates Film Jockeys,' 7 July, Berlin. http://artconnectberlin.com/mindpirates/events/2608 [accessed 12 September 2013].

Moner, William J. 2011. 'Undercompensated Labor in *Life in a Day*,' *Flow* 14.1. http://flowtv.org/2011/06/crowdsourced-labor-in-life-in-a-day/?utm_source=Flow+TV+Journal+List&utm_campaign=aa45b6e369-New_Issue_of_Flow_Volume_14_Issue_01-6_12_2011&utm_medium=email [accessed 12 September 2013].

Murch, Walter. 2004. *The Conversations: Walter Murch and the Art of Editing Film*. New York: Alfred A. Knopf.

Navas, Eduardo. 2010. 'Regressive and Reflexive Mashups in Sampling Culture,' in Stefan Sonvilla-Weiss, ed., *Mashup Cultures*. Mörlenbach: Springer-Verlag/Wien.

Pasolini, Pier Paolo. 1967. 'Observations on the Long Take.' Translated by Norman MacAfee, Craig Owens. *October* 13 (1980): 3–6.

Poschardt, Ulf. 1998. *DJ Culture*. London: Quartet Books.

Raskin, Richard. 1998. 'Five explanations for the jump cuts in Godard's BREATHLESS,' *POV*, no. 6. http://pov.imv.au.dk/Issue_06/section_1/artc10.html [accessed 12 September 2012].

Schiller, Jakob. 2012. 'Photo Project Aims to Capture a Day in the Life of the World,' *Wired*, 13 April. www.wired.com/rawfile/2012/04/photo-project-aims-to-capture-a-day-in-the-life-of-the-world [accessed 20 December 2013].

Sonesson, Göran. 1998. 'The Concept of Text in Cultural Semiotics,' in Peeter Torop, Michail Lotman and Kalevi Kull, eds, *Sign System Studies 26*. Tartu: Tartu University Press: 88–114.

Sonvilla-Weiss, Stefan. 2010. 'Introduction: Mashups, Remix Practices and the Recombination of Existing Digital Content,' in Stefan Sonvilla-Weiss, ed., *Mashup Cultures*. Mörlenbach: Springer-Verlag/Wien.

Tryon, Chuck. 2009. *Reinventing Cinema: Movies in the Age of Media Convergence*. Piscataway, NJ: Rutgers University Press.

29

THE PROFESSIONALISED FANDOM OF CAREERS IN CULT

"Passionate work" within academia and industry

Matt Hills

Cult film has become an established part of academic analysis, often linked to a "subcultural ideology" (Jancovich et al. 2003: 1) of fan distinctions (Jancovich 2002). As I.Q. Hunter affirms in *Cult Film as a Guide to Life*, the "current integration of cult into academia [has occurred] within pretty strictly defined parameters – as transgressive texts to be understood in relation to subcultural fans" (2016: 20). But these parameters have not only emphasised subcultural fans, they have also raised the question of cult fandom entering "a realm of intersection" (Roach 2014: 36) by becoming part of what's been termed "aca-fandom" or "scholar-fandom" (Hills 2002). How are cult fan identities intertwined with the scholarly labour of professional academics studying cult? And beyond academia, what of "petty producers" (Abercrombie and Longhurst 1998: 140) who combine fandom with related industry work, perhaps in "paratextual industries" (Consalvo 2007: 183) such as fan presses or specialist DVD/Blu-ray labels? So-called fantrepreneurship (Carter 2017) highlights the pertinence of I.Q. Hunter's rhetorical question: "what better ambition could there be for a cultist than to make a career out of what you love?" (2016: xiii).

I want to complicate the notion that aca-fans and fantrepreneurs are straightforwardly engaged in a "labour of love" (Carter 2017) by drawing on critical labour studies. Such work – carried out by Casey Brienza (2016), Brooke Erin Duffy (2017), Peter Fleming (2009), and Angela McRobbie (2016) – has not explicitly focused on cult film. Nor has it been widely applied in cult media studies; I will be deploying it to illuminate aca-fandom and fantrepreneurship in novel ways. I will contextualise these cult fan-professional intersectionalities not simply as valorisations of fan expertise, but as practices informed by the mainstreaming of neoliberalism.

Neoliberal culture can be defined as a set of externalised and internalised values whereby institutions are increasingly turned "into markets ... redefining all human action as instances of the use of human capital (i.e., as *capital investments in one's personal future*)" (Busch 2017: 18). Competitive individualism thus becomes "the essence of neoliberal governmentality: governing means promoting competition, while self-governing means promoting one's own competitive-ness" (Bröckling 2016: 60) via a "Project Me self", made up of a kaleidoscope of work and leisure "projects" (Bröckling 2016: 189). The aca-fan, like the tellingly named fantrepreneur, may in fact be readable not only as capitalising on their fan passions, but also as conforming to the neoliberal subjectivity of "the entrepreneurial self" (ibid.). To figure the aca-fan as engaged "in ... a war ... against 'neo-liberalism'" (Hunter 2016: 38), however provocatively, may be to miss the psychological and cultural contexts in which such professionalised cult fans now operate, i.e. within a "normalisation of the self as resource" (Reckwitz 2017: 127).

I will consider the aca-fan case in more detail next, before addressing the fantrepreneur's situation. I will argue for the need to do more than read the careers of professionalised cult fans as simple success stories (converting subcultural capital into cultural/economic capital) and "labours of love". Reading professionalised cult fandom critically means considering how its deployment, as a non-work identity/affect within spheres of formal work, can seek to confer authenticity on forms of labour (Fleming 2009) at the very same time that questions of authenticity surrounding cult status have increasingly become problematic (Sexton 2014; Hills 2015).

The cult "aca-fan" and neoliberal conversions of capital (I)

Scholar-fandom has typically been viewed as a useful melding of scholarly frameworks and fan knowledge (Jenkins 1992; Hills 2002), but such a stance has generally treated fandom and academia monolithically, validating aca-fan work. Recent analysis of aca-fan identity concludes, however, that "a strict definition of the aca-fan's position in terms of the characteristics of their discourse … appears impossible" (Cristofari and Guitton 2017: 716). This is because rather than homogeneously combining academic and cult fan subjectivities, "both academics and fans might be perceived as occupying a variable position along different axes, such as rationality – emotionality, professional-amateur, and so on …, and differences are more individual than collective" (ibid.). Here, Cécile Cristofari and Matthieu J. Guitton strike at the heart of a narrative positing aca-fandom as a singular class of cult media scholarship, arguing that "looking at the aca-fan's position in terms of where they stand within both communities is more fruitful. … Understanding what an aca-fan is thus amounts to localising their relative positioning" (ibid.). Cristofari and Guitton are interested in exactly *what kind of academic and cult fan identities are being brought into dialogue* via fandom's professional appropriations.

This perspective can enable us to helpfully revisit debates surrounding cult aca-fandom. For instance, I.Q. Hunter's work has been significant, given that a highly self-reflexive 1990s chapter he wrote about being a "fanboy" of the cult movie *Showgirls* (reprinted in Hunter 2016) gave rise to feminist critique of the "masculinity of cult" and the "cult of masculinity" (Hollows 2003; Read 2003) in scholarship and fandom alike. Joanne Hollows argued that

> for some … subcultural capital will be converted into economic capital through the pursuit of subcultural 'careers' in magazines, retailing and distribution. … The rewards of cult fandom are thus open to those who have the most mastery of its masculine dispositions. Other fans may opt to convert their subcultural capital into 'proper' or legitimate cultural capital which … is why subcultural ideologies are frequently reproduced in academic accounts of cult.
>
> (Hollows 2003: 48–49)

Here, the cult aca-fan is depicted as quite separate from the fan entering media/paratextual industries, and as elevating fannish "subcultural capital" – which has value only in the eyes of relevant other cultists (Thornton 1995: 11) – into "proper" cultural capital, that is, an academic career and authority. However, this focus on the "rewards" of cult fandom doesn't fully consider how any such conversion of subcultural capital corresponds to a neoliberal subjectivity of "Project Me" (Bröckling 2016: 189), where tastes become not merely markers of distinction but, more fundamentally, part of a normalised, competitive self-as-project "that perpetuates … the model of expressive self-realization" (Reckwitz 2017: 234).

Jacinda Read focuses more directly on Hunter's work by responding directly to his *Showgirls* essay, but retains a focus on its alleged conversions, this time "from feminized fan-boy to academic bad-boy" in Hunter's self-representations:

> what appears to be at stake here is a ... 'politics of incorrectness'.... Thus, while Hunter repeatedly claims that neither the film nor his reading of it is politically transgressive or subversive, what *is* politically transgressive or subversive for Hunter is *liking* the film.... I would suggest that by describing his fondness for *Showgirls* as both 'perverse'... and 'pathological'.... Hunter characterizes *himself* as the 'delinquent misreader'.
>
> (Read 2003: 65)

For Read, Hunter's performance of cultish aca-fandom "functions to construct distinctions within academic culture rather than blur the boundary between fan and academic" (2003: 66), at the same time as othering the "feminine associations of the fan and the failed masculinity of the nerd in favour of a characterisation of himself not as a fan-boy but as an academic bad-boy" (ibid.).

These feminist readings do not view Hunter's work as a matter of individualised aca-fandom, however, responding to such performativity as replaying structuring masculinised dispositions of subcultural authenticity within academia (see Hunter 2013: 27 and a related reading offered in Hills 2015: 105–106). The emphasis on *conversion* is especially important, I would argue, since this views aca-fandom not as a hybrid or "straddling" position between/across academia and fandom (Brennan 2014:219), but as a claim that works on fandom, transforming its pre-existent investments into new kinds of professional assets. As such, cult fandom becomes a reserve of (non-work) value here, capable of being profitably drawn into the academic work environment. Hunter's self-account shows him very much "getting a life" as an "academic bad-boy" rather than a feminised fan/nerd or a potentially disempowered academic subjected to the neoliberal/RAE/REF system, just as Peter Fleming has argued that:

> the call for authenticity is ... indicative of a 'lack' that defines the work situation. ... It is a lack of power, lack of control ...; to put it rather telegraphically, a lack of a life [in and through work]. ... This appropriation draws upon forms of social life that forever lie beyond capitalism, what I shall ... call ... *the commons*.
>
> (2009: 5)

Rather than academia offering a privileged position, as in Hollows' reading, it is entirely feasible that its (relatively) contemporary manifestations may be experienced not as an idealised space of autonomous intellectualism, but as a precarious, competitive and individualised domain in which academics are expected to perform via self-branding and the "aspirational labour" of career rewards to come (Duffy 2017: 4, 231). Set against this, aca-fandom may hold out the promise of (subcultural/fan) authenticity converted into work "authenticity" (Fleming 2009) via neoliberal norms of "passionate work" (McRobbie 2016: 107). However, there is an irony here: academia's neoliberal precarity may be resisted, in this instance, not only by holding on to a non-commodified "experience" (of cult subculture and fandom) but also *by pitting neoliberal work strategies against a broader neoliberal work context* (Busch 2017). As Casey Brienza has argued, "the standard account of doing it for 'love' ... leaves workers vulnerable to exploitation" (2016: 130) despite holding out "the promise of having one's truest self ... validated in the context of professional life" (2016: 131).

I.Q. Hunter's recent return to his *Showgirls* analysis even depicts academia as an explicit source of anxiety rather than a "legitimacy" to be enjoyed, discussing the "careerist need, even in a fan-press book, to talk the academic talk 'rigorously' enough to get entered into the research assessment exercises that … intermittently blight our professional lives" (Hunter 2016: 38). Here, cinephilia is represented as a yearned-for space of personal authenticity, albeit one which cannot be fully imported into academia due to its neoliberal "research assessment" pressures. There can never be quite enough fandom in aca-fandom, it would seem. Yet Hunter also repeats his earlier othering of (feminised) fandom, this time rejecting the "fanboy" label altogether, both on grounds of age (2016: 39) and because he ponders whether he lacks "the credentials for serious fandom, at any rate as they are written up in academic research"; these are said to involve not just "liking a film (a lot)" but "being considerably more active and productive" via social media, for instance, or through the creation of fanfiction etc. (ibid.). He rejects fan studies at the same time: specialised fan studies' work is critiqued for not accounting for all audience types and experiences rather than just fandom, when there are, of course, other forms of audience studies and memory studies' scholarship exploring varied audience experiences perfectly well.

Hunter's attack on fan studies hinges on his discursive displacement of fandom via cinephilia, as if this means that he is no longer a "fan". The feint equates fandom *tout court* with one way of being a fan, just as early debates on aca-fandom presumed one monolithic version of fan "immersion" in their self-justifications (Hills 2002). But it also fails to consider how, and to what extent, discourses of cultish "cinephilia" may simply resemble another way of being a fan. As Iain Robert Smith notes, given "that Hunter's own work so often returns to the question of aesthetic likes and dislikes, this position on fan studies may strike the reader as a little inconsistent" (2017: 402). In another sense, though, it is all-too-consistent, yearning for neoliberal "passionate work" that is somehow untainted by the neoliberal contexts of contemporary higher education.

Angela McRobbie suggests that the fashion industry has been the "professional field of work most closely aligned with this passionate *dispositif*" (2016: 108), arguing that such affective labour acts as a middle-class-oriented "mode of gender re-traditionalization" (2016: 110):

> the idea of work corresponding to one's inner dreams or childhood fantasies also banishes, to some separate realm entirely, the idea of organized labour (despite the unionization of white-collar work in the last decades). Passionate work is then inherently individualistic and conservative. It is identifiably 'girlish' and enthusiastic.
> (McRobbie 2016: 107; see also Duffy 2017: 9)

However, McRobbie subsequently observes a "managerial brand of passionate work … heavily tilted towards the male workforce" (cf. Fleming 2009), and I would argue that aca-fandom, which has previously offered an individualistic, masculinised narrative of cultish "passionate work", has now become increasingly "'girlish' and enthusiastic" as well, even whilst remaining likely to skew towards middle-class self-validation (McRobbie 2016: 36; Hunter 2016: 38).

If accounts of cult aca-fandom can be complicated by articulating its "conversions" (of capital and self-identity) with neoliberal subjectivities, work strategies and contexts, then what of professionalised cult fandom that stays closer to media/paratextual industries in the form of the "fantrepreneur"? I'll now consider how this offers a related take on cult "authenticity" processed into "authentic" labour.

The cult "fantrepreneur" and neoliberal conversions of capital (II)

Fans-turned-producers have been previously theorised in fan/audience studies (e.g. Abercrombie and Longhurst's 1998 model), but the position of the cult "fantrepreneur" has been explored in depth most recently by Oliver Carter (2017). The emergence of cult-oriented video/DVD/ Blu-ray labels has allowed a number of cultists to enter the "formal" economy of cult film distribution by establishing companies such as Something Weird Video or Vinegar Syndrome (Lobato and Thomas 2015: 3; Church 2016: 153). And scholars have studied other cult-oriented labels such as Third Window and Arrow (Wroot 2017a, 2017b; Hills 2017b) which, alongside fan presses such as FAB, mean that cultists can entrepreneurially engage in niche commercialism. As Virginia Crisp has observed, there is "a [fan] recognition that specialist distribution is not necessarily a profitable pursuit, and that small distributors are doing a good job in the face of conditions that make the release of certain films in particular territories economically unviable" (2015: 167). This contrasts with cult fans' more common "disdain towards Hollywood", demonstrating that cultists are not always opposed to commercialism, only to specific versions of it (Mathijs and Sexton 2011: 62).

Oliver Carter argues that the "owners of fan enterprises ... adopt a more 'authentic' and considered approach to the artefacts they produce and distribute, drawing on their own fan knowledge to aid their production practices" (2017: 198). He considers "how the fantrepreneur has to negotiate the tensions between profit and pleasure. While a typical entrepreneur may be driven by the desire to maximise profit, the fantrepreneur is not" (2017: 204), given that they wish to create "authentic" releases that will be valued by fellow cultists. However, nor can they "be purely motivated by their fandom; they also have to consider the financial viability of releasing such a product" (ibid.). This means that they remain "as producers, ... as much at the mercy of structural [market] forces as the consumers at the other end of the continuum" (Abercrombie and Longhurst 1998: 140). Ultimately, Carter reproduces the same narrative as Casey Brienza's (2016: 130) respondents who worked in the US manga publishing industry, asserting that for fantrepreneurs, "this is more a labour of love rather than one that seeks to solely economically benefit from ... cultural production" (Carter 2017: 204). Brienza, however, heard "talk about doing it for 'love' ... so often, recited so glibly" across her fieldwork that she "began to mistrust it" (2016: 130) as a kind of rehearsed self-justification for cultists' sacrifices and lack of financial remuneration. She eventually concludes that cultural workers utilising their fandom within Japanese manga's US domestication take "great pleasure in superimposing themselves upon it ... [T]here are numerous ... subtle ... cases of self-insertion" (2016: 132), ranging from adding "secret messages" to book samplers, to drawing on personal knowledge about the East Coast and West Coast of America in story adaptation, to having one's likeness included in manga artwork (Brienza 2016: 132–133). This process of "self-insertion" is summarised as follows:

> feeling like one has become a part of the final product itself is such a powerful reward, so craved and sought after, that some laborers will accept that in lieu of any upfront economic reward whatsoever. ... *It is ... the neoliberal ethos at its finest* – the [publishing] organisation's capitalist ambitions made personal.
>
> (Brienza 2016: 133, my italics)

A related scenario is set out both in David Church's (2016: 159) discussion of Mike Vraney's establishment of cult label Something Weird Video (SWV), and in Oliver Carter's (2017: 204) analysis of Joe Rubin's co-founded label, Vinegar Syndrome (VS), which specialises in releasing cultified vintage pornography (Church 2016: 153). The case of SWV demonstrates how Vraney's

> background as a comic book collector and 16mm print collector since the 1970s inspired his business strategies. Much as comics collectors seldom seek out individual titles in their own right and instead prefer to amass large runs of multiple series, Vraney banked on fellow fans' completism.
>
> (Church 2016: 162)

Although this is not, perhaps, an obvious "self-insertion", it nevertheless involves Vraney's fandom making a mark upon his unusually completist commercial release strategies (without any emphasis on the textual or source quality of the material). Church concludes that, as a result,

> SWV is one of the most important video labels … making available an extensive cata-logue of not just adult and exploitation films, but also African American race films, 1930–1940s American B films, 1960s–1970s European and East Asian genre films; and all manner of ephemeral and nontheatrical short subjects.
>
> (Church 2016: 164)

Similarly, Carter argues that the "model Vinegar Syndrome uses differs considerably to the dominant one used by other independent home video labels" by virtue of their in-house "side-line business scanning and restoring films. It also relies on Rubin and [co-founder Jay] Upson's fan knowledge, mostly releasing films that are either orphaned [i.e. have no copyright protec-tion] or in the public domain" (Carter 2017: 211). By integrating fan knowledge – aimed at recovering, restoring and respectfully making cult films available as well as supporting other niche cult labels by scanning titles for them – with good business sense then capitalist ambitions are again "made personal" here, in Brienza's neoliberal sense.

As I've argued elsewhere (Hills 2017a), such mergers between "passionate work" and niche commercialism mean that cult cinema can readily become aligned with entrepreneurial practices of distribution. However, this "new spirit of capitalism" (Boltanski and Chiapello 2005), where work becomes playful (Hills 2017a: 81), does not merely involve the conversion of subcultural capital into economic capital, *contra* Hollows 2003. I would argue that a crucial aspect in terms of securing cult fans' sense of authenticity is precisely the combination of durable subcultural capital alongside the enduring economic capital of an ongoing commercial presence – that is, these niche cult video/DVD/Blu-ray labels become objects of subcultural trust for fans rather than being remembered as brief experiments or failed business ventures.

As a form of competitive neoliberal subjectivity, "the entrepreneurial self must market its human capital" via "customer orientation" (Brockling 2016: xvii). Hence the compound of subcultural and economic capital permits cult fans' recognition of fantrepreneurs' ongoing, successful "orientation" towards fandom as a simultaneous market and community. For example, Something Weird Video was founded in 1990, and has outlived Mike Vraney himself, who passed away in 2014. Vinegar Syndrome launched far more recently, in early 2013, but it is surely no accident that Oliver Carter's commentary stresses how it has "consistently releas[ed] four or five films per month" (2017: 211), thereby establishing itself as a staple and stable presence on the cult film scene. Writing for *Medium*, Jason Coffman argues that:

> since launching their imprint, Vinegar Syndrome has proven themselves repeatedly to be one of the most important companies in a crowded market of specialized labels

releasing cult and exploitation films. Their releases are distinctly different from the output of other labels, frequently giving lost and forgotten films their first release on home video or giving films that have been previously released a new life with thorough restoration.

(Coffman 2015)

These sentiments are borne out by the aca-fan analyses of Church (2016: 153), stressing VS's articulation with "quality" releases in place of simply furnishing "access" to cult material, and Carter (2017: 203), who also emphasises the fantrepreneurial "authenticity" of VS's work.

Fantrepreneurs are not restricted to the domain of "formal" distribution, however. Brigid Cherry has considered how commodified cult fan production can occur in micro-businesses where "e-commerce sites (Etsy, for example) are used to convert fan cultural capital into economic capital by allowing entrepreneurial fans to sell handicrafted fan-themed objects" (2016: 164). In *Cult Media, Fandom, and Textiles: Handicrafting as Fan Art*, Cherry analyses how female cult fans have set up their own businesses selling custom-dyed yarn inspired by cult media texts:

Though the micro-economy of fan handicrafting does work in ways that commodify fandom, its business model is often designed to deliver the raw materials of fan production – patterns and yarns, in this case – directly to the fans. The dyers and pattern designers are fans themselves and interact within the fan community as fellow fans, their peers ... are also their customers.

(Cherry 2016: 176)

Within this micro-economy some dyers' "yarns develop a cult status in their own right" (Cherry 2016: 166). And knitted figures using these kinds of yarn are themselves handmade, working against the economy of scale required for commercial production or licensed merchandising. The entrepreneurially fan-targeted yarn collected by fan-consumers is simultaneously the raw material for their creative productivity (Cherry 2016: 173).

The experiential turn in cinema has similarly traded on fantrepreneurial activity, with cinephile entrepreneurs such as Secret Cinema's Fabien Riggall reconceptualising movie screenings as immersive, material-cultural events. E.W. Nikdel demonstrates that Secret Cinema's staging of films such as *The Empire Strikes Back* can "mirror the way that cult fans isolate particular moments or scenes for special attention" (2017: 114) as well as "[l]ike cult audiences of the past, ... intersect[ing] with notions of public performance, distinction and collective engagement" (2017: 113) and embodying "the late Umberto Eco's claim that cult films 'must provide a completely furnished world' ... which will envelop its fans" (2017: 114). However, Nikdel distinguishes Secret Cinema from cult fandom by arguing that it doesn't go

beyond the mainstream, something that helped cult films and fandom emerge in the 1970s. For instance, whilst the audience at *The Empire Strikes Back* responded to the film's classic moments with a collective rapture, they are hardly indicative of cult's defiance of mainstream Hollywood. ... Secret Cinema events are more driven by a form of nostalgia rather than the culture of ... discovery that partly defined the cult scene of the 1970s and 1980s.

(Nikdel 2017: 115)

Thus fantrepreneurial activity appears to work against cult "authenticity" in this case, unlike the labour of cult distributors, resulting in "a more diluted form of cult fandom … without the non-mainstream attraction of 'true' cult" (Nikdel 2017: 119). But it is difficult to see how "good" and "bad" objects of cult commerce and entrepreneurialism can be separated out so clearly; Secret Cinema remains niche rather than mainstream in the sense that its productions have a very limited run, never to be repeated. They can attract the same "retro" subcultural capital as now-defunct cult cinema venues like the Scala in London – you had to be there at the time to accumulate fan cultural capital which is no longer available in the present moment (Hills 2015: 105–106; Nikdel 2017: 117). And any notion of "true" cult, even protected by scare quotes, is surely problematic at best, given contemporary cult's discursive multiplicity (Barefoot 2017: 70–91).

Although it doesn't feed as strongly into fans' co-creation of brand-related material culture, fantrepreneurial activity has also emerged around cult film soundtracks. These have attracted their own specialist reissue labels (Sexton 2015: 14), demonstrating that, like cult fan handicrafting, cult films can inspire intermedial traces such that "film cultification processes take place not merely within film culture but amongst other different media cultures" (Sexton 2015: 26).

Thus far, I have separated out the aca-fan and the fantrepreneur, but it should be noted that these categories can themselves intersect. Catherine Roach puts forward the term "*aca-fan-writer* … to capture the multiplicity of identity … wherein I occupied simultaneously the position of the academic outsider, studying the genre; the fan consumer, reading it; and the inside practitioner, writing it" (2014: 39). Similarly, one might theorise the tripled hybridity of the aca-fantrepreneur such as Xavier Mendik's work on Cine-Excess "cult content creation" for DVD/Blu-ray releases (www.cine-excess.co.uk/cult-content-creation.html), or aca-fans whose freelance commercial work can involve compiling liner notes or supplying commentaries. Here, aca-fan identities entrepreneurially engage with paratextual industries, rendering the cultural capital of scholarship another element that can be incorporated into accumulations of "authentic" self-branding, also mediated through subcultural capital.

In this chapter I've considered how aca-fans and fantrepreneurs have both played out a neoliberal "normalisation of the self as resource" (Reckwitz 2017: 127). Rather than simply living out their dream jobs, such aca-fans and fantrepreneurs – along with hybrids of these hybrids – have converted forms of capital by "making a project of themselves" (Nikolas Rose in Bröckling 2016: 189) in line with neoliberalism. Although it may be tempting to celebrate the self-realisations, scholarly justifications, and community mediations on display, cult remains caught up here in a wider cultural politics of work, with conversions/compounds of subcultural capital demarcating customer orientation as much as taste distinction. Indeed, just as cult "authenticity" has become ever more questionable (Hunter 2016: 20–21), cult film has taken on the (problematic) role of recuperating one strand of "authentic" labour and "passionate work".

References

Abercrombie, Nicholas, and Brian Longhurst. 1998. *Audiences*. London: Sage.
Barefoot, Guy. 2017. *Trash Cinema: The Lure of the Low*. London and New York: Wallflower Press.
Boltanski, Luc, and Eve Chiapello. 2005. *The New Spirit of Capitalism*. London: Verso.
Brennan, Joseph. 2014. 'The Fannish Parergon: Aca-Fandom and the Decentred Canon,' *Australasian Journal of Popular Culture*, 3.2: 217–232.
Brienza, Casey. 2016. *Manga in America*. New York: Bloomsbury Academic.
Bröckling, Ulrich. 2016. *The Entrepreneurial Self: Fabricating a New Kind of Subject*. London: Sage.
Busch, Lawrence. 2017. *Knowledge for Sale: The Neoliberal Takeover of Higher Education*. Cambridge, MA: MIT Press.

Carter, Oliver. 2017. 'A Labour of Love: Fantrepreneurship in Home Video Media Distribution,' in Jonathan Wroot and Andy Willis, eds, *DVD, Blu-ray and Beyond Navigating Formats and Platforms within Media Consumption.* London: Palgrave Macmillan: 197–213.

Cherry, Brigid. 2016. *Cult Media, Fandom, and Textiles: Handicrafting as Fan Art.* London: Bloomsbury Academic.

Church, David. 2016. *Disposable Passions: Vintage Pornography and the Material Legacies of Adult Cinema.* New York: Bloomsbury Academic.

Coffman, Jason 2015. '10 Definitive Vinegar Syndrome Releases,' in *Medium,* April 15. Available online at https://medium.com/@rabbitroom/10-definitive-vinegar-syndrome-releases-dee206520aa2, accessed 10/1/18.

Consalvo, Mia. 2007. *Cheating: Gaining Advantage in Videogames.* Cambridge, MA: MIT Press.

Crisp, Virginia. 2015. *Film Distribution in the Digital Age: Pirates and Professionals.* London: Palgrave Macmillan.

Cristofari, Cécile, and Matthieu J. Guitton. 2017. 'Aca-fans and Fan Communities: An Operative Framework,' *Journal of Consumer Culture,* 17.3: 713–731

Duffy, Brooke Erin. 2017. *(Not) Getting Paid to Do What You Love: Gender, Social Media, and Aspirational Work.* New Haven: Yale University Press.

Fleming, Peter. 2009. *Authenticity and the Cultural Politics of Work.* Oxford: Oxford University Press.

Hills, Matt. 2002. *Fan Cultures.* London and New York: Routledge.

———. 2015. 'Cult Cinema and the "Mainstreaming" Discourse of Technological Change: Revisiting Subcultural Capital in Liquid Modernity,' *New Review of Film and Television Studies,* 13.1: 100–121.

———. 2017a. 'Transnational Cult and/as Neoliberalism: The Liminal Economies of Anime Fansubbers,' *Transnational Cinemas,* 8.1: 80–94.

———. 2017b. 'A "Cult-like" Following: Nordic Noir, Nordicana and Arrow Films' Bridging of Subcultural/Neocultural Capital,' in Jonathan Wroot and Andy Willis, eds, *Cult Media Re-packaged, Re-released and Restored.* London: Palgrave Macmillan: 49–65.

Hollows, Joanne. 2003. 'The Masculinity of Cult,' in Mark Jancovich, Antonio Lázaro-Reboll, Julian Stringer and Andy Willis, eds, *Defining Cult Movies: The Cultural Politics of Oppositional Taste.* Manchester: Manchester University Press: 35–53.

Hunter, I.Q. 2013. *British Trash Cinema.* London: BFI Publishing/Palgrave Macmillan.

———. 2016. *Cult Film as a Guide to Life: Fandom, Adaptation, and Identity.* London: Bloomsbury Academic.

Jancovich, Mark. 2002. 'Cult Fictions: Cult Movies, Subcultural Capital and the Production of Cultural Distinctions,' in *Cultural Studies,* 16.2: 306–322.

Jancovich, Mark, Lázaro-Reboll, Antonio, Stringer, Julian, and Willis, Andy. 2003. 'Introduction,' in Mark Jancovich, Antonio Lázaro-Reboll, Julian Stringer and Andy Willis, eds, *Defining Cult Movies: The Cultural Politics of Oppositional Taste.* Manchester: Manchester University Press: 1–13.

Jenkins, Henry. 1992. *Textual Poachers.* New York: Routledge.

Lobato, Ramon, and Julian, Thomas. 2015. *The Informal Media Economy.* Malden: Polity Press.

Mathijs, Ernest, and Jamie Sexton. 2011. *Cult Cinema.* Malden: Wiley-Blackwell.

McRobbie, Angela. 2016. *Be Creative: Making a Living in the New Culture Industries.* Cambridge, UK: Polity Press.

Nikdel, E.W. 2017. 'Cult Fandom and Experiential Cinema,' in Jonathan Wroot and Andy Willis, eds, *Cult Media Re-packaged, Re-released and Restored.* London: Palgrave Macmillan: 105–123.

Read, Jacinda. 2003. 'The Cult of Masculinity: From Fan-Boys to Academic Bad-Boys,' in Mark Jancovich, Antonio Lázaro-Reboll, Julian Stringer and Andy Willis, eds, *Defining Cult Movies: The Cultural Politics of Oppositional Taste.* Manchester: Manchester University Press: 54–70.

Reckwitz, Andreas. 2017. *The Invention of Creativity.* Cambridge: Polity Press.

Roach, Catherine M. 2014. '"Going Native": Aca-Fandom and Deep Participant Observation in Popular Romance Studies,' *Mosaic* 7.2: 33–49.

Sexton, Jamie. 2014. 'From Bad to Good and Back to Bad Again? Cult Cinema and Its Unstable Trajectory,' in Claire Perkins and Constantine Verevis, eds, *B is for Bad Cinema.* Albany: State University of New York Press: 129–145.

———. 2015. 'Creeping Decay: Cult Soundtracks, Residual Media, and Digital Technologies,' *New Review of Film and Television Studies,* 13.1: 12–30.

Smith, Iain Robert. 2017. 'Media,' *The Year's Work in Critical and Cultural Theory,* 25.1: 398–417.

Thornton, Sarah. 1995. *Club Cultures.* Cambridge: Polity Press.

Wroot, Jonathan. 2017a. 'Letting the Fans Be Involved: Third Window's Cultivation of an Audience for Disc Releases,' in Jonathan Wroot and Andy Willis, eds, *DVD, Blu-ray and Beyond: Navigating Formats and Platforms within Media Consumption*. London: Palgrave Macmillan: 73–91.

———. 2017b. '*Battle Royale* as a One-Film Franchise: Charting a Commercial Phenomenon through Cult DVD and Blu-ray Releases,' in Jonathan Wroot and Andy Willis, eds, *Cult Media Re-packaged, Re-released and Restored*. London: Palgrave Macmillan: 11–29.

PART VI

Music and sound

Sound and music in cult film

Music has played a key role within many areas of cult cinema. A number of cult films are renowned for their soundtracks and some cult films feature music from acts who may already have accrued their own cult followings. A number of chapters and articles on the subject do exist, such as our own survey of music and cult film (Mathijs and Sexton 2011), Cherry's overview of cult film and music (2013) and her article on music videos inspired by cult film (2009), Conrich's chapter on cult film musicals (2006), and Sexton's chapter on cult film soundtracks and retro-media (2015). Such work, however, is relatively sparse, so the chapters in this section are crucial contributions to this field. In our own chapter on the topic, we listed a number of overlaps between cult film and music: cult films which feature extensive pop and rock music (in which music is used as an audience attraction and/or narrative driver, and which may also feature specific musical performances); cult films which feature musicians in acting roles – such as David Bowie in *The Man Who Fell to Earth* (Roeg, 1972); musical films which have gained cult reputations; and soundtracks to cult films which have gone on to become cult artefacts themselves.

Such categories are certainly not exhaustive, however. As noted by Brigid Cherry (2009), cult films can influence musical subcultures in a number of ways. Analysing in particular how the Beastie Boys' 'Body Movin' (1998) music video pastiches *Danger Diabolik* (Bava, 1968), she further notes how artist and song names, lyrics and sampled audio have drawn on cult cinema. Such connections show no signs of slowing down – Julia Holter's recent music video for 'Les Jeux to You' (2019), for example, is an acknowledged tribute to Alejandro Jodorowsky's *Fando and Lis* (1968) – and are even beginning to make a mark on more mainstream areas of music culture. Hence Kanye West's stage designs for his 2013/14 'Yeezus' tour being heavily indebted to Jodorowsky's *The Holy Mountain* (1973).

The musical is a long-standing genre that has also been associated with cult cinema, as outlined by Ethan de Seife in his chapter. As de Seife notes, we can broadly distinguish between two different types of cult musicals: musicals which self-consciously draw on, and/or position themselves as examples of, cult cinema; and musicals that were made during the classical era of Hollywood which later were taken up ironically as cult texts. As more unintentional cult texts, the latter set of films – such as the films Busby Berkeley was involved in choreographing (and sometimes directing), or films featuring stars such as Gene Kelly or Judy Garland – could be received by cultists as forms of alternative filmmaking even though they emerged from within the Hollywood system. As de Seife argues, these films often revelled in their artifice and were perceived by many cult audiences as subversive and campy. More recent musicals which have been considered examples of cult cinema tend to be more aware of cult cinema as a phenomenon and are designed to appeal to more alternative audience formations. De Seife also looks at a number of such films, which include one of the most prominent examples of a cult film, *The Rocky Horror Picture Show* (Sharman, 1975), in his overview, as well as arguing that perhaps we might also want to think about the possibility of Disney musicals such as *Frozen* (Buck, Lee, 2013) as cult films, albeit with a largely younger audience, due to the obsession and repeat viewings that many of these films garner.

James Wierzbicki looks as the musical soundtrack and the cult film. Surveying previous articles on the subject – specifically discussing Mathijs and Sexton (2011) and Cherry (2013) – he notes how little agreement there seems to be on what constitutes a cult film, which also applies to cult film music. Troubled by the subjective nature of opinions regarding cult films, Wierzbicki attempts to present a more objective perspective, and looks at the use of previous soundtracks within films as a particularly important factor in cult film music. Discussing this with specific reference to *Halloween*, Wierzbicki notes how rare the reusing of previous soundtrack material is and argues that when music soundtracks intertextually catalyze collective memories through their placement within a film, then such examples can be considered instances of cult film music.

If cult film music has only been intermittently studied, then the non-musical dimension of cult soundtracks has generated even less academic attention. As such, Nessa Johnston's chapter on (non-musical) sound in cult film is a much-needed overview of this particular issue. While studies of the soundtrack are largely devoted to music, the soundtrack also consists of sound effects and dialogue, the latter registering specific types of vocal inflections. Work on non-musical aspects of the soundtrack are now gaining quite a bit of attention but, as Johnston notes, very little of this focuses on cult film. Johnston also contends that quotation and homage in relation to other soundtrack elements are important factors to consider in discussing examples of cult sound (in terms of quotable dialogue, imitation of distinctive actors' vocal mannerisms, or through reusing stock sounds). She looks at three main areas of cult film sound – a 'good' cult film with 'bad' sound, a 'good' cult film with 'good' sound, and a 'bad' cult film with 'good' sound – which she elaborates through case studies of *Pink Flamingos* (Waters, 1972), *Eraserhead* (Lynch, 1976), and *Star Wars* (Lucas, 1977). In addition to de Seife's and Wierzbicki's chapters, this speculation on the sounds of cult therefore opens up new avenues to explore in relation to cult cinema's sonic dimensions.

References

Cherry, Brigid. 2009. 'From Cult to Subculture: Reimaginings of Cult Films in Alternative Music Video', in Iain Robert Smith, ed., *Cultural Borrowings: Appropriation, Reworking, Transformation: A Scope e-Book*: 124–137. www.nottingham.ac.uk/scope/documents/2009/culturalborrowingsebook.pdf. Accessed April 2019.

Cherry, Brigid. 2013. 'Cult Films and Music', in J. Edmondson, ed., *Music in American Life: An Encyclopedia of the Songs, Styles, Stars, and Stories That Shaped Our Culture*, vol. 1. Santa Barbara, CA: Greenwood Press: 322–325.

Conrich, Ian. 2006. 'Musical Performance and the Cult Film Experience', in Ian Conrich and Estella Tincknell, eds, *Film's Musical Moments*. Edinburgh: Edinburgh University Press: 115–131.

Mathijs, Ernest, and Jamie Sexton. 2011. *Cult Cinema: An Introduction*. Malden, MA: Wiley-Blackwell.

Sexton, Jamie. 2015. 'Creeping Decay: Cult Soundtracks, Residual Media, and Digital Technologies', *New Review of Film and Television Studies*, 13, 1: 12–30.

30

CULT MUSICALS

Ethan de Seife

Introduction

Some of the most ardent and long-lived movie cults are those that take as their objects musical films. The cult surrounding *The Rocky Horror Picture Show* (1975) – perhaps the *ne plus ultra* of cult films, period – is about as devout as cults get; other noteworthy musicals with devoted cult followings include *The Wizard of Oz* (1939), *Singin' in the Rain* (1952), and *Myra Breckinridge* (1970), to name just a few.

Yet *Rocky Horror*, and many of the cult musicals made in its wake – from *Rock 'n' Roll High School* (1979) to *Hairspray* (1988) to *Repo! The Genetic Opera* (2008) – are self-conscious about their cult statuses. In that many of them were designed to appeal to fringe subcultures and/or midnight-movie audiences, they offer admirers multiple points of specialized entry beyond the merely musical: challenging comedy, outré social attitudes, intentional campiness, inside jokes. What, then, of the "normal" musicals that have attracted loyal followings? Many musicals from Hollywood's studio era have become cult classics: *Gentlemen Prefer Blondes* (1953), *West Side Story* (1961), *The Sound of Music* (1965), as well as nearly the entire *oeuvres* of Judy Garland, Esther Williams, Gene Kelly, Doris Day, and Busby Berkeley. The cults for these mainstream films are no less avid than those of more self-conscious musicals.

The chief reason that musical films have inspired ardent admirers is right there in their genre's name. The music that musicals necessarily use to convey narrative and emotional content has long provided viewers with a particularly powerful and memorable means to access and enjoy the films. Of just such stuff are cult followings born.

Human emotion, memory, and even physical behavior are profoundly affected by music. Though too great a subject to address here, an oft-cited remark by Arthur Schopenhauer aptly summarizes the uniquely deep relationship between the human species and the music we have created for tens of thousands of years:

> The inexpressible depth of all music, by virtue of which it floats past us as a paradise quite familiar and yet eternally remote, and is so easy to understand and yet so inexplicable, is due to the fact that it reproduces all the emotions of our innermost being, but entirely without reality and remote from its pain. ... The seriousness essential to it ... is to be explained from the fact that its object is not the representation ... but that

this object is directly the will, and this is essentially the most serious of all things, as being that on which all depends.

(Schopenhauer 2012: 170)

Fascinatingly, Schopenhauer, though writing in the nineteenth century, touched on several topics that are germane to the study of cult musicals: music's universal, yet ineffable, appeal; its deep emotional resonance; and that there must always be a representational distance between the music and the idea it reflects. Musical films – be they the mainstream kind or the self-conscious kind – have, since the advent of film sound, taken advantage of these fundamental, "built-in" features of their genre to forge particularly close relationships with their viewers.

The first wave of film musicals employed music not just to create appealing, memorable scenes, but to sell sheet music, records, and concert tickets. Later cult musicals employ music for similar purposes, *and* as a means of rendering their challenging content more approach-able, often in an ironic manner. Yet all cult musical films, regardless of their vintage, share an important quality with *all* musical films. They use music to make their stories more meaningful, their emotional content more deeply felt, their stars' performances more appealing, their jokes funnier, their tragedies more affecting. For all musicals, music is an *intensifier*; for cult musicals, music's intensifying power is all the stronger. Music renders a cult film's effects – intentional or unintentional, sincere or ironic, patent or latent – more powerful. Every cult musical's cult is inseparable from its music.

Busby Berkeley and the cultists' *lagniappe*

Most film genres emerged from traditions in other narrative media: novels of the Old West pre-date film westerns, just as ghost stories predate horror films. In that human beings have enjoyed musical performances and musical theater for millennia, the musical film is no different in this regard. Yet, unlike nearly every other genre, the film musical could never have existed without the development of specific filmmaking technologies. Musicals are nothing without music, and films were silent until the late 1920s.

The novelty of talking pictures engendered a bump in audience figures, which in turn spurred Hollywood studios to produce musicals in great numbers. J. Hoberman, in his mono-graph on *42nd Street* (1933), writes that, by 1929, fully a quarter of the studios' output belonged to the musical genre (Hoberman 1993: 15). Yet musicals' popularity should not be construed as a broad-based cult following. Cultists attach their admiration to a single text, or to a single artist's body of work, not to an entire genre.

In retrospect, the earliest film musicals that may usefully be viewed through the lens of cult fandom would seem to be the kaleidoscopic, pulchritudinous, all-singing-all-dancing extravaganzas helmed by Busby Berkeley. Berkeley, a former Broadway choreographer, assumed the same role for several films in the early 1930s; his first solo credit as a film director was the much-beloved *Gold Diggers of 1935* (1935).

For the next two decades, Berkeley asserted his unique aesthetic as strongly as any other Hollywood *auteur*. Enamored of geometric compositions and the synchronized movements of his performers, Berkeley made films that verged into the avant-garde, so committed are they to privileging visual design over narrative. The director's signature crane shots transform dancers into flower petals, filigrees on a gigantic cake, or, more aptly, pure abstractions of color and movement.

The lavish art design and choreography of Berkeley's musicals is the root of their cult followings (though the skimpy costumes don't hurt). The films offer viewers a main course – coherent, if lightweight, stories peppered with catchy tunes – as well as *lagniappe*: a little something extra, an essential ingredient for cultists. The alternative readings that are encouraged by the visually splendid *lagniappe* of the Berkeley films are specifically predicated on music. Only the singing-and-dancing scenes in Berkeley's films receive the special visual treatment that is the essence of their cult followings. Indeed, the "normal" scenes in his films are just that: utterly conventional.

Yet Berkeley's spectacles of flesh and song are cult films chiefly because audiences of later eras, upon reconsidering them, found them to be surreptitiously subversive in their disdain for narrative and their celebration of the body. In this way, cult readings of Berkeley's remarkable films may set the tone for cult readings of many other mainstream musicals. Latter-day cults of "classic," mainstream musicals are generally predicated on alternative, against-the-grain readings that consider these films to be subversive, campy, ironic, or self-conscious. Musicals were generally not tailor-made for cult audiences until several decades after Busby Berkeley's symmetrically arrayed hoofers shuffled off to Buffalo.

Cult musical stars of Hollywood's Golden Era

The cults surrounding Busby Berkeley's musicals do not typically fixate on the films' stars, brimming though these films are with talented and beloved performers. Yet many mainstream musicals of the 1940s, 1950s, and 1960s have acquired cult followings precisely because of the "cults of personality" of their lead performers. This is an important shift in the development of the cult musical.

The nameless chorines of the "backstage musicals" of the 1930s may look terrific when arrayed into a Tinseltown mandala, but they possess little star power as individuals. As musicals grew in popularity – and in economic significance to their studios – the genre gave birth to many stars. The cults that have arisen around several of those stars have, in many cases, extended their enthusiasm to the musicals in which the performers appear. In many – but not all – cases, the cultish adulation of these stars and their musicals is, like that of the cults of the Berkeley films, grounded in subversive readings.

Several of the most important and bankable stars of the Hollywood musical are also the objects of some of its most ardent cults: Judy Garland, Esther Williams, and Doris Day are key examples. Of these, Williams is to some extent an outlier, as her cult overlaps with that of Busby Berkeley, who directed and/or choreographed her in three features. Oddly, though, only two of those collaborations belong to the niche subgenre of which Williams is the chief cult object. Williams appeared in some 26 features from 1942 to 1963, yet her cult reputation rests on her dozen or so "aquamusicals." These curious films – including *On an Island with You* (1948), *Million Dollar Mermaid* (1952), and *Dangerous When Wet* (1953) – combine music, dancing, and, of all things, synchronized swimming.

Perhaps it is for their very oddity that these are regarded as cult films; perhaps cultists ironically appreciate the baroque narrative twists by which the films conspire to get Williams's characters into the water: a dunk tank in *Texas Carnival* (1951), a dip with Hannibal himself into Roman waters in *Jupiter's Darling* (1955). The films' visual styles also have their cult appeal: in all of the aquamusicals, even the ones untouched by Berkeley, the musical numbers are staged with kaleidoscopic, synchronized splendor.

Though more strongly identified with Williams, Busby Berkeley worked with Judy Garland more often, collaborating with her on seven musicals. Yet Garland's star burned more brightly than Williams's. Unquestionably the most important and arguably the most talented female performer in the history of the American film musical, Garland is also the object of a cult that

Figure 30.1 Esther Williams and a bevy of bathing beauties in *Neptune's Daughter* (Buzzell, USA, 1949). Metro-Goldwyn-Mayer. Image courtesy of George Eastman House

values not just her talent but the complex and camp meanings embedded in her star persona – a subject taken up in great detail by Steven Cohan in his essay in this volume.

Performing a camp reading of nearly any studio-era Hollywood star is not particularly challenging. Such readings require little more than the ability to mockingly celebrate what Susan Sontag famously called "failed seriousness" (Sontag 1964). Camp is a fundamentally ironic process that affords alternative avenues of fandom for non-mainstream audiences. As such, it is often a key component of films' and stars' cult followings; as Steven Cohan demonstrates, Garland's cult following is crucially grounded in camp.

However, some of Garland's musicals have garnered cults for reasons that do not necessarily overlap with camp/gay readings of them. Viewed through a camp lens, *The Wizard of Oz* is a rich text, indeed. Yet, at the same time, few films provide a better example of a "mainstream cult" than does *The Wizard of Oz*, which, since regular US television broadcasts in the 1950s and 1960s, has been an object of special fondness for a multigenerational audience of hundreds of millions of people.

Ernest Mathijs has memorably called *The Wizard of Oz* "the United Nations of cultism," as it has "attracted a complex mosaic of cult receptions that carry radically different implications yet appear to coexist tolerantly" (Mathijs 2011: 231). Yet nearly every member nation of that cult gives special regard to music. Ross Semple, in an article in *Gay Times*, takes the film's camp value as a given. "What's camp about Garland in *The Wizard of Oz*?" he asks. "The answer: a tune about a rainbow. … Like Dorothy, gay people dream of finding that place – beyond the rainbow – where we can be truly comfortable in our own skin and accepted by those around us" (Semple 2015). Another segment of that cult celebrates the film for the way its actions appear to "synch up" with Pink Floyd's 1973 album *Dark Side of the Moon* when the two texts are played simultaneously. Inasmuch as the film is a mainstream cult, that reputation rests in large part on such unforgettable songs as "Follow the Yellow Brick Road," "Ding-Dong! The Witch Is Dead," and "We're off to See the Wizard." Music is at the heart of the cult reputation of *The Wizard of Oz*. The same is true of many of Judy Garland's other films, notably *Meet Me in St. Louis* (1944), *Easter Parade* (1948), and *A Star Is Born* (1954).

Like those of many of Garland's films, the cult followings for the films of Doris Day – especially the musicals – are at least partly rooted in the extracinematic. Though her singing career began in the late 1930s and her acting career in the late 1940s, Day is best known to cultists for her trio of films with Rock Hudson. These colorful, buoyant musical romantic comedies – *Pillow Talk* (1959), *Lover Come Back* (1961), and *Send Me No Flowers* (1964) – so emphatically emphasize Day's squeaky-clean, girl-next-door image as to nearly beg for alternative readings. Cultists have based such readings on Rock Hudson's homosexuality. (Perhaps that is why 1963's *The Thrill of It All*, in which the uncontroversially heterosexual James Garner is the male lead, offers diminished pleasures.) If Day's characters were so head-over-heels in love with characters played by a gay man, then it is the smallest of leaps to view Day as a stand-in for a gay man, and her (and her characters') sexuality as gayness just barely concealed by a surfeit of overly enthusiastic heterosexuality. The cult potential in these rich ironies is evident.

Day's musicals convey that emphatic heterosexuality, so easy to read as "bearding," largely through song. As in all musicals, the songs in Doris Day's musicals are special sites of emotional truth and meaning. More than spoken dialogue, songs are the way that characters in musicals reveal their innermost feelings. In other words: if it's sung, it's true. "Possess Me," a song from *Pillow Talk*, is illustrative in this regard. Day's character, Jan Morrow, "sings" this song in her head as she takes a nighttime drive with Brad Allen (Hudson). As Jan moves closer to Brad, the audience is granted access to her thoughts and feelings, which are so passionate as to take musical form. "Possess Me" offers plenty for the cultist to appreciate, from its brazen sexual content (evident in its title) to quaint, giggle-inducing euphemisms like "make love" to the syrupy string section that swells to accompany the exchange of polite-yet-randy glances. Viewed through the lens of the open secret of Hudson's homosexuality, the song manages to convey sincerity as well as irony – exactly the kind of shifting, semi-contradictory meanings that attract audiences for whom *lagniappe* is a crucial part of cult fandom.

The cults that admire Judy Garland, Doris Day, and their films are largely predicated on against-the-grain readings that incorporate elements of camp. Yet the cults of Hollywood's two biggest male musical stars, Gene Kelly and Fred Astaire, are not particularly focused on any apparent subversiveness in their films. The cults of Kelly and Astaire seem to be comprised of especially avid admirers of these performers, different from run-of-the-mill fans in their ardor, not their reasoning.

The *oeuvres* of Astaire and Kelly may, in fact, be the exceptions that prove the rule that cult musicals earn that mantle chiefly for their music. Though they are both excellent and underrated singers, Astaire and Kelly are celebrated by their admirers mainly for their dancing abilities. In that their musicals are cult films, it is chiefly for this reason. Then again, every time these performers dance, it is in accompaniment to music. The title number of *Singin' in the Rain* is celebrated not just for Kelly's graceful splashing but for the catchiness of the song (even if it was nearly 25 years old by the time of the film's release). The number is perhaps the best example in the entire genre of a character using music (and dance, music's physical expression) to reveal his most profound feelings. Don Lockwood would not be singin' in the rain – that is, expressing joy in a stereotypically bleak setting – were he not profoundly and joyfully in love with Kathy Selden.

"New musicals" and the conscious cultivation of camp and cult

Film scholar Thomas Schatz has famously proposed a four-stage cycle of development through which all film genres pass. In the "experimental" stage, genres find their footing by accreting the conventions that define it. A film in the "classic" stage represents its genre at a point of maturity and stability, when conventions are firm and familiar. In the "refinement" stage, genre films reach their apotheoses by emphasizing every convention to the nth degree; such films do not challenge their genres, but lavishly and even excessively celebrate their conventions. In the final, "baroque" stage, genre films exhibit mannerist tendencies. Films at this stage knowingly acknowledge audiences' awareness of the genre's conventions; for this reason are they often regarded as deconstructionist or parodic texts (Schatz 1981: 36–41). Often, a genre evolves from the baroque stage by return to the classic phase, having first assimilated any new conventions proffered by recent baroque films. So the cycle resumes.

The films of Astaire, Day, Garland, Kelly, and Williams belong squarely to the "classic" stage of the development of the Hollywood musical. Several operatically inclined films of the early to mid-1960s, such as *West Side Story* and *The Sound of Music*, are usefully considered as "refined" texts, but are no less the object of cult affection for it. Still, the refinement stage may be seen to represent a last-ditch effort to pull out all stops before the genre train crashes spectacularly. One standard version of the history of the American film musical argues that train crashes in the form of such films as *Paint Your Wagon,* the 1969 western/comedy/musical that tries to be all things to all people and just winds up seeming ... square (Delamater 1981: 174–175). The 31 musicals starring Elvis Presley, too, are objects of cult followings – mostly for ironic reasons having to do with "failed seriousness," though also to celebrate Presley himself. But these joyless affairs are, arguably, evidence enough that the mainstream musical was dying or dead by the end of the 1960s.

A less extreme view to the genre's development at this time is that its definition had expanded. While it is apposite to regard cult concert films like *Monterey Pop* (1968), *The Concert for Bangladesh* (1972), and *Wattstax* (1973) as documentaries, they are at least equal parts musicals: movies whose structures are determined by their music, and whose chief appeals to their audiences are their musical performances. Here, again, the cults of such films overlap with the cults of their performers – Jimi Hendrix, George Harrison, Isaac Hayes.

Another way in which the musical genre developed at this time is that "excessive" conventions, formerly the hallmark of baroque musicals, found their way into the DNA of the classic musical. Marvelously representative of this tendency are two films by Jacques Demy, *The Umbrellas of Cherbourg* (1964) and *The Young Girls of Rochefort* (1967). *The Young Girls of Rochefort*, in particular, suggests that the musical genre can find exciting avenues for advancement by plumbing its own past. Demy's joyful, particolored film draws on musicals of the classic phase (by casting Gene Kelly and embracing a vivid, Technicolor-like palette), as well as on those of the refined era (by casting *West Side Story* star George Chakiris, and by leavening its central love stories with a subplot about murder).

The musical numbers in *The Young Girls of Rochefort* convey, as per convention, characters' most sincere and profound emotions. Yet they also convey, with appealing melodies and multi-colored *mise-en-scène*, intentionally banal story information. "We are twin sisters / Born under the sign of Gemini / Mi fa sol la mi re / re mi fa sol sol sol re do," sing Cathérine Deneuve and Françoise Dorléac in "Chanson des Jumelles," one of the film's catchiest tunes. The film owes its cult following in part to its unusual, tacit claim that everyday life is no less worthy of musical celebration than are extraordinary events.

Figure 30.2 Grover Dale (left) and George Chakiris (right) lead a colorful dance through Rochefort's town square in Jacques Demy's *Les Demoiselles de Rochefort* (Demy, France, 1967). Parc Film/Madeleine Films

Self-consciousness of one type or another would play a significant role in defining the cult musical for the next several decades. Many musicals from the mid-1970s forward may be considered "baroque" for the ways in which they anticipate and cater to a camp/cult response. The central text in this regard is surely *The Rocky Horror Picture Show*. The film caters to a cult audience by foregrounding and celebrating "deviant" sexuality – anticipating the "Judy Garland response." Equally importantly, its overall tone is an ironic one that invites audiences to enjoy the film on several levels: on its own terms; as a none-too-serious work of glorious imperfection; as an irreverent yet loving parody of classic musicals.

Many cult musicals of the 1970s rely on ostensibly transgressive content to foster their cult audiences, as if the mere existence of musicals about, say, Weimar-era gay culture (*Cabaret* [1972]), or a longhaired savior (*Jesus Christ Superstar* [1973]), or even hippies (*Hair* [1979]) was shocking enough to reconfigure the genre. Yet genre conventions run deeper than subject matter; on reflection, many of these films appear fairly "straight." A more complex musical from this era is Brian De Palma's *Phantom of the Paradise* (1974), which offers viewers multiple, semi-contradictory access points. The film combines, updates, and "musicalizes" the stories of *Faust*, *The Phantom of the Opera*, and *The Picture of Dorian Gray*, unspooling a musical narrative within the *milieu* of the contemporary record industry. Not just parodic but satirical, *Phantom of the Paradise* uses music to convey an ambivalence about music's own value. The film's songs, written by costar Paul Williams, are as tuneful as any by Betty Comden and Adolph Green, yet they espouse a profound cynicism about trust, love, and art. Misunderstood upon its initial release (except, curiously, in Winnipeg), *Phantom of the Paradise* has seen its cult grow in recent years, with audiences attracted to its oddball humor, cynical attitudes, and witty songs.

Figure 30.3 Soon-to-be-undead glam-rock star Beef (Gerrit Graham) mesmerizes his admirers in Brian De Palma's *Phantom of the Paradise* (De Palma, USA, 1974). Harbor Productions

Musicals from the 1980s and beyond

Many of the post-*Rocky Horror* musicals that would acquire cult followings did so on the grounds of their ironic or postmodern approaches. Peter Jackson's *Meet the Feebles* (1989), for example, is actually a fairly conventional backstage musical, yet it also ironizes that subgenre by the fact that it is performed entirely by puppet animals who engage in heroin abuse and coprophagy, among other peccadilloes. Lars Von Trier's alternately joyful and harrowing *Dancer in the Dark* (2000) celebrates *and* eviscerates musicals of the classic, refined, *and* baroque stages, and utterly annihilates the musical convention of the happy ending. *Repo! The Genetic Opera* (2008) updates the operetta – a hoary old subgenre whose last icon was Jeannette MacDonald in the 1930s – to address such topics as organ harvesting, drug abuse, and ultraviolence. More than any other modern musical, *Hedwig and the Angry Inch* (2001) modeled its cultivated cult on that of *Rocky Horror*. The film borrows from its predecessor the tropes of glam rock and non-mainstream sexuality.

An ironic approach seems to have been "built in" to many of the musicals made since the mid-1970s. It is true of the musical films of director Baz Luhrmann – *Strictly Ballroom* (1992), *William Shakespeare's Romeo + Juliet* (1996), and *Moulin Rouge!* (2001) – which have cultivated cult followings by using an ironically anachronistic, frenetic style to delve musically into "historical" scenarios. The same claim may be made even more strongly for the potty-mouthed yet oddly reverential musical films of Trey Parker and Matt Stone, notably *Cannibal! The Musical* (1993) and *South Park: Bigger, Longer & Uncut* (1999).

Even relatively "straight" post-1970s musicals – such as *Purple Rain* (1984), *Hairspray* (1988; remade in 2007), and *Spice World* (1997) – are objects of cult affection for sincere as well as ironic reasons. The cult of *Purple Rain* loves the movie's remarkable music, yet howls with derision at its ham-handed narration; director John Waters courted the cult of *Hairspray* with danceable rock 'n' roll chestnuts and a championing of several stripes of counterculture; the cult of *Spice World* revels in the film's wink-wink acknowledgment of the designed-by-committee personae of its stars, the prefab pop group the Spice Girls.

But the film musicals with the greatest cultural currency are the animated features that Disney releases with astonishing regularity. For decades, Disney's animated films – from *Beauty and the Beast* (1991) to *Pocahontas* (1995) to *Frozen* (2013) – have cultivated fandom as much through song as through appealing character design and compellingly straightforward narration. Disney has perfected the process of using music to inspire audience devotion.

Frozen is the highest grossing animated feature of all time, bringing in more than a billion dollars for its studio (Huddleston). Its soundtrack was the biggest album of 2014, selling more than 10 million copies that year alone (PA 2015). Most of the enthusiasts of the film and the soundtrack may be young children, but why should a cult have an age restriction? As with every other cult musical, *Frozen* uses musical numbers to present its characters' most heartfelt emotions as well as its most narratively salient moments – often, these are one and the same.

If a film's cult status is measured by the ardor of its admirers, *Frozen* has nearly every other musical beat. But even though *Frozen*'s is a cult following of a radically different order than those of *Rocky*, *Hedwig*, and *Repo!*, it is nevertheless founded on an admiration for the film's music.

Conclusion

My stepfather informed me, years ago, that he does not care for musicals. Barely able to imagine such an opinion, I asked him how he'd arrived at it. He replied that he could not "get past" the genre's inherent unreality: that people just break into song all of a sudden, accompanied by nondiegetic music, no less. For him, this convention of the genre so thoroughly compromises any musical's diegesis as to render the whole film unpalatable. Yet this convention is fundamental to the musical. With the exception of a few subgenres (the backstage musical, the "rockumentary," the "mockumentary," certain music videos) "breaking out into song" is *what happens* in musicals. Disliking musicals because they have nondiegetic musical numbers is akin to disliking cheese because it's made of milk. My stepfather may never "get" musicals, but his opinion of them hints at a key reason that certain musicals have developed cult followings.

As Barry Keith Grant writes, "The film musical, perhaps more than any other genre, has always foregrounded its nature as a generic construct and has thus demanded the greatest suspension of disbelief from the viewer." Even though the musical's spontaneous singing and dancing are no more or less "real," he writes, than the western genre's convention of the gunfight on a dusty street, Grant grants that it "seems more of a contrivance" (Grant 3–4). In other words, a certain degree of artifice and irony is "built in" to the musical. In this way, the musical genre is exceptional. The most foundational of its conventions highlights the genre's artificiality and compromises the coherence of its films' diegeses. No other genre possesses this tendency.

Fascinatingly, the musical numbers of even the more self-conscious cult musicals are special sites of sincerity and emotion. *The Rocky Horror Picture Show*, which hardly ever ceases winking knowingly at its audience, nevertheless uses such songs as "Touch-A, Touch-A, Touch Me," "Once in a While," and "Rose Tint My World" to signal major narrative pivots and/or to communicate characters' most honest feelings.

As we have seen, cults usually, but do not *always*, attach themselves to musicals because of the films' perceived ironic qualities, be they campy or otherwise. In particular, the cult followings of many classic Hollywood musicals center instead on the luminous personalities of their stars. Yet the great majority of musical-film cults have picked up on this underlying irony in one way or another, amplified it, and celebrated it. In their natural disregard for the construct of the coherent fictional world, musicals invite audiences to view them from a certain critical or ironic distance.

Another fundamental musical convention – the very fact that they necessarily contain music and lyrics – also contributes to the creation of a critical viewing distance. A catchy tune can "cloak" subversive lyrics so that their transgressiveness is not necessarily immediately apparent. Schopenhauer himself hinted at this most remarkable of music's features when he described music as "so easy to understand and yet so inexplicable."

Many studio-era Hollywood musicals slipped potentially objectionable content past the censors by couching it within a jaunty tune. Only because he sings about it could Bob Hope, for instance, refer obliquely to his own gender uncertainty in "Buttons and Bows," in the Western/musical/comedy *Son of Paleface* (1952): "When I was 12 / Oh, what a joy / Mom told me I was a boy." This extra layer of musical "padding" allows audiences of later eras to revisit such films, find in them the subversive content that has been semi-concealed by a musical treatment thereof, and use that subversiveness as the basis of cult followings.

From at least the 1960s onward, many cult musicals haven't bothered to use music to conceal subversive content – quite the opposite. The songs in the 1976 cult film *The First Nudie Musical*, for instance, refer directly to orgasms, dildos, and cunnilingus. In such musicals, music does not conceal subversive content but, rather, *enhances* it, thereby inviting a different but no less ardent mode of cult adoration. Whether cult musicals use music to conceal or to boast about their subversive content – or even if they contain nothing subversive at all – music is necessarily the most important element of these films' cult followings. Without a musical score that offers viewers some kind of *lagniappe*, no musical can be a cult musical.

References

Delamater, Jerome. 1981. *Dance in the Hollywood Musical*. Ann Arbor, MI: UMI Research Press.

Grant, Barry Keith. 2012. *The Hollywood Film Musical*. Malden, MA: Wiley.

Hoberman, J. 1993. *42nd Street*. London: British Film Institute.

Huddleston, Jr., Tom. 2015. "*Frozen* Heats up Disney's Earnings." *Fortune*, 3 February. fortune.com/2015/02/03/disney-quarterly-earnings. Accessed 29 July 2019.

Mathijs, Ernest. 2011. "*The Wizard of Oz*," in Ernest Mathijs and Xavier Mendik, eds., *100 Cult Films*. London: Palgrave Macmillan: 230–232.

PA. 2015. "Frozen Soundtrack Named 2014's Biggest Album." *The Telegraph* (London), 14 April. www.telegraph.co.uk/culture/disney/11535770/Frozen-soundtrack-named-2014s-biggest-selling-album.html. Accessed 29 July 2019.

Schatz, Thomas. 1981. *Hollywood Genres: Formulas, Filmmaking and the Studio System*. New York: Random House.

Schopenhauer, Arthur. 2012. *The World as Will and Representation*, Vol. 1. Quoted in Bart Vandenabeele, ed., *A Companion to Schopenhauer*. Malden, MA: Wiley.

Semple, Ross. 2015. "Camp Sites: *The Wizard of Oz*." *Gay Times*, 26 September. www.gaytimes.co.uk/culture/8905/camp-sites-wizard-oz. Accessed 29 July 2019.

Sontag, Susan. 1964: "Notes on Camp." http://faculty.georgetown.edu/irvinem/theory/Sontag-NotesOnCamp-1964.html. Accessed 29 July 2019.

31

CULT SOUNDTRACKS (MUSIC)

James Wierzbicki

In John Carpenter's 1978 *Halloween*, the kids being minded by the hapless babysitter through most of the film are doing what kids do naturally. The eye of Carpenter's observant narrator rarely shows us footage from the several 'scary' movies that the kids watch, but its ear eavesdrops often on those movies' soundtracks. Indeed, what comes out of the TV set's tiny loudspeaker forms the sonic backdrop for the one environment in *Halloween* that, all things considered, remains relatively safe. Sometimes as pervasive as would be the aroma of popcorn had *Halloween* been equipped with 'smell-o-vision,' this sonic backdrop includes an occasional pitch from the TV station's host and an occasional scrap of dialogue from one or another of the movies, but by and large it keeps spoken words to a minimum, and most of its content comes in the form of sound effects and underscore. If Carpenter had wanted nothing more than to depict kids watching TV on Halloween night, he could easily have borrowed from any of countless horror films. As it happened, he chose Christian Nyby's 1951 *The Thing from Another World* and Fred McLeod Wilcox's 1956 *Forbidden Planet*.

It may be that Carpenter opted for these two films because, as is noted often in interviews with Carpenter, they were especially influential on him during his childhood. It may also be that Carpenter opted for these films in particular because, as is sometimes suggested in the academic press, he felt them to be precursors to the 'modern' stalker film of which *Halloween* was arguably the first representative (Dika 1990: 137), or because segments of their dialogue having to do with invisible threats touch on *Halloween*'s rather obvious main plot (Cumbow 2000: 54), or because the theme of 'monsters from the id' that is explicit in *Forbidden Planet* and implicit in *The Thing from Another World* relate in various ways to *Halloween*'s tantalizing subplot about a nubile young woman who fears for her life and at the same time fairly throbs with repressed sexual desire (Dika 1990: 51; Muir 2005: 81–82; Cherry 2009: 99). These are sensible and credible reasons for why Carpenter, in his second outing as a filmmaker, might have made overt reference to these two films. But perhaps there is another, simpler, explanation.

Members of *Halloween*'s audience can be divided into three categories. On one end of the scale are those who have absolutely no experience with the two films that play on the television; vis-à-vis *The Thing* and *Forbidden Planet*, these naïve audience members are as virginal as is *Halloween*'s central female character, and thus they will hear in the soundtracks only background music that is suitably creepy but which otherwise, for them, carries no special meaning. On the other end of the scale, certain members of the audience – a small group, to be sure, but doubtless much larger today than when *Halloween* was fresh – can be said to be intimate not just with the soundtracks but with everything else about these two films; the members of this elite set are dedicated and deeply knowledgeable fans of 1950s sci-fi movies, and surely more than a few of them will 'read between the lines' and come up with interpretations comparable to those summarized above. Between these two extremes is the vast majority of filmgoers, a group that might be described as being to a certain extent cinematically literate but hardly 'geeky' in its approach to cinema trivia; probably these more or less 'normal' audience members, as much today as in 1978, will pay far more attention to *Halloween*'s unfolding plot than to plots of old movies that they may or may not remember, yet probably they will be aware – not so much because of what they fleetingly see as because of what they persistently hear – that the 'scary' movies the kids watch on TV are at least vaguely familiar.

Halloween indeed features images from *The Thing* and *Forbidden Planet*. For the most part, though, the cameo appearances go to isolated fragments of these films' soundtracks. In order to make their dramatic effect, these fragments do not need to be identified. All that is necessary to draw audience members into the domestic scenes, to make filmgoers feel as if they are not merely observing the scenes but are participating in them, in ways perhaps reminiscent of their own childhoods, is that the largely wordless soundtrack fragments 'ring a bell.'

★★★★

Ineffability is a concept common to the relatively vast literature on cult cinema. We all know that cult films exist, and each of us can come up with long lists of examples, yet it seems that no one can say what a cult film actually is. The elusiveness that characterizes most definitions of cult cinema applies as well to definitions of cult-film music, whether the sources of that music are originally composed scores or compilations of pre-existing materials. Just as the term 'cult film' covers "a wide-ranging and eclectic group of films that can be drawn from almost any genre, any time period and any national cinema," writes Brigid Cherry in her entry on "Cult Films and Music" in an encyclopedia on music in American culture, so the "music in cult film is equally diverse" (Cherry 2013: 322). In a chapter titled "Cult Cinema and Music" in their *Cult Cinema: An Introduction*, the co-editors of this *Routledge Companion to Cult Cinema* similarly celebrate not only the diversity of music-related cult films and music related to cult films but also the range of musical-filmic traits that "can never be exhaustively categorized" (Mathijs and Sexton 2011: 182).

Except for mentions of clearly measurable attendance figures for off-hours screenings of certain music-rich films, Mathijs and Sexton, like Cherry, offer no real criteria for determining the 'cult' status of film music of any sort. They do, however, offer numerous examples of films whose music arguably qualifies for that status, and they divide these films, roughly yet more or less systematically, into 'musicals,' films featuring music by established performers, films with compiled soundtracks, and films with original scores. The lists sometimes overlap, and it is at the very least interesting to note how a film classified a certain way in one listing occasionally gets classified a different way in the other. It is more interesting, because it illustrates how subjective are the very ideas of the cult film and cult-film music, to note how much the listings do *not* overlap.

The sections on 'musicals' in both "Cult Films and Music" and "Cult Cinema and Music" have in common their mentions of *The Sound of Music* (1965), *Rocky Horror Picture Show* (1975), *Grease* (1978), and *Hairspray* (2007); Mathijs's and Sexton's much longer chapter also mentions *Footlight Parade* (1933), *The Wizard of Oz* (1939), *Singin' in the Rain* (1952), *Rock 'n' Roll High School* (1979), *Annie* (1982), *Forbidden Zone* (1982), *Streets of Fire* (1984), and *Cry-Baby* (1990). Cherry indeed mentions *Forbidden Zone* and *Streets of Fire*, but she classifies them not with 'musicals' but with "films that have achieved cult status" largely because they star "bands and musicians [respectively, Oingo Boingo and The Blasters] with cult followings" (Cherry 2013: 324); Mathijs's and Sexton's comparable list of band-specific films includes *A Hard Day's Night* and *Help!* (1964 and 1965, both featuring The Beatles), *Tommy* and *Quadrophenia* (1975 and 1979, featuring The Who), *The Song Remains the Same* (1976, featuring Led Zeppelin), *The Wall* (1982, featuring Pink Floyd), and *Stop Making Sense* (1984, featuring The Talking Heads), and it includes as well such star-studded documentary films as *Monterey Pop* (1968), *Woodstock* (1970), and *Gimme Shelter* (1970).

As for soundtracks whose compilations of mostly rock music seem to have attained 'cult' status independent of the films that gave birth to them, the only items common to Cherry's list and the list put together by Mathijs and Sexton are the musically diverse soundtracks from *Reservoir Dogs* (1992) and *Donnie Darko* (2001); Cherry's list also includes the music from *Animal House* (1978), *Fast Times at Ridgemont High* (1982), and *Ferris Bueller's Day Off* (1986), while Mathijs's and Sexton's longer list also includes the music from *Wild in the Streets* (1968), *Easy Rider* (1969), *Vampyros Lesbos* (1971), *Repo Man* (1984), *Pulp Fiction* (1994), *Trainspotting* (1996), and *Death Proof* (2007).

As for 'cult' soundtracks consisting for the most part of original material from a single composer, the only scores common to both lists are those for Gordon Parks's *Shaft* (1971, with archly 'funky' music by Isaac Hayes), David Lynch's *Eraserhead* (1977, with atmospheric music, or 'sound design,' by Lynch and Alan Splet), and Ridley Scott's *Blade Runner* (1982, with electronic music by Vangelis). Along with these, Cherry's highly subjective list includes the soundtracks for Carol Reed's *The Third Man* (1949, with zither music by Anton Karas), Robert Wise's *The Day the Earth Stood Still* (1951, with a theremin-flavored orchestral score by Bernard Herrmann), Alejandro Jodorowsky's *El Topo* (1970, with Jodorowsky's own generic 'Western' music), and Dario Argento's *Suspiria* (1977, with persistently gritty music by Argento and the Italian group Goblin). The equally subjective list offered by Mathijs and Sexton includes the soundtracks for Stanley Kubrick's *A Clockwork Orange* (1971, with electronic compositions and arrangements by Walter Carlos), various films by Werner Herzog (e.g., the 1972 *Aguirre, Wrath of God* and the 1976 *Heart of Glass*, with music by the German avant-garde band Popul Vuh), Godfrey Reggio's *Koyaanisqatsi* (1983, with 'minimalist' music by Philip Glass), and, collectively, the Hammer Studio's horror films from the 1950s, 1960s, and 1970s (with orchestral music by such composers as Don Banks, James Bernard, Tristram Carey, Paul Giovanni, and Basil Kirchin); in a paragraph devoted to scores that have attracted cult followings at least in part because their composers were also their films' directors, Mathijs and Sexton cite (along with Lynch's weird music for *Eraserhead* and Herschell Gordon-Lewis's unabashedly tacky music for his 1963 *Blood Feast*) Carpenter's simple yet highly effective music for *Halloween*.

Apropos of *Halloween*, it seems more than coincidence that each of these extended commentaries, in their discussions of original scores that in effect have taken on cult-fueled lives of their own, mention one or the other of the two 'movies-within-the-movie' whose easily recognized visual images flash only for moments on the diegetic TV screen but whose soundtracks, within the narrative, linger for long whiles.

★★★★

Since the standards remain so loose and so subjective, it can hardly be said that Carpenter's slasher classic, or anything else mentioned in this *Routledge Companion*, in fact *is* a cult film. It is most certainly a fact, though, that many experts on cult film *consider* Carpenter's opus to be a stellar example of the type. It is likewise a fact that Carpenter's film features clips from two older films whose soundtracks have been identified by at least some commentators, as noted above, as the focus of 'cult' attention. And all this raises questions about a possible set of criteria by which to measure candidates not for 'cult' status in general but for a special kind of 'cult' status.

All it takes for a film to be a 'cult' film, really, is that it be "a movie with a following" (Kawin 1991: 18). The tautology applies as well to certain soundtracks for cult films, such as those that Ennio Morricone composed for various of Sergio Leone's 'spaghetti Westerns' (e.g., *A Fistful of Dollars* (1964), *For a Few Dollars More* (1965), *The Good, the Bad, and the Ugly* (1966), and *Once Upon a Time in the West* (1968)) and those that the members of the Italian fusion-rock group Goblin, either together or as individuals, provided for a host of so-called *giallo* films (e.g., along with the above-mentioned *Suspiria*, such other Argento films as *Profondo Rosso* (1975), *Tenebre* (1982), and *Phenomena* (1985), and such lesser-known thrillers as Joe d'Amato's *Buio Omega* (1979), Bruno Mattei's *L'altro inferno* (1981), and Michele Soavi's *La Chiesa* (1989)). The tautology applies, too, to those rare soundtracks – such as Alex North's for *Unchained* (1955), or Max Steiner's for *A Summer Place* (1959), or Jack Nitzsche's for *Performance* (1970) – that seem to have been "accorded [cult] status even when the film is not" (Donnelly 2015: 31).

But what about mere fragments of soundtracks, like the bits and pieces of the soundtracks from *Forbidden Planet* and *The Thing from Another World* that are heard in *Halloween*? For a fragmentary cultural object to be a 'cult' object, is it enough that it be somehow recycled? In the case of filmic objects, is 'cult' status in effect guaranteed simply because some component of the film is quoted, or paraphrased, or alluded to, in a later film? In the case of soundtracks, should 'cult' status be awarded for no other reason than because a portion of a soundtrack finds its way into some other film's *mise en scène* or underscore?

The quick answer to these questions should be in the negative, and for evidence that quotation alone is not enough to confer 'cult' status upon a soundtrack one need look no further than the various off-shoots of the film that has thus far been at the center of this discussion. Numerous of the sequels offer variations on the idea of a 'scary movie on TV,' but usually the imitations pale in comparison with Carpenter's original effort.

Rick Rosenthal's 1981 *Halloween II*, for example, includes audio-visual quotations from George Romero's 1968 *Night of the Living Dead*, and Steve Miner's 1998 *Halloween H20: 20 Years Later* includes scenes of people watching Ed Wood's 1959 *Plan 9 from Outer Space* and Wes Craven's 1997 *Scream 2*. Paying obvious homage both to the fountainhead of the franchise and to the first of the sequels, the 2007 and 2009 remakes by Rob Zombie (né Robert Bartleh Cummings) of *Halloween* and *Halloween II* give 'cameo' appearances not just to clips from *The Thing from Another World* and *Forbidden Planet* but also to the soundtrack from *Night of the Living Dead*. Additionally, Zombie's 2009 *Halloween II* includes clips from a 1931 Ub Iwerks cartoon titled *Spooks* and a made-for-the-movie music video featuring a band called Captain Clegg and The Night Creatures; his 2007 *Halloween* includes clips from William Castle's 1959 *House on Haunted Hill* and – perhaps for no other reason than that its title is the name of the heavy metal band with which the director performed before turning to filmmaking – Victor Halperin's 1932 *White Zombie*.

Probably most persons browsing through this book will not hesitate in granting 'cult' status to Romero's *Night of the Living Dead* and to Wood's famously pathetic *Plan 9 from Outer Space*. But likely they would not award such status to these films' soundtracks, or to the soundtrack for *White Zombie*. Not unlike certain of their films' blank-faced characters, these soundtracks have no 'personalities' of their own, all three of them being compilations of pre-existing material or library commodities. *White Zombie* uses stock music recycled from earlier RKO-Pathé productions; *Plan 9 from Outer Space* uses production music rented from the commercial Video Moods and Impress libraries; *Night of the Living Dead* uses a hodge-podge of music borrowed from such decidedly 'B-grade' films as *Teenagers from Outer Space* (1959) and *The Devil's Messenger* (1961) and from such ephemeral early 1960s television series as *Ben Casey* and *Naked City*.

Because it is so ineffectual in all three of its usages in the *Halloween* cycle, the banal sound-track from *Night of the Living Dead* is especially deserving of a bashing. It should be remembered that within the narrative of Carpenter's film the audience for *Forbidden Planet* and *The Thing from Another World* comprises children genuinely involved in the movies' plots, and these children are on edge at least in part because of the movies' 'edgy' soundtracks. Within the narrative of Rosenthal's *Halloween II*, the only persons exposed to a telecast of *Night of the Living Dead* are a sleepy old couple and a group of bored employees at the local hospital, and the only important characters in the two Zombie films positioned within earshot of the soundtrack are one of the virginal protagonist's friends (as she has perfunctory sex with a boyfriend) and the virginal protagonist herself (as she wakes from a bad dream). Whereas the kids in the original film – and in Zombie's remake thereof (Roche 2014: 151–152) – pay keen attention to what spews sonically as well as visually from their TV set, in the later films no one seems interested in any aspect whatsoever of the *Night of the Living Dead*. At least in part because the kids are shown to care about them (but perhaps also in part because they are worth caring about), the soundtracks from *Forbidden Planet* and *The Thing from Another World* in the Rob Zombie remake as much as in the original film ring true; at least in part because none of the films' characters care in any way about them (but perhaps also in part because, really, there is nothing to care about), the soundtrack of *Night of the Living Dead* falls flat. The author of a monograph on Carpenter was addressing only the 1981 sequel, yet he astutely anticipated the future remakes, when he wrote: "Instead of amplifying the thematic and stylistic impact of the film, the Romero quote here amounts to little more than a throwaway" (Cumbow 2000: 66).

★★★★

Throwaways of all sorts – sonic, visual, verbal – abound in horror-film spinoffs and spoofs, especially in the richly intertextual more recent offerings. Not only are these quotations commonplace; they are typically devoid of meaning, except to those cinephiles especially steeped in horror-film trivia. If one were to concentrate only on this fan-oriented and often campy genre, one would be right to conclude that, as suggested above, the mere fact of a filmic object's being quoted is hardly enough to warrant bestowing upon that object the perhaps coveted mantle of 'cult'-hood.

But if one broadens the field of survey to include the whole of cinema, and if one forgets about *Halloween* and focuses on the real subject of this essay, one notices that soundtrack quotation is quite rare. Indeed, the quotation of even a fragment of soundtrack is *so* unusual that the mere fact of its existence – so long as it is not so subtle as to go unnoticed – is likely to be an indicator of at least some sort of 'cult' status. In the wide world of cinema in general, the relationship between quotation and the 'cult' status of the quoted material is clearer, and more teleological, than it is within the parochial confines of horror-film remakes. In the bigger picture, a soundtrack or excerpt thereof does not *become* a candidate for 'cult' status because it is quoted; rather, the soundtrack music is quoted because it already *is* an object of 'cult' attention.

It is important to distinguish here between music that is quoted and a soundtrack that is quoted. Cinematic use of pre-existing musical material has long been ubiquitous (Inglis 2003; Kubernick 2006; Powrie and Stilwell 2006; Goldmark et al. 2007), and just because pre-existing music used in one film is used again in a later film does not mean that the later film quotes the soundtrack of the earlier film. The "Ode to Joy" from the last movement of Beethoven's Symphony No. 9 figures often in films, for example, but the tune as heard in Peter Weir's 1989 *Dead Poets Society* or in Ang Lee's 1994 *Eat, Drink, Man, Woman* has nothing at all to do with the soundtracks of, say, Stanley Kubrick's 1971 *A Clockwork Orange* or Frank Capra's 1941 *Meet John Doe*. Similarly, although fruitful comparisons might indeed be made between the implications of "Love Is Strange" in a variety of filmic contexts, it would take a considerably stretched

311

imagination to argue that the iteration of this cloying 1956 pop song in a season-two episode of the HBO series *The Sopranos* somehow makes reference to the soundtracks – and, by implication, to the narratives – of Martin Scorsese's 1997 *Casino*, Emile Ardolino's 1987 *Dirty Dancing*, or Terrence Malick's 1973 *Badlands*.

The situation is altogether different when music recycled in a later film is linked inextricably with an earlier film. In such a case the recycled material transcends the sonic nature of music: in addition to being whatever it is in terms of harmony, melody, and so on, the material functions as a symbol of the earlier film, or of a particular scene, or situation, contained within that earlier film. Like a logo for a successfully marketed soft drink or make of automobile, music of this sort not only reminds listeners of a specific 'product' but also evokes an array of ideas and emotions related to that 'product.' To make this powerful psychological effect, of course, the music needs to be truly iconic, which is to say that in the context of the newer film its reincarnation must be instantly recognized and associated, at least to some extent, with its source. Importantly, the recognizing and associating must be experienced by an audience much larger than one made up only of specialists; in order for the soundtrack reference to be not just a throwaway but a meaningful example of what the late Italian thinker Umberto Eco called "intertextual dialogue" (Eco 1985a: 172), the referenced material must be recognized by members of the proverbial 'general audience.'

Near the end of Ron Underwood's 1991 *City Slickers*, the three New Yorkers who play cowboy for a summer are amazed that, against formidable odds, they have actually succeeded in wrangling a herd of cattle to its destination; just before he leads the group in a gallop down to the ranch, the city slicker played by Billy Crystal looks wryly at his mates and encourages them to join him in singing "bum, budda-bum, budda-bum, budda-bum, budda-bu-u-m bu-u-u-u-um … ." Probably only moviegoers of a certain age would identify this straightaway as the theme for the long-running (1959–1973) American television show *Bonanza*, and probably only screen-music scholars would know, or care to know, that the tune was concocted (originally with genuine lyrics) by the prolific songwriting team of Jay Livingston and Ray Evans, that the lyrics were scrapped even before the pilot aired, and that the instrumental version was arranged and orchestrated, respectively, by Hollywood veterans Billy May and David Rose. But I would wager that the vast majority of first-time viewers of *City Slickers*, whether in 1991 or nowadays, and regardless of their age or country of origin, would find that this soundtrack quotation, like the soundtrack quotations in Carpenter's *Halloween*, is at least vaguely familiar, and that it calls to mind ideas not just of exuberant horsemanship but also – always dominant in the *Bonanza* scripts – of triumph and camaraderie. If it were not such a sure bet as to be unsporting, I would also wager that filmmaker Underwood and his crew were absolutely convinced that the quotation would indeed be interpreted, by the 'general audience,' in the way I just described; had they not been so convinced, the gesture would hardly have been worth the effort, let alone whatever money had to be paid for use of copyrighted material.

This logic applies to virtually all soundtrack quotations, including quotations that take place not in other soundtracks but in real life. Bernard Herrmann's music for Alfred Hitchcock's 1960 *Psycho* is justifiably celebrated, and the entire score has long had a fan club. But only the cue that accompanies the shower scene has developed enough of what Eco, in a 1985 essay on cult cinema in general, called "archetypal appeal" for it to be counted among "the catalyzers of collective memories" (Eco 1985b: 3), and thus only the shower-scene cue gets regularly recycled in films and TV shows or performed live, usually in tandem with mock-violent hand gestures, by conversationalists making sarcastic comments about acquaintances who they think have gone a little cuckoo. Likewise for the seemingly innocent tune that the one-eyed murderess whistles at the start of Quentin Tarantino's 2003 *Kill Bill: Vol. 1* (although most listeners today would know it from the Tarantino film, the tune in fact derives from Herrmann's score for Roy Boulting's 1968 *Twisted Nerve*). And likewise for that repeating four-note figure for electric guitar, a piece of stock music by the French composer Marius Constant, that between 1960 and 1964 introduced television viewers to *The Twilight Zone*.

These musical 'objects' are simply too iconic to be referenced in throwaway fashion; the baggage that they carry is too well known, and too densely packed, for them to be used for any reason other than to make an effect. Sometimes the effect that filmmakers try to make with their references to these and comparably resonant "catalyzers" is poignant, as when the achingly lonely zither music for *The Third Man* fills the room as the movie is watched on television by the title character in Nicolas Roeg's 1976 *The Man Who Fell to Earth*. Sometimes the effect is ironic, as when the title songs from Robert Wise's 1965 *The Sound of Music* or Henry King's 1955 *Love Is a Many-Splendored Thing* are woven into the narrative of Baz Luhrmann's 2001 *Moulin Rouge!* Sometimes the effect is just creepy, as when the *Twisted Nerve/Kill Bill* melody resurfaces as a mobile-phone ringtone in Tarantino's 2007 *Death Proof*. Sometimes – indeed, often – the effect is comedic: Herrmann's shower-scene music is by this time so deeply embedded in the cultural consciousness that an imitation of it in a serious horror movie would be a laughingstock, but a parody can still make for a good joke.

The sole point of the sharply stabbing music in *Psycho* is to startle the audience; the main point of more or less the same music in many subsequent films (e.g., Mel Brooks's 1976 *High Anxiety* or Harold Ramis's 1983 *(National Lampoon's) Vacation*) and television shows (e.g., the 1990 episode of the *Mr. Bean* series titled "The Curse of Mr. Bean" or the 1997 episode of *The Simpsons* titled "The Springfield Files") is that it be recognized and associated, however vaguely, not necessarily with Hitchcock's *Psycho* but only with the general idea of 'startle.' Recognition combined with association is similarly the main point of the other examples of quoted music discussed above, for unless the music is immediately linked with some basic concept any hoped-for dramatic effect – whether that be comedy, creepiness, irony, or poignancy – is impossible. Some quotations, of course, are indeed mere throwaways, and some are so 'hidden' as to be meaningful only to the clever persons who selected them. But in most musical instances of what Helle Kannik Haastrup calls "explicit intertextuality" the referenced material is indeed "part of popular culture and therefore familiar to the mainstream film audience"; familiarity is crucial to the interaction, for "the use of intertextuality in film is not about excluding people ... but about including as many as possible" (Haastrup 2014: 88).

★★★★

That an entire soundtrack be not so much popular as intensely loved is sometimes offered as the single condition for the soundtrack's having 'cult' status. Fair enough, but this condition depends hugely on the subjective responses of relatively small and self-selected audiences. And it hints at a circular argument, one that proposes that a soundtrack is a 'cult' soundtrack because certain people treat it as a 'cult' soundtrack.

The more objective criterion for 'cult'-hood suggested throughout this essay applies not to entire soundtracks but only to those small but precious bits of soundtracks that are, to repeat Eco's phrase, "catalyzers of collective memories." Participation in the 'cult' of such a soundtrack excerpt does not require emotional involvement on the part of the moviegoer. Affection, or animosity, might indeed enhance the 'cult' experience, and so might whatever associations the hearing of the excerpt triggers. But all that is necessary – and this is a *sine quo non* – is that the moviegoer acknowledge, consciously or not, the fact that the excerpt is something that he/she has previously encountered.

James Wierzbicki

References

Cherry, Brigid. 2009. *Horror*, New York: Routledge.

Cherry, Brigid. 2013. "Cult Films and Music," in Jacqueline Edmondson (ed.), *Music in American Life: An Encyclopedia of the Songs, Styles, Stars, and Stories That Shaped Our Culture*, Volume 1, Santa Barbara, CA: Greenwood Press: 322–325.

Cumbow, Robert. 2000. *Order in the Universe: The Films of John Carpenter*, Lanham, MD: Scarecrow Press.

Dika, Vera. 1990. *Games of Terror: Halloween, Friday the 13th and the Films of the Stalker Cycle*, Cranbury, NJ: Farleigh Dickinson University Press.

Donnelly, K.J. 2015. "Music Cultizing Film: KTL and the New Silents," *New Review of Film and Television Studies* 13, no. 1: 31–44.

Eco, Umberto. 1985a. "Innovation and Repetition: Between Modern and Post-Modern Aesthetics," *Daedelus* 114, no. 4: 161–184.

Eco, Umberto. 1985b. "*Casablanca*: Cult Movies and Intertextual Collage," *SubStance* 14, no. 2: 3–12. (Reprinted in *Travels in Hyperreality*, New York: Harcourt, pp. 197–211.)

Goldmark, Daniel Ira, Lawrence Kramer and Richard Leppert, eds. 2007. *Beyond the Soundtrack: Representing Music in Cinema*, Berkeley: University of California Press.

Haastrup, Helle Kannik. 2014. "Storytelling Intertextuality," *Film International* 12, no. 1: 85–97.

Inglis, Ian, ed. 2003. *Popular Music and Film*, New York: Wallflower Press.

Kawin, Bruce. 1991. "After Midnight," in J.P. Telotte (ed.), *The Cult Film Experience: Beyond All Reason*, Austin: University of Texas Press: 18–25.

Kubernick, Harvey. 2006. *Hollywood Shack Job: Rock Music in Film and on Your Screen*, Albuquerque: University of New Mexico Press.

Mathijs, Ernest and Jamie Sexton. 2011. *Cult Cinema: An Introduction*, Chichester: Wiley-Blackwell.

Muir, J.K. 2005. *The Films of John Carpenter*, Jefferson, NC: McFarland.

Powrie, Phil and Robynn Stilwell, eds. 2006. *Changing Tunes: The Use of Pre-existing Music in Film*, Farnham: Ashgate.

Roche, David. 2014. *Making and Remaking Horror in the 1970s and 2000s: Why Don't They Do It Like They Used To?*, Jackson: University Press of Mississippi.

32

SOUNDING OUT CULT CINEMA

The 'bad', the 'weird' and the 'old'

Nessa Johnston

What is the sound of cult cinema? Can we speak meaningfully of such a thing, given the widely discussed conceptual slippages at play in any definition of cult? Writings on cult cinema, both popular and academic, lack much engagement with cult cinema's sonic elements. It is difficult to conceive of the 'sound' of cult cinema without initially thinking of music, given that some cult cinema scores have simultaneously a cult following for the musicians along-side a cult following for the film or film's director (examples include the Italian progressive rock band Goblin and their association with Italian horror, or the funk and soul soundtracks of Blaxploitation). However, music in cult cinema is discussed elsewhere in this volume by James Wierzbicki. This chapter therefore provides an opportunity to consider other elements of the sound of cult cinema, including dialogue, sound effects, and non-narrative/non-semantic aspects such as noise.

In academic circles, there is little intersection between studies of cult cinema and studies of film sound, at first glance. This chapter will uncover and highlight relevant past work that explicitly, and (more often) implicitly considers sound in cult cinema, or cult cinema in sound studies. The potential difficulties of defining cult cinema have been widely discussed in earlier volumes; yet for the purposes of this chapter, let us accept as best as we can that there are established underground/cult film scenes, historical moments, and cult canons that exist as influential cultural formations. So, what is there to gain from discussion of 'cult sound'? Is it a way of forging an alternative 'sounding out' of a cult canon? Conversely, is talking about 'cult sound' a way to cast a 'cult' eye (or more accurately, ear) on film sound studies, a field preoccupied with Hollywood sound, 'serious' arthouse cinema, and a few 'sound auteurs'?

As well as revaluating film sound studies work from a cult perspective, this chapter takes earlier attempts to map out definitions of cult cinema and shifts these definitions to focus upon cult cinema's sonic properties. Mathijs and Mendik delineate four major elements that combine to help designate a cult film. These are 'anatomy', 'consumption', 'political economy' and 'cultural status' (Mathijs & Mendik 2008: 1). They further delineate 'two major philosoph-ical perspectives on cult cinema' – ontological and phenomenological (Mathijs & Mendik 2008: 15). A 'sounding out' of cult cinema can be achieved through the use of these elements and perspectives as a starting point, but as this chapter builds it shall demonstrate just how entangled they are with each other, especially in any discussion of the sonic. So while my discussion of cult sound and genre attempts an ontological approach it rapidly becomes phenomenological, because what dominates discussion and examples are films celebrated for having 'weird' sound, 'bad' sound, and (perhaps to a lesser extent) 'old' sound – and whose terms are these? Although these classifications can be discussed within an anatomical approach (focusing on genre and genre's sonic conventions), they constantly return to consider reception contexts and discussion of the cultural status of sound and the soundtrack. Furthermore, the nostalgia inherent in appreciation of particular kinds of 'old' film sound places elements of the cult canon in a more historical context of now obsolete production technologies and past exhibition spaces, mixing the 'consumption', 'political economy' and 'cultural status' outlined earlier.

Cult sound and the cult 'canon'

The cult 'canon' tends to be dominated by genre films, and as I have argued elsewhere, the dominant characteristics of a film's soundtrack can cite it within particular genre conventions, that is, certain types of sounds are associated with certain genres (Johnston 2012). For example, much has been written on the types of sounds that characterise science fiction (Hayward 2004; Whittington 2007; Johnston 2012) and horror (Spadoni 2007; Coyle 2008; Hayward 2009; Whittington 2014). These anatomical characteristics must be acknowledged but limit our understanding. More interestingly, William Wittington's work on science fiction sound puts forward an overriding argument regarding the evolution of the genre and the evolution of sound effects design and the associated job title of 'sound designer' as symbiotic, with science fiction sound in particular providing a means of showcasing new technologies of sound reproduction and exhibition. His later work on horror argues that the 'respectable' title of 'sound designer' is less associated with horror, suggesting that this is due to the apparently 'lower status' of the horror genre (Whittington 2014: 174). Neither work considers these genres' association with cult cinema, despite discussion of many films that feature in the critical canon of cult. However, his reference to budgetary constraints and 'status' in his discussion of horror sound implies questions of taste – more specifically sonic taste frameworks – that are relevant. Indeed, this discussion is more relevant than any anatomical approach to the characterising sounds of horror and sci-fi. Horror and sci-fi films were historically more closely associated with lower budget, less reputable film production. In his landmark study of B-movies and exploitation cinema of the post-war period *Bold! Shocking! Daring! True!* Eric Schaefer mentions "poor recording and matching" as a characteristic of exploitation films that were "made cheaply, with extremely low production values, by small independent firms", alongside "shoddy standing sets [...] continuity errors [...] the simplest camerawork and the most basic editing" (Schaefer 1999: 5). Hence sound tends to be discussed in this context in terms of its 'badness', and as a marker of production values, rather than as an area for imaginative creativity or sonic innovation. Sound is often positioned as a technically objective aspect of such production values – the sound is 'good' (clear, intelligible) or the sound is 'bad' (distorted, unintelligible). Hence, the need to consider 'bad' sound in relation to 'badness' in cult cinema.

Electronically-generated sounds have been associated with sci-fi since the post-war period, mainly in the realm of film music (Hayward 2004: 9–10), long blurring the distinction between noise and music, sound effects and score. The strange, inorganic sound of electronic instruments such as the Theremin moved from the world of avant-garde concert music to the less rarefied world of sci-fi films such as *The Day the Earth Stood Still* and *The Thing from Another World* (both 1951), providing an aural match for the dread of alien invasion. *Forbidden Planet* (1956), (later cultified in the lyrics of the *Rocky Horror Picture Show*'s [1975] opening number "Science Fiction Double Feature"), featured a pioneering electronic score by Bebe and Louis Barron, credited as 'electronic tonalities' rather than 'electronic music' as a means of avoiding conflict with the musicians' union (Leydon 2004: 66–67). Anatomy and political economy intersect here: the types of 'strange' sound associated with the strange world of 1950s alien invasion and space exploration movies disrupts industrial and economic categories of music and sound. Hence, the need to consider 'strange' sound in relation to 'strangeness' in cult cinema.

Much as the canon of cult cinema did not spring into the world fully formed and packaged as 'cult', but rather became cult through patterns of consumption and cultural formation, the status of certain types of sound in cult films becomes cultified over time. The strange-ness of electronic sounds just discussed has shifted over time to become associated with particular types of film genres of particular eras. Andy Birtwistle argues that the otherworldly Theremin of the 1950s no longer sounds strange or futuristic but instead sounds vintage and quaint (Birtwistle 2012: 126–183). Although he focuses more on musical scores than on sound, Jamie Sexton considers the relationship between older formats and technologies associated with past decades, such as vinyl and VHS tape which "take on renewed meanings within a digital age". Collectors of cult films and film soundtracks treasure releases on older non-digital release formats which "become enhanced within cult communities" (Sexton 2015: 12). Older technologies of sound reproduction and exhibition become imbued with nostalgia for the past. This is consolidated and exemplified in recent films which pay homage to earlier eras of filmmaking and exhib-ition, such as Quentin Tarantino and Roberto Rodriguez's *Grindhouse* (2007) which adds fake crackles, pops and bloops reminiscent of a scratched optical soundtrack to its opening, and also *Berberian Sound Studio* (2013): "the setting of the film in a sound studio signals the importance of the sonic, whilst the analogue nature of the sound studio foregrounds its retro-dimensions via mise-en-scene" (Sexton 2015: 23). The analogue sound equipment of the studio's setting is depicted via intense close-ups and detailed sound design that foregrounds the clicks, hums and whirrs of its analogue mechanics, in contrast to the cold 'silence' of contemporary digital sound equipment:

> If digital technologies are valued for their use value (more mobile, more 'spread-able' and accessible), then analogue technologies, like the 'vintage' film content that is revalued by these cultures, also attain a cultish aura, prized for their almost sacred nature.
>
> (Sexton 2015: 27)

Berberian Sound Studio can be understood as what Philip Drake, in his work on *Jackie Brown* (1997), terms "retro cinema"; the sounds of technology in Joakim Sundström's sound design for *Berberian Sound Studio* function like the songs in *Jackie Brown* to "re-key narrative events, evoking an associational structure of feeling of the period" (Drake 2003: 193). Hence, the need to consider 'old' sound in relation to the 'old' (that is, nostalgic) aspects of cult cinema.

Cult sounds? Sonic quotation, parody and transcultural exchange

The examples of Tarantino and Rodriguez's faked sonic parody of the distorted 'grindhouse' soundtrack, and *Berberian Sound Studio*'s analogue sonic homage, point to the important role of quotation and parody in any discussion of cult film sound. Beyond homage to old sound technology and its associated non-signifying noises, there are many cases of particular sound-track elements (voice, dialogue and sound effects) that could be considered 'cult'. In fact, 'quotable' dialogue is perhaps the most important sound element of any cult film and worthy of a more systematic and detailed study beyond the scope of this chapter. In addition, there are types of voice and vocal performance that can be considered cult, in the context of cult stardom, cult characters and cult actors. While Umberto Eco's seminal essay on *Casablanca* (1942) might refer to the audience practice of quoting revered lines of dialogue from the film, Barbara Klinger's more recent work (2015) uncovers "pre-cult" transmedial aspects of Humphrey Bogart's stardom across film, radio, television and beyond. Klinger combines sound studies with cult film studies to highlight "transmedial Bogey's" distinctive heavily accented nasal voice and dialogue delivery as having a contemporaneous cult following, as well as later becoming associated with, and widely parodied, as a characterising sound of 1940s Hollywood detective drama and film noir. Arguably, all cult actors, characters and stars have voice as an element of their cult performance, however some are especially celebrated for the distinctiveness of their voice and vocal delivery, for example Christopher Walken and Werner Herzog. An unusual and notable example of a cult sound effect is the "Wilhelm scream" – a series of male screams originally recorded during the production of Warner Bros *Distant Drums* (1951), added to Warners' sound effects library, and later reused to such an extent that it developed its name and became a 'quotable' sound effect amongst professional sound designers, appearing in hundreds of feature films and television programmes (*Hollywood Lost and Found* 2010). Beyond being a professional in-joke, there is wide awareness of the "Wilhelm scream" amongst film buffs and fans of historical Hollywood, as evidenced by the circulation of YouTube video compilations of the scream.

Voice, technology and political economy intersect when discussing non-Anglophone cinemas with cult status amongst Anglophone audiences – consider how Hong Kong and Italian popular cinema have been celebrated and parodied as characterised by poor lip-synching. In his essay on sound and music in Hong Kong cinema, Gary Needham highlights a sequence in *Wayne's World 2* (1993) which switches into an audiovisual parody of Hong Kong martial arts movies, complete with poorly dubbed and poorly sychronised English-language dialogue. Needham eloquently describes how this Anglophone perception of Hong Kong popular cinema arose from the circulation of cheaply re-dubbed English language versions which in no way reflected the slicker, more professional quality of typical sound post-production in Hong Kong in the 1970s. Moreover, in his earlier discussion of Italian *giallo*, Needham points out "the limitations of genre theory built primarily on American film genres [and] the need for redefinition concerning how other popular film-producing nations understand and relate to their products" (2008: 295). The 'cult' descriptor is slippery, and encompasses many genres, cycles and conceptual categories which are in themselves difficult to delineate; furthermore, acknowledging the limitations described by Needham further highlights the problem of defining the terms of 'cult sound' for the purposes of this chapter.

It is important to acknowledge therefore that my discussion of cult sound is very much informed by a Western Anglophone 'ear' for the soundtrack and contextualised mainly by English language criticism and scholarship on the topic. In this respect, Nezih Erdogan's work on sound in popular Turkish cinema stands out as a landmark intersection of film sound studies and non-Anglophone cult film studies. In his work on the use of post-production dubbing in Yeşilçam films of the 1970s he notes how the disunity of voice and body, through poor lip-synching, though generally associated with 'low'/sloppy production values creates a melodramatic excess, with the voice functioning almost as an interior voice (Erdogan 2002: 239) or the voice of a sort of puppet master in which the actor is "be-spoken" (Erdogan 2002: 243). Refreshingly, Erdogan moves analysis of sound in these films away from a banal discussion of 'good' and 'bad' sound, finding useful ways to theorise the Yeşilçam soundtrack away from the Anglophone bias in film sound studies.

Regarding film sound, the 'bad', the 'old' and the 'weird' are complex and culturally contingent categories which contribute to questions of taste, better understood as sonic taste frameworks. These frameworks have a counterpoint in critical approaches to cult cinema – as well as there being a cult 'canon', cult cinema can be understood as oppositional to a more respectable art house 'canon' or Hollywood 'canon'. As a way to consider how these frameworks converge and diverge, I shall finish by considering three brief case studies: a 'good' cult film with 'bad' sound, a 'good' cult film with 'good' sound, and a 'bad' cult film with 'good' sound.

Pink Flamingos (1972)

The early films of director John Waters, 'the Pope of trash', have been long established within the 'canon' of cult cinema, with *Pink Flamingos* (1972) exemplifying his greatest (or lowest) excesses. The plot, in which two sets of characters (played by an ensemble of Waters regulars, most prominently Divine) compete for the title of 'filthiest people alive', self-reflexively celebrates bad taste in an oppositional fashion to mainstream or good taste. However, its trashiness or 'bad'-ness is invested with (sub)cult(ural) capital by the voiced intentions of its director, who distinguishes between "good bad taste" versus "bad bad taste".

> It's easy to disgust someone; I could make a ninety-minute film of people getting their limbs hacked off, but this would only be bad bad taste and not very stylish or original. To understand bad taste one must have very good taste.
>
> (Waters 1995: 2; quoted in Mendik and Schneider 2002: 204)

Hence, *Pink Flamingos* is a 'good' cult film, but with 'bad' sound.

'Bad' sound in this context can be understood as sound that is technically limited, or sound that falls short of a professional/Hollywood standard. By his own admission, Waters had problems with dialogue intelligibility in his early films; *Pink Flamingos'* predecessor *Multiple Maniacs* (1970) was recently digitally restored to include "dialogue that I've never even heard before because the sound was so bad" (Waters, interviewed in Brady 2016). His early films used a single system film camera obtained cheaply, of a type typically used in news reporting rather than professional feature filmmaking, which meant that the sound (as Waters's producer Robert Maier recalls):

> had always been a problem for John's films. Single system film was not meant for duplication and was a pain to edit. It is a miracle that *Pink Flamingos* survived with any sound. The single system news camera recorded sound on a thin magnetic strip on the side of the film. To add music or narration, John had to record directly onto the film. If he missed a cue, he would record over the original dialogue and it would be lost forever.
>
> (Maier 2012)

However, working with technological limitations contributed to the flourishes and excesses that have come to characterise the sound of Waters's early films. *Pink Flamingos'* soundtrack lacks subtlety and is characterised by over-the-top shrilly delivered voiceover, 'mute' sequences with non-diegetic music and little or no added sound effects or location sound, and abrupt jumps from music sequences to sequences with location sound. Waters effectively brags about the technical limitations in which he was working: "I edited [*Pink Flamingo*] in the attic of my house with the most pitiful tools imaginable. [...] The extra sound was recorded directly onto a magnetic projector that sometimes worked" (Waters 1995: 17), in keeping with the somewhat romanticised picture of the maverick low-budget filmmaker, the cult figure of the 'Pope of

Trash' in waiting, battling the technical and budgetary odds. Sound that is 'bad' compared with Hollywood sound becomes a trashy low-budget badge of honour in this instance.

Waters has recently admitted that he would instruct the actors to "scream and overreact [...] we were using really bad sound equipment, I just wanted to make sure people could hear the dialogue" (*HMV.com* 2017). He contrasts the tone of performance in his later films with that of his earlier films: "I mean take Mink [Stole], who in *Serial Mom* [1994] gives this beautifully natural and funny performance, in this movie [*Multiple Maniacs*] she's yelling and screaming and being crazy" (*HMV.com* 2017). Hence, the technical limitations of low-budget filmmaking contribute to the sound aesthetic and by extension a performance aesthetic that is central to Waters's early films' appeal. In an article positing *Pink Flamingos* as a key piece of resistant queer filmmaking, Anna Breckon celebrates Divine's "high-pitched monotonous shriek" in the execution scene near the end of the film, proclaiming victory "in the name of filth" (2013: 516). The shrieks of Edith Massey's voice, Divine's voice, and the hysterical vocal performances throughout *Pink Flamingos* may have been borne out of technical problems but deliver a key pleasure of the film's sound.

Eraserhead (1977)

Pink Flamingos, and the next case study, David Lynch's *Eraserhead* (1977), share an association with the midnight movie cinema exhibition scene of the 1970s and 1980s; indeed in 1985 *Eraserhead* was described as "one of the most persistent and successful cult films of the midnight and art house circuits" (Godwin quoted in Todd 2012: 25). In his introduction to the foundational edited collection *Sound Theory, Sound Practice* (1991), Rick Altman calls for a shift towards the study of "cinema as event" and away from "film as text", a tantalising glimpse into how film sound studies and cult film studies could converge. Following from Altman's argument, an ear for cult sound recognises the importance of exhibition contexts to the process of cultification, and the associated sound environment and use of sound technology as contributing a particular sonic ambience. It considers the differences between viewing a scratched print of *Eraserhead* with optical sound at midnight in a downtown movie theatre in early 1980s New York City, on VHS at 3 A.M. at a house party in Dublin in the late 1990s, or watching a digital file via a laptop with headphones at home in 2018. It considers the material dimensions of the technologies of storage and exhibition of the film (including its sound), as well as the sonic dimensions of the exhibition experience.

The era of midnight movies coincided with the decline of the downtown areas of major US cities as a result of 'white flight' and suburbanisation. Small downtown cinemas, operating on narrow margins with deteriorating facilities, started to cater for more niche tastes, and the midnight movies catered for a more student and bohemian crowd, as opposed to the more family-oriented suburban cinemas (Waller 1991). Little is written about the sound exhibition conditions in these cinemas, but a particularly insalubrious sub-set that screened pornographic films, known as the 'pornies' (as depicted in contemporaneous films such as *Midnight Cowboy* [1969] and *Taxi Driver* [1976]), have been described as having particularly poor sound: "The dialogue of the films is absolutely incomprehensible, and the easy-listening music that predominates is distorted and wobbly beyond belief, like something coming from underwater" (Stevenson 1996: 31). This is an extreme example of the sub-optimal sound exhibition conditions associated with run-down downtown movie theatres of the 1970s, yet as the example of *Grindhouse* demonstrates, there is an affection for the specific types of noise and 'bad' sound associated with the midnight movie circuit of that time.

Watching the films of that era now, via digitally restored prints, will therefore be a different kind of sonic experience (just as Waters's claim that he can now hear previously unheard lines of dialogue in *Multiple Maniacs* strongly implies). Yet there remain other kinds of noise in the audioviewing experience of these film texts. While both *Eraserhead* and *Pink Flamingos* have 'noisy' soundtracks, *Pink Flamingos'* 'noisy' soundtrack is a product of the technical ignorance of Waters and his inexperienced crew, whereas sound in *Eraserhead* is the work of acclaimed sound designer Alan Splet. Splet was given greatly extended time to work on the sound in the film and remained a close collaborator with David Lynch until Splet's untimely death in 1994. As Liz Greene explains, Splet held "a privileged position within the film industry" and was certainly not "a typical example of a sound designer and music editor"; instead he "is a great example of what could be possible" through his collaborative relationship with Lynch (Greene 2016: 19).

Eraserhead is a strange film to experience, set in a bleak dystopian rendition of a dark run-down urban post-industrial wasteland, perhaps mirroring the surroundings of viewers in the dilapidated downtown theatres of the midnight movie circuit. The world of the film is experienced via the perspective of its bewildered lead character Henry, in which the relentlessly noisy industrial soundscape plays a crucial role:

> In the film a complex relationship between synchronous and asynchronous sound exists due to the strange world Lynch creates. [...] The industrial wasteland is visually shown in an early sequence, but it is the soundscape that continues this industrial bed of noisiness throughout the film, the noisy low-end rumbling hum continues and rarely ceases. The industrial warehouses are not seen again, but the soundtrack asynchronously provides the disturbing mood to the domestic settings of Henry's home life. The world sounds menacing to Henry: it is a horror film based in a surreal world.
>
> (Greene 2016: 22)

Unlike *Pink Flamingos,* the soundtrack of *Eraserhead* embraces noise artistically. *Eraserhead* stands out as a hybrid 'art-cult' feature, compared with *Pink Flamingos* 'trash' status: similarly, the film contrasts with *Pink Flamingos* by virtue of the artistry of its sound design. *Eraserhead*'s sound blurs boundaries between sound design and score, to the extent that the strange noise of the sound design has become highly influential upon underground 'noise' musicians, indicative of "prior cultist attachments to films and soundtracks, involving cross-media interactions between film and music" (Sexton 2015: 22). Hence, sound in *Eraserhead* is a key element of its cult appreciation: *Eraserhead* is therefore a 'good' cult film with 'good' sound.

Star Wars (1977)

Star Wars (1977) is an example of "mass cult" (Grant 1991: 122), rather than the more obscure and underground films more typically treated as cult 'canon'. It is one of the most popular films in the world, yet has earned a (contested) status as cult by virtue of the cult adoration of its fans, manifested by the prevalence of *Star Wars* conventions, the personal (and financial) investment of fans in the franchise, and so forth. It is of interest here by virtue of its celebrated sound design by Ben Burtt, working in collaboration with director George Lucas, which moved away from the theremin-driven bleeps and bloops of earlier sci-fi towards a more 'natural' sound aesthetic. It also features what Kevin Donnelly defines as sound "stars" such as the distinctive buzzing hum of the lightsabre, and the tweets and chirps of R2D2 (quoted in Hills 2011: 29). Burtt is also credited with using the "Wilhelm scream" discussed earlier at strategic points in the film, which further invests *Star Wars* with sound-specific cult status. As "mass cult", *Star Wars* is therefore a 'bad' cult film with 'good' sound.

Writing in 1978 (and republished in 1985), Charles Schreger describes 1970s America as "sound obsessed", with a hugely successful music and record industry embracing hi-fi technologies, and cinema exhibition comparatively lacking good quality sound (Schreger 1985; see also Wurtzler 2009). The late 1970s saw a few directors embrace the potential of Dolby noise reduction technology, initially used in music, then concert films (such as *The Grateful Dead* [1977] and *Tommy* [1975]). The release of *Star Wars* has been celebrated in film sound studies as one of several high-profile watershed releases of the period that embraced the creative and technological potential of sound design (see also Sergi 2004). This is partly attributed to the creative freedom afforded to Burtt – who is said to have spent six months experimentally collecting sound recordings for use in the design of well-known *Star Wars* characters (Schreger 1985: 352) – as well as Dolby noise reduction technology's capacity for reproducing greater sonic detail. In the words of Walter Murch, whose work on *Apocalypse Now* (1979) has been similarly celebrated: "*Star Wars* was the can opener that made people realize not only the effect of sound, but the effect that good sound had at the box office" (Murch, in Biskind 1998: 335). Not only is this an example of what Whittington describes as the symbiotic relationship between sound technology and science fiction sound design, with a fantastical special-effects driven blockbuster such as *Star Wars* providing the ideal showcase for sound design 'whooshes' rendered in Dolby stereo, it also demonstrates a correlation between the rise of the sound designer, the rise of Dolby, the rise of the multiplex, and the rise of the blockbuster; an interrelationship between production technology, aesthetics, exhibition technology and film genre. Gianluca Sergi argues that

> contemporary sound is one of the leading Hollywood exports in technological, aesthetic and financial terms. [...] American companies have established a virtual domination of the world market insofar as sound technology is concerned. Thus there is little doubt that Hollywood ought to be identified as the home of contemporary sound [...].
>
> (Sergi 2004: 5)

Conclusion

In this chapter I have attempted to 'sound out' cult film studies, as well as use cult film studies as a way to highlight gaps and biases in film sound studies. Given Altman's 1991 plea to shift from "film as text" to "cinema as event", there is an affinity between the two fields, and although I have highlighted some works that bring the two together, it is surprising how 'deaf' cult film studies is to the soundtrack, especially the non-musical soundtrack.

Questions of taste, especially of 'good' and 'bad' sound, have been at the forefront of my discussion. I have used these categories playfully rather than definitively, as a way of getting away from the idea of sound as being a purely technical process which can be objectively measured as 'good' or 'bad', much as 'bad'-ness in cult film generally is a complex descriptor, yet one that is intrinsic to the cult cinema fan. In celebrating 'bad' sound and its integral role in cult cinema appreciation, I am wary of the danger of devaluing the craft of sound personnel and the art of the sound designer, given the extent that the work of sound professionals is typically devalued in the film industry. My discussion of the celebrated work of Ben Burtt and Alan Splet is meant to ameliorate this danger to some extent. Nevertheless, just as cult cinema's appreciation of 'trash' acts as a corrective to 'art' cinema's serious aspirations, an exploration of 'bad' sound is designed to act as a corrective to a perhaps idealised discussion of the soundtrack's creative possibilities, taking in a whole swathe of sonic representations and experiences not previously considered.

References

Altman, Robert, ed. 1991. *Sound Theory, Sound Practice*. New York: Routledge.

Biskind, Peter. 1998. *Easy Riders, Raging Bulls*. New York: Simon and Schuster.

Brady, Tara. 2016. "John Waters: The Filth and the Funny," *Irish Times*, 9 November 2016. www.irishtimes.com/culture/film/john-waters-the-filth-and-the-funny-1.2858154 (accessed 31/7/2017).

Breckon, Ann. 2013. "The Erotic Politics of Disgust: *Pink Flamingos* as Queer Political Cinema," *Screen*, 54.4: 514–533.

Birtwistle, Andy. 2012. *Cinesonica: Sounding Film and Video*. Manchester: Manchester University Press.

Coyle, Rebecca. 2008. "Spooked by Sound: *The Blair Witch Project*," in Hayward, Peter, ed., *Terror Tracks: Music, Sound and Horror Cinema*. London: Equinox: 213–228.

Drake, Philip. 2003. "'Mortgaged to Music': New Retro Movies in 1990s Hollywood Cinema," in Grainge, Paul, ed., *Memory and Popular Film*. Manchester: Manchester University Press: 183–201.

Eco, Umberto. 2008. "*Casablanca*: Cult Movies and Intertextual Collage," in Mathijs, Ernest, and Mendik, Xavier, eds, *The Cult Film Reader*. Maidenhead: Open University Press: 67–75.

Erdogan, Nezih. 2002. "Mute Bodies, Disembodied Voices: Notes on Sound in Turkish Popular Cinema," *Screen*, 43.3: 233–249.

Grant, Barry Keith. 1991. "Science Fiction Double Feature: Ideology in the Cult Film," in Telotte, J.P., ed., *The Cult Film Experience: Beyond All Reason*. Austin: University of Texas Press: 122–137.

Greene, Liz. 2016. "From Noise: Blurring the Boundaries of the Soundtrack," in Greene, Liz, and Kulezic-Wilson, Danijela, eds, *Palgrave Handbook of Sound Design and Music in Screen Media: Integrated Soundtracks*. Basingstoke: Palgrave Macmillan: 17–32.

Hayward, Philip. 2004. *Off the Planet: Music, Sound and Science Fiction Cinema*. London: John Libbey.

Hayward, Philip. 2009. *Terror Tracks: Music, Sound and Horror Cinema*. Sheffield: Equinox.

Hills, Matt. 2011. "Listening from Behind the Sofa? The (Un)earthly Roles of Sound in BBC Wales' *Doctor Who*," *New Review of Film and Television Studies*, 9.1: 28–41.

HMV.com. 2017. "It was a punk movie before anyone knew what punk was…" hmv.com talks to John Waters about *Multiple Maniacs*." www.hmv.com/video/john-waters-interview-mulitple-maniacs-criterion-collection (accessed 31/7/2017).

Hollywood Lost and Found. 2010. "The Wilhelm Scream." http://hollywoodlostandfound.net/wilhelm.html (accessed 30/8/2017).

Johnston, Nessa. 2012. "Beneath Sci-fi Sound: *Primer*, Science Fiction Sound Design, and American Independent Cinema," *Alphaville: Journal of Film and Screen Media* 3. www.alphavillejournal.com/Issue%203/HTML/ArticleJohnston.html (accessed 31/7/2017).

Klinger, Barbara. 2015. "Pre-Cult: *Casablanca*, Radio Adaptation, and Transmedia in the 1940s," *New Review of Film and Television Studies*, 13.1: 45–62.

Leydon, Rebecca. 2004. "*Forbidden Planet*: Effects and Affects in the Electro Avant Garde," in Hayward, Philip, ed., *Off the Planet: Music, Sound and Science Fiction Cinema*. London: John Libbey.

Maier, Robert. 2012. "Divine's Lost Underground Baltimore Movie-'Vacancy'," *Rober Maier* [blog/website]. http://robertmaier.us/2012/08/31/divines-lost-underground-baltimore-movie-vacancy/ (accessed 31/7/2017).

Mathijs, Ernest, and Mendik, Xavier, eds. 2008. *The Cult Film Reader*. Maidenhead: Open University Press.

Mendik, Xavier, and Steven Jay Schneider, eds. 2002 *Underground U.S.A.: Filmmaking beyond the Hollywood Canon*. London: Wallflower Press.

Needham, Gary. 2008. "Playing with Genre: An Introduction to the Italian giallo," in Mathijs, Ernest, and Mendik, Xavier, eds, *The Cult Film Reader*. Maidenhead: Open University Press: 294–300.

Needham, Gary. 2009. "Sound and Music in Hong Kong Cinema," in Harper, Graeme, Doughty, Ruth, and Eisentraut, Jochen, eds, *Sound and Music in Film and Visual Media: A Critical Overview*. London: Bloomsbury: 363–374.

Schaefer, Eric. 1999. *Bold! Daring! Shocking! True! A History of Exploitation Films, 1919–1959*. Durham, NC: Duke University Press.

Schreger, Charles. 1985. "Altman, Dolby and the Second Sound Revolution," in Weis, Elisabeth, and John, Belton, eds, *Film Sound: Theory and Practice*. New York: Columbia University Press.

Sconce, Jeffrey. 1995. "'Trashing' the Academy: Taste, Excess, and an Emerging Politics of Cinematic Style," *Screen*, 36.4: 371–393.

Sergi, Gianluca. 2004. *The Dolby Era: Film Sound in Contemporary Hollywood*. Manchester: Manchester University Press.

Sexton, Jamie. 2015. "Creeping Decay: Cult Soundtracks, Residual Media, and Digital Technologies," *New Review of Film and Television Studies*, 13.1: 12–30.

Spadoni, Robert. 2007. *Uncanny Bodies: The Coming of Sound Film and the Origins of the Horror Genre*, Berkeley: University of California Press.

Stevenson, Jack. 1996. "The Day They Turned the Lights Up: A Tribute to the Late Great American Porn Theatre," in Jaworzyn, Stefan, ed., *Shock: The Essential Guide to Exploitation Cinema*. London: Titan: 23–31.

Todd, A. 2012. *Authorship and the Films of David Lynch*. London: I.B. Tauris.

Waller, Gregory A. 1991. "Midnight Movies, 1980–1985: A Market Study," in Tellotte, J.P., ed., *The Cult Film Experience: Beyond All Reason*. Austin: University of Texas Press.

Waters, John. 1995. *Shock Value: A Tasteful Book about Bad Taste*. New York: Thunder's Mouth Press.

Whittington, William. 2007. *Sound Design and Science Fiction*. Austin: University of Texas Press.

Whittington, William. 2014. "Horror Sound Design," in Benshoff, Harry M., ed., *A Companion to Horror Film*. Oxford: Wiley: 168–185.

Wurtzler, Steve. 2009. *Electric Sounds: Technological Change and the Rise of Corporate Mass Media*. New York: Columbia University Press.

PART VII

Aesthetics and intermediality

Cult film aesthetics

Since cult films are often described in terms of 'openness', and as 'mad', weird' and 'wonderful', it is no surprise that their looks and style are called extraordinary. Often extravagant, cult films appear as if they are all over the place: inspired by too many loosely organized efforts for expressing ideas that are impossible to contain in a single film text and affected by desires for innovation and experimentation frequently outmatching filmmakers' abilities. Overall, 'waste' is a key feature.

This section aims to look beyond some of the elements of look and style of cult cinema that have been discussed elsewhere (see Mathijs and Mendik 2008, for a summary of cult cinema's anatomy). Several elements remain at the forefront, because they influence every debate about the aesthetics of cult cinema: hyperbole, excess, and roughness (or 'un-finishedness'). Above all, this section aims to 'ground' these key characteristics in practices and routines (or sometimes lack of protocol) used to make cult films. The idea of 'making' here is to be understood as an effort that occurs on the side of the production culture (talent and crew involved in the manufacturing and presentation of the film) and the side of reception culture (audiences, fans, friends and foes, and society as a whole).

As John Thornton Caldwell (2008) has pointed out, film production culture is characterized by hyperbole, excess, and self-reflexivity. Filmmakers and crews have a high degree of awareness about the value of their work (sometimes an inflated sense of entitlement), and the way labour is organized in the various corners of the film industry is often wasteful – not only in terms of equipment, machinery, and engineering (powering a film set is expensive), but also, importantly, in terms of 'wasting' human resources. Mathijs and Sexton have noted (2011) that this is all the more the case with cult cinema. Films are often works of love where labour, in a wide variety of applications, is produced generously, often with little financial or meritorious reward. As such, cult cinema labour fits the proverbial 'labour of love' tag, which Andrew Ross (1989) assigns to it in his study of camp aesthetics and its sociological significance – both in making and in enjoying the work.

This section looks at the aesthetics of cult cinema as a result of techniques, tactics, accidents, and experiments of labour – of work as the result of effort fuelled by intentions and imaginations. The issue of achievement is almost incidental in this perspective. Cult films often set out to be high quality, and as demonstrations of skill and talent, in terms of how they are made and how ideas are executed, but often they do not achieve such goals (cult films are still frequently 'failures'), and equally often the reception (the area where a film's cult status is decided) does not match the production intentions or efforts, and certainly not the aesthetic imaginations of the crews who devoted their time and labour to it. If one looks at the production histories of *Freaks* (Browning, 1932), *Casablanca* (Curtiz, 1943), *Plan 9 From Outer Space* (Wood, 1959), *The Rocky Horror Picture Show* (Sharman, 1975), or *The Room* (Wiseau, 2003), they are marked by incidental events, unplanned occurrences, and haphazard situations.

Viewers work too, by completing a film and turning it into a cultural object. In cult cinema, reception labour is highly significant, because audiences, often of wildly diverse plumage (and equally often unintended audiences), mine films for significance against the aesthetics offered to them – viewers read into film, and in the case they read against the grain, against protocols and routines assigned to them (-for instance by watching at times not usually associated with 'proper' spending of effort. In other words: a waste of time (see Mathijs 2010). I.Q. Hunter's arguments about the diverse interpretations of *Blade Runner* (Scott, 1982) and the mining of the work of Stanley Kubrick (through *Room 237* [Ascher, 2012]) are cases in point.

The first three chapters in this section discuss specific techniques of aesthetic labour, as expressed in special effects, character representations, and costumes and props design. Working from extensive empirical research into the production of special effects, Leon Gurevitch discusses how cult cinema aesthetics are often governed and inspired by 'practical effects.' Unlike digital effects, which have become the norm for the film industry, and hence for much of production culture, practical effects rely on analogue technology and – above all – on physical sets (set design, make up, creatures, dummies, backgrounds, light flares …) that give a film a feeling of being grounded in 'real imagination' (as opposed to computer- or algorithmically generated imagery and soundscapes). In terms of labour, Gurevitch notes, this attitude matches an expression of a desire for control over a creation as well as demonstrations of craftsmanship. *Even when* this attitude does not diminish these artists excitement of working with digital effects (an example of the wastefulness of generosity and desire typical for cult cinema), the 'labour of the real' is seen as 'way cooler' than that of digital effects. In the chapter on props and costumes, Tamao Nakahara moves from production culture to 'production play' in order to pronounce the mutual efforts of producers and fans in making meaning of films as cultist actions – acts in search of completest desires, for instance, and for multilevel interpretations. In this sense, costumes and props, as they appear in films are ammunition for viewers to 'play' with texts, wastefully (also see the chapter by Lynn Zubernis, which emphasizes cult collecting in particular). Nakahara zooms in on Harry Potter props, but also highlights costumes, rooms, and accessories from *The Rocky Horror Picture Show* as well as soap operas and comedy to illustrate how the labour involved in production play intimately connects the physical placement of material objects in films with the mental moving of those objects by viewers in an effort to give meaning to them. In the conclusion of her chapter, Nakahara mentions the 'acting body' as a site of cult aesthetics. This site is examined in detail in the chapter by Jörg Sternagel on 'mad characters'. In using the performance of Heath Ledger as The Joker as a case study, Sternagel reminds us that in cult cinema, often, the performance is not an acting body, but a textual property, that, as he puts it, "does not allow any opportunity to retreat from what is happening on screen". The act of unbalanced representation as a technique of aesthetics in cult cinema is one that puts 'mad' characters at the forefront of their appeal. Our section on cult cinema and acting (section IX) elaborates further on these aesthetics by presenting them as a fugitive item across and beyond texts: if one takes one look at how the performances and reputations of Judy Garland Dennis Hopper, Barbara Steele, Klaus Kinski, Bruce Lee, Crispin Glover, or Heath Ledger (to return to Sternagel's case study), as expressed in fandom, criticism, or biographical accounts, exists 'mad' becomes a more general term, even if guised as 'extravagant, 'excessive', 'hyperbolic' or veiled in identity political terms such as 'macho', 'intense', 'brute', 'hysterical', 'scream queen', 'foreigner', 'childish', and equally often diverted into positions of cultural rebellion such as 'outsider', 'misfit' or 'outcast'.

The last two chapters, by I.Q. Hunter and Stacey Abbott, extend the aesthetics of cult cinema to other media, novels and television, respectively. As I.Q. Hunter argues, novels that have received cult status (he singles out H.P. Lovecraft and William Burroughs, amongst others) often generate different kinds of cults than the films that adapt such texts, yet as remediations and intertextual re-interpretations (in other words, though the labour of the reader) they both single out aesthetics – look and style as a form of openness that activates that reader. Similarly, Abbott singles out the textual (and indeed multitextual) plenitude of cult television, and a decided focus on 'looks', as a shared characteristic of cult television and cult cinema, one that demands interpretive labour on behalf of the viewer. Abbott notes that cult films as remakes of already existing cult television series generate confusion with fans, often creating the impression that some cult television is "indigenous" to that medium. In particular, the serial openness of television, or its ability to open up aesthetic avenues across credit sequences and episodes (and sometimes deliver entire chunks of a season situated, and therefore, looking as 'elsewhere) can make series such as *Star Trek* and *Twin Peaks* stand separate from their film companions. However, more recently, Abbott writes, increases in cross-media productions (series based on films on series etc., or serialized stories appearing across platforms) have created a fluidity that, typically for cult, can be seen as a stimulator for both fan labour and the labour of productions (and the fluidity of boundaries between them) – an 'endless openness' as it were.

Whether open wide, mad, play-ish, or cool in how they connect the labour of producers to that of audiences, cult cinema aesthetics retain the overall feeling that they are used beyond the bounds of moderations – wastefully.

References

Caldwell, John Thornton. 2008. *Production Culture: Reflexivity and Critical Practice in Film and Television.* Durham, NC: Duke University Press.

Mathijs, Ernest. 2010. "Time Wasted." *Flow TV: A Critical Forum on Media and Culture* (March 29): online at: www.flowjournal.org/2010/03/time-wasted-ernest-mathijs-the-university-of-british-columbia/. Accessed April 2019.

Mathijs, Ernest, and Xavier Mendik (eds). 2008. *The Cult Film Reader.* New York: McGraw-Hill.

Mathijs, Ernest and Jamie Sexton. 2011. *Cult Cinema.* New York: Wiley.

Ross, Andrew. 1989. *No Respect: Intellectuals and Popular Culture.* London: Routledge.

33

INSIDE AN ACTOR'S SCRAPBOOK

Heath Ledger's aesthetic practice of *unbalancing*

Jörg Sternagel

From Conrad Veidt's starring role in Paul Leni's *The Man Who Laughs* (1928) to Jared Leto's brief appearance as the Joker in David Ayer's *Suicide Squad* (2016), one permanent possibility for human subjectivity has moved into visibility through actors: *madness*, which illuminates human nature as such, picturing that subjectivity cannot be genuinely comprehended, and would not be what it is, as Jacques Lacan reminds us, "without madness as the limit of its freedom" (2006 [1947]: 144). Madness is "freedom's most faithful companion, following its every move like a shadow", rather than "resulting from a contingent fact – the frailties of his organism – madness is the permanent virtuality of a gap opened up in his essence" (ibid.: 144). It is exactly this gap that is also opened up by actors, in "mad" or "insane" acting, through altered states, seemingly uncontrolled by reason or judgement, ruinously imprudent and/or extravagantly, wildly foolish, carried away, filled with enthusiasm, excited and exciting, infatuating and infatuated. These openings are especially performed by actors who dare to grasp their meaning, to treat them, like Maurice Merleau-Ponty describes, as "modalities and variations of the subject's total being" (Merleau-Ponty 2002: 123–124). Think of Nicolas Cage, Danny Glover, Klaus Kinski, Juliette Lewis, Margot Robbie, Gena Rowlands, Romy Schneider, or Tommy Wiseau, who all achieve to make visible a *phenomenology of madness* as an expression of the subject's total being that pays reverential homage to the permanent virtuality of the gap opened up in the essence of freedom and has therefore produced several works of art that might be categorized as "cult", especially if this gap is also filled with the addition of the subjectivity of a clown, a pantomime or harlequinade, a fool or jester as a stage or screen character, but also as an ambiguous, mysterious and even uncanny being on the screen. Think of Tim Curry as Pennywise on the TV screen in the mini-series *Stephen King's It* (Tommy Lee Wallace, 1990) or John Carroll Lynch as Twisty in the fourth season of *American Horror Story* titled *Freakshow* (Ryan Murphy, 2014), or go off screen and remember Ronald McDonald welcoming you at his restaurants, or Cindy Sherman's photographs of clowns displayed in galleries (2014), and return to the cinema screen and watch the ensemble in *Balada triste de trompeta* (Alex de Iglesia, 2010), Andy Powers in *Clown* (John Watts, 2014), or Heath Ledger in *The Dark Knight* (Christopher Nolan, 2008):

Opening Heath Ledger's scrapbook

Almost at the end of the German documentary *Too Young to Die: Heath Ledger* (Dag Freyer, 2012), we finally see Heath Ledger's father taking us inside his son's diary, a colorful scrapbook that he made preparing his iconic role of the Joker in *The Dark Knight*: compiling pictures, magazine cuttings, sketches, hand-written notes and more, Heath Ledger briefly guides us through his creative process of bringing a character on screen, where his aesthetic practice of acting with disposition, movement and timing turns out to be a precise practice of *unbalancing* for the purpose of the role of the Joker: Ledger's version of the Joker does not allow any opportunity to retreat from what is happening on screen. Ledger enters as a Joker with long, dark, partly green and greasy hair, an imperfect and sweaty clown's makeup, black gloves and the obligatory purple zoot jacket combined with corresponding vest, shirt and trousers. His threat is experienced via the detailed face, the moving body and its often interrupted rhythm, the changing voice, the wild expressions and turbulent gestures. What Ledger achieves throughout the film is to create a perceptual field that captures situations in which his own subjectivity is pictured as *pathological*. The actor shows a loss of plasticity, distinctive for madness, and thereby visualizes the relation of madness to human existence as such: madness is a constant possibility concerning a subject's vital areas. Inside this actor's scrapbook then means to extract elements from these vital areas, *migrating gestures*, with which we find (1) *repetition and difference* fleshed out of a semiotics of clowning, leading to (2) *performative modalities* cast in dialectical forms including the histrionic and the quotidian, having a body and being a body, providing (3) *paradigms of visibility*, where the first paradigm, *the visibility of the spectacle*, deals with the celebrity Ledger off screen, while the second, *the visibility of recognition*, centers the delight in watching his performance on screen, and the third, continuing with the spectator's experience, within contexts of affect, *pathos* and the performative, renders *the visibility of being*.

Repetition and difference

As soon as Heath Ledger's father, Kim Ledger, takes his son's scrapbook out of a box, laying it on a table for us to see, we become aware of this book as the one where the actor wrote down his notes in preparing his role of the Joker, which is also his chosen scrapped title on the cover of the popular American "eeBoo Elephant & Nemo Composition Notebook" he used (see Figure 33.1). Kim Ledger then successively skips through seven select double pages of the book of which we can briefly catch a glimpse, while pausing the documentary, from double page to double page, frame by frame, allowing us a closer, if partly blurry sight on them: getting inside this actor's scrapbook develops to an extraction of elements from vital areas, *migrating gestures*, that the actor makes visible on screen in the film *The Dark Knight*.[1] These gestures enable us to find patternings of repetition and difference, also fleshed out of a semiotics of *clowning*. In the process of his preparation, Heath Ledger compiles, cuts, sketches, writes, highlights, underlines and scribbles, emphasizes what he finds, (re-)discovers, imagines and remembers from other films, TV, magazines, comics and more. The seven double pages show this work; they appear as an occasional collage of what he pictures as the Joker, a close characterization of an ambiguous figure famous as the antagonist and nemesis of the Batman, drawn from within an ongoing comic universe initiated by the creative team Bill Finger, Bob Kane and Jerry Robinson in 1940, and taken from out of screen adaptations like the TV series *Batman* (1966–1968), directed by Oscar Rudolph and others with Cesar Romero, and the film *Batman* (1989), directed by Tim Burton with Jack Nicholson. No clipping stands alone, no pasting is isolated, every image and every word is followed by another image and another word. The overall impression is that of an actor's characterization of his role to play, which is rich in detail and associative in its combination of image and word, where the word overwrites the image, and conveys a new meaning, as especially on the second double page, where a screen grab is glued on the left page: we see an extreme close up of the actor Malcolm McDowell's face, in character as Alex in *A Clockwork Orange* (Stanley Kubrick, 1971), on which Ledger writes "My psychological makeup is radically different to others". From an outside perspective, Ledger's look on McDowell's face, his expression and gaze, to an inside reflection,

Ledger's thoughts on McDowell's depiction of Alex, as hand-written in the picture by Ledger, we witness a part of a makeup of the Joker himself: repeating notions of the ambiguity of McDowell's variation of Alex, who appears to be wavering in conduct to others, Ledger's version of the Joker learns from this interpretation in creating his character in difference to others. "What's it going to be then, eh?", as an opening question from McDowell, leading to the counterquestion of Ledger, "Why so serious?", guiding both figures through processes of differentiation, containing elements of surprise, unpredictability and uncertainty, leading to constant threats to others. "It is simple: Kill the Batman", we read on another page that is juxtaposed again with an image of McDowell as Alex, this time along with his three fellow actors, the "Droogs", in the infamous Korova milk bar that provides both the setting for Kubrick's establishing shots and a corresponding commercial with McDowell in character of which we also see a scrap by Ledger: "Got Milk?", McDowell's Alex asks, turning toward us with an evil smile. It is about face (see Figure 33.2).

Figure 33.1 Still from *Too Young to Die: Heath Ledger* (*Heath Ledger: Liebling der Götter*, Freyer, GER, 2012), Broadview TV

Figure 33.2 Still from *Too Young to Die: Heath Ledger* (*Heath Ledger: Liebling der Götter*, Freyer, GER, 2012), Broadview TV

From here, Ledger's Joker chooses a "killer smile", as Daniel Wallace remarks in his *Visual History of the Clown Prince of Crime*, while "[c]ritics praised Ledger's portrayal of the Joker as a bringer of anarchy. 'Madness is like gravity,' he says in the film. 'All it takes is a little push'" (Wallace 2011: 196). And, indeed, this push originates in the visual history of the character Ledger embodies, and to whom he especially refers to through select comic panels in his scrapbook, his *Joker log*, with which specifically Alan Moore's and Brian Bolland's 1988 DC comic *Batman: The Killing Joke* comes to mind, where the art and colors of Bolland are combined with the texts of Moore to another variation of a scrapbook: in one panel, we see the Joker's antagonist Commissioner Gordon sitting in his apartment and pasting clippings on Catwoman and the Joker, while in dialog with his daughter Barbara, who points to a possible more professional filing system for these memories on paper (and is later killed by the Joker). In another panel, we see Gordon captured by the Joker, as he shares a contemplation on memories:

> Can we live without them? Memories are what our reason is based upon. If we can't face them, we deny reason itself. Although, why not? We aren't contractually tight down to rationality! There is no sanity clause! So when you find yourself locked onto an unpleasant train of thought, heading for the places in your past where the screaming is unbearable, remember there's always madness. Madness is the emergency exit. You can just step outside, and close the door on all those dreadful things that happened. You can lock them away … forever.

It is the background of the Joker that started his "unpleasant train of thought". In several episodes, we learn that he quit his job as a lab assistant to become a comedian, but missed a punchline in the act, and failed to pursue. Living subsequently in poverty, he gets on a fast track to delinquency, while feeling guilty towards his pregnant wife Jeannie, who later dies of an electric shock by accident testing a baby-bottle heater. "If you hurt inside, get certified, and if life treat you bad … don't get ee-ee-even, get mad!", the Joker then exclaims, as standing in the arena of a circus, addressing his audience.[2] While the character's introspection is supposed to develop as radically different to others, his external observation by others is rendered visible in the same manner: it is in the face. In Ledger's face, we see a clown's face. The facial makeup is drawn from the practice of *clowning*, compared to what Paul Bouissac highlights in the process of facial transformations in clowns:

> The face of the clown is a live mask. It is a mask inasmuch as its makeup hides the identity of the person who has applied it to his or her face. It is alive because, in contrast to a solid mask, it allows the production of all the meaningful muscular contractions that characterize the semiotics of the human face. However, the makeup significantly modifies the natural features to the extent that the communicative potential of the face is constrained in certain aspects. Some elements of the face are enhanced; others are played down. Also, artificial parts are often added.
>
> (Bouissac 2015: 23)

A clown's makeup undergoes a process of crafting that Bouissac exemplifies with the makeup of an Auguste clown, a happy, red type whose facial transformation goes through six stages: beginning with the man behind the clown, the first stage is the "selective reddening of the facial background and painting of a red circle on the chin", the second, "adding patches of white to enhance the signaling properties of the upper teeth and the sclera", continued by taking the color black "to artificially enlarge the pupils as the face will be perceived from a distance by the audience", followed by "augmenting and rounding the upper face to complete the neotonic configuration", "adding the red nose", and finally "capping the skull with a round hat" (Bouissac 2015: 25–32). The Joker's makeup, however, undergoes a process of crafting that uses this example, but modifies it, while similarly the facial transformation goes through six, but very different stages: beginning with Ledger behind the clown, the first stage is the selective whitening of the facial background and using lots of red lipstick around the mouth, the second adding scars of red to enhance the signaling properties of the upper teeth, continued by taking the color black to artificially enlarge the pupils as the face will be perceived close-by from the audience, followed by leaving the upper face as it is, without any augmenting or rounding its upper part, without a red nose, or even a hat, but, instead, with long, dark, partly green and greasy hair. The mask of Ledger's Joker is not thick and impermeable, as if shaped in plaster. The surface of Ledger's face, his mask, is thin and permeable, as if painted in watercolors. Ledger's makeup fades, and his smile stays on (Sternagel 2012: 130). He is visible through the white makeup, as his features literally sweat through it, enhanced through the scars around his mouth that render a permanent smile. It is a lively face allowing the production of muscular contractions indeed, especially when the smile turns to laughter, when all is moving in this face and nothing is played down. In this fashion, Ledger repeats what is familiar in a semiotics of clowning, as the choice of color and design of the makeup, but successively modifies it and manages to act out a difference in the process: neither his own face nor his face of a clown as a live mask allow any retreat when confronting him or being confronted by him. He is in the face of others, of yours and mine, always ready for his close-up. His clown play is a threat, "putting things inside out and upside down" – metaphors that Bouissac uses to describe the ways in which "clowns toy with the norms grounding the personal and social lives of their audience (Bouissac 2015: 175). The Joker toys wrongly though, since his *ludic mode* has serious consequences, it evokes chaos. "Do I really look like a man with a plan?", he asks, "You know what I am? I am a dog chasing cars. I wouldn't know what to do with one if I caught it. You know, I just 'do' things …"

Performative modalities

This line, "I just 'do' things", serves as a trajectory for bringing us back inside this actor's scrapbook, and leads us to the question of what *things* the actor is doing from where. In other words, it inspires to take a closer look at his artistic practice of acting, of showing us who he brings to the screen, who it is who we perceive up there in the theatre. The notes on another of the book's double pages briefly show us excerpts from what might be both lines from the screenplay by Jonathan and Christopher Nolan and/or Ledger's own words, sentences that bring us closer to one particular scene of the film in which Ledger acts out what we have so far become familiar with in the film: the surprising, unsettling, and hardly uncategorizable appearance and incorporation the actor plays out in the scene titled "The Hospital Room", as headlined in the notebook and shown in full in the documentary. It is a scene where, within the diegesis, the Joker meets one of his antagonists Harvey Dent as Two-Face, depicted by Aaron Eckhart, after Dent became Two-Face, losing half of his face in an attack with fire and gasoline initiated by the Joker. "I don't want there any hard feelings between us, Harvey". He, the Joker, does not have a plan, however, he just does things: "Introduce a little anarchy, upset the established order, everything becomes chaos, I am an agent of chaos. And you know the thing about chaos: It's there!" It is the strive for unsettling, for *unbalancing* the established order, and Ledger reflects upon this drive of his character by broadening his *repertoire*: not only does he continue what he has shown in the scenes before, his variation of a clown, but instead adds another costume to the costume he already wears. In the hospital room, he appears as a hospital nurse, in a white uniform, with a clown's makeup, and blurs the lines between anything familiar even further (see Figure 33.3). He does not only achieve another variation of his characterization but deepens the utter confusion of watching him on screen. This variation of the Joker is performed as a primordial matter, from which anything and anybody are shaked inside out and upside down. This variation, though, is in itself brought to the screen not as chaotic at all. It is an act that requires the precision of the actor Ledger to bring this presence to life, to be obliged to the particular moment on set, in a scene, in this scene in the hospital, through the internal attitude of himself, his training, his reflection, as well as through external impulses as provided by the script, the direction and fellow actors, as Eckhart the antagonist in the hospital scene. And this precision is visible not only in the film, but also in its preparation from which we catch a glimpse in his scrapbook, where he writes down, clips, and chooses what adds to his Joker, where certain performative modalities come into play: those modalities as aspects of his things which relate to his ludic mode, in which he wanders between the possible and the impossible, the necessary and the contingent, relating to his faculties of sense, giving his character a personality by inventing ways of behaving.

These ways change from the histrionic to the quotidian and back, they combine hyperbolic gestures of intimidation with small gestures of daily life, where a laugh might be something casual, but is always on the verge of anything out of line, of everything evoking disturbance towards others, an impossible gesture to cope with. As Lesley Stern notes, "Gestures migrate between everyday life and the movies, but where the gestural often goes unnoticed in the everyday, in the cinema (where it travels between the quotidian and the histrionic) it moves into visibility" (2001: 328–329). This acting, leading to this very character, these migrating gestures of the actor's body, his posture, his "body language" are nothing to be locked in any register though, because they move so many registers into visibility at once. The *repertoire* of Ledger here is an open source of influences and inspiration. While the process of *clowning*, with the predecessors, the films and the graphic novels, develops to a process of gaming, *toying* with several possible modalities, the very instance of what Ledger achieves is the Joker as a bearer of confusion. He cannot be pursued, but grasped in his playful fashion, which is anything but harmless, it is harmful, threatening, and very violent. What Ledger evokes is partly a *coulrophobia*,

Figure 33.3 Still from *The Dark Knight* (Nolan, USA, 2008). Warner Bros

a fear of clowns, since he appears to be *disturbing* with his imperfect and sweaty clown's makeup, black gloves and the obligatory purple zoot jacket combined with corresponding vest, shirt and trousers.[3] His threat is experienced via the detailed face, the moving body and its often interrupted rhythm, the changing voice, the wild expressions and turbulent gestures (Hassoun 2015: 3).[4] With Ledger's Joker, we experience a voice that is constantly interrupted by smacking lips, and behold a wild, nervous face, terrifying gazes, threatening postures, quick, turbulent gestures and sudden moves (Hassoun 2015: 13–14).[5] "Ooohhh. You want to play. Come on!", the Joker demands.

Paradigms of visibility

The Joker's demand to play is brought to the screen by Ledger who acts it out within three *paradigms of visibility*.[6]

Visibility of the spectacle

Before the film, Ledger, the actor works up interests in the work, in his fellow-actors, in props and set designs, in the camera, to bring, at least in part, the Joker to life. In sum, his interest, at least on an artistic level, would be to create a role. Before the film, I, in turn, work up an interest for Heath Ledger, as have I experienced him in numerous films before, as in *Monster's Ball* (Marc Forster, 2001), *The Brothers Grimm* (Terry Gilliam, 2005), *Brokeback Mountain* (Ang Lee, 2005), and *I'm Not There* (Todd Haynes, 2007), and therefore decide to be at the movies with him, to watch him in another film. In sum, my interest, on an experiential level, would be to meet again. During the film, Ledger offers variations of his art, variations I am partly familiar with like the tone of his voice, his pronunciation of words, his facial expressions: here, the focus is on the situation of perception during the film, a situation that is also influenced by experiences before or after the film. This is where *the visibility of the spectacle* develops, pointing successively lesser and lesser to Ledger's familiar performing choices and my experience of them, but more and more to his star or celebrity functions. Such a paradigm could be further scrutinized with Richard Dyer, for example, and his thoughts about *Heavenly Bodies*, where the economic importance comes into play and the star is also presented as being fashioned "out of the raw material of the person", where "make-up, coiffure, clothing, dieting and body-building can all make more or less of the body features they start with" (Dyer 1986: 5). Or, it could be interpreted with Guy Debord and his approach in the *Society of the Spectacle* (1962), where I am separated from the celebrity or star in everyday life as the images I see with him, from him are detached from life and only propose an illusionary form of life's unity, where Ledger is "the spectacular representation of a living human being, embodying this banality by embodying the image of a possible role" (Debord 1995: 60).

Visibility of recognition

Whenever actors enter the scene in a film, their depictions and performances also rely on patterns of recognition. Certainly, Nolans's film, too, in his making, to follow James Naremore in *Acting in the Cinema*, is dependent on "a form of communication whereby meanings are acted out", where, once it is released in cinema, my "experience of watching them involves not only a pleasure in storytelling but also a delight in bodies and expressive movement, an enjoyment of familiar performing skills, and an interest in players as 'real persons'" (Naremore 1988: 2). Here, the visibility of the spectacle shifts to *the visibility of recognition* as "the interest in players as 'real persons'" remains influential, while the "delight in bodies and expressive movement" becomes central. The film's decision is to offer a basis for orientation from which a "delight in bodies and expressive movement" can develop. This basis, this center is the face of Ledger. He acts out either familiar or different meanings prominently via his face, while being always ready for the close-up. In his scenes, Ledger's moving, altered face frequently appears at the center of attention whenever he enters and offers both an orientation and a dis-orientation. Here too, "something sharper than a mask is looming", "something sharper", that Roland Barthes sees in the face of actress Greta Garbo, "a kind of voluntary and therefore human relation between the curve of the nostrils and the arch of the eyebrows; a rare, individual function relating two regions of the face" (Barthes 2004: 589–590).

Visibility of being

There is a process of force, of exhaustive search in depicting the Joker's adversary, the anarchical villain, prominently through and with the face of Ledger, with an attention to detail carrying affects at the level of presence, *the visibility of being* as a force of becoming: from out of the face, its expressions, onto the body parts, up and down, sideways, develop a bodily uneasiness with what is rendered visible on screen, centered on and around Ledger's full body, following his bodily traces in a slippery realm of film experience, where unresolved affects might prevail, as the face of Ledger and his body develop to be unraveling – causing uncertainties of how to act within the visual, auditory, and tactile field between the screen, Ledger, and me, for example.[7] The coexistence with the film actor is challenged, and the bodily link to the actor is shakened. The form which is common to both the actor's and the spectator's visual and tactile perceptions is occasionally shattered, the form that both actor and spectator possess, where, according to Merleau-Ponty, "all happens as if the intuitions and motor performances of the other are founded in a kind of internal encroachment, as if my body and the other's form a system" (Merleau-Ponty 2010: 452). The form is my body, and what I learn to consider as the other's body is a possibility of movements for me; thus, as Merleau-Ponty put it: "we can say that the actor's art is only a deepening of an art that we all possess" (ibid.: 453). Ledger's body, his voice impress us as an incident, whereas both our listening and watching, is always a listening *to* and a watching *at*, corresponding to be affected by: we enter the dimension of response, as we respond to what is not ours, what interferes, what is owned by the other. The film experience then evokes *pathos*; it relates to something that is striking and surprising, that is passionate. With Ledger, our acting subject, his performative body, in expressive modality, mobilizing affects, we enter an experience that inflicts itself on ourselves – and this infliction appears, while we are responding to it, in-between the screen, him and us, in-between the other, and ourselves, neither following a scheme of stimulus and reaction nor a principle of cause and effect, as the effect precedes the cause and points to a gap of impossibility as soon as our own sense-making and sensual possibilities are overcome. There is no resolution. "BYE, BYE", he writes in capital letters over one of the last pages of his scrapbook and leaves us *be*.

Notes

1 Lesley Stern (2014) asks:

> What does it mean to speak of gesture in the cinema? Is there any use, any conceptual mileage, to be gained from such a phrase as 'cinematic gesture'? Can we itemise a repertoire of actorly gestures that are cinematically specific, can we describe the semantic content of each, the affect attached, the effect produced?

2 This episode does not take place in a circus, but in a tunnel of horror, where Gordon is sent by a ghost train and welcomed by the Joker. The place of this clown appears to be one of terror and fear.

3 Outside circuses and off screens, clowns have become threatening sightings spreading across the United States and Europe. Therefore, "nobody laughs at clowns anymore." See, for example, *The Guardian*, accessed October 25, 2016: www.theguardian.com/culture/2016/oct/05/clown-sightings-south-carolina-alabam.

4 In a comparative acting analysis between Romero, Nicholson, and Ledger, Dan Hassoun (2015: 13) emphasizes a similar notion while describing Ledger's performance: "the Joker's facial and vocal fluctuations rhetorically function to imply a complexity extending beyond the mask." Ledger's fluctuations indeed go beyond the mask as noted above, but they function not only as rhetorical, since they present themselves as *corporeal*. First set pictures and clips point to a similar approach by Joaquin Phoenix in the latest rendition of the *Joker*, directed by Todd Philips, to be released in 2019.

5 Hassoun also points to Ledger's use of his voice: "His vocal tone shifts registers at unexpected beats, conveying an odd mixture of narcissism, pain, sarcasm, and deathly seriousness from moment to moment. His eyes, which tend to roll back or dart sideward, further sell an image of introspection." Again, there is more, since the actor's introspection transgresses to his fellow actors and us, the spectators, to their and our external observation.

6 These paradigms are suggested as *visibility regimes* by Andrea Mubi Brighenti (2010) in the context of studies of art and surveillance. They provide a useful approach to scrutinize the actor's art and its perception further.

7 A comparable slippery realm of film experience originates from the fragmentized, partly digitalized body of Helena Bonham Carter in Tim Burton's *Alice in Wonderland* (2010), where also different aspects of acting can be highlighted within the three paradigms of visibility. See Jörg Sternagel (2016).

References

Barthes, Roland. 2004. "The Face of Garbo," in Leo Braudy and Marshall Cohen, eds, *Film Theory and Criticism: Introductory Readings*, 6th edition. Oxford: Oxford University Press.

Bouissac, Paul. 2015. *The Semiotics of Clowns and Clowning. Rituals of Transgression and the Theory of Laughter*. London: Bloomsbury.

Brighenti, Andrea Mubi. 2010. "Artveillance: At the Crossroads of Art and Surveillance," *Surveillance & Society*, 7.2: 175–186. www.capacitedaffect.net/2010/Brighenti-2010-Artveillance.pdf.

Debord, Guy. 1995. *The Society of the Spectacle*. New York: Zone Books.

Dyer, Richard. 1986. *Heavenly Bodies. Film Stars and Society*. New York: St. Martin's Press.

Hassoun, Dan. 2015. "Shifting Makeups: The Joker as Performance Style from Romero to Ledger," in Robert Moses Peaslee and Robert G. Weiner, eds, *The Joker: A Serious Study of the Clown Prince of Crime*. Jackson: University Press of Mississippi.

Lacan, Jacques. 2006 [1947]. "Presentation on Psychical Causality," in *Écrits*. New York: Norton.

Merleau-Ponty, Maurice. 2002 [1945]. *Phenomenology of Perception*. London: Routledge.

———. 2010. "The Experience of Others," in *Child Psychology and Pedagogy. The Sorbonne Lectures 1949–1952*. Evanston: Northwestern University Press.

Moore, Alan, and Brian Bolland. 2008. *Batman: The Killing Joke. The Deluxe Edition. Introduction by Tim Sale*. Burbank: DC Comics.

Naremore, James. 1988. *Acting in the Cinema*. Berkeley: University of California Press.

Stern, Lesley. 2001. "Paths That Wind through the Thicket of Things," *Critical Inquiry*, 28.1: 317–354.

———. 2014. "Putting on a Show, or The Ghostliness of Gesture", *LOLA*, 5 November. www.lolajournal.com/5/putting_show.html [Accessed October 25, 2016].

Sternagel, Jörg. 2012. "'Look At Me!': A Phenomenology of Heath Ledger in *The Dark Knight*," in Aaron Taylor, ed., *Theorizing Film Acting*. London: Routledge.

———. 2016. "Performative Modalities of Otherness," in David J. Gunkel, Ciro Marcondes Filho and Dieter Mersch, eds, *The Changing Face of Alterity: Communication, Technology and Other Subjects*. New York: Rowman & Littlefield: 65–86.

Wallace, Daniel. 2011. *The Joker: A Visual History of the Clown Prince of Crime. With an Introduction by Mark Hamill*. New York: Rizzoli.

34

SPECIAL EFFECTS AND THE CULT FILM

Cult film production and analogue nostalgia on the digital effects pipeline

Leon Gurevitch

In 2012 British Hollywood film director Christopher Nolan gave an interesting interview. In an article published in the Directors Guild of America Quarterly (amongst other places) Nolan responded to a question from reporter Jeffrey Ressner as to why he was "among the last holdouts who shoot on film in an industry that's moved to digital", explaining that, while he had felt under increasing pressure over the past ten years to move to digital, he remained with celluloid and the techniques of "practical effects" (also seemingly referred to interchangeably as "physical effects") as much as possible. Explaining his reasoning, Nolan stated that:

> The thing with computer-generated imagery is that it's an incredibly powerful tool for making better visual effects. But I believe in an absolute difference between animation and photography. However sophisticated your computer-generated imagery is, if it's been created from no physical elements and you haven't shot anything, it's going to feel like animation.
>
> (Ressner 2012)

Likely unknown to Nolan, his appeals to both the "physical elements" of pre-digital cinematography, and his distinction between "animation and photography" powerfully echoed theoretical arguments put forward regarding the limits of animation and the importance of photographic cinematography by Siegfried Kracauer some 52 years earlier in his tellingly titled book *Theory of Film: The Redemption of Physical Reality*. Right from its very preface Kracauer argued, in what reads like a statement made by Nolan himself (minus the normative dismissal of colour), that:

> It would be fair to advise the reader at the outset that this book does not include all the things he may be looking for. It neglects the animated cartoon. ... Its exclusive concern is the normal black-and-white film, as it grows out of photography. The reason I confine myself to it is rather obvious: Film being a very complex medium, the best method of getting at its core is to disregard, at least temporarily, its less essential ingredients and varieties.
>
> (Kracauer 1960: vii)

Kracauer's opening here, written in 1960, demonstrates the historical degree to which notions of the "physical" and indexical in image capture have been prioritized over apparently "less essential" non-indexical animated production (at least during the twentieth century).[1] But comparing Nolan's proclamations with Kracauer's is interesting for another reason. Writing in the 1960's Kracauer was doing so in a cultural context in which indexical photography reigned as the predominant form of moving image production. Kracauer here casts other forms of image production aside as subcategories that would not lead him to the theoretical heart of film. By contrast, Nolan's interviews (of which there are many) all hold a very different tone: in most of them he presents himself as a craftsman who has been doggedly holding onto his materials and production processes in the face of industrial pressure to move to digital. Nolan makes clear that he is very much in a minority in an industry that has already made the transition away from the physicality of film.

Following on from Nolan, in 2015, J.J. Abrams announced that he had turned to physical effects for his direction of *Star Wars*, stating that the production was governed by physical sets rather than digital effects and explaining that fans, "wanted it to be legitimate. Building as much as we could was a mandate. ... Even before ILM gets started, you can watch the movie and see what it is" (Burns 2015). As with Nolan's words, Abrams reference to legitimacy here was telling: it may have seemed that, in comparison to Kracauer's thinking of fifty years earlier, *physical reality* was once again being "redeemed", what Abrams really claimed to be redeeming here was the *Star Wars* franchise itself, through the "legitimacy" that the physical reality of practical effects apparently brought. As Abrams' production designer on *Star Wars* later explained:

> J.J.'s mandate from day one was authenticity and being as true to the original trilogy as possible. And he felt the prequels were flawed by the fact that they had every [CG] tool known to mankind and used everything at their disposal. I use the metaphor of disco when the synthesizer came about and everyone was using it in any way possible. And I think J.J. wanted to reconnect with how the original films were made (Burns 2015).

Both Nolan and Abrams stated adherence to practical effects are not isolated cases. They mark a general trend toward the claim that "practical effects" should govern, or *increasingly are* governing Hollywood movie production. Alongside the *Star Wars* marketing the internet was quickly awash in 2015 with videos demonstrating the degree to which *Mad Max Fury Road* had involved practical stunts (both acrobatic and automobile). The reasons why this should have happened are both multifaceted and the subject of current scholarship amongst the likes of Dominik Schrey (2014), Jason Sperb (2015), and Lisa Bode (2018). Crucial to this shift has been, as Schrey notes, an explicit axis of nostalgia. Referring to Laura Marks, Schrey notes that nostalgia for an analogue past is both a feature of our new media landscape and simultaneously a consequence of it. In a claim that bears striking relevance to Abrams claims that his motivations for turning to practical effects were based in the philosophical belief that is was:

> really important, that the movie, in a way, go backwards to go forwards. ... I wanted it to look and feel the way the original trilogy did – which is to say, when I saw those two droids in the desert of Tatooine, that was real (Burns 2015).

Marks notes that inherent in what she calls "analogue nostalgia" is "the brave attempt to re-create immediate experience in an age when most experience is rendered as information" (Marks 2002: 153).

We might say, then, that nostalgia and legitimacy were the X and Y axis of factors driving Abrams' relegation of digital effects to last place ("even before ILM gets started, you can watch the movie") in the hierarchy of the cult film franchise resurrection business. Interestingly, nostalgia and legitimacy have long been factors that figured large in the cult film franchise business. Certainly, nostalgia – and the legitimacy that is drawn from it – has been a key factor in the formation and entry of many films into the cult status canon. That being the case, the question of where newly emergent digital effects practices and processes fit into the geography of cult films was never likely to be straightforward.

Resurrecting the cult film in the age of digital VFX

Since its reconfiguration as a large scale digital industry in the 1990s, visual effects production has been a site at which both older cult film franchises have been refreshed (*Star Wars*, *Star Trek*, *Planet of the Apes*, *Mad Max*, *King Kong*, *Tron*) and new cult film franchises have emerged (*Lord of the Rings*, *The Hobbit*, *Avatar*). The implications of CG visual effects upon a cult franchise are multifaceted and ever publicly played out. During the mid-1990s and early 2000s the possibility that Hollywood studios might bring to bear the power of their deep pockets to resurrect cult film franchises multiplied by the power of contemporary digital effects capabilities were often greeted with much excited anticipation. Perhaps the textbook case of this was George Lucas' decision to return to the *Star Wars* franchise with disastrous results in the eyes of many fans (witness Simon Pegg's character traumatized fan figure in Edgar Wright's British TV series *Spaced* as a popular cultural example of the pain it caused amongst fans as he burns his merchandise and cries to Bill Bailey that "it still hurts"). Lucas' apparently disastrous focus on digital visual effects have now become the textbook example of the corrupting effects of computer generated imaging upon the avid cult film fans right to unadulterated nostalgia.

While VFX are frequently identified as the source of all that is wrong with failing cult franchises (of which *The Phantom Menace* was only the most high-profile example), the VFX industry itself is staffed with intensely committed cult film fans, many of whom are engaged in the process of creating spectacular effects for the very films directors are claiming to take a "VFX lite" approach to. Drawing upon extensive interviews from visual effects professionals whose careers have spanned Weta Digital, Industrial Light and Magic, Digital Domain, Dreamworks and many more, this chapter will consider the way in which for better or worse, the VFX pipeline is now central to the production of Hollywood cult films. With a globally mobile army of VFX professionals who inhabit a privileged geography as committed cult film fans working on the "inside" and as socially networked film project promoters in public, theories of cult film must encompass the VFX pipeline and the increasingly nuanced treatment of digital visual effects as a site of craft and equally the imagined location at which such craft is undermined.

The nuance revolves around an emergent discursive relationship between correlated notions of craft, physicality, authenticity and reality that are bundled up with the nostalgia of past sites of media consumption. In this heady mix, it seems, digital VFX, regarded as symptomatic of corporate and economic studio influence and a loss of past forms of craft, have become a focal point of frustration for many cult film fans nostalgic for an earlier time. I want to argue in this chapter that the turn toward what is being termed "practical effects" is part of a wider turn toward a nostalgia for the physicality of analogue that encompasses much more than just film production practice and can be found more broadly in what Charles Acland (2006) has termed Residual Media.

While Acland, talks of media forms in his work, he also describes "the broader appeal of popular pleasures that revel in the rediscovery of vintage artifacts and styles" (Acland 2006: xiv).

In the current context, however, I would suggest that this appeal has now broadened out still further to encompass not only the rediscovery of vintage artefacts but also to the reverential return to production processes by which such artefacts were made. Any walk through the gentrified part of a modern city reveals a nostalgia for, and resurrection of, all things analogue and with it the fetishization of craft and its physicality. From craft beer and ice cream to wood carved cell phone covers (ironically mass-produced via laser cutting technology), furniture production, vinyl and physical photography the past is returning to consumer production in a way that suggests a shift in the philosophy of consumption as much as production.

Most importantly, and somewhat ironically, this return to the fetishization of physical production and craft is even something that has entered the production pipelines of the digital VFX industry. In the rest of the chapter I will consider the contradictions that follow from the fact that many of the people in the VFX industry who work on the cutting edge of CGI production are often intense cult film fans at the same time as they are also intense analogue fetishists themselves. Interviewing digital visual effects artists in this environment provokes all sorts of questions regarding the contradictions of the narratives Hollywood now constructs around its professed return to the legitimacy of practical effects. Ultimately, I will argue that this so-called return to practical effects has as much to do with marketing the cult film to fans as it does with the reality of contemporary filmmaking.

Physical vs digital: Nostalgia, materiality and the cult of craft

Where did the rapid and seemingly pervasive discourse of "physical effects" originate in relation to cult film production? It was not long ago that the industry press was proclaiming each new cult film franchise to be dusted off and given the electro-shock therapy of big studio VFX budgets with excitement. In the last few years, however, the idea that large scale VFX represents a magic pixie dust has fallen rapidly out of favour. In its place has come a nostalgia for the notion of a lost authenticity located in a seemingly better filmmaking past. Around this nostalgia has orbited interconnected concepts of cultural capital, taste, the philosophy of quality and, most importantly, notions of craft. As we shall see throughout this chapter, the concept of quality, craft and authenticity are the conceptual threads that run through discourses of nostalgic return and are particularly worth interrogating because there is no apparent reason why such notions should be automatically aligned with analogue production over digital production. In other words, there is a false opposition created in discourses around "practical effects" that align analogue technologies and physical materiality with notions of craft while digital production, by implication, is left to represent soulless mass production.

Retracing our steps back to earlier notions of craft it is interesting to consider the manner in which they are constructed and contextualized. Perhaps the best and most revealing articulation of the values embodied in notions of "craft" were outlined by designer and film maker, Ray Eames at the first annual conference of American Craftsmen in 1957. There Eames described his notion of a "craftsman-like" object as something that had a "tremendous amount of thought and work" spent on its preparation. Similarly, a "craftsmanlike guy" referred to at the conference was described in terms of his "terrifically humble attitude to the materials that he works with and to the problems that surround him". These descriptions were not as simple in their construction as they looked (though there was a degree of deliberate simplicity to Eames' words typical of the values often espoused in the field of design). What Eames was describing here was a philosophy toward the act of fabrication: a discourse crucial to our own understanding of the way in which digital VFX are positioned in cult film production today, as we shall see, not least because in their perceived "demateriality" digital effects are treated as a form that runs contrary to notions of "craft".

The origins of the discursive tendency to associate digital production with a loss of craft in specific relation to the VFX industry were very presciently laid out in Michele Pierson's 2002 book *Still in Search of Wonder*. In it, Pierson outlined a conceptual obstacle frequently raised in the construction of digital production as a craft-based form:

> Even though there have been attempts to conceive of craft outside the reduc-
> tive association of craft with "handicraft" before now, craft has traditionally been
> associated with artisanal forms of production. Against the standardization of mass
> production processes it has stood for a "workmanship of risk." Not just the applica-
> tion of a technics – a body of knowledge, a set of skills – craft has traditionally been
> defined by an intuitive relation to the materials of its making. This way of thinking
> about craft – with its emphasis on the haptic dimension of workmanship and the
> construction of material artifacts – poses some obvious problems for transposing
> craft into the digital realm.
>
> (Pierson 2002: 140)

Here Pierson outlines a number of conceptual frameworks within which notions of "craft" have been wrapped: not simply skills and knowledge but also the physicality of materials, resulting tangible artefacts and individuated artisanal production in a direct relationship between the human hand and the resulting output. By contrast with this, the production of digital visual effects spawned a global industry over the last thirty years that was based upon ever cheaper computational power, ever more sophisticated levels of simulation and ever greater levels of distributed, Fordist production labour. In this context, digital processes that involve simulation of "materials" and increasing complexity of production were necessarily going to face resistance in a cultural environment seeing a swing back toward analogue as a site of nostalgic certainty.

Anybody involved in the production of VFX movies during the pre-digital days will (and does – as we shall see) point out that special effects production was always a complex process involving many thousands of people. But it seems that in recent times, the lack of a haptic dimension to digital visual effects production (and many other forms of digital production and distribution) has put it in the crosshairs of a culture nostalgic for analogue.

In my own interviews in the visual effects industry I have encountered precisely such sentiment many times. One Visual Effects Supervisor, Simon (effectively the head of the depart-ment that oversees a team of animators responsible for the very technical and creative mix of simulation and spectacle), couched his nostalgia for the old days in response to the protests over the infamous Rhythm and Hues VFX company bankruptcy. In that instance, VFX animators around the world protested that they were undervalued and without them, VFX movies could not be made. They did this by sharing a meme on social media that contained a picture of the set of *Life of Pi* featuring the main character on the boat in a blue key water tank (minus the famous CG tiger) and the caption "your film without VFX". Referring to this Simon argued for moderation on the part of the digital effect industry, tellingly arguing that:

> Yeah the tiger's front and centre but so is the boat he's in that some set dresser has gone
> and built. When I was doing animatronics, the actual satisfaction was making the thing.
> We did this Loch Ness with its head dancing. We made this massive hydraulic 40 foot
> Loch Ness monster. It was awesome.[2]

Simon's professed love for the physicality of working with materials and taking joy in the process of crafting an animatronic monster recalls Pierson's assertion that this "way of thinking about craft – with its emphasis on the haptic dimension of workmanship and the construction of material artefacts – poses some obvious problems for transposing craft into the digital realm". And indeed it did for Simon, who, by contrast with his nostalgic earlier days making animatronics, complained that on the modern digital VFX pipeline, "we don't have any control. We are all sort of technicians in this big process".

Simon's complaints regarding a large and immensely complex digital visual effects production pipeline as a place in which the craft of practical visual effects were stripped from him and his colleagues, and with it the ability to take joy in the fabrication process, chimes with a complaint Ray Eames made of industrial design and the capacity of its production processes to strip design of its craftsmanship. For Eames, as for Simon, craftsmanship and satisfaction in the act of craftsmanship came from a one to one relationship between the crafter and the materiality of the output. By contrast, in a complex industrial organization, especially one whose output is primarily mass produced, Eames argued that designers and makers increasingly surrendered their responsibility for making decisions to layers of management and analysts further up the chain. As Eames complained:

> Because of this [increasing industrial complexity], the responsibility for a decision-aesthetic, practical and connected with craft-has to be set back in the industry itself. So we have the designer in industry feeding back basic responsibility to management, to the purchasing agent, to the engineer, to the analyst.
>
> (Eames 1957)

Likewise, Simon's suggestion that "we are all just technicians in this big process" echoes Eames' suggestion that increasing industrial complexity in the industrial process of design more generally removed the designer from her craft by taking away direct decision making.

High concept cult film and the marketing logic of "practical effects"

We must be cautious here, however, of falling into the trap of creating a narrative that sees digital VFX houses pitted in opposition to directors who eschew digital effects as "craftsman". Notions of craft as they apply to "practical effects", now so frequently marketed in interviews and press material for new blockbusters, are largely and explicitly associated with directors in service of a Hollywood star system deployed in service of selling the film. A great deal of store has been placed in recent years in maintaining positive fan relationships. Since the advent of "high concept Hollywood" (Wyatt 2003) and the rise to prominence of marketing across all levels of the film inception and production process, studios have understood that excited fans are worth their marketing weight in gold. And in a context of contemporary social media landscapes that elevate fans to the level of networked mini-marketers, marketing departments have realized that claims to be resurrecting the production techniques of their fan bases nostalgic childhood's is a smart PR move if nothing else.

The suggestion that the return to practical effects somehow simplifies the film making process and allows for more direct decision-making, interaction with materials and by extension a return to the capacity for craftsmanship is problematic at best. When interviewing VFX animators (as in many other qualitative research scenarios) one is frequently struck by the degree of contradiction present in one's interviewees' answers. In the case of Simon, no sooner had he stopped decrying the increased complexity of the VFX pipeline and the loss of direct decision-making than he turned to an acknowledgement of the fact that the old days of physical movie production were not much different:

> In movie production as well you … actually build a set and light it and roll a camera in front of it and practice in front of it; there's incredible breadth of disciplines required. VFX, because we touch all these different areas like going to make a CG Whitehouse and blow it up; you end up with this big cross section of skill sets as well. You might have an architect building your thing. It's almost like a microcosm of the actual film itself because you do require people that; because you've got to build different objects you've got to understand the physics of certain things and fluids and muscles and then how light transport works. You end up with this mad array of people. I think it's kind of similar. I think on a film set you've got an incredible breadth of people. There's just so many different disciplines to put together.[3]

Simon's description here, makes clear that any movie requiring complex visual effects is subject to similar levels of division of labour and therefore subsequent levels of complexity in which decision-making is necessarily distributed across a wide range of professionals. But such a reality does not fit well in a cultural context in which the value and sanctity of craft has returned as a driving discourse in the ideology of discerning consumption. In this context, digital effects have come to stand for lack of craft.

Ironically, as a highly skilled and high wage industry, the digital VFX industry contains precisely the demographic of people who fetishize notions of craft and increasingly decry mass production. As highly mobile and often young tech industry professionals with abundant spare income, many VFX professionals set up design oriented businesses in their spare time that take them back to various analogue crafts while others devote spare time to indy projects looking for VFX expertise that will not require Hollywood budgets to achieve.

In his excellent work on the animation industry and the nature of authorship, Matt Stahl (2005) outlines the degree to which modern work and labour practice alienates animators from the fruits of their own labour. Stahl describes a work environment in which animators contribute a great deal of the creative labour for any given production but can lay claim to none of the credit (financial or otherwise). In such an environment resentment is rife and, he suggests, encourages professionals to work as production line robots. It stands to reason, then, that under such circumstances visual effects professionals of all flavours in their spare time might seek to undertake work where they could feel more directly involved, able to wield agency and decision making symptomatic of a craft. This is the significance of Simon's comparison above: he argues that the digital VFX pipeline alienates him because of its size and complexity and then goes onto acknowledge that practical visual effects productions of the past were subject to the same industrial logic. In this sense, what he says is not a contradiction but entirely consistent with an industry that currently seeks to associate director auteurs and their preferences for practical effects with notions of craft, quality and legitimacy. The important point here is that this narrative is a commercial and ideological one, not something that reflects the reality of contemporary industrial blockbuster cult film production.

Most digital VFX professionals I have interviewed spend some proportion of their time on personal projects undertaken for the love of a sense of ownership and craft that they point out large production environments lack. Take for instance Ignacio who worked in the "pre-vis" department (at the beginning of the visual effects production pipeline). Ignacio acknowledged that he had enjoyed working on *The Hobbit* movies but suggested he might like to move into the games industry - a sentiment expressed by a significant number of interviewees. For Ignacio, the appeal of working in a games company lay in its potential to offer a reconnection between personal input and seeing tangible results from labour expended. As he explained when he revealingly segued from plans for a career in the games industry to his hopes for a future in creative writing:

> I want to work on cool projects. ... I'd love to work at a game company or working on a series that I love. I don't want to work in games for the sake of games. I'm looking to take a year off because I got accepted doing a postgrad in creative writing. *For me personally to have something creative that's my own. ... I need something that's mine.* At the moment I'm taking a year off to do that knowing full well that I do enjoy my job and I would like to continue to be able to financially support myself doing something fun. So I'm looking to see if I maybe pick up some work in London for a bit while I am in that area. [emphasis added][4]

For Ignacio then, working in a large visual effects production company had become less important than that he could work on "cool projects". In this context it quickly becomes apparent that "cool" is measured in part by the capacity to feel a sense of ownership. In the same spirit, another artist (Kevin in the textures department), when asked if he regarded himself as an artist or computer technician answered that:

> It depends on the project and it depends on who I'm working for. I still get to be an artist sometimes but not most of the time. They're so particular for the look of something that you get some concept and you match it and then they change it 100 times and then you go back to version one and then you change it a few more times. And then the janitor at the studio sees it and has a comment. Everybody has a comment. ... It changes a million times and it becomes no longer fun.[5]

It seems that what constitutes "cool" for Ignacio is described as "fun" by Kevin. Kevin's description of the visual effects pipeline production process that sucks all the "fun" out of his work here is powerfully reminiscent of Eames' earlier description of design industries increasingly governed by remote decision-making processes. Though he was deliberately exaggerating for comic effect when he disdainfully described the impact of the janitor upon the process, Kevin's example is telling: his complaint, like Ignacio's and even Simon's, is that decision making has been dispersed and is frustratingly opaque. Interestingly, this suggests that, even within the VFX production pipeline the idea of a single auteur with a singular vision of what she would like to craft would be welcomed, and Kevin even says so directly:

> It's no longer fun ... unless there's a really good art director and a really good person at the top that knows what he wants and he actually has a good concept bought off on before the work starts. But that's not what happens any more. Now it's like, "here's a concept and let's explore every option in the known universe and then we'll go back to version one and then we'll see how it goes."[6]

Tellingly Kevin's description betrays a problem borne of the way digital effects production, subject to the huge cost reductions rendered by Moore's Law, now allows for a proliferation of iterative prototyping at every level: "let's explore every option in the known universe".

However, Simon, Ignacio and Kevin's experiences may not be so unique to digital VFX as they might first appear. Ignacio's decision especially to pursue a creative outlet in which he can make something that is "his own", like many other VFX professionals I interviewed, turns out to be a common feature of the industry more broadly, and not just now but historically too. Ernest Mathijs, for instance, has written about "Horror Effects Auteurs" of the 1970s and 1980s: "a small but increasingly significant group of HFX-artists whose reputation has become so important (both aesthetically and as a marketing tool) that it has come to overshadow some of the more traditional elements within the horror genre" (2010: 158). While Mathijs description here bears uncanny echoes of the ways in which Nolan and Abrams are positioned by Hollywood marketing at the beginning of this chapter, his account of how HFX-auteurs rose to prominence is no less telling. Mathijs describes the professionals of KNB-EFX studio who maintained their cult street cred by volunteering to work for small-scale indie-horror productions such as *Ginger Snaps*. What Mathijs argued characterized horror effects production in the 1970s and 1980s could now be said to play out across contemporary VFX movie production where digital effects professionals similarly contribute to small-scale productions of all kinds.

Something striking about Mathijs' account of the development of practical/animatronic HFX is his description of its transition from a personalized and DIY culture in the 1970s through to a more professionalized industry in the 1980s. By the 1980s this professionalized horror effects industry will have been more significant in scale and, therefore, more complex in its division of labour. Revealingly, Mathijs' description of an industry in which "HFX-auteurs" rose to prominence on the back of work they undertook on low budget productions in their spare time suggests that the desire to work in small-scale and small-budget environments is not something specific to digital production. That being the case we could argue that it is not something specific about the digital VFX industry that strips effects professionals of the capacity to engage in "craft", rather, that large-scale effects industries (practical and digital) separate their employees from a sense of direct authorship and therefore notions of immediacy and craft, leading them to seek a creative outlet elsewhere. For both practical HFX professionals and their contemporary digital VFX equivalents, it is not *the media or material they work with* that effects their connection to their sense of craft but rather *the scale at which they are working and the complexity of decision making in their production environment*.

Conclusion: Crafting production or producing craft?

Regardless of the way in which digital effects have come to be treated as an ailment of contemporary Hollywood movies, what really appears to be the problem is the dispersal of decision making and the lack of direction in the production process. The reason that this complaint (heard over and over in the VFX industry) is so significant to us is that it demonstrates something crucial from both within the VFX industry and from without: that visual effects per se are not the problem for workers or audiences looking to reconnect with film in ways that they used to in their past. Rather, it is lack of clarity in decision making and lack of ownership over decision making that seems to alienate VFX production staff. Indeed, it is perhaps no coincidence that the sharp rise in hostility toward visual effects amongst major studio marketing departments happened to follow the large and global digital VFX protests of 2013 in which "your movie without VFX" memes were shared virally across social networks (marketing poison for the major studios who had spent years turning the far less powerful VFX houses into the feudal serfs of Hollywood's corporate environment (-for more detail on this episode, see Gurevitch 2015).

At the level of consumption too, it seems that audiences are alienated by a similar lack of clarity and coherence: the chief criticism of George Lucas' VFX "renovation" of the original *Starwars* trilogy was that it contradicted the aesthetic coherence of the films and violated the sanctity of the movies. It was perhaps no surprise, then, when his *Phantom Menace* prequels were seen to multiply this crime. Specifically, Lucas was criticized (and Peter Jackson has faced similar charges since) for allowing digital VFX to overwhelm the craft of filmmaking by filling the screen with too much material. It seems fitting that the battle scenes in these movies (and the choice of where to look) are as confusing to audiences as the VFX production pipeline is to its artists, who seem unsure of where to derive managerial coherence. But it is somewhat disingenuous to blame this development on the materiality of digital as a medium per se. Rather, it is the consequence of a shake up in the production logic of image making facilitated by a switch over to digital technologies (and herein lies the difference). As Pierson argued with typical prescience much earlier in this process:

> Digital technologies have not just transformed the filmmaking process at the level of technical operations. They have also transformed the way the people who make films physically and mentally engage in the production of artifacts. Coming to terms with the materiality of these transformations necessitates being able to theorize digital production positionally and relationally. This means being able to think of digitality in relation to particular filmmaking practices, each with its own mode of organizing, training, and accrediting people to perform specific tasks. Furthermore, these practices in turn need to be situated in relation to the diverse contexts that give films a public life.
>
> (Pierson 2002: 139)

In light of this it is more accurate to understand digital effects as a production technology that changed the filmmaking process, and, after an initial burst of uncontained enthusiasm (as is so often the case with new production technologies), are settling into a film production landscape in which they constitute varying degrees of the onscreen material depending on economics, directorial preference, generic requirements and fan demands.

To relegate the digital effects to the exile of a discursive space in which they stand for corporate short-sightedness or the deadzone of an alienating and craftless industry intent on mass production and mass profits risks missing the point: Hollywood, from the very earliest days, has always been an industry founded on the logic of the Fordist production line. Indeed, ironically, because they are subject to Moore's Law like every other computational entity, there is ample evidence that digital effects present an opportunity to liberate film production from the industrial monopoly of Hollywood as much as they might appear to represent the worst excesses of its budgetary industrial formula. To take a classic example of this, the current director of *Star Wars: Rogue One* (Gareth Edwards) made his way into Hollywood on the back of a low budget cult movie (*Monsters*, 2010) he made with editor Colin Goudie. *Monsters* catapulted Edwards into Hollywood on the back of bespoke VFX that Edwards himself made in his bedroom, the story of which is reminiscent of a digital era *Rebel without a Crew* (Rodriguez, 1996).[7] Ironically then, while HFX may have witnessed a move from DIY outfit in the 1970s to a complex professionalized industry in the 1980s, and with it a transition to more alienated forms of effects labour, ever cheaper and more freely available digital effects could well lead to a proliferation and democratization of more DIY based and less alienated VFX production.

Rather than presenting digital effects as the enemy of the cult film (or any kind of film for that matter) it is perhaps more accurate to understand it as a complex and nuanced new (relatively speaking) image fabrication form (perhaps more akin to an infinitely malleable material) the parameters of which are still being explored and the implications of which, not just for film making but for film theorizing too, are only just beginning to be understood.

Notes

1 As is now pointed out in scholarship so often that it seems redundant to do so again but across a wider (pre-twentieth century) span of time the majority of our visual culture has not been indexical.
2 Simon Clutterbuck, in interview.
3 Ibid.
4 Ignacio Pena, in interview.
5 Kevin Norris, in interview.
6 Ibid.
7 Rodriguez Robert (1996). Plus, personal correspondence with the author.

References

Acland, Charles, ed. 2006. *Residual Media.* London: University of Minnesota Press.
Bode, Lisa. 2018. '"It's a Fake!" Early and Late Incredulous Viewers, Trick Effects, and CGI,' *Film History: An International Journal*, 30.4: 1–21.
Burns, Chris. 2015. 'Star Wars Practical Effects: J.J. Abrams Speaks on the Standard, In Slash Gear.' www.slashgear.com/star-wars-practical-effects-j-j-abrams-speaks-on-the-standard-16379432 [accessed 01/10/2016].
Eames, Ray. 1957. 'The Making of a Craftsman,' Speech made at The First Annual Conference of American Craftsmen. www.eamesoffice.com/scholars-walk/the-making-of-a-craftsman [accessed 10/01/2016].
Gurevitch, Leon. 2015. 'The Straw That Broke the Tiger's Back? Skilled Labour, Social Networks and Protest in the Digital Workshops of the World.' In Richard Maxwell, ed., *Routledge Companion to Labour and Media.* London: Routledge: 190–201.
Kracauer, Siegfried. 1960. *Theory of Film (1997 edition).* Princeton, NJ: Princeton University Press.
Marks, Laura. 2002. *Touch: Sensuous Theory and Multisensory Media.* London: University of Minnesota Press.
Mathijs, Ernest. 2010. 'They're Here! Special Effects in Horror Cinema of the 1970s and 1980s.' In Ian Conrich, ed., *Horror Zone: The Cultural Experience of Contemporary Horror Cinema.* London: I.B. Taurus: 153–173.
McKnight, Brent. 2015. 'The Extreme Lengths JJ Abrams Went to Connect the Force Awakens to the Original Star Wars Trilogy.' www.cinemablend.com/new/Extreme-Lengths-JJ-Abrams-Went-Connect-Force-Awakens-Original-Star-Wars-Trilogy-72581.html [accessed 01/10/2016].
Pierson, Michele. 2002. *Special Effects: Still in Search of Wonder.* New York: Columbia University Press.
Ressner, Jeffrey. 2012. 'The Traditionalist,' The Directors Guild of America. www.dga.org/craft/dgaq/all-articles/1202-spring-2012/dga-interview-christopher-nolan.aspx [accessed 01/10/16.]
Schrey, Dominik. 2014. 'Analogue Nostalgia and the Aesthetics of Digital Remediation.' In K Niemeyer, ed., *Media and Nostalgia: Yearning for the Past, Present and Future.* London: Palgrave Macmillan: 27–38.
Sperb, Jason. 2015. *Flickers of Film: Nostalgia in the Time of Digital Cinema.* London: Rutgers University Press.
Stahl, Matt. 2005. 'Nonproprietary Authorship and the Uses of Autonomy: Artistic Labor in American Film Animation, 1900–2004,' *Labor Studies in Working-Class History of the Americas*, 2.4: 87–105.
Wyatt, Justin. 2003. *High Concept: Movies and Marketing in Hollywood.* Austin: University of Texas Press.

35

PRODUCTION PLAY

Sets, props, and costumes in cult films

Tamao Nakahara

Cult, fandom and play

This chapter aims to contribute to the study of film sets, props, and costumes, an area to which film studies has given valuable, yet limited, attention. In the growing area of cult film studies, while scholars may scrutinize specific objects and backdrops within the frame, surveying the place and mechanics of sets, props, and costumes across various fan film viewing and engagement practices could advance our understanding of film production methods, fan theory, and broadly of how micro-cultures interact with media texts. This chapter aims to proffer key ways in which these film-production objects can function to broker relationships between movie productions and fan experiences.

Fans and fan communities engage with visual media in several ways; and, for the purposes of this project, I use as my starting point the assumption that most audiences engage with a film within a certain duration with a clear start and end, whether they are watching a movie in its entirety or in parts. At some point, the active viewing period ends and spectators either move on to other activities or may contemplate what they saw further. In this way, the film-viewing experiences usually have set spatio-temporal coordinates with a start and end, and it is notable that sociologist Johan Huizinga particularly called out the stage and screen when examining the spatio-temporal boundaries of play:

> [...] the third main characteristic of play [... is ...] its limitedness. It is "played out" within certain limits of time and place. It contains its own course and meaning. [...] The arena, the card-table, [...] the stage, the screen, [...] are all in form and function play-grounds [...].
>
> (Huizinga 1980 [1949]: 9–10)

The reason that Huizinga's theorizations of play have been fundamental to fields such as cultural and visual studies is that he addresses concepts that led to current understandings of meaning creation within activities of play. Even the most "passive" of movie-watchers relate to media on different levels of meaning creation. Similarly, in other areas of reader/viewer research, discourses have examined levels of reader involvement and spatio-temporal delineations such as implied readers who are asked to "suspend disbelief" (Todorov 1978 [1990]), specific genre consumers who are "actively involved" and interacting with the constructed nature of films, the role of counterfactuals (Dannenberg 2008), and the application of carnival for participatory rules of engagement (Bakhtin 1984). All of these practices of play shed light on the spaces and times of meaning creation. The kinds of spaces and places relevant to these works' understandings of play are often those that feature in cult films: tables, props, décor, accessories, living rooms (how the audiences of *The Room* (Wiseau 2003) build emotional relationships with the arrangement of the eponymous room and its mysterious occurrences of spoons), set stages and labyrinthine rooms (numerous spaces in *The Rocky Horror Picture Show* (Sharman 1975)), and the arrangements of furniture made in those spaces, whether it is for dancing, dining, seducing, celebrations, or confrontations (and both aforementioned films have numerous instances). If one adds to the spoons of *The Room* the seven-piece set of cutlery of *The Rocky Horror Picture Show*, and the abundance of alcoholic drinks in *Casablanca*, or the presence of rabbits in *Harvey*, *Psycho*, *El Topo*, and *Pulp Fiction* (all of which are commented on by viewers), then it is necessary to discuss the intersection between having such staging elements in a film, and how audiences use them to create meaning. Audiences read those props into the films as part of their enjoyment of (or frustrations with) the films. "Cult films," that is films that receive that adjective, arguably pique viewers' interest even after the exhibition period has ended (and "exhibition" here includes any type of format from theater to cell phone viewings). Movies that gather a cult following arguably leave their fans with a type of emotional residue, an experience that they tend to contemplate well after the viewing duration has ended. An initial assumption may be that the attraction is positive and that the fans continue to reflect on one or many aspects of the film that they enjoyed: immersive narrative worlds, suspense, favorite script lines, their well-timed deliveries, charismatic actors, erotic moments, or dynamic action-packed scenes.

The residue left by props, costumes, and sets may also feed social and historical needs as scholars have been persistently pointing out. For example, Judith Hess Wright argues that viewers return to genres that provide "comfort and solace" as well as a means to accept the status quo instead of take social action (Wright 2012 [1986]: 60). Similarly, Mark Jancovich shows how some science fiction has reflected social concerns with the sciences, scientists, and dehumanizing rationalism (Jancovich 1996). Finally, Amanda Ann Klein examines how American film cycles "provide audiences with versions of the same images, characters, and plots that they enjoyed in previous films" (Klein 2011: 6). For instance, Klein shares how

> [...] Judd Apatow's comedies of the 2000s, such as *The 40 Year Old Virgin* (2005) and *Knocked Up* (2007), focus on schlemiel protagonists who end up winning over audiences as well as the girl of their dreams. Audiences who regularly seek out these films are paying to see these particular elements replicated in film after film.
>
> (Klein 2011:12)

During this process, viewers pay attention to details, and those essential details include particular clothing and material elements.

As Henry Jenkins has noted for television culture, viewers may equally continue to think about a movie because of how it provokes negative sensations:

> The fans' response typically involves not simply fascination or adoration but also frustration and antagonism, and it is the combination of the two responses which motivates their active engagement with the media. Because popular narratives often fail to satisfy, fans must struggle with them, to try to articulate to themselves and others

unrealized possibilities within the original works. Because the texts continue to fascinate, fans cannot dismiss them from their attention but rather must try to find ways to salvage them for their interests.

(Jenkins 1992: 24)

"[T]he texts continue to fascinate," as Jenkins states – that is, the fan experiences exist along multiple spatial and temporal periods that do not align at the same start and end. The "non-alignment" between the duration of the film and the duration of its emotional impact is core to the fans' emotional residue. Metaphorically, one might think of a scenario in which a passenger vehicle comes to an abrupt stop, but the passengers' bodies still sense the momentum of the forward movement. Even though the viewing period has a distinct start and end, the physical and emotional conditions for each audience member do not abide by the same limits; they continue until they are "played out." Because of this, the viewer's absorption in aspects of the movie could continue for minutes to months after the initial exhibition. Huizinga states that

Play is distinct from "ordinary" life both as to locality and duration. [...] Play begins, and then at a certain moment it is "over". It plays itself to an end.

(Huizinga 1980: 9)

For cult fans (and arguably other fan communities), there is, instead, more than one bracketed period of play: creative play of the viewing period (shouting and yelling included) is one arena for absorption and meaning creation, but potentially viewers explore other levels of play that encompass the emotional residue and its outlets. Fan behaviors show that play and meaning creation can endure quite a bit outside of the viewing period through fan behaviors. The wealth, industriousness, and visibility of that output has led to much of the current discussion and arguably has helped launch and grow fan studies as a discipline.

Consumptive and productive fetish play

The fan outlets and output take on several forms of play, but here I will examine two broad categories that are consumptive and productive: (1) the consumption of related fetish objects or (2) the prolific production of such objects. On the consumptive end, audience members may rewatch the film (or part of it) multiple times, seek peripheral cinematic options within the genre, cycle, or franchise, find intertextually related media by the same director or with the same actors, or seek paratexual information about the movie (its history, production, cast and crew, reviews, extras on DVD). Fans might collect materials related to their object of desire: posters, paraphernalia, trinkets, action figures, costumes, and other similar items that can be purchased online or at specialty store chains such as Forbidden Planet. Some fans may financially afford original set components, props, or costumes from the shoot through eBay or auctions (Geraghty 2014). Fans may also participate in public activities such as conventions (*Star Trek* [Roddenberry, 1966–1969] and horror movie conventions), original location visits (*The Lord of the Rings* tours in New Zealand), tours that showcase original sets, props, and costumes (the Warner Bros. Studio Tour London - The Making of *Harry Potter*), and visits to original "relics" or locations that inspired constructed sets or CG-animated scenes. Some of these activities may come together in a way for fans to engage in private or at these community events. A prop (say, a weapon or talisman) from a cult film can be used in playful situations outside of the film's viewing duration (a *Star Trek* fan might purchase and zap a blaster at a convention). Alternatively, an item can be used "against" its original intentions (e.g. fans may enact divergent scenes from *The Lord of the Rings* with a ring). (For more on this, see the chapter by Lynn Zubernis in the section on fandom in this volume.) In several cases, this consumptive play is a side-effect of a fetish fascination with the totemic potential of props and costumes.

On the productive end, fans equally can produce and wear in private, or share in public. Viewers may participate in activities such as discussions (oral or written), and produce fan letters, fan fiction, fan drawings of characters and scenes, cosplay clothing that they tailor, crafts, and other output that expresses the creative period of play that endures after the watching the movies. In these cases, as Jenkins states:

> [...] fans actively assert their mastery over the mass-produced texts which provide the raw materials for their own cultural productions and the basis for their social inter actions. In the process, fans cease to be simply an audience for popular texts; instead, they become active participants in the construction and circulation of textual meanings.
>
> (Jenkins 1992: 24)

In this way, fans can practice productive behaviors for themselves and for others. (They write for themselves or share fan fiction when they cannot wait for the next installment, alter the narrative outcome of the film and find others who share the same frustrations, or make and sometimes sell clothes or accessories tailored after a character's attire for themselves or others). In many of these cases, the images of the sets, props, and costumes play an integral part in the ways that viewers manage their emotional residue and in the ways that they build a relationship with the film and its production *socially*.

Production play

As mentioned, for some fans the first step in fan behavior may be to repeat the initial viewing experience through follow-up viewings. On one level, fans may bring their proxy props and ludic readings to the films in the form of passions, creativity, immersive viewings, and discussion. Throwing spoons in the air during screenings of *The Room* is one ludic example. But on another basic level, repeated viewings *statistically raise the probability* that the fans may (1) take note of other recurring tropes, sets, props, or costumes, as well as inter- and intra-narrative connections, and (2) may potentially find or create deeper meanings from those observations.

According to Andrew Horton, (leaning on Ludwig Wittgenstein) some comedy audiences take on the "gamelike activity" with which they discover "a network of similarities" that they digest or discuss with others for understanding or meaning (Horton 1991: 9). Developing this idea further, Matt Hills leverages Winnicottian and other psychoanalytic theories to explore how affective play (which can involve this type of gamelike activity) connects individual fans (to whom a film text is a "proper transitional object") to other fans (with the same PTO relationships) and, as a result, they together build their fan community (Hills 2002: 108–113). As they build that fan base, they also start developing individual and shared knowledge about the cult film.

This gamelike expression and knowledge can broadly touch on a wide variety of areas as detailed above, but some of the most readily visible methods of building fan knowledge is through knowing personal and professional details of the cast and crew, or of the labor and physical challenges that went into its construction. Scholars of star studies have given the former robust attention, but the latter could use further investigation into how fans build a fantasy of connectivity to a film through knowledge of the production process. As C. Lee Harrington and Denise Bielby describe of soap opera culture, certain practices foster the "illusion of intimacy between celebrities and fans" such that fans feel closer to their beloved film when they amass knowledge about the people, processes, and objects that went into making the movie (Harrington and Bielby 1995: 152). While repetitively viewing part or all of a film as an outlet for emotional residue, fans similarly build up recognition of and familiarity with not only the characters and celebrity actors, but also of the material items that went into the final product. This leads them to an illusion of intimacy with the set and costume design, and that fantasy is part of what I call the "production play."

The discussion here of the "production play" is part of a larger project of exploring how viewers' ability to recognize and engage with the constructed nature of a film and its production details help to shape the breadth with which they might explore different subject positions, modes of reading, and perspectives. For this chapter, I focus on how sets, props, and costumes broker fans' connection to the production aspects of the film and contribute to the production play. A core part of that brokering is from the way that fans build the "illusion of intimacy" through their knowledge of the set and costume design, and the meanings that they imbue into those objects.

When fans gain production knowledge from repetitive viewings and a sort of detective work of sets, props, and costumes, they can gain an emotional attachment to the related objects that they consume and collect. Their connectivity to the films is through loosely alternating attachments, for example, between emotional attachments to the narrative or immersive worlds as well as knowledge attachments to the illusion of authenticity imbued in the film objects. The sets, props, and costumes perform as referents that have been captured on celluloid or in data. The images of those items are the visual index to an authentic moment in the production process that viewers may experience: the actors were on set, they wore those specific costumes, they posed or moved against particular backdrops, and they engaged with or were in the vicinity of props with potential significance. Fans can build illusions of intimacy with the film-making process and its resulting product through familiarity with and knowledge of the items that they see. In this way, the objects receive great scrutiny, become markers of meaning, and they broker the relationship between the fans and the film through their role as index to authenticity. The fantasy of authenticity is further developed (often through commodified resources such as interviews with cast members while in character costume and make-up, blooper reels, "making of" videos with footage of cast and crew on set, in front of green screens, and interacting with special effects machinery, as well as audio commentaries with film-makers sharing anecdotes of shooting schedules, on-set challenges, number of takes, and other subjective production information) (Fraade-Blanar and Glazer 2017).

A particularly keen example of the sliding between emotional attachments and knowledge attachments is the presentation of the Warner Bros. Studio Tour London – The Making of *Harry Potter*. The tour initiates with markers of authenticity about the in-studio work that went into making the films. Visitors must take a train and then bus to the suburbs of London that drops them off at one part of the studio lot (as opposed to, for example, an "inauthentic" museum that might be constructed more accessibly in the heart of London). Before reaching the studio sets, visitors watch a video narrated by the three key protagonists/actors, who explain that the tour is just as much about the process of movie-making as it is about the *Harry Potter* universe (both the books and films). Once visitors are allowed into the studio area, they see a mixture of sets, props, and costumes on display with video explanations of the hard labor that went into each tangible result. Especially for the sets, the scaffolding and back sides are visible to reveal the constructed nature of the whole world. In addition, much of the tour and its presentation of sets and objects also indulges in the magical fantasy of the narrative world for fans. Attendees are invited to switch rapidly between the constructed authenticity of the studio ("the set rooms were created here," "Daniel Radcliffe worked here," "they wore these exact costumes," "this is how Radcliffe played with his wands," etc.) and the constructed fantasy world of the book and movie ("this is where Harry Potter lived," "this is the bridge to Hogwarts," "this is Diagon Alley where the characters walked amongst bustling shoppers"). As a result, the tour volleys between lot tour and theme park encouraging visitors to explore both fantastical practices. Even in parts of the tour where the original sets no longer exist, they borrowed qualities of originality or authenticity from other items. For example, the train station with the Hogwarts Express that appears on the tour is not the original set from the film, but a recreation. To account for this "lack of authenticity," the tour takes pains to displace the discourses of authenticity onto discourses of labor (explaining how many sets rotate quickly on the lot as part of business, showing an accompanying time-lapse video of crews building and tearing down the original train station), and onto discourses of historic originality (of how the British steam locomotive no. 5972 "Olton Hall," was transported to the studio and used for the film and tour). Visitors can walk through the train from 1937 and engage in simultaneous or alternating experiences of knowledge authenticity as well as emotional imagination into the world of the story and the characters who rode the train.

A large part of fan knowledge relies on this type of visual evidence of material referents as a type of primary text. Fans then have license to investigate the film for further clues: viewing the film multiple times, freezing the frame into a type of photograph for reflection, and investigating "secondary sources" such as interviews, DVD commentaries, production materials, and photos. Through this, fans seek a truth from both the primary and secondary sources; and the primary film, when combed through using the apparatuses for recording and exhibition, provides the illusion of authenticity much in the way that Walter Benjamin famously describes photography – it "can bring out those aspects of the original that are unattainable to the naked eye yet accessible to the lens" (Benjamin 2004 [1936]: 239). Repetitive viewings and freeze-framing a film become part of the detective work that helps the objects speak about the production process.

The films speak, for instance, about how budgetary constraints or vendor relationships might affect the reappearance of the same sets, props, and costumes – the precise referential objects on which fans base much of their knowledge and illusion of intimacy. When Italian 1960s and 1970s popular and low budget productions reused sets to lower costs or rent costumes from the same vendor, for example, fans could rejoice in their recognition of the recurrence and in their reinforcement as experts. Similarly, part of the cult status of Roger Corman's early 1960s Edgar Allan Poe adaptations comes from the fact that fans point out recurrent sets used in the films such as *The Haunted Palace* and *The Terror*. Even big budget Disney animations reveal a range of possibilities: from the ability to insert numerous references to earlier movies (as they did with *Moana* (2016) and several other Disney products) to the inclusion of a previous Disney animal purely because they did not have the resources to character design a new animal for a brief scene.

In addition to brokering connections to the production through film objects, cinema itself, one could argue, is a revealing medium of its own construction. Horton, for example, argues that film comedy is about its own unmasking compared to other genres such as tragedy:

> Tragedy is also necessarily dialogic (a system of interrelated discourses among creator/text/contemplator). But [...] tragedy (and other noncomic forms) seeks to isolate or at least reduce the number of "discourses" in order to imply a sense of "fate" and

inevitability as opposed to an awareness of potentiality and "unfinalizedness" (Mikhail Bakhtin's term). And tragedy has traditionally performed this role by effacing a direct awareness of contact between creator and contemplator.

(Horton 1991: 9–10)

In reference to his comment, all genres are necessarily dialogic, both engaging with their viewers and revealing their own mechanics. Benjamin, through Miriam Hansen's interpretation of the lost version of this Artwork essay, saw cinema not only on the side of semblance and illusion, but more strongly on the side of revealing its own workings. For Benjamin, play represents the subtle balance between the dangers and benefits of technology and, in the context of cinema, between the inhuman limits of the apparatus and the harnessing of that apparatus in the name of human expression. As actor Holly Hunter has stated, "the stage is the actor's medium and film is the director's medium," and along those lines, Benjamin feels an awareness of the actor's performance to show humanity in the face of the factory of make-up, costumes, lighting, framing, and other ways that technologies discipline the actor's body:

> To perform in the glare of arc lamps while simultaneously meeting the demands of the microphone is a test performance of the highest order. To accomplish it is to preserve one's humanity in the face of the apparatus.
>
> (Benjamin in Hansen 2011: 111)

Benjamin, it could be argued, performed his own type of production play, attempting to create his own illusion of intimacy as he imagined the actor's laboring body, being paid to emote and express humanity while under the duress of various film devices, positioned to capture the image (and sound) of what may later, for fans, become a referent for fan knowledge.

Given the wide range of examples from obscure to Hollywood industry films, and from "bad" to "good" films that have gained cult followings, it is worth addressing Hills' concerns with Harrington and Bielby's examination of the "illusion of intimacy" (Hills 2002: 107). He states,

> But this specific point is highly problematic: ludic reading is viewed here as something which can be directly encouraged by industry machinations, despite that fact the transitional phenomena are both 'created and found'. This contradiction – which is central to Winnicott's account – is therefore overruled in Harrington and Bielby (1995) by a logic of ideological coercion where 'an illusion of intimacy' is created by TV industry strategies. And this occurs despite the authors' earlier statement that 'ideological' explanations of play and fan pleasure should be avoided. There is a shift in the logical model that Harrington and Bielby use; at moments they remain focused on affective play, but then fall back into a model of theoretical over-rationalisation.

One could argue that despite any industrial star-making machines, fans still own and appropriate the illusions of intimacy on their end even through the consumption of products intended to nurture precisely that "created and found" experience.

Despite Hills' combing through logical inconsistencies within Harrington and Bielby's use of D.W. Winnicott's theories, from a standpoint of 15 years after the publication of *Fan Cultures*, it seems that if we strictly cohere with the concept of the transitional phenomena of being both "created and found," we lose a way to read the extensive data that exists today on how a fans engage with a wide range of movies and marketing in both consumptive and productive ways. Ed Wood fans sew costumes to mimic the characters of *Plan 9 from Outer Space* (1959), James Cameron's *Avatar* (2009) fans purchase badges, magicbands, and other souvenirs at the end of the Disney Pandora Park visit, or art film fans explore an immersive *Battle of Algiers* (Pontecorvo 1966) production by Secret Cinema in the tunnels of London. In all of these examples, fans construct ebbing and flowing scenarios of consumption, production, creation, and discovery, whether those ludic engagements are Winnicottian, Huizingan, or other forms of play that need further exploration. Because of the powerful illusion of intimacy through the production play, many fans will engage with the material elements that they see on screen (costumes, magicbands, and the structure of the Casbah) whether those interactions are backed by industry marketing and merchandizing, or not. Jeffrey Weinstock has remarked that it was not the film *The Rocky Horror Picture Show*, but the display of its props in a record store that "initiated" his curiosity in the film (Weinstock 2007). Likewise, exhibitions of artwork associated with the films of David Cronenberg include the *actual, physical presence* of props from *Videodrome* (1983) (the television set, or the VHS stomach slit), *Naked Lunch* (1991) (the bug-typewriter), or *The Fly* (1986) (Brundlefly's teeth). A statue from Paul Verhoeven's *RoboCop* (1987) finds a permanent home after fans organize a Kickstarter campaign and work to place it in Detroit's Michigan Science Center (DeVito 2018). As the examples of storefronts, exhibitions, and city statues show, the potential for dialogic relationships between makers and readers is high and diverse. It has increased with communication platforms on the internet as well as personal information that fans readily volunteer (such as on Facebook and Twitter). In the past, industry-based genre practices existed on the levels as described by Steve Neale in terms of genre as a form of "a set of [audience] expectations" (Neale 1980: 51) or Rick Altman, who sees genre as a step in the "Producer's Game" to "[a]nalyse the film in order to discover what made it successful" (Altman 1999: 38). As a result, they contributed their own form of repetition that fans could recognize within genres or as playing against genre conventions. Whether the films are no-budget, exploitation, independents, or Hollywood blockbusters, especially since the mass use of the internet, there have been increased ways in which makers and viewers can have multi-directional dialogic relationships. For instance, *Manos: The Hands of Fate* (Warren, 1966) was essentially a lost "bad" film that found resurgence when the television show, "Mystery Science Theater 3000" (MST3K) (Hodgson, 1988–1999), featured the movie in a 1993 episode. As a result of MST3K's bringing the film to light, the film now has a cult following, a restoration on Blu-ray, and a Kickstarter campaign in which fans and supporters are funding a sequel that went into production in 2016.

Conclusion

Production play addresses the constructed and productive fantasies between film producers and fans. "Play" has occupied a place in various theoretical discourses, but the key areas of overlap refer to experiences of bracketed time and space, where both absorption and creativity can form with lowered limitations. For fans of beloved films, play is the mechanism behind repeated viewings, for scouring the visual plane for "clues" to meaningful readings, and for bolstering the fantasy of connecting with the "original" production and producers, cast, and crew. The process of the production play is a critical part of enriching the understanding of the term, "cult."

References

Altman, Rick. 1999. *Film/Genre*. London: British Film Institute.

Bakhtin, Mikhail. 1984. *Rabelais and His World*. Bloomington: Indiana University Press.

Benjamin, Walter. 1936 [2004]. *The Work of Art in the Age of Mechanical Reproduction*. New York: Random House. 217–253.

Dannenberg, Hilary. 2008. *Coincidence and Counterfactuality: Plotting Time and Space in Narrative Fiction*. Lincoln: University of Nebraska Press.

DeVito, Lee. 2018. "Finally, Detroit's RoboCop Statue Has a Home." *Detroit Metro Times*. https://www.metrotimes.com/the-scene/archives/2018/05/02/finally-detroits-robocop-statue-has-a-home (accessed August 8, 2019).

Fraade-Blanar, Zoe, and Aaron Glazer. 2017. *Superfandom: How Our Obsessions Are Changing What We Buy and Who We Are*. New York: W.W. Norton.

Geraghty, Lincoln. 2014. *Cult Collectors: Nostalgia, Fandom and Collecting Popular Culture*. London: Routledge.

Hansen, Miriam. 2011. *Cinema and Experience: Siegfried Kracauer, Walter Benjamin and Theodor Adorno*. Berkeley: University of California Press.

Harrington, C. Lee, and Denise Bielby. 1995. *Soap Fans: Pursuing Pleasure and Making Meaning in Everyday Life*. Philadelphia: Temple University Press.

Hills, Matt. 2002. *Fan Cultures*. London: Routledge.

Horton, Andrew. 1991. *Comedy/Cinema/Theory*. Berkeley: University of California Press.

Huizinga, Johan. 1980. *Homo ludens: A Study of the Play-element in Culture*. London: Routledge.

Jancovich, Mark. 1996. *Rational Fears: American Horror in the 1950s*. Manchester: Manchester University Press.

Jenkins, Henry. 1992. *Textual Poachers*. London: Routledge.

Klein, Amanda Ann. 2011. *American Film Cycles: Reframing Genres, Screening Social Problems and Defining Subcultures*. Austin: University of Texas Press.

Neale, Steve. 1980. *Genre*. London: British Film Institute.

Todorov, Tzvetan. 1978 [1990]. *Genres in Discourse*. Cambridge: Cambridge University Press.

Weinstock, Jeffrey. 2007. *The Rocky Horror Picture Show*. New York: Columbia University Press/Wallflower Press.

Wright, Judith Hess. [2012 [1986]]. "Genre Film and the Status Quo." In Barry Keith Grant (ed.), *Film Genre Reader II*. Austin: University of Texas Press: 41–49.

36

CULT FILM AND ADAPTATION

I.Q. Hunter

The term "cult novel" is as tendentious as that of cult film.[1] Cult novels are in fact harder to define than cult films as they lack any equivalent to that foundational period of "midnight movies" in the early 1970s which instituted a canon of cult films adopted by countercultural audiences and subsequently check listed in books like Stuart Samuels's *Midnight Movies* (1983) and Danny Peary's *Cult Films* trilogy (1982, 1983, 1989). Novel-reading, unlike cinema-going, is generally a solitary experience, at least before its cult pleasures could be shared in reading groups and in online forums, and determining a novel's cult status and reputation is therefore unavoidably speculative. One simple but unsatisfactory rule of thumb might be that a cult novel belongs to that elusive discursive category if it is repeatedly inserted into it by, for example, reviews of reprints, on book jackets and in publishers' catalogues, or in Wikipedia entries, journalistic surveys, and online listicles that address "what is a cult novel?" In that sense "cult" is no less debatable as a descriptor than "classic," a category into which many cult novels are ultimately inducted.

Extrapolating from the sources mentioned above, one finds that cult novels do seem to cohere as a kind of genre or modality. Typically they are underground, Romantic, transgressive, and touch on the borders of avant-garde, trash and genre writing (Calcutt and Shepherd 1998: x). Their appeal, moreover, according to the only comprehensive guide to cult novels, is to

> people who feel somehow cut off, socially disenfranchised, deprived of their rightful community of man. Much as they may lament this condition publicly, many secretly prefer alienation, taking curious comfort in the knowledge that they are not alone in their loneliness.
>
> (Whissen 1992: xxvii)

Cult novels not only interpolate and comfort their readership of outsiders but spur them to action: "A cult book must, above all, serve as the mirror in which the alienated see themselves reflected – and rejoice" (Whissen 1992: xxx). Inspired by encountering their reflection, readers modify their behaviour, dress, habits, and view of the world, usually in the direction of unconventionality. Sara Alegre makes a further distinction between readers' and authors' cult novels:

readers' cult novels [like Frank Herbert's *Dune*] depend essentially on the reader's identification with a strong individual character of mythical dimensions, whereas writers'
cult novels [like *Naked Lunch*] are enjoyed because the author is admired by aspiring or
established authors due to his or her condition as a highly original (Romantic) artist.
This explains, in addition, why cult books are found at either side of the canonical
divide and why they cannot simply be identified with pulp or popular fiction.

(Alegre 1999: 141)

The novel's fascination is often enhanced by that of its author, whose arresting or lurid biography may secure the novel's cult status. William S. Burroughs's history as a drug-addicted
uroxicidal Beat lends an aura of outsider authenticity to the paranoid fantasies of his *Naked
Lunch*. Burroughs, like Sade, Rimbaud, Bukowski, Pynchon, Fr. Rolfe (Baron Corvo), Ayn
Rand, and Michel Houellebecq, are cult writers as much as authors of cult texts, and their biographical legends (or tantalising anonymity in the case of Pynchon) are inextricable from the
allure of their writing.

Cult novels by definition appeal, at any rate initially, to a limited exclusive readership of
enthusiasts, though as with cult films it is anyone's guess how many cultists make for a "legitimate" cult. While the Golden Age of cult films' reception as cult began in the late 1960s, that of
the highest profile cult novels was post-war America (Whissen 1992: x), the age of the Beat and
underground novel (*On the Road*), ambitious science fiction (*Dune, Stranger in a Strange Land,
Atlas Shrugged*), novels about youthful alienation (*The Catcher in the Rye*) and life at the sexual
margins (*Last Exit to Brooklyn*). The counterculture of the mid to late1960s, which made cult
hits out of *Easy Rider* (1969) and *El Topo* (1970), resurrected and appropriated earlier novels,
such as *Siddhartha, Steppenwolf,* and *The Lord of the Rings*, and inspired their adaptation into films
in the 1970s.

There is, on the face of it, no special relationship between cult films and screen adaptation
simply because the majority of films are adaptations and cult novels do not seem to be adapted
more often than any other kind of novel. As it happens, the original wave of midnight movies in
the 1970s, such as *El Topo*, tended not to be adaptations, but that is largely because many of them
were exploitation or trash movies and such films are rarely directly sourced from pre-existing
material other than the box office hits they may have ripped off. Even so, numerous canonical
cult films since then have been adaptations of one sort or another. *The Rocky Horror Picture Show*
(1975) was of course adapted from a stage musical, and novels were the sources of *Get Carter*
(1971), *The Holy Mountain* (1973), *Blade Runner* (1982) and many others, however quirky and
"unfaithful" those adaptations turned out to be. Not too many of these cult films, however,
were adapted from cult novels, though cult status may have been retrospectively conferred on
the novel because of the cult prestige of their adaptations. By contrast, properties with a large,
visible and exploitable fandom, such as *The Lord of the Rings* (cult in the 1960s but mainstream
by the 1990s (Hunter 2007)), *Twilight, Fifty Shades of Grey* and comic books, will be picked out
or even fast-tracked into adaptation for the same reason of commercial viability as any other
exceptionally popular novel. Adapting a cult novel therefore follows the same logic as any other
adaptation. The adaptation is intended to attract a readymade audience, which being already
familiar with the material is in less need of orientation. Like remakes and sequels, adaptations
draw on "pre-sold" narratives and take advantage of audiences' pre-knowledge of a text and its
culturally sedimented significance, both of which make the film easier to stand out and sell in
a crowded market. One key difference, however, between cult novels and either bestsellers or
books with substantial fan followings is that cult novels generally accrue their reputation slowly
and unevenly over many years and often in spite of commercial failure and critical indifference

or hostility. Adaptations inspired by novels' gathering cult visibility will therefore tend to appear long after initial publication and frequently in the guise of homages tailored to the novels' later cult reputation (and readership) rather than their initial contexts of production and reception. When that occurs, as with *Steppenwolf* (1974) (based on a 1927 novel whose cult peaked among hippies in the 1960s, which explains its adaptation as a "head film"), *The Sheltering Sky* (1990), and *Naked Lunch* (1991), the novel's cult reputation will shadow the adaptation in a way that an adaptation made before a cult develops is unlikely to.[2]

As already mentioned, with most cult films, including adaptations, their cult status does not usually depend on their sources also being cult. Indeed, adapting a novel whose cult status is not only recognised but liable to be invoked in discourses around the film is very different from adapting a novel without any such impedimenta. Not all adaptations are, as it were, "Adaptations," where the fact of adaptation and the priority of the original text are flagged up as significant and a special adhesive relationship is struck with the source. This is equally true for classics like *The Great Gatsby*, against which any adaptation will be measured and probably found wanting, as for cult novels like *On the Road*. Cult novels, however, might pose special problems of adaptation. For instance, one quality that seems to define cult novels is "unfilmability." Many canonical cult novels, such as *The Catcher in the Rye*, *The Dice Man*, *The White Hotel*, and *The Secret History* have resisted adaptation, and those that have been adapted have often seen their adaptations classed as artistic as well as commercial failures (*The Lord of the Rings* (1978), *Dune* (1984), *Fear and Loathing in Las Vegas* (1998), *On the Road* (2012), *Atlas Shrugged* (2013)). Although purists will argue that all "good" novels are unfilmable, cult novels tend to be imperviously so because they are, for example, about internal states (*Against Nature*), hyperliterary or stylistically opaque (*Finnegans Wake*, *Atrocity Exhibition*), or adrift from conventional plot and characterisation (*On the Road*, *Hadrian the Seventh*). Indeed their very oddity and difference may be part of their cult glamour. But it may also be that they are simply very long (*Gravity's Rainbow*, *Atlas Shrugged*, *In Search of Lost Time*, *Infinite Jest*), extravagantly transgressive (*American Psycho*, finally tamed and adapted after many missteps in 2000 as an arty black comedy), or so closely tied to the period, subculture, or biographical legend that "cultified" them that successful adaptation is thwarted by the very different contexts of cinema.

The obvious problem with adapting properties with a significant cult fandom is that fan expectations may need to be managed or even explicitly catered to, if it is sensed that negative fan reaction or anticipation might work against the film's reception and commercial chances. This is evidently true of novels with significant mainstream fandoms, whose protective impulses towards the novels may inhibit or indeed sometimes enhance the adaptation's success:

> the Rottweiler-like fans of the film's source material – comic book, video game, young adult novel, whatever – who can be relied on to show up out of a mixture of loyalty and curiosity, then rabidly promote and defend it on social media, no matter how dire the reviews may be.
>
> (Collins 2016)

With cult novels, generally regarded as having small but vociferous and protective fan followings, the fans may be less of a problem simply because niche fandoms can be more easily ignored, but the cult status of the novel may still need to be protected so as not to alienate the cultists. At the same time, the fact that a film is adapted from a cult novel may boost its distinctiveness in the marketplace sufficiently to make it worthwhile conserving whatever is cult about the source. To say the least, then, cult novels need special handling.

One thing, however, that adaptation scholars tend to agree on is that "fidelity" is not an especially good gauge of whether a film is a "good" adaptation and that judging it by its faithfulness doesn't uncover what makes it work or fail as a film. Theoretically, this is watertight. There is nothing necessarily superior about a faithful adaptation, which is anyway a practical impossibility given the differences between novels and films. That a film is an adaptation is rarely the most interesting thing about it. Putting fidelity aside has the advantage too of short-circuiting the usual tiresome conclusion that "the book is always better," with its insinuation that film itself is a lesser medium, at least compared with literary novels, and that adaptation is a matter of strenuous damage control. The problem with discarding fidelity, however, is that, in spite of scholarly remonstrations, audiences and readers (and not just fans) emphatically *do* care about relationships of fidelity and adequacy to the original. To reiterate, this is equally the case with adaptations of novels with fandoms as it is with literary classics. Rare will be the review of the next Jane Austen film that does not start by comparing it with the source novel, generally to its detriment. Audiences – some, not all – do *care*, for one of the pleasures of adaptation for those invested in the original novel lies precisely in comparison. If you have read the novel, even if you have forgotten everything about it, you may enjoy your memory being jogged, recalling reading the novel, and talking about the relationship afterwards. Deviating from the novel or getting it "wrong" may have the force of personal betrayal. This is heightened with cult novels (and indeed with remakes of and sequels to cult films). Cultists may worry not only about the film "ruining" the novel but also commercialising it and making it too accessible to wider audiences ignorant of the special pleasures, contexts and meanings of the original (rather as fans of Japanese horror films like *Ringu* (1998) were agitated by the American remakes (Hills 2005)). Fidelity is therefore not to be lightly discarded, as it remains a key way in which audiences relate to and judge films. In fact, this is something that adaptation studies can learn from cult and fan studies: emotional investment matters, as do the multiple pleasures of intertextual comparison.

To complicate matters, adaptations of cult novels if they gain cult status may – in fact undoubtedly will – acquire a *different* cult or fan following from that of the originals. Cult films have many different entry points for their cultists, who may be fans of the soundtrack, special effects, or a cult actor rather than the film *per se*, and who may thereby dislocate the film from the original novel. So an adaptation such as *Dune*, generally regarded as a disaster, has acquired a cult reputation as a troublesome outlier among David Lynch's films, a reputation quite distinct from its supposedly secondary relationship to the novel (even though *Dune* is one of the least "cultish" of Lynch's films). William Goldman's 1973 novel, *The Princess Bride*, is a rare example of a cult novel whose adaptation has also become cult. Fidelity to the novel's curious combination of genres which, according to the film's director Rob Reiner, "for fifteen years had been the story that no studio would touch," managed to reproduce those aspects which made it cult (Elwes and Layden 2014: 1). The novel has a significant fan base, but the 1987 film's cult, which took off on VHS, nevertheless seems to be independent of the novel's, even though the film, adapted by Goldman himself, is exceptionally close to the novel's plot, tone and characterisation. But with most adaptations of a cult novel, the point about fidelity holds. Comparing *Blade Runner* to Philip K. Dick's *Do Androids Dream of Electric Sheep* (and there is no reason why *Blade Runner* cultists should also be Dick cultists) misses out on much of what made Ridley Scott's film, as opposed to the novel, cult – its elaborate wraparound visuals, relation to *film noir* and the fascination of its textual cruxes, multiplied over the numerous different cuts of the film.

Adaptations are therefore rarely just adaptations; they remediate the novel, and it is the sometimes convoluted or thwarted process of remediation that may establish the film's cult. The messy failure of Lynch's *Dune*, which cultists interpret as a visionary *auteur* struggling in the confines of blockbuster filmmaking, contributes to its status as a cult *film maudit*. Failure is not

I.Q. Hunter

necessarily off-putting to cultists, who often revel even in disasters, especially when the result is a compelling ruin or, like Jodorowsky's earlier aborted effort to adapt *Dune*, a masterpiece of fragments ripe for imaginative reconstruction. To put it another way, no film, even a cult one, is *only* an adaptation of a novel. Adaptations never just adapt a single source, even if that is what is centred in discourses around the film. Adaptation is a process of accretive *intertextuality*, a term that adaptation scholars prefer to adaptation, as it signals that textual commerce is much wider than just between "original" and "copy." As James Naremore has said, in a key statement about adaptation:

> the study of adaptation needs to be joined with the study of recycling, remaking, and every other form of retelling in the age of mechanical reproduction and electronic communication. By this means, adaptation will become part of a general theory of repetition, and adaptation study will move from the margins to the center of contemporary media studies.
>
> (Naremore 2000: 15)

Intertextuality is possibly still more complicated with cult films. For one thing, films become cult for reasons not related to their sources – extratextual reasons, specific to the fan base or period of production, or the vagaries of the film's release. Cultishness exists in the unanticipated, quirky relationship between text and audience. While there may be a set of cultish characteristics or textual markers shared by cult novels and cult films, it is not necessarily the case that they are easily transferable between the two forms. Adapting a cult novel may require special strategies of radical adaptation to cope, for example, with its supposed unfilmablility, which foreground the process of intertextual commentary in order to update and use the novel in ways that make it accessible and relevant. This is true of cult films adapted from "ordinary" novels as well as cult ones. Indeed, cult *films* tend to be, insofar as they have shared characteristics, highly intertextual, and this interferes with any sense of fidelity. They are often revisionist, mischievous, generically hybrid, and frequently auteurist, an adaptation "performed" by a director, where adaptation is an appropriation as much as a transference. Anyone approaching Kubrick's *The Shining* (1980) strictly as an adaptation of Stephen King's 1977 novel rather than as a typically elusive and wayward Kubrick film is likely to overlook both what matters about the film and what triggered the florid cult over-interpretations archived in the documentary *Room 237* (2013). The differences and similarities will undoubtedly be arresting and illuminating, just as comparing any novel with its adaptation will teach you much about what "works" (or could work) on screen, but a list of the changes Kubrick and his collaborators made to the novel hardly explains or argues against the reasons for those changes. It is true that pursuing an adaptation from screen treatment through multiple drafts to final screenplay will throw up numerous insights into adaptation as an exercise and technique of problem-solving, and as a process. But what made Altman's *The Long Goodbye* (1973), for example, into a cult film was its hard swerves *away* from Raymond Chandler's 1953 novel, its elaborate visuals, correction of *film noir*, and so on – its approach of *anti*-adaptation, if you like. Similarly, Paul Verhoeven adapted Heinlein's cult *Starship Troopers* by comprehensively satirising its gung ho fascism in a deliberate refusal of fidelity. While the conditions that make a novel cult – such as its being taken up by a particular subculture sometimes years after its publication – make reproducing its "cultness" difficult, the methods of adaptation employed by cult directors such as Kubrick, Altman and Verhoeven, who are intent on wrenching the novel into their own worlds, works against any notion of fidelity.

As an example of the complex relations between cult and adaptation, take H.P. Lovecraft, who wrote stories and novellas rather than novels. Lovecraft was an American writer of horror

362

and science fiction stories in 1920s and 1930s pulp magazines, who, though long regarded as marginal or even bad, became influential on genre writers such as Stephen King. He created a usable world, the "Cthulhu Mythos," which other writers could appropriate, as much as he did a series of adaptable standalone texts. Since the 1960s, when his cult seems to have become established, his stories have been adapted numerous times, though not always with much sense of fidelity or commercial benefit from attachment to his works, and the films are best understood as slotting into the generic cycles and tropes of the period in which they were made. His work is "unfilmable" in that his technique trades in the unsayable and the unshowable, not to mention what Michel Houellebecq calls a deep-seated racial hatred that "provokes in Lovecraft the trancelike poetic state in which he outdoes himself by the mad rhythmic pulse of cursed sentences" (2008: 107).

The first Lovecraft adaptation was *The Haunted Palace* (1963), which was based on his 1941 novella *The Case of Charles Dexter Ward*, but the film's title was taken from a poem by Edgar Allan Poe, so that the film might pass as one of Roger Corman's series of Poe adaptations for American International Pictures. Positioning the film as a Lovecraft adaptation, at a time when his cult was not worth exploiting, was evidently less important as a selling point than its similarity to the other Vincent Price films in the Poe cycle. AIP went on to make an adaptation of Lovecraft's 1927 story "The Colour Out of Space" as *Die, Monster, Die!* (1965) (*Monster of Terror* in the United States), a US/GB production, in which Lovecraft's town of Arkham was relocated to England. Comparisons with the original story (whose reputation was again insufficient to warrant retaining its title) elide the film's overriding debt to the Poe films (the director, Daniel Haller, was production designer on some of them) and indeed to Hammer's horror films, emphasised by some exteriors being filmed at Oakley Court, site of many Hammer films. As so often, reading *Die, Monster, Die!* as an adaptation enables us to highlight interesting points of similarity and different, but such a narrow focus detracts from the key determinants of the production, which are bounded by the state of the genre in the mid-1960s. AIP's psychedelic *The Dunwich Horror* (1970), also directed by Haller, is a "closer" adaptation of Lovecraft in that it retains the genre-friendly title of Lovecraft's 1929 story and draws explicitly on his mythos about the Great Old Ones. But while the storyline retains the original's focus on Wilbur Whateley (Dean Stockwell) attempting to revive the Old Ones with a copy of the "evil book" *The Necronomicon*, the film is more explicable as a reworking of Roman Polanski's *Rosemary's Baby* (1968) (Migliore and Strysix 2005: 55). The climactic mountain-top sex scene, for example, plays much like the rape by the Devil in *Rosemary's Baby*, and arguably it is to the satanic cycle which that film inspired that *The Dunwich Horror* truly belongs.

Since then the most frequent adapter of Lovecraft has been Stuart Gordon, with *Re-Animator* (1985) (from Lovecraft's "Herbert West: Reanimator" stories), *From Beyond* (1986) and *Dagon* (2001) among others. These are much more obviously "cultish" films, made when Lovecraft had become a recognised cult author, but the mode in which the stories are adapted adheres closely to, first, contemporary genre tropes and, second, the means by which low-budget horror films attract cult audiences of "gorehounds" with gruesome special effects, outrageous comedy, and self-conscious trashiness. Even so, as Ken Hanke has remarked, the films are carefully tailored to respect the Lovecraft cult through knowing references to the mythos. This is essayed most successfully in *Re-Animator*, a key trash horror comedy of 1980s, which

> could charm the Lovecraft purist with its in-joke savvy (even if it would have certainly appalled the puritanical Lovecraft), while appealing to a far broader type of audience. The more casual viewer could revel in the film's countless excess and off-the-wall

humor. The scholarly were treated to references to Miskatonic University and the Lovecraftian town of Arkham, Massachusetts.

(Hanke 1991: 313)

Indeed, by the 1980s, Lovecraft's world-building mythos was frequently alluded to in many horror films, such as *The Beyond* (1981) and *The Evil Dead* (1981), in which the "Necronomicon" appeared, but these films were "Lovecraftian" rather than attempts at faithful adaptation. The most "Lovecraftian" of them all was John Carpenter's *In the Mouth of Madness* (1995), a cultish, intertextually rich homage, which as Andrew O'Hehir says, "isn't a Lovecraft adaptation, but something more like a postmodern mashup of Lovecraftian themes" (2012). It is reasonable to conclude that, as Stephen Jones says, "Lovecraft's stories have never been successfully transferred to the movies – perhaps because his uniquely cosmic and twisted visions still surpass Hollywood's technical abilities to recreate them" (1990). But if Lovecraft's stories resist adaptation, the "Lovecraftian," as an intertextual resource, has proved irresistible. Most recently, the H.P. Lovecraft Historical Society has embarked on radio adaptations and short DVD versions of the stories set roughly in the period of the stories and in the style of pre-war Universal horror: *Call of Chthulu* (2005) and *Whisperer in Darkness* (2011). These are fan films, adaptations by and for cultists, where a specific kind of authenticity is all important. The films are designed for comparisons and to be viewed knowledgeably *as* adaptations with the originals kept firmly in mind.

These films might be called "cult adaptations," a means of adaptation that is intended to preserve whatever is "cultish" about the original text and to require a special kind of viewing by self-selecting audiences. Elsewhere I have tentatively suggested that there is indeed such a thing more widely in contemporary film culture as a "cult adaptation," in which a cult novel, or cultish novel, is adapted in a manner that appropriates the novel's cult aura and presents the film as potentially cult (Hunter 2016). Films such as Terry Gilliam's *Fear and Loathing in Las Vegas* and David Cronenberg's *Naked Lunch* (perhaps the archetypal cult adaptation) are not fan productions but rather art house films that fit the category of prospective cult film and whose cult status is further burnished by their relative commercial failure. Here "cult adaptation" amounts to a kind of genre or at least template for independent films by directors with cult reputations, aimed at literate "cultish" audiences potentially familiar with the cult source novels, and which pay tribute to the novels by aggressively foregrounding their unfilmability and often the biographical legend of the writer. Made years after the novel's publication, the films are offered as homages as much as adaptations, with the novel's author emphasised in publicity, and the director positioned in ancillary materials as a fan of the novel to emphasise the film's authenticity. An aspect of vanity production often surrounds the film, as with Ben Wheatley's *High-Rise* (2016), based on J.G. Ballard's 1975 novel, which is not only cultish in its approach and address but pays homage to Cronenberg's similarly plotted *Shivers* (1975). But even here the film aims to be "Ballardian" as much as a detailed transference of the novel.

In relation to cult and indeed fandom, adaptation in fact requires a much broader definition. The study of cult adaptations might better focus on adaptations *from* cult films, such as remakes, novelisations, spin offs, comic books, franchising, fan fiction and films, staged resurrections such as theatrical versions of *Dirty Dancing* (1987), which appeal to the nomadic fannish delight in entering intertextual worlds. To get a clearer sense of how all of this functions would, however, need detailed descriptions beyond the scope of this chapter of cult practices as they pertain to specific films through case studies of their production, distribution, and reception. Textual analysis isn't necessarily the best approach. It is true that adaptation studies has been bedevilled by having the case study as its default mode, which militates against general overviews of adaptation as an industry practice or adaptation itself as a series of discrete sub-genres, but it at least acknowledges that the process of adaptation, like that of cultification, may have very specific determinations with each novel and film.

Notes

1 This essay will focus on cult novels, though comic books (*Watchmen, Judge Dredd*), LPs (The Who's *Tommy* and *Quadrophenia*, Pink Floyd's *The Wall*), autobiographies and many other kinds of text also inspire films, which may or not emerge as cults.

2 An example of adaptations that happen immediately but which are not inflected by cult are novelisations, which are commercial spin offs produced during a film's production. Cult films from *2001: A Space Odyssey* (1968) to *Performance* (1970) and *Taxi Driver* (1976) were novelised but, by definition, were in no sense inspired by the films' later cult reputation or adapted in ways that paid homage to the reasons for the cult. (Such novelisations may, however, be reissued years later to cash in on the film's cult.)

References

Alegre, Sara Martín. 1999. "Cult Novels on the Screen: *Dune* and *The Naked Lunch*," in Fernando toda Iglesia, Juan A. Prieto Pablos, María José Mora and Teresa López Soto, eds, *Actas Del XXI Congreso Internacional AEDEAN*. Seville: Secretariado de Publicaciones de la Universidad de Sevilla: 141–146.

Calcutt, Andrew and Richard Shepherd. 1998. *Cult Fiction: A Reader's Guide*. London: Prion Books.

Collins, Robbie. 2016. "Why It's Time to Blow Up the Summer Blockbuster," *Telegraph*, 18 June [online]: www.telegraph.co.uk/films/0/why-its-time-to-blow-up-the-summer-blockbuster/ [Accessed 19 June 2016].

Elwes, Cary with Joe Layden. 2014. *As You Wish: Inconceivable Tales from the Making of* The Princess Bride. New York: Touchstone.

Hanke, Ken. 1991. *A Critical Guide to Horror Film Series*. London: Routledge.

Hills, Matt. 2005. "Ringing the Changes: Cult Distinctions and Cultural Differences in US Fans' Readings of Japanese Horror Cinema," in J. McRoy, ed., *Japanese Horror Cinema*. Edinburgh: Edinburgh University Press: 161–174.

Houellebecq, Michael. 2008. *H.P. Lovecraft: Against the World, Against Life*, trans. Dorna Khazeni. London: Gollancz.

Hunter, I.Q. 2007. "Post-classical Fantasy Cinema: *The Lord of the Rings*," in Deborah Cartmell and Imelda Whelehan, eds, *The Cambridge Guide to Literature on Screen*. Cambridge: Cambridge University Press: 154–166.

Hunter, I.Q. 2016. *Cult Film as a Guide to Life: Fandom, Adaptation, and Identity*. New York: Bloomsbury.

Jones, Stephen. 1990. "Haunters of the Dark," *Fear* 22 (October): 25–27.

Migliore, Andrew and John Strysix. 2005. *Lurker in the Lobby: A Guide to the Cinema of H.P. Lovecraft*. Portland: Night Shade Books.

Naremore, James. 2000. "Introduction: Film and the Reign of Adaptation," in J. Naremore, ed., *Film Adaptation*. Piscataway, NJ: Rutgers University Press: 1–16.

O'Hehir, Andrew. 2012. "Beware the Flying Lobsters from Yuggoth!," *Salon*, 3 August [online]: www.salon.com/2012/08/03/pick_of_the_week_beware_the_flying_lobsters_from_yuggoth [Accessed 17 June 2016].

Peary, Danny. 1982. *Cult Movies*. London: Vermilion.

Peary, Danny. 1983. *Cult Movies 2*. London: Vermilion.

Peary, Danny. 1989. *Cult Movies 3*. London: Sidgwick & Jackson.

Samuels, Stuart. 1983. *Midnight Movies*. New York: Macmillan.

Whissen, Thomas R. 1992. *Classic Cult Fiction: A Companion to Popular Cult Literature*. Westport, CT: Greenwood Press.

37

CULT FILM – CULT TELEVISION

Stacey Abbott

Film and television are distinct media, each possessing a distinguished history, as well as different production contexts and industrial infrastructures that lend themselves to divergent approaches to authorship, consumption, fandom, genre and storytelling. Yet there is an established tradition of adapting successful television texts to the cinematic screen such as Hammer's version of the *Quatermass* serials; spyfy series *The Avengers* (1961–1969); action adventure shows such as *The A-Team* (1983–1987); British comedies like *On the Buses* (1969–1973), *Absolutely Fabulous* (1992–2012), *The League of Gentlemen* (1999–2002), and *The Thick of It* (2005–2012); and science fiction series such as *Dr. Who* (1963–89, 2005–) and *Star Trek* (1966–1969). Similarly, there are occasions when a successful, or not so successful, cinema feature is translated to television such as *Young Indiana Jones* (1992–1993), *Buffy the Vampire Slayer* (1997–2003), *Stargate: SG-1* (1997–2007), and *Fargo* (2014–). These works can take the form of adaptation, remakes, reboots, sequels, prequels, or the continuation of an ongoing narrative. The primary industrial appeal of such adaptations is the potential for a pre-existing product to draw an established audience from one media to another.

When considering this approach to adaptation in relation to cult media, the concept becomes somewhat complicated. It is not that cult film and television cannot make the transition across media, in fact many of the titles listed earlier would be considered cult. Rather the commercial objective for the production of such remakes or reboots does not fit with the traditional perception of cult media as being 'marginal' or of interest to a small but loyal audience. If a product is perceived to have 'failed', then there is questionable commercial benefit to adapting it to a new media. Even if the creative desire is to continue the story of a cult text cut short by cancellation, it is a challenge to locate the incentive for the studios or distributors to fund such a project.

Adapting a cult television series to cinema (or vice versa) does not necessarily guarantee that the film will share the series' cult appeal, as the nature of cult is often defined quite differently depending upon the media. Most cult scholars agree that the cult-ness of a text, whether film or television, is partly defined by the actions and behaviour of its audience rather than something that is necessarily embedded within a text (Jancovich and Hunt 2004: 27). Scholars however also recognise that certain textual factors might appeal to cult audiences. For instance, Sara Gwenllian-Jones and Roberta E. Pearson argue that 'cult television's imaginary universes support an inexhaustible range of narrative possibilities, inviting, supporting, and rewarding close textual analysis, interpretation, and inventive reformulations' (2004: xii). The cult TV series encourages and rewards fan engagement and creativity, as television writer Jane Espenson argues: 'if you force viewers to *participate* in order to mine the most enjoyment from a show, then they will feel invested, and if they enjoy what their effort exposes, they will become the cult you're looking for' (2010: 45; italics in the original). Furthermore, Ernest Mathijs and Xavier Mendik argue that cult film audiences are often attracted to a selection of features within their cinema, including: innovation, badness, transgression, genre, intertextuality, loose strands, nostalgia, and gore (2008: 2–3). The behaviour of the fans and the types of texts that inspire such actions can, however, be quite different. Many cult film fans are drawn to texts that are rarely screened or which are best viewed collectively, involving performed behaviour and rituals, such as dressing up and throwing rice or spoons in *The Rocky Horror Picture Show* (1975) or *The Room* (2003). In contrast, cult television is often easily available to view, broadcast directly into the home, and is associated not with public exhibition but domestic viewing rituals, such as watching *Twin Peaks* while eating cherry pie and drinking coffee.

Notions of quality can also distinguish how cult film and television are perceived. Ernest Mathijs and Jamie Sexton explain that

> many cult [film] reception contexts explicitly refer to the films as 'bad,' as poor or distasteful filmmaking ... celebrated because of their representations of transgression, abjection, freakery, grossness, gore, misogyny, or cruelty. ... This badness is as frequently approached ironically as it is carried as a sign of pride.
>
> (2011: 18)

So John Waters' *Pink Flamingos* (1972) is celebrated for its tastelessness while Ed Wood's *Plan 9 from Outer Space* (1959) is loved because of its perceived amateur qualities, described for many years as 'The Worst Movie of all Time'. Cult film fans and scholars often celebrate those texts that challenge a perceived cinematic canon, undermining traditional notions of quality (see Hunter 2008). Roberta Pearson, however, points out that 'cult television fans position themselves against the mainstream partly by arguing for the quality of their programmes' (2010: 16). For instance, Rhonda V. Wilcox has made a case for the 'quality' of aesthetics within recent cult television, arguing that cult TV series are often characterised by a 'textual plenitude' which 'support[s] aesthetic analysis' (2010: 31). Mark Jancovich and Nathan Hunt similarly argue that cult TV 'privileg[es] form over function' while opposing 'itself to the easy and transparent readings that distinguish popular taste' (2004: 28). Cult film is, therefore, often seen by its audiences as standing in opposition to hierarchies of quality within cinema, while cult TV fans position their favourite texts (*Buffy the Vampire Slayer, Supernatural* [2005–2020]) against the perceived mediocrity of mainstream television. There are, therefore, significant differences between cult film and TV that impact upon the transmutability of cult across media. Of course, numerous examples of cult television series have been adapted to film but many, such as David Lavery, have argued that the transition resulted in a loss of those qualities that made the text special:

> *The X-Files* was briefly reincarnated for the second time, in 2008 in a pedestrian, forgettable movie, *The X-Files: I Want to Believe*, reminding us yet again (as had *Buffy, League of Gentlemen, Star Trek, The Twilight Zone, Stargate,* and *Dr. Who* before it) that some cult universes are indigenous to television.
>
> (2010: 6)

Similarly, the reimagining of *The Rocky Horror Picture Show* as a television event in Fox's *The Rocky Horror Picture Show: Let's Do the Time Warp Again* (2016) has been criticised for the loss of the original cult text's frankness and transgressive sexual politics as a result of it being broadcast on television (Fienberg 2016; Moylan 2016).

Despite concerns over the transmutability of cult, there are established examples of texts that have successfully transitioned while maintaining, sometimes arguably, their cult status. The longest running example of a cult cross-media franchise that is considered by many to be cult in both its televisual and cinematic form is *Star Trek* (1966–). This franchise began on television in 1966 and for over fifty years has repeatedly oscillated between television and film, sometimes existing as both a cinematic and television franchise simultaneously. For instance, the *Star Trek* movies featuring the original television cast were made between 1979 and 1991, briefly overlapping with the first spin-off series *Star Trek: The Next Generation* (1987–1994). *Star Trek*, arguably, represents the quintessential American cult TV series. The original show's ratings were low, but it fostered a loyal fandom that fought to keep it on the air when it was under threat of cancellation after its second season. These fans kept *Star Trek* alive after its eventual demise in 1969, through obsessive reviewing of episodes in syndication, joining fan clubs, writing fan fiction and attending conventions (Hark 2008: 3). As Lincoln Geraghty has demonstrated, the fandom grew not only from a shared love of the show but also a recognition and celebration of creator Gene Roddenberry's utopian vision for the future (2007: 5).

The existence of this fan base influenced the decision to bring *Trek* back as an animated series in 1973–1974 and, according to Roberta Pearson, led 'Paramount executives, impressed with the fans dedication and, more importantly, with their disposable income, [to] reviv[e] *Trek* in film form in 1979', notably on the heels of the blockbuster success of *Star Wars* (2010: 10). Paramount Studios' re-conception of *Star Trek* from television to cinema involved bringing in Robert Wise, the Academy Award winning director of *The Sound of Music* (1965) and *The Andromeda Strain* (1971), while special effects artist Douglas Trumbull, renowned for his work on *2001: A Space Odyssey* (1968) and *Close Encounters of the Third Kind* (1977), was recruited to visually transition the series from its low budget TV origins to a big screen science fiction spectacular. The aim of this production was to re-imagine the series as cinematic epic, particularly through Trumbell's eye-popping effects put on display via 'long, contemplative, gliding shots of various forms of mysterious space hardware' (Nichols 1984: 131). While receiving mixed reviews from both fans and critics, a trend that has continued with *Trek* movies into the twenty-first century, *Star Trek: The Motion Picture*'s opening weekend domestic intake of $11,926,421, leading to a total domestic box office of $82,258,456, ensured that the once-struggling cult series was successful enough, given its $35 million budget, to warrant a sequel. For *Star Trek II: The Wrath of Khan* (1982), the budget was reduced, achieved by using the Paramount television crew to make the film. To satisfy fans, greater links to the series were established by bringing the popular villain, Kahn, from 'Space Seed' (1.22) to the big screen. The film also built upon the emotional relationship between the primary characters, Kirk, Spock and Dr. McCoy as established in the series, which culminated in Spock's death at the film's end, leading to fan discussion and theories about the possibilities for Spock's return. In addition to being a fan favourite, the film, made for a budget of $11.2 million, earned a domestic box office income of $78,918,963, making it an unqualified commercial success. This led to a further four sequels featuring the original cast. Furthermore, according to Pearson, 'the success of the film franchise, together with ongoing fan activities such as conventions persuaded the studio to similarly resurrect *Trek* television in 1987' (10), a trend that has been repeated with the success of the cinematic reboot franchise (2009, 2013, 2016) leading to the return of *Star Trek* to television in 2017 with the series *Discovery*, after a twelve-year gap in the franchise's televisual presence.

Through *Star Trek*'s movement back and forth between television and film, the franchise has straddled the cult/blockbuster divide, reinforced by the reboot franchise, which has split *Trek* fans. For instance *Star Trek: Into Darkness,* which was a box office success (with a domestic gross of $228,778,661), was voted the 'worst Star Trek film in the entire canon' by fans with some arguing that 'by rebooting the series in 2009 as an action-oriented, fast-paced, big-budget blockbuster proposition, Abrams and his team have completely alienated the hardcore *Star Trek* audience' (Child 2013). For many fans, critics and scholars, blockbuster success immediately disqualifies a text from consideration as cult. While the global popularity of the *Star Trek* franchise negates notions of marginality, the manner in which fans continue to engage with *Trek* highlights, however, its continued cult credentials. Matt Hills argues, with regard to *Star Wars*, that

> the need to distinguish fan culture from a 'mass' audience when the cult alibi of 'obscurity' remains impossible results… in … 'overconsumption' or repeat viewings. … *Repetition* thus stands in for *rarity* of viewing where the fan distinctions of the cult blockbuster are concerned.
>
> (Hills 2003: 184)

This approach applies to *Star Trek*, and not simply the overconsumption of the text but also the consumption of ancillary products, merchandise and events. Yet despite the size of the audience, the Trekkie remains the quintessential cult TV fan as evidenced by the cinematic parody *Galaxy Quest* (1999) which, while never directly mentioning *Trek*, clearly models its fictional SF TV series on *Star Trek,* lampooning cult celebrities, fans and conventions. *Star Trek* conventions occur globally while *Star Trek* stars, from across the range of series and films, continue to appear at Comic-cons around the world. In 2017, CBS began streaming the new series *Discovery* globally via the on-demand service Netflix, while also making the back catalogue for each *Star Trek* series available to be watched and rewatched, fostering the continued overconsumption of this blockbuster cult text across film and television (Bradley 2016).

Star Trek is a distinct example of cult cross-media adaptation that has blossomed into a blockbuster franchise, fuelled by the fans as well as the commercial drives of Paramount Studios, seeking to maximise the franchise's televisual and cinematic presence. While the transition from TV to cinema often conveys commercial imperatives, it is also responsive to factors surrounding fans' and creators' passion for, and love of, a particular product. This transition is, however, marked by varying degrees of success such as in the cases of *Twin Peaks* (1990–1991) and *Veronica Mars* (2004–2007).

Twin Peaks

If *Star Trek* embodied a cult series within the network era, struggling against the perceived need within American television for networks to vie for the highest ratings, *Twin Peaks* is situated at a transitional moment within television in which a quirky and unusual series became desirable by standing apart from the mainstream. Robert J. Thompson argues that *Twin Peaks* marked a significant moment when the major networks sought to compete with one another through 'innovation' by 'looking for shows that would defy the very rules that [the networks] had so stubbornly adhered to throughout most of the medium's history' (1996: 153). *Twin Peaks,* co-created by television writer/producer Mark Frost and art-house cinema director David Lynch, seemed to offer the desired lightning in a bottle. Modelled on the televisual soap opera, *Twin Peaks* was built around the investigation into the murder of high school prom queen Laura

Palmer within the northwestern town of Twin Peaks, offering a glimpse, in *Blue Velvet*-fashion, into the comic, disturbing and surreal underbelly of small town America, mixed with infusions of supernatural and real-world horror. The series interwove melodramatic and stylistic excess within the matrix of familiar televisual formats and was marked by quirky, often unexplained, behaviour and dialogue.

The airing of the first season totalling eight episodes, as a mid-season replacement in the spring of 1990 led to a cultural phenomenon surrounding the series, as the cast and crew were elevated to celebrity status, appearing on the covers of *Time Magazine, Vogue, Rolling Stone* and *Playboy*. Audiences became consumed with the question: who killed Laura Palmer? For its second season, the creators were given a complete run of twenty-two episodes but as the narrative was stretched over a longer arc audience figures began to flag and the show was moved around the schedule and put on hiatus before eventually being cancelled – a familiar story for many cult TV fans (Lavery 1995: 1–2). Despite its mainstream popularity, the show had garnered cult appeal from the start with the publication of the fan magazine *Wrapped in Plastic,* the emergence of the group C.O.O.P. (Coalition Opposed to Offing Peaks), the repetition and circulation of familiar catch phrases among fans, the consumption of ancillary products such as *The Secret Diary of Laura Palmer* (1990), and *Diane: The Twin Peaks Tapes of Agent Cooper* (1990), and the popularity of Twin Peaks viewing parties in which copious amounts of coffee and cherry pie were consumed. David Bianculli describes the show as 'the cult TV show to end all cult TV shows' while Miles Booy and Sergio Angelini argue that

> *Peaks* was packaged as cult before anyone had even seen it. If *Trek* had developed a world ripe for both immersion and appropriation more or less without realising it, the town of Twin Peaks, where characters speak in instantly quotable dialogue and come complete with props (the log, the Dictaphone, Nadine's eye-patch), seems consciously built for such a purpose.
> (Bianculli 2010: 299; Angelini and Booy 2010: 23)

The series, cancelled after the airing of the season two finale directed by Lynch and characterised by his signature nightmarish surrealism, was left unresolved, as Jeffrey Weinstock explains:

> the finale of *Twin Peaks* left us with a world broken: Cooper compromised, Ben Horne, now revealed to be Donna's (Lara Flynn Boyle) father, possibly dead on the floor of the Hayward home; Audrey (Sherilyn Fenn) seemingly blown to bits …; Leo (Eric DaRe) tenuously holding in place with his teeth a suspended box of tarantulas. … The series went off the air with a literal bang that fans received as – and with – a whimper – and has remained suspended, like the box of tarantulas over Leo's head, in time ever since.
> (2016: 8)

After cancellation, when Lynch announced that he would be returning to *Twin Peaks* in cinematic form, fans of the series were delighted that their favourite show would live on but embedded within this exultation was the belief, by many, that these narrative questions would be answered.

The resulting film *Twin Peaks: Fire Walk With Me* (1992) however confounded many fans in terms of its relationship to the original series. The film opens with an extreme close up of a blue snow-filled screen accompanied by Angelo Badalamenti's recognisable Noir-ish score as the title card and credits appear. As the names scroll by, the camera slowly pulls back to a medium shot to reveal that the snowy image is in fact on a television set. Suddenly the TV is smashed and a woman's screams are heard from off camera, before the scene fades out and back in to a long shot of a body wrapped in plastic floating down the river as the subtitle 'Theresa Banks' appears, deliberately reminiscent of the discovery of Laura Palmer's body in the television series, also wrapped in plastic, on the bank of a river ('Pilot' 1.1). This opening both establishes the film's connection to the show through the music, the body, and the river, but clearly disrupts the text's relationship to its televisual predecessor, smashing the TV as if declaring a violent break from the parent text. Narratively, this opening also disrupts expectation of a continuation of the plot for in the pilot to the series, Dale Cooper tells Sheriff Truman that the body of Theresa Banks had been found a year earlier, thus establishing that the film is in fact set prior to the show. Furthermore, as the investigation of Banks' murder unfolds, like in the series, an FBI agent arrives in a small town, but it is not fan-favourite Special Agent Cooper and his trusty, if acerbic, forensic coroner Special Agent Albert Rosenfield, but rather new characters Special Agent Chester Desmond and Special Agent Sam Stanley. While Cooper's relationship with local Sheriff Harry Truman was cooperative and emotionally bonding, Desmond faces distrust, resistance and abuse from the local authorities. Finally, it takes a total of thirty-four minutes before the film introduces the iconic *Twin Peaks* theme music over the image of the 'Welcome to Twin Peaks' sign, posted alongside the road into town and with the titular mountains looming in the back of the image. This opening seems designed to unsettle the *Twin Peaks* fan rather than cater to their desires for the film.

The smashing of the television also takes place just as Lynch's name appears on the screen, asserting Lynch's authorial stamp. While Lynch was a key figure on the series and has subsequently been attributed with the creative authorship of the show by fans and scholars, he was *co-creator* and executive producer along with Frost. He only directed a total of six out of thirty episodes, including the pilot, the season two opening episode and the show's finale (episode 29). As I have argued elsewhere, Lynch's directorial contribution was significant but Lynch and Frost deliberately encouraged a range of directorial styles as a means of developing *Peak's* quirky and innovative approach (Abbott 2016). The film, however, clearly positions itself as a Lynch film, highlighting his narrative and stylistic preoccupations. Unlike the series, which despite its quirkiness had a strong narrative drive in which the murder mystery was interwoven with a range of domestic, romantic and political narrative strands, *Fire Walk With Me*, tells the story of the last week of Laura Palmer's life. That she is destined to be a murder victim is known by anyone, whether fan or casual viewer, familiar with the series. But it is also clearly signalled to anyone who may watch the film without knowledge of the show, when Special Agent Cooper, investigating the sudden disappearance of Agent Desmond, makes the following comments:

> Diane, this case gives me a strange feeling. Not only has Special Agent Chester Desmond disappeared without a trace but this is one of Cole's blue rose cases. The clues that were found by Special Agent Desmond and Agent Stanley have led to dead ends. The letter that was extracted from beneath the fingernail of Theresa Banks gives me the feeling that the killer will strike again. But as the song goes, who knows where – who knows when.

The film then cuts to the Twin Peaks title sequence, accompanied by the show's theme music, with the subtitle 'one year later', followed by a medium close up of Laura Palmer, clutching her schoolbooks on her way to school. These shots are an answer to Cooper's question. As such the film is not interested in mystery or even story. While the series is modelled on the televisual soap opera format, built around a range of narratives and an ensemble cast, the film is modelled

Figure 37.1 Agent Cooper investigates the disappearance of Agent Desmond. Still from *Twin Peaks* (ABC, USA, 1990–1991)

on the cinematic horror film, offering an affective experience, mixing extreme horror along-side hyperbolic melodrama, of Laura's final days. This approach frustrated many fans looking for answers to the show's unresolved questions but also seeking the familiarity of the show's quirky humour and strange group of characters. This frustration with the lack of resolution has been addressed by fans through social media and fan fiction, in which they develop their own vision of the series. For instance, Rebecca Williams explains how the Twitter account @TheLodge encourages the production of fanfiction about 'an imagined third season', allowing 'fans to deal with an unsatisfactory ending and enable[ing] [the] continuation of a beloved narrative world' (2016: 146).

While the film was met with boos at Cannes, a sometimes hostile sometimes lukewarm response from critics and disappointment from many fans, it has since been heralded as one of Lynch's most masterful and uncompromising films (Collin 2014). It prefigures his increasingly experimental and surreal approach in films such as *Lost Highway* and *Inland Empire*. The mixing of horror and melodrama alongside the focus on Laura's story, rather than the other inhabitants of the town, FBI agent Cooper, or even her father, connects the film to Lynch's cinematic pre-occupations, as Robbie Collin explains: 'Like *Blue Velvet*'s Dorothy Vallens, *Mulholland Drive*'s Rita and *Inland Empire*'s Nikki Grace, Laura is a classic Lynchian woman in trouble' whose soul is revealed to be lost, 'long before she met her grisly end in an abandoned railway car' (2014). In this manner, the reception of the film upon its initial release distanced the film from its cult television predecessor but as time has passed has contributed to the film's status as an auteurist cult film, in keeping with Lynch's standing as a cult director. As such the film marks a notable tension between the transition of a cult television text to cinema and the emergence of diverse reading strategies.[1]

Veronica Mars

While *Twin Peaks* highlights a potential tension between the cult TV fans and the creator/auteur, *Veronica Mars* embodies the perceived collaboration of creator and fans in making the transition from television to film possible. The notion of fans contributing to the revival of a loved cult series after it has been cancelled has a long history, from *Star Trek* to *Arrested Development*, *Quantum Leap* to *Roswell*, in which fans' protests, or the success of a series in syndication, contributed to decisions to restore the failing shows. In most of these cases, the shows were revived on television. Joss Whedon's *Firefly*, like *Star Trek* before it, embodied the, albeit rare, possibility that a cancelled television series could be adapted to cinema due partly to the sales of the series on DVD and fan activism in establishing a highly visible and vocal fandom known as the Browncoats. When the film was eventually made, Whedon openly acknowledged and thanked the fans for their contribution to the process at a preview screening of an incomplete version of the film at San Diego Comic-con.

> The people who made the show and the people who saw the show…fell in love with it a little bit too much to let it go. Too much to lay down arms when the battle looked pretty much lost. In Hollywood people like that are called unrealistic, quixotic, obsessive. In my world they're called Browncoats. … This movie should not exist. Failed TV shows don't get made into major motion pictures, unless the creator, the cast and the fans believe beyond reason. It's what I've felt. It's what I've seen in the DVD sales, the booths at the cons run by fans, the websites and the fundraisers. All the work the fans have done have helped make this movie. It is, in an unprecedented sense, your movie. … They tried to kill us. They did kill us and here we are. We have done the impossible and that makes us mighty.

This statement was both a thank you and an attempt to galvanise the fans' enthusiasm for the series and film in order to boost box office receipts. Here creator, cast and fans are presented as a united front, collaborators in making and promoting the film to the uninitiated.

Rob Thomas, creator-writer-producer of *Veronica Mars*, Film Noir/teen detective series cancelled after its third season on WB/CW, took this collaborative relationship between creators and fans a step further. When compared to *Twin Peaks* and *Firefly*, *Veronica Mars* was a more successful cult series, managing to stay on the air for three seasons and comprising a total of sixty-four episodes.[2] Despite this comparative longevity, the show was eventually cancelled in 2007. In 2013, Thomas proposed launching a Kickstarter campaign in which the fans would fund a feature film based on the series. Thomas negotiated a deal with Warner Brothers, who agreed that if the crowdsourcing reached its minimum target of $2 million, the studio would market and distribute the film. The campaign was launched on 13 March 2013 with a high-profile video promotion that circulated via social media. Funders were offered a range of rewards for their donation, which included digital copies of the script and the film, DVDs, t-shirts, tickets to the premiere, and speaking parts in the film. Against their own expectations, the campaign exceeded its minimum target within the first twenty-four hours and by its end, it had reached a total of $5,702,153 donated by 91,585 fans. The film began production in the summer of 2013 and was released in cinemas in the spring of 2014, as well as being made available digitally around the globe.

This particular approach to reviving a cancelled series as a cinematic feature has generated praise for its innovation and engagement with fans as well as criticism for the ethical implications of the production model. Kristina Busse notes that this 'merging of fan and industry interests often ends up shifting costs and risks onto the fans' (2015: 112) and Luke Pebler questioned the ethical implications of this merging of fan and industry, suggesting that this campaign was:

> Setting a precedent wherein studio-owned IP gets seed funding from Joe-Schmoe-fifty-bucks-a-head. … As it stands, the only way I see this as an ethical gambit is if

Thomas uses this outpouring as leverage to get the movie green-lit by the studio …
and then gives everyone their money back when he sends them their thank-you gifts.

(2013)

In contrast, Bertha Chin raised the spectre of fan agency, challenging those critics who suggest that fans have been duped into funding this project and asserting that this project also presents a model based upon fan 'choice' and 'power':

Frustratingly, fan agency always gets left out in arguments which purports concern that fans are being duped by studios and networks. Perhaps, rather than assuming that fans are being duped into donating towards a studio film, thought should be given to implications the success of this campaign might bring to Hollywood's system; or more importantly, the power fans can wield if they decide a *Veronica Mars* movie is deserving to be made.

(2013)

Bethan Jones similarly argued that 'fans are well aware that they are donating to a large studio – the difference is that *it doesn't matter*. The investment is in the text, not the studio'.

Veronica Mars presented a model in which creators and fans collaborated in order to get the project off the ground, empowering fans by providing an opportunity for them to contribute to the film's production. This discourse continued to surround the production, in which contributors were sent regular updates about the status of the film, announcements about casting including the return of favourite characters/actors from the series, and importantly distribution plans to ensure that all contributors would be able to see the film either in cinemas or online by its global release date. During the production many fans identified filming locations in advance and gathered around the locations in the hopes of catching a glimpse of anyone associated with the film. Rather than keeping their distance, cast and crew came out to meet the fans, signing autographs and taking photos and thanking them all for their support. Cinema screenings on opening night were sold out celebratory events filled with funders, wearing their VM t-shirts, exuding a sense of community and ownership over their film.

With this strong sense of fan ownership, there was an obligation for the film to meet fan expectations and in this manner it did. In contrast to *Fire Walk With Me,* the film was replete with references to the series; acknowledgement of established story lines; the return of a broad selection of major and minor characters from the show, populating the screen with familiar faces; a sharply written script with the snappy dialogue associated with the show; a continuation of key themes and relationships, in particular the love story between Veronica and bad-boy Logan Echols, the emphasis upon Veronica's relationship with her father Keith Mars, and the evocation of a long history of class segregation and police corruption within the town of Neptune, California. Most importantly, the film featured the return, and return to form, of its strong and fierce female heroine Veronica Mars, last seen walking away in the rain, having – most likely – caused her father to lose the election that would have seen him return to the position of Neptune Sheriff. While *Fire Walk with Me* refused to resolve the unanswered questions of the series, *Veronica Mars* concludes with Veronica deciding to stay in town, taking over her father's detective agency, and resuming her part in the Neptune class wars, declaring to the audience,

This is where I belong, in the fight. It's who I am. I've rolled around in the mud for so long, wash me clean and I don't recognize myself. So how about I just accept the mud and the tendency I have to find myself rolling in it.

Figure 37.2 Veronica Mars walking in the rain at the end of series three. Still from *Veronica Mars* (UPN, USA, 2004–2006)

First and foremost, Thomas delivered a film that would satisfy the fans of the series, the funders and collaborators in this project, potentially at the expense of drawing in the uninitiated. The world-wide gross for the film was $3,517,027, although this does not include the sales of digital downloads available through iTunes and Amazon. The film was deemed enough of a success by Thomas and Warners and led to the production of a new online series *Play It Again Dick* (2014) aimed once again at the show's cult fans. In many ways, whether the film made money at the box office is irrele-vant as its primary global release was within the digital realm effectively negating the distinction between cult film and television. For the fan of *Veronica Mars*, the film was both the conclusion to the series that they had been denied through cancellation and a gateway to future adventures in the form of the *Veronica Mars Revival*, an eight-episode limited series for Hulu (2019).

Conclusion

Star Trek, Twin Peaks and *Veronica Mars* each embody diverging approaches and results from adapting a cult television series to cinema, evoking very different relationships with the fans and raising different issues of transitioning from TV to cinema. There has in recent years been an increase in cult films, such as *The Evil Dead* (1981), *From Dusk Till Dawn* (1996) and *Wolf Creek* (2005), being adapted to multi-episode serialised television, partly in response to the increasingly popular presence of horror on television. In the network era, cult film audiences were generally too small to attract the ratings required for television and the network's 'Least Objectionable Viewing Strategy' in which programmes were designed to be as inoffensive as possible, seemed diametrically opposed to the often transgressive and confrontational nature of cult film. A serialised television adaptation of *The Evil Dead* would have been difficult to imagine in the 1980s and 1990s. In a digital, multichannel landscape, however, loyal cult audiences are precisely the target market for a rising number of cable channels or on demand services such as Netflix. This increasingly competitive market has seen a relaxation of censorship, resulting in growing presence of graphic and transgressive material appearing on the television screens as evidenced by the graphic body horror on display in *Ash vs Evil Dead* (2015-2018) and *Wolf Creek* (2016-). These changes in the nature of television raise questions about the evolving nature of cult in film and television and the relationship between the two. Perhaps, in a post-cinema/post-television world where films and TV series are consumed across a multitude of media platforms (cinemas, television, computers, tablets, phones), the distinction is becoming blurred or no longer relevant with potential for fans to more fluidly move between media as they pursue the challenging and transgressive material that fuels their fandom.

Notes

1 It is of note that the return of *Twin Peaks* in 2017, in the form of the long-awaited third season co-produced by Lynch and Frost, shared *Fire Walk With Me*'s narrative and stylistic approach designed to confound fan expectations. While many of the series regulars returned, the series refused to answer many narrative questions.
2 As compared to *Twin Peaks* thirty episodes and *Firefly's* fourteen.

References

Abbott, Stacey. 2016. "'Doing Weird Things for the Sake of Being Weird": Directing *Twin Peaks*', in Jeffrey Weinstock and Catherine Spooner, eds, *Return to Twin Peaks: Approaches to Materiality, Theory, and Genre on Television*. New York: Palgrave Macmillan: 175–191.
Angelini, Sergio, and Miles Booy. 2010. 'Members Only: Cult TV from Margins to Mainstream', in Stacey Abbott, ed., *The Cult TV Book*. London: I.B. Tauris: 19–27.
Bianculli, David. 2010. '*Twin Peaks*', in David Lavery, ed., *The Essential Cult TV Reader*. Lexington: University Press of Kentucky: 299–306.
Bradley, Laura. 2016. 'Netflix Will Stream the New *Star Trek* Series Around the World', *Vanity Fair* (18 July). www.vanityfair.com/hollywood/2016/07/star-trek-cbs-netflix-stream-globally. Accessed 20 November 2016.
Busse, Kristina. 2015. 'Fan Labor and Feminism: Capitalizing on the Fannish Labor of Love', *Cinema Journal* 54. 3: 110-115.
Child, Ben. 2013. 'Into Darkness Voted Worst *Star Trek* Film by Trekkies', *The Guardian online* (14 August). www.theguardian.com/film/2013/aug/14/star-trek-into-darkness-voted-worst. Accessed 20 November 2016.
Chin, Bertha. 2013. 'The Veronica Mars Movie: Crowdfunding – Or Fan-Funding – At Its Best?', *On/Off Screen* (13 March). https://onoffscreen.wordpress.com/2013/03/13/the-veronica-mars-movie-crowdfunding-or-fan-funding-at-its-best. Accessed 20 November 2016.
Collin, Robbie. 2014. '*Fire Walk With Me*: The Film That Almost Killed *Twin Peaks*', *The Telegraph* (13 October). www.telegraph.co.uk/culture/film/film-news/11153925/Fire-Walk-With-Me-the-film-that-almost-killed-Twin-Peaks.html. Accessed 15 November 2016.
Espenson, Jane. 2010. 'Playing Hard to "Get" – How to Write Cult TV', in Stacey Abbott, ed., *The Cult TV Book*. London: I.B. Tauris: 45–53.
Fienberg, Daniel. 2016. "'The Rocky Horror Picture Show: Let's Do The Time Warp Again": TV Review', *The Hollywood Reporter* (17 October). https://www.hollywoodreporter.com/review/rocky-horror-picture-show-lets-938951. Accessed 5 January 2017.
Geraghty, Lincoln. 2007. *Living with Star Trek: American Culture and the Star Trek Universe*. London: I.B. Tauris.
Gwenllian-Jones, Sara, and Roberta E. Pearson. 2004. 'Introduction', in Gwenllian-Jones and Pearson, eds, *Cult Television*. Minneapolis: University of Minnesota Press: ix–xx.
Hark, Ina Rae. 2008. *Star Trek*. London: BFI/Palgrave Macmillan.
Hills, Matt. 2003. '*Star Wars* in Fandom, Film Theory, and the Museum: The Cultural Status of the Cult Blockbuster', in Julian Stringer, ed., *Movie Blockbusters*. London: Routledge: 178–189.
Hunter, I.Q. 2008. 'Beaver Las Vegas! A Fan-Boy's Defence of *Showgirls*' in Ernest Mathijs and Xavier Mendik, eds, *The Cult Film Reader*. Maidenhead: McGraw-Hill/Open University Press: 472–481.

Jancovich, Mark, and Nathan Hunt. 2004. 'The Mainstream, Distinction and Cult TV', in Sarah Gwenllian-Jones and Roberta E. Pearson, eds, *Cult Television*. Minneapolis: University of Minnesota Press: 27–44.

Jones, Bethan. 2013. 'Fan Exploitation, Kickstarter and Veronica Mars', The X-*Files* (15 March). https://bethanvjones.wordpress.com/2013/03/15/fan-exploitation-kickstarter-and-veronica-mars. Accessed 20 November 2016.

Lavery, David. 1995. 'Introduction: The Semiotics of Cobble *Twin Peaks' Interpretive Community'*, in David Lavery, ed., *Full of Secrets: Critical Approaches to Twin Peaks*. Detroit: Wayne State University Press: 1–21.

Lavery, David. 2010. 'How Cult TV Became Mainstream', in David Lavery, ed., *The Essential Cult TV Reader*. Lexington: University Press of Kentucky: 1–6.

Mathijs, Ernest, and Xavier Mendik. 2008. 'What Is Cult Film?', in Ernest Mathijs and Xavier Mendik, eds, *The Cult Film Reader*. Maidenhead: McGraw-Hill/Open University Press: 1–11.

Mathijs, Ernest, and Jamie Sexton. 2011. *Cult Cinema*. Oxford: Wiley-Blackwell.

Moylan, Brian. 2016. 'The Fan Rituals that Made Rocky Horror Picture Show a Cult Classic', *The Guardian* (19 October). https://www.theguardian.com/culture/2016/oct/19/rocky-horror-picture-show-fan-rituals-fox-remake. 5 January 2017.

Nichols, Peter. 1984. *Fantastic Cinema*. London: Ebury Press.

Pearson, Roberta. 2010. 'Observations on Cult Television', in Stacey Abbott, ed., *The Cult TV Book*. London: I.B. Tauris: 7–17.

Pebler, Luke. 2013. 'My Gigantic Issue with the Veronica Mars Kickstarter', *Revenge of the Fans*. www.suzanne-scott.com/2013/03/15/guest-post-my-gigantic-issue-with-the-veronica-mars-kickstarter/. Accessed 20 November 2016.

Thompson, Robert J. 1996. *Television's Second Golden Age: From Hill Street Blues to ER*. Syracuse, NY: Syracuse University Press.

Weinstock, Jeffrey. 2016. '"It Is Happening Again": New Reflections on *Twin Peaks'*, in Jeffrey Weinstock and Catherine Spooner, eds, *Return to Twin Peaks: New Approaches to Materiality, Theory, and Genre on Television*. New York: Palgrave Macmillan: 1–25.

Wilcox, Rhonda V. 2010. 'The Aesthetics of Cult TV', in Stacey Abbott, ed., *The Cult TV Book*. London: I.B. Tauris: 7–17.

Williams, Rebecca. 2016. 'Ontological Security, Authorship, and Resurrection: Exploring *Twin Peaks'* Social Media Afterlife', *Cinema Journal*, 55.3: 143–147.

PART VIII

Auteurs

Cult auteurs

The beginnings of auteurism are often connected to the *Cahiers du Cinema* critics (such as Truffaut, Godard and Rivette) in the 1950s. Significant directors had long been hailed as creative forces before the intervention of the *Cahiers* critics, but it was their specific debates – underlined by a passionate and often iconoclastic tone – that have become most privileged within histories of auteurism and cinema. At the time, this approach was considered by some as cultist because it was promoting a cult of the individual within cinema production, and because it often located artistic excellence across the work of a number of Hollywood directors' films – such as Howard Hawks and Alfred Hitchcock – which had previously been perceived as entertainment rather than art (see Sexton 2014). Following the adoption and wider dissemination of such ideas beyond France – as in the works of the British *Movie* critics, or the American critic Andrew Sarris (which titled one of his collections *Confessions of a Cultist*), the idea of considering the director of different types of films as an author has become less controversial and hence less cultist, even if debates underpinning the philosophical dimensions of authorship within a collective medium such as film continue.

Cult authorship (or auteurism) can now be distinguished from more traditional and established authorship, although there are certainly grey areas and cases which seem to blur such distinctions. There are some directors, for example, who could be considered both either established and/or mainstream, on the one hand, yet maintain a cultist dimension, on the other. In this section, the figure of Joss Whedon is someone who has worked within the mainstream of film and television production, but who has been considered cult because of the intense fandom he has garnered. As Erin Giannini notes in her chapter, Whedon can be considered an example of 'mainstream cult', in particular through his association with the Marvel Cinematic Universe, having directed *Avengers Assemble* (2012) and *Avengers: Age of Ultron* (2015), as well as being involved in creation of the television series *Agents of S.H.I.E.L.D.* (ABC, 2013 –). Giannani argues that Whedon's background was important in being hired to work on *Avengers Assemble* – particularly his experience in creative transmedia narratives (narratives which carry over into different media), as well as his close relationship with many fans, which helped him to create and publicize *Serenity* (2005), a film version of the cancelled television show *Firefly* (Fox, 2002–2003).

Other case studies in this section are less mainstream in nature, fitting more traditional ideas of cult cinema as existing on the margins of, or totally outside of, the mainstream industry. Out of these, David Lynch is the most well-known and critically established figure. Lynch can be considered a cult director who also enjoys the status of an art film auteur, as evidenced by the frequent articles on him and his work in art-focused publications, and through the numerous awards he has received. Yet he began his feature film career with *Eraserhead* (1977), which gained a cult reputation through screenings on the American midnight movies circuit, while his work has attracted significant fan devotion. In his chapter on Lynch, Jeffrey Weinstock delves into the work of Lynch and identifies some of its defining characteristics, including his play with identities and temporality, self-reflexivity, the importance of musical performance, and a very open approach to character and narrative which results in his films being difficult to fully explain. This latter approach in particular has fuelled the cult following of his work, as some fans become obsessed with interpreting details and enigmas in his work in the absence of any such explanations from Lynch himself.

The other three case studies in this section focus on auteurs who have mostly gained followings outside of the mainstream or legitimate channels. Such forms of cult authorship tend to construct notions of artistic excellence in different ways than more traditional approaches, but they also share a male bias. One factor leading to such biases is the sheer number of males in directing roles in comparison to females; however, this factor itself stems from systemic sexism within the industry, while male biases have also been considered prevalent within forms of cult consumption (see Hollows 2003; Klinger 2010). Recently – particularly since the rise of the #MeToo movement and the exposé of numerous sexual harassment incidents by men – there has been a renewed intensity to challenge male biases within film criticism and scholarship. One result of this is an attempt to challenge the 'canon' of films and filmmakers regularly lauded as artistic high-points, and to bring female filmmakers – many who have been marginalised or outright neglected – into more prominent positions. As such, we considered it important to include female auteurs within this section and to focus on figures who have yet to be written on extensively.

Alexander Heller-Nicholas explores the work of Roberta Findlay, a female director working within the male-dominated exploitation industry. Unlike Doris Wishman, who has been subject to scholarly analysis (e.g. Bowen 1997; Luckett 2003; Modleski 2007), Findlay has been largely overlooked. As Heller-Nicholas explains, this is partly due to her association with former husband Michael Findlay, whose films she worked on (usually as cinematographer) before moving into directing. Findlay is, as Heller-Nichols argues, a difficult director to approach and judge, as her films will often offend the contemporary viewer through their regressive sexual politics; yet the very nature of her working prolifically within a disreputable, male-oriented mode of filmmaking is itself worthy of consideration. While her films fit into a cultist vein of celebrating wild, outlandish cinema which does not conform to mainstream aesthetic conventions.

Jennifer O'Meara looks at a very different kind of female cult director, Anna Biller, whose work does draw on elements of the exploitation film but in a more critical fashion. As O'Meara notes, Biller has only directed two feature films so far – *Viva* (2007) and *The Love Witch* (2016) – which goes against the idea of cult reputations building up over time. But in the contemporary era films and filmmakers can build up cult status in more marked ways than in previous eras, and O'Meara investigates how Biller's films are infused by a cult aura not only via their references to previous forms of cult cinema, but also through the ways that her films are promoted, screened and received by a largely female set of fans. Biller's films can also be considered a form of retro-cinema with their references not only to previous cult films but also to more classical forms of female cinema, and through Biller's avoidance of digital filmmaking. Unlike many of the more prominent forms of retro-cult cinema, though, which are largely male, Biller offers a more feminine mode of retro-cult, in which she critiques the masculinist gender politics of some of the exploitation films she draws upon.

As O'Meara notes, Biller has referred to herself as a 'minoritarian' subject due to her mixed heritage (she has a Japanese American mother). So whilst most of the writing on Biller has looked at her as a female filmmaker, her interstitial status is also important in distancing her from another norm within cult authorship: not only are men dominant, but they tend to be men from North America or Western Europe. There are a number of exceptions to this, and within cult cinema there has been a longstanding interest within some areas outside of these spheres, particularly within East Asia (notably Hong Kong, Japan and South Korea). As such, we considered it important to include a director outside of the more privileged cult regions. Alejandro Jodorowsky is a good example of a non-Western cult director: a director who has a big reputation within cult circles but who is largely unknown outside of them. Jodorowsky's cult status did burgeon particularly within the United States when his film *El Topo* (1970) became a midnight movie sensation. While born in Chile, he is a particularly international director: he lived in France for many years, made his first features in Mexico, gained a cult reputation in America, and has since made films in different parts of the world. In his chapter on Jodorowsky, Antonio Lázaro-Reboll looks beyond the director's reception in the United States, particularly his films' reception on the midnight movie circuit, which have been well documented. Instead he provides an account of Jodorowsky's reception in Spain, where he has also become a revered cult director but in different ways. Lázaro-Reboll notes that his cult profile in Spain became particularly marked in the 1990s and was heightened by Jodorowsky's activities outside of film: tarot readings, book projects and personal media appearances all helped to maintain his profile when he was not directing. He also mentions how Jodorowsky's cult status has fluctuated through time and that interest in the director became prominent again in the mid-2000s following official releases of many of his films on DVD. Likewise, Jodorowsky's status – and that of other directors – has manifested differently in Spain than in the United States, even if he is considered cult in both regions. This points to the complex nature of cult reputations, which are always subject to spatial and temporal shifts and never entirely fixed.

References

Bowen, Michael J. 1997. 'Embodiment and Realization: The Many Film-Bodies of Doris Wishman', *Wide Angle*, 19.3: 64–90.

Hollows, Joanne. 2003. 'The Masculinity of Cult', in Mark Jancovich, Antonio Lázaro-Reboll, Julian Stringer and Andy Willis, eds, *Defining Cult Movies: The Cultural Politics of Oppositional Taste*. Manchester: Manchester University Press: 33–52.

Klinger, Barbara. 2010. 'Becoming Cult: *The Big Lebowski*, Replay Culture and Male Fans', *Screen*, 51:1: 1–20.

Luckett, Moya. 2003. 'Sexploitation as Feminine Territory: The Films of Dorish Wishman', in Jancovich et al., eds, *Defining Cult Movies*: 142–156.

Modleski, Tania. 2007. 'Women's Cinema as Counterphobic Cinema: Doris Wishman as the Last Auteur', in Jeffrey Sconce, ed., *Sleaze Artists: Cinema at the Margins of Taste Style and Politics*. Durham, NC: Duke University Press: 47–70.

Sexton, Jamie. 2014. 'From Bad to Good and Back to Bad Again? Cult Cinema and Its Unstable Trajectory', in Claire Perkins and Constantine Verevis, eds, *B is for Bad Cinema: Aesthetics, Politics, and Cultural Value*. Albany: State University of New York Press: 129–145.

38

"IT'S A STRANGE WORLD"

David Lynch

Jeffrey Andrew Weinstock

In the penultimate episode of *Twin Peaks: The Return*, the 2017 Showtime continuation of David Lynch and Mark Frost's seminal series that first aired on ABC in 1990 and 1991, FBI Special Agent Dale Cooper, played by Kyle MacLachlan, revisits the Washington state town of Twin Peaks where the original series was set (episode 17, "The past dictates the future," original air date September 3, 2017). Having himself only recently "returned" from a kind of twenty-five-years stasis, Coop discovers his evil doppelganger, the malicious Mr. C. (also MacLachlan), prostrate on the floor of the sheriff's office and witnesses a supernatural confrontation as a glowing orb containing the face of BOB, the malevolent spirit from the original series (Frank Silva) squares off with a green-gloved young man with super strength (Freddie Sykes, played by Jake Wardle) who shatters the orb. And then things get strange.

BOB seemingly vanquished, Cooper bids adieu to FBI director Gordon Cole (played by Lynch himself) and his assistant Diane (Laura Dern) – telling them, "I'll see you again at the curtain call." With the help of otherworldly spirits – a one-armed man (Al Strobel), a surreal skeleton of a tree with a sort of talking brain, and an equally bizarre steam-punkish giant teapot that apparently was once rogue FBI agent Phillip Jeffries – Cooper travels back in time, apparently to attempt to prevent the death of Laura Palmer, the precipitating event of the original series. As he takes Laura's hand (Sheryl Lee, both in the original series and *The Return*) and leads her through the woods away from the assignation that would result in her death however, she disappears with a scream.

The final episode of *The Return* (episode 18, "What is your name?" airdate September 3, 2017) confirms for us that in the world of David Lynch, there are no tidy conclusions, no easy answers, and no unvarnished tranquility. In this episode, Cooper begins a quest to find Laura and bring her home to Twin Peaks. Along the way, the scrupulously straight-laced Cooper has a disquieting sexual encounter with Diane that seems to satisfy neither of them; in the morning, he finds her gone, and discovers in her place a note that confusingly refers to him as Richard and her as Linda. In Odessa, Texas, Cooper (or is it Richard?) tracks down a woman (played by Sheryl Lee) who he believes is Laura Palmer – she, however, insists her name is Carrie Page and has never been to Twin Peaks. She also appears to have shot a man in the head on her sofa. The FBI lawman, bizarrely ignoring the murder, travels with Laura/Carrie to Twin Peaks, taking her to the house in which Laura grew up, but she does not recognize it, and Laura's mother, Sarah Palmer (Grace Zabriske), isn't living there. Confused and disoriented, the always-confident

Figure 38.1 Laura/Carrie screaming in *Twin Peaks* and *Twin Peaks: The Return*. Stills from *Twin Peaks* (ABC, USA 1990–1991) and *Twin Peaks: The Return* (Showtime, USA, 2017)

Cooper falters, asking what year it is; then, suddenly, Carrie/Laura screams: it is *The Scream*, the scream Laura gives in the original television series and Lynch's prequel film *Fire Walk With Me* (1992) when she is being killed by BOB, the scream she or her doppelganger gives in the Black Lodge, the scream she gives in the woods as she is wrenched away from Cooper who is trying to take her home. The house goes dark, there is a blinding burst of bright light, and the series concludes not with *The Scream*, but with *The Whisper* – with the image of Cooper in the Black Lodge as Laura Palmer whispers in his ear that he'll see her again in twenty-five years. The credits role quickly over a solemn music bed and the series ends.

I have recapitulated the conclusion to 2017's *Twin Peaks: The Return* at some length because, with its many twists and turns, odd characters and events, and bleak, unnerving conclusion, the series can serve as an extremely useful lens through which to consider director (as well as writer, producer, actor, sound designer, painter, and so on) David Lynch in relation to the idea of "cult" media. Liberated from concerns related to budget and the conventional cinematic constraints on length, *The Return*, shot continuously from one long shooting script and then edited into episodes, is essentially an eighteen-hour-long Lynch film – one that draws upon imagery and conceits present across Lynch's body of work. With all due respect to *The Return* co-writer Mark Frost, *The Return* is clearly "Lynch on steroids," a concatenation of Lynchian tropes and preoccupations including doppelgangers, metatextual self-reflexiveness, temporal extension and deformation, surreal imagery, and a mix of horror and humor connected to both the beauty, tragedy, and absurdity of life. Not only has *The Return* arguably expanded the parameters of the televisual medium, but it is perhaps the fullest possible expression of a mature filmmaker's personal vision and aesthetic, reprising and elaborating on Lynch's characteristic preoccupations. Through consideration of *The Return*, therefore, much of Lynch's career comes into focus, as do the "cultic" features and challenges characteristic of his work that endear some viewers while alienating others.

"When you see me again, it won't be me": Splintered identity

In the final episode of the first run of *Twin Peaks* (episode 29, "Beyond Life and Death," first aired June 10, 1991), Agent Cooper, who has entered the Black Lodge, a part of the spirit world, is confusingly told by The Man From Another Place – the famous sort-of-but-not-really backward-talking red-suited little person played by Michael J. Anderson – that, "When you see me again, it won't be me." And this indeed turns out to be the case as The Man From Another Place is apparently replaced in *The Return* by something akin to a denuded silver Christmas Tree with a speaking brain. This cryptic statement concerning "a me that isn't me," however, holds broader significance for Lynch's oeuvre in general, especially his more recent work, which has increasingly – and often confusingly – featured characters transforming or splitting into others. In Lynch's work, the "me" often turns out to be multiple and/or fluid. As Audrey Horne (Sherilyn Fenn) puts it in *The Return*'s episode 13 ("What story is that, Charlie?" airdate August 5, 2017): "I'm not sure who I am, but I'm not me."

The doppelganger motif is at the center of *The Return* as there are not just two Agent Coopers, but at least three and perhaps even four. Good Coop, we understand, has been confined to the Black Lodge for the past twenty-five years while his evil twin, the doppelganger Mr. C. – apparently a physical incarnation of the evil spirit BOB – has been at large, causing mischief in the world. Among the chaos sown by Mr. C. is the creation of another doppelganger of Cooper, Dougie Jones, who lives his life as an insurance salesman in Las Vegas until he is forcibly returned to the Black Lodge in place of Mr. C. The real Dale Cooper, released from his long confinement, takes Dougie's place, but remains unaware of his true identity and mostly non-responsive almost until the end of series' run. *The Return* is thus not only a return to *Twin Peaks*, the original series, but takes as its focus the return of Dale Cooper to himself. Or does it?

The last two episodes of *The Return* – possibly – undermine the entire narrative of Cooper and his return. First, as the green-gloved superhero Freddie Sykes battles glowing orb BOB, Lynch superimposes Cooper's face over the action, giving us in essence two "good" Coopers: one present in body and one somehow observing unseen. Then the finale introduces the confusion related to Richard and Linda. Is Dale Cooper really someone named Richard who has dreamed the entire series? Are good Coop, Mr. C., and Dougie Jones all parts or manifestations of this Richard? Or has Cooper somehow literally become someone else in the end? In typical Lynch fashion, there are many theories but no answers to these questions.

What we do know from Lynch's body of work is that people do actually transform at times into other people. This is certainly the case in *Lost Highway* (1997) when, after having been convicted and sentenced for murdering his wife, Fred Madison (Bill Pullman) literally transforms in his prison cell into young auto mechanic Pete Dayton (Balthazar Getty). Pete then becomes romantically involved with the mistress of the local mob boss, Alice Wakefield, who is played by Patricia Arquette – who also plays Fred's wife Renée who gets murdered early on. Near the end of the film, after a sexual encounter with Alice in the desert, Pete transforms back into Fred. No explanation for the transformations is ever offered by the film.

People become or turn out to be other people as well in both *Mulholland Drive* (2001) and *Inland Empire* (2006). In *Mulholland Drive*, we are first introduced to Betty (Naomi Watts), an enthusiastic ingénue just arrived in Hollywood seeking to be discovered, only to learn later that Betty apparently is just a dream conjured into being by Diane Selwyn (also Watts), a failed actress suicidal over a bad break-up with her lover. Amplifying this confusion still further, the main plot of *Inland Empire*, arguably the most elusive and dreamlike of all Lynch's feature films, focuses on actress Nikki Grace (Laura Dern), who wins the lead role of Sue in a film called *On High in Blue Tomorrows*. As the film progresses, however, any sense of a stable, coherent self begins to unravel as Nikki's identity seems to splinter into several different people. As with *Lost Highway*, no explanations are provided by the film for the proliferating Nikkis; rather, in his typically suggestive and oneric way, Lynch leaves it to the viewer to try to try to piece together his elusive puzzle and to make connections among segments and subplots.

The recurring presence of doppelgangers, and the transformation of characters into other characters in Lynch's work, of course compels the questions of "what does it mean?" and "how do I make sense of this?" And there has been no shortage of scholars ready to proffer theories, usually adopting a psychoanalytic approach.[1] The long and the short of it, however, is that Lynch has been remarkably reserved when it comes to offering explanations of his own films and has left it up to viewers and critics to develop their own interpretations, frustrating viewers who seek closure and rational explanation.

"No hay banda": Music and self-reflexive performativity

Perhaps even more insistent – and characteristically Lynchian – than doppelgangers and splintered identity is Lynch's foregrounding of diegetic music and performance, the staged quality of which then often self-reflexively foregrounds the medium of conveyance, metatextually reminding us that what we are watching are performances and cinematic sleight of hand. This functions most prominently in *The Return* through the performances at the Bang Bang Club, the local Twin Peaks bar and music venue. Music of course played an important role in the original *Twin Peaks* series, notably through composer Angelo Badalamenti's haunting score and singer Julee Cruise's dreamy live performances at the Roadhouse. *The Return* ups the musical ante so to speak by having most episodes end with a musical performance. Some of these performances are nods to the original run of the series – Julee Cruise ends episode 17 by singing "The World Spins," a song she sang in the second season of the original run, and the character James Hurley (James Marshall) performs the song "Just You," one which he sings with the characters Donna (Lara Flynn Boyle) and Maddy (Sheryl Lee) in season 1 of the original series. Other performers are rock artists and bands in what amount to music videos – performances by Nine Inch Nails and Pearl Jam singer Eddie Vedder stand out in this respect, but Lynch also featured contemporary alternative rock bands with the kind of retro rock sound he tends to favor (Chromatics, The Cactus Blossoms).

Most characteristic of Lynch however, and saturated with allusions to Lynch's body of work, is the performance by Mexican American singer Rebekah Del Rio of the song "No Stars" – a song co-written by Lynch – at the end of episode 10 ("Laura is the one," airdate July 15, 2017) of *The Return*. Sung as a sorrowful ballad in both English and Spanish, the song's lyrics mourn the inability to go back to a more innocent time – and, as such, seem to foreshadow the series' conclusion in which Coop seeks unsuccessfully to change the course of time by preventing Laura's death. As one watches the performance, however, it is clear that something is off. As Del Rio emotes, her head moves way back and forward, the distance between her lips and the microphone changes substantially, but the sound remains entirely consistent. Del Rio, we discover, is lip-synching. This performance in front of a live audience is not a "live" performance. It is staged – and this conclusion reminds us that all of this is staged, none of it is "real."

This is precisely the insight that Lynch forces on us much more explicitly in another musical performance by Del Rio, one alluded to Del Rio's performance of "No Stars" in *The Return*. In what may well be the most memorable scene from *Mulholland Drive* – and indeed perhaps from Lynch's entire body of work – Betty/Diane and Rita/Camilla go to a late-night performance at a theater named Club Silencio. As they enter, a rather satanic MC (listed as "The Magician" in the credits and played by Richard Green) on a stage backed by Lynch's favorite red velvet curtain announces, "No hay banda. There is no band! Il n'est pas de orquestra." And yet, he points out, we hear music – apparently coming from nowhere. A white-jacketed trumpeter emerges from behind the curtain, appearing to play, but then lifts his trumpet high in the air while the music continues. "It is all recorded," The Magician tells us, seemingly summoning bursts of music – and then thunder and lightning – out of the ether, before disappearing in a cloud of smoke. In his wake, Rebekah Del Rio emerges from behind the curtain, walks unsteadily to a microphone, and performs a heart-breaking a cappella rendition in Spanish of Roy Orbison's 1962 hit "Crying." Only she doesn't make it all the way through. Instead, she collapses – while the singing continues unabated. No hay banda, no hay cantante, no band, no stars. It is all stagecraft, smoke and mirrors – Lynch's cinematic take on Magritte's *This Is Not a Pipe*. The stage and the cinema are pure artifice – and Lynch, we realize, is the Magician who through BOB's enigmatic invitation in the original *Twin Peaks* run, invites us to walk with him between worlds and through fire.

One can trace this metatextual thread from *The Return* back to the beginning of Lynch's work. Not only is *Inland Empire* a film about the making of a film (in which we cease to be able to discern where the film ends and "real life" starts), but it features interspersed segments of a bizarre television sitcom starring rabbit-headed performers, as well as an unexpected musical number in which a troupe of mysterious girls perform Little Eva's 1962 "The Locomotion"; in *Lost Highway*, Fred is a saxophone player who we see perform near the start and who later, as Pete, discovers Alice is a porn performer as a loop of her having sex plays during a botched robbery attempt; in *Wild at Heart* (1990), not only do Sailor Ripley (Nicolas Cage) and Lulu Pace (Laura Dern) go to hear speed metal band Powermad play at a club, but Sailor twice performs Elvis songs – the first time, Powermad unexpectedly yields the floor to him as he sings "Love Me" and we hear girls screaming and crying. Later, he serenades Lula with a rendition of "Love Me Tender." Performance is absolutely central to *Blue Velvet* (1986) as Dorothy Vallens (Isabella Rossellini) is a mediocre lounge singer while Ben (Dean Stockwell) lip-synchs a performance of Roy Orbison's "In Dreams" (1963) – the song to which the villain Frank (Dennis

Figure 38.2 Rebekah Del Rio performing in *Mulholland Drive* and *Twin Peaks: The Return*. Stills from *Mulholland Dr.* (Lynch, USA, 2001) and *Twin Peaks: The Return* (Showtime, USA, 2017)

Hopper) later beats Jeffrey Beaumont (Kyle MacLachlan); *The Elephant Man* (1980) concerns a deformed freak-show performer who is rescued and later develops a love for the theater; and, going all the way back to Lynch's first feature, a central role in *Eraserhead* is played by The Lady in the Radiator (Laurel Near), a Betty Boop-ish character with oddly bloated cheeks who sings and dances on a stage.

Through these performances insistently foregrounding the act of performing, Lynch in an almost Brechtian way directs his viewers to reflect on the artifice of film. His films become films about films – part of their strangeness is that, at moments, they estrange us from cinematic absorption, alienate us from uncritical consumption. These are moments that challenge conventional viewership positions and practices, reminding us that, though we hear music, there is no band. In this way, Lynch puts us on guard against the all-too-easy assumption that cinema presents "life as it is."[2]

"Is it future or past?" Lynchian temporal deformation

Near the end of episode 7 of *The Return* ("There's a Body All Right"; airdate June 17, 2017), more or less where we've been taught by preceding episodes to expect a musical performance, we are instead treated to a scene of a man sweeping up peanut shells and dirt off the floor of the Bang Bang Club – for two and a half minutes. He sweeps and sweeps and sweeps and sweeps some more – and there seems to be no larger purpose to his sweeping other than to clean up. How viewers respond to watching a man sweep for two minutes likely is indicative of whether or not they are Lynch fans because the sweeping is characteristic of what we could refer to as Lynchian temporal deformation, a playing with time that Lynch develops in two ways: through scenes of "excessive" duration and through the scuttling of narrative chronology.

In Lynch's films, time often slows down in scenes with minimal dialogue full of long pauses and repetitions, and actions that extend well beyond conventional expectations based on Hollywood filmmaking. In what we might refer to as Lynch's deformed temporality of the extended moment, scenes "go on too long" and test the patience of viewers eager to see the plot progress. In some cases, such as the man sweeping in *The Return*, the scenes seem perversely purposeless, included solely to frustrate viewers impatient to see what happens next.[3] More often in Lynch, this extended temporality combined with awkward silences and affectless dialogue appears intended to evoke a particular mood – often one of dreamlike confusion generally tinged with horror. This characterization of Lynchian deformed temporality applies to the whole of *Eraserhead* for example, a film featuring almost entirely affectless characters, minimal dialogue, and often-disturbing surreal imagery. This deformed temporality of the extended moment, combined with the absence of affect also characterizes much of *Dune* (1984), with its extensive use of voice-overs – which may explain in part why the film failed at the box office. And one can draw a direct line from the nightmarishly surreal and slow-moving *Eraserhead* to black-and-white scenes in *The Return* that take place in what may be perhaps the counterpart to the Black Lodge, the White Lodge, in which more benevolent spirits dwell. These scenes are defined by their *slowness*. In episode 8 ("Gotta light?" airdate June 25, 2017), a twelve-minute segment devoid of dialogue and almost entirely in black and white has a matronly woman (listed in the credits as Señorita Dido, played by Joy Nash) and her giant counterpart (Carel Struycken, who played the Giant in the original *Twin Peaks* run) in a kind of 1930s drawing room receive news of human atomic testing and, apparently, the birth/release of evil spirit BOB; in response, they slowly send what seems to be the spirit of Laura Palmer to earth. Everything in this scene almost happens in slow motion, which – as with the twenty-five-year stasis of Cooper in the Black Lodge – suggests that time, as in dreams, functions differently in the spirit world.

In addition to the deformed temporality of the extended moment however, Lynch also enjoys complicating and undoing narrative chronology altogether. *The Return* repeatedly calls into question the linear progression of time through the character of Phillip Gerard (Al Strobel), the one-armed man of the spirit world who on three separate occasions asks Cooper whether it is future or past. Cooper's final line in *The Return* is then to question what year it is. *Mulholland Drive* and *Lost Highway* complicate chronology further, suggesting what Jennifer Hudson in relation to the former has characterized as a kind of Möbius strip conception of time (2004: 18). In *Mulholland Drive*, Betty and Rita see the body of a suicide victim several days dead who the film suggests is Diane – the dreamer of the dream (if it is a dream). *Lost Highway* begins with Fred receiving a cryptic message that he himself is shown delivering at the end of the film. Fred from the future delivering a message to himself is echoed by the bifurcation of The Mystery Man (Robert Blake) who speaks to Fred at a party while also apparently speaking to him on the phone from inside Fred's house. *Inland Empire* then exaggerates this temporal slippage even further, complicating or discarding chronological order altogether and moving back and forth between Poland in the 1930s and the present day.[4]

As with his characteristic splintering of identity, Lynch's temporal deformations act as provocations to the viewer that interrupt conventional viewing practices. Extended scenes and moments retard narrative development while temporal loops and discontinuities frustrate the desire for explanation and closure. These dilations and interruptions of time, together with the assault on singular identity and self-reflexive performativity, are part and parcel of Lynch's strange world, his vision of a universe that resists the imposition of determinate meaning.

"It's a strange world": The surreal, tragic, and absurd

Lynch's self-reflexivity and playing with identity and temporality finally culminate in a dark vision of cosmic absurdity in which normalcy is always a façade obscuring a more complicated and chaotic reality – one that resists the imposition of rational meaning or linear development. The original *Twin Peaks* was of course always about the strange, dark, and tragic lurking just below the surface of the mundane. Laura Palmer was a dual person: Ivory girl beauty queen by day, drug-using prostitute at night, and the two options given us by Lynch to explain her murder – either raped and murdered by her father or by the evil spirit BOB – are equally unsettling. What Agent Cooper's investigation into her murder reveals in the original run is just how saturated the seemingly wholesome town is with petty double-dealing and nefarious activity ranging from Leo's (Eric DaRe) drug dealing and domestic abuse of Shelly (Mädchen Amick) to Ben Horne (Richard Beymer) and Catherine Martell's (Piper Laurie) scheming.

This is the implication as well of the famous opening sequence to *Blue Velvet* in which the nostalgic vision of white picket fences and wholesome suburban life set to the strains of Bobby Vinton's 1963 version of "Blue Velvet" quickly gives way to a darker vision of death and decay as Tom Beaumont (Jack Harvey) collapses while watering the flowers and the camera descends into the grass and then into the dirt where insects swarm. Accentuating the horror here is the fading out of "Blue Velvet" as the music is replaced by the sound of machinery, a low hum, growls, and what sounds like chewing and rending.[5] The message is clear: beneath the idyllic surface of suburban normalcy is a shifting substrate of horror, decay, and perversion. This message is reinforced after clean-cut Jeffrey Beaumont finds a severed human ear crawling with ants and is amplified after having infiltrated Dorothy Vallens' apartment (initially disguised as an exterminator of course), he observes Dorothy's masochism, villain Frank Booth's perverse sadism, and ultimately confronts his own sadistic impulses. Walking with Sandy (Laura Dern) and describing what he has discovered related to Vallens, Jeffrey offers a comment that can be taken to summarize Lynch's entire oeuvre: "It's a strange world."

Lynch's films distort time and undo coherent identity as part of a project of reframing reality – his vision twists our focus away from the "normal" world and forces us to focus on the strange, a kind of shifting substrate of affect and experience that defies empiricism and linear time. Some of this is circus sideshow with Lynch as carnival barker. Lynch, for example, repeatedly introduces both grotesque and famously quirky characters into his work: the chipmunk-cheeked Woman In the Radiator and the horribly deformed baby of *Eraserhead*; the Elephant Man (John Hurt); the corpulent and diseased Harkonnens of *Dune*; the laconic and sexually ambiguous Ben in *Blue Velvet*; multiple characters including the Log Lady (Catherine E. Coulson), The Man from Another Place, and The Giant in the original *Twin Peaks* run; Bobby Peru's (Willem Dafoe) decayed teeth in *Wild at Heart*; the Mystery Man in *Lost Highway*; and a whole range of characters in *The Return* including not just the spirits of the Black and White lodges, but a little person hitman ("Ike the Spike," played by Christopher Zajac-Denek), a flighty chorus girl (Amy Shiels), a drug-addled hippy (David Patrick Kelly), and a green-gloved superhero. The absurdities of these characters sometimes provoke laughter (Candie the showgirl whacking her mob boss with a TV remote control), sometimes horror (the malformed baby in *Eraserhead*), sometimes just befuddlement (the dancing Man from Another Place), but all point to the larger theme of the absurdity of existence itself in a world where not everything makes sense and which lacks any transcendental signified, any stable anchor guaranteeing meaning.

Lynch scrupulously resists giving us explanations; instead, meaning is replaced by *energy* that circulates – power that transforms and is transformative, and that cannot be destroyed. In *Eraserhead*, sparks fly as the Man in the Planet (Jack Fiske) manipulates his levers; these sparks ignite in *Wild at Heart* with its recurrent image of a match being struck, and then the spirits of *Twin Peaks*, the evil ones who feed on pain and sorrow, present us with the cryptic invitation to walk with them through fire. In *Lost Highway*, Fred, having experienced visions of a cabin engulfed in flames, transforms into Pete during a thunderstorm. In *The Return*, the spirit world is directly associated with electricity – Cooper, after a kind of vision quest through the stars, returns by way of an electrical outlet. The most striking example of Lynch's holistic vision of the circulation of energy is the acclaimed episode 8 of *The Return*, which features an extended, stunning sequence of a nuclear explosion in which the camera takes us into the heart of a mushroom cloud. Set to the jarring strains of Krzysztof Penderecki's *Threnody for the Victims of Hiroshima*, the scene of swirling smoke and fire, of chaos and destruction, is one of both creation and destruction as the explosion seems to unleash BOB on the world.

In the nuclear test scene, the machinic pulse or thrum characteristic of Lynch's sound design builds to a fever pitch as immense force is unleashed, reordering the universe; quieter, but in some ways no less stunning, is the scene of a young boy who is struck and killed by a motorist in *The Return*'s episode 6 ("Don't Die," airdate June 10, 2017). In what may well be the most heart-wrenching scene in Lynch's entire body of work, the camera is unflinching in its documenting of the moment of impact and the bloody aftermath. As the distraught mother (Lisa Coronado) holds her son (Hunter Sanchez) to her chest, we see what appears to be the boy's soul leave his body and ascend into the sky, passing through overhead electrical wires on the way. There is no larger reason the boy was struck and killed beyond being in the wrong place at the wrong time; the implication, however, is that the boy's energy has been reabsorbed into something larger. He is not gone but transformed.

In Lynch, there is electricity that flows throughout the world and those who can tap into it are the heroes, lovers, villains, and magicians. Stepping back from rational explanation, linear time, and coherent, singular identity, Lynch constructs a cinematic universe around the strangeness of oneiric transformation and of energy coalescing in new forms. Like the spice in *Dune*, energy, Lynch seems to say, must flow and, in its flowing, it bends time and distorts space. The human condition finally for Lynch is a precarious one. Those who seek to obstruct the flow of energy are damaged and destroyed, like Lula's mother Marietta (Diane Ladd) in *Wild at Heart*; those who embrace it fully are dissolved, like Henry at the end of *Eraserhead*. The answer that Lynch gives us then – liberating to some, frustrating to others – is only to "go with the flow" and to contemplate with wonder the absurd, tragic, glorious strangeness of the universe, aware that there will be no final answers except those we make ourselves.[6]

Notes

1 See, for example, Žižek on *Lost Highway* and McGowan's Lacanian analysis of Lynch's body of work.
2 Kaleta and Schneider address alienation in Lynch, with an emphasis on *Eraserhead*, through a reflection on excess.
3 *Twin Peaks* fans may remember as well the scene from the original run when, after Agent Cooper has been shot) in Episode 8 ("May the Giant Be With You"; airdate September 30, 1990), a doddering old waiter (Hank Worden), unable to appreciate the gravity of events, stands over the prostrate, incapacitated lawman with a glass of warm milk for what seems like ages!
4 Žižek sees the temporal loop in *Lost Highway* as "the loop of the psychoanalytic treatment" (2000: 18). Nieland observes that critics have linked the "nonlinear, recursive temporality" of *Inland Empire* to the affordances of digital technology (2012: 140–141). See also Zegarlinska.
5 Atkinson in his study of *Blue Velvet* emphasizes the way this scene reveals "dark, unstoppable natural forces at work under the careful veneer of small-town America" (1997: 20). On sound in Lynch's early work, see particularly Michael Chion.
6 This perspective is developed most fully by Nochimson, who writes in *The Passion of David Lynch* that his films "encourage spectators to perceive the hollowness of linguistic structure and then discover a more complex form of connection through the subconscious" (1997: 7).

References

Atkinson, Michael. 1997. *Blue Velvet*, London: British Film Institute.
Chion, Michel. 1995. *David Lynch*, Trans. Robert Julian, London: British Film Institute.
Hudson, Jennifer A. 2004. "'No Hay Banda, and yet We Hear a Band: David Lynch's Reversal of Coherence in *Mulholland Drive*," *Journal of Film and Television*, 56.1: 17–24.
Kaleta, Kenneth. 1993. *David Lynch*, New York: Twayne.
McGowan, Todd. 2007. *The Impossible David Lynch*, New York: Columbia University Press.
Nieland, Justus. 2012. *David Lynch*, Urbana: University of Illinois Press.
Nochimson, Martha. 1997. *The Passion of David Lynch: Wild at Heart in Hollywood*, Austin: University of Texas Press.
Schneider, Steven Jay. 2004. "The Essential Evil in/of *Eraserhead* (or, Lynch to the Contrary)," in Erica Sheen and Annette Davison (eds.), *The Cinema of David Lynch: American Dreams, Nightmare Visions*, London: Wallflower Press.
Zegarlinska, Magdalena. 2014. "'In the Darkness of Future Past': Time in David Lynch's Films," in Barbara Lewandowska-Tomaszczyk and Krzysztof Kosecki (eds.), *Time and Temporality in Language and Human Experience*, Frankfurt: Peter Lang: 407–413.
Žižek, Slavoj. 2000. *The Art of the Ridiculous Sublime: On David Lynch's Lost Highway*, Seattle: Walter Chapin Simpson Center for the Humanities.

39

"YOU GUYS ALWAYS BRING ME THE VERY BEST VIOLENCE"

Making the case for Joss Whedon's *The Avengers* and *Serenity* as mainstream cult

Erin Giannini

Can a film that grossed $1.5 billion worldwide be considered cult? Marvel's *The Avengers* was one of the highest grossing films in Hollywood history ("All-Time Box Office"), featuring (fairly) famous faces, superheroes, loud explosions, and the near-total destruction of New York City, using cutting-edge special effects, and a budget of $220 million.

Further, *The Avengers* was meant to anchor and advance the Marvel Cinematic Universe (MCU), referencing the narratives the previous films (*Iron Man* and *Iron Man 2*, *The Incredible Hulk*, *Thor*, and *Captain America: The First Avenger*), as well as setting up what was known as "Phase Two": *Iron Man 3*, *Thor: The Dark World*, *Captain America: The Winter Soldier*, *Guardians of the Galaxy*, *Avengers: Age of Ultron*, and *Ant-Man*). The success or failure of *The Avengers* would certainly have major repercussions for Disney/Marvel, as well as for whomever was chosen to helm the film.

With those factors in mind, why then would Kevin Feige, CEO of Marvel Studios, pick Joss Whedon, a man known primarily for cult television series such as *Buffy the Vampire Slayer*, *Firefly*, *Angel*, and *Dollhouse* – as well as the (relative to the MCU) small-budgeted film *Serenity* and then-unreleased horror film *The Cabin in the Woods* – for a project on which so much narrative, and money, had been spent? By the metrics of Hollywood blockbusters, such as project should require, at the very least, a known quantity to Marvel Studios, such as Jon Favreau (*Iron Man*), and ideally, a brand-name director that could draw in a large audience solely on the basis of previous work.

Matt Hurd makes a compelling argument was to why Whedon represented the best choice for directing *The Avengers*, including his ability to work with large casts and production teams, his focus on character, and his long-standing knowledge of the source material (Hurd 2012: 447–454). Indeed, it is these elements, particularly the former two, that made *The Avengers* so successful; the story could resonate for the viewer with or without the knowledge of the previous films because of the seemingly organic interaction between the characters. (It should also be noted, however, that Marvel Studios makes a practice of hiring low-priced directors, or, as Adam Rogers explains it in his article about Whedon "Marvel Studios has a reputation for cheapskatery on talent" [Rogers 2012]).

For *The Avengers*, perhaps the smartest decision Whedon made was to make the premise of the character's interaction the difficulty of that interaction; four of the five central characters of *The Avengers* – Thor (Chris Hemsworth), Tony Stark/Iron Man (Robert Downey Jr), Bruce

Banner/The Hulk (Mark Ruffalo), and Steve Rogers/Captain America (Chris Evans) – each had at least one MCU film focused on their origins or adventures. None seemed likely, within the film, of giving up the power or control of the spotlight; thus, much of the plot of the film focused on the competing egos and challenges of super-powered individuals sharing their power – a concept, incidentally, that Whedon first examined in the final season of his series *Buffy the Vampire Slayer* ("Chosen").

While I'm not arguing that such a narrative decision is one that only Joss Whedon could have made, it does indicate his understanding of narrative and character dynamics. Whedon's work within cult television, the transition of his property *Firefly* to the film *Serenity*, and his continued, small-scale work (*In Your Eyes*, *Much Ado About Nothing*) through his production company Bellwether Films, put both Whedon and his work in a fairly unique position of what Matt Hills has dubbed "mainstream cult" (Hills 2010a: 67–73). In this chapter, I'll examine the ways that in which *Firefly/Serenity* paved the way for the choice of Whedon for *The Avengers*, with a view to a conclusion that both the narrative and the production of *The Avengers*, despite its high budget and high box office returns, also fits into Hill's concept of "mainstream cult" through both its use of a transmedia narrative and its selection of cult television auteur Whedon.

In the introduction to *The Cult Film Reader*, Ernest Mathijs and Xavier Mendik argue that cult film is defined by "four major elements: anatomy ... consumption ... political economy", and "cultural status". That is, how it's put together, how it's received by the audience, how it's financed, produced, and promoted, and how it fits within the broader culture in which it's released (Mathijs and Mendik 2007: 1–11). On a narrative level, they argue, cult films contain some elements of innovation, transgressive narrative choices, and aesthetic or moral "badness", as well as fitting primarily into a genre (sci-fi, horror, etc.) (Mathijs and Mendik 2007: 15). For cult television, as Roberta Pearson points, much of the discourse around its definition seems to focus primarily on its reception (Pearson 2003); it's cult if either the audience defines it as such, or the audience itself does not fit into the mainstream. Mark Jancovich and Nathan Hunt argue that "[c]ult TV is defined not by any feature shared by the shows themselves, but rather the ways in which they are appropriated by specific groups" (Jancovich and Hunt 2003: 27), although as both Pearson and Jancovich and Hunt – as well as numerous non-academic sources – have agreed, cult television, by definition, exists outside of the mainstream (Pearson 2010: 9).

Yet, as Pearson argues, the concept of "marginality" as a defining criteria of cult television is a feature of the past. The appropriation of cult signifiers such as genre and heavily serialized narratives into popular, major network series such as *Lost* and *Heroes*, "signal a fundamental reconfiguration of the American television industry – the mainstream as the new cult" (Pearson 2010: 9–14). In the same volume, "mainstream cult" is a concept that Hills examines in depth, arguing not only that cult can serve as an "industry bellwether" in Pearson's term (Pearson 2010: 9), but in fact that the "notion of cult TV appreciation as a resolutely grassroots and non-commercial audience activity set against industry machinations" (i.e., Henry Jenkin's "textual poaching"), "makes little sense in the contemporary TV marketplace, where cult fans have become one niche market amongst others to be surveyed, understood, and catered for" (Hills 2010a: 69), a conclusion Angelini and Booy also reach in their analysis of the shift of cult's features into mainstream programming (Angelini and Booy 2010: 19–27). Fan's textual poaching thus becomes simply an enlistment of the fan audience as de facto publicizers, in which "the fan serves not as an invited guest, but rather as domestic help, invited in so as to perform labor" (Johnson 2007: 78). That is, rather than representing an oppositional culture against mainstream tastes and interests, cult has transmogrified into just another brand for media companies to offer and their audiences to promote.

In this respect, viewing *The Avengers* as a film that, at the least, shares features with cult as a generic definition, becomes more tenable. If, as Mathijs and Mendik argue: "[c]ult films rely on reputations, and reputations are the result of specific types of presence in a public sphere" (Mathijs and Mendik 2007: 7), the choice of Whedon to write and direct the tentpole feature of the MCU becomes more understandable. Matthew Pateman ties Whedon's brand of "critical and cultural capital" (Pateman 2014: 167) to Fox's decision to move forward with Whedon's short-lived series *Firefly*, in the hopes that Whedon could reproduce the franchisability not only of departed Fox series *The X-Files*, but Whedon's own creations: *Buffy the Vampire Slayer* and its spin-off *Angel* (Pateman 2014: 154–156). These desires, on the part of the network, Pateman argues, "compromised" the series' chances of success.

> It was not clear that Whedon's style of television writing (long form, story arced, supernatural or science fiction) would fit with a channel that had largely favored, even in its quality output, mainly anthology-style dramas … or domestic realism.
>
> (Pateman 2014: 167)

In a previous article, I also briefly discussed the challenges of the competing brands of Whedon, Fox, and the series *Firefly*, reaching a similar conclusion to Pateman that the "intersecting nexus of histories, industrials contexts, financial imperatives … and business and sponsorship practices" (Pateman 2014: 168), were a "deluge that ultimately sank the series" (Giannini 2014).

"Can't stop the signal": Serenity as test case

Yet, seemingly, these same qualities that position Whedon as a cult auteur (Lavery 2014: 1–16) also drew Marvel to Whedon, with far more success than Whedon's relationship with Fox. In this section, I'll address the transmedia transition of *Firefly* from television to film as a precursor, or test case, for the choice of Whedon to anchor the transition from Phase One to Phase Two of the MCU.

Numerous analysis have been written as to why *Firefly*, as a series, failed on Fox (Buchanan 2005; Yeffeth 2005; Abbott 2008; Lubin 2014; Pateman 2014), pointing to unrealistic ratings expectations, the decision to air the series' episodes out of order, and the unforeseen length of the 2002 Major League Baseball season, which pre-empted *Firefly* twice during its first month of airing. While the former can be attributed to the industrial/network conditions that existed in 2002 within Fox (see Pateman 2014 for a full analysis), and the latter an unexpected complication, it is the second reason that holds the most interest in terms of my analysis. Whedon's brand is perhaps best shared as a word-of-mouth phenomenon. With the rise of the DVD format in the late 1990s/early 2000s, as well as the ubiquity of fan communities and connections through the Internet, Whedon's work benefitted from brand proselytizers; that is, engaged viewers/fans who would recommend his work to others, and were able to introduce said work through, as per example, loaning DVD sets to others.

As will be clear, this type of brand proselytizing would eventually work to the series benefit, but not in time to gain *Firefly* additional seasons on television. One of Whedon's signatures is generic hybridization; in the case of *Firefly*, which blended two genres (sci-fi and western) that had not been successful on network television for more than 20 years (Pateman 2014: 158), the series needed to at least gain Whedon fans, whom could thus recommend it to other viewers. Instead, Fox chose to air the episodes out of their planned order, eliminating another signature of Whedon's work; that of consistent narrative and character development. As I wrote in a previous piece, there was a particular logic to Fox's choice, in line with the series pre-debut advertising campaign ("Out There? Oh, It's Out There!"); they front-loaded the episodes that were high on both humor and action (Giannini 2014), to the detriment of narrative consistency.

The documentary *Done the Impossible* (2006) focused on the fan efforts to either resurrect the series on a different network (as had happened with *Buffy the Vampire Slayer*), or transition it to another medium entirely. A further indication that Fox should have perhaps trusted Whedon's fanbase in terms of publicity and gaining viewership was the clear understanding of the process on display within the documentary. When *Firefly* was released on DVD in 2003, one of the most successful fan efforts involved purchasing several copies of the DVDs and giving them away to friends and family. The DVD sales were reported to be a significant factor in Universal Studio's decision to pick up the property as a film (Chonin E1); they subsequently enlisted fan communities to publicize *Serenity*, as well as offering pre-screenings (which had not been done before) months before the film was released (Russell 2005). These pre-screenings of the (mostly) finished film were only available in selected cities and through limited ticket sales, positioning them as both a gift to fans (Whedon recorded a thank-you message that ran before each screening; cast members from the film appeared at various locations) and underscoring the film's cult status as a "specialist event" with "limited access" (Mathijs and Mendik 2007: 7–8).

While the film itself didn't have a large opening weekend box-office (approximately $10 million), the film made back its budget with both domestic and international box office (Box Office Mojo 2016a, 2016b). Further cementing its positioning as a more "cult" property, the film has been screened globally on June 23 of each year (Whedon's birthday), with the proceeds from the screenings donated to Whedon's favorite charity, Equality Now.

In terms of the transmedial transition from television to film, Whedon's narrative challenges for *Serenity* were significant. The film needed to be accessible to a broader audience while not alienating fans of *Firefly* with unnecessary exposition or out-of-character portrayals, in what Whedon himself referred to as the "most difficult script" he'd written (Abbott 2008: 228). Certain characterizations were necessarily shifted; contrary to the television series, the character of Simon Tam (Sean Maher) was re-imagined as more action oriented (see the series pilot episode "Serenity" vs the opening scene of the film), and the interpersonal dynamics between the characters of Mal (Nathan Fillion) and Inara (Morena Baccarin) shifted from Inara's desire to keep their relationship professional ("Heart of Gold") to Mal's inability to connect with anyone. Such shifts were seemingly necessary for the shift in format; the film's running time was insufficient to tease out these more complex character developments.

Serenity did manage, however, to represent a transmedia property on both an extrinsic and intrinsic level. On the surface, *Firefly/Serenity* is the same story told in multiple mediums: television (*Firefly*), comic books (*Those Left Behind*, which filled in the narrative blanks between the television series and film), and film (*Serenity*). Stacey Abbott, however, points out that the film itself did not disavow, either narratively or aesthetically, its television roots. "[T]he film does not sacrifice the intimacy of the television form, but within the constraints of its running time maintains the emphasis upon complex characterization and story over spectacle" (Abbott 2008: 232), through the film's emphasis on character development, as well as technical decision such as the use of hand-held cameras and close-ups. Abbott argues that Whedon's use of close-ups, most notably with the character of River Tam (Summer Glau), within the film not only recalls the "extreme close-up of Charles Foster Kane's lips speaking the word 'Rosebud'", but also "highlights how Whedon places spectacle at the service of characterization and story … interweaves the stylistic conventions of film and television" (Abbott 2008: 236).

This ability to balance spectacle and characterization, style and substance, and an ensemble cast, arguably made Whedon a strong candidate for helming *The Avengers*.

Erin Giannini

"Puny god": Cult meets mainstream in the MCU

Henry Jenkins opens his analysis of *The Matrix* trilogy as a transmedia property by citing Umberto Eco's points regarding how films become cult artifacts, including extensive world-building, positioning the property as an "encyclopedic" work to be "mastered by devoted consumers", space for viewer's fantasy creation, and the ability to be pushed into different directions (Jenkins 2006: 97). While Eco's analysis may not be applicable to all cult properties – several cult horror franchises, such as *Saw* or *Nightmare on Elm Street*, either dispense with elements such as world-building, or directly contradict their own characterization/origin stories in service of the franchise (see *Nightmare on Elm Street 2: Freddy's Revenge*, which remains an outlier within that franchise) – *The Avengers*, and the MCU as a whole, is by its nature an extensive, decades-long work that may be impossible for even devoted consumers to "master".

In that respect, I'm limiting my discussion to the MCU, rather than the comic books, which themselves are often full of contradictions, reversals, and odd characterizations (see, as per example, the recent furor over Marvel comics' decision to make Captain America a member of Hydra [Holub 2016]).

The MCU, starting with *Iron Man*'s release in 2008, currently consists of the films based primarily on a single character (Iron Man, Thor, Captain America, Captain Marvel, Doctor Strange, Ant-Man, Spider-Man, Black Panther, or The Hulk); four Avengers films (*The Avengers, The Avengers: Age of Ultron, Avengers: Infinity War,* and *Avengers: Endgame*), and the television series *Agent Carter* (2015–2016), *Agents of S.H.I.E.L.D.* (2013–2020), *Daredevil* (2015–2018), *Jessica Jones* (2015–2019), *Luke Cage* (2016–2018), *The Defenders* (2017), *Inhumans* (2017), *The Punisher* (2017–2019), and *Cloak and Dagger* (2019–present). The single-character films that were released from 2008 to 2012, terminating with the release of *The Avengers* in May 2012, are known collectively as "Phase One"; that is, the "world-building" of the MCU. Phase Two, which included additional Iron Man, Thor, and Captain America films, as well as introducing new single-character or single-universe characters such as Ant-Man (Paul Rudd) or the crew in *Guardians of the Galaxy*, expanded both characterizations and cast, anchored again by another Avengers film directed by Whedon. Phase Three, which began with a third Captain America film (*Captain America: Civil War* [2016], featuring nearly all of the cast, with some additions, that appeared in *The Avengers* films, making it a de facto Avengers installment) added additional single character films, some of which were sequels and others introducing new characters (Black Panther, Captain Marvel, Doctor Strange, Wasp), terminating with a final Avengers installment (*Avengers: Endgame* [2019]).

Phase Two, which also included the simultaneous debuts of Marvel's now-numerous television projects, unequivocally positions the MCU as a transmedia property, operating within at least three different mediums. Jenkins notes the difficulty of creating a true transmedia narrative, in which the narrative only becomes coherent when the viewer/consumer engages with each medium in which the narrative is situated. The attempt on the part of *The Matrix* trilogy, which Jenkins analyzes as a test case, was successful in as far as its narrative was built into different mediums: online games, an animated series, comic books, and the films themselves. It was perhaps less successful in that engagement with all of these elements was necessary to make the films' narratives comprehensible. It thus prized the highly engaged fan over the casual viewer in a way that no film before or since has quite managed to do (Jenkins 2006: 126–127). While Jenkins refers to *The Matrix*'s transmedia narrative as a "flawed experiment, an interesting failure", that nonetheless doesn't "detract from the significance of what it tried to accomplish" (Jenkins 2006: 97), the placement of the fan over the average moviegoer positions *The Matrix* as a cult property despite its high box office returns, large budget, and cutting-edge visual aesthetics.

Matt Hills, however, interrogates Jenkins reading of *The Matrix* trilogy as one that operates under the same binaries of "mainstream" (casual viewers) and cult (fans) that are growing more difficult to sustain within both the film and the television mediums (Hills 2010a: 71). Hills' own reading of "mainstream cult" – in which cult properties in both film and television aren't required to position themselves as "anti-commercial or anti-mainstream" (Hills 2010a: 70) – offers a better fit for analyzing Whedon's role within the MCU (as well as Whedon's previous output). The blending of a cult sensibility with a mainstream budget, aesthetic, and release seen within *The Matrix* trilogy thus offers the same opportunity to position *The Avengers/The Avengers: Age of Ultron* as mainstream cult.

As ambitious, however, as the MCU appears to be, with its television, film, and comic book properties as part of its encyclopedia of shared knowledge, it has not thus far attempted the type of narrative split employed in *The Matrix* trilogy. That is, while viewing the single-character films, the Avengers films, and the television series may create a richer narrative experience for the viewer, the plot is not rendered incomprehensible if the viewer chooses a more casual level of engagement. As per example, the release of *Captain America: The Winter Soldier*, shifted the narrative of season one of Marvel's *Agents of S.H.I.E.L.D.*, a co-production of Marvel and Whedon's Mutant Enemy production company, from a more "monster-of-the-week" format to a longer arc involving S.H.I.E.L.D.'s nemesis Hydra. The film revealed that Hydra had long infiltrated the organization, a narrative arc that played out over multiple seasons of the television series. In this case, rather than making one element of the transmedia enterprise required viewing to understand the developments in another medium, the MCU has been able to use its television properties to tell longer-form stories not possible within the film format, such as *Agent Carter*, offering more backstory for Peggy Carter (Hayley Atwell), Steve Rogers' love interest from the first film, as well as historical background for the development of S.H.I.E.L.D. and Hydra. (It is arguable, however, that *Agents of S.H.I.E.L.D.*'s first season suffered from having to introduce such a narrative arc late in the season ["Turn, Turn, Turn"] due to concerns over spoiling the film.)

There are thus numerous reasons why Whedon would be chosen to both write and direct the two Avengers films, predicated on his reputation as a cult television auteur. There is the early transition of his 1992 film *Buffy the Vampire Slayer* being reimagined/rebooted for television in 1997, a medium in which it created far more of a cultural impact, as well as the aforementioned transition of series *Firefly* into the film *Serenity*. It is the particular features, however, of these cult phenomena, that hold the key to the choice of Whedon. Previous to the release of *The Avengers*, Hurd, as mentioned above, explicated the numerous reasons why Whedon was the obvious choice, including his understanding of group dynamics (each Whedon series featured an ensemble cast that [more or less] were given significant narrative arcs of their own), and his facility with generic hybridity (horror/comedy/bildungsroman for *Buffy*; horror and noir for *Angel*; sci-fi and western for *Firefly*; and sci-fi/technological thriller/corporate intrigue for *Dollhouse*) (Hurd 2012). As Hills writes:

> [A] range of popular contemporary TV shows seem to be engaged in deconstructing the cult versus mainstream binary, presently commercially driven TV drama which self-consciously draws on discourses of authorship, sophistication, and quirkiness which have been more traditionally linked to cult TV in its telefantasy mode.
>
> (Hills 2010a: 73)

As I've indicated throughout this chapter, it is easy to expand Hills' definition beyond television to encompass the multi-platform transmedia text of the MCU. Eco has indicated that it is nearly impossible to view any cult property with fresh eyes within our postmodern media landscape (Eco 1986: 200–201), but rather than a cause for concern for the MCU, that is seemingly their operating principle. *The Avengers* was required to reference and build upon the films leading up to it and set up the next series of films, and, unlike *The Matrix*, do so without alienating the casual viewer, all of which *The Avengers*, according to most critics (the film has a 92% fresh rating on review aggregator Rotten Tomatoes), pulled off successfully. While Whedon's name was not strongly touted as part of the publicity leading up to the film's release, certain signatures present in his work were obvious in both films, including the aforementioned ability to work with ensemble casts and hybridized forms (superhero film/war film [see Guffey 2014: 280–293 for an analysis of *The Avengers* as a war film]), as well as a more significant role and characterization for the sole female lead Natasha Romanoff/Black Widow (Scarlett Johannson), touches of humor, and even references to Whedon's other series: in a battle between Loki (Tom Hiddleston) and the Hulk, the Hulk smashes the demi-god into the floor and walks away with a dismissive "puny god", a reference to the *Buffy* episode "Triangle", which featured a super-strong troll smashing "puny receptacles" – among other things – with a hammer eerily similar to the one Thor wields.

There is also the persistent question, asked of Nick Fury (Samuel L. Jackson): "What is Phase Two"? This is a metanarrative moment par excellence; in the film, it refers to a plan to weaponize alien technology, yet it's also is the term used to refer to the second series of Marvel films that *The Avengers* was required to set up. It thus becomes a question asked both diegetically and extradiagetically (characters and audience).

It should be noted, however, that *The Avengers* could be viewed as at least a dual-authored text: Marvel and Whedon. As Mary Ellen Iatropoulos argues, since *The Avengers* script "was developed in consultation with Kevin Fiege ... the argument could be made that Fiege ... holds ultimate authorship over all Marvel properties", never mind Stan Lee, who created the characters in the first place (Iatropoulos 2015). Whedon's signatures, combined with the MCU creates, she argues, a "sort of interpretive adaptation rooted in a sense of appreciation and respect" (Iatropoulos 2015). Iatropoulos argues that Whedon's recent work in both the MCU and his micro-budget adaptation of *Much Ado About Nothing* position Whedon as both "fan and creator" – touching on a similar argument made by Jonathan Gray, in which he explicated the ways in which Whedon must kill himself as author through this dual positioning as fan and showrunner (Gray 2010: 113) – and unsettles notions of authorship. I would further suggest that these porous interpretive boundaries within Whedon and the MCU more firmly positions *The Avengers* as "mainstream cult"; it "may not easily or cleanly fit into oppositions such as cult versus mainstream, but by drawing on the binary of authored versus manufactured ... the culture versus commerce binary underpinning the cult versus mainstream distinctions can instead find a variant outlet" (Hills 2010a: 70). That is, *The Avengers/The Avengers: Age of Ultron* has elements of both Whedon's style (e.g., the fight scenes, "bringing the funny", "turning on a dime", language, and "giving the devil his due" [Lavery 2014: 191–194]), and the necessary products of the MCU film-producing machine: spectacle, toyetic potential, and action. In that respect the Marvel/Whedon authorship relationship resembles that of the rebooted *Dr. Who*, which in Hills' analysis of the series is both multi-authored and, in the case of the reboot, featuring long-term fans (Russell T. Davies and Stephen Moffat) – as Whedon was of Marvel – as showrunners (Hills 2010b).

There is a significant amount of critical debate as to whether *Avengers: Age of Ultron* was equally successful in that regard, and Whedon himself left Marvel following its release, citing, among other things, the pressure of Marvel's transmedia requirements (Robinson 2015). Yet Whedon's involvement with Marvel did not preclude other work, including his adaptation of *Much Ado About Nothing* following the end of filming *The Avengers* and featuring Whedon alums such as Sean Maher and Nathan Fillion from *Firefly*, Clark Gregg from *The Avengers*, Fran Kranz and Reed Diamond from *Dollhouse*, and Amy Acker and Alexis Denisof from *Angel*, as well as writing and producing *In Your Eyes* though his micro-budget production company Bellwether Films. Further, Whedon's horror film *The Cabin In the Woods* (held up by MGM's financial issues) was released within weeks of *The Avengers* release. The nearly simultaneous release of these films, both of which featured Chris Hemsworth in a leading role, operate as bookends of Whedon's role as a mainstream cult auteur. Both *The Cabin in the Woods* and *The Avengers* share particular features of cult films; most importantly, the diegetic awareness of the large body of material both are drawing from. As stated above, the MCU/Marvel has morphed into a transmedia enterprise, with various (and sometimes competing) storylines across multiple platforms. While *The Cabin in the Woods* is nowhere near *The Avengers* in terms of scale, it does similarly draw on a large corpus of material; in this instance, horror films, which serve both narratively and visually as the driving engine of its story (see Canavan 2014 for an analysis of *The Cabin in the Wood*'s metacommentary on the horror genre, and Lipsett 2014 for the differing reactions to the film from horror fans).

Conclusion

Viewing Whedon, then, as writer/director who comfortably straddles the cult/mainstream binary offers the ability to view, at least on a narrative level, his work within the MCU as sharing features with both. Its high production values, large budget, and massive ancillary and promotional materials are beyond the dreams of most films normally viewed as "cult", and yet it is shameless in its borrowing of these features to, oddly enough, appeal to a broader swath of the viewing audience. Even Whedon's follow-up, *Avengers: Age of Ultron*, which debuted to mixed reactions from both fans and critics, fits into Eco's criteria for the features of cult film, in as far as its overabundance of characters (new and old), the juggling of disparate storylines to set up Phase Three of the MCU, and even its metatextual play that references both Disney's *Pinocchio* ("I've Got No Strings") as well as the "puppet narratives" of Whedon's *Angel* (Masson 2013: 43–67), *Dollhouse*, and *The Cabin in the Woods*, lack the coherence of both the first Avengers film and Whedon's other work. As Eco points out, coherence isn't necessary for cult films; they can sustain several ideas as "a disconnection series of images, of peaks, of visual icebergs" (Eco 1986: 198).

From the film *Buffy the Vampire Slayer*, to whatever lies beyond Whedon's relationship with the MCU, it is clear that Whedon's ocuvre, despite the medium, represents a clear, if sometimes messy, blending of the aesthetics and mediums of both mainstream and cult.

References

Abbott, Stacey. 2008. "'Can't Stop the Signal": The Resurrection/Regeneration of *Firefly*', in Rhonda V. Wilcox and Tanya R. Cochran (eds), *Investigating* Firefly *and* Serenity: *Science Fiction on the Frontier*. I.B. Tauris, London: 227–238.
Boxofficemojo. 'All-Time Box Office.' 15 May 2016.
Boxofficemojo. 'Serenity.' 15 May 2016.
Angelini, Sergio and Miles Booy. 2010. 'Members Only: Cult TV from Margins to Mainstream', in Stacey Abbott (ed.), *The Cult TV Book: From* Star Trek *to* Dexter: *New Approaches to TV Outside the Box*. Soft Skull Press, New York: 19–27.

Buchanan, Ginjer. 2005. 'Who Killed *Firefly?*', in J. Espenson (ed.), *Finding Serenity: Anti-heroes, Lost Shepherds, and Space Hookers in Joss Whedon's* Firefly. BenBella Books, Dallas: 29–36.

Canavan, Gerry. 2014. '"Something Nightmares Are From": Metacommentary in Joss Whedon's *The Cabin in the Woods*', *Slayage: The Online Journal of the Whedon Studies Association*, 10.2/11.1 (36/37). Available from: www.whedonstudies.tv/uploads/2/6/2/8/26288593/canavan_slayage_10.2–11.1.pdf. Accessed 12 March 2019.

Chonin, Neva. 2005. 'When Fox Cancelled *Firefly*, It Ignited an Internet Fan Base Whose Burning Desire for More Led to *Serenity*', *San Francisco Chronicle*, 8 June, E1. Available from: www.sfgate.com/cgi-bin/article.cgi?f=/c/a/2005/06/08/DDGQJD4D2O1.DTL&hw=firefly&sn=001&sc=1000. Accessed 12 March 2019.

Eco, Umberto. 1986. *Travels in Hyperreality*. Harcourt Books, New York.

Giannini, Erin. 2014. '"It Doesn't Mean What You Think": River Tam as Embodied Culture Jam', *Slayage: The Online Journal of the Whedon Studies Association*, 13.2, no. 42. Available from: www.whedonstudies.tv/uploads/2/6/2/8/26288593/giannini.pdf. Accessed 12 March 2019.

Gray, Jonathan. 2010. *Show Sold Separately: Promos, Spoilers, and Other Media Paratexts*. NYU Press, New York.

Guffey, Ensley. 2014. 'Joss Whedon Throws His Mighty Shield: Marvel's *The Avengers* as War Movie', in Rhonda V. Wilcox, Tanya R. Cochran, Cynthea Masson and David Lavery, (eds), *Reading Joss Whedon*. Syracuse University Press, Syracuse, NY: 280–293.

Hills, Matt. 2010a. 'Mainstream Cult', in S. Abbott (ed.), *The Cult TV Book: From* Star Trek *to* Dexter: *New Approaches to TV Outside the Box*. Soft Skull Press, New York: 67–73.

Hills, Matt. 2010b. *Triumph of a Time Lord: Regenerating* Doctor Who *in the Twenty-First Century*. I.B. Tauris, London.

Holub, Christian. 2016. 'New Captain America Comic Explains the Hydra Reveal', *Entertainment Weekly*, 29 June. Available from: www.ew.com/article/2016/06/29/new-captain-america-comic-explains-hydra-reveal. Accessed 16 October 2016.

Hurd, Matthew. 2012. 'Six Reasons Why Joss Whedon Is the Perfect Director for *The Avengers*', in Mary Alice Money (ed.), *Joss Whedon – The Complete Companion: The TV Series, the Movies, the Comic Books, and More*. Titan Books, London: 447–454.

Iatropoulos, Mary Ellen. 2015. 'Of Whedonverse Canon and "Someone Else's Sandbox": Marvel, Much Ado, and the Great Auteur Debate", in Valerie Estelle Frankel (ed.), *After the Avengers: From Joss Whedon's Hottest, Newest Franchises to the Future of the Whedonverse*. PopMatters, Chicago.

Jancovich, Mark and Nathan Hunt, N. 2003. "The Mainstream, Distinction, and Cult TV", in Roberta Pearson and Sarah Gwenllian-Jones (eds), *Cult Television*. University of Minnesota Press, Minneapolis: 27–44.

Jenkins, Henry. 2006. *Convergence Culture: Where Old and New Media Collide*. New York University Press, New York.

Johnson, Derek. 2007. 'Inviting Audiences in: The Spatial Reorganization of Production and Consumption in "TVIII"', *New Review of Film and Television Studies*, 5.1: 61–80.

Lavery, David. 2014. *Joss Whedon, a Creative Portrait: From* Buffy the Vampire Slayer *to* Marvel's The Avengers. I.B. Tauris, London.

Lipsett, Joe. 2014. '"One for the Horror Fans" vs. "An Insult to the Horror Genre: Negotiating Reading Strategies in IMDB Reviews of The Cabin in the *The Cabin in the Woods*', *Slayage: The Online Journal of the Whedon Studies Association*, 10.2/11.1: 36–37. Available from: www.whedonstudies.tv/uploads/2/6/2/8/26288593/lipsett_slayage_10.2–11.1.pdf. Accessed 12 March 2019.

Lubin, Gus. 2014. 'It's Amazing How Badly Fox Screwed up Joss Whedon's *Firefly*', *Business Insider*, 22 September. Available from: www.businessinsider.com/fox-screwed-up-firefly-2014-9. Accessed 1 November 2016.

Mathijs, Ernest and Xavier Mendik. 2007. 'Editorial Introduction: What Is Cult Film?', in Ernest Mathijs and Xavier Mendik (eds), *The Cult Film Reader*. Open University Press, Berkshire: 1–11.

Masson, Cynthea. 2013. 'Break Out the Champagne, Pinocchio: *Angel* and the Puppet Paradox', *Studies in Popular Culture*, 35.2: 43–67.

Pateman, Matthew. 2014. '*Firefly*: Of Formats, Franchises, and Fox', in R.V. Wilcox, T.R. Cochran, C. Masson, and D. Lavery (eds), *Reading Joss Whedon*. Syracuse University Press, Syracuse, NY: 153–168.

Pearson, Roberta. 2003. 'Kings of Infinite Space: Cult Television Characters and Narrative Possibilities', *Scope: An Online Journal of Film and Television Studies*, 5.4. Available from: www.nottingham.ac.uk/scope/documents/2003/november-2003/pearson.pdf. Accessed 1 November 2016.

Pearson, Roberta. 2010. "Observations on Cult Television', in S. Abbott (ed.), *The Cult TV Book: From* Star Trek *to* Dexter*, New Approaches to TV Outside the Box*. Soft Skull Press, New York: 7–17.

Robinson, Joanna. 2015. 'Joss Whedon Says His Battle with Marvel Got "Really Unpleasant"', *Vanity Fair*, 5 May. Available from: www.vanityfair.com/hollywood/2015/05/joss-whedon-fight-marvel-studio. Accessed 15 November 2016.

Rogers, Adam. 2012. 'With *The Avengers*, Joss Whedon Masters the Marvel Universe', *Wired Magazine*, 30 April. Available from: www.wired.com/2012/04/ff_whedon/. Accessed 1 December 2016.

Rotten Tomatoes. 2016. "Marvel's The Avengers (2012). Available from: www.rottentomatoes.com/m/marvels_the_avengers/. Accessed 1 December 2016.

Russell, M.E. 2005. 'The Browncoats Rise Again: The Best Sci-Fi Series You've Never Seen Has Gone from Cancellation to the Big Screen: Will a Never-Tried Marketing Strategy Work for "Serenity"?', *The Weekly Standard*, 25 June. Available from: www.weeklystandard.com/Content/Public/Articles/000/000/005/757fhfxg.asp. Accessed 14 March 2018.

Yeffeth, Glenn. 2005. 'The Rise and Fall (and Rise) of *Firefly*', in Jane Espenson (ed.), *Finding Serenity: Anti-Heroes, Lost Shepherds, and Space Hookers in Joss Whedon's* Firefly. BenBella Books, Dallas: 37–46.

40

ANTI-AUTEUR
The films of Roberta Findlay[1]

Alexandra Heller-Nicholas

"Taste classifies, and it classifies the classifier", Pierre Bourdieu once famously stated (1984: 6). Chances are he probably hadn't intended the statement to be used in reference to pornographer and horror director Roberta Findlay, but in terms of her cult appeal it's a useful starting point to begin thinking through the work of a filmmaker whose broader *oeuvre* can be best summarised by that most hackneyed of critical terms, "problematic". Staking a claim as a Findlay "fan" implies a complex ideological positioning: on one hand a seemingly progressive alignment through the championing of a woman filmmaker, yet this lies at odds with the inescapable fact that this same filmmaker is the driving force of some of the nastiest and inescapably regressive exploitation and pornographic films of the late-twentieth-century American cinema.

From her early roughies like *Her Flesh* trilogy (1967–1968) and the notorious *Snuff* (1976) made with her ex-husband Michael through to hardcore classics like *Honeysuckle Rose* (1979) and *Glitter* (1983) to later-era horror films like *Blood Sisters* (1987) and *The Oracle* (1985), much of the cult appeal of Findlay's work stems from the narrative that strings together these three different parts of her directorial career. She and Michael split after the *Snuff* debacle (discussed further shortly) and she committed more wholly to pornography, an industry she left to make horror films after her attempt to cash-in on the suicide of *Glitter's* star Shauna Grant in *Shauna: Every Man's Fantasy* (1985) allegedly made her a pariah in the world of adult entertainment. In part, it is the overarching story that unites her films that render her an object of cult fascination as much as how strongly the films on their stand-alone "merits" (for want of a better word) as such.

Roberta Findlay is an important cult film director because despite the fact that few would attempt to defend her work as necessarily "great", the aggressive, unrelenting tastelessness, rawness and general spirit of don't-give-a-fuckness that marks her films is for many of us unparalleled. These films are marked by a unique blend of sleazy honesty: they are what they are, and never seek to apologise for it. They may not be perfect or even very good, but the films of Roberta Findlay are all the things that cult film at its best should be: shocking, confrontational, and fundamentally *wild*. For all the pouty, sassy bad-girl posturing of 90s postfeminism, this is a woman who – if her work is anything to go by, at least – suggests they were made by someone genuinely untouched by conservative morality. And keeping in mind that no women directors appear on Andrew Sarris's foundational so-called "pantheon" of great directors, then surely at its

Figure 40.1   *Blood Sisters* (Findlay, USA, 1987). Reeltime Distribution Corporation

most basic level what does or does not define a great woman director – in the domain of cult film, at least – is still very much open for debate.

From this perspective, how do we begin to figure Roberta Findlay – or Doris Wishman, or Stephanie Rothman, or Jackie Kong – as a cult auteur? In 1971, Linda Nochlin wrote a foundational essay called "Why Have There Been No Great Women Artists?", positing that an assumed male bias is entrenched deeply within in the disciplinary psyche of art history. Sparked by the spirit of second wave feminism, she argued that it was in large part the task of feminist art historians to challenge and discredit this bias, the question of her essay's title itself a deliberate sexist provocation. Getting to the heart of the matter, Nochlin pulls no punches: this is, she makes clear, the wrong question, ignoring as it does the institutional and broader cultural and social factors that have for so long diminished the work of women artists, particularly in the context of the professional art scene. There is of course an impressive range of women artists – from Artemesia Gentileschi to Georgia O'Keeffe to Tracey Moffatt – but historically at least, Nochlin raises the point that many women artists who have risen to prominence did so through their general proximity to men. Which leads us to Michael Findlay.

Roberta Findlay's filmmaking career effectively began when she met Michael. She loved Joan Crawford movies, and in her first career overview published in 1978, Gerald Peary described her as a devoted cinephile who fell in love with cinema – and her soon-to-be husband – when she was a seventeen-year-old music student at the City College of New York and the Manhattan School of Music. They both belonged to the Theodore Huff Film Society, a group dedicated to b-grade cinema of the 1930s and 1940s in particular (Peary 28). Roberta only went because she was "in love with Michael and … felt that anything he did was fabulous and spectacular", and she described the movies that she saw as mostly "wacko … a kind of word for it was 'very esoteric'". But feeling excluded by the pretensions of the group, Michael began his own film society that focused on European silent cinema, where Roberta would record musical accompaniments that were played at screenings (Peary 29).

She loved music, but realistically knew that a career as a concert pianist was unfeasible. When Michael suggested she join him making films, the choice was simple: "I have to do something or else I'll have to work all the time" Peary (29). Roberta Findlay started making movies because she was in love with Michael, but she also loved cinema itself: as she told Peary, her favourite films during this period were as far from the future Findlay filmography as can be imagined, including *The Crowd* (King Vidor, 1928), *The Passion of Joan of Arc* (Carl Theodor Dreyer, 1928), *The Thief of Bagdad* (Raoul Walsh, 1924), *I Married a Witch* (René Clair, 1942) and Orson Welles's *A Touch of Evil* (1958) (Peary 29–30).

With her signature frankness, Roberta has stated that her first steps into adult film were simply because she was nervous Michael would "succumb to his leading ladies" if she wasn't around (Peary 28). But her passion was for photography, and as Briggs noted on the 2004 Media Blasters commentary for *Blood Sisters*, "Roberta Findlay was primarily a cinematographer, and so sometimes you do find these beautiful images in her work even if the narrative stuff around them is a little shabby". Roberta herself added in an interview on this same *Blood Sisters* home entertainment release, "I'm nuts about lighting, so I spent most of the time cutting down lights". Evoking – consciously or not, who knows – the notion of Alexandre Astruc's infamous *caméra-stylo*, she talks about "painting with light", adding that "we were always very, very careful about lighting". Identifying herself from the early days on her work with Michael as a "cameraman" (Peary 28), the gender fluidity of how she perceived her work on film is telling regarding her personal politics: less attempting a radical gender reclamation of supposedly traditional male roles, for Roberta, it was simply what the job was called. She was a cameraman because she worked the camera. Similarly, claims for her as a celebrated "woman director" do not neatly adhere to – and, in fact, openly rebel against – the orthodox ways the label has been critically configured.

The mythology surrounding Roberta Findlay as a kind of forgotten woman auteur is tempting as a site for retrospective canonisation, but the reality of her practice makes such missions difficult to say the least. While a number of her hardcore films were released with male aliases, as Gerald Peary noted in 1978, an unnamed American film critic announced at an international conference on psychoanalysis in Italy that Findlay's own name appearing on *Angel Number 9* was "an obvious pseudonym", as the film clearly could only have been made by a male director (Peary 28). But Molly Haskell, disagreed: in her 1975 article "Are Women Directors Different?", she argued *Angel Number 9* could only have been directed by a woman because of its casual reference to pregnancy: Peary quoted Haskell from her piece "Are Women Directors Different?" from 3 February 1975 in *The Village Voice* that this image was a "no-no in sexploitation movies, a definite downer to Don Juan fantasies of quickie, no-fault sex" (Peary 28). Yet even this kind of utopian vision of Findlay's practice seems to fly in the face of the basic economic realities that drove her work as a filmmaker. Time and time again, without hesitation, Findlay made her motives explicit: she did it for the money.

Findlay is therefore an essential figure to consider in reference to E. Ann Kaplan's question in 2003; "is the gender of the filmmaker more significant than the values or political perspectives a film espouses?" (15). While wider debates about women's filmmaking tend to be framed as progressive simply because the very act of women making movies is in itself a subversion of the dominant straight-white-male auteurist paradigm, Findlay has herself explicitly rejected attempts to revive her status as a "feminist" filmmaker. She was frank in the 1970s that she had "no interest in women's lib" (Peary 30) and has only continued to reject the "rescuing" of her professional reputation as a kind of feminist innovator. In an interview with J.R. Taylor, she confesses "I did that once. … It was so embarrassing. I went out around '88 or '90 with some X-rated film … under the pretence – their pretence – that I was some kind of artist/feminist.

Nonsense". Again, the financial motivation for Findlay was clear: "It was very silly, but if that's what I'm supposed to be, fine, as long as I get paid" (Taylor n.p.). She has even less time for her fans, particularly in terms of her earlier work: "People who like those old movies seem to have deep psychological problems" (Taylor n.p.).

Further attempts to force Findlay into a traditional "auteurist" mold become more difficult when faced with the fact that even a solid, conclusive list of her filmography is almost impossible to pin down. She has herself struggled to remember what jobs she did on what films, but on the *Blood Sisters* commentary Briggs makes a brave guess and suggests that in one capacity or another, her output probably sits around the fifty-film mark. Across these, she appeared both in front of and behind the camera, with Taylor noting the apparent contradiction in her frankness admitting she starred in a sex scene in Michael's 1966 film *Take Me Naked*, but simultaneously refusing to admit that she had a small role as a cleaning woman in her hardcore film *Raw Footage* (1977). A look at her IMDb.com profile lists a stream of uncredited acting performances (or, alternatively, credited as "Anna Riva") but it also is evidence of a person who was clearly very hands-on when it came to the grunt-work of low-budget filmmaking: her credits include editing, composing, camera operating as well as directing. But curiously, in terms of some of the films that her name linked to so closely (the *Her Flesh* trilogy in particular) she has suggested that she had little to do with them:

> My husband was making those films, and I guess I knew about them. I'm not in them. I was in school. I wasn't quite married to him yet, but I left home at 16 and moved in with Michael, and he was making these pictures. I don't even know if I was on the set. Maybe I did voiceovers. I would say if I had done anything more. I don't mind talking about this. It's just that people expect me to be something I'm not.
>
> (Taylor n.p.)

But Landis and Clifford effectively contradict this, claiming that the collaboration was marked by a more equal professional partnership between the husband and wife:

> Mike directed and edited the films, Roberta did the photography. ... Mike was always the lead. Roberta did everything from voiceovers to playing floozies and masochistic victims. Roberta's female co-stars were one-shot transient strippers who generally disappeared after the filming. Mike essentially wrote the films, although some scenes are semi-improvised.
>
> (29)

This is, to put mildly, strikingly at odds with mainstream film culture where individuals often clamour for recognition, and even in cult film circles directors effectively become brand labels: David Lynch, Quentin Tarantino, John Waters, and so on. Roberta Findlay stands in sharp, and perhaps even perversely refreshing contrast. J.R. Taylor has suggested that attempts to label her as a driving creative force behind these films happened sometime after Michael's death in a helicopter accident in 1977: a mythology began to emerge around Roberta as a woman responsible for distinctly "unladylike" films. She became "the focus point of freaks who'd really like to know a femme mind who could come up with such sickness worthy of *Her Flesh*. As a result, Roberta quickly lost interest in cultivating a fanbase" (Taylor n.p.).

As noted, Roberta Findlay began her career as the cinematographer and miscellaneous on-set sidekick to husband Michael. As Joe Bob Briggs has noted, Roberta Findlay was far from the first woman filmmaker behind the sexploitation camera – Doris Wishman comfortably predated her – but with Michael, her work (whatever it was) on the 1964 film *The Body of a Female* launched what Briggs has defined as "some of the weirdest, sleaziest, most perverted" films of the era. Beginning making so-called "roughies" for the grindhouse circuit with Michael in the 1960s, Mike Watt has pithily described this subgenre as "ill-tempered 'nudies', with an equal amount of violence and sex throughout the running time. S&M, bondage and general slapping around were par for the course with the nudity in these" (24). After the notorious controversy surrounding her and Michael's 1976 film *Snuff* and its exposure as a 'real death' hoax, Roberta shifted between horror and pornography until she retired from the industry altogether when her 1989 punk-comedy *Banned* could not get a distributor. Her assessment of this industrial climate was typically frank: "there were no more video companies left to sell garbage to" (Taylor n.p.).

After his films *The Sin Syndicate (1965)*, *Take Me Naked* (1966) and the Yoko Ono-vehicle *Satan's Bed* (1965), Michael moved onto his most famous films of the period with the roughie *Her Flesh* trilogy (*The Touch of Her Flesh* (1967), and *The Kiss of Her Flesh* and *The Curse of Her Flesh*, both from 1968). Attaining astronomical success on the grindhouse circuit, the *Her Flesh* films are as canonical as roughies get, important not only because as Bill Landis and Michelle Clifford noted "they were a married couple who made extreme, sexually motivated movies" (29), but also because as "an intense study in S&M sinema as it veered towards hardcore, the *Flesh* series defined sleazoid aesthetics for a generation of moviegoers" (37).

As Briggs suggests in the *Blood Sisters* commentary, the decline of roughies with the rise of hardcore in the late 1960s saw the couple move towards horror, although they were still producing hardcore films in the early 1970s, attempting to avoid legal problems by utilising the old Kroger Babb trick of framing their films as quasi-documentaries with a surface veneer of 'educational' value (Peary 28). The Findlays happily dropped this pretence with their move towards what Peary has eloquently termed more explicit "'fuck-suck' hardcore" (29). According to Roberta, her first film as both director, screenwriter and editor was the now-lost *Erotikon*[2] (date unknown), recalling that Michael surrendered control of the project to her simply because he couldn't drive the Belgian-made project as, unlike her, he couldn't speak French. With Bela Bartok on the soundtrack, Roberta has described it warmly as a hardcore art film: "it was my own film and I was very proud of that picture" (Peary 30).

In 1971, she made *The Altar of Lust*, re-released in loving detail by boutique cult restoration/distribution company Vinegar Syndrome as a double with Findlay's *Angel of Fire* (an alternate name for *Angel Number 9*) in 2014. For Findlay, *The Altar of Lust* was

> a hard-core feature with a very slim script and no sync sound. I was the producer and the director and the cameraman and the editor. It was the first picture I had ever done all by myself. I don't know what possessed me. I had nobody to turn to. Then I wrote another script, produced and directed it, and cut it. Again, it wasn't much. It was just a stupid series of loops, later retitled *The Doctor Knows Best*.
>
> (Peary 28)

But contending with a flooded hardcore market, Michael and Roberta made the horror film *Shriek of the Mutilated* (1974) as the result of a business strategy, simply because the kind of pornography they were making was no longer the guaranteed profit-maker it had once been. Then – for better or for worse – the *Snuff* story began. Originally titled *The Slaughter*, according to Roberta herself it shelved "because it was so awful" (Peary 30). As she tells it, Michael intended the film to be a loose retelling of the Manson family murders with a political angle, "because in Argentina, there are these German Nazis living there". She continues, "this Charles

Manson character makes a speech about killing all these German people. And he asks if that isn't the same thing as the Israelis supplying guns to the Arabs. Now, I never understood what that meant". Neither, it seems, did the Motion Picture Association of America, who told Michael and Roberta in no uncertain terms that the film was "disgusting", and that they "couldn't be making films about Charles Manson that were favourable to him" (Peary 30).

The Slaughter would have vanished completely if not for distributor Allan Shackleton who in 1976 tacked footage of what he promoted as the "real" murder of a woman crew member onto the end of *The Slaughter* and release it under the provocative, taboo-breaking title *Snuff*. Much has been written about the *Snuff* controversy and the role it played in the then-mobilising anti-pornography feminist movement in the United States.[3] *Snuff*, from this perspective, was evidence of a very real market-value of screen depictions of violence against women, a claim not weakened with the revelation that Shackleton's promotional campaign was a massive hoax. From Shackleton's perspective, it was a financial success, but the Findlay's saw little of the profits: Roberta said she made nothing from *Snuff*, and that Michael made no more than $1500 (Peary 30).

Roberta and Michael had separated by this stage, and according to grindhouse director/producer John Amero until then "Roberta sort of walked quietly in Mike's shadow". He continued, "After the divorce she became very assertive. She had learned the business and became a hardcore director" (Landis and Clifford 43). As for why she turned to directing in a more dedicated manner, by 1978 at least Roberta herself still seemed unsure. She told Peary that it was possibly related to the collapse of her marriage: "I left Michael. I don't know why but I just left. I don't know why to this day. And I started making films myself. I went to a film distributor and said 'I can make you a film really cheap, and I'll make you a lot of money'" (30).

Without Michael in the picture, as a pornographer Roberta Findlay worked hard and her output was prolific. Aside from *Honeysuckle Rose* with John Holmes in 1979 and *Glitter* with Shauna Grant in 1983, Findlay directed a steady stream of films including *Teenage Milkmaid* (1974), *The Clamdigger's Daughter* (1974), *Anyone But My Husband* (1975), *From Holly With Love*

Figure 40.2 *Snuff* (Michael and Roberta Findlay, USA, 1976). August Films/Selected Pictures

(1978), *Mystique* (1979), and *Angel Number 9*. Findlay's last hardcore film *Shauna: Every Man's Fantasy* (1985) reunited her with Grant, but in circumstances many both within the industry remember with some distaste. Born Colleen Marie Applegate, Grant was a cheerleader-turned-runaway from rural Minnesota who – after working with key industry figures including the legendary Suze Randall, a fellow woman pornographer during the era – made over thirty adult films between the age of 18 and her death at 20. Despite earning a number of nominations at both the Erotic Film Awards and the Adult Film Association Awards (the latter found her seated next to Francis Ford Coppola), Grant quit the business, unhappy with her chosen career path and struggling with substance abuse issues. She shot herself in the head and died on 21 March 1984.

As Briggs has stated, *Shauna: Every Man's Fantasy* was "pretty controversial within the porn industry". It brought together archival footage of Grant's hardcore work with actual home movies from her youth and structured this material around a quasi-journalistic investigation into the question "Did pornography kill Shauna Grant?". Intercut between this archive material was "interviews" with many of Grant's colleagues, who combined dialogue with explicit hardcore performances. Franklin Mark Osanka and Sara Lee Johan pulled few punches in their consideration of Findlay's hardcore swansong:

> Heartlessly crass and cynical porn industry cash-in on Shauna Grant's suicide directed by that veritable wellspring of humanity, Roberta Findlay. See porn actors and actresses talk about their memories of Shauna while they're fucking and sucking each other. See these same lowlifes gamely attempt to squeeze out an honest emotion only to fail miserably. Hear Shauna being showered with such touching compliments as "she had that wet-behind-the-ears innocence that never failed to arouse a crotch." There's even a mock interview with a female 'psychiatrist' who analyzes Shauna's unwillingness to deep throat pecker as being an indication of her sexual inhibition, before doing a raunchy, incestuous role-playing number with creepy George Payne.
>
> (87)

So offensive was Findlay's "memorial", they added, that "the only thing this lacks is a scene of Ron Jeremy screwing poor Shauna's exit wound on the morgue examining table" (Osanka and Johan 87). But for Grant's friend and fellow actor Kelly Nichols, the loss was both personal and real. "Shauna was the first publicized porn death. There were a couple of earlier ones, but this was the biggie because porn was just starting to get more accessible through the VCR". She continued,

> It just had tabloid written all over it. And Shauna was a beautiful girl. She made great print. Any time a girl dies, it's like a little piece of us dies. It feels a little like, *if we're not careful, that could be us.*
>
> (McNeil and Osborne 364)

It was in this context that *Shauna: Every Man's Fantasy* became effectively Findlay's last hardcore movie, her professional reputation allegedly stained by the ethically tone-deaf "tribute" to the tragically deceased Grant.

With Findlay herself noting on the extras for the 2004 *Blood Sisters* DVD that the only real difference between horror and porn was the colour of the bodily substances involved, returning to horror seemed a logical progression. She collaborated now with Walter Sear and together they turned towards cheap horror film production for the then-blossoming straight-to-video market in the early-1980s (Watt 24). There is little point denying that Findlay's latter horror work fluctuates between the banal, the ludicrous and the sometimes outright offensive, yet it is its very audacity alone that – for certain audiences, at least – also renders it wholly captivating. *The Oracle* (1985) combines the haunted house sugbenre with a marital melodrama; *Prime Evil* (1988) explores the satanic cult trope while her last released horror movie – 1988's *Lurkers* – is a ghost story. But even by 1987's *Blood Sisters*, on the DVD release for that film Findlay clearly stated that she held no pretences to what motivated her to make movies: her "inspiration" was that she didn't get "caught out on her tax". A sexy-sorority-hazing-ritual-meets-unexpected-supernatural-complications movie, *Blood Sisters* is perhaps the weakest of Findlay's work during this period, but less a typical horror movie than a visceral action-exploitation film, Findlay's *Tenement* from 1985 is the most memorable of her directorial output during this era. A vicious movie set in an isolated South Bronx apartment building, it tracks a feral, blood-thirsty rampage through the eponymous building. *Tenement* is a grotty, unforgiving film that feels more 70s than 80s – a grindhouse classic that came out in the midst of the VHS era – but it is driven by such an intense spirit of exploitative pluck that it remains one of Findlay's most unforgettable films.

With the failure to secure distribution for 1989's *Banned* – a film screenwriter Jim Cirile envisioned as "a punk-rock *All of Me*" (Watt 66) – Findlay stopped making films, and today it seems highly unlikely that she will return. But as Joe Bob Briggs noted the 2004 DVD release of *Blood Sisters*, "Roberta is a pioneer, a ground-breaker", and the warmth in his voice alone indicates that this isn't snark or sarcasm. No matter how hard we try to push her, Findlay resists orthodox auteurist frameworks, even those we tweak and modify for the often gonzo-ridden outlaw terrain of cult filmmaking. Her "filmography" (itself an unstable concept) and the drastically different production contexts in which she worked deny us any such critical comforts. But if depravity is an art form, Findlay excelled. "Sleaze was her strong point", Briggs enthused, while for Taylor, as key figure in American extreme exploitation, Findlay was involved in myriad ways "with masterpieces of oppression that Abel Ferrara would envy". Yet even this attempt to elevate her name to the status of a more familiar (male) auteur seems to fly in the

Figure 40.3   *Tenement* (Roberta Findlay, 1985)

face of Findlay's *own* relationship to her movie career. She never wanted adoration, to provoke audiences to think about the world in new ways. While hardly tasteful as such, Findlay's films were marked by an undisguised frankness about her motivations that challenges the frequently essentialised discourse surrounding women directors as necessarily "progressive". Findlay was always clear on this point: her films were not intended to open our hearts or minds, but our wallets.

Notes

1 This chapter is a variation of my previously published article "What's Inside a Girl?: Porn, Horror and the Films of Roberta Findlay", *Senses of Cinema*, 80 (September 2016) sensesofcinema.com/2016/ american-extreme/porn-horror-roberta-findlay/ Many thanks to Jack Sargeant for his invaluable feedback and suggestions on this earlier piece.
2 A title which, considering Findlay's early interest in European silent cinema, seems to be a curious reference to Mauritz Stiller's 1920 film of the same name.
3 For more information, see my previous article: "Snuff Boxing: Rethinking the *Snuff* (1976) Coda", *Cinephile: The University of British Columbia Film Journal*. 5.2 (2009) http://cinephile.ca/archives/ volume-5-no-2-the-scene/snuff-boxing-revisiting-the-snuff-coda/.

References

Bourdieu, Pierre. 1984. *Distinction: A Social Critique of the Judgement of Taste*. Cambridge, MA: Harvard University Press.
Kaplan, E. Ann. 2003. "Women, Film, Resistance: Changing Paradigms," in Jacqueline Levitin, Judith Plessis and Valerie Raoul (eds), *Women Filmmakers: Refocusing*. New York: Routledge, pp. 15–28.
Landis, Bill and Michelle Clifford. 2002. *Sleazoid Express: A Mind-Twisting Tour Through the Grindhouse Cinema of Times Square*. New York: Simon and Schuster.
Nochlin, Linda. 1988. *Women, Art and Power and Other Essays*. Boulder, CO: Westview Press.
Osanka, Franklin Mark and Sara Lee Johann. 1989. *Sourcebook on Pornography*. Lexington: Lexington Books.
Peary, Gerald. 1978. "Woman in Porn: How Young Roberta Findlay Finally Grew Up and Made Snuff," *Take One*, September, pp. 28–30.
Taylor, J.R. 2008. "The Curse of Her Filmography: Roberta Findlay's Grindhouse Legacy," *New York Press*, 20 July 2005, accessed 30 March 2008, www.newyorkpress.com/18/29/film/JRTaylor.cfm.
Watt, Mike. 2013. *Fervid Filmmaking: 66 Cult Pictures of Vision, Verve and No Self-Restraint*, Jefferson, NC: McFarland.

41

ANNA BILLER

Jennifer O'Meara

It is a testament to Anna Biller's singularity as a filmmaker and artist that, with only two features and a handful of shorts to her name, she has rightfully earned a place in this collection. Biller began making shorts in 1994 after studying for a BA in art at UCLA, and an MFA in film and video at the California Institute of the Arts. It was the originality of her feminist revision of the sexploitation genre in *Viva* (2007) that first signalled her potential to be labelled a cult auteur, a category which, historically, has been male-dominated. Biller's labour-intensive work processes involve not only writing, directing and editing her features, but also designing costumes and sets and producing their music. It would thus be a further nine years until her second feature, *The Love Witch* (2016). Both independent films focus on the complicated sexual fantasies of their leading ladies. *Viva* explores the life of Barbi (played by Biller), a 1970s housewife who is attempting to take part in the sexual revolution, to mixed effect. *The Love Witch's* Elaine (Samantha Robinson) is more extreme still, using spells and potions to attract men into her sensuous, gothic Victorian world.

Biller's initiation into cult cinema might appear to be premature or at least accelerated, after all, such cinema is often defined by its rich afterlife among fans. However, the distinctiveness of her features, in terms of style and content, seems to invite such a reception. In terms of time periods and generic conventions both films are positioned ambiguously. *The Love Witch's* horror is merged with the femme fatale figure of *film noir* while, as Beth Johnson explains when label-ling *Viva* a 'murky melodrama', it is also more overtly a 'socially satirical' sexploitation film (2012: 267; 265). Johnson highlights the symbolic resonance of *Viva* as 'a text that refuses to "fit" with generic representations associated with gendered texts' (267–269). It is perhaps this play with genre conventions and tone that aligns Biller's work most closely with cult cinema. At the same time, in terms of formal influences within these divergent genres, Biller's work gains consistency: it is inflected with rich colour palettes that recall Dario Argento's 'Giallo' horrors, but also Douglas Sirk's Technicolor melodramas.

In certain respects, *Viva* and *The Love Witch's* cult potential seems tied to their anachronism and fetishistic attention to past media cultures and formats (such as the 1960s and 1970s sex-ploitation genre and 1950s Technicolor palettes). At the same time, Biller's digital presence on platforms like Twitter signals an acute understanding of social media's ability to foster an ongoing relationship between filmmaker and fan— one that has enabled her to quickly build up the kind of loyal following associated with cult auteurs. Born in California to a Japanese American mother and an American father, Biller's combined training in art and film is apparent from her distinctive stylistic approach. Her racial identity also influences her approach to gender and feminism, including the decision to cast herself in the central role in *Viva*. As Elena Gorfinkel notes in her study of the film's provision of a 'retrospective life' for sexploitation cinema (2011), Biller has stated her desire to creatively rewrite a moment of history by 'put[ting] herself, as a minoritarian subject, into the film historical picture' (124). Biller's strategy for tapping into cinema's 'retrospective' lives is another way in which her work aligns with cult media contexts. Retro tendencies in cult cinema tend to be quite male in tone, as exemplified in Robert Rodriguez and Quentin Tarantino's graphically violent *Grindhouse* (2007) double-feature. In contrast to this, Biller's retro-tendencies are often unapologetically feminine; treating costumes and objects, rather than woman, as the subject of the camera's gaze. After now outlining Biller's distinctive aesthetic, I will return to the (gender) politics of her work and her digital media presence – thus arguing that it is a combination of the style, content and reception of her work that quickly lent her films a cult sensibility.

Manicured and technicoloured: Biller's laborious aesthetic

Pictured in the extravagant headpiece she wears in *Viva*, Biller appears on the cover of David Andrews's *Theorizing Art Cinemas: Foreign, Cult, Avant-Garde, and Beyond* (2013). While her work is only briefly discussed in the book itself, Andrews positions Biller with the traditions of art cinema, and away from those cult films that result from 'the fetishization of directorial incompetence' (105). Because although Andrews does still group *Viva* with 'campy, so-bad-they're-good cult movies' (alongside the likes of *Pink Flamingos* and *House*), he cites an 'intentional camp irony' and 'complicated aesthetic effects that their creators intended' as reasons why such films should not be labelled '"bad" in any straightforward sense' (105–106). Specifically, Andrews stresses the control of the auteur (in this case Biller) over the unconventional aesthetic, something that separates them markedly from the ineptitude of other cult directors: instead, such filmmakers 'found a way to do what they wanted to do' (106).

Biller's 'complicated aesthetic effects' are apparent from watching even a short clip from her work. Hard key lighting is often used to emphasize the heavily saturated colours of Biller's intricate costumes and meticulous sets. In interviews and on social media, Biller also reveals her wilful drive to achieve these effects. In an online article for *Stuff*, titled '*The Love Witch*: The Technicolor dream that almost became a logistical nightmare', Biller explains how her determination to shoot and cut on celluloid meant she had to convince one of the few remaining film editors to come out of retirement and fly him back to Los Angeles: 'I had to beg him to cut the negative and he had to take his equipment out of storage (Croot 2017)'. In other words, to use Andrews' description, she worked hard to *find a way* to achieve an unconventional style and effect.

Biller's use and discussion of Technicolor is distinctly in line with Jack Stevenson's account of 'The Cult of Technicolor: a séance' in his book on the B-movie (2003). Writing at the start of the 21st century, Stevenson ends his tongue-in-cheek chapter with a summary of contemporary 'followers' of the cult:

> Today, a cult of true believers persist, plugging their ears to the heresies of soulless modern technologists who tell the people that our only hope for good colour in the future lies with digital technology. Burn them! These true believers gaze into a night sky that isn't quite black enough […] and they know that Technicolor will come to earth again.
>
> (Stevenson 2003: 75)

Biller's status as a 'true believer' in Technicolor is reinforced each time she answers a question about whether all the trouble of using film was 'worth it'. As she stresses to interviewer James Croot (2017): 'Oh, yes. The colours are richer and deeper than a digital print and the blacks are blacker.' As both Stevenson and Biller suggest through their references to shades of black, film colour is tied not just to tone and palette, but to contrast. Biller's love of colour is married to a corresponding interest in darkness (literal and figurative), that spills across her films both visually and thematically.

A meticulous attention to the details of mise-en-scene and production design, and an unwillingness to take shortcuts, are a recurring theme in the filmmaker's discussion of her processes. In this respect, Biller's cult auteur status parallels that of contemporaries like Wes Anderson. And while Anderson has been described by Joseph Aisenberg as having the calculation of a museum curator (2008), Biller's sourcing and/or recreating of period details in both *Viva* and *The Love Witch* takes this further. She crafts stories that allow her to bring historical, museum-worthy objects to the screen itself.

Biller's approach is also more hands on than Anderson's, as well as being proudly equated with branches of film labour that have historically been associated with women (such as costume, make-up and production design). Biller literally hand-pulled a pentagram rug for *The Love Witch* (see Figure 41.1), while she describes her aim of making cinema that is 'a complete sensual experience' (Stigler 2017). As she explains when asked to discuss her ideas on what constitutes a female gaze in relation to desire and pleasure: 'I love it when objects are treated erotically. You know, when a glass has a beautiful sparkle on it' (Stigler 2017). She expands further: 'I love colour, I love interior decorating, I love objects, I love faces. And so for me a female gaze is about gazing at the things that I find interesting.'

Figure 41.1 Elaine (Samantha Robinson) lying on top of the pentagram rug that Biller hand-pulled for *The Love Witch* (Biller, USA, 2016). Image shot by M. David Mullen, courtesy of Anna Biller Productions

Writing on *Viva,* Gorfinkel identifies the power inherent in this kind of treatment: 'Biller rescues and elevates the details of a mass cultural erotics, making these elements the privileged sites of female spectatorial pleasure and engagement rather than the spectacle of sexual display' (101). Biller takes aesthetic and revisionist pleasure in the material objects of the past, and by working them into complex sets she invites an imagined (female) viewership to as well. Those critical of Biller's work might accuse it of being overly manicured, or focused on style over substance, without understanding the social critiques that are woven into her intricate shots and tableaux-like staging. Like the claustrophobic domestic spaces in which Douglas Sirk placed his stifled women in 1950s melodramas, Biller's female protagonists are both master and victim of the dense spaces in which they exist and their stylized self-presentations (Figure 41.2). The director alludes to this in interview with Brittany Stigler, explaining that:

> I think women, or most women, have a fantasy about a perfect world they can live in. [...] We all want to fantasize about living in this kind of world of aesthetic pleasure. So I like to create that in a movie sometimes. [...] But not to make it fake or silly. But to kind of contrast that with the interior world of a woman that's really untidy.

In allowing her women to exist in fantastic material worlds, particularly domestic ones, Biller underscores the tendency for women's control to be limited to historically feminine spaces (like the home or, in *The Love Witch,* the tearoom). It is perhaps no coincidence then that *The*

Figure 41.2 Anna Biller as Barbi in *Viva* (Biller, USA, 2007), with the character's costume and pose highlighting overlaps between her stylized space and body. Image shot by Steve Dietl, courtesy of Anna Biller Productions

Love Witch's Elaine rents a room from a female landlady, Trish (Laura Waddell), an agreement negotiated over fine china in the pink tea room, or that Trish later 'tries on' Elaine's physical identity, in the form of her wigs, makeup and clothing, when she enters her bedroom. Trish's status as a landlady – in control of many of the film's stylized physical spaces – is thus linked to her ability to master the stylized 'space' of her tenant's body.

Given the importance Biller attributes to these fantasy spaces, it follows that sourcing objects for these worlds is made a priority. The practice departs from the norm she has criticized for objects in film sets to be 'afterthoughts': 'People hire a prop master [at] the last minute, and they don't have enough time and scramble things together at the last minute, and they're not important' (Stigler 2017). Biller's time-consuming sourcing of meaningful objects – ones she deems appropriate to the female characters she has similarly crafted – thus becomes a kind of respectful act: like buying thoughtful gifts for the (fictional) women in her life, rather than forcing them to live in a world that has been 'scramble[d] together'.

A symbiosis between aesthetic pleasure and critical discourse is noted by Johnson in relation to *Viva*. As she explains, the film is 'a very serious, striking commentary which seeks not only to visually seduce the contemporary viewers, but significantly, to mentally stimulate them' (2012: 264). Like Gorfinkel, the author of the only other sustained research on Biller's films, Johnson interprets Biller's work as both politically informed and educational (264–265). (As I will discuss later in this chapter, these traits are also present, at a personal level, on Biller's Twitter's account.) Unlike the sexploitation films of the 1970s, which sought to sexually arouse and titillate an assumed male and heterosexual audience, *Viva* foregrounds the male body. With Barbi's husband Rick (Chad England) frequently presented shirtless, and so 'situated and exhibited as the object of the gaze' (Johnson, 266), it is understandable that scholars like Gorfinkel also interprets the film as highlighting 'the uses of sexploitation films for contemporary female spectators' (99–100). As Gorfinkel elaborates, Biller 'bind[s] the charge of the obsolete details of mise-en-scène and sexploitation's generic codes to a decidedly feminist gestural *ecriture*' (99–100).

Although *The Love Witch* is perhaps less explicit in its feminist agenda, it nonetheless renegotiates politics around erotic forms of looking. As played by the classically beautiful Samantha Robinson, Elaine is offered up as an object of the gaze. Yet viewers are also invited to see her appearance as a constructed masquerade, as when Elaine is repeatedly shown putting on or removing her long dark wig. Since it is merely an enhanced version of her natural hair (longer, thicker, shinier) the illusion of Elaine's exceptional appearance is revealed as just that. In the process, and continuing Johnson's view that *Viva* both mentally stimulates and visually seduces, we are encouraged to see Elaine's self-presentation as a complementary form of magic to her witchcraft.

Niche exhibition spaces

The cultish nature of Biller's cinema is confirmed further when one considers the exhibition spaces in which her films are shown. Although screened at a variety of festivals and in some arthouse cinemas, *Viva* was programmed by a number of niche festivals that implicitly encourage audiences to experience it as a cult work. It was screened, for example at the B-Movie Underground Trash Film Festival (the Netherlands, September 2007); the Lausanne Underground Film Festival (Switzerland, October 2007); the Amsterdam Alternative Erotic Film Festival (the Netherlands, November 2007); the Mix Brasil Festival of Sexual Diversity (Sao Paulo, November 2007); and the Cine-Excess Film Festival (London, September 2008). Similarly, *The Love Witch* was programmed at a number of underground and horror film festivals: the Porn Film Festival, Berlin (October 2016); the Scream Queen Film Fest in Tokyo

(October 2016); the Slash Film Festival, Vienna (October 2017); and the Chicago Underground Film Festival (June 2017). Being screened at festivals such as these further aligns Biller's cinema with the margins of mainstream taste, and the kind of cult following associated with fans of the horror and porn genres.

Biller's films have also quickly made the shift to non-theatrical venues, as when the Museum of Sex in New York screened both films as part of their 2017–2018 exhibition, *NSFW: Female Gaze*. In certain ways, the exhibition and its title is fitting culmination for Biller's work to date: the 'not safe for work' (NSFW) acronym signals the supposed explicitness of Biller's films, which dare to revisit and revise earlier representations of female sexuality – both in the short-lived sexploitation genre, and in mainstream cinema that prioritizes the 'male gaze'. Here, the term applies both to Laura Mulvey's conception of it and to the more generalized way that the term has since come to been used. Furthermore, the 'female gaze' is a term that Biller is explicitly asked about in interviews, likely because her films are both so visually dense (in terms of colour, costume, mise-en-scene) and because they are so focused on women's perspectives. Or, as the Museum of Sex put it in their programme notes for the exhibition, 'The artists in *NSFW Female Gaze* both reclaim and break out of women's historical roles as muse and object. The exhibition showcases a fearless new visual language of desire that defies social norms and expectations.' When Biller directs herself as the star of *Viva* she becomes her own muse, dressed in the costume she has made for herself, and shot by the Director of Photography who follows Biller's own instructions. Biller then edits her own performance. And while Biller has spoken about the difficulties she felt when promoting the film at festivals, when she was encouraged to pose provocatively leading her to feel objectified, up until that point, she – rather than any man or male perspective – was shaping her presentation in her own film.

In addition to Biller's work being embraced by festivals with overtly niche or subcultural directives, there is a distinctly cult sensibility to related fan events. In March 2018, Biller attended and helped coordinate a 'High Tea Party' at The Mystic Museum in Burbank, California, an event that was inspired by *The Love Witch* and which Biller and the film's star, Samantha Robinson attended. Although taking place only two years after the film's initial release, the event was layered with markers that the film has already achieved a devoted cult following. Attendees were encouraged to attend in costumes inspired by the film (and for which there was a competition) and there were photo and signing opportunities with Biller and Robinson (see Figure 41.3). As well as being encouraged to buy merchandise directly tied to the film (DVDs and posters to be signed), the event featured a tie-in with 'Demonic Pinfestation', a largely digital distributor of niche pop cultural pins; in this case, they were packaged alongside 'spell kits' inspired by the love potions Elaine uses in the film. Upon entering the event, which I attended during a research trip to Los Angeles, we were also given a single tarot card – a nod to their role within the narrative. The card featured the film's distinctive pink and black iconography and an image of Samantha, alongside the message 'Bright Blessings' and the names and symbols of both The Mystic Museum and Demonic Pinfestation.

As even the names of these collaborators suggest, both the museum and the craft company 'Demonic Pinfestation', align closely with *The Love Witch*'s style and content, as well as Biller's work more broadly. The Bearded Lady's Mystic Museum, to give it its full-name, was launched in 2016 with a focus on 'the history of fortunetelling, spiritualism and other mystical arts' (Derrick 2018). The museum showcases taxidermy, spirit boards, and a range of fortune-telling devices, including teacups and tarot cards. Like *The Love Witch* and *Viva*, it thus shows reverence towards material cultures of the past. As Gorfinkel notes of *Viva*, 'the film resignifies the broader period's consumer objects and artefacts into bearers of retrospective affect' (102). For Gorfinkel, Biller's attention to recreating the material world of sexploitation and the period in which it emerged

Figure 41.3 Poster promoting *The Love Witch* 'High Tea Party' in Los Angeles, March 2018. Reprinted with permission from Anna Biller. Poster credit: Demonic Pinfestation, with photography by Richard Foreman

(in terms of costumes, make-up, and decor) demonstrates a 'fascination with the object, with the negligible things that clutter the frame of film history' (102). The Mystic Museum similarly raises objects of fortune-telling and spiritualism to the status of 'permanent exhibition', treating them with the same kind of reverence that more mainstream, and state-funded, museums would treat more 'worthwhile' artefacts tied to organized religions. With its displays of fortune-telling devices, the museum is also reflective of the kind of Southern Californian Wiccan lifestyle to which the film's protagonist, Elaine, belongs. According to the museum's website, their frequent events include 'ghost investigations, movie nights, witch craft classes, [and] séances'.[1] In other words, they hold precisely the kind of events that *The Love Witch*'s Elaine would be interested in. Even the museum's location described by journalist Lisa Derrick (2018) as being the section of Burbank that 'has always had a *Twilight Zone* freaky small-town vibe' – recalls *The Love Witch*'s setting. Much of the film was shot in Eureka, a city in California's Humbolt County that is known for its preserved, Victorian-era architecture.

Given the symbiosis of the event venue, its location, and the involvement of Biller and Robinson, it is unsurprising the event was completely sold out. The crowd, many of whom were dressed in the kind of dark wigs, large floral hats and colourful dresses as Robinson as Elaine, were mostly young and female. They seemed invested in Biller's status as a (burgeoning) cult auteur: invested financially, in terms of costumes, and emotionally, in terms of joining a long queue to get a picture or a signature. And though there were men, and even a few children, in attendance, Biller's ability to attract a significant following of mostly women parallels her social media following.

Biller's ambivalent attitude to digital media

Biller is a prominent figure in the Twitter film community, where she has built up roughly twenty-seven thousands tweets and close to twenty thousand followers through her handle, @ missannabiller.[2] The content Biller posts ranges from standard promotional materials for her films and production anecdotes, to specialized knowledge on film history (such as summaries of Sergei Eisenstein's predictions on cinema, complete with reading recommendations).[3] She also shares personal, scathing takes on different aspects of the media, particularly as they relate to gender. Biller's use of Twitter thus benefits from, and contributes to, the strong community of feminist media accounts on the platform. Her gender-focused tweets are frequently retweeted by feminist websites like *Bitch Flicks* (@BitchFlicks), *Bust Magazine* (@bust_magazine) and *Jezebel* (@Jezebel). Given that Biller tweets in an individual capacity from a personal account, her presence is perhaps closer to that of other prominent, female media figures on Twitter, like Melissa Silverstein (@melsil), the founder and publisher of the website *womenandhollywood.com* (Twitter handle: @womenahollywood). Just as Silverstein's website aims to 'educate, advocate, and agitate for greater gender diversity in Hollywood and the global film industry', Biller's use of social media is both informative and disruptive. Furthermore, many of feminist media sites are overt about their need to advocate for more intersectional forms of feminism. Biller's Asian-American ancestry thus makes her an even more fitting commentator on these issues. In this regard, her Twitter presence shares common ground with actor Constance Wu (@ ConstanceWu). After Wu's breakout role in *Fresh of the Boat* (ABC, 2015—), the Taiwanese American performer quickly became an articulate advocate for addressing the marginalization of Asian experiences and actors in the US media.

While Biller is far from a luddite, with a well-maintained website (www.lifeofastar.com) in addition to her strong Twitter presence, she is bluntly provocative about her views on digital cinema. Thus, another way to view Biller's work as it relates to an 'Otherness' that attracts a cult following, is as a reactionary form of independent American cinema in the digital era. As Geoff King examines in *Indie 2.0: Change and Continuity in Contemporary American Indie Film* (2013), digital technologies, platforms and culture have altered the landscape of American indie cinema in the twenty-first century. The ubiquity of digital cameras (both stand-alone and phone-based), along with digital editing software have provided would-be filmmakers with 'a whole new realm of micro— or virtually no-budget production' (King 2013: 78). Meanwhile, platforms like YouTube, Vimeo and Kickstarter have provided the channels through which to distribute and/or to raise funds.

Although, as King takes care to point out, not all American independent cinema reflects such new technological trends, one formal development in this time was the rise of blurred footage, hand-held camera work, and the 'desktop aesthetic'. For example, films like *Tarnation* (Jonathan Caouette, 2003) and *Four Eyed Monsters* (Susan Buice and Arin Crumley, 2005) embrace the aesthetic style of their own computer's software programmes, such as iMovie's tonal tinting and 'in-square' facility, 'through which images can be replicated in numerous grid-works of squares across the screen' (King 2013: 226). Unlike the indie filmmakers grouped under the label of 'Mumblecore', Biller is not concerned with social commentary on contemporary relationships using contemporary technologies, or in following dominant digital cinema practices.

Instead, in March 2017, Biller posted a tweet that accompanied a close-up of Moira Shearer in Technicolor classic *The Red Shoes* (Powell and Pressburger, 1948) with the following emphatic message: 'I spoke to the head of Kodak, who said, "Film is 3D – light hits different colors at different times." And, "WE ARE AT WAR WITH THE PIXEL."' Just as Biller does not disclose her date of birth publicly, her distaste for producing digital media suggests a desire not to be automatically tied to the (cinematic) norms of her generation. Put differently, like the Head of Kodak she quotes, she is 'at war' with the pixel and relates cinematic practices, such as digital colour grading. Indeed, it is perhaps telling that she instead aligns herself with the unnamed Head of Kodak (Jeff Clark is the current CEO): in the past, such a figure would have held more weight. In the twenty-first century, Biller herself has become one of film's most informed and forthright ambassadors. Biller's ability to make film fashionable again also benefits from certain conflations between the filmmaker, her stylish or Wiccan female characters, and the medium itself. With both emerging and established media makers increasingly unfamiliar with analogue processes, there is a certain wizardry to those who achieve otherworldly effects by non-digital means. Discourse of this nature can centre around Biller and her work, as in an *American Cinematographer* article entitled 'The Magic of Hard Lighting for *The Love Witch*' (Mullen 2016). Written by M. David Mullen, the film's cinematographer and Biller's former class mate at CalArts, he highlights the 'magic' of *The Love Witch*'s technical processes, including achieving the qualities in Figure 41.4 using a kaleidoscope lens and colour gels (Mullen 2016).

A luxurious, confident cult cinema

No-one observing Anna Biller's multi-layered worlds could describe her as a minimalist. Yet, when it comes to producing feature films, the director is a proponent of the less-is-more approach. In August 2017, Biller used her website and Twitter account to share an essay on the aims and influences for her next project, *Bluebeard*, a 35mm feature film.[4] Biller describes it as 'a serial killer film in the style of the classic women in peril pictures, for modern audiences', and she cites diverse influences from *Sudden Fear* (David Miller, 1952) to the Hammer *Horror of Dracula* (Terence Fisher, 1958) and pulp gothic novels. Despite these comprehensive details no timeline was proposed. Presumably, Biller is slowly but surely crafting *Bluebeard*'s universe and convincing funders it's worth the investment.

Like many cult auteurs before her, Biller continues to play with the norms of genre conventions, as well as the norms of (contemporary) taste and style. *Bluebeard*'s planned merging of the woman-in-peril picture with the serial killer film continues on from Biller's mixing of melodrama with sexploitation in *Viva*, and horror with *noir* in *The Love Witch*. What separates

Figure 41.4   Elaine/Samantha Robinson in *The Love Witch* (Biller, USA, 2016), as captured using a kaleidoscope lens and colour gels. Image shot by M. David Mullen, courtesy of Anna Biller Productions

Biller, from many, earlier cult filmmakers, is both her gender and her willingness to share the public (and Twitter) stage with her work. Biller is confident of the intervention her films are making and she is willing to defend them, much as she defends broader causes – when advocating for film stock, as well as for more diverse offerings for, and by, women in cinema.

Notes

1 The museum's website is available at https://squareup.com/store/BeardedLadysMysticMuseum (accessed 21 August 2018).
2 As of August 2018.
3 @missannabiller, Tweet. 12 August 2018. https://twitter.com/missannabiller/status/1028719932937 101312.
4 http://www.lifeofastar.com/Bluebeard_Movie.html.

References

Aisenberg, Joseph. 2008. 'Wes's World: Riding Wes Anderson's Vision Limited', *Bright Lights Film Journal*, No. 59, February, www.brightlightsfilm.com/59/59wesanderson.php (accessed 28 July 2018).

Andrews, Dudley. 2013. *Theorizing Art Cinemas: Foreign, Cult, Avant-Garde, and Beyond.* Austin: University of Texas Press.

Croot, James. 2017. "The Love Witch: The Technicolour Dream that Almost Became a Logistical Nightmare", *Stuff*, July 20, Available at www.stuff.co.nz/entertainment/film/94908435/the-love-witch-the-technicolour-dream-that-almost-became-a-logistical-nightmare (accessed 9 August 2018).

Derrick, Lisa. 2018. 'Friday the 13th Gets Magical at the Bearded Lady's Mystic Museum Speakeasy', *LA Weekly*, April 11, available at www.laweekly.com/arts/friday-the-13th-meets-the-shining-at-the-bearded-ladys-mystic-museum-speakeasy-9352421 (accessed 9 August 2018).

Gorfinkel, Elena. 2011. "'Dated Sexuality': Anna Biller's *Viva* and the Retrospective Life of Sexploitation Cinema", *Camera Obscura*, Vol. 26, No. 3: 95–135.

Johnson, Beth. 2012. "Semblance and the Sexual Revolution: A Critical Review of *Viva*," in X. Mendik, ed., *Peep Shows: Cult Film and the Cine-Erotic*. New York: Wallflower Press: 264–274.

King, Geoff. 2013. *Indie 2.0: Change and Continuity in Contemporary American Indie Film*. New York: Columbia University Press.

Mullen, M. David. 2016. 'The Magic of Hard Lighting for *The Love Witch*', *American Cinematographer*, November 1, available at https://ascmag.com/articles/the-magic-of-hard-lighting-for-the-love-witch, accessed 22nd August 2018.

Stevenson, Jack. 2003. *Land of a Thousand Balconies: Discoveries and Confessions of a B-Movie Archaeologist*. Manchester: Headpress.

Stigler, Brittany. 2017. "Interview: Anna Biller & The NSFW Female Gaze," *ScreenSlate.com*, July 6, available at www.screenslate.com/articles/29, accessed 9 August 2018.

42

ALEJANDRO JODOROWSKY AND *EL TOPO*

Antonio Lázaro-Reboll

How does one approach the artistic trajectory of a uniquely charismatic, controversial and idio-syncratic character whose multifaceted work on both sides of the Atlantic spans more than sixty years? American film critic Roger Ebert recalls his encounter with Alejandro Jodorowsky in Cannes in 1988 thus:

> he handed me a typewritten autobiography: 'was born in Bolivia, of Russian parents, lived in Chile, worked in Paris, was the partner of Marcel Marceau, founded the "Panic" movement with Fernando Arrabal, directed 100 plays in Mexico, drew a comic strip, made "El Topo" and now lives in the United States – having not been accepted anywhere, because in Bolivia I was a Russian, in Chile I was a Jew, in Paris I was a Chilean, in Mexico I was French, and now, in America, I am Mexican.'
>
> (2007)[1]

Certainly, 'Jodorowsky is a hard man to pigeonhole' (2006: 16), as Ben Cobb stated in *Anarchy and Alchemy. The Films of Alejandro Jodorowsky*, the first English-language volume devoted to his cinema: '[He] is a graphic novelist, mime artist, psychologist, Tarot reader, author, philosopher, composer, actor, mystic and theatre impresario [...] a showman, a clown, a self-proclaimed clown' (2006: 15–16), as well as the director of eight feature films.[2] His films and his figure have polarized critical opinions across the decades. Notably, the initial reception of *El Topo* (1970) in the New York midnight movie circuit divided the critical establishment. Reviews in *The New York Times* signalled equivocal views: while Vincent Canby asked 'Is "El Topo" a Con?' (1971), Peter Schjeldahl wondered 'Should "El Topo" Be Elevated to "El Tops"?' (1971). Twenty years later, the British TV documentary *Jonathan Ross Presents For One Week Only* summed up critical reactions to Jodorowsky in the Anglo-Saxon world:

> For some, he is a genius, a poet of the film world creating vivid, exciting pictures filled with religious and cultural symbols; to others, he is a pretentious fake, dressing up his second-rate melodrama with over-the-top violence and surreal claptrap.
>
> (1991)

Such idiosyncratic autobiographical template, versatile approach to artistic creation and ability to divide opinion are magnified by a larger-than-life and charismatic personality. In 'Producing and Explaining Charisma: A Case Study of the Films of Alejandro Jodorowsky', Jeremy Guida argues that his charismatic authority 'can be attributed to the polysemous nature of his films' religious signs, his baffling success despite screening risky images' (2015: 548) and 'the unique setting and viewing practices associated with the midnight screenings' (2015: 546). For many today, he is 'a spiritual guru, tweeting tarot-card readings and "psychomagical" advice [a tarot-derived form of therapy] to his nearly one million followers' (Benson 2014) (1.7 million at the time of completing this chapter). Certainly, the protean trajectory of Jodorowsky and the cultural significance of his diverse yet interrelated cultural output demands to be written as part of a larger project which goes beyond the aims of this chapter.

Given the focus of this volume on cult cinema, my chapter addresses the film that readily associated the name Jodorowsky to cult status, *El Topo*. Cult film scholarship of the last ten years has yielded a familiar account of the reasons that have made *El Topo* a cult film par excellence (Mathijs and Mendik 2008; Mathijs and Mendik 2011; Mathijs and Sexton 2011): its centrality to the midnight movie phenomenon, the textual and symbolic properties of the film, and the perceived excessive and transgressive nature of its themes. But conspicuously absent from US and European cult film scholarship, as well as from most fannish accounts of *El Topo*, for instance, are references to the film's unique position within the historical context of the Mexican industry at the turn of the 1970s since readings of the film take its commercial and critical success in the midnight movie circuit as the default point of departure for discussion.[3] Censorship reports on *El Topo* – a total of eight – echoed wider institutional preoccupations within Mexico over the promotion of experimental cinema, the liberalisation of the film industry, the distribution of Mexican films abroad to open new markets and to project a more progressive image of the country, and, above all, the kind of cinema that ought to be supported by Mexican institutions. As in the case of his first film *Fando y Lis*, which had a polemical opening at the 1968 Festival of Acapulco, controversy surrounded the production and the exhibition of *El Topo*. As one of the censorship reports stated, while the film as a whole is 'an excellent production' which displays 'truly beautiful colour cinematography' and a distinct 'attempt to produce a new type of cinema', 'the blood, the violence, scatology, blasphemy and abnormality shown in the film', as well as those scenes featuring 'lesbianism, sadism and other unconventional sexual practices' ought to be censured (cited in Algarabel 2012: 209) for their immorality. Nonetheless, the censors concluded that

> should [*El Topo*] be eventually approved it will probably be one of the crudest films ever to be authorized and it will set a precedent for the future. However, if it is banned, there will be a questioning of how far the *Dirección General de Cinematografía* promotes the renewal and the improvement of our national cinema.
>
> (cited in Algarabel 2012: 210)

Eventually, *El Topo* was rated *Categoría 'C'* – that is, suitable for adults over 21 – and its exhibition authorized on August 1970, although it would not be commercially released until 15 April 1971. But, after all the problems he experienced with the commercial release of *Fando y Lis*, Jodorowsky decided that *El Topo* would premiere in New York on 18 December 1970. The rest is (cult film) history.

Rather than focusing on the exhibition and critical reception in the midnight movie circuit, which is well documented in histories of cult cinema (Hoberman and Rosenbaum 1983), this chapter proposes to look at another non-Anglophone context of exhibition, consumption and reception: Spain. By focusing on the contingencies which shaped the trajectory of *El Topo* in

Spain at different times and in different contexts from the mid-1970s to the turn of the twenty-first century, the chapter seeks to tell other stories of the transnational circulation and reception and the shifting cultural status of *El Topo*. First, I chart my evolving relationship with *El Topo* from my initial viewing experience in the early 1990s to current object of academic study. A detailed examination of the fractured exhibition trajectory of the film follows in order to track down *El Topo*'s exhibition history and its various waves of critical reception in Spain over a period of more than three decades, from the mid-1970s to the mid-2000s. A discussion of the shifting cultural contexts in which *El Topo* circulated reveals a film with the potential to appeal across different generations of viewers and to cut across the highbrow, the middlebrow, and the lowbrow. Throughout the chapter, the trajectory of *El Topo* is charted vis-à-vis the development of Jodorowsky's media profile in Spain.

Personal sights of *El Topo*

My first (affective) encounter with *El Topo* was, to a certain extent, a local midnight-movie experience. To be more precise, well beyond midnight in a small, noisy and sultry bar called "Electric" in my hometown in Spain back in 1990. While the garage and psychobilly rock music of The Cramps and The Fuzztones was being played by a local DJ, my eyes were drawn to the images being shown on the two screens placed at either end of the venue. Its parodic western scenarios, the pools of blood filling up the frame, and its suggestive imagery had an extraordinary visual impact on me that night despite the bootleg quality of the tape being played and the images acting as a visual backdrop to the music. The "Electric" had been organizing garage and psychedelic special nights accompanied by the silent screening of exploitation movies – many of which were already cult movies in specific geographical and social contexts of reception. In these weekend rituals I also had the pleasure of discovering Santo el Enmascarado de Plata and Zé do Caixão (a.k.a. Joe Coffin). Subsequent encounters with *El Topo* were mediated through video bootlegs and through local and foreign fanzines, among them American *European Trash Cinema*, British *Eyeball*, and Spanish *2000maniacos*. When issue 7 of *European Trash Cinema* arrived in the post that same year, it included coverage of *Santa Sangre* (1989) and a brief interview with Jodorowsky and producer Claudio Argento (Bissette 1991: 4). Jodorowsky and *Santa Sangre* also featured in the second issue of *Eyeball* where its editor Stephen Thrower raved about the director and the film: 'His is a primal cinema. [...] Far away from sterile academic clichés, SANTA SANGRE throbs with a vital energy. The same-life force characterizes the man himself' (1990: 5). In the interview Jodorowsky irreverently reflected on his filmmaking practice:

> when I make pictures – even when I am shooting it's a scandal. The other day, to make a scene [...] I had to slap the executive producer! I had to because he couldn't understand my images. I'm not logical, my logic is broken. I'm broken in the logic of continuity, of editing, of matching ... logic is stupidity.
>
> (Jodorowsky cited in Thrower 1990: 5)

Santa Sangre generated renewed interest in Jodorowsky in the horror film fanzine scene, as well as in the genre festival circuit across Europe. Imagfic (Festival Internacional de Cine de Madrid), held in April 1990, afforded me the opportunity to view the film on the big screen.

The revival of Jodorowsky in cult film circuits in Spain, nevertheless, did not materialize until the early 2000s when the San Sebastián Horror and Fantasy Film Festival and *2000maniacos* joined forces. As part of the programme "Perversa América Latina", the 2002 edition of the festival included a retrospective of Jodorowsky's films.[4] The fanzine provided a comprehensive journey through the uncharted territory of Latin American exploitation cinemas, featuring an extensive interview with the director ranging from tarot to comics to the possibilities of digital technologies (Palacios 2002). By then, my acquired taste for the films of Jodorowsky converged with my academic involvement in a cult movies working group at the University of Nottingham, which led to conference and eventually to a co-edited volume, *Cult Movies. The Cultural Politics of Oppositional Cinema* (2003). Concurrent with this line of research and my particular interests in Spanish and Latin American films and figures which had achieved cult status in US and British contexts of reception and consumption, I followed with great interest the gradual development of Jodorowsky's media profile in Spain. When ABKCO and Allen Klein finally permitted the release *El Topo* and *The Holy Mountain* in 2007, Tartan acquired the distribution rights in the UK and commercialized them as part of the 'Alejandro Jodorowsky Boxset', a six-disc DVD pack which inevitably I had to buy.[5]

Jodorowsky's inroads into the Spanish marketplace

While Jodorowsky may have 'languished into obscurity' (Rose 2009) for British audiences after the making of *Santa Sangre*, he progressively carved out a niche in the Spanish book market and the media reaching specific readerships and audiences throughout the 1990s and the early 2000s, in particular through the publication of his autobiographical novels and writings about Tarot and his own therapeutic practice psychomagic. The Casa de América, a public institution which regularly hosts prominent Latin American figures in Spain, held the presentation of his memoir *La danza de la realidad* (2001) and the film season 'Alejandro Jodorowsky, el cine y sus raíces psicomágicas' in February 2002 in Madrid. The book presentation 'filled the Casa de América auditorium to overflowing and left more than 200 in the street' (Ortega Bargueño, 2002), unable to attend a public session of psychomagic. He was also popular and charismatic in his TV appearances, both in late-night round-table discussions – Spanish *tertulias* – and cultural programmes which can be traced back to programmes like *La tabla redonda* (La 2, 1990–1993), *Los unos y los otros* (TVE1, 1994–1995), *Negro sobre blanco* (La 2, 1997–2004), or *Saló de lectura* (Barcelona Televisió, 2001–2006). Of his participation as a guest host in *Saló de lectura*, the television critic Víctor S. Amela wrote, 'throughout two hours [Jodorowsky] responded to spectators' questions live with his tarot cards on the table and his artistic imagination bursting forth. Television surrendered to [...] his poetic therapy' (2002: 8). Jodorowsky's psychomagic connected positively with segments of the Spanish public at the turn of the twenty-first century. *La danza de la realidad* topped the best-selling book lists in 2003, as did *Psicomagia* and *El maestro y las magas* in 2004 and 2005, respectively.

As far as the commercial and media exposure of Jodorowsky in Spain is concerned, the year 2003 was a turning point in his fortunes when FNAC España – the large transnational retailer of cultural goods and electronics – started a commercial and cultural partnership with Jodoroswky. On 22 April 2003, Jodorowsky launched in the Barcelona FNAC store his official homepage, alejandro-jodorowsky.com. (The domain is no longer available.) 'As of today', announced the FNAC website, 'you will be able to explore the universe of one of the most heterodox creators in the world from the click of a mouse'. Visitors of the Jodorowsky universe – or *Canal Jodorowsky* as the website described it – could navigate through his literary, filmic and comics art output, access previously unpublished texts, keep up to date with his multiple activities, and even receive psychomagical advice by interacting online with Jodorowsky himself. Jodorowsky also provided an eleven-point *sui generis* guide-cum-manifesto on how to make films, "Cómo hacer cine". FNAC became a platform from which Jodorowsky's unconventional and fertile creativity reached a wider Spanish market and contributed to an intensification of his presence in the media, which revolved primarily around his own distinctive brand of pyschomagic, the principles of Tarot-card reading and the therapeutic value of art. Jodorowsky was the main guest in talk-shows such as *Buenafuente* (Antena 3, 2005) and *El loco de la colina* (TVE, 2006), and the host of cultural programme *Carta Blanca* (TVE, 2006). The Jodorowsky I had come to see in the DIY pages of alternative publications devoted to lowbrow genre production was a decade later not only a regular talk-show guest and a familiar face in many a cultural supplement but had also become a cultural good neatly located in the clicks-and-mortar commercial structure of FNAC.

It is worth dwelling briefly upon some of the cultural, commercial and critical implications of Jodorowsky's integration within the commercial operations and cultural initiatives of a transnational company like FNAC. Housed online in the ClubCultura.com pages of FNAC, Jodorowsky shared the site with some of the most relevant contemporary Ibero-American authors, among them novelists Isabel Allende and Julio Cortázar and filmmakers Pedro Almodóvar and Tomás Gutiérrez Alea. To be sure, with this type of initiative FNAC acts, as Triana-Toribio has argued, as 'a platform for cultural products to permit the "cultural flow" of Ibero-American" culture' (2008: 266) founded on a common language and a shared cultural history. Furthermore, the ClubCultura website facilitates the creation and perpetuation of 'a cult of personality around individual auteurs' (2008: 270) making them 'more accessible to the wider public' (2008: 276) and effecting 'an artistic canonization through criteria that are designed to appeal to middlebrow taste' (2008: 266). Following Bourdieu's views on the relationship of the petite bourgeoisie to culture in *Distinction*, Triana-Toribio concludes that '[T]he entire enterprise of ClubCultura can be read as a middlebrow venture' which provides '[the petite bourgeoisie] accessible versions of avant-garde experiments' (2008: 266). From 2003 to 2007, when Jodorowsky's unavailable cult films were commercialized by FNAC as a boxset ('Pack Alejandro Jodorowsky'), his work entered the mass market. Indeed, 2007 was a remarkable year in the rekindling of the director's cult filmography worldwide and in the process of Jodorowsky's (re)cultification.[6]

The circulation of *El Topo* in Spain

The circulation of *El Topo* in the midnight movie circuit and its critical reception in the United States is well documented. Reviews by Canby, Greenspun and Schjeldhal in *The New York Times*, O'Brien in the *Village Voice*, and Kael in *The New Yorker* acted as frames of reference through which the film would be cultified; Hoberman's and Rosenbaum's chapter in *Midnight Movies* regulated much of its subsequent reception, as far as cult film scholarship is concerned (1991: 93–102). Consigned to international bootleg networks through which the film illegitimately came to the surface, *El Topo* re-emerged in a range of legitimate institutional contexts in Spain throughout the second half of the 1970s and the early 1980s. Such contexts, far removed from the midnight movie circuit and its bourgeoning cult in associated contexts of consumption and spectatorship, allow us to examine its cultural significance and its critical performance in other film cultures, which are not necessarily linked to cultism.

Due to censorship, *El Topo* did not reach Spanish screens until 1976 during the historical period known as *Transición* which followed the end of the dictatorship after the death of General Francisco Franco on 20 November 1975. First screened as part of the second edition of the Festival de Cine IberoAmericano held in Huelva in 1976 (6–12 December), it shared the programme with a group of eleven films representative of the New Mexican Cinema which included works by Felipe Cazals and Arturo Ripstein, among others. The Mexican connection was further accentuated by the festival's tribute to Spanish exile Luis Buñuel whose influence was visible in some of the directors associated with the new currents in contemporary Mexican cinema. The event, conceived to act as a commercial and cultural 'bridge between countries on the other side of the Atlantic and Europe' (Leblic 1976: 19), featured a total of fifty films from thirteen Latin American countries as well as Portugal and Spain. *El Topo* was placed therefore as part of the wider promotion and showcasing of new cinematic trends coming out from Latin American territories, and, more specifically, as an example of the experimental films encouraged by the liberal government of Echeverría in the early 1970s to push the exhibition of New Mexican cinema abroad (Almost three decades later, it might be argued, FNAC returned *El Topo* and Jodorowsky to its original circulation in Spain, a shared Ibero-American film culture). While coverage of the festival focused primarily on the presence of Buñuel's first return to Spain after his self-imposed exile, *El Topo* still caught the attention of the mainstream press. Reports of the festival in *La Vanguardia Española* and *El País* give a sense of its initial reception among festival-goers and, above all, the reaction of films critics. According to *La Vanguardia Española, El Topo* 'received a warm ovation of approval' from the audience (Jordan 1977: 34), and, together with Luis Alcoriza's *Las fuerzas vivas* (1975) and Miguel Littín's *Actas de Marusia / Letters from Marusia* (1976), it delivered 'the highest quality [and] appeal of the [Mexican] lot' (Jordan 1977: 34). *El País'* report on the festival included the first review of *El Topo* to be published in Spanish. Its title, '"El Topo" insólita y genial película', anticipated to the national daily readers the extraordinary and brilliant character of the film. The review itself, brief yet compelling, is a reflection on the difficulties of reviewing it: *El Topo* 'cannot be narrated or told, let alone analysed' (1976), wrote Ángel S. Harguindey. Harguindey was astounded and perplexed by the challenging nature of the text ('[it] transcends the limits of what we understand by culture in the Western world'), the impossibility of containing the potential meanings of the film ('the author demonstrates a competent knowledge of biblical texts, Eastern philosophy and all the elements associated with counter-culture'), and, above all, the impotence of translating into words what he had seen on screen ('[an] aesthetic instinct which, in my opinion, is linked to hallucinatory experiences and episodes associated with irrational modes of knowledge'). The attempt to evaluate and convey the *El Topo* experience seemed to be beyond the faculties of this film correspondent, who admitted that the film lent itself to 'all kinds of interpretations, as many as spectators viewing it' (1976). Beyond the festival, the film reached a very small audience for it was only shown once at the Madrid and Barcelona cinémathèques on 25 January and 4 February 1977, respectively.

Three years later, *El Topo* was exposed to a very different sociocultural moment in the history of Spanish cinema. With the abolition of censorship in 1977 and the implementation of a revised classificatory system, *El Topo* entered the unique experiment in adult cinema which took place in Spain between 1977 and 1982, the "S" category. This category was ascribed to all those products whose content or theme could damage the spectator's sensibility.[7] The "S" rating was not only attached to softcore pornography but also to material deemed potentially offensive on account of extreme violence or incendiary politics. S-Rated pictures could be exhibited in any cinema, their box-office receipts were taxed like any other films, and their publicity was unrestricted.[8] When *El Topo* premiered in Madrid in February 1980 and thereafter in other metropolitan areas across Spain such as Barcelona, Seville and Valencia, the promotional material exploited its "S" status. The ads placed in *ABC*, for example, accredited the "S" to the film's 'violent scenes' and described it as 'the apotheosis of violence'. The film's long-standing ban from Spanish screens and its "American" provenance were also highlighted: 'A mythical title of American cinema … long awaited'. (Its exhibition in the US midnight movie circuit may explain the mistake regarding its industrial origin, American rather than Mexican.) The trade press forewarned prospective exhibitors of the commercial and moral dangers of showing a film like *El Topo*. According to the trade journal *Cine Asesor*, the film displays 'a number of sequences packed with the kind of sadist realism that produces nausea even to the strongest of stomachs' (1980). In addition to the physical effects the film may have on the spectator, *Cine Asesor* also alerted that the film may either 'assault the healthy and natural taste of the spectator or provoke his laughter' (1980). Overall, it predicted the film's commercial performance as 'average' with a real prospect of 'decreasing notably if the problematic trajectory of its director and its distribution is not known' (1980). In fact, exhibitors did little to fill in audiences with the circumstances surrounding the production, distribution and exhibition of *El Topo* in its native Mexico or in the US midnight movie context. As one of the film reviewers indignantly pointed out, 'not even a hand programme or a simple synopsis are provided to facilitate an understanding of this film' (Fernández Santos 1980).

If coverage of *El Topo* in 1976 had been circumscribed to the general chronicling of a festival devoted to Ibero-American cinemas, reviews on *El Topo* in 1980 circulated in a range of publications, from the mainstream press to cultural magazines to popular film magazines. Within this widespread critical reception, it is possible to identify a series of recurrent themes. While Harguindey had been at a loss for words to interpret *El Topo*, film critics in the early 1980s framed Jodorowsky and his film through the director's artistic trajectory as part of the Grupo Pánico,[9] recognizable artistic traditions (namely, surrealism), and the intricate web of symbolic and intertextual references on display. The dominant critical opinion from the mainstream press was that the film had failed to translate on to the screen the strategies and techniques of the Grupo Pánico Lázaro: *ABC*, for example, stated that, despite its potential status 'as the flagship film of panic surrealism', *El Topo* shows 'an absolute contempt for the most basic rules of cinema' (1980). And, despite the film's display of surrealist sensibilities through the lens of the western, *El Topo* failed in its ultimate attempt to '*épater les bourgeois*' (Martialay 1980), as *El Álcazar* put it. Its use of multiple symbols and cultural references exasperated the *ABC* critic: not only 'tiresome and irritating for their obviousness' but also 'disconcerting for the vast majority of the audience [due to] the accumulation of biblical allusions, surrealist quotations and references' (Crespo 1980). Martialay went further by asserting that *El Topo* was 'of little interest for the average spectator' but that 'it had some interest for cinephiles' (1980). Other publications such as the popular film magazine *Fotogramas* and the religious weekly *Vida Nueva* praised the concept at the core of the film – a journey of initiation – and encouraged prospective viewers to engage with and be transformed by the film: for *Fotogramas*, the film appealed to the emotions through confronting and shocking images like 'the best examples of Theatre of Cruelty' (Guarner 1980); *Vida Nueva* described the whole gamut of emotions felt while viewing the film 'dissent, applause, fascination and repulsion, nausea, breeze of mystery' (Pérez Gómez 1980). Most reviews reveal more about contemporary Spanish film cultures than about *El Topo*, in particular the reading protocols of a generation of critics whose discursive practices privileged a critical habitus typified by high-brow references informed by cinephilia.

By the 1990s and 2000s critical reception of *El Topo* must be seen as a constellation of contextual factors shaped by previous critical reception, the increasing popularity of Jodorowsky's commercial and media profile, the emergence of a new generation of 'fan cult' critics writing for fanzines devoted to lowbrow genres, and, of course, the availability of the film on DVD – the 'Pack Alejandro Jodorowsky' distributed by Cameo Media for the Spanish market – which renewed its cult status and, at the same time, made his work available in the mainstream market and, by extension, a broader target audience. The conflation of lowbrow and middlebrow might be said to be at work during the 2007 edition of the San Sebastián film festival when the organizers of a niche genre film festival linked to cult fandom joined forces with FNAC to exhibit the films of a multifaceted creator; as the catalogue announced, 'during the festival, FNAC will screen three movies directed by the playwright, filmmaker and shaman Alejandro Jodorowsky' (2007: 117). In the review of the DVD pack, the specialist cinephile magazine *Dirigido por* concluded that the recuperation of Jodorowsky's cinema 'reminds us of a way of understanding and making film which has now disappeared' (Freixas, 2007: 80).

Blinded by the underground burrows of the midnight movie circuit, cult film scholarship on *El Topo* has paid little attention to other contexts and practices of distribution, exhibition and critical reception across other film cultures. This chapter has dug into the Spanish context and into the different historical contingencies channelling the circulation of *El Topo*. Jodorowsky's film has circulated as an example of Latin American cinema in the mid-1970s, a category "S" film in the early 1980s, and as a cult film in film genre festivals and fanzines from the 1990s onwards. In forty years it has occupied and moved across different categorical spaces in Spanish film cultures, initially associated with a high-brow avant-garde tradition via its exhibition in a festival, shortly after classified as a low-brow "S" product, and, more recently, relocated within a middlebrow framework. Historicizing four decades of the reception, consumption and repackaging of *El Topo* may resonate with readers who have had comparable encounters with this and other cult movies. And, all along, Jodorowsky keeps cultivating his maverick art and placing his products in the marketplace trading in scandal, psychomagic or cult.

Notes

1 By then, this was a well-rehearsed autobiographical template that was repeated time and again by Jodorowsky in interviews and in pressbooks and reproduced in writings about Jodorowsky.
2 For the first Spanish-language book devoted to his films, see Moldes (2011).
3 As Dolores Tierney aptly has put it, *El Topo's* cult status and reputation 'is predicated on US-based (or, indeed, European-based) consumption and/or spectatorship, [namely] its New York midnight screenings' (2014: 131). Exceptions to this dominant approach in English-language scholarship can be found in David Church (2007) and Josetxo Cerdán and Miguel Fernández Labayen (2009).
4 See Lázaro-Reboll (2009) for a detailed discussion of "Perversa Amérca Latina" and the reception of Latin American exploitation cinemas in contemporary Spanish subcultures.
5 The 'Alejandro Jodorowsky Boxset', released on14 May 2007, includes three films with audio commentaries from the director on *Fando and Lis*, *El Topo* and *The Holy Mountain*, the soundtracks for *El Topo* and *The Holy Mountain*, the short *La cravate*, and a ninety-minute documentary entitled 'Constellation Jodorowsky'. Tartan also released *El Topo* and *The Holy Mountain* as standalone discs. In the United States, Anchor Bay distributed the boxset 'The Films of Alejandro Jodorowsky', whereas in France Wildside distributed 'L'universe de Alejandro Jodorowsky'.
6 Among the tributes in specialist film genre festivals, the Festival Internacional de Cinema Fantàstic de Sitges (2006) and the San Sebastián Horror and Fantasy Film Festival (2007).
7 The Spanish government instituted a four-tiered rating system for film products: (1) all audiences; (2) over 14 years of age; (3) over 18; and (4) "S" rating.
8 Over 130 films came under the category 'S'. Titles as different as *In the Realm of the Senses* (Nagisa Oshima, 1976) and *Sex is Crazy* (Jesús Franco, 1981) attest to the diversity of films that came under this category.
9 The *Grupo Pánico* or *Movimiento Pánico* was the avant-garde performance arts movement created by Jodorowsky in conjunction with Spanish playwright Fernando Arrabal and French artist and writer Roland Topor in Paris in 1962. Jodorowsky dissolved it in 1973.

References

n.a. (1980) '"El Topo", de Alejandro Jodorowsky', *ABC*, 22 February, n.p.
Algarabel Rutter, Nimbe Montserrat. 2012. Cine y Poder. Reconstrucción de los discursos de la censura y el escándalo en México (1968–2002), PhD Thesis, Mexico DF: Centro de Investigaciones y Estudios Superiores en Antropología Social.
Amela, Víctor A. 2002. 'Poesía y fútbol', *La Vanguardia. Vivir*, 29 April, 8.
Benson, Eric. 2014. 'The Psychomagical Realism of Alejandro Jodorowsky', *New York Times Magazine*, 14 March. www.nytimes.com/2014/03/16/magazine/the-psychomagical-realism-of-alejandro-jodorowsky.html (accessed 19 August 2016).
Bissette, Stephen R. 1991. 'Interview with Jodorowsky', *European Trash Cinema* [Collector's issue]: 52–54.

Bourdieu, Pierre. 1984. *Distinction: A Social Critique of the Judgment of Taste* (trans. Richard Nace), Cambridge, MA: Harvard University Press.

Canby, Vincent. 1973. 'Is "El Topo" a Con'?, in *The New York Times Film Review 1971–1972*, New York: New York Times and Arno Press: 70.

Cerdán, Josetxo, and Fernández-Labayen, Miguel. 2009. 'Arty Exploitation. Cool Cult, and the Cinema of Alejandro Jodorowsky', in Victoria Ruétalo and Dolores Tierney, eds, *Latsploitation, Exploitation Cinemas, and Latin America*, London: Routledge: 102–114.

Church, David. 2007. 'Alejandro Jodorowsky', *Senses of Cinema*, 42. sensesofcinema.com/2007/great-directors/jodorowsky/ (accessed 14 December 2007).

Cine Asesor. 1980. 'El Topo', n.p.

Cobb, Ben. 2006. *Anarchy and Alchemy: The Films of Alejandro Jodorowsky*, London: Creation Books.

Crespo, Pedro. 1980. '"El Topo", de Alejandro Jodorowsky", *El País*, 22 February: 54.

Ebert, Roger. 2007. '*El Topo*', 6 October, www.rogerebert.com/reviews/great-movie-el-topo-1970 (accessed 14 December 2007).

Fernández Santos, Jesús. 1980. 'Entre el absurdo y la provocación', *El País*, 22 February, n.p.

Freixas, Ramón. 2007. 'Jodorowsky seminal', *Dirigido por*, September, 370: 78–81.

Gorina, Alejandro. 1980. 'El Topo', *El Noticiero Universal*, 22 February, n.p.

Greenspun, Roger. 1971. '"El Topo" Emerges: Jodorowsky's Feature Begins Regular Run', in *The New York Times Film Review 1971–1972*, New York: New York Times and Arno Press, 5 November: 167.

Guarner, José Luis. 1980. 'Película de la semana: El Topo', *Fotogramas*, 5 March: 17.

Guida, Jeremy. 2014. 'Producing and Explaining Charisma: A Case Study of the Films of Alejandro Jodorowsky', *Journal of the American Academy of Religion*, 83(2): 537–553.

Harguindey, Ángel S. 1976. '"El Topo", insólita y genial película', *El País*, 12 December, n.p.

Hoberman, J., and Jonathan Rosenbaum. 1991. *Midnight Movies*, second edition. New York: Da Capo Press.

Jancovich, Mark, Antonio Lázaro-Reboll, Julian Stringer and Andy Willis, eds. 2003. *Cult Movies: The Cultural Politics of Oppositional Cinema*, Manchester: Manchester University Press.

Jordan. 1977. 'Cine Tercer Mundista en Huelva', *La Vanguardia Española*, 8 January: 34.

Kael, Pauline. 2000 (1975). 'El Poto-Head Comics', *Deeper into Movies: The Essential Kael Collection: From '69 to '72*, London and New York: Marion Boyars: 334–340.

Lara, Fernando. 1976. 'Ha llegado Buñuel …', *Triunfo*, 25 December: 44–45.

Lázaro-Reboll, Antonio. 2009. '"Perversa América Latina." The Reception of Latin American Exploitation Cinemas in Spanish Subcultures', in Victoria Ruétalo and Dolores Tierney (eds.), *Latsploitation, Exploitation Cinemas, and Latin America*, London: Routledge: 37–54.

Leblic, Rafael. 1976. 'Convocatoria iberoamericana de cinematografía', *ABC*, 23 November: 19.

Martialay, Félix. 1980. 'El Topo', *El Álcazar*, 13 March, n.p.

Mathijs, Ernest, and Xavier Mendik, eds. 2008. *The Cult Film Reader*, New York: Open University Press/ McGraw-Hill Education.

——— eds. 2011. *100 Cult Films*, London: BFI.

Mathijs, Ernest, and Jamie Sexton. 2011. *Cult Cinema*, Oxford: Wiley-Blackwell.

Moldes, Diego. 2011. *Alejandro Jodorowsky*. Madrid: Cátedra.

O'Brien, Glenn. 1971. 'Midnight Mass at the Elgin', *The Village Voice Film Guide*, 25 March: 268–269.

Ortega Bargueño, Pilar. 2002. 'Pasta de almendras para los desengaños', elmundo.es, 20 February. www. elmundo.es/elmundo/2002/02/18/cine/1014048133.html (accessed 14 December 2007).

Palacios, Jesús. 2002. 'De charla con el judío errante', *2000maniacos*, 26: 36–41.

Pérez Gómez, Ángel. 1980. 'El Topo. Un western iniciático', *Vida Nueva*, 1 March: 7.

Rose Steve. 2009. 'Lennon, Manson and Me: The Psychedelic Cinema of Alejandro Jodorowsky', theguardian.co.uk, 14 November (accessed 19 August 2016).

Ross, Jonathan. 1991. *Jonathan Ross Presents for One Week Only*, Channel X.

Schjeldahl, Peter. 1973. 'Should "El Topo" Be Elevated To "El Tops"?', *The New York Times Film Review 1971–1972*, New York: New York Times and Arno Press: 78–79.

Thrower, Stephen. 1990. 'Fantastic Crimes & Broken Logic. Alejandro Jodorowsky interviewed by Stephen Thrower', *Eyeball. The European Sex & Horror Review*, 2: 5–7.

Tierney, Dolores. 2014. 'Mapping Cult Cinema in Latin American Film Cultures', *Cinema Journal*, 54(1): 129–135.

Triana-Toribio, Núria. 2008. 'Auterism and Commerce in Contemporary Spanish Cinema', *Screen* 49(3): 259–276.

PART IX

Actors

Cult cinema acting

The cover of this volume is graced by Pam Grier, one of the quintessential performers of cult cinema. Her appearance, and demeanor, in films from *Beyond the Valley of the Dolls* (Meyer, 1970) and *The Big Doll House* (Hill, 1971) via *Foxy Brown* (Hill, 1974) to *Jackie Brown* (Tarantino, 1997), exemplifies cult acting – a term to be understood here as 'acting cultishly' as well as 'acting in cult films'. Excessiveness ('doll') and exoticism ('brown') typify the film titles of the stories Grier acts in, in ways that make many cringe about their political correctness (they signal exploitation fare). But they also raise the issues of specialty skill and uniqueness ('beyond', 'foxy') – of a different form of performing. Grier was initially cast for her looks, as a beautiful, exotic lady, and gradually grew out of exploitation film to become a respected actress whose skills in playing sly, cunning, graceful and determined women characters earned her respect beyond the exploitation circuit, and an enduring fan following. As has become common for the ways in which cult films since the 1970s have become overly self-reflexive, she has continued to perform similar characters, sometimes as a homage to earlier performances – her skills at portraying someone escaping the law are a marker of that. One could say that that also makes her a marker for cult film at large: always the fugitive.

If we take Pam Grier as our exemplar, the three keywords in cult acting are aesthetics, recognition, and reputation. The aesthetics of cult acting refer to the ways in which cult acting embraces the look of the body as a non-normative presence, with actions and gestures that stand separate form those regularly seen as standard for actors. Partly, this comes down to stature and body make-up. As Linda Williams (1994) has noted, performances of bodies involve, in equal ways, the looking of the body, and the looking at the body. This is all the more the case in cult acting. Rosenbaum and Hoberman (1983), Mathijs and Sexton (2011: 97–107), Taylor (2012), and Pomerance (2019) have noted how in cult films the body-look frequently involves bodies that are (or are presented as) transgressively and freakishly out of sort compared to what are seen as 'normal' proportions. The actor of short stature, for instance, recurs in numerous cult films (there is a revealing self-reflexive discussion of this kind of acting in the cult classic *In Bruges* (McDonagh, 2008). Such representations also include bodies of varying skin colour and complexion (scars), highly sexualized bodies, bodies in peril, bodies whose integrity is violated, and exaggerated athletic bodies – and sometimes all of these at the same time. Beyond the composition of the body the aesthetics of cult acting also include excessively hyperbolic or somnambulistically minimalist expressions and gestures, such as fists, hand motions, eye stares, grins and smiles, trances, fixed postures, and super tense and cramped positions. Each of the actors profiled in this section exemplifies these.

Of course, to a large extent, cult acting bodies are managed through acting skills, and this is where recognition comes in, in two ways. First, there is the coordination of body movements. Directed by skills derived from talent and training, often involving exhaustive choreographing, cult acting stands out through its exploration of the limits (and the exhaustion) of what is humanly possible, without resorting to deception. Or, to paraphrase Divine in *Pink Flamingos* (John Waters, 1972): "the real thing," whether it is fighting, dancing, doing the splits, swimming, taking punches, fainting, picking up a milk shake sliding across a counter, or holding a monkey in religious ecstasy while balancing on a sinking raft. Costumes too play an important role, and cult acting is known for its exuberance in adornment and accessories, as well as in body modification beyond the bounds of normativity: be they super-firm six packs, messy beards, luscious eye lashes, blood-shot eyes, or breathalyzers. Uniqueness is key here, and cult acting stands out not only because of the non-normative or innovative skill and talent involved, but also because of how this leads to actions that appear to spring out of nowhere, by surprise or instinct. Regardless the origin, the action sets a limit for a particular kind of template. Put differently, the way Barbara Steele performs a damsel in distress became the template for the 'scream queen.' And James Monaco (1977) has convincingly shown how Judy Garland's outfit from *The Wizard of Oz* (Fleming, 1939), clicking heels in red shoes and all, can never be done again. And yet, the second part of recognition is exactly that: doing it again. Here, recognition is more a mode of reception, as its significance lies outside the actual performance. Cult acting is known for what can be described as 'referentiality': a way of acting or presentation that draws attention to, or allows viewers to recognize in one performance images of and references to other performances by the same person – a breeze of 'something else' inside one performance that may or may not actually be there. This means that cult acting opens itself up to 'reading into' a performance what a fan is eager to see reflected. To an extent, this involves positioning and managing acts so that this is possible, and gestures such as open arms (in itself a cultish gesture) accommodate that. They provoke that aura. So do wide-open eyes, cheeky glances, suppressed smiles and nudges – they all give the impression that something is going on *beyond* the character arc. Repeating gestures across films and performances, such as a dance move, or licking an object (or one's own wounds), are also signals of referentiality. Extraordinary body movement and intertextual referentiality form the core of cult acting's recognition.

Finally, cult acting distinguishes itself through the reputations of the actors that are associated with it. A great deal of that reputation relies of the resumé or career of the performer, and as Mathijs and Sexton (2011: 76–85) have observed, shortened, abrupt, and fractured trajectories help form cult reputations, the origins of which are searched for in the performances of the actors involved – as if the characters reveal or express real-life struggles. At its most banal, this means typecasting, but in the case of most cult acting it is an archeological technique to connect often extraordinary life stories to performances. The reputations of Judy Garland, Klaus Kinski, and Bruce Lee (plus Heath Ledger, who is a case study in this volume's section on Aesthetics) are inevitably intertwined with their lives, because of the high visibility of their struggles. In the cases of Dennis Hopper and Crispin Glover, the proxy association of their performance choices, often side by side with or in support of other performers of note, or in ensembles, has given them an enhanced reputation as performers (they make perfect subjects for a 'six degrees of separation' game, based on John Guare's play of the same name). And in the case of Barbara Steele, and Pam Grier, a trajectory that moves from exploitation film, intertwined with arthouse and indie films, towards esteem and homage, has helped cement their solid cult reputations. At its largest, cult acting comes to stand for a 'type' of subcultural positioning, with the combinations of acting and extracurricular activity and cultural identity becoming totemic for ways in which performances have 'talked back' to the world. Grier has found herself emblematic for resourceful women performers of colour, without it doing injustice to her skills and talent. Lee, Hopper, and Garland too have become symbols for causes, and their acting has been given larger prominence through their achievements and sufferings.

References

Mathijs, Ernest, and Jamie Sexton. 2011. *Cult Cinema*. New York: Wiley.
Monaco, James. 1977. *How to Read a Film*. Oxford: Oxford University Press.
Pomerance, Murray. 2019. *Virtuoso: Film Performance and the Actor's Magic*. London: Bloomsbury.
Rosenbaum, Jonathan, and J. Hoberman. 1983. *Midnight Movies*. New York: Da Capo Press.
Taylor, Aaron (ed.). 2012. *Theorizing Film Acting*. New York: Routledge.
Williams, Linda. 1994. 'Learning to Scream', *Sight and Sound*, 4 (12): 14–17.

43

JUDY GARLAND

Steven Cohan

Frances Ethel Gumm was born in Grand Rapids, Minnesota, on June 10, 1922. Very early in her life, Frances, or "Baby" as she was called, performed professionally in vaudeville with her two elder siblings as the Gumm Sisters. At Chicago's Oriental Theatre in 1934 headliner George Jessel introduced the singing act as "the Garland Sisters" because their surname was getting laughs from the audience. By the following year the sisters were consistently using Garland for their act's name, and Frances took a different first name, becoming "Judy Garland," known as the little girl with a powerful grown-up voice. Also in that momentous year of 1935 Judy auditioned for Metro-Goldwyn-Mayer, which signed her to a long-term contract albeit with six-month renewals; at her audition, moreover, she met composer and music arranger Roger Edens, who would turn out to be an influential mentor and life-long friend. By 1937, Judy was singing in short subjects and feature-length films, appearing on radio, and had started her recording career at Decca. Her first big hit was "Dear Mr. Gable, You Made Me Love You," which Edens partly wrote and arranged for her. First sung to great acclaim at a studio birthday party for MGM star Clark Gable (and to show off Judy to studio executives), the song was included in *Broadway Melody of 1938* (1937) and it became one of her signature tunes. As well as costarring in several MGM features as the studio developed her screen persona, Judy played Betsy Booth, the proverbial girl next door, in three of the studio's Andy Hardy series of films starring Mickey Rooney.

Judy Garland became an MGM star in 1939 with the release of *The Wizard of Oz,* the film for which she is now best known, and *Babes in Arms*, a bigger hit at that time that saw her costarring again with Rooney. While *The Wizard of Oz* gave Garland the song with which she would forever be identified, "Over the Rainbow," *Babes in Arms* was the first of four "barnyard musicals" she and Rooney, a popular onscreen teen couple, did for studio producer Arthur Freed and his assistant, Edens. The Freed production unit at MGM would become well known for its musical films. By 1942 the more adult Garland received sole above-the-title billing for *For Me and My Gal*, which featured Gene Kelly in his first role at MGM; and thereafter she headlined a string of MGM hits produced by Freed, notably *Meet Me in St. Louis* (1944), *The Harvey Girls* (1946), and *Easter Parade* (1948).

During her tenure at MGM, the studio gave Garland addictive prescription drugs to control her weight, others to give her energy for the long hours of filming, then still others to allow her to sleep so she could start over again the next day. Although she was a pretty young woman,

Figure 43.1 Judy Garland sings "Over the Rainbow". *The Wizard of Oz* (Fleming, USA, 1939). Metro-Goldwyn-Mayer

she was not considered glamorous like the studio's sirens, Lana Turner and Hedy Lamarr, her two costars in *Ziegfeld Girl* (1941). Studio head Louis B. Mayer reportedly called her his "little hunchback." In her early films, moreover, the young Garland was given songs alluding to her "in between" status. Along with the drugs and a rigorous diet, her nose was fitted with plugs to modify its shape, her teeth were capped, and the studio costumers tried multiple ways to disguise her tiny (4'11") short-waisted body. Nonetheless, after *Meet Me in St. Louis* she was considered a major film star with a huge fan base and was closely identified with MGM's lush, expensive, high-grossing Technicolor musicals.

However, as the decade came to a close, the addictive drugs began to affect Garland's body and her psyche adversely. As her behavior became more erratic and her absences from the set more commonplace, Garland was replaced by Ginger Rogers, Betty Hutton, and Jane Powell in several high profile musicals originally intended for her, *The Barkleys of Broadway* (1949), *Annie Get Your Gun* (1950), and *Royal Wedding* (1951), respectively. Despite those setbacks, Garland still had big successes with *In the Good Old Summertime* (1949) and her final MGM film, *Summer Stock* (1950), which yielded another signature song for her, "Get Happy." MGM suspended Garland after she failed to show up for rehearsals for *Royal Wedding*, and Garland made a well-publicized suicide attempt afterward, although the cut to her throat turned out to be superficial. A few months later she asked to be released from her MGM contract, which still had two years left on it.

The following decade was a series of comebacks for Garland. She rebounded in 1951 from what looked like the end of her career by returning to her vaudeville roots, first with a set at the London Palladium and then in a four-week engagement that was extended to a record-breaking nineteen weeks at the Palace Theatre on Broadway. This success led to a return to films with *A Star Is Born* (1954) at Warner Bros. While a personal triumph for her and with still another signature song, "The Man that Got Away," this comeback film had an overlong, over-budget shoot; then the studio decided to cut a half hour from the three-hour running time after its first-run engagements so the film would fit more easily on a double bill when it went into general release. Nominated for an Academy Award for Best Actress and expected by many to win, her loss of this prize, coupled with stories about her tardiness and illnesses while making *A Star Is Born*, diminished further interest in her by Hollywood; although her name was mentioned in connection with several upcoming film musicals, nothing came of them. From this point on, Garland went back to live performing in nightclubs and theaters, reinventing herself as a major concert artist. She also signed with Capitol Records and released several well-received albums.

During the fifties Garland battled with frequently visible weight gains. In November 1959 she was hospitalized for acute hepatitis, the source of her extreme weight gain to 180 pounds at that time, and doctors told her she would never perform again. However, she recovered, recorded a new album, and developed her two-act concert format, which would henceforth become the gold standard of her live performing. As part of a tour of big US cities, Garland's third big comeback was a solo concert at Carnegie Hall on April 23, 1961, before a star-studded audience, which yielded a Grammy-winning, best-selling, two-disc record album recorded live, *Judy at Carnegie Hall*. Building on this success and looking svelte and in good health, Garland did some television specials and guest shots, two dramatic films, and what would be her final musical, *I Could Go On Singing* (1963), playing a character much like herself. CBS signed her to a weekly television series for the 1963–1964 season, but after several format and costar changes the network canceled her variety show. For the remaining years of her life Garland struggled with her finances, needing to pay debts accrued by the various men managing her career, as her drug addictions took their toll on her health and her voice, and gossip about her erratic behavior kept her in the news. She died of an accidental overdose of barbiturates in London on June 22, 1969.

Figure 43.2 Judy Garland sings "The Man that Got Away" on *The Judy Garland Show* (CBS, 1963–64)

Judy Garland was a mainstream star during her lifetime but is considered a cult figure today. Most famously, she is a gay icon, the result of several intersecting factors. On the day of her funeral, the drag queens at the Stonewall Inn, gathering there in her memory, got fed up with police harassment and their active resistance started a riot that many consider the inauguration of the gay liberation movement. Whether factual or not, the association still adheres to Garland's legend as a cult star with a strong gay male following.

Why her by-now indelible identity as a gay icon? To begin with, Garland was associated with gay men in her private life. She married three men – Vincente Minnelli, Mark Heron, Mickey Deems – who were rumored to be bisexual, and her father was also said to have had hookups with younger men. Her daughter, Liza Minnelli, married a gay man, Peter Allen, whom she met when he worked with Garland in Australia. Furthermore, the Freed unit at MGM was informally known as "Freed's fairies" due to the number of gay men who worked for Freed and MGM in various capacities. Garland had long-standing personal as well as professional relationships with many of those gay men, who groomed her to stardom, notably but not only Edens, director Charles Walters, and choreographer Robert Alton. Walters, for instance, not only directed her in *Easter Parade* and *Summer* Stock but did the same for her Palace vaudeville act. Edens also worked with Garland to develop her act for the Palace Theater after leaving MGM, writing new arrangements and lyrics for her, and, since he was still contracted to MGM, he provided routines and arrangements for *A Star Is Born* without taking a credit. Alton staged her return to the Palace in 1957.

These factors from her biography are circumstantial, however. A more salient reason for Garland's appeal to gay fandom as a cult star has to do with her filmography, on one hand, and her concert performing, on the other. The two present somewhat contrasting views of Garland but intersect in her gay fandom, which was already large and visible during her lifetime. The musical genre has long had a strong gay following for its utopian spirit, its over-the-top displays of lavish spectacle, its gender-bending play and performativity in numbers, and its projection of liberated male and female bodies moving in space through song and dance. Musicals were often built around female stars like Garland, and her singing gave voice to a strong expression of subjectivity that appealed to gay men as an alternative to the more conventional macho displays of heterosexual masculinity in action genres like the Western and war film.

Conversely, Garland's later concert appearances came to be read either as her triumphant resilience given the suffering in public that marked her private life since leaving MGM or, especially at her low points, as symptomatic evidence of her ongoing abjection due to her addictions, implied by her tardiness in getting on stage on time and her hoarseness and mumbling. As far as writers of the sixties were concerned, she represented for gay men a grotesque figure of pathos whose display of suffering on and off stage they could identify with (Goldman 1984: 3–8). Now Garland's singing of "Over the Rainbow," which typically closed out her set list, was a torch song about lost youth or lost innocence, a song less about longing for that yellow brick road and more about reaching for those final high notes of an iconic song and, as often as not in her last years, failing to do so.

Film scholar Richard Dyer expands upon these points to offer an even more nuanced account of Garland's legendary appeal to gay fans. He argues that her appeal rested on three interconnected qualities of her stardom that worked in conjunction with her star-is-born/star-is-worn biography: her ordinariness, her androgyny, and her camp attitudes. The basis of her meaning for gay men, according to Dyer, builds from but then exceeds the superficial disparity between her MGM and post-MGM stardoms. "To turn out not-ordinary after being saturated with the values of ordinariness structures Garland's career and the standard gay biography alike," he writes (Dyer 2004: 153).

Such difference-in-normality was already the basis of her MGM persona, moreover. As Dyer explains, while her filmic characters are all ordinary young women who tend to live in small towns, Garland bears "a special relationship to ordinariness" (152). He points to two elements of her screen persona at MGM that bring out this connection. First is Garland's lack of glamour; her films render it as proof of her normality, but this trait also registers insecurity on her handlers' part behind the cameras, and eventually Garland herself, about her femininity and hence about the stability of normative gender roles. Second is Garland's emotional intensity as a singer; whether in upbeat peppy tunes or plaintive torch songs, her powerful voice surpassed both her biographic age when she began in films and the restraint of her characters' small-town lives, further signifying "an essence of emotional difference akin to the idea of gayness born within normality" (159).

Additionally, as she matured during the forties Garland was often an androgynous figure in some of her musical numbers, wearing, for instance, a tuxedo jacket and fedora in "Get Happy" in *Summer Stock,* a clown costume in "Be a Clown" in *The Pirate* (1947), and a tramp get-up in "A Couple of Swells" in *Easter Parade* (a number that was featured in her Palace comeback and a 1955 TV special). The androgyny added an element of theatricality and gender play to Garland's star persona, and her apparent ease when wearing male clothes heightened the sense of "difference-in-normality" personified by her characters and the intensity of her singing.

Finally, in her vocal inflections, as when reciting comic dialogue in her films, and her off-camera fame as a funny, sometimes bawdy, often self-deprecatory storyteller, Garland was not an object of camp appreciation or deprecation, but a star who exhibited and shared with

Figure 43.3 Judy Garland and Fred Astaire perform "A Couple of Swells" in *Easter Parade* (Walters, USA, 1948). Metro-Goldwyn-Mayer

pre-Stonewall gay men their camp outlook. This was especially apparent when she reflected anecdotally upon her own life in her concerts or on late night talk shows. One can account for her camp attitudes by recalling what I have already mentioned: how, starting as a young teen, she worked with gay men at MGM like Edens, Alton, and Walters, who not only influenced her performing style for the screen, but shared a camp viewpoint that she made her own on and off screen.

Garland's camp performances on film and delivery of some songs on stage involved more than her simply being funny. For instance, her dance numbers often surrounded her with a male ensemble that, as in her sole number in *Ziegfeld Follies* (1946), represents them as "a queer entourage" and even made them viewable to some spectators as a "contingent of [her] adoring fans" (Tinkcom 2002: 58). Similarly, Garland's performance in other numbers produces a "camp affect" through "the distancing stance [she] takes toward glamour," as in *Ziegfeld Girl* (Cohan 2005: 105). Finally, her solo singing, whether the song is torched or belted, plays with the dualism of camp wit and its strong emotional affect, which celebrates theatricality and authenticity, and irony and intensity, as two sides of the same coin. In her singing and its staging, this is to say, one quality passes as and so implies the other in dialectic tension, as in her performances of the torchy "Man that Got Away" or the belting "Trolley Song," another standard number in her concert repertoire from *Meet Me in St. Louis* (Cohan 2005: 24–36).

Even without knowing much about her career or her life, the film most people identify with Garland, *The Wizard of Oz*, has strong queer resonances, contributing to her gay and even lesbian cult status from another perspective. Consider that the three friends who travel with Dorothy on the yellow brick road are three effeminate or "sissy" males who need her direction, and that the narrative arc is a tale of a young girl fighting a "bad" mother figure in the Wicked Witch and desiring to return to Auntie Em, the "good" mother figure back home in Kansas, which the Good Witch Glinda helps Dorothy to do. In fact, Alexander Doty convincingly reads the film, a rare Hollywood production lacking a heterosexual couple, as a lesbian fantasy on Dorothy's part. As she travels with those sissy male comrades down the yellow brick road to Oz, Dorothy deals with a fraudulent patriarch (the Wizard) while negotiating her way amongst strong female figures, the butch Wicked Witch and femme Glinda, each attractive in negative or positive ways to Dorothy's adolescent sexuality (Doty 2000: 49–78).

In much the same vein, the song from *The Wizard of Oz* most identified with Garland as her theme, "Over the Rainbow," shows Dorothy yearning for the escapist Technicolor, utopian world of a musical – or, as Doty argues, the song posits the urban queer world of Oz in contrast to the sepia toned, black-and-white landscape of repressed sexuality in Kansas. It therefore follows that common lore still believes that the rainbow flag of gay pride alludes to Garland and Oz, just as a common phrase to connote gay people, "Friends of Dorothy," refers to those three sissy males whom she meets in Oz (although in point of fact, the term probably refers to the witty writer of the 1930s, Dorothy Parker).

The Wizard of Oz has therefore generated another type of cult following for Judy Garland, namely, straight as well as queer girls and women. Her female fans of various ages and sexual orientations have identified with Garland's marginality or her difference-in-normality, especially as personified by Dorothy. Garland was very popular among women during her MGM days and women were also dedicated fans during her concert years, with a group of them, self-named "the Bench Wenches," faithfully attending weekly tapings of her TV series in Los Angeles. Since then, at least judging anecdotally from fan pages on the Internet by girls and women and the large number of female Garland fans who have taken my course on the Hollywood musical over the past fifteen years, the star continues to have cult value for young women. In fact, the three qualities singled out by Dyer – Garland's unstable relation to ordinariness, her androgyny, and her camp attitudes – may apply to this fan formation too, although in a different social context. For as well as responding to the emotional intensity of her powerful voice, Garland as Dorothy, I think it is safe to say, represents what is now a post-feminist stance toward the limitations of conventional femininity, especially as a standard imposed upon women and girls by patriarchy. These female fans may discover Garland through *The Wizard of Oz* but their interest extends to her other films and/or her recordings, too.

Garland fandom, then, is multifaceted, which also contributes to her cult status even if some mainstream viewers and listeners now consider her a "niche" taste. To be sure, there are many fans whose fandom takes in her entire career, but others fan formations focus more exclusively around *The Wizard of Oz*, or her MGM musicals, or her recordings, or her concert performances, or her TV series. Still another fan formation may accrue around Garland's biography, especially as it recounts a narrative about her troubled and troubling ungovernable body in relation to female labor in an industrial setting like Hollywood.

That is, while one perspective of Garland's career emphasizes how her love of performing compensated for whatever travails and tragedies marked her life off-screen and off-stage, another perspective on her life sees her as a victim of her stage mother, LB Mayer and her studio, and her managers who stole her earnings or invested them poorly, and it takes seriously Garland's voiced wish at times not to have to perform to keep her family in food, clothes, and lodgings. This double context contributes to her camp affect, accounting for her self-deprecating wit, to be sure; but it also illuminates how her absences and tardiness, her weight gains and losses, and the insecurity about her looks resulting from the studio's treatment of her, all posit Judy Garland as not simply being victimized by studio regulation; rather, in her "unprofessional" behavior she may have been actively resisting it too. Given how men who saw Garland as a prized commodity dominated Hollywood and the concert industry, her behavior can be viewed in this light. Many reasons factored into her "bad" conduct at work when she failed to show for rehearsals or a day's shooting or delayed the start of a performance for an hour or more. Given accounts of her quickness in taking direction and learning complex routines, it is also possible Garland only felt comfortable performing when she could give one hundred and ten percent of herself, and whatever private demons or drugs caused her to lose confidence in her ability, that may have been another reason for what the press reported as her increasing lack of professionalism.

In *A Star Is Born* Norman Maine's (James Mason), decline as a movie star parallels the rise of Esther Blodgett (Garland). The studio head tells Maine:

> They can't afford you any more, Norman. You're too big a risk. Those big fat flush days when a star could get drunk and disappear and hold up production for two weeks are over. Even if you hadn't slipped a little, they still wouldn't take the chance. Your record's too bad. No one can afford it anymore.

MGM's Dore Shary, Mayer's successor, said much the same retrospectively when commenting about the studio's decision to let Garland go in 1950. In 1954 fans already read Esther and Norman as composite representations of Garland's own career, and this interpretation still holds fast. As movie attendance decreased and the government forced the studio's divestment of its profitable theater chain, MGM, like the other major studios, ceased indulging in excessive star behavior like Garland's. But her passive-aggressive behavior as a laborer in the entertainment industry may have been the only way she knew, even if not consciously, how to exert some degree of control over her working conditions, suggesting that her "deviant" body, which gave MGM so much trouble and which gossip columnists in the fifties focused on in their obsessions with her weight, symptomatically registered her resistance.

Garland's gay fandom may now seem generational, even an embarrassment to some gay men of the post-Stonewall era, as new cult formations have risen around Cher, Bette Midler, Barbra Streisand, Madonna, Britney Spears, Christina Aguilera, Lady Gaga, and Beyonce (Gross 2000). Nevertheless, numerous books continue to be written about Garland's life and her output of movies, records, and TV appearances (Tormé 1970; Deans and Pinchot 1972; Edwards 1974; Finch 1975; Frank 1975; Sanders 1990; Shipman 1992; Luft 1998; Clark 2000). As the dates of these books and those listed for further reading indicate, the wave of publications about Garland in the years after her death was followed in the last decade of the past century by a second and larger wave of biographical reconsiderations of her life and legacy. Furthermore, while her song repertoire was never infinite but confined to show tunes, ballads, torch songs, marches, and other forms of early to mid-twentieth century popular music, new masters or newly discovered alternate versions of the same songs, or new configurations of them (all Harold Arlen songs, say, or songs done multiple times at different times and in different arrangements) continue to be issued as "new" CDs. Her life story, or portions of it, has been filmed for television, dramatized for the stage, and fictionalized. Her currency on the Internet remains unabated. A holograph concert, using footage of her singing from her TV series, has been talked about but has yet to materialize.

Decades after her death, in other words, Judy Garland continues to come back. Her immortality, in this respect, is probably the ultimate sign of her cult status today. Whereas cult stars like James Dean and Marilyn Monroe died young, so their imagery remains ageless, much like Elvis Presley, imagery of Judy Garland juxtaposes young and old: the innocent, desiring Judy of *Wizard of Oz* fame versus the mature, sometimes drunk or drugged Garland of her last years. But in between those two poles are images of this star in her twenties from her MGM musicals and in her thirties from *A Star Is Born* and her concerts and TV shows. Garland was all of these personae: each one in its own way visualizes a tiny woman with a powerful voice and great sense of humor, especially about herself and her life, which she never saw as tragic.

References

Clark, Gerald. 2000. *Get Happy: The Life of Judy Garland.* New York: Random House.
Cohan, Steven. 2005. *Incongruous Entertainment: Camp, Cultural Value, and the MGM Musical.* Durham, NC: Duke University Press.
Deans, Mickey and Pinchot Anne. 1972. *Weep No More, My Lady.* New York: Hawthorn Books.
Doty, Alexander. 2000. *Flaming Classics: Queering the Film Canon.* London: Routledge.
Dyer, Richard. 2004. *Heavenly Bodies: Film Stars and Society,* second edition. London: Routledge.
Edwards, Anne. 1974. *Judy Garland.* New York: Simon & Schuster.
Finch, Christopher. 1975. *Rainbow: The Stormy Life of Judy Garland.* New York: Ballantine Books.
Frank, Gerold. 1975. *Judy.* New York: Harper & Row.
Goldman, William. 1984. *The Season: A Candid Look at Broadway.* New York: Limelight Editions.
Gross, Michael Joseph. 2000. "The Queen Is Dead," *Atlantic Monthly* (August): 62–70.
Luft, Lorna. 1998. *Me and My Shadows: A Family Memoir.* New York: Pocket Books.
Sanders, Coyne Stephen. 1990. *Rainbow's End: The Judy Garland Show.* New York: Zebra Books.
Shipman, David. 1992. *Judy Garland: The Secret Life of an American Legend.* New York: Hyperian.
Tinkcom, Matthew. 2002. *Working Like a Homosexual: Camp, Capital, Cinema.* Durham, NC: Duke University Press.
Tormé, Mel. 1970. *The Other Side of the Rainbow with Judy Garland on the Dawn Patrol.* New York: William Morrow.

44

FROM THE OTHER SIDE
OF THE WIND

Dennis Hopper

Adrian Martin

What determines the parts that an actor gets to play on screen? An intricate, sometimes barely fathomable alchemy of factors: his/her potentialities and limitations – or at least how these are perceived and construed by the film industry; specific movie successes that suddenly give the actor a bankable association and create an image; the fact that any durable screen persona is usually a dynamic amalgam of various, even contradictory facets that can be used and combined differently in any given film; how the actor's gender, age, physique, at any given stage of life, mesh (or fail to mesh) with a certain repertoire of standardised, narrative movie types; and, hovering over all of this, a certain, always powerfully influential force of the felt cultural meaning of this actor (if he or she has had any career longevity) as some kind of icon, some sign of his or her times.

Dennis Hopper (1936–2010), a prolific, energetic, charismatic performer in A grade and B grade films alike, in popular cinema and in art cinema – and a ubiquitous media celebrity – also came loaded (more than most contemporaneous actors) with a past. Out of the 1950s: James Dean and *Giant* (1956). Out of the 1960s: *Easy Rider* (1969), which he also directed. And then everything that followed these brilliant origins: the 1970s burn-out (when, in fact, he never stopped working around the world) and the mid-1980s comeback heralded by his role as Frank Booth in *Blue Velvet* (1986). As the years and decades roll by, the names, creators and iconic figures with which Hopper was associated, either on or off screen, also shifted and changed in a dizzying procession: from Dean, Natalie Wood and Roger Corman, to Wim Wenders, Francis Coppola, Charles Bukowski and William Burroughs; from David Lynch, Neil Young, Christopher Walken, Quentin Tarantino and Barbara Hershey to Sean Penn, Keanu Reeves, Abel Ferrara, Asia Argento and Kevin Costner.

His image changed, too – most notably from the Gothic, noir and Tarantino associations of the '80s and '90s (*Blue Velvet*, *Red Rock West* [1992], *True Romance* [1993] and his own *The Hot Spot* [1990]), what he himself enthusiastically dubbed the "Blood Lust Snicker Snicker in Wide Screen" phenomenon, or the "new wave of violence in movies" (Hopper & Tarantino 1994: 13–14), to a closer identification in the general media-sphere with a role he had long played in real life. This was Hopper the connoisseur and collector of modern art since his friendship with Dean; art photographer and painter; fixture of *Interview* magazine; distinguished (if quirky and sometimes deliberately self-mocking) talking head in numerous TV documentaries (on Marcel Duchamp, Andy Warhol, and the UK series *This Is Modern Art*); and a type of self-conscious performance artist in films of a much-touted wave of narrative features by celebrated New York artists (Julian Schnabel's *Basquiat* [1996] and David Salle's *Search and*

Destroy, aka *The Four Rules* [1995]). Tailored elegance – a far cry from the earlier, vintage, cowboy-hippie look – comes to the fore in the Hopper incarnation of the 1990s (it is a prime element in Schrader's *Witch Hunt* [1995]); his characters' costumes were increasingly supplied by Armani or Hugo Boss, and his haircuts invariably short and sharp. At the end of the '90s, the disquieting B movie *MichaelAngel* (1999) brought together the psychosis of Frank Booth with this carefully nurtured art world association: Hopper plays a serial killer whose artfully gruesome blood splatterings at the scenes of his crimes bring him perverse recognition as "a brilliant abstract expressionist".

Bringing along these various associations to each new role of the 1980s and '90s – and cast in part because of them – Hopper faced the risk of becoming merely a "convocation of all that he had previously done (…) an emblem, a citation, a monument – to the point of becoming a museum-piece". But, as Jean-Marc Lalanne goes on to comment in his analysis of the career of Jean-Pierre Léaud, what such a process can overlook, obscure and constrain is an emblematic figure's "extraordinary possibilities as an actor" (Lalanne 1997: 55). It is the aim of this survey to speculate on the logic underpinning Hopper's career moves as an actor, especially from the start of the 1980s up to his death at age 74. Of course, commentators like myself are prone to find logic where, in the flow of an actor's life, there is only a volatile mixture of opportunity, advice, luck (good and bad), timetabling clashes, hunches, deals, and maybe – somewhere, somehow, through all of that – the fragile thread of a personal vision. Nonetheless, this chapter emphasises the striking coherence of Hopper's films as an actor, when viewed from a particular angle. For the most part, I am placing biographical and journalistic sources to one side. And only fleeting allusions will be made to Hopper's directorial career, covering seven features from *Easy Rider* to *Chasers* (1994), plus several shorts.

Looking at Hopper from different methodological perspectives has the effect of creating multiple, sometimes overlapping, sometimes incommensurable Hoppers. This essay recognises three: Hopper as an emblem of 1960s counterculture (his place in a history of popular culture); Hopper as a screen actor (his skills and limitations, and the way these relate to a given film's stylistics); and Hopper as male anti-hero (within the changing social values of his times).

Hopper 1: 1960s emblem

Dennis Hopper is a creature of the 1960s – indelibly associated with that decade in the form in which it has been so relentlessly mythologised, de-mythologised and re-mythologised by the mass media ever since (see Orlean et al. 2010). Part of Hopper's appeal – in career terms, probably both a fortune and a curse – lies in the fact that he not only embodied a certain cultural history, but also had to perpetually re-enact it (in various explicit or implicit ways) in most of his roles. His work offers a way of remembering and negotiating the 1960s. The shape of Hopper's later career – 1970s burn-out, 1980s comeback, 1990s success – easily bolsters many different or contradictory versions of what the 1960s might mean to us today, depending which part of that narrative is stressed, how it is alluded to and reflected upon in any one of his films. Hopper is, all at once, the 1960s "without apology" (see Sayres et al. 1984) or smothered in regret, a post-Beat relic or a pre-punk role model, the living spirit of an era or its ravaged ghost. Through him, different interest groups can work out – in that shared, imaginative space provided by cinema – something of their relation to that tumultuous decade of social change.

Other actors are similarly emblematic, like Hopper's *Easy Rider* confreres Peter Fonda and Jack Nicholson, or the national stars created by the various New Waves of the 1960s all around the world (Léaud, Lou Castel, Zbigniew Cybulski, David Warner). But to none of these has the 1960s identification stuck so persistently or tenaciously as it did to Hopper. This has to do not only with the parts that Hopper got, but also the kind of sensibility he embodied and projected on screen. Hopper exhibits an identifiably 1960s energy, according to standard pop culture lore: the rebel, the anarchist, the good-hearted doper and drinker, the wild and crazy guy with a brimming libido and a manic, instantly recognisable laugh.

Hopper's countercultural 1960s persona is nostalgically indulged in the teen comedy *My Science Project* (1985) and the trading-places plot of *Flashback* (1990) – not forgetting Robert Altman's little-seen *O.C. & Stiggs* (1987), with its homage to Hopper's role in *Apocalypse Now* (1979). On another level, his persona receives an upbeat, "back to the future" workout when projected into the worlds of *The American Way* (aka *Riders of the Storm*, 1986) and *Space Truckers* (1996). These films, like *Waterworld* (1995), deftly marry Hopper's trademark 1960s look with the punk bricolage, scavenger mode of costume popularised by the *Mad Max* films (1979–2015).

But if Hopper sometimes carries with him the dream of the 1960s, ultimately, he does not embody a utopian yearning or aspiration. Failure, death-drives and burn-out shadowed him from the start, from the James Dean association through to the inaugural moment of generational error – "we blew it" – in *Easy Rider*. So, those Hopper dramas that involve explicit, sometimes elaborate references to the '60s – from his own *The Last Movie* (1971) and *Tracks* (1976) to *Apocalypse Now*, *River's Edge* (1986), *The Indian Runner* (1991) and *Jesus' Son* (1999) – are usually sad, ugly affairs, tales of genocide, cultural devastation, suicide and betrayal. Hopper, in the long run, is less an emblem of the 1960s, frozen in time, than an embodiment of the continuing legacy of that era, of the wear and tear visited by the vicissitudes of personal and public history upon its dreams and ideals – a living test of its ability either to survive as inspiration, or die pathetically, as if to reveal its inherent bankruptcy, its status as a historical "original sin" against the social order.

The television film *Doublecrossed* (1991) elegantly offers, in the course of its true-life story of Barry Seal, the full mélange of Hopper's 1960s-related images. He is wild and crazy, lawless, reckless Dennis – a devil-may-care dope smuggler bonding with his best male friend as he pilots his plane into Latin American and Third World hot spots with abandon. He is manic, but not wilfully self-destructive – fondly remembering how, in the "peace and love" days, drugs were merely used for pleasant "recreation". Likewise, while he is a naturally anarchic soul, he is not deceitful or manipulative. "This may come as a surprise to you", as he says to the government agents who eventually nab him, "but I'm an honest man". Finally, when the bureaucrats have left Seal out to dry, and even his best friend has gone down in a last run, he drives ritually, stoically, to the place where he knows a rendezvous with death awaits him.

The 1960s countercultural legacy had another, paradoxical outcome for Hopper as an actor. Like Rip Torn or Donald Sutherland, he ended up often playing exactly the reverse of what his former association with radicalism would decree: law enforcers (*Nails* [1992], *Road Ends* [1997], *The Prophet's Game* [1999]), corporate "suits" (*Black Widow*, 1987), money men (the wealthy art dealer and Warhol patron Bruno Bischofberger in *Basquiat*), the self-appointed capitalist king of a post-apocalyptic Chicago (*Land of the Dead*, 2005), and even a cultural-conservative hero, Frank Sinatra (*The Night We Called It a Day*, 2003). A certain mode of agit-prop satire is clearly brought into play by such casting – although, by the 1990s, Hopper grew into such roles so well, and on such a grand scale thanks to the success of *Speed* (1994), that the political irony may have disappeared. In his private and public life, Hopper himself veered increasingly to the right after the 1980s, eventually participating in the frankly propagandistic, anti-Michael Moore satire, *An American Carol* (2008).

In popular perception, Hopper became a standby "heavy" or villain, in either the cartoonish, artificial, generic mode of *Waterworld* and *Super Mario Bros.* (1993) – abstracted even further in his voice work for video games such as *Deadly Creatures* (2009) – or the more naturalistic dramatic mode of *Paris Trout* (1991). So, in the cinema of the 1990s and 2000s, Hopper came to represent a figure of evil. But what complexion of evil, exactly? Although Hopper's villains can be shady and even omnipotent, it is hard to imagine him as the sort of cold, steely, Nietzschean intellectual portrayed by, for example, Jeremy Irons in *Die Hard With a Vengeance* (1995). The reason for this is simple: Hopper always plays men of impulse, driven beings. Anti-intellectualism comes naturally to him: in *Search and Destroy* he rails against the "intellectuals" and "guardians of our culture" who trashed his last book; in *The Last Days of Frankie the Fly* (1996) he sneers at an amateur filmmaker as "Mr NYU"; and in *MichaelAngel* he advises: "Never hire a model who thinks she's an art critic". His own characters do not merely feel or express emotions – they are gripped, possessed by them.

Hence the trance-like quality of many Hopper performances. His characters trust their feelings and are spurred into action by them; their only imaginable program is one powered by lust, greed or revenge, not by abstract principle. Even when Hopper mouths statements of ideology (as in *Paris Trout*), he delivers them in a glazed, robotic way, as if such rationalisations of pure emotion were simply for the benefit of the world, not the key to understanding his animating, inner will. In *Blue Velvet*, the fact that Booth's extravagantly histrionic psychosis (manifested in bursts of violence, fabric fetishism and ceaseless, bizarre verbal obscenities) resembles the exhibited symptoms of Tourette's Syndrome, serves implicitly to "absolve him from guilt somewhat" (Routt 1987: 51).

Hopper 2: Screen actor

Was Dennis Hopper a good actor? There is an unfortunate, dimly understood myth or cliché that needs to be hurdled before any real answer to this question can be given. Hopper is caricatured in many places as a typical Method actor. In the annals of received, media-fed wisdom, Method performers are in some sense not reflective, craft-based actors at all (which is far from the truth): unable to create any distance between themselves and their role, they immerse themselves in pure emotion, they "become" their parts through various rituals that are regularly the butt of satire. A capsule entry in the *Time Out Film Guide* on *Tracks* summarises this easy line on Hopper: his performance is a "terminal piece of Method acting" (Pym 2000: 739).

The image of Hopper as a Method-induced raver slides easily into the judgment that he is a bad actor – or, at the very least, an over-actor. Leonard Maltin's entry on *King of the Mountain* (1981) in his *Movie & Video Guide* determines that Hopper "overacts outrageously" (Maltin 1999: 739). Cult fans invert such a verdict – but tacitly agree with the terms of its evaluation – when they praise the actor's excess, his spectacular circus turns that leap out of the narratives containing them. Tarantino's appreciation is typical:

> One of your performances that's one of my favourites – it's a wacky, kooky performance – is in *The Glory Stompers* [1967]. I *loved* you in that. You know, that *is* the beginning of you as Frank Booth in *Blue Velvet* right there (…) *The Glory Stompers* is really cool, because it looks like you're improvising it throughout the whole thing. (…) You have this one line which is *so* fucking funny in it: when you're fighting this guy, you beat him up, and then you look around and say: "Anybody got anything else to say? Turn it on, man, just turn it on" (Hopper & Tarantino 1994: 21–22).

Intimately related to this prevailing perception of Hopper is the assumption that he only ever really played himself – and that such a mode of performance constitutes his evident limit, his lack of range as an actor. But what are the real limits of Hopper's acting range, if any? It is true that, for instance – unlike Al Pacino, say – accents are not his bag; his adoption of different American idioms (as in *Frankie the Fly*), a European lilt (*Basquiat*) or a Russian growl (in the hit TV series *24*) sound somewhat tentative. There is also the intriguing fact that Hopper is rarely cast in period pieces (*Samson and Delilah* [1996] and *Jason and the Argonauts* [2000] notwithstanding). When he is used in this way, the period is not very far away in time (*Paris Trout*), or there is virtually no attempt to mould and integrate the star's performance into the period – most spectacularly the case in the zany Australian bushranger Western *Mad Dog Morgan* (1976).

Being perceived as always playing oneself in cinema means, essentially, being identified by a repertoire of mannerisms. Hopper's mannerisms are, without a doubt, prodigious. Physically, they include: his way of using hands (either fingers pointing or wielded as outstretched palms) and arms in broad, extravagant, punchy movements that underline key words and points; his manic, nervy way of nodding, often with the entire top half of his body, and of shuffling from side to side, from foot to foot; his full-out register, involving bulging, wide-open eyes and shouting – usually reached via the vocal intermediary of an exasperated question asked in a raised pitch.

Verbally, Hopper's inventions – and clearly he had a creative hand in writing or rewriting a good number of them – are frequently astounding. A degree of improvisation, stream-of-consciousness or free-association governs the wildest linguistic flights in his oeuvre. Beyond the inescapable 1960s-era markers (the ubiquitous use of "man" as verbal punctuation), Hopper uses a Beat poetry or jazz-inspired way of breaking down and repeating the parts of a line in several phrases or sentences – "Get some money, man. Go! Get money!" (*Search and Destroy*), "New York. Actresses go there. That's the place actresses go" (*Frankie the Fly*) – and a wholly individual way of stressing or stretching out certain words or syllables in a phrase ("*home* is *where* you *haaang* yourself", *Eye of the Storm* [1991]). The soliloquy in Ferrara's *The Blackout* (1997) – where his performance as the director of an audio-visual "happening" is based on personal memories of Nicholas Ray making *We Can't Go Home Again* (1973) – is classic Hopper at his most freeform, mannered and exhibitionistic:

> Since film was too expensive for us, and we *video artists*, as we like to call ourselves, who're gonna regenerate the world, and pay for our own *film videos*, you know what I mean, *vidiots* that we are, *freaks* to the light, freaks to the light, freaks, freaks that record our own image, freaks that record our own image, man, whoa, alright, alright.

But does this all indicate that Hopper was undirectable, a personality just "let go" in front of a camera? Every individual acting style implies, allows or encourages a certain *mise en scène* that will best render it. Some filmmakers (Tony Scott in *True Romance* and Bigas Luna in *Reborn* [1984]) take a recognisably Godardian approach to capturing Hopper's physical mannerisms: they deliberately "deframe" bits of his body language just beyond the boundaries of the screen, as if his energy can scarcely be contained there; they shove him off-centre or into zones of blur, or film him from the back. Others (like Stephen Gyllenhaal in *Paris Trout*) carefully contain the familiar gestures and isolate them, using the pointing fingers and raised voice as "steps" or vectors within the dramaturgy of a scene.

The obvious fact that Hopper learned his lines and hit his marks in so many films (and that, as a director, he ably guided others to do so) testifies beyond doubt to his professionalism. *Carried Away* (1996), because of its vast difference from every other Hopper film, provides ample evidence of how actorly, in a conventional sense, he could be when someone took a chance on him. Bruno Barreto's film is a melancholic, reflective portrait of a precarious rural community. Hopper is cast against type as "a mediocre teacher and a worse farmer", visibly showing the strain of age. All of the actor's mannerisms have been pared back and his typical look (for the '60s or for the '90s) radically altered via old-fashioned glasses, a pipe and baggy, unglamorous costume. Instead, the role comes decked out with some classic signs of acting dexterity – such as the walking stick he uses to limp around on.

Hopper is a far more controlled and focused performer than he is sometimes taken to be. One endlessly enthralling sign of Hopper's skill is his ability to listen to other actors who share a scene with him; this is a significant test of any performer. The famous encounter between Hopper and Walken in *True Romance*, for instance, is a model demonstration of different ways of listening. Walken (like Meryl Streep) is a histrionic listener; in every shot where he does not speak, he rolls his shoulders, widens and narrows his eyes, and looks ostentatiously around the room for reactions from others. Hopper, by contrast, is a supportive, ensemble player, intensely fixed on the utterances, facial expressions and overall body language of his fellow players. He performs listening with a director's instinct: his gaze, his gestures of touch, his relay of other actors' energy, are all ways of aiding and guiding the essential dramaturgical lines of a scene.

Hopper 3: Male anti-hero

From out of the '60s, Hopper brought a brooding air of violence, often psychotically tinged, and also a difficult-to-manage kind of sexuality – latent qualities which Lynch cannily made manifest in *Blue Velvet*. Not for Hopper the middle-age career as "cheeky devil" or sly romantic that Jack Nicholson has so richly enjoyed and cannily guided from film to film. An uncomfortable oddness dogs Hopper's roles, fed by the typically inequitable paradoxes accompanying age and gender in actors' careers: in *Carried Away* a star of his own generation, Julie Harris, who began in Hollywood only a few years before Hopper, is now cast as his mother; and in *Space Truckers*, the futuristic plot contrives to pair him with a woman his own age but cryogenically suspended in her youthful beauty.

Hopper is often a solitary figure in his movies – no partner, no family, no tribe. Sex scenes are strikingly rare in his filmography and tend to be deliberately perverse or shocking when they do appear (as in *Blue Velvet*, *Backtrack*, *Carried Away* and *Lured Innocence* [1998]). In *The Piano Player* (aka *The Target*, 2002), the spectacle of Hopper's character gazing at his sexy, adult daughter asleep has nothing paternal about it. Kinky foreplay with Hopper completely clothed, directing the action like an elegant, elder libertine, displaces sex scenes in *The Blackout* and *MichaelAngel*. "Feel good" specials like *Hoosiers* (1986) and *Chattahoochee* (1990) – in which Hopper reforms his self-destructive ways, overcomes his demons, integrates himself into a community, and succeeds or enables others to succeed – are rarer still.

All this implies that Hopper, although he was some kind of star, and regardless at times of his top billing in the credits, was rarely a "leading man", and almost never a hero – certainly not a romantic hero. In *The Palermo Shooting* (2008), Wenders went so far as to cast him as "The Death"! By the same token, it began to seem impossible for movies to successfully slot Hopper into the standard roles available for older actors. Prime example: Hopper never cuts it as a conventional, reassuringly symbolic "father figure". Rather, he played a patriarchal emblem of a particularly dark, diseased sort – in the sense that "his" 1960s begat the world with which younger characters underneath him now struggle (this is especially strong in *River's Edge*). When cast as a real, biological father, Hopper is either entirely dysfunctional and troublesome (*Out of the Blue* [1980], *The Pick-Up Artist* [1987], *The Piano Player*), or he is more like a strange brother, friend or even double to his child (in *True Romance* he kisses his son's fiancée and then muses to himself as he drives off that she "tastes like a peach").

Either way, he is rather uncivilised and uncivilisable – and that sets him apart from male stars ranging from Cary Grant to Harrison Ford. Many of the fascinations, contradictions and complexities contained in Hopper's aggregate screen persona arise from the consequences of the fact that his specific maleness is hard to place or tame. It was logical, in this light, that Hopper would end up appearing in Isabel Coixet's 2008 adaptation of Philip Roth's novel *Elegy* as a Pulitzer-winning poet who, before dropping dead from a heart attack, counsels his best friend to enjoy some "sex on the side" of his respectable marriage, with younger women. Hopper's expert turn as the 1970s Sinatra in *The Night We Called It a Day* – a surprising but inspired piece of casting – highlights all at once the cool, sinister, charming, garrulous, perverse and difficult aspects of the Hopper persona.

Blue Velvet is unquestionably the central event of Hopper's later career. The film gave him, simultaneously, an association with a burgeoning genre – the neo *noir* erotic thriller – and an ambiguous, troubling, multiple role inside the genre's model scenario. On the one hand, *Blue Velvet* placed Hopper squarely into the symbolic father role of many a *noir* film: powerful, controlling, violent, the leader of a criminal mob or system, and – most importantly – intensely possessive of a younger woman. Invariably, his claim over that woman will be challenged by a younger man who enters this world and brings about its downfall – the classic, Oedipal triangle of father, mother and son. Such a Freudian "family romance" plays itself out, post-*Velvet*, in *Eye of the Storm, Midnight Heat* (1991), *Top of the World* (1997), *Paris Trout*, in the subtext of *MichaelAngel* (where Hopper's nemesis is a sexually repressed priest), and as sci-fi comedy in *Space Truckers*.

By the same token, Booth in *Blue Velvet* has a decidedly peculiar and unstable relation to his own sexual identity. In his famous, inaugural scene with Dorothy (Isabella Rossellini), he is both the "Daddy" who barks commands and brutally beats his female slave, and the "baby" who "wants to fuck". In other words, he is both father and child, and whenever he switches roles he re-casts Dorothy as either daughter or mother (Creed 1988: 108). However, Booth hardly seems to master (except through sudden violence) this circuit of identity-switching and sadistic-masochistic polarities. His apparent dominance in this perverse relationship is complicated by his massive insecurity (he cannot bear to be looked at), his dependence on external stimulants (the blackly comic "reveal" of his oxygen mask) and his suggested impotence – as well as, in a later scene, a strong dose of homoerotic or polysexual desire.

Homosexuality (repressed or otherwise) will rarely pop up again in Hopper's subsequent screen persona. But childishness of various sorts will be ever-present – capped by one of his final credits, a voice performance for the animated children's film *Alpha and Omega* (2010). In *Black Widow*, his cameo as a rich magnate has him hovering over a children's toy whose controls he cannot comprehend, yelling: "I'm five fucking years old!" In *Doublecrossed* he is so childlike that the film cannot see its way clear to show a scene of Seal as an apparently devoted father interacting with his kids. *Paris Trout* is structured around short, intense, mysterious scenes of Hopper standing over his senile, comatose mother, anxiously asking "Are you there?" – and finally deciding to kill her so as to "end all my connections with everything that came before": an epitaph that would fit many Hopper characters.

Is there pathos in Hopper's ageing screen persona? Many of his roles in the 1980s and 1990s hark back to the type of parts Robert Mitchum took in his later years on screen: the once-glorious guy on a last run, taking a last chance on a last job, as he reflects on passing time and the waning of his energies. The crime genre is a natural locus for such character types, and Hopper specialised in playing the small-time, low-life crook or operator – the little man, the loser – in such films as *Boiling Point* (1993), which gave him an immortal exit line, as he throws up his hands before a flank of cops and whines: "You never win!"

Male pathos slid easily into male comedy near the closing stages of Hopper's screen career. This gave him – especially for his age, and given his tortuous personal and professional history – a lightness that we do not associate with, for instance, the advanced age roles of Jason Robards or James Coburn. One striking index of the comic dimension of Hopper's roles in the '90s and beyond: it is hard to think of another actor of his vintage who was glimpsed so often, and with so little glamour, in his underwear (*Frankie the Fly, Carried Away, Eye of the Storm* – and in *Chasers*, a cameo as a "perverted underwear salesman" [Maltin 1999: 233]).

Hopper's size served the comic side of his acting well: the quick, agile movements he executes of walking, bending, nodding, ducking and weaving build a quietly humorous and utterly infectious aura around his tough, little body (see the set-piece in *Doublecrossed* where Hopper works a room of stiff, static government agents). It is through such lightness that Hopper connects, even in the midst of otherwise dramatic roles, with that hovering quality of childishness. A line from a brief, autobiographical memoir by Hopper is resonant: "I was Errol Flynn and Abbott and Costello" (Hopper 1980).

And perhaps some trace of that beguiling amalgam I have evoked here – charmer and clown, avant-garde hippie and consummate professional, rebel and reactionary, innocent child and crazed pervert – will be evident in the one, small Dennis Hopper role we finally now can see: as a garrulous representative of the "New Hollywood" circa 1972, in Orson Welles' *The Other Side of the Wind* (2018)… a film which stands as a posthumous triumph for many of its dear, departed participants.

References

Creed, Barbara. 1988. "A Journey Through *Blue Velvet*: Film, Fantasy and the Female Spectator", *New Formations*, 6 (Winter): 97–117.

Hopper, Dennis. 1980. "Personal Bio", quoted in Andrew Burden, "*The Texas Chainsaw Massacre 2*", http://www.rottentomatoes.com. Date accessed: 6 January 2018.

Hopper, Dennis & Quentin Tarantino. 1994. "Blood Lust Snicker Snicker in Wide Screen", *Grand Street*, 49 (Summer): 13–14.

Lalanne, Jean-Marc. 1997. "Léaud the First", *Cahiers du cinéma*, 509 (January): 14–15

Pym, John, ed. 2000. *Time Out Film Guide*, eighth edition. London: Penguin.

Maltin, Leonard. 1999. *Movie & Video Guide*. New York: Signet.

Orlean, Matthieu, Jean-Baptiste Thoret, Bernard Marcade & Pierre Evil. 2010. *Dennis Hopper and the New Hollywood*. Paris and Melbourne: Flammarion and Australian Centre for the Moving Image.

Routt, Bill & Diane Routt. 1987. "*Blue Velvet*", *Cinema Papers*, 62 (March): 51.

Sayres, Sohnya, Anders Stephanson, Stanley Aronowitz & Fredric Jameson. 1984. *The 60s Without Apology*. Minneapolis: University of Minnesota Press.

45

BARBARA STEELE

Nia Edwards-Behi

In this chapter I will offer an overview of Barbara Steele's career as an actress, with a focus on those films which confirm her position as a cult star. While best known for her essential presence in Italian Gothic cinema of the 1960s, Steele also boasts several films later in her career which confirm her cult stardom. In many ways, Steele's cult status seems inextricably linked to her roles in Italian Gothic films, including foremost her dual role as Asa and Katia in Mario Bava's *The Mask of Satan* ('La Maschera del Demonio', 1960). This star-making role set the precedent for the interpretation of the majority of Steele's subsequent (mostly Italian) horror film roles. Her roles in Italian Gothic films were often dual – at once playing a monstrous figure and an innocent victim. In some ways this duality is reflected in her cult status too – while initially known and loved for her Gothic films, the later part of her career is notable for a string of appearances in a variety of cult films. More recently, Steele has been featured in several films which have utilised her position as a cult star as representative and iconic of the films for which she is best known.

Steele and the Italian Gothic

The Italian Gothic film is itself a sub-genre that lends itself to cult appreciation. Seemingly appearing out of nowhere in 1957, Ricardo Freda's *I Vampiri* was arguably the first Italian horror film of the sound era (Di Chiara 2016: 35). Though often referred to as a subgenre of the horror film, the Italian Gothic horror films of the 1960s are, in the context of Italian film production, more accurately a *filoni* (a 'vein') than a cycle or subgenre, as outlined by Francesco di Chiara (2016: 33–35). *I Vampiri* was not an initial success, but following the popularity of Britain's Hammer Horror, and *The Mask of Satan*'s international success in 1960, in a new cut titled *Black Sunday*, the Gothic horror film flourished in Italy as a popular mode of filmmaking. The Italian Gothic would prove modestly successful in Italy but found greater success in foreign markets, particularly in the United States. The continued availability of these films after theatrical runs could be difficult, particularly due to the many different versions of films – different cuts and different soundtracks often existing for one film. This sort of multifarious releasing of the films, especially over time, implied and lent itself to cult fan behaviour such as collecting, cataloguing and comparing versions. In some modern releases of such films, different versions are included to present the films in as definitive a release as possible. For example, Arrow Video's 2013 Blu-ray release of *Black Sunday* includes two versions of the film as well as three different audio versions.

451

Italian Gothic cinema has also been used as a way of differentiating between casual fans of horror and more committed, 'authentic' fans of the genre. Knowledge of Italian Gothic cinema is generally revered above knowledge of, say, Italian gore cinema, and further above knowledge of, say, American slashers (Cherry 2012: 26). This is even though the Italian Gothic cycle is, arguably, rooted in the commercial aim of cashing in on the success of *Black Sunday* abroad and similarly the success of Hammer's gothic output. This commercial framework would define the production context of horror in Italy for decades to come, as summarised by director Luigi Cozzi, who has claimed that producers in Italy didn't "ask what your film is like, they ask what film your film is like" (in Baschiera & Hunter 2016: 6). However, there are stylistic and formal elements of the Italian Gothic that set it apart from the sorts of films it might first have been emulating; Tim Lucas goes so far as to claim that Bava's "unique sensibilities would evolve a new visual vocabulary of Gothic cinema" (Lucas 2013: 56). Certainly, its emergence in a nation which otherwise lacked a Gothic tradition made it even more notable.

Barbara Steele herself can be considered a defining feature of the Italian Gothic cinema and so by that very extension alone she might be considered a cult star. Her work with many of the most notable directors, and in some of the most notable films, renders her an iconic element of the *filoni*. This is particularly true when considering the way in which work on Italian Gothic, or Gothic cinema more broadly, is illustrated. Images of her punctured face feature heavily – be it through film stills or various poster artworks for *Black Sunday*. For example, the BFI companion *Gothic: The Dark Heart of Film* includes a short section on Italian Gothic, which is headed by a half-page illustration of the *Black Sunday* quad poster, which prominently features an artistic rendition of Asa's wide-eyed face (Lucas 2013: 55–56). The front cover of Troy Howarth's extensive monograph *The Haunted World of Mario Bava* is a large detail of the French poster artwork for *Black Sunday*, depicting Asa staring down the encroaching mask (and immediately inside is a full-page still image of Steele as Katia). Further demonstrating her position as a key figure of the Italian Gothic, Severin Films' Blu-ray release of *Nightmare Castle* not only declares Steele, on the front cover, to be 'Queen of Horror', but also includes two further Italian Gothic films featuring Steele – *Castle of Blood* and *Terror-Creatures From The Grave*. This denotes the *filoni* as an important part of horror, and Steele a further important star in relation to it. Danny Shipka goes so far as to suggest that since her pivotal appearance in *Black Sunday*, "Gothic heroines strived to imitate Steel's characteristics. [...] if Steele wasn't available, producers would choose from a variety of international actresses that fit the Steele mould" (2011: 37).

Following *The Mask of Satan*, Steele starred in *The Pit and the Pendulum*, another Gothic film but this time for Roger Corman in the United States. It's likely that Steele was cast in the film after American International Pictures' distribution of *Black Sunday* in the United States. Indeed, the trailer for *The Pit and the Pendulum* declares Steele to be "more blood-chilling than in *Black Sunday*." Di Chiara has noted that AIP was vital in "providing Italian producers with an important commercial outlet for their genre productions" (2016: 39). In 1962, Steele starred in Riccardo Freda's *The Horrible Dr. Hichcock*, playing the second wife to the titular scientist. Here, Steele plays a rare, straight-forward victim role, as the would-be blood-donor for the revival of Dr. Hichcock's dead first wife. A year later, Steele reprised her role as the second Mrs. Hichcock in *The Ghost*, part-sequel to *The Horrible Dr. Hichcock* and part-Gothic reimagining of *Les Diaboliques*. In 1964, Steele starred in two Gothic horror films for Antonio Margheriti: *Castle of Blood* and *The Long Hair of Death*. In *Castle of Blood* her role is that of a woman not quite dead and not quite living, while in *The Long Hair of Death* she plays a dual role of two avenging daughters of a wrongfully killed woman. In 1965 Steele appeared in *Terror-Creatures from the Grave*, as the wife of a recently deceased man, and *Nightmare Castle*, in another famous dual role as a murdered woman and her half-sister. In 1966 Steele made her final Italian film, *An Angel for*

Satan, playing a woman seemingly possessed by a malicious spirit. That same year she also starred in *The She-Beast*, as another woman possessed by the spirit of a witch, a film notable for being the debut of British director Michael Reeves. Steele rounded off her appearances in horror films during the decade in 1968, with the British production, *The Curse of the Crimson Altar*, alongside such venerable horror stars as Boris Karloff and Christopher Lee. The film indicates the move from Gothic 'terror' to the more titillating blend of horror and sex, as a man looks for his brother at a country mansion, where it emerges that a cult is still secretly operating. The film is garishly coloured and perhaps more indicative of its time, being set in the present and featuring an extensive party scene as well as rituals and witchcraft.

When beginning her career Steele was under contract to Rank in the UK, who eventually sold her contract because she was "too exotic looking to be believably cast as the girl next door" (Lucas 2007: 293). These same features are what made her such a distinctive star. When Steele is written about, either in a scholarly or a journalistic context, her physical features are often described, or otherwise an appraisal of her beauty is offered. For example, Kim Newman describes her face as "haunted" (2011: 254), Tim Lucas describes her as a "large-eyed sphinx of a brunette" (2013: 57), while Barry Forshaw describes her beauty as "fatal" (2013: 102) and Mathijs and Sexton describe it as "mysterious" (2011: 84). Those she worked with have also passed comment on the distinctiveness of her features, and implicitly their importance to her Gothic roles. Freda reportedly claimed that "there are times, in certain conditions of light … when her face assumes a cast that doesn't appear to be quite human" (in Wright 1995: 145), while Corman has said that "she has a great otherworldly quality – her bone-structure, her face. […] I was struck by it and used it as much as I possibly could" (in Barker & Jones 1997: 130). More recently, journalist Martyn Conterio keeps things succinct, simply exclaiming: "That face! Those eyes!" (Conterio 2015: 31)

Steele's eyes are arguably one of her most defining features, and the focus on them is clear in the Gothic films she starred in. As Upchurch has written, "her beauty suggests both the fragility of a defenceless animal and the fierceness of a beast of prey" (1993: 53), and her eyes are a major part of this "exotic duality" (Upchurch 1993: 53). Freda, director of *The Ghost*, has described Steele's eyes as "metaphysical, unreal, impossible" (in Barker & Jones 1997: 126), seemingly ideal attributes for her dual roles. While her eyes might at times signify her position as powerful, alluring and dangerous, they are also framed in such a way that they can denote vulnerability and victimhood. In *The Mask of Satan*, Steele's dual performances as the witch Asa and her innocent descendant Katia are marked by her use of her eyes as a key part of her performances. In the famous opening scene, we first see Asa only from behind, as she is branded on her back. When she turns her head to face her executioners, her wide eyes are framed centrally and emphasised by the close-up shot of her face. While initially the wideness of her eyes denotes a sense of vulnerability, Asa then becomes defiant, taunting and cursing the men as they approach her with the mask. Now, her eyes are no longer wide, but narrowed, and her face takes on a harder look to complement her words. Later, when we first meet Katia, her eyes are also emphasised. Again, she seems to express herself, in this scene, only with her eyes – the rest of her face and body is incredibly still. She is calmer than we have seen Asa, but the importance of her eyes as reflective of her disposition is clear. Examples occur throughout her Gothic films, where her eyes are framed centrally, or in close-up, and often emphasised through dramatic lighting. For example, in a key moment in *An Angel for Satan*, Roberto (Anthony Steffen) confronts Harriet (Steele), who is unaware that she has been behaving strangely under the influence of the ghostly Belinda (also Steele). They embrace, but as they do a nearby clock strikes midnight, and in a swift cut, we are shown Harriet's eyes peering over Roberto's shoulder, in extreme close-up, indicating a reaction to the time and that she is now possessed by the spirit of Belinda.

Later Italian horror filmmakers, such as Dario Argento or Lucio Fulci, would be noted for obsessively destroying or torturing eyes in their films, from *Terror at the Opera* to *Zombie Flesh Eaters*. However, while these films are known for being particularly graphic and gory, the Italian Gothic, while at times gruesome, certainly emphasised terror over horror. Indeed, the emphasis of the films' narratives tend to be on uncanniness and a sense of disquiet, rather than outright monstrosity or extreme violence. There was also an emphasis on sensual and erotic concerns, with the films often featuring narratives driven by dysfunctional or perverse sexuality. Steele and her characters have often been written about in relation to this aspect. Indeed, her attractiveness is often at the forefront of appraisals of her roles and appreciations of her cult status, as outlined above. Joe Dante describes her as a "sexy monster," her duality appealing to "kids who were beginning to get interested in sex but were still more interested in monsters" (in Barker & Jones 1997: 126). By contrast, former *Fangoria* editor Chris Alexander claims his attraction, as a youth, to Steele was "cereberal" rather than "sexual," as it was with other female horror stars, and he goes on to truly elevate Steele above others, describing her as "supernatural [...] unusual, unlike any other living thing on screen" (2015: 6). Elsewhere, Steele's characters and performances have been used as a sort of figurehead in the re-appraisal of the Italian Gothic cycle with a more feminist approach, by writers such as Carol Jenks and Patricia MacCormack. Jenks writes about Steele specifically in relation to her role in *The Mask of Satan*, using it as an example of her body of work in Italian horror, and the way she is fetishised both by filmmakers and critics (Jenks 1996). MacCormack has written of this fetishisation of Steele's image in relation and comparison to the figure of Giovanni Lombardo Radice, a similar cult figure who, as a man, is written about very differently (MacCormack 2002, 2004). Steele herself has expressed her understanding of her characters in terms verging on scholarly, sympathetically noting of her 'sexy monster' characters that "the dark goddess can't just go on wreaking hubris and havoc ad infinitum, she gets her comeuppance, too" (in Barker & Jones 1997: 126).

In this same period, Steele also starred in Federico Fellini's *8 ½*, a film she herself has written about as a 'cult' film, though of a very different sort to her Gothic work. When discussing her own career in interviews, *8 ½* is often the only non-genre film which is mentioned, presumably due to its prominent position as one of an Italian *auteur's* most well-known films. In an interview for Severin Films, Steele says "Of course, I made tons of films that weren't horror stories," but notes that they're never remembered or talked about (Gregory 2009). Steele's love for Italy – often expressed in interviews – and her romanticised view of the country during the 1960s, particularly in comparison to her unhappy experiences working in Britain and the USA, contribute to the high profile of the Gothic films she starred in. Steele describes Fellini as a "cult director" after pondering that "perhaps none of his films are cult films" (Steele 1994); presumably due to her recollection of his personality and her desire at that time to work with him, she valorises the director himself over his films. In much the same way, Steele recalls Margheriti, Freda and Bava in interviews, and describes working with them and their different personalities. Likewise, these directors' relationship to Steele is recounted – and so her personality during the period is shaped in turn by the recollections of others. Conterio has noted that Steele is an "unreliable narrator" (Conterio 2015: 32) when it comes to recounting her past career and collaborators, and Lucas has outlined at length some of Steele's apparent mis-remembering of certain details of working on *The Mask of Satan* (Lucas 2007). This tendency contributes to her status as a cult star, in that her stories and recollections become part of the myth-making around these films which she was a part of. Chris Alexander has celebrated Steele's knack for storytelling, writing that "*no one* on the glowing green Earth talks like Barbara Steele" (2015: 6).

The Italian Gothic Film seemed to fall out of fashion and stop production almost in-line with Steele's own roles in them. As with the decline of Hammer Horror's Gothic production, and indeed AIP's Poe adaptations, the Gothic horror cycle proper seemed to flourish and languish in the 1960s. With this decline in the genre, and changes in her personal life, Steele returned to America, but found the industry much less satisfying than it had been in Italy – calling her return there "a ghastly mistake" (Gregory 2009). Although she did not actively pursue an acting career in Hollywood, she continued to appear in some films, followed by a new-found career as a producer. Steele's cult reputation would continue thanks to her appearances in some high-profile cult films during this period. In addition to these films' own cult status – as the products of particular genres and directors – her own involvement with them not only contributes to their status as cult films, but the manner of her casting in these also reflects back upon her status as a cult star.

Continued cultification

In the 1970s, Steele worked with Jonathan Demme, David Cronenberg and Joe Dante. While Steele's cult films of the 1960s all broadly fall under the category of the Gothic, her films for these directors are varied, spanning the women in prison film (*Caged Heat*), the body horror film (*Shivers*) and the exploitation film (*Piranha*, essentially a pastiche or rip-off of *Jaws*). Even though the genres are varied, they might all be classified together as cult films. Their cult status primarily emerges from their genres, their directors, their stars, and the manner of their release, or a combination of these reasons. Contributing to Steele's own cult status in relation to these texts is her own recollection of them, particularly the details of her casting in these roles. Dante has explicitly outlined the importance of Steele's stardom in her continued presence in the genre, claiming that Cronenberg, Demme and himself wanted her for their films "based on the fact that we had all seen her when we were growing up and that she had made an indelible impression on us that a lot of people who were her contemporaries didn't" (in Barker & Jones 1997: 130).

In 1974, Steele starred in Jonathan Demme's directorial debut, the women-in-prison film *Caged Heat*, made for Roger Corman's AIP. In the film she plays the role of the wheelchair-bound and tyrannical warden of the prison, McQueen. Although since becoming a more main-stream director with Oscar-winning films such as *The Silence of the Lambs* and *Philadelphia*, Demme began his career working for Roger Corman as a writer and moved to directing with *Caged Heat*. As with many who began careers with Corman, Demme maintained an affection for those films and the period in his career (for example, see Demme 2014). Steele recalls that she was offered the part of McQueen in the film by Demme as she walked along Sunset Boulevard, and the director jumped out of his sports car, begging her to accept the role (Steele 1994).

In 1975, Steele played a minor, though iconic, role in David Cronenberg's breakthrough film, *Shivers*, in which parasites cause the residents of a tower block to experience lethal levels of sexual desire. Steele plays Betts, friend and would-be lover of Janine (Susan Petrie), and gets to feature in one of the film's most memorable scenes, in which she is attacked by parasite while taking a bath. Cronenberg would continue to make films which emphasised bodily breakdown, the mistrust of authority, and scientific experimentation. His reputation as a cult auteur is closely tied to the generic obsessions of his early work, as later films such as *Videodrome* and *Scanners* cemented this reputation, while his more recent films have shifted to emphasise more real-world horrors. Again, Steele has recounted the story of her casting in *Shivers*, whereby Cronenberg visited her personally, delivering a bunch of marigolds and spending hours convincing her to take the part (Steele 1994). Cronenberg has also recalled meeting Steele, referring to her as a "horror queen" (Grunberg 2005: 31), though he recalled their meeting a little differently, "sitting on the beach and we're eating some salad or something, and Barbara is drinking a glass of wine" (Grunberg

2005: 31). In both cases, these recollections of their meeting bring together two cult personas, he as a then-young director meeting an icon of the genre, and she as someone able to draw the attention of young and exciting filmmakers. Steele's position as notable amongst the rest of the cast is evidenced in the opening credits of *Shivers*. Even though the film features other genre regulars, such as Lynn Lowry as Nurse Forsythe, it is Steele who is awarded the final position in the credits, singling her out amongst the secondary characters: "Barbara Steele as Betts".

A few years later in 1978, Steele would play a small but important role in Joe Dante's *Piranha*, another Roger Corman production. The film is a parody of the hugely successful *Jaws*, only this time killer piranhas terrorise the local population. Steele plays the role of a shady government operative and is even afforded the final line of the film. Dante not only has a reputation as a cult director, but he also actively promotes the appreciation of films which might be considered cult, particularly through his *Trailers From Hell* website and in his journalistic career writing for publications such as *Famous Monsters of Filmland*. Steele recounts a less flamboyant story of her casting in this case – she says that Dante simply had to ask, and that he "bought me three martinis and I said yes!" (Garris 1979).

Steele's roles in these films also place her alongside other actors who might be considered as cult icons, due to their frequent appearances in films that are considered cult. For example, many of the other women who star in *Caged Heat* have cult reputations of their own, from Erica Gavin, known for her brief acting career primarily due to her key roles in Russ Meyer films, and Roberta Collins, who starred in horror films such as *Eaten Alive* and *The Witch Who Came From the Sea*. From *Shivers*, Lynn Lowry is arguably a more recently created cult star. Her roles in films in the 1970s, including *Shivers* and the horror films *I Drink Your Blood* and *The Crazies*, are now remembered as cult titles, and she has now made many appearances in contemporary independent horror films, often made by self-proclaimed fans of 1970s horror, such as James Balsamo, a self-proclaimed "gorehound and all around [sic] movie geek" (Hallam 2014). However, none of these actors might be considered a cult icon in quite the same way as a figure like Steele. Her position as a cult star is not only due to her appearances in cult films, but also due to her own construction of her stardom. Her stories about her casting in these three films particularly relate to this, but so does her rejection of the Hollywood system. Her relatively infrequent appearances since her Italian career attests to this: she has chosen sparse roles, and doesn't shy away from expressing her dissatisfaction with the Hollywood industry. She has characterised this as temperamental – claiming in one interview that she couldn't take the rejection and auditioning process of Hollywood (Gregory 2009). If the notion of cult is traditionally related to opposing mainstream systems of production and mainstream product, then Steele's career very much conforms to this opposition.

In 1979, Steele starred in what would be her 'final' role for some time, in the semi-slasher *Silent Scream*. With *Silent Scream*, Steele all but retired from acting. During the 1980s and early 1990s, Steele's career moved primarily to television. Steele worked as a producer on the mini-series *The Winds of War* (1983) and *War and Remembrance* (1988), the latter of which won her a Primetime Emmy award. Following many years working behind the scenes on television productions, her most notable television work would come for one of her most frequent collaborators at the time, Dan Curtis – her starring role in the revived *Dark Shadows*. A remake of the popular gothic-soap which originally aired in the late 60s to the early 70s, the series was short-lived. While the original soap dealt in all manner of gothic and supernatural tropes, the revival series focused on what was arguably its most popular and memorable plot-line, that of the vampire Barnabas Collins and his arrival at the modern-day Collins household. The series continued to emphasise a gothic sensibility within its soap-opera format, from its mansion setting to the inclusion of vampires and witches. Steele's involvement with the series not only ties her to a cult franchise (following on from the original series), but also contributes her own presence and reputation to the production. Perhaps underlining Steele's aversion to Hollywood is her refusal of a cameo in Tim Burton's 2012 feature film version of the series (Conterio 2015: 86), and her claim that the film was "overdone and overwrought" (Salmon 2016: 16).

Contemporary era

In recent years Steele's status as an iconic cult star has been central to her casting in films, namely 2008's *The Boneyard Collection*, 2011's *The Butterfly Room* and 2014's *Lost River*. In low-budget anthology film *The Boneyard Collection* she appears in a cast featuring many other cult horror icons, including Tippi Hedren, Kevin McCarthy and Forrest J. Ackerman. Steele's brief cameo role involves several references to her past work, including her writer character suggesting that she might set her next work in a 'haunted Italian castle' with what might as well be a wink to camera. Ryan Gosling's critically-mauled directorial debut *Lost River* concerns a family in a desolate town in the United States, who struggle to make ends meet, with mother Billy (Christina Hendricks) taking on dangerous work to support her children, while her teen son, Bones (Iain de Caestecker) and his friend Rat (Saoirse Ronan) find themselves attempting to unravel the town's hidden mythology. Steele plays the minor role of Grandma, a Miss Havisham-esque relation of Rat, who is mute and immobile. *Lost River* is aesthetically inspired by European genre filmmaking, and David DelValle goes so far as to claim that Steele's character "represents Gosling's homage to the Italian Gothic Cinema of the 1960s" (DelValle 2015: 48) in a film that was frequently criticised by reviewers for presenting a mash-up of influences rather than a coherent film of its own (see, for example, McCarthy 2014; Collin 2015; Barber 2014; Romney 2015).

Of her most recent films, *The Butterfly Room* most prominently showcases Steele as both an actress and as an icon. *The Butterfly Room* is a thriller about a lone, older woman, Ann (Steele), and the mysterious motherly relationship she strikes up with two girls, and her estrangement from her own daughter (Heather Langenkamp). As well as frequently paying homage to Steele's iconic status, the cast of *The Butterfly Room* highlights Steele's position as a cult star. The many other women in the film are also played by actresses known for their work in horror films, from Langenkamp and Erica Leerhsen in the main cast, to cameos from PJ Soles, Camille Keaton and Adrienne King. While these actresses might be considered 'scream queens' and associated with slasher films, and although Steele has certainly also been referred to as a scream queen herself, her cult stardom pre-dates the popularity of the term, which was cemented by the success and density of the slasher cycle of films. Indeed, a recent profile of the actress in *Fangoria* poses the question: "Why do we saddle her with diminishing monikers like 'scream queen'?" (Riccuito et al. 2015: 42), suggesting that Steele's stardom is more authentic compared to that of a 'scream queen'.

One of the central concerns of both the study of stardom and the study of cult texts is that of authenticity. While earlier studies of more traditional conceptions of stardom figure authenticity as, generally, a sense of the 'ordinary' (eg. Dyer 1986), in relation to cult stardom the sense of authenticity varies a great deal, and can refer to irony, over-acting, and even the *extra*-ordinary can be valued as authentic attributes (Egan & Thomas 2013, 8). Steele has been instrumental in maintaining her own sense of authenticity, in relation both to the roles she chose and directors she's worked with, and those she has rejected. Barbara Steele's cult stardom is similar in some ways to the stardom of Ingrid Pitt, as established by Egan in her study of the actress, in so far that her "status as a cult icon [...] can be attributed to a number of factors external to her roles" (2013, 212). While the way in which Pitt and Steele are figured as cult stars is slightly different, the notion of authenticity in their off-screen personas is vital to the solidification and continued status of their stardom. That is not to say that the films Steele has starred in play no role in this. In some ways, Barbara Steele's status as a cult star is reflective of the formative films which thrust her to that position: a status filled with dualities. The gothic horror of the 1960s can boast Steele as a defining icon. Her magnetism in these films ensured a generation of young filmmakers in the 1970s sought her out for their own tentative steps into making what would become cult bodies of work. Through these films, Steele's own cult stardom has been sustained in the years following the body of work she is, arguably, most famous for, and particularly Steele's own discerning selection of such roles, and her recollections of those choices, further contributes to her cult status.

Steele's continued cultivation of her own cult persona – as one who rejected Hollywood from the beginning of her career, quite literally – means her more recent career is defined by films which either implement her as an icon, or are an homage to her work. Although it is her association with horror and other genre films which have resulted in her cult stardom, it is Steele herself who has arguably ensured that stardom has endured, even while seeming to, at times, disparage it.

References

Alexander, Chris. 2015. "First Rites," *Fangoria* 342: 6.

Barber, Nicholas. 2014. "Cannes Review: Ryan Gosling's Lost River", *BBC.com*, http://www.bbc.com/culture/story/20140520-if-ryan-gosling-made-blue-velvet [accessed 25/08/2016].

Barker, Clive, & Jones, Stephen. 1997. *Clive Barker's A-Z of Horror*, London: BBC Books.

Baschiera, Stefano, & Hunter, Russ. 2016. "Introduction" in Stefano Baschiera and Russ Hunter, eds, *Italian Horror Cinema*, Edinburgh: Edinburgh University Press: 1–14.

Cherry, Brigid. 2012. "Beyond *Suspiria*: The Place of European Horror Cinema in the Fan Canon" in Patricia Allmer, Emily Brick and David Huxley, eds, *European Nightmares: Horror Cinema in Europe Since 1945*, Chichester: Wallflower: 25–34.

Collin, Robbie. 2015. "Lost River: Review," *The Daily Telegraph*, http://www.telegraph.co.uk/film/lost-river/review/ [accessed 25/08/2016].

Conterio, Martyn. 2015. *Black Sunday*, Leighton Buzzard: Auteur.

Del Valle, David. 2015. "Down the Lost River," *Fangoria* 342: 48–49.

Demme, Jonathan. 2014. "Roger Corman," *Interview Magazine*, http://www.interviewmagazine.com/film/roger-corman/ [accessed 25/08/2016].

Di Chiara, Francesco. 2016. "Domestic Films Made for Export: Modes of Production of the 1960s Italian Horror Film" in Stefano Baschiera and Russ Hunter, eds, *Italian Horror Cinema*, Edinburgh: Edinburgh University Press: 30–44.

Dyer, Richard. 1986. *Heavenly Bodies: Film Stars and Society*, Basingstoke: Macmillan.

Egan, Kate & Thomas, Sarah, eds. 2013. *Cult Film Stardom: Offbeat Attractions and Processes of Cultification*, Basingstoke: Macmillan.

Forshaw, Barry. 2013. *British Gothic Cinema*, Basingstoke: Palgrave Macmillan.

Garris, Mick. 1979. Fantasy Film Festival: Joe Dante, Barbara Steele & Paul Bartel, https://www.youtube.com/watch?v=pukpsGMIvdM [accessed 25/08/2016].

Gregory, David. 2009. "Barbara Steele in Conversation" on *Nightmare Castle Bluray*, Severin Films, 2015.

Grunberg, Serge. 2006. *David Cronenberg: Interviews with Serge Grünberg*, London: Plexus.

Hallam, Scott. 2014. "Indie Filmmaker James Balsamo Talks Mutants, B-Movies and More" in *Dread Central*, www.dreadcentral.com/news/53788/indie-filmmaker-james-balsamo-talks-mutants-b-movies-and-more-for-catch-of-the-day/ [accessed 25/08/2016].

Howarth, Troy. 2002. *The Haunted World of Mario Bava*, Godalming: FAB Press.

Jenks, Carol. 1996. "The Other Face of Death: Barbara Steele and La Maschera Del Demonio," in Andy Black, ed., *Necronomicon Book One*, London: Creation Books: 88–101.

Lucas, Tim. 2007. *Mario Bava: All the Colours of the Dark*, Cincinnati: Video Watchdog.

Lucas, Tim. 2013. "Bava and the Italian Gothic" in James Bell, ed., *Gothic – The Dark Heart of Film*, London: BFI: 56–57.

MacCormack, Patricia. 2002. "Barbara Steele's Ephemeral Skin: Feminism, Fetishism and Film," *Senses of Cinema*, 22, http://sensesofcinema.com/2002/feature-articles/steele/ [accessed 25/08/2016]

MacCormack, Patricia. 2004. "Masochistic Cinesexuality: The Many Deaths of Giovanni Lombardo Radices" in Ernest Mathijs & Xavier Mendik, eds, *Alternative Europe: Eurotrash and Exploitation Cinema Since 1945,* London: Wallflower: 106–116.

Mathijs, Ernest, & Sexton, Jamie. 2011. *Cult Cinema: An Introduction*, Chichester: Wiley-Blackwell.

McCarthy, Todd. 2014. "Lost River: Cannes Review," *Hollywood Reporter*, www.hollywoodreporter.com/review/lost-river-cannes-review-705908 [accessed 25/08/2016].

Newman, Kim. 2011. *Nightmare Movies: Horror on Screen since the 1960s*, London: Bloomsbury.

Riccuito, Daniel, Cairns, David, & Matsui, Jennifer. 2015. "Barbara Steele: The Beauty of Terror," *Fangoria* 342: 42–46.

Romney, Jonathan. 2015. "Lost River Review," *The Guardian*, www.theguardian.com/film/2015/apr/12/lost-river-review-ryan-gosling-christina-hendricks-matt-smith [accessed 25/08/2016].

Shipka, Danny. 2011. *Perverse Titillation: The Exploitation Cinema of Italy, Spain and France, 1960–1980*, London: McFarland.

Steele, Barbara. 1994. "Cult Memories." *The Perfect Vision* 6.23. http://www.anangelforsatan.com/articles/cult-memories/ [accessed 25/08/2016].

Salmon, Will. 2016. "Afterlife: Barbara Steele," *SFX*, Issue 273: 16.

Tweedle, Sam. 2009. "Reluctant Scream Queen: A Conversation with Barbara Steele", *Confessions of a Pop Culture Addict*, http://popcultureaddict.com/interviews/barbarasteele/ [accessed 25/08/2016].

Upchurch, Alan. 1993. "The Dark Queen," *Film Comment* 29.1: 53.

Wright, Bruce Lanier. 1995. *Nightwalkers: Gothic Horror: Movies The Modern Era*, Dallas: Taylor.

46

BRUCE LEE
Cult (film) icon

Paul Bowman

I write these words on the 44th anniversary of the death of Bruce Lee (July 20, 1973). When he died I was two years old. Lee was at the height of his fame. At the time of his death, his fourth martial arts film, *Enter the Dragon*, was being released internationally. He was already well known around the world: in Asia he was stellar; in the West his films had a growing cult status (Hunt 2003; Lo 2005; Teo 2009). For all audiences, he was becoming the exemplar of a new type of masculine cool invincibility – a simultaneously impossible yet (*possibly – almost*) achievable ideal (Chan 2000; Nitta 2010). It was impossible because Lee was invincible, but it seemed (quasi) achievable because Lee's invincibility was always shown to be the product of dedicated training in kung fu. So, his image wasn't *simply* fictional. His image wasn't *merely* fake. He wasn't *magic*. He was simply *a kung fu expert*. This meant that all you had to do to be like him was *train*. Anyone could train. Everyone could train. So, very many people did. And this became known as the 'kung fu craze' of the 1970s (Brown 1997).

At the time of his death, *Enter the Dragon* was about to push Lee into the mainstream of global popular consciousness. If up until this point he had achieved 'cult' status in the West, he was about to attain the status he had already attained across Asia: superstardom. But this would not involve selling out or dampening down any of the 'cult' features that characterised his kung fu films. Rather, Lee's success would amount to the international explosion of martial arts film and martial arts practice: its leaping out from the shadowy margins and into the bright lights of the mainstream.

This explosion is still referred to as the kung fu craze of the 1970s. Bruce Lee was the image and the name that exemplified this 'craze'. There were other martial arts stars, of course, both before and after Bruce Lee; but he was and remains the quintessential figure. His name still sells books. Documentaries are still being made about him (Webb 2009; McCormack 2012). Martial arts magazine issues that have his image on the cover still sell more copies than those which don't. Blog entries about him still generate spikes.[1] He is still credited as an inspiration by athletes, boxers, UFC and MMA fighters, and martial artists of all stripes (Miller 2000; Preston 2007). YouTube continues to throw up new Bruce Lee homages and montages. Computer games still have Bruce Lee characters. He is still used in adverts. He is universally regarded as having been a key figure for non-white film and TV viewers of the 1960s and early 1970s – a kind of oasis in a desert of white heroes and (at best) blaxploitation (Prashad 2003, 2002; Kato 2007; Bowman 2010; Chong 2012). He was immediately (and remains) a complex and important figure for diasporic ethnic Chinese the world over (Marchetti 2001, 1994, 2012, 2006; Hiramoto 2012; Teo 2013). And he forged the first bridge between Hong Kong and Hollywood film industries.

There is so much more to say about all of this. I could go on with this list. But I have said much of this before (Bowman 2010, 2013). So instead, having set the scene, however fleetingly, let's pause to reflect on whether this makes Bruce Lee a 'cult' figure.

In order to focus principally on Bruce Lee as a cult icon, we cannot undertake too much of a digression into a fully elaborated discussion of the controversial and problematic term 'cult' in film and cinema studies (Mathijs 2005; Mathijs and Mendik 2008; Shepard 2014). Suffice it to say that in and around film studies the ongoing academic disputes about the notion of 'cult' centre on the question of what makes something a cult object. Is the thing that makes an object (normally a film but sometimes an actor, director or even genre) into a 'cult' object to be found in the properties of the object itself, or in the status of that object in relation to other objects, or in an audience's response to it?

There is a lot of disagreement about this. My own sense is that cult is principally a useful descriptive term, but that it is less useful analytically. Nonetheless, in attempting to think about Bruce Lee through this lens, some hugely stimulating insights can emerge. In what follows, I will principally concern myself with responses and relations to the cinematically constructed image of Bruce Lee, rather than with attempting to adjudicate on the matter of whether this or that feature of his films (Barrowman 2016) or his cinematic, media or spectacular image fit into this or that categorisation or definition of 'cult' or 'not-cult'. So rather than worrying about taxonomies, I will translate the ideas and associations of the word 'cult' into the sense of a variably manifested passionate relation to or with something – in this case, the textual field of objects known as 'Bruce Lee'.[2]

I do this because there is not now and there never has been a single or singular cult of Bruce Lee. It has always been cults, plural. The ideas, ideals, injunctions and aspirations associated with Bruce Lee were always multiple. In effect, there have always been several Bruce Lees – different Bruce Lees for different people. Lined up side by side and viewed together, the 'Bruce Lee' constructed by each group, audience or constituency often appears, on the one hand, partial and incomplete, yet on the other hand, larger than life and impossibly perfect. There are biographical, technological and textual reasons for this.

Firstly, Lee died unexpectedly, very young, in obscure circumstances, and for a long time afterwards much of his life remained shrouded in mystery – a mystery that largely arose because of a lack of reliable, verifiable information about him, his life, and the circumstances of his death. It is arguably the case that his family, their advisors, and his estate made a series of less than ideal decisions around the dissemination of information about Bruce Lee both in the immediate aftermath of his death and in the subsequent years and even decades (Bleecker 1999). These decisions all seem to have arisen from a desire to paint Bruce Lee hagiographically, as a perfect figure, a kind of saintly genius. Somewhat predictably, then, other voices have more than once come out of the woodwork to make somewhat contrary claims and to paint Bruce Lee in rather different lights. Through all of the mist and murk, one of Lee's many (unauthorised) biographers, Davis Miller, makes an important point when he observes in his 2000 publication, *The Tao of Bruce Lee*, that surely there has been no other twentieth-century figure, so globally famous, about whom so little was actually known for so long (Miller 2000; Bowman 2010).

The film theorist André Bazin might have disputed such a claim, however. For, as he argued when discussing the cinematic images of Joseph Stalin, the cinematically constituted, disseminated and experienced image does much to create a kind of double or doubling effect (Bazin 1967: 1–14). Of course, there may be a world of difference between Bruce Lee and Joseph Stalin, but Bazin's observations can be applied to the figure that viewers felt they experienced when they experienced Bruce Lee. Indeed, it can be extended to apply to many other cinematic or media experiences of many other kinds of celebrity image too. The logic is this. Firstly, the cinematic image can make the figure seem larger than life. Baudrillard would call this 'hyperreal': more real than real (Baudrillard 1994). But Bazin also notes that the image on the cinema screen is, in a way, already dead, absent, out of reach, 'mummified'. Yet, at the same time, and paradoxically by the same token, the nature of the cinematic image can make us feel we personally have intimate, personal, access to the person we are watching (Bazin 1967: 1–14; Chow 2007: 4–7).

These kind of observations about the cinematic image can serve as an entry point into thinking about the 'technological' reasons why there has never simply been *one* cult of Bruce Lee, but always more than one. We each see a very distant, larger than life figure, and yet we can also come to feel that we have an intimate insight into him – whatever that may be. He is there, and we can see what he is saying and doing; but he is gone, and we have to construct an interpretation.

This is where the textual or semiotic dimension becomes fully active. For, like any other media image, 'Bruce Lee' is essentially and irreducibly *textual*. When we think of or speak about Bruce Lee we are dealing not with one single or simple thing, but with complex pieces of textual material, woven into different textual constructs (films, documentaries, books, magazines, posters, anecdotes, memories). In fact, taken to its most 'radical' extreme, the theory of textuality essentially dispenses with the need for there to be an actual 'text' (such as a film, a book or a magazine article) in front of us at all. For, as elaborated by Jacques Derrida, the theory of text-uality (aka deconstruction), holds that for each and every one of us the entire world is a text. We relate to *everything* the same way we relate to texts: we look, we listen, we think, we try to interpret, to make sense, to extract or establish meaning, and so on. According to the infamous phrase of Derrida (who was the most famous proponent of textuality as an approach to more or less everything), 'there is nothing outside the text' (Derrida 1976: 158–159).

Whether we go this far or not, according to most theories of text and textuality, the meaning of any given text is produced in the encounter with the reader. So, although the creators of any given text (literary, cinematic, TV, radio, etc.) will have had intentions, and will have wanted to create certain effects and induce certain responses, the buck stops with the reader, or the person who experiences these devices and combinations of elements. Accordingly, whilst some viewers may watch Bruce Lee's filmic fights with his opponents and find them thrilling, tense, exciting, brilliant, even tragic, other viewers may find them boring, turgid, unintelligible, or even comical, and so on. Elsewhere in his acting, where some may perceive 'cool' others may see 'wooden'; where some may perceive genius others may see idiocy.

Nonetheless, despite the range of meanings that could be attached to any aspect of Bruce Lee, it is certain that he had a massive impact. Although many in the Western world had seen 'Asian martial arts' on TV and cinema screens more and more since the 1950s (most famously perhaps in the TV series *The Avengers* and the James Bond film, *Dr No*), the effect of Bruce Lee on many viewers was instant and transformative. More than one documentary about the impact of Bruce Lee contains newsreel footage showing children and young teenagers leaving cinemas and movie theatres in the United Kingdom and United States and performing the cat-calls, poses and attempting to do the flashy moves and kicks of Bruce Lee (BBC4 2013). In fact this scenario has come to constitute something of a 'creation scenario' in stories about the birth of what has long since been referred to as the 'kung fu craze' that swept through the United States, Europe and much of the rest of the world, starting in 1973 (Brown 1997).

This was the year of the box office release of *Enter the Dragon* – a film that is notable because it was the first Hollywood and Hong Kong co-production, the first Hollywood film explicitly framed as a 'martial arts' film, and perhaps the first 'formal' introduction of many Westerners to the imagined world of Asian martial arts (Bowman 2010). It is also the year that Bruce Lee died in obscure circumstances. In many countries news of Bruce Lee's death came out shortly before the film was actually released (Hunt 2003). All of which immediately made both the film and the man extremely intriguing. It is true that this was not the first martial arts film that had been available to audiences in the West. Several Hong Kong martial arts films had been successful in the United States before. Indeed, it was their increasing success that had given Hollywood producers the confidence that this venture could be successful in the first place. But *Enter the Dragon* is without a doubt the most important martial arts film of the period, precisely because of its *mainstreaming* of Asian martial arts.

There are perhaps no rigorously scientific ways of establishing 'importance', 'effect' or 'influence' in the realms of media and culture (Hall 1992), but it can be said (with the benefit of hindsight) that from the moment of the release of *Enter the Dragon* it was absolutely clear that Bruce Lee was not merely *influential* but actually *epochal*. The historian, philosopher and cultural critic Michel Foucault came up with the notion of a 'founder of discursivity' (Foucault 1991). For Foucault, a founder of discursivity is something or someone that generates a whole new discourse, or that radically transforms an ongoing discourse. Although not discussed by Michel Foucault, my contention is that Bruce Lee should definitely be accorded the status of founder of discursivity.

The meaning of the term 'discourse' in this sense is quite precise. In the tradition of Foucault, a discourse is also but not only a conversation. Discourses in this sense also involve actions. For example, the discourse of architecture is not only the conversations and arguments of architects, town planners, residents' associations, lawyers, and so on. The discourse of architecture also refers to the processes, practices and results of these conversations and arguments: what buildings look like, how they are made, the changes in their styles and configurations, and so on. In Foucault's sense, there are discourses in and of all things: law, religion, science, fashion, music, taste, you name it. So, a founder of discursivity may be identified in a person (for example, Elvis or Jimi Hendrix), or in a technological change (the electrification of music). The point is, we are dealing with an intervention that disrupts and transforms states of affairs. Bruce Lee was precisely such a disruption and transformation.

Let us return to the mythic scene of our origin story: the excited or excitable young viewers of a new Bruce Lee film, who have just left the cinema. They are not merely *discussing* the films. They *make* cat-calls. They try to throw kicks and punches in ways that two hours previously were completely unknown to them but to which they have just very recently been introduced and instantly become accustomed. What is there to say about this scene or situation?

Bruce Lee made only four and a half martial arts films before he died. He only used his signature screams and cat-calls for dramatic cinematic effect within those films. There is no evidence that he made his signature noises off-screen. Moreover, few cinematic or actual martial artists ever really followed Bruce Lee in using these kinds of noises in fight scenes, never mind in sparring or in competition. If and when such mimicry occurs, it is always in some sense what Judith Butler would call a 'parodic performance'. And yet, to this day, when children in the playground strike improvised/invented 'kung fu' poses and throw what they think might be cool kung fu shapes, they still very often make the Bruce Lee cat-calls, screams and kiais – in performances that are in one sense parodic but in another sense completely sincere.

Evidence for this claim is anecdotal, of course. But I often observed it personally at my own children's primary school, four decades after Bruce Lee's death. At the same time, people from both my own and other countries have recounted the same observation to me. Of course, there may be various kinds of confirmation bias at play here. I may actually only be remembering a highly select few instances, and blowing them up, out of all proportion, while forgetting or ignoring cases where children's martial arts play is not accompanied by Bruce Lee sounds. Similarly, my interlocutors may be telling me what they think I want to hear. But, unlike trying to establish 'influence' and 'effect' directly, perhaps a research project could be constructed that could explore what children 'do' when they strike 'martial artsy' poses. And my hypothesis would remain that they very often make noises that can directly and unequivocally be traced back to no one other than Bruce Lee. The fact that few such children are likely to have any conscious knowledge or awareness of Bruce Lee makes this even more interesting. But, in such a situation, are we still dealing with a *cult*? And what is the relation of any such conscious or unconscious cult with 'cult film'?

Bruce Lee's films constituted an intervention, definitely. A transformation, certainly. In the realms of film, Bruce Lee's fight choreography changed things, raised the bar, set new ideals in film fight staging. But this remains in the realm of what we might call 'film discourse' or 'film intertextuality', relating as it does to the 'internal conversations' and changing practices and conventions within, across and among films. But we are not yet really dealing with the effects of these films on actual people – or at least actual people other than film fight choreographers.

To turn our attention to 'real people', we might refer back to our creation scenario one more time, and ask what happened to all of those impressionable and impressed boys and girls who left the cinema with a newly inculcated desire for this new 'ancient' thing called kung fu. As a range of commentators and historians have remarked, the scarcity and rarity of Chinese martial arts schools in Europe and the United States forced people who desired to learn kung fu 'like Bruce Lee' to take up the much more readily available arts of judo and karate. There were comparatively more judo and karate clubs in Europe and the United States than kung fu clubs. This disparity has geopolitical and historical causes that are too complex to cover adequately here. Suffice it to say that kung fu clubs gradually emerged in response to the demand. But the first big explosion in participation in Asian martial arts in the wake of the 'kung fu craze' was an uptake of judo, karate, and taekwondo, not kung fu. The films that inspired the interest came from Hong Kong, but the Asian martial arts on offer in the West came from Korea and Japan, generally via some connection to the military.

Over time, more was learned about Bruce Lee's art. He had trained in *wing chun* kung fu as a teenager in Hong Kong. Wing chun is a close range fighting art with short punches, locks, grapples, and a preference for low kicks. When he moved to the United States at the age of 18, he was definitely a competent martial artist, and apparently blessed with incredible speed and grace of movement. His speed reputedly impressed even very senior and well established Chinese martial artists. Famously, however, his iconoclasm didn't (Russo 2016).

Stories about and studies of Bruce Lee's iconoclasm, irreverence and various fights and tussles abound. Rather than recounting them here, the point to be emphasised in this context is that when Bruce Lee gradually began to enter into the TV and movie business, first as a trainer, then choreographer, and supporting actor, he clearly knew that what mattered most on screen was drama. Hence, his screen fights always involved high kicks, jumps, and big movements. Everything was exaggerated and amplified (although those closest to him have claimed that he really struggled to move slow enough to enable the camera to capture his techniques).

Because of the complexity of this chiasmus, Bruce Lee can be said to have always sent his 'followers' moving in one of two or more directions. First, his *Chinese* kung fu sent people flocking into *Japanese* and *Korean* style dojos and dojangs. Second, Bruce Lee publicly disavowed formal stylistic training – first claiming to have abandoned *wing chun*, then naming his approach 'jeet kune do', then coming to regret giving it a name at all (Inosanto 1994; Tom 2005). Nonetheless, fans flocked to find wing chun classes. Others sought jeet kune do classes. Others took his message of 'liberate yourself from styles' or 'escape from the classical mess' to mean that one should reject any and all formal or systematic teaching and work out how to 'honestly express yourself', as Lee was fond of saying (Lee 1971).

Furthermore, within the jeet kune do community itself, a sharp divide appeared immediately after Lee's death. Some of his students felt that they should continue to practice and teach exactly what Bruce Lee had practiced and taught with them. Others felt that the spirit of his jeet kune do was one of innovation, experimentation and constant transformation, and that what needed to be done, therefore, was to continue to innovate and experiment in line with certain principles or concepts. Hence a rift emerged among Lee's closest friends and longest students. It continues to this day.

As such, all different kinds of people with all different kinds of orientation believed and continue to believe that they are 'following' Bruce Lee, that they love him and honour him and respect him. Yet they are all doing very different things and adhering to very different images and ideas. For all of them, Bruce Lee was 'The Man'. I use this term because I have heard these words – and words like them – in many countries and contexts, from many different kinds of people, the world over.

The most memorable occasion was in Hong Kong, after a kung fu class. The style we were practicing was *choy lee fut* kung fu. This is very different to the wing chun kung fu that Bruce Lee studied as a teenager in Hong Kong, and a world away from the jeet kune do style that he devised as an adult in the United States. In fact, choy lee fut is often positioned as wing chun's nemesis. It is certainly the style that is mentioned most frequently in the various versions of mythical stories of the young Bruce Lee in Hong Kong. In these stories we are told that wing chun students and choy lee fut students would often have formal style-versus-style duels on the city's rooftops. Sometimes in these stories Bruce Lee is depicted as the scourge of all rivals. In other versions, an innocent young Bruce Lee is depicted as starting his first rooftop fight and immediately recoiling in pain and shock, before being told to get back into the fray, doing so, and emerging victorious.

In all of the Hong Kong–based wing chun kung fu stories about Bruce Lee, choy lee fut kung fu comes off badly. Perhaps this is the reason for the frequent animosity that exists between wing chun and other styles of kung fu in Hong Kong. I certainly witnessed some of this during a visit there in 2010. The sense among practitioners of other styles of kung fu seemed to be that wing chun kung fu *only* became famous *because* of Bruce Lee's fame. In this sense, the global success of wing chun itself could be regarded as a kind of cult formation that is indebted to Bruce Lee (Bowman 2010; Judkins and Nielson 2015). Certainly, I was also told in Hong Kong that among the 'traditional' Chinese martial arts community of Hong Kong, wing chun was regarded as simply *too new* and *too local* to deserve the global fame it had achieved in the wake of Bruce Lee.

Knowing this is doubtless what made my choy lee fut colleague's declaration that 'Bruce Lee was *the man*' so significant for me. On the one hand, Bruce Lee popularised a *rival* style of kung fu, and stories about his martial arts encounters often involved the disparagement of other styles (specifically choy lee fut). But on the other hand, for all who had eyes to see, Bruce Lee was unequivocally brilliant – amazing to watch, astonishing, inspiring, graceful, powerful, elegant. So, even practitioners of 'rival' styles, even traditionalists who may disparage either or both wing chun and jeet kune do, could easily concede Bruce Lee's brilliance and their admiration for him.

Of course, some may say that none of the examples of influence and importance that I have so far given really fall into the category of 'cult' as it is normally used, either conversationally, colloquially or as technically conceived within film studies. Neither children parroting and copying moves after a cinema visit, nor an expansion of martial arts classes as part of an international boom, nor the elevation of a once obscure southern style martial art constitute evidence of a 'cult' – certainly not one organised by devotion to a personality or a celebrity. Nonetheless, my claim is that all such examples are *ripples* that attest to a significant and generative intervention.

For, in the end, Bruce Lee most often functions as a kind of muse (Morris 2001). People have been inspired by Bruce Lee in myriad ways: musicians, athletes, artists, thinkers, performers, dancers, and others, have all referenced Bruce Lee as an inspiration. In the realms of martial arts practice and film fight choreography, Bruce Lee arguably dropped a bomb, the effects of which are still being felt. But, being forever absent, forever image, forever a few frozen quotations, what we see are a diverse plurality of *practices of citation*.

The different ways in which bits and pieces of 'Bruce Lee' are picked up and used (and abused) attest to the nature of his intervention. Before Bruce Lee, one could dream of being any number of things – footballer, athlete, rock star, and so on. After Bruce Lee, one more gleaming new option was definitively out of the box, on the table, in the air, everywhere: *martial artist*. This is why the impact and importance of Bruce Lee has always exceeded the world of film and seeped into so many aspects of so many lives. This is another way in which Bruce Lee can be said to be like water.

Notes

1 I have been told this numerous times by editors of martial arts magazines and bloggers, both UK, US, and transnational/online.
2 I discuss the ways in which the term 'Bruce Lee' organises a complex field of images, ideas, citations and allusions in *Beyond Bruce Lee* (Bowman 2013).

References

Barrowman, Kyle. 2016. 'No Way as Way: Towards a Poetics of Martial Arts Cinema,' *JOMEC Journal*, 0.5. https://jomec.cardiffuniversitypress.org/articles/abstract/10.18573/j.2014.10263/
Baudrillard, Jean. 1994. *Simulacra and Simulation*. Ann Arbor: University of Michigan Press.
Bazin, André. 1967. *What Is Cinema? Vol. 1*. Berkeley: University of California Press.
BBC4. 2013. 'Everybody Was Kung Fu Fighting: The Rise of Martial Arts in Britain, Series 12, Timeshift – BBC Four'. *BBC4*. February 24. https://www.bbc.co.uk/programmes/b01p2pm6 [Date accessed, 31 July 2019.
Bleecker, Tom. 1999. *Unsettled Matters: The Life and Death of Bruce Lee*. Lompoc, CA: Paul H. Crompton Ltd.
Bowman, Paul. 2010. *Theorizing Bruce Lee: Film-Fantasy-Fighting-Philosophy*. Amsterdam: Rodopi.
———. 2013. *Beyond Bruce Lee: Chasing the Dragon through Film, Philosophy, and Popular Culture*. New York: Columbia University Press.
Brown, Bill. 1997. 'Global Bodies/Postnationalities: Charles Johnson's Consumer Culture'. *Representations*, 58 (Spring): 24–48.
Chan, Jachinson W. 2000. 'Bruce Lee's Fictional Models of Masculinity'. *Men and Masculinities*, 2.4: 371–87.
Chong, Sylvia Shin Huey. 2012. *The Oriental Obscene: Violence and Racial Fantasies in the Vietnam Era*. Durham, NC: Duke University Press.
Chow, Rey. 2007. *Sentimental Fabulations, Contemporary Chinese Films: Attachment in the Age of Global Visibility*. New York: Columbia University Press.
Derrida, Jacques. 1976. *Of Grammatology*. Translated by Gayatri Chakravorty Spivak. Baltimore: Johns Hopkins University Press.
Foucault, Michel. 1991. *The Foucault Reader*. London: Penguin Books.
Hall, Stuart. 1992. 'Cultural Studies and Its Theoretical Legacies'. In Cary Nelson and Paula Treichler Lawrence Grossberg, eds, *Cultural Studies*, New York: Routledge: 277–94.
Hiramoto, Mie. 2012. 'Don't Think, Feel: Mediatization of Chinese Masculinities through Martial Arts Films'. *Language & Communication*, 32.4: 386–99.
Hunt, Leon. 2003. *Kung Fu Cult Masters: From Bruce Lee to Crouching Tiger*. London: Wallflower.
Inosanto, Dan. 1994. *Jeet Kune Do: The Art and Philosophy of Bruce Lee*. London: Atlantic Books.

Judkins, Benjamin N., and Jon Nielson. 2015. *The Creation of Wing Chun: A Social History of the Southern Chinese Martial Arts*. New York: SUNY Press.

Kato, T.M. 2007. *From Kung Fu to Hip Hop: Revolution, Globalization and Popular Culture*. New York: SUNY Press.

Lee, Bruce. 1971. 'Liberate Yourself from Classical Karate'. *Black Belt Magazine*.

Lo, Kwai-Cheung. 2005. *Chinese Face/Off: The Transnational Popular Culture of Hong Kong*. Chicago: University of Illinois Press.

Marchetti, Gina. 1994. *Romance and the 'Yellow Peril': Race, Sex, and Discursive Strategies in Hollywood Fiction*. Oakland: University of California Press.

———. 2001. 'Jackie Chan and the Black Connection'. In Matthew Tinkcom and Amy Villarejo, eds, *Keyframes: Popular Cinema and Cultural Studies*. London: Routledge.

———. 2006. *From Tian'anmen to Times Square: Transnational China and the Chinese Diaspora on Global Screens, 1989–1997*. Philadelphia: Temple University Press.

———. 2012. *The Chinese Diaspora on American Screens: Race, Sex, and Cinema*. Philadelphia: Temple University Press.

Mathijs, Ernest. 2005. 'Bad Reputations: The Reception of "Trash" Cinema,' *Screen*, 46.4: 451–72.

Mathijs, Ernest, and Xavier Mendik, eds. 2008. *The Cult Film Reader*. Maidenhead: Open University Press.

McCormack, Pete. 2012. *I Am Bruce Lee*. Documentary.

Miller, Davis. 2000. *The Tao of Bruce Lee*. London: Vintage.

Morris, Meaghan. 2001. 'Learning from Bruce Lee'. In Matthew Tinkcom and Amy Villarejo, eds, *Keyframes: Popular Cinema and Cultural Studies*. London: Routledge: 171–184.

Nitta, Keiko. 2010. 'An Equivocal Space for the Protestant Ethnic: US Popular Culture and Martial Arts Fantasia,' *Social Semiotics*, 20.4: 377–392.

Prashad, Vijay. 2002. *Everybody Was Kung Fu Fighting: Afro-Asian Connections and the Myth of Cultural Purity*. Boston: Beacon Press.

———. 2003. 'Bruce Lee and the Anti-Imperialism of Kung Fu: A Polycultural Adventure,' *Positions*, 11.1: 51–90.

Preston, Brian. 2007. *Bruce Lee and Me: Adventures in Martial Arts*. London: Atlantic.

Russo, Charles. 2016. *Striking Distance: Bruce Lee and the Dawn of Martial Arts in America*. Lincoln: University of Nebraska Press.

Shepard, Bret. 2014. 'Cult Cinema by Ernest Mathijs and Jamie Sexton. Walden, MA and Oxford: Wiley-Blackwell, 2011,' *Quarterly Review of Film and Video*, 31.1: 93–97.

Teo, Stephen. 2009. *Chinese Martial Arts Cinema: The Wuxia Tradition*. Edinburgh: Edinburgh University Press.

———. 2013. *The Asian Cinema Experience: Styles, Spaces, Theory*. London: Routledge.

Tom, Teri. 2005. *The Straight Lead: The Core of Bruce Lee's Jun Fan Jeet Kune Do*. North Clarendon, VT: Tuttle Publishing.

Webb, Steve. 2009. *How Bruce Lee Changed the World*. Documentary.

47

ALL HE NEEDS IS LOVE

The cult of Klaus Kinski

Ian Cooper

Looking at his lengthy filmography, it is not hard to see the cult appeal of Klaus Kinski. Indeed, he specialized in genres that traditionally draw devoted, even obsessive, followings: *Krimis*, Spaghetti Westerns, *gialli* and horror films. But like a number of other stars with consider-able cult followings – Frances Farmer, Timothy Carey, Oliver Reed – the films are only part of the story. There were the angry appearances on TV chat-shows, the tabloid gossip, the live performances, notably the short-lived *Jesus Christ Erloser* (*Jesus Christ Saviour*) tour as well as his well-documented rages on set and in press conferences. Then there was the scandalous auto-biography – well, autobiographies, given that there were three versions; the hard-to-find *Ich bin so wild nach deinem Erdbeermund* from 1975, *All I Need Is Love* (1988) which was withdrawn after copyright disputes and threatened libel actions and the (comparatively) toned-down re-release called – without any apparent irony – *Kinski Uncut* (1996). And perhaps most important of all, there's that face, described breathlessly – but not inaccurately – by David Thomson:

> Its intensity speaks of desperation and the ordeal of survival; its fierceness comes from
> a life so threatened that ego, need and will have carried it close to madness. But it is
> a beautiful face too, especially intriguing because of the way it slips from cruelty to
> gentleness, from conquistador to visionary.
>
> (Thomson 1984: 71)

Elsewhere, Thomson called it 'one of life's more amazing faces' (2002: 470), one 'that had seen hell' (2002: 471). The praise Kinski earned throughout his career was overshadowed by his oft-expressed dismissal of most, if not all, of the films he made. This dismissive attitude and his fre-quently caricatured rages and tantrums have led many to regard him as a bit of a ham, although Kinski was far more over-the-top on talk shows and in press conferences than he ever was on screen. Peter Bradshaw alluded to this reputation for excess in his review of the re-released *Aguirre der Zorn Gottes/Aquirre Wrath of God* (1972), calling the actor's performance 'remarkable' before adding he's 'not nearly as hammy as you might expect' (2001). Kinski's performances of deranged, obsessive men are mirrored by his off-screen antics and vice versa and it becomes increasingly hard to separate the man from the roles. He frequently claimed to work solely for mercenary reasons, openly admitting in his autobiography, 'I do flicks only to make money' (Kinski 1996: 244) but the director Peter Geyer has noted how:

Whatever he did, he was always totally passionate and fanatical about it. For example, if you watch *Aguirre* you get the feeling that he was exceptionally obsessed with that role, but the truth is that he actually didn't want to shoot *Aguirre* in the first place.

(in Jahn 2008)

A large part of the Kinski myth is this apparent contradiction, an actor who seems completely committed to his roles while at the same time loudly and frequently proclaiming that he couldn't give a shit. This mixture of dedication and disdain is reminiscent of Brando, another iconic performer. Indeed, Werner Herzog has compared the two, writing that 'working with Marlon Brando must have been like kindergarten compared to Kinski' (in Cronin 2002: 88).

Arthur Penn wants me for a film. I turn him down. I've turned down Fellini and Visconti and Pasolini as well as Ken Russell and Liliana Cavani – usually because of the money. And I'd have turned down Eisenstein and Kurosawa for the same reason. By now I've made over 250 movies and turned down over a thousand.

(Kinski 1996: 307)

There's a tendency to divide Kinski's work into two groups – roles in prestige fare by name directors and low-rent genre films. The first group includes not only his frequent collaborator Herzog but also David Lean (*Doctor Zhivago* [1965]), Billy Wilder (*Buddy, Buddy* [1981], a film dismissed by the actor – not unfairly – as 'that piece of Hollywood shit' [Kinski 1996: 266]) and Sergio Leone (*For a Few Dollars More* [1965]). But there are a number of problems with this approach. Firstly, a number of these supposed hacks including Jess Franco and Joe D'Amato have acquired considerable critical followings over the years so it's become much harder to dismiss their strange, oddly personal genre films out of hand. Secondly, while Herzog can certainly claim to have gotten the most out of the actor, it's hard to argue convincingly that Kinski's performances in his more acclaimed films are better than his inspired turns in the Euro genre netherworld. Yes, he is electrifying as the gulag-bound anarchist in *Doctor Zhivago* but it's virtually a cameo and his performance in the lacklustre late Wilder pales next to his eponymous turn in the determinedly down-market *Jack the Ripper* (1976). Kinski also worked with a number of wayward talents who fall somewhere between the two categories; James Toback (*Love and Money* [1982]), Sergio Corbucci [*Il Grande Silenzio/ The Great Silence* [1968]) and Andre Zulawski [*L'important c'est d'aimer/ That Most Important Thing:Love* [1975]), the visionary Polish director whose *Possession* (1981) managed to win an award at Cannes while also being banned as a Video Nasty in the United Kingdom.

Kinski was born Klaus Günter Karl Nakszynski in 1926 in Zoppot, then part of the semi-autonomous Free City of Danzig, now in Poland. His father was an opera singer-turned-pharmacist, his mother a nurse and the family moved to Berlin in 1931. One of the challenges in writing about Kinski is the difficulty in separating the man from the myth. Certainly, many commentators – notably 'best enemy' Herzog – have suggested Kinski was prone to exaggeration and fabrication. In his autobiography, for example the actor goes into harrowing detail about his impoverished background – fighting rats for the last piece of bread, sleeping on subway grates to keep warm – but as Herzog puts it, 'he grew up in a relatively well-to-do middle-class pharmacist's household' (Cronin 2002: 289). He was drafted into the *Wehrmacht* in 1943 and wounded before being captured by the Allies, although according to Kinski, he had always planned to desert. He ended up in a British POW camp in Colchester where he claims to have drank urine, eaten cigarettes and stood naked in the rain in an attempt to get sick so he would be sent back to Germany.

Kinski was entirely self-taught as an actor and worked hard, particularly on his voice, although he was fond of claiming his talent was innate. As Herzog claims in his documentary *Mein Liebster Fiend/My Best Enemy* (1999) the actor saw himself as 'a genius who had fallen straight from heaven and who had obtained his gift by the grace of god'. He performed on stage in Berlin and Vienna, although his unpredictable nature meant he spent long periods out of work. In 1950 he was hospitalized in a psychiatric clinic after a couple of suicide attempts and an attack on a former lover. Records released in 2008 reveal after a preliminary diagnosis of schizophrenia, his doctors decided he suffered from psychopathy, noting:

> His speech is violent. In this, his self-centred and incorrigible personality is evident as one that can't blend in civil circumstances. He remains consistent to his egocentric world view and declares all others prejudiced [...] The patient hasn't had a job in one year, but still speaks confidently of the new film in which he will star.
>
> (Anon. 2008)

He was released after three days. In Vienna he reinvented himself as a monologist, performing works by Villon, Shakespeare and Rimbaud. He seems to have adopted elements of the latter's vagabond poet persona, combining it with the myth of the misunderstood genius: at one point in his autobiography, for example, he has what sounds very like a panic attack which climaxes in his having to 'dash out of Amsterdam's Van Gogh Museum. I have to puke in the street. I mustn't end up like that!' (Kinski 1996: 227). He would also at various times compare himself to Hitler ('I would have been better than Adolf Hitler. I could have delivered his speeches a lot better... that's for certain' [Naha 1983: 41]) and Christ (with the aforementioned Jesus Tour).

Although there were a couple of notable film roles early in his career including the Douglas Sirk war story *A Time to Love and a Time to Die* (1958), Kinski became known for his frequent appearances in German *krimis*. These horror-tinged crime and mystery thrillers were inspired by the prolific English writer Edgar Wallace and proved enormously popular in West Germany from the late 1950s to the early 1970s. Stories of masked killers and sinister red herrings in various atmospheric settings – country houses, seedy night clubs and girl's schools – they antici-pate the more acclaimed Italian *gialli* and Kinski appeared in many of them, unsurprisingly cast as shady characters, creepy butlers or small-time crooks.

> The street kid in me says, "Grab the money and run - who cares who it's from! Don't think about whatever you have to do for it or when you have to do it!"
>
> (Kinski 1996: 289)

Herzog may have cast doubt on Kinski's impoverished childhood but as he became better-known, the actor's attitude to money certainly suggests a morbid fear of destitution. He was not only interested in large paychecks (memorably turning down *Raiders of the Lost Ark* [1981] in favor of the vaguely silly mamba-on-the-loose drama *Venom* [1981]) but was also fond of exploitation films, what with their short shooting schedules and up-front payments. This was surely a factor in his move to Rome in the late 1960s where he appeared in an impressive amount of Euro horrors, cop thrillers and Spaghetti Westerns:

> Westerns. One after another. They get shittier and shittier, and the so-called directors get lousier and lousier.
>
> (Kinski 1996: 210)

While many of these films were poor and Kinski's appearances could amount to little more [CE:Add the word 'than' here] glorified cameos, they did little to dilute the actor's cult status. On the contrary, they seemed to exemplify his contempt for film-making while also contributing to his reputation as an artistic outsider – for every *Doctor Zhivago* there were a handful of exploitation pictures with such memorable titles such *Slaughter Hotel* aka *Asylum Erotica* (1970), *The Hand That Feeds the Dead* aka *Evil Face* (1974) and *Death Smiles at a Murderer* (1973). The latter film, the directorial debut of Joe D'Amato is surely notable for the fact that Kinski is one of the most restrained things about it, in the small role of a doctor in a demented tale of sexual obsession and necrophilia which borrows heavily from Poe. Similarly, the actor's presence in the chilly and enigmatic *Footprints on the Moon* (1975) is almost distracting, a small (if ultimately typically sinister) role which could have been played by any half-way decent actor. Among the many Westerns, there are some jewels among the formulaic dross and Kinski is at his best as the twitchy hunchback taunted by Lee Van Cleef in *For a Few Dollars More* and the terrifying Loco in Sergio Corbucci's remarkable *The Great Silence*. One unintended consequence of his churning out European genre fare was the loss of his distinctive and expressive voice through dubbing. There is some irony in the way that an actor who became famous for his readings and recordings spent a considerable part of his career dubbed with a series of characteristically bland mid-Atlantic voices.

Kinski's dedication to European exploitation films seems almost heroic, churning out a bewildering number of cheap genre movies which veer from the remarkable to the slapdash. Although the actor is best-known for his work with Herzog, he may ultimately have more in common with Jess Franco, who he worked with often. Franco's filmography is even more impressive – at least 160 films – and they often demonstrate a kind of weird demented poetry, a frenzied creativity which must have appealed to Kinski.

In the early 1970s, Kinski consolidated his growing cult status, with the aforementioned *Jesus Christ Saviour* tour (filmed by Peter Geyer and released in 2008) and his first collaboration with Herzog. Kinski had wanted to perform the New Testament on stage since 1961, although it would be ten years before he appeared live on stage at the Deutschlandhalle in Berlin. The show was intended as the start of a world tour taking in more than a hundred venues but this didn't happen and Geyer's film makes it clear why. Kinski, alone on a bare stage in the vast theatre, casts Christ very much in his own image, describing him as 'the freest and most modern of all men', an angry visionary with 'anarchistic tendencies'.

The idea of Christ as a radical political figure may have been a very timely one (as evidenced by the many references to Vietnam) and Kinski's seemingly sincere performance is often spellbinding. But a significant proportion of the youthful audience seems to have come along solely for the purpose of heckling him and it isn't hard to see why, this wealthy film star preaching against greed and materialism and espousing non-violence while shoving and screaming at anyone who walks onto the stage. As Nick Schager puts it:

> Kinski becomes a bipolar figure, at once justified in his rage and clear-sighted in his condemnations and yet the anti-thesis of the very virtues he extols.
>
> (2011)

The fact that the actor had served in the *Wehrmacht* in World War II doesn't help matters and the crowd respond to his having a stage invader removed by chanting 'Kinski is a fascist'. His career in popular genres also works against him – when a heckler shouts 'it's just like an Edgar Wallace movie', another responds with 'or a Spaghetti Western'.

Figure 47.1   Klaus Kinski as the title character in *Aguirre, the Wrath of God* (Herzog, W. Germany/Peru/Mexico, 1972). Werner Herzog Filmproduktion/Hessischer Rundfunk

Herzog is a miserable, hateful, malevolent, avaricious, money-hungry, nasty, sadistic, treacherous, cowardly creep...He doesn't care about anyone or anything except his wretched career as a so-called filmmaker.

(Kinski 1996: 222)

Sure, the man was a complete pestilence and a nightmare to work with but who cares? What is important are the films we made together (Herzog in Cronin 2002: 91)

Unquestionably, the most acclaimed Kinski performances are his collaborations with Werner Herzog – *Aquirre, Wrath of God, Nosferatu: Phantom der Nacht/Nosferatu the Vampyre* (1979), *Woyzeck* (1979), *Fitzcarraldo* (1982) and *Cobra Verde* (1987). It can be hard work trying to cut through the layers of myth and hyperbole surrounding the Herzog/Kinski relationship. As noted above, Kinski was not averse to exaggeration and outright fabrication but Herzog too has been a keen self-mythologizer, the risk-taking Teutonic autocrat who once ate his own shoe on stage transformed with age into a playfully gloomy, soft-spoken eccentric.(Indeed, it's hard to imagine any other European arthouse director appearing as the villain in a Tom Cruise action thriller, voicing a character on *The Simpsons*, inspiring an internet meme offering spoof motivational quotes ['I believe the common denominator of the universe is not harmony but chaos, hostility and murder'] and playing a thinly-disguised self-portrait in the sit-com *Parks and Recreation*.)

It's often been noted that the Herzog/Kinski films with their focus on madness and obsession can be regarded as a kind of dual autobiography, although obsession takes many forms and Kinski's befuddled, muted title role in *Woyzeck* or his lonely vampire in *Nosferatu* are very different to the megalomaniac visionaries of *Aquirre* and *Fitzcarraldo*. But while these driven dreamers and doomed romantics could easily have led Kinski to indulge in the kind of scenery-chewing he is sometimes accused of, his performances are nuanced, even subtle. This may be down to Herzog's patience or it might be the case that despite his frequent bitching, Kinski saw a kindred spirit in the director.

Aguirre Wrath of God is a remarkable film, a surreal, often blackly funny trip down river into a heart of darkness which uncannily prefigures *Apocalypse Now* (1980). The moments which are most familiar – and featured prominently in *Mein Liebster Fiend* – are from the end of the film, as Kinski's Aguirre goes insane and proclaims his omnipotence to an audience of corpses and chattering monkeys (and it is hard to avoid Hitler comparisons, the pathetic end of a ranting dictator deluded to the last).

But for most of the film, Kinski is unusually contained, watching, listening and scheming, a weird mix of Macbeth and Richard III (the latter an obvious comparison given the character's twisted body and limp, although the real Aquirre did actually have an injured leg). Even when he has attained power, he condemns a man to death without raising his voice ('That man is a head taller than me. That may change').

Nosferatu the Vampyre is Herzog's reworking of Murnau's landmark 1922 horror film with Kinski as the eponymous vampire. It's a beautiful, extremely atmospheric take on the Dracula story, full of haunting images such as the mummified corpses at the opening, the unmanned boat sailing up a canal, the dinner party in the streets held by plague sufferers. Kinski's Count is more sympathetic than Max Schreck's vampire yet also more repulsive. He not only looks grotesque but also sounds it – his obscenely heavy breathing and his noisy feeding when he finally gets to bite Lucy (Isabelle Adjani, looking like she's just stepped out of a silent movie). Kinski's performance is typically physical, as in the moment he suddenly lurches forward, his body contorted to suck the blood from Harker's thumb. These odd jerky movements are combined with great gentleness, his soft voice and the moment when he appears in Lucy's bedroom with a seemingly sincere 'Excuse me for not knocking'. The one weak spot in Herzog's film is Renfield, played like a bad parody of Dwight Frye by the novelist Roland Torpor, whose performance is even more lamentable when set alongside Kinski's Renfield in Franco's *Count Dracula* (1970).

Woyzeck is the elliptical, grueling adaptation of Georg Buchner's unfinished drama about a lowly soldier driven crazy by the infidelity of his partner, Marie (Eva Mattes). Herzog originally wanted to cast Bruno S, the troubled self-taught musician turned actor who played the leads in *Jeder fur sich und Gott gegen alle/ The Enigma of Kaspar Hauser* (1974) and *Stroszek* (1977) before turning to Kinski. As in *Aguirre*, the actor conspicuously plays down the character's growing mental instability and there is a very oppressive quality to the story as life piles agonies onto the protagonist – his mistreatment by his superiors, the bizarre experiments he subjects himself to for extra money (including a diet consisting solely of peas) and the aforementioned cuckolding. The climactic murder of Marie comes over as inevitable and Herzog depicts it as operatic spectacle, the repeated plunging of the knife, Woyzeck's contorted face, Marie's terror and the splashing of blood (the fact that a – presumably unplanned – fly appears during the scene is oddly fitting, given the director's use of animals throughout his filmography). In marked contrast – and befitting his status as underdog – Woyzeck's death isn't shown with him wandering off even more dazed than usual away from the camera and into the water.

Fitzcarraldo may be the most celebrated of the Herzog/Kinski films, although again the director considered a number of other actors for the titular role. The film began with Jason Robards in the role and after he became ill, Herzog thought of Jack Nicholson and even at one point considered playing the role himself. Kinski isn't an obvious choice to play the Irish opera obsessive-turned-rubber baron who carries a boat over a mountain in Peru, but his performance is not only impressive but also oddly sweet. The scenes of Fitzcarraldo with his brothel owner lover (Claudia Cardinale) are extremely affecting and although there is great danger in the mission, the character's dream of an opera house in the jungle is far from the murderous lunacy of Aquirre. *Fitzcarraldo* is clearly a film about film-making and the ending is a triumphant one, as Fitzcarraldo, 'the Conquistador of the Useless' sails past an adoring public surrounded by opera singers, smoking a cigar and beaming with joy.

Cobra Verde is the least of the Herzog/Kinski films and the one time the director lets the actor rely on his trademark snarling and ranting. Based on a novel by Bruce Chatwin, it's the story of a bandit who is sent on what is supposed to be a suicide mission into West Africa but ends up as a Kurtz-ish slave trader living in splendid isolation. Kinski's character resembles the kind of morally dubious anti-heroes he played in Italian Westerns and Verde is sexually promiscuous, mercurial and frequently admirably unsympathetic, traits he shares with the actor playing him. The ending of this last collaboration between director and star is appropriately final, as Verde tries to pull a boat into the sea before collapsing and dying as the tide comes in. While Fitzcarraldo could move a boat over a mountain, Verde can't even get a lifeboat down the beach into the sea.

Herzog has worked with a number of oddball cult actors including Bruno S., Brad Dourif and Michael Shannon, indicating a clear identification between the director and his lead actors. In contrast, his female leads – including Mattes, Cardinale, Adjani and Nicole Kidman tend to be much less idiosyncratic – if no less accomplished. The bug-eyed David Lynch regular Grace Zabriskie who appears in *My Son, My Son, What Have Ye Done?* (2009) may be the only female performer in his films who comes close to possessing the weird intensity of his male leads.

The Herzog films also serve as a corrective to Kinski's oft-cited claims to be motivated solely by money. It isn't just the demanding, often dangerous and lengthy shoots in Peru, Brazil, Columbia and Ghana (just how many cheap European horrors could Kinski have made if he hadn't followed the director to such far-flung climes?) There are also the four-hour make-up sessions for *Nosferatu* and the long takes and some unsimulated brutality in the emotionally

Figure 47.2 Klaus Kinski as the crazed landlord in *Crawlspace* (Schmoeller, USA/Italy, 1986). Empire Pictures

exhausting *Woyzeck* (which started shooting a mere five days after *Nosferatu* wrapped). Indeed, contrary to the vitriol he heaps on the director in his autobiography, *My Best Enemy* contains footage of an unusually relaxed Kinski telling an interviewer with something like pride how he and Herzog go 'as far as possible'. (Kinski's claims in his autobiography to have directed some of these films don't hold water, especially in the light of the one film he is credited with directing, *Paganini*, a fascinating muddle which nevertheless pales next to even Herzog's minor work.)

In the 1980s, and despite the acclaim which came from the Herzog films, Kinski refused to become respectable, appearing in the disparate likes of *Fruits of Passion* (1981), a French-Japanese adaptation of the *Story of O, Code Name Wild Geese* (1984), an Italian war drama with no connection to the 1978 Andrew V. McLaglen film and *The Little Drummer Girl* (1984), a Le Carré adaptation starring Diane Keaton.

As he got older and more grizzled, there were a handful of low-budget horror and sci-fi films where he played mad scientists, creeps and killers. *Crawlspace* (1986) shows just how much Kinski could elevate a routine horror flick into something much weirder. He plays Karl Guenter, son of a Nazi war criminal and insane landlord who has kitted out his apartment building as a voyeur's paradise with an array of peepholes, secret passages and death-dealing devices. In many ways it is a generic early 80s horror film, with a series of vaguely anonymous female characters stalked and skewered, although it's often unusually tasteless.

Guenter keeps a female prisoner in a cage in his room and not only has he removed her tongue but her shaved head and uniform are clearly intended to invoke the Holocaust. Kinski's performance is remarkable, from his array of hideous jumpers – usually worn with a tie – to his louche manner. He barely raises his voice, instead employing a lazy, lounge-lizardy whisper and indulges in some very dry humor – at one point his cat is killed after wandering into one of his death machines and he picks up the severed tail and tosses it aside with a deadpan, 'Sorry kitty'. He treats his slave to lengthy autobiographical anecdotes, applies a face-full of smeared make-up, dresses up in a SS uniform and plays Russian roulette using a bullet streaked with his own blood which literally has his name on.

His descent into a very gothic madness serves if nothing else to remind us of just how controlled his excesses were in the Herzog films. The moment he gives a Nazi salute and cries out 'Heil Guenter' has a particular frisson, not only given the actor's comment that he would have been a better Fuhrer but also because Günter was his middle name. Director Schmoeller went on to make the short film, *Please Kill Mr. Kinski* (1999). As well as the familiar rages and confrontations (six fist fights by the third day of shooting, demands that the director refrain from saying cut or action), Schmoeller relates how the film's producers suggested killing their star for the insurance money.

As noted earlier, Kinski's scandalous autobiography is a vital part of his appeal. After lawsuits and some re editing, *Kinski Uncut* was finally published in 1996, five years after the actor's death. The book isn't really concerned with his acting, what with most of his films – and especially their directors – dismissed out of hand. Rather there's a focus on his formative years and his experiences in World War II, his obsessive love for his son Nanhoi (born in 1976 and now an actor using the name Nikolai) and an awful lot of very graphic sex. Indeed, the majority of the text is taken up by semi-pornographic Henry Miller-esque romps with literally dozens of women which all start to blur into one well before the book is over. Kinski also writes about his aforementioned committal to a psychiatric hospital and if the diagnosis of psychopathy was indeed correct, this surely complicates his status as a ranting prima donna, instead casting him as mentally ill and therefore meaning the excessive behavior as chronicled by Herzog, Schmoeller and others should be regarded as a kind of Bedlam performance.

Given the view he had of himself as a kind of tortured genius, it's little wonder that Kinski was attracted to playing the Italian violinist Niccoló Paganini, who is as well-known today for his gambling and womanizing as he is for his music. *Paganini* (1988) aka *Kinski Paganini* was clearly a labor of love for the actor, who as well as starring, wrote, directed and edited it while the cast includes his then-girlfriend Debora Caprioglio - billed as Debora Kinski – and young son Nikolai.

As a film, it isn't very good, even in the longer 'Director's Cut' (which is 13 minutes longer than the version originally released), fragmented, rambling and repetitive. But it's invaluable as a companion piece to Kinski's autobiography, an overheated, almost incoherent blend of art and sex. Indeed, the violinist and the actor become almost inseparable – an opening voiceover from a breathless woman talks of 'his ugly head and his terrible face and his twisted cynical mouth' but this doesn't get in the way of his amorous encounters. He has panting groupies, women masturbating while listening to his music and a number of – very loud – sex scenes. More troubling in the light of recent allegations (discussed later) is Paganini's (Kinski's?) desire for underage girls which is mentioned a number of times, with one character noting that, 'given the chance he would rape every girl he meets, especially the ones under age' (and one may get similar twinges at the mentions of father-daughter incest in *Aquirre* and the under-age sex in *Cobra Verde*). Paganini and Kinski also share an obsession with money arising from a poverty-stricken childhood and are fixated on their only son (played predictably by the 13-year-old Nikolai). The most affecting scenes are those of the boy mourning his father and these scenes are all the more powerful in the light of Kinski's death only three years later.

Since 1991 the cult has grown stronger, with a touring exhibition, *Ich Kinski* (2001–2002), a number of lavishly-illustrated books and even a Kinski Cologne. The image of the actor as a sex-crazed libertine has, for some, been complicated by recent claims by his eldest daughter Pola that he sexually abused her for 14 years starting when she was five years old. She stated that she decided to tell her story principally because, "I can't hear it anymore: 'Your father! Great! A genius! I always liked him," she said. "The idolization has only gotten worse since his death" (in Roxborough 2013) but surely her revelations relate to him as a father and a man, not as an actor. It might be hard to tarnish the memory of someone who admits to incestuous sex with his mother and sister (although like so many Kinski statements this has been challenged, to put it mildly) but only time will tell. Already, the fan-site *Du Dumme Sau* (in German, 'you stupid sow', named after an insult the actor flings at a [male] heckler in *Jesus Christ Erlöser*) has shut down in the wake of the revelations. Arno Frank may be slightly premature when he writes of 'A film idol's fall' (Frank 2013) but he does accurately identify Kinski's strange allure:

> Two questions are enough to reveal the deep complexity of German actor Klaus Kinski's appeal: Why are we so fascinated with him? And why are we simultaneously so repelled?
>
> (Ibid.)

Frank goes on to consider how the Kinski cult will cope with the allegations and suggests that given the actor's 'unique genius for providing an unobstructed glimpse into his disturbed soul, the confirmation of evil somehow fit [*sic*] seamlessly into our overall image of him' (Ibid.) This 'deep complexity' shows no sign of going away. It may well just get even deeper and even more complex.

References

Anon. 2008. 'Asylum records confirm Klaus Kinski's madness', *The Local*. www.thelocal.de/20080722/13215. Accessed May 1, 2015.

Bradshaw, Peter. 2001. 'Aquirre Wrath of God', *The Guardian*. www.theguardian.com/film/2001/aug/17/culture.peterbradshaw1. Accessed April 25, 2015.

Cronin, Paul. 2002. *Herzog on Herzog*. Faber & Faber: London.

Frank, Arno. 2013. 'Monstrous Talent: A Film Idol's Fall,' *Speigel Online International*. www.spiegel.de/international/zeitgeist/sexual-abuse-revelations-change-our-view-of-klaus-kinski-a-877039.html. Accessed May 2, 2015.

Jahn, Pamela. 2008. 'Jesus Christ Saviour: Interview with Peter Geyer,' *Electric Sheep*. www.electricsheepmagazine.co.uk/features/2008/08/03/jesus-christ-saviour-interview-with-peter-geyer. Accessed May 1, 2015.

Kinski, Klaus. 1996. *Kinski Uncut*. Bloomsbury: London.

Naha, Ed. 1983. 'The Master of Screen Depravity Speaks,' *Fangoria* (28): 41–43.

Roxborough, Scott. 2013. 'Klaus Kinski's Daughter Claims He Sexually Abused Her,' *The Hollywood Reporter*. www.hollywoodreporter.com/news/klaus-kinski-daughter-sexual-abuse-410213. Accessed May 2, 2015.

Schager, Nick. 201. 'Film Comment Selects 2011: Jesus Christ the Savior,' *Slant Magazine*. www.slantmagazine.com/house/article/film-comment-selects-2011-klaus-kinski-jesus-christ-the-savior. Accessed May 1, 2015.

Thomson, David. 1984. 'Klaus Kinski: A Face to Conjure With,' in *Movies of the Seventies*. Orbis: London: 70–71.

Thomson, David. 2002. *The New Biographical Dictionary of Film*. Little, Brown: London.

48

CRISPIN GLOVER

Sarah Thomas

Innovative in his artistic outlook, marginal in his success, transgressive in his oddness, and excessive in his performances, Crispin Glover embodies cult stardom. A true cult auteur in many regards, one of his most recent endeavours is an internationally-toured live show called 'Crispin Glover's Big Slide Show', an event described in one press release as 'bewildering, unnerving, surreal, and blackly comic', and 'unsuitable for children' (Hodgson 2014). It mixes screening and live performance, showcasing Glover's own directorial effort *What Is It?* (2005), a film with a cast of actors with Down's Syndrome and described by Glover as 'Being the adventures of a young man whose principal interests are snails, salt, a pipe and how to get home as tormented by an hubristic racist inner psyche'.[1] A further feature of the Slide Show are readings and illustrations from Glover's re-working of 19th Century books, accompanied by an earnest over-the-top commentary which tends to be greeted with nervous laughter and rapturous applause.[2] Aside from his own offbeat projects, much of his conventional fame stems from his early role as George McFly in *Back to the Future* (1985). Since then he has occupied a significant space in alternative independent cinema and cult television with scene-stealing supporting roles in *River's Edge* (1986), *Wild at Heart* (1990) and the Starz network's adaptation of Neil Gaiman's *American Gods* (2017), and embellished mainstream productions with elaborate eccentricity, such as insisting his character in *Charlie's Angels* (2000) be reworked as mute.

Beyond the screen his outsider cult status was affirmed by an event at New York's Museum of Arts and Design which positioned him as

> A unique voice ... and pioneer within the cult cinema for his character actor roles in Hollywood blockbusters, the eponymous character in the remake of *Willard* ... and directing a series of independent feature films that explore alternative perspectives on contemporary life.[3]

Part of his cult identity has been consolidated via an unconventional approach to music, producing the album, *The Big Problem ≠ The Solution. The Solution = Let It Be* in 1989, which incorporates readings from a self-published book (*Oak-Mot*), a cover of 'These Boots are Made for Walking' and 'Clowny Clown Clown' (the latter's bizarre music video now archived on YouTube).[4] Signifiers of his cult star persona abound elsewhere: his father Bruce Glover is also a cult character actor; Crispin has renovated a dilapidated chateaux in the Czech Republic; he has a cult look that is never deviated from (a black suit and narrow tie); and other cult figures (such as Juliette Lewis) interview him, confirming and extending their own offbeat status.[5] What Glover projects (and is projected upon him) is more 'cult aura' than 'cult image', even cameoing as Andy Warhol in Oliver Stone's *The Doors* (1991).

But, whilst Glover personifies an auratic identity rooted in the cult and alternative, he remains an actor with a distinct presence in Hollywood filmmaking. Within Glover lies a constant negotiation between the mainstream, the familiar, the niche and the subcultural and between industry and independence, but unlike other cult stars, this is not necessarily one of conflict. My chapter will emphasise the increasing significance of industrial and economic sites for this, but Glover's cult status certainly exists at the cultural and ideological level that is typical to cult stardom. An article in *The New Yorker* (McGrath 2006) illustrates the wide gamut of Glover's movie star existence. A profile of the late YouTube star Stevie Ryan, it characterises a meeting between Ryan and Glover as a crossing of new and traditional worlds – 'a YouTube star landing a feature-film role, and a Hollywood star joining the YouTube community'. The meeting leads to a sketch on Ryan's YouTube channel, where her online persona (Little Loca) happens across Glover at his home amidst the affluent trappings and vintage Bentleys. She exclaims 'Hey wait a minute. You look like McFly, fool. … Look at this house and these cars… you ain't Crispin Glover the *movie star*?' He responds 'Movie star. *That* guy? That guy's an *idiot*'. Recounted in a widely circulated but niche high-end magazine, successfully adapting to ground-breaking (in 2006) social media practice, here Glover simultaneously dismisses the traditional movie star identity as well as confirming it (he *is* George McFly and he *is* a Hollywood success: that *really is* his own collection of extraordinary and expensive cars).

The production and [re]circulation of cult status

In public discourse, Glover is *always* orientated to the reader/viewer via mainstream Hollywood, but as that fabricated exchange with a subcultural online star illustrates, this too occurs through cult discourse. There is a hierarchy of 'cultness' in both by which he is made accessible and recognisable; first through his supporting roles in the major films, *Back to the Future*, *Charlie's Angels*, and *Alice in Wonderland* (2010). Secondly, through his appearances in key films of American independent cinema of the 1980s and 1990s, *River's Edge*, *Twister* (1989) and *What's Eating Gilbert Grape* (1993), alongside other iconic American cult actors (Johnny Depp, Harry Dean Stanton and Dennis Hopper). His work with seminal independent auteurs is also cited; David Lynch (*Wild at Heart*), Gus Van Sant (*Even Cow Girls Get the Blues* [1993]) and Jim Jarmusch (*Dead Man* [1995]). Then his work in low-grade mainstream fare: *Epic Movie* (2006) and *Hot Tub Time Machine* (2010), and a notorious appearance on David Letterman in 1987. Finally, if at all, his own projects *What Is It?* and *It Is Fine. Everything is Fine!* (2007) or his leading roles in cult films, *Willard* (2000) and *Bartleby* (2001) are acknowledged. This is ironic, as the primary aim of his public appearances are to publicise the latter category.[6]

We might discern an obvious trajectory through Glover's chronology; mainstream breakthrough in quirky supporting roles in the 1980s, consolidation of cult status during American independent cinema of the 1990s, opportunistic leading roles in minor films in the early 2000s, and a mix of minor-mainstream films with his self-directed projects post-2006. The quality and box-office success of the mainstream work and how it utilises the cult screen personality of 'Crispin Glover' declines as his personal pursuit of surrealist projects increases. However, off screen the cult star status of Glover is well-circulated in articles, interviews, podcasts and his own social media. Now more than ever, unusually for such an offbeat marginal figure, he is an accessible cultural presence in the international public domain with features and reviews in *The New York Times*, *Rolling Stone*, *The Guardian* and the accolade of a true star, a *Daily Mail* commentary on his lack of aging.[7] The contemporary 'knownness' of Glover-as-cult-star has been partly cultivated away from his control, most notably through the repositioning of *Back to the Future* as a cult text through audience nostalgia (Pett 2013) and he has become the cast member with the most sustained profile in contemporary extratextual material. Whilst willing to reflect on the film, his focus is usually his lawsuit with the producers for hiring another actor as George McFly and using prosthetics to disguise him as Glover in *Back to the Future II* (1989). Although Michael J. Fox and Christopher Lloyd recently appeared in a number of sketches on American television to celebrate the 30th anniversary of the film, neither participate in many interviews anymore. So, whilst, as Colin McEnroe noted before interviewing Glover, 'his body of work is very much at odds with *Back to the Future* and all the mainstream success it symbolizes' (2013), this distance is eroded by the cultification of the trilogy by fans, which Glover's existing cult status (and contentious history with the film) contributes to. No longer standing apart from the film text due to the obvious differences of his eccentric cult identity and performance style, both the film trilogy and Glover's 'cultness' are continually shifting.

Away from nostalgic reappraisals of this cult blockbuster, it is primarily Glover's non-naturalist performance style that first produced and then characterised his cult status. This style is apparent in his appearance as McFly where, compared to the other actors, he is overly mannered in his delivery and exaggerated in his physicality. His co-star Lea Thompson described his rehearsal technique was 'awesome' but 'weird' (Parker 2015). Such an approach typifies his work in his mainstream and independent films, notably as Layne in *River's Edge*, a performance described as 'seem[ing] out of sync with the less stylized behavior of the film's other actors' (Geeslin 1987). I have written elsewhere about how Glover's stylised acting supports mainstream performance, helping to emphatically define and ground leading characters (as stars) as 'ordinary' and 'normal' in response to him, characteristic of the function of character actors more widely (Thomas 2012: 44–45).

Beyond this, Glover's excessive acting adds to the atmosphere required by films that require audiences to suspend disbelief outside genre expectations, such as the time-travel elements in *Back to the Future* – ostensibly a teen film. This is particularly true of *River's Edge* which dramatises the murder of a young girl and its aftermath, committed and covered up by members of an offbeat small-town clique. An ambiguous film that offers no easy answers to the crime or the cover-up, its unpredictable mood is anchored and intensified by the disruptive performances of Glover and other significant cult star, Dennis Hopper. Through Glover's performative choices in these films (*River's Edge* to *Willard* and beyond) these texts position themselves as cult artefacts, the acting working in conjunction with other formal elements such as narrative, soundtrack and mise en scène that are used in unconventional ways. As such, Glover's acting can be defined as 'formalist' whereby its production *and* value lies in the self-conscious artificiality of its excess. In Glover's case, this sits comfortably within films that also strive to unsettle, rather than standing against the film as 'hammy' performance does (Mathijs and Sexton 2011: 82–84). This creates continuity between the oddness of his characters and the mode by which he depicts them, rather than the distancing bathos or 'self-reflexivity' of other cult acting that relies on displaying the cult of personality onscreen. By favouring a style that, though formalist (not naturalist) technique, enables Glover to embody (or disappear into) the character, each characters' weirdness is represented as more authentic and therefore more believable within each film's odd storyworld. Glover characterises his acting in this way defining it as 'heightened reality', stating he does not believe naturalism with its underplayed small gestures 'reflects the truth of drama or psychology'. Instead, his 'heightened reality' shows the 'intention of the character to its fullest extent' at the same time as allowing the 'skill of the actor' to be observed.[8]

The intensity and acute characterisation of Glover's acting remains key to the actor's cult status, negating the *very* mainstream work he has undertaken. Returning to the dissemination of

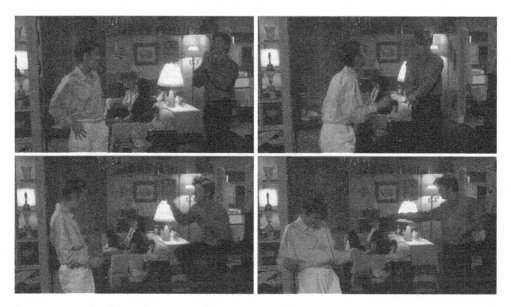

Figure 48.1 Crispin Glover's dancing moves from *Friday the 13th: The Final Chapter* (Zito, USA, 1984). Paramount Pictures/Georgetown Productions/Sean S. Cunningham Films

Glover's stardom via contemporary social media, in 2016 the YouTube channel 'No Small Parts' (filmmaker, actor and cult fan, Brandon Hardesty) produced an episode on Glover. Normally short commentaries of 30 minutes or less on actors 'that nobody knows about, but have a recognisable face', the extended Glover episode (46 mins) acknowledged his wider fame, but that 'his phenomenal acting work' of 'strange and unique performances' necessitated a full deconstruction of the '100% original' man. It is this unique performance style and commitment to embodying a role that explains much of Glover's public celebrity (and its image of eccentricity) as it was showcased to a mainstream American television audience in 1987 with Glover's bizarre appearance on *Late Night with David Letterman*. Dressed, as would be revealed four years later on the film's eventual release, as the character Rubin from *Rubin and Ed* (1991), Glover appeared incoherent and confrontational, attempting to kick Letterman in the head. A search for 'Crispin Glover' on YouTube reveals that this is by far the most uploaded clip of the actor, and apart from *Back to the Future*, likely to be many peoples' first encounter with him. Glover is constantly asked about this incident but refuses to clarify whether he was acting in-character: 'I have neither confirmed nor denied in media whether or not that was me on the 1987 *Late Night with David Letterman* appearance'.[9] It has come to be considered as a performance art stunt; a precursor to Joaquin Phoenix's extended 'in-character' public appearances for the mockumentary *I'm Still Here* (2010), reinventing it as another of the 'pleasures' of Glover's acting and subversive cult identity in its constant online recirculation.[10]

Whilst these on- and off-screen performances by Glover emanate from his own deliberate artistic intent, his contemporary cult status is also maintained by other producers and users, especially via social media. Although not through his own active agency, they contribute to his subcultural identity and can be seen neatly in the fan-produced video which loops a short, almost negligible sequence from Glover's appearance in *Friday 13th: The Final Chapter* (1984).[11] For over five minutes, it rewinds and repeats a moment of Glover dancing in an exaggerated manner (10 seconds in the original film). This clip is heavily recirculated around internet platforms and has become a meme, changing its form as other users have adapted and extended into gifs. In line with early summations of online media's shifting of conceptions of stardom, 'Crispin Glover' has become a hyperlink 'connecting the many and various contexts of star presence' (McDonald 2003: 42); a personality created by online users and adding to his star identity.

The *Friday 13th* meme has the opposite effect to Glover's intent in the sequence where overtness of form is employed in service of character psychology and, in his words, 'truth'. Gifs and other online texts displace the gesture from the diegetic narrative, distancing the viewer from any conception of the character, showcasing only the 'oddness' of Glover himself, reifying him and his performance through the lens of the 'cult of personality'. However, there is little tension between Glover (as niche artist) and these examples of more populist celebrations of the actor (also including appreciation of his mainstream films), even if they (and elements of his star persona) exist outside his control. Instead, when asked to reflect on the meme, Letterman, *Charlie's Angels* or *Back to the Future*, Glover always engages with the topics and texts of his past, often citing these as favourite performances. When it is referenced in *The New Yorker* article that 'YouTubers have watched the [Letterman] incident more than a quarter of a million times', he merely reflects 'It's interesting now that there's this whole new life for it' (McGrath 2006).

These patterns of exchange, appreciation and [re-]circulation between Glover and his fans, and the role of social media platforms in sustaining his cult identity, position Glover as an exemplar of the postmodern subcultural celebrity. He has adapted to the digital landscape effectively, and if anything, the accessibility of this niche figure has only increased his star status. Glover maintains his own website (crispinglover.com), keeps updated Facebook, Instagram and Twitter accounts, and frequently participates in content-creation on major online community sites such as Nerdist podcasts and Reddit AMAs (Ask Me Anything). These processes align to Elizabeth Ellcessor's argument for 'a new kind of star system' where 'the workings of a star text of connection are formed through complicated interactions of media platforms, texts, audiences, and industries, facilitated by digital and social media' (2012: 75). The circulation and exhibition of Glover's stardom also illustrates Henry Jenkins et al.'s examination of contemporary hybrid content circulation in *Spreadable Media* where 'a mix of top-down and bottom-up determine how material is shared across and among cultures in far more participatory (and messier) ways' (2013: 1), utilising online communication tools that create and circulate context in easy-to-share formats. This contrasts with models of traditional distribution, whereby now the public are no longer seen as consumers of pre-constructed messages, but as those who shape, share, reframe and remix media content 'not as isolated individuals but within larger communities' (ibid.: 2). However, Glover is a more complex case study of cult /subcultural stardom than this alone would suggest and the next section will discuss another element of Glover's professional life; the management of his own filmmaking projects, drawing on his use of both unconventional and traditional methods of distribution.

The distribution of cult status

To introduce 'spreadable media', Jenkins et al. redefine conventional definitions of the term 'circulation' to illustrate how convergence cultures have changed the media landscape. The old use of 'circulation' is 'really talking about distribution' where 'distribution' is defined as a broadcast model where [corporate] 'producers create discrete and finished products for a mass audience' (ibid.). This section considers how Glover produces, manages and distributes his own material and his close economic control over this. Whilst Glover does not create products for a 'mass audience', his working practices mirror Jenkins et al.'s further contextualisation of traditional distribution 'where the movement of media content is largely – or totally – controlled by the commercial interests producing and selling it' (ibid.).

As a figure who constantly refers to himself as 'a working actor' (i.e. that acting is a job dependent on labour, economies and institutions as much as it is an artistic, personal vocation) Glover is quick to discuss finance and employment in interviews, reflecting on his place in an industrial landscape. He is open about his financial motivation for making *Charlie's Angels*, declaring that 'I recognized in 2000 and 2001 that I really needed to make as much money as I could in order to fund my own filmmaking', prompting the interviewer to declare 'just because a man's eccentric doesn't mean he can't also be pragmatic' (Freeman 2015). He articulates the processes of Hollywood (from product to publicity), his position in this corporate system and the duties therein, telling another interviewer 'I have respect at this point in my career as to what media is for as a businessperson and a filmmaker. I was paid to be in the movie. I enjoyed working with everybody. So, I'm here to do my job and I appreciate talking to you. My way of thinking about publicity is probably very different than it was 25 years ago' (Ryan 2012). '25 years ago' was the Letterman appearance, and it becomes clear in these publicity interviews that as Glover's star status and use of digital media has expanded, so too has his development of the way his work, stardom and career exists within a wider structure of economic realities.

Glover uses the term 'corporate' when talking about the mainstream Hollywood industry and modes of production, distribution and exhibition. In line with the auratic nature of his cult self-image this is always in conversations about his own projects, *What Is It?* And *It Is Fine. Everything Is Fine!* As well as its original intention of promoting the casting of performers with Downs Syndrome, Glover positions *What Is It?* as his 'psychological reaction to the corporate constraints that have happened with corporately funded distributed films' (ibid.), and articulation of his feelings towards the damaging influence of business interests on cultural production and how funding and distribution opportunities are limited for with films uncomfortable elements. It began as a project with the potential for corporate backing with 'various actors attached to it, David Lynch was going to be executive producer' but fell through when the corporate entity had questions about the viability' of making a movie with a predominantly Downs Syndrome cast (Bonner 2013). His later film also explores extreme subject matter (psychosexual fantasy) though and beyond disability into the crime/murder genre, adapting the autobiographical script of its main performer, cerebral palsy sufferer Steven C. Stewart. In terms of content and distribution, these films were conceived as challenges to mainstream industrial practice allowing Glover to 'put my artistic passions and questions into my own filmmaking' (Carter 2015), play the rebellious outsider and self-finance films unlikely to gain any conventional distribution. Indeed, the most orthodox exhibition of *What Is It?* and *It Is Fine. Everything Is Fine!* were their selections for the Sundance Film Festival in 2005 and 2007.

I say 'unlikely' because apart from Sundance, Glover has never actually offered these films for conventional distribution or exhibition. Instead he has implemented a tightly controlled practice in which he meticulously manages every aspect of production, distribution, exhibition, and promotion. This positions them differently to other types of cult texts, from the repositioning of mainstream into cult (*Back to the Future*), the spreadable bottom-up circulation of fan-favourites (*The Big Lebowski*), semi-restricted circulation via midnight cinema and television screenings and/or niche label DVD releases (*The Room, Pink Flamingos*), and even those that have been officially removed from circulation by the litigious actions of other institutional powers against the filmmakers/distributors, but may be acquired in through bootlegs (*Superstar: The Karen Carpenter Story*). The only way to see Glover's films is to attend his screening/Q&A events that tour art cinemas worldwide, such as 'Crispin Glover's Big Slide Show' and according to

Figure 48.2 Crispin Glover in *Willard* (Morgan, USA, 2003). New Line Cinema/Hard Eight Pictures

his website 'Any other current means of viewing his films other than at his live shows is not approved'. He explains this decision as one determined by economic necessity; the films are self-funded and this personal investment requires a good financial return, which he believes is best generated from the 'Slide Show' exhibition format. This restricted distribution prevents breach of copyright of the films, which is a major priority of Glover's. Whilst happy for the 'bottom-up' recirculation of mainstream content like the Letterman appearance, the prospect of a YouTube bootleg of his films is 'something I would be very litigious about' (McGrath 2006). He has commented 'I am in control of the distribution and personally supervise the monetary intake of the films that I am touring with. I also control piracy in this way because digital copy of this film is stolen material and highly prosecutable' (Douglas 2012). As one interviewer emphatically declared, Glover is 'a man who owns his own work'.[12]

The unsettling nature of films and Glover's strategy of self-distribution are framed as anti-corporate stance, driven by artistic integrity. It is certainly this, but in his singular management of production, distribution and exhibition it is also a means of control that mimics a mainstream corporate strategy; the vertical integration of the classical Hollywood studio system. It remains recognisably bound by a 'cult' identity and the financial returns are much smaller, but it remains a coherent business model that enforces strict legislative control and circulation of product. He even self-regulates admitting only over 18s, calling this 'a good law'.[13] Glover describes the 'Slide Show' experience as akin to classical practices: '[Prior] to the 1950s, people exclusively saw films in movie theaters. The films were able to recoup and profit at that time in that fashion' (Carter 2015). His practice is reminiscent of the blockbuster roadshow format of Hollywood exhibition of the 1950s, where prestigious or extraordinary films were showcased in limited runs on an exclusive reserved-seat basis, often with supplementary programme material, and where 'the goal was to keep the picture in circulation for as long as possible in order to tap its maximum box-office potential' (Hall and Neale 2010: 160). Glover has been touring *What Is It?* for ten years, mainly exhibiting in exclusive theatres in major urban areas, often multiple times. Returning to Jenkins et al. on contemporary modes of circulation, here Glover's circulation of cult product, stardom and identity has moved away from concepts of participation, hybridity and community back towards the traditional definition of 'distribution' as media content controlled by the interests producing and selling it. Glover aligns himself with this traditional mode, stating 'distribution, of course, means to make available to the public, which I most certainly have done' (Carter 2015). It resembles what Jenkins et al. call the 'stickiness model' of circulation, which 'privileges putting content in one place and making audiences come to it so they can be measured' (2013: 5).

The juxtaposition of Glover's cult, offbeat identity with his firm control over all elements of production suggests almost a cult parody of the classical mogul. He positions himself within and without the contemporary Hollywood system, using its desire to cast him in eccentric character roles, conforming to promotional duties *and* challenging it through his unsettling non-mainstream works and microcosm of economic organisation and monopolistic power. This power even extends to publicity material; theoretically Glover is open and accessible, willingness to discuss anything from using Hollywood for his own benefit, approaches to acting, and his conflict with *Back to the Future's* Bob Gale. However, whilst this creates a sense of intimacy authenticity, its method of delivery is unusual and also about maintaining control over content, and therefore how it should be interpreted. The majority of Glover's responses to questions across his interviews are remarkably similar, often literally word-for-word. This is because, as he occasionally discusses, he relies upon a 'crib sheet' with pre-prepared and memorised answers to frequently asked questions. As he describes it,

> I normally answer questions from a 1600 word page document that I have saved from my written interviews over the last 9 years of touring with my live shows and feature films I have directed. This means I can use that resource to answer certain commonly asked questions and respond in more detail to less commonly asked questions.[14]

From this self-curated archive he has become his own studio publicity department, recycling stock answers and wholly in charge of content creation. He even restricts the visual imagery of himself, distributing a limited set of publicity photographs with the same black and white head shot of Glover illustrating numerous interviews: one example is captioned 'A photo Crispin Glover emailed to *The Australian* of himself' (Douglas 2012). For a man who collects vintage Bentleys and lives in a Czech castle, this is unlikely to be due to the expense of updating high quality head-shots.

Typical of celebrity practice and Hollywood manufacture of classical stardom these encounters provide 'the illusion of intimacy' (Schickel 1985: 4) and is symptomatic of how Glover carefully adopts and adapts systemic 'corporate' practices and applies them to cult/artistic projects and his own management of his cult star persona. He engages, but on his own artistic and economic terms and distributes a coherent, unwavering star image; the cult aura of 'Crispin Glover'. This production of stardom works together, and apart from, the participatory user-generated online content recirculated by Glover aficionados. As such, Glover is very much anchored to mainstream Hollywood; it helps orientate the public to him, notably *a specific public*; cult audiences who have embraced his embodiment of that image and who have in turn repositioned what 'cult' is and how Glover is placed in this context. In the industry's employment of him, Hollywood showcases his eccentricity by making overt his 'heightened reality' on and off screen, and also enabling the financing of his own alterative, independent works. Although the embodiment of the excessive, offbeat, uncontrolled cult star personality, in his carefully considered business model and management strategies that cohere production, distribution, exhibition and promotion, Glover is also indicative of longevity of the traditional Hollywood economic system, albeit now maintained through cult channels. He stands as an authentic cult star, but one concurrently and nuancedly embedded within mainstream Hollywood.

Notes

1 www.crispinglover.com/statement.htm.
2 http://crispinglover.com/slideshow.htm.
3 http://madmuseum.org/series/it-crispin-hellion-glover.
4 www.youtube.com/watch?v=rH6b_lSQst0.
5 'Into the Night': Juliette Lewis interviews Crispin Glover, 2011. www.youtube.com/watch?v=Vuow8wlWwdk.
6 For example, an interview with *The Guardian* focuses on *Back to the Future* at length and then briefly mentioning the DVD release of *The Carrier* (renamed *The Bag Man*). Only the end line reveals Glover is screening *It Is Fine. Everything is Fine!* at the ICA in London (Freeman 2015).
7 Eleanor Gower 2013.
8 All quotes from YouTube interview with ExploreTalent.com 2008. www.youtube.com/watch?v=GAwTdcYwp3s.
9 Reddit AMA (Ask Me Anything) 2014. www.reddit.com/r/IAmA/comments/1ywe62/crispin_hellion_glover_actor_and_filmmaker_more/.
10 Glover continued to appear on mainstream talk shows in the 1980s and 1990s, even returning to Letterman three weeks later as 'himself'.
11 Uploaded by jaybauman, 12 April 2012. www.youtube.com/watch?v=0UkJl8FmiMk.
12 YouTube interview, Mad Bros Media, November 2015. www.youtube.com/watch?v=YIANCEug6OY.
13 Ibid.
14 Reddit AMA (Ask Me Anything) 2014.

References

Bonner, Michael. 2013. '"I Met Andy Warhol at Madonna and Sean Penn's Wedding": An Interview with Crispin Glover', *Uncut*: 7 January. [online] https://blackboard.aber.ac.uk/webapps/portal/execute/tabs/tabAction?tab_tab_group_id=_55_1 [Accessed 5 July 2016].
Carter, Spike. 2015. 'Everything Is Fine with Crispin Glover', *Vanity Fair*: 2 October. [online] www.vanityfair.com/hollywood/2015/10/everything-is-fine-with-crispin-glover [Accessed 1 August 2016].
Douglas, Tim. 2012. 'Interview with Crispin Glover', *The Australian*: 6 July. [online] www.theaustralian.com.au/arts/full-interview-with-crispin-glover/story-e6frg8n6-1226418067115 [Accessed 13 August 2016].
Ellcessor, Elizabeth. 2012. 'Tweeting @feliciaday: Online Social Media, Convergence, and Subcultural Stardom', *Cinema Journal* 51:2: 46–66.
Freeman, Hadley. 2015. 'Crispin Glover: When you raise questions people think, "You're crazy"', *The Guardian*: 30 July. [online] www.theguardian.com/film/2015/jul/30/crispin-glover-the-carrier-interview [Accessed 31 July 2016].
Geeslin, Ned. 1987. 'Crispin Glover of *River's Edge* Emerges as King of the Oddballs', *People Magazine*: 22 June. [online] www.people.com/people/archive/article/0,,20096575,00.html [Accessed 31 July 2016].
Gower, Eleanor. 2013. 'Who Needs a Time Machine? *Back To The Future* Star Crispin Glover Looks Nearly as Youthful as 1985 Alter Ego George McFly (but a LOT Scruffier)', *Daily Mail*: 15 January. [online] www.dailymail.co.uk/tvshowbiz/article-2262580/Back-To-The-Future-star-Crispin-Glover-looks-nearly-youthful-1985-alter-ego-George-McFly-LOT-scruffier.html [Accessed 26 August 2016].
Hall, Sheldon, and Steve Neale. 2010. *Epics, Spectacles and Blockbusters*, Detroit: Wayne State University Press.
Hodgson, Barbara. 2014. 'Hollywood Comes to Newcastle', *The Journal*: 26 April. [online] www.thejournal.co.uk/culture/film-news/hollywood-comes-newcastle-actor-crispin-7035785 [Accessed 5 April 2016].
Jenkins, Henry, Sam Ford and Joshua Green. 2013. *Spreadable Media: Creating Value and Meaning in a Networked Culture*, New York: New York University Press.
Mathijs, Ernest, and Jamie Sexton. 2011. *Cult Cinema*. Chichester: John Wiley & Sons.
McDonald, Paul. 2003. 'Stars in the Online Universe: promotion, nudity, reverence', in Thomas Austin and Martin Barker (eds.) *Contemporary Hollywood Stardom*, London: Arnold: 29–44.
McEnroe, Colin. 2013. 'Act of Odd: An interview with Crispin Glover', WNPR: 7 March. [online] http://wnpr.org/post/act-odd-interview-crispin-glover#stream/0 [Accessed 5 April 2016].

McGrath, Ben. 2006. 'It should happen to you: the anxieties of YouTube fame', *The New Yorker.* 16 October. [online] www.newyorker.com/magazine/2006/10/16/it-should-happen-to-you [Accessed 26 January 2016].

Parker, Ryan. 2015. 'Lea Thompson Recalls Weird Time a 'Back to the Future' Co-Star Invited Her to His All-Black Apartment', *The Hollywood Reporter.* 20 October. [online] www.hollywoodreporter.com/news/back-future-lea-thompson-recalls-832472 [Accessed 5 April 2016].

Pett, Emma. 2013. "Hey! Hey! I've Seen This One, I've Seen This One. It's a Classic': Nostalgia, Repeat Viewing and Cult Performance in *Back to the Future*', *Participations* 10:1. [online] www.participations.org/Volume%2010/Issue%201/11%20Pett%2010.1.pdf [Accessed 4 July 2016].

Ryan, Mike. 2012. 'Crispin Glover's Letterman Appearance Explained; Michael Jai White's 'Spawn' Issues: A 'Freaky Deaky' Q&A', *The Huffington Post.* 27 April. [online] www.huffingtonpost.com/2012/04/27/crispin-glover-letterman-interview_n_1458004.html [Accessed 5 July 2016].

Schickel, Richard. 1985. *Intimate Strangers: The Culture of Celebrity.* New York: Doubleday.

Thomas, Sarah. 2012. 'Marginal Moments of Spectacle': Character Actors, Cult Stardom and Hollywood Cinema', in Kate Egan & Sarah Thomas (eds.), *Cult Film Stardom: Offbeat Attractions and Processes of Cultification*, Basingstoke: Palgrave Macmillan: 37–54.

INDEX

Abar, the First Black Superman 136–137
Abbott, Stacey 60, 327, 366–377, 394–395
abjection 34, 48, 51, 168, 367, 438
Abrams, J.J. 339–340, 346
Absolutely Fabulous 366
aca-fandom 255, 285–288, 291–292
acting 28–29, 30, 45, 73, 85, 135, 145, 147, 212,
    254, 295, 301, 326, 329–330, 333–336, 405,
    431–433, 446–450, 455–457, 462, 471, 475,
    480–483, 485
Adjust Your Tracking 223–224
aesthetics 2, 4–5, 8, 12, 17, 19, 21, 26–29, 33–36,
    40, 48, 50, 52–56, 73, 78, 85–86, 92–93,
    163–164, 167, 171, 175, 196, 204, 206, 208,
    218–221, 228, 255.6, 267, 275, 278, 281, 288,
    298, 320–322, 325–327, 329–330, 343, 346,
    367, 380, 384, 393, 406, 412, 414–415, 419,
    427, 431–432, 457
Aguirre, the Wrath of God 309, 468–469, 472–473
Akira 115, 121
Alfredson, Tomas 37
Alice in Wonderland 479
American International Pictures (AIP) 12, 132,
    135–136, 217, 363, 452, 455
An American Werewolf in London 204
An, Jinsoo 112, 114
Andreini, Isabella 71
Andrews, David 8, 20, 33–39, 123, 171, 173, 412
Anger, Kenneth 4, 25–27, 30, 140, 161, 162,
    164–166, 203
anime 17, 85–86, 121–130, 238, 257, 261
Anno, Hideaki 125
Antichrist 37, 180, 184
Ant-Man films 12, 392, 396
Apocalypse Now 1, 322, 445, 473
Aragon, Louis 72

Argento, Dario 17, 18, 37, 38, 76–79, 81–82,
    309–310, 411, 454
Armstrong, Robert Plant 282
Arnett, Sandra 123, 129
Arrabal, Fernando 166, 422, 429
arthouse/art-house 2, 16, 18, 31, 34, 163, 182, 185,
    186, 216, 245, 255, 315, 369, 415, 432, 472
Arzner, Dorothy 145
The A-Team 366
Audition 38, 118
Austin, Bruce 211, 216–218
Austin-Smith, Brenda 136, 139, 146–151
auteur (approach, status and concept) 3, 14, 16–20,
    35–39, 42, 44, 48, 50–52, 54–56, 92–93, 100,
    118, 123, 139, 140, 145–146, 161, 164, 184 204,
    298, 315, 344–346, 361–362, 372, 379–431,
    454–455, 478–479
Avatar 340, 356
The Avengers 207, 366, 379, 392–401, 462
Azuma, Hiroki 114, 122

Back to the Future 154, 205, 280, 478–483, 485
Bacon-Smith, Camille 254, 255
Badlands 312
bad taste (includes badfilm) 8, 33, 36–37, 40–49,
    60, 162, 319
The Bakavali Flower 105
Bakhtin, Mikhail 70–71, 73, 262, 350, 355
Barbarella 159, 268
Barjatya, Sooraj 109
Barker, Martin 209, 210, 254
Barthes, Roland 1, 254, 336
Bartlett, Becky 8, 40–49
Baschiera, Stefano 80, 452
Basket Case 226
Batman 205, 206, 211–212, 330–332

Baudrillard, Jean 65, 102, 462
Bauman, Zygmunt 155, 158, 255
Bava, Mario 17, 37, 38, 41, 76–79, 81–82, 295, 451–452, 454
Bazin, André 461, 462
The Beast of Yukka Flats 40, 44
The Beatles 309
Beausoleil, Bobby 161, 165
The Beehive 100
Begotten 168
Behind the Green Door 38
Bellow, Saul 100
Benjamin, Walter 4, 70, 77, 254, 354–355
Benshoff, Harry M. 86, 131–138, 148, 324
Berberian Sound Studio 317
Bergson, Henri 72–73, 162, 168
Berkeley, Busby 296, 297–299
Besson, Luc 114
A Better Tomorrow 114
Betz, Mark 28, 82
The Beyond 248
Beyond the Valley of the Dolls 431
Biancolelli, Caterina 71
The Big Lebowski 35, 173, 190, 212, 483
Bijou 38
Biller, Anna 20, 36, 380, 381, 411–421
The Bird with the Crystal Plumage 76, 82
Birdemic: Shock and Terror 45–47
Birdemic 2: The Resurrection 45–47
Biskind, Peter 52–55, 322
The Black Belly of the Tarantula 79
Black Christmas 158
Black Devil Doll from Hell 223, 225, 230
The Black Godfather 131
Black Sabbath 38
Black Swan 190–191, 194, 195–196
Blacula 132, 135–135
Blade II 93
Blade Runner 60, 65, 115, 309, 326, 359, 361, 398
The Blair Witch Project 51–52
blaxploitation 20, 86, 90, 113–114, 119, 131–138, 315
blockbuster 5, 54–55, 109, 138, 182, 205–207, 211–212, 254, 282, 322, 343–344, 356, 361, 368–369, 392, 478, 480
Blockbuster Video store 182, 226, 240
Blood and Black Lace 38
Blood Cult 223–231
Blood Feast 12, 35, 51, 227, 268, 309
Blood on Satan's Claw 164
Blood Sisters 405–409
Bloodsucking Freaks 147, 172, 229
Blue Velvet 25, 370, 372, 387, 389–390, 443, 446, 448–449
Boardinghouse 225, 230
Bollywood 86, 100
Boltanski, Luc 290

The Boneyard Collection 457
Bong Joon-ho 37
Bould, Mark 8, 59–68
Bourdieu, Pierre 4–5, 41, 48, 53, 402, 410, 426, 430
Bowman, Paul 460–467
Brakhage, Stan 26, 35–36
Brando, Marlon 469
Brass, Tinto 18, 38
The Breakfast Club 95
The Brood 55
Brooker, Will 211–212, 254
The Brothers Grimm 335
Browning, Tod 18, 52, 172, 326
Buffy, the Vampire Slayer 279, 366–367, 392–399
Bukowski, Charles 359, 443
The Bunny Game 186
Buñuel, Luis 18, 25, 35, 426–427
Burroughs, William S. 167, 168, 283, 327, 359, 443
Burton, Tim 135, 330, 457
The Butterfly Room 457

The Cabin in the Woods 392, 399
The Cabinet of Dr. Caligari 35
Cage, Nicholas 329, 387
Caged Heat 455, 456
Caldwell, John Thornton 255, 325
Call of Chthulu 364
camp 2, 4, 19, 20, 26, 29–30, 36–37, 42, 46, 52, 55, 66, 75, 107, 114, 133, 146, 152–154, 159, 164–165, 190–197, 204, 207, 208, 218, 228–229, 284, 296, 297, 311, 325, 356, 373, 374, 395, 407, 412, 438–442, 469; camp and music 299–303, 305
Cannibal Holocaust 20
Cannibal Hookers 229
capitalism 3, 62–63, 162, 220, 287, 289–290, 445
Captain America films 392, 395, 397
Cardona, Rene 93–94
carnival/carnivalesque 1, 35, 70, 73, 109, 116, 148, 262, 350, 390
Carnival of Souls 51
Carpenter, John 35, 52, 250, 307, 309–312, 364
Casablanca 95, 103, 153–154, 159, 209, 254, 318, 326, 350
La Casa Muda (The Silent House) 89
Cassel, Vincent 194
Castle, William 18, 211, 248, 310
Castle of Blood 452
Chandler, Raymond 64, 362
Chaplin, Charlie 31, 69, 71–72
Charlie's Angels 478, 482, 483
Chelsea Girls 25, 28
Cherry, Brigid 147, 291, 295–296, 307–309, 452
La chiave 38
Church, David 20, 79, 81, 133, 176, 199, 215–222, 223, 229, 230, 289–291, 429
Cinemageddon (website) 200, 235–242

cinephilia 100, 105–106, 114, 132, 144, 219, 233, 245, 276, 280, 282, 288, 428
Citizen, Robyn 17, 86, 111–120
Citizen Kane 47
Claire, René 25, 404
Cleopatra Jones 135
A Clockwork Orange 35, 309, 311, 330
Clover, Carol 147
Cobra Verde 472, 474
Coen, Joel and Ethan (Coen Brothers) 35, 192
Coffy 131
Cohan, Steven 300, 435–442
Cohen, Larry 18, 60, 132, 158
comedy 8, 17, 35, 37, 45, 69–75, 80, 92, 94, 99, 101, 113, 118, 132, 133, 136–137, 191–192, 204, 217, 270, 280, 297, 301, 302, 306, 313, 326, 350, 352, 354, 363, 366, 397, 406, 445, 449; black comedy 45, 360
Conrich, Ian 149, 228, 295
conventions 30, 124, 207, 257–265, 266, 268–269, 271, 321, 351; Comicon 259–261; Daicon conventions 124–125; Star Trek conventions 259–260; *Star Wars* conventions 321; Stripper Convention 271; Worldcon 259; World Science Fiction convention 259, 261
Cook, Pam 15, 20, 152
Cooley High 132
Cooper, Ian 468–477
Coppola, Francis 18, 408, 443
Corbucci, Sergio 17, 469, 471
Corman, Roger 12, 18–19, 38, 55, 90, 135–136, 146, 163, 354, 363, 443, 452–453, 455–456; *Masque of the Red Death* 38
cosplay 200, 253, 255, 257, 261–263, 352
Count Dracula 473
counterculture/countercultural 2, 26, 44, 52–55, 57, 140, 162, 172, 203–204, 255, 304, 358–359, 444–445
Crash 35
Craven, Wes 18, 38, 52–53, 310
Creeping Terror 40, 47
Cronenberg, David 18, 35, 53, 55–57, 60, 61, 356, 364, 455
Cronos 93
Crowley, Aleister 162, 164–165, 168
Cry-Baby 308
cultification/cultify 2, 36, 86, 121, 123, 128, 180, 183, 185, 187, 199, 206, 208–212, 290, 292, 316–317, 320, 360, 365, 426, 455, 485
Curry, Tim 191, 329
Cypher 61

Dafoe, Willem 390
D'Amato, Joe 17, 18, 237, 310, 469, 471
Dance, Girl, Dance 145
Danger Diabolik 295
Dans ma peau 38

Dante, Joe 12–13, 16, 18, 55, 454–456
Darabont, Frank 208
Dark, Gregory 20, 39
The Dark Knight 205, 329–330
Darktown Strutters 136–137
Dark Victory 149
Daughters of Darkness 148
Daumal, Rene 166
Davis, Bette 149, 158
Davis, Glyn 7, 8, 24–32, 91
Dawn of the Dead 56
Day, Doris 297, 299, 301
Dead End Drive-In 218, 219
Dead Man 479
Dead Poets Society 311
Dean, James 101, 442–443, 445
Deep Red 77–78, 224
Deleuze, Gilles 161–162
Del Toro, Guillermo 93
Demme, Jonathan 12, 18, 51–52, 455
Demoiselles de Rochefort 302–303
Demy, Jacques 302
Denison, Rayna 17, 85–86, 121–130, 238
Deodato, Ruggero 19, 20
De Palma, Brian 4, 303, 304
Deren, Maya 25, 166–167
Dern, Laura 383–385, 387, 389
Derrida, Jacques 102, 462
The Descent 250
De Seife, Ethan 295, 296, 297–306
Detention 61
De Valck, Marijke 244, 246–248
The Devil Rides Out 164
The Devil is a Woman 193
Dick, Philip K. 65, 361
Die Hard with a Vengeance 446
Dietrich, Marlene 191, 193
Dika, Vera 152, 307
Dionysus 70–71, 161, 168
Dirty Dancing 154, 207, 312, 364
The Disaster Artist 47
Disco Godfather 137
Disney 218, 296, 305, 354, 356, 392, 399
Divine 1, 29, 31, 319–320, 432
Djalil, H. Tjut 112
Doctor Gore 227
Doherty, Thomas 16, 18
Donnie Darko 35, 36, 60, 204, 212
Dracula 52
Dracula 39, 52, 105, 107–108, 419, 472–474
Driller Killer 227
drive-in theatres 215–221
Dr. No 463
Dr. Who 127, 147, 256, 366–367, 398
Dr. Zhivago 469, 471
Duchamp, Marcel 25, 166, 275, 443
Dune 361–362, 388, 390–391

Durgnat, Raymond 74
DVD 14, 16, 30, 64, 80–81, 91, 100, 110, 116–117,
    122, 166, 182, 184, 186, 200, 220, 225, 230,
    234–236, 239–240, 246–247, 285–290, 351,
    354, 364, 373, 381, 394–395, 408–409, 416, 425,
    428, 483; DVD/Blu-ray 285–290, 292
Dyer, Richard 30, 335, 438–440, 457

Easter Parade 301, 435, 438–439
Easy Rider 54, 268, 309, 359, 443–445
Ebert, Roger 53, 229, 422
Eco, Umberto 1, 24, 46–47, 98, 153, 274, 291,
    312–313, 318, 396–399
Edwards-Behi, Nia 249, 451–459
Egan, Kate 20, 81, 100, 176, 223, 457
Ehrenreich, Barbara 1, 268, 274
Eisenstein, Sergei 276–277, 279, 418, 469
elegance 444–445, 448, 465
El Topo 2, 27, 35, 93, 203–204, 207, 245, 268, 309,
    350, 359, 381, 422–429
Emmanuelle 17, 145
Empire 26, 28
Enter the Dragon 113, 119, 480
Eraserhead 1, 28, 35, 203–204, 207, 212, 296, 309,
    320–321, 380, 388, 390–391
Esper, Dwain 16, 19, 57
ethnicity 115, 119, 460, 462; *see also* race
Eurotrash 14, 17
Everything is Fine 483
Evil Dead 29, 35, 237, 364, 375–376
excess/excessive 5, 8, 21, 43, 47–48, 62, 81, 133,
    149, 172, 204, 206, 254, 302, 318–319, 325, 327,
    347, 363, 370, 388, 423, 431–432, 441, 446, 468,
    475, 478, 480, 485
The Exorcist 51–52, 54
exploitation 1–2, 7–8, 11–23, 24, 28, 31, 39, 42,
    46, 53, 82, 86, 89–90, 91–94, 105–106, 108, 115,
    131–132, 138, 143, 145, 147, 162, 175, 199, 203,
    215–219, 220–221, 223–224, 229, 237, 255,
    272, 287, 290–291, 316, 356, 359, 380–381,
    402, 409, 424–425, 431–432, 455, 470–471;
    sexploitation 30, 105, 109, 146, 404–405,
    411–412, 415–416, 419

Faces of Death 229
The Family Stone 155–156
fandom 3, 9, 13, 14, 41–42, 51–52, 59, 100, 102,
    111–112, 114, 118, 121–123, 125–129, 147, 158,
    161, 173, 176, 200, 204, 215, 219–221, 228, 233,
    235–236, 239, 241, 244–247, 250, 253–294, 298,
    300–301, 305, 326, 349, 352, 359, 361, 364–365,
    366, 368, 373, 376, 379, 423, 428, 438, 441, 442
Fando y Lis 298, 423
fantasy 30, 59, 81, 89, 92–94, 105, 131, 196, 219,
    224, 244–245, 255, 259, 262, 352–354, 356,
    396–397, 402, 414–415, 424, 440, 483
fantrepreneur 285, 289–292

Farhadi, Asghar 102
Fargo 366
Faster, Pussycat, Kill! Kill! 38
Faust 162–163, 303
Fear and Loathing in Las Vegas 364
Fellini, Federico 82, 100, 454, 469
femininity 145, 191, 268, 439, 445
feminism 112, 135, 143–145, 147–149, 196, 268–8,
    402–404, 407, 411–412, 415, 418, 441, 459;
    postfeminism 402, 441
Ferrara, Abel 19, 409, 443, 447
Ferris Bueller's Day Off 205, 280, 309
festivals 14, 37–38, 81, 94, 98, 100–101, 116,
    153, 156, 200, 205, 244–251, 255, 415, 423,
    424, 426–429, 483; Abertoir Horror Festival,
    Aberystwyth 248, 249; Brussels International
    Fantastic Film Festival (BIFFF) 245, 249;
    Cannes Film Festival 244–245; Cine-Excess
    Film Festival 81, 172, 292; Kurja Polt Genre
    Film Festival, Ljubljana 244, 246
file-sharing 15, 91, 183, 230, 235–241, 263,
    281, 342
film noir 38, 62, 77, 81–83, 318, 361–362, 370,
    373, 397, 411, 419, 443, 449; Italian noir 77;
    neo-noir 60, 449; Nikkatsu Noir 116;
    Scandinavian noir 18
Findlay, Roberta 20, 90, 380, 402–410
Firefly 373, 376, 379, 392–395, 397, 399
Fisher, Terence 164, 419
Fist of Fury 113
Fitzcarraldo 472–474
Flaming Creatures 26–29, 203
The Fly 56
Fonda, Peter 444
Footlight Parade 308
For a Few Dollars More 310, 469, 471
Forbidden Planet 307–308, 310–311, 316
Forbidden Zone 308
42nd Street 15, 216, 219–221
42nd Street (1933) 193, 298
Fotamecus Film Majik 168
Foucault, Michel 156, 178, 463
Franco, Jess 12, 36, 39, 47, 237, 429, 469, 471, 473
Frankenstein 60
Frankenstein Girl 119
freakery 116–117, 172, 367
Freaks 5, 18, 35, 172, 203, 206, 211, 326
Freeway II: Confessions of a Trickbaby 20–21
Freud, Sigmund 194, 449
Friday the 13th films 147, 224, 226, 228, 237,
    481–482
Friedkin, William 52, 54
Friedman, David 19, 143
Fritz the Cat 73
From Dusk Till Dawn 375
Frost, Mark 369–371, 383–384
Frozen 205, 296, 305

Fulci, Lucio 18, 81, 225, 248, 454
Fuller, Samuel 38
futurism/futurist 66, 86, 114, 317, 448

Gainax 121–130
Galaxy Quest 369
Galbraith, Patrick 123, 127–128
Galindo, Rubén 90
Game of Death 113
Ganja and Hess 86
Garbo, Greta 195, 336
Garland, Judy 4, 296–297, 299–303, 326, 432–433,
    435–442
gender/gender role 3–4, 8, 20, 27–29, 30,
    77, 111–112, 115, 132, 135, 139, 143–151,
    190–191, 193–194, 219, 255, 258, 262,
    266–267, 272, 288, 306, 404, 411–412,
    418, 420, 438–439, 443, 448; cis-gender
    111, 272; gender politics 8, 279, 381
Ghost in the Shell 115, 259
Ghost World 205
giallo 9, 17, 39, 76–84, 310, 318, 411
Giannini, Erin 379, 392–401
Gilliam, Terry 335
Gimme Shelter 309
Ginger Snaps 148, 346
The Glamorous Life of Sachiko Hanai 38
Glen or Glenda 43, 47–48, 204
Glitter 402, 407
Glover, Crispin 31, 326, 432, 478–487
Goblin (band) 309, 310, 315
Godzilla 17, 115
Goleh, Fereydoun 100
The Golem 162–164
Gorfinkel, Elena 19, 72, 143, 216, 235, 276, 412,
    414–416
Gosling, Ryan 457
Gothic (aesthetic) 108, 147, 162, 164, 411, 419,
    443, 451–458, 475
Grant, Barry Keith 29, 85, 101, 171–172, 177, 204,
    208, 212, 305, 321
Grant, Shauna 402, 407–408
Grease 207, 308
The Greasy Strangler 246
The Great Silence 469, 471
Gremlins 12, 55–56
Grier, Pam 1, 133, 134–135, 431–432
Grindhouse (*Planet Terror, Death Proof*) 36, 220,
    313, 317
Grossberg, Lawrence 254, 257, 262
grotesque 73, 116, 172, 180, 184, 390,
    438, 473
Grotesque 180, 184–186
Guardians of the Galaxy 392
Guerrero, Ed 132–134, 137
Gunbuster 125
Gurevitch, Leon 255, 326, 338–348

Hairspray 297, 304, 308
Halloween (holiday) 105, 154, 158, 207
Halloween films 52, 147, 224, 226, 296, 307–312
Hammer (studio) 17, 39, 309, 363, 366, 419, 451,
    452, 454
Hamoon (*Hamoun*) 100–101
Hansen, Miriam 4, 147, 215, 355
Hantke, Steffen 8, 17, 50–58
The Happiness of the Katakuris 149
Harakiri 114
Hard Boiled 38, 114
A Hard Day's Night 309
The Harder They Come 203–204, 207
Harold and Maude 73, 206
Harrington, C. Lee 352–353, 355
Harrington, Curtis 25
Harry Potter (franchise and tours) 205, 207, 328,
    351, 353–354
Hate Crime 180, 186
Hated: GG Allin and The Murder Junkies 177
The Haunted Palace 363
Haute Tension 38
Hawkins, Joan 5, 92, 223, 225
Haynes, Todd 41, 335
Hebdige, Dick 1, 85
Hedwig and the Angry Inch 304
Hellboy films 93
Heller-Nicholas, Alexandra 380, 402–410
Henenlotter, Frank 35, 37, 60
Herbert, Daniel 223–226
Her Flesh (trilogy) 406
Hernández, Gustavo 89
Herzog 100
Herzog, Werner 4, 309, 318, 469–475
Hill, Jack 132, 135
Hills, Matt 60–61, 73, 85, 121–124, 127–129, 140,
    147, 176, 183, 187, 204–205, 208, 210, 234, 247,
    254–256, 258, 261–262, 279, 285–294, 321, 352,
    355, 361, 369, 393, 397–398
Histoire d'O 38
Hitchcock, Alfred 45, 52, 76, 312–313, 379
The Hobbit (trilogy) 209, 253, 340, 344
Hoberman, J. 28, 42–43, 70, 85, 140, 203, 204,
    206–207, 209–210, 236, 298, 423, 426, 431
Hollows, Joanne 30, 139, 144, 149, 158, 367,
    286–287, 290, 380
Hollywood 2, 7, 14, 18, 28–29, 34, 36, 38, 51,
    55, 112, 131–138, 145–146, 149, 158–159,
    164–165, 204, 207, 216–218, 220, 269,
    271–272, 282, 289, 291, 296–298, 305–306,
    312, 315, 318–320, 338–339, 340–344,
    346–347, 355, 364, 373–374, 376, 379,
    385, 388, 392, 418, 437, 440–441, 448,
    455–458, 460, 462–463, 469, 478–479,
    483, 484–485; Hollywood classics 40–41,
    44, 55, 99, 152–154, 295, 299–300, 484;
    New Hollywood 52–54, 100, 138, 450

The Holy Mountain 93, 165–166, 245, 295, 359, 425
home video *see* video
Hooper, Tobe 12, 29, 38, 52, 55, 57, 245
Hopper, Dennis 268, 326, 388, 432–433, 443–450, 479–480
horror 2, 4, 8–9, 30, 35, 37–38, 40, 46, 50–57, 59–60, 69, 73, 77, 80, 89, 92–94, 99, 105–106, 108, 112, 132, 164, 171, 184–185, 191, 200, 204, 206, 211, 223–229, 240, 244–250, 280, 298, 307, 309, 311, 313, 346, 351, 362–364, 370, 372, 375–376, 388–390, 392–393, 396–397, 399, 402, 406, 408–411, 415, 419, 424, 451–458, 468, 470, 473–475; horror exploitation 12–20; horror and gender 146–149; horror and sound 315–316, 321; horror and transgression 174, 175–176, 178; J-horror 116–117, 184, 245, 361
The Horror of Dracula 419
Horrors of Malformed Men 116–117
The Host 37
Hostel 38, 118, 184
Hot (Hot Neighbour) 109
The Hot Spot 443
House (Hausu) 36, 115–116
House on Haunted Hill 73
House of Psychotic Women 219
The Howling 12, 55
Huizinga, Johan 349, 351, 356
Hum Aapke Hain Kaun (Who am I to You?) 109
The Human Centipede II 180, 185–186
The Hunger 148
Hunter, I.Q. 45, 46, 48, 172–173, 285–288, 292, 326, 327, 358–365, 367
Hunter, Russ 145, 200, 233, 244–251, 452
hyperbole 21, 148, 254, 325, 327, 334, 372, 432, 472

Ichi the Killer 118, 184
Imanjaya, Ekki 123
immigration (migrant work) 90–92, 105, 111, 133, 215
The Incredible Hulk 392, 393, 396
In the Mouth of Madness 364
The Indian Runner 445
Inland Empire 372, 385, 387, 389
Inspector Montalbano 77
intertextuality 2, 29, 33, 71–73, 101, 114, 162, 166, 206, 279, 296, 311–313, 327, 351, 361–362, 364, 367, 432, 464
internet 47, 65, 91, 100, 102, 106, 109, 156, 186, 233–238, 253, 258, 339, 356, 394, 440, 442, 472, 481
Interview with the Vampire 148
Invocation of my Demon Brother 165
Iordanova, Dina 244, 246
Irani, Ardeshir 98
Iron Man 206, 392

The Isle 112
I Spit on Your Grave 225
Ito, Mizuko 123–124
It's a Wonderful Life 154

Jackie Brown 135, 317, 431
Jackson, Peter 18, 60, 253, 304, 347
Jackson, Samuel L. 398
Jameson, Fredric 152
Jancovich, Mark 14, 34, 41, 81, 92, 121, 123–124, 155, 173, 177, 208, 224–225, 228, 234–235, 285, 350, 366–367, 393
Jarmusch, Jim 479
Jaws 51, 55, 138, 209, 455–456
Jenkins, Henry 71, 121, 255, 258, 261, 279, 286, 350–352, 393, 396–397, 482, 484
Jodorowsky, Alejandro 1, 18, 21, 27, 93–95, 165–166, 203, 245, 268, 295, 309, 362, 381, 422–429
Jodorowsky's Dune 21
Johnson, Dwayne (The Rock) 64–65
Johnston, Nessa 296, 315–324
Joker 326, 329–337
The Joker 337
Jordan, Neil 101
Juan de los muertos 94

Kael, Pauline 41, 426
Kaji, Meiko 115
Kannas, Alexia 9, 76–84
Kaufman, Lloyd 19, 35
Keaton, Buster 31, 71–72
Kelly, Gene 296–297, 30–32, 435
Kelly, Richard 35, 60–61
Khooni Dracula 108
Kierkegaard, Søren 100
Kill Bill (Vol. 1 and 2) 115, 312–313
The Killer 38, 114
Kill List 168
Kim Ki-duk 112, 119
King, Adrienne 457
King, Geoff 71, 73, 418–419
King, Henry 313
King, Martin Luther 136, 137
King, Stephen 56, 329, 362–363
King, Zalman 20
King Kong (1933) 4, 18, 148, 190, 340
King of the Mountain 446
Kinski, Klaus 326, 329, 432, 468–477
Kiss Me Deadly 61, 62–63
Klein, Allen 166, 425
Klein, Amanda Ann 255, 266–274, 350
Klinger, Barbara 61, 154, 183, 200, 211, 318, 380
Koven, Mikel 76–80, 82, 131, 234
Kracauer, Siegfried 4, 82, 215, 338–339
Kristel, Sylvia 30, 145
Krzywinska, Tania 162–164, 167

Index

Kubrick, Stanley 35–36, 54, 59, 61, 280, 309, 311, 326, 330–331, 362
Kuchar, Mike and George (Kuchar Brothers) 26, 29–30

LaBruce, Bruce 190–191
Labyrinth 205, 207
Lady Gaga 190, 442
Lady Snowblood 115
Lady Terminator 112
Lamarre, Thomas 126, 128
Langdon, Harry 31, 72–73
Larsen, Katherine 255, 260
The Last Dragon 113
Last House on the Left 38, 53
The Last Movie 445
The Last Seduction 35–36
Lavery, David 140, 367, 370, 394, 398
Lázaro-Reboll, Antonio 235, 381, 422–430
Lazarus, Tom 39
Ledger, Heath 326, 329–337, 432
Lee, Ang 311, 335
Lee, Bruce 17, 112–114, 118–119, 237, 326, 432, 433, 460–468
Lee, Christopher 164, 453
Lee, Sheryl 383, 386
Lenzi, Umberto 81, 247
Leone, Sergio 17, 310, 469
Lewis, Hershell Gordon 12, 18, 35, 51, 53, 57, 224, 268, 309
Lewis, Juliette 329, 478
Life in a Day 281–282
Lifeforce 55
Lindberg, Christina 1, 246
The Lizard 101–102
Lobato, Ramon 175, 230, 236, 240, 289
The Long Hair of Death 452
Looper 61
The Lor Girl 98–99
Lord of the Rings 66, 205, 253–254, 340, 351, 359–360
Lost Highway 372, 385, 387, 389–390
Lovecraft, H.P. 59, 327, 362–364
The Love Witch 411–420
Lucas, George 8, 54, 296, 321, 340, 346–347
Lucas, Tim 15, 239, 452–454
Lucifer Rising 161, 165
Luckett, Moya 20, 146, 380
Lugosi, Bela 167, 204
Lunch Meat 228–229
Lupino, Ida 145
Lust for Dracula 39
Lynch, David 28, 35, 296, 309, 320–321, 361, 369, 370–372, 380, 383–391, 405, 443, 448, 474, 479, 483

MacCormack, Patricia 454, 460
MacDonald, Kevin 281
machinima 255, 256, 276
Macias, Patrick 116–117
MacLachlan, Kyle 383, 388
Mad Dog Morgan 447
Mad Max 339, 340, 445
The Magician 163–164
Magic Mike 255, 266–268
Magic Mike XXL 266–273
Magritte, Rene 387
Malick, Terrence 312
Maltby, Richard 72
Man Bites Dog 73
The Mansion of Madness 91
The Man Who Fell to Earth 295, 313
The Man Who Laughs 329
Margheriti, Antonio 19, 452, 454
El Mariachi 94
Marins, José Mojica (Coffin Joe) 18, 92–93
Mars Attacks! 135
Marshall, Neil 250
Marsiglia, Tony 39
Martin, Adrian 72, 73, 234, 241, 276, 443–450
Martin, Eugenio 250
Martino, Sergio 78, 80
Martin, Steve 71
Martyrs 38
Marvel 61, 205, 379, 392–394, 396–399
Marx, Karl 62
masculinity 19, 30, 59, 100, 108, 114–115, 135, 139, 144–147, 149, 181, 192–193, 219, 267–272, 286–288, 381, 438, 460
Massey, Edith 31, 320
Matango: Attack of the Mushroom People 245
Matinee 12–13, 21
The Matrix trilogy 61, 205, 396–398
Maut (Death) 110
McCarthy, Melissa 71
McCullough Richard 43, 45, 208
McRobbie, Angela 285, 287–288
Mead, Taylor 24, 31
Medved, Harry and Michael (Medved Brothers) 41–43
Meet Me in St. Louis 154–155, 301, 435–436
Mehrjui, Dariush 100
Mekas, Jonas 25–28, 31
melodrama 29, 50–51, 80, 92, 99–100, 108, 114, 146, 149, 164, 318, 370, 409, 411, 414, 419, 422
Mendenhall, Julia 190–197
Méndez, Fernando 89
Mendik, Xavier 14, 16, 17, 27, 33, 35, 40, 69–70, 74, 146, 152, 210, 292, 315, 319, 325, 367, 393–395, 423, 461
Merhige, Elias P.
#Metoo 380
Metzger, Radley 18–19, 22, 38

Meyer, Russ 18–19, 29, 36, 38, 431, 456
MichaelAngel 444
Mickey Mouse 72
Middlemost, Renee 139, 140, 152–160
midnight movie/midnight screenings 2, 4, 7–8, 25, 27–28, 30, 35, 60, 85, 112, 144, 148, 161, 166, 191–192, 199–200, 203–212, 215, 234–235, 244, 297, 320–321, 358–359, 380, 381, 422–424, 426–429, 483
Miike, Takashi 38, 118–119
Million Dollar Mermaid 299–300
Mirbaqeri, Davoud 101
mockery 17, 21, 42, 65, 133, 144–145, 206, 219, 267, 300, 305, 312, 443, 481; mockbuster 14; mockumentary 305, 481
Moctezuma, Juan Lopéz 91, 94
Modleski, Tania 20, 146, 380
Mondo Cane 20
Monster A-go Go 44
Monterey Pop 302, 309
Monty Python and the Holy Grail 73, 204
Morocco 190
Motamen, Farzad 101
Moulton, Carter 200, 203–214
Mraovich, Sam 44
Mr Nobody 61
Much Ado About Nothing 393, 398–399
Mulholland Drive 372, 385–387, 389
Multiple Maniacs 207, 319–321
multiplex 204, 218, 220, 322
Mulvey, Laura 145, 147, 269, 416
Murnau, Friedrich Wilhelm 163, 473
musical 98–99, 113, 132, 138, 149, 191, 269, 271, 278, 295–308, 311, 313, 317, 322, 359, 380, 386–388, 403, 435–442
Myra Breckinridge 297
Mystery Science Theater 3000 40, 91, 356, 359, 363, 366, 368, 394
mysticism 5, 66, 161–169, 416–417, 422
Mystics in Bali 112

Nakahara, Tamao 17, 326, 349–358
Naked Lunch 356, 359, 364
Naremore, James 82, 335, 362
Natali, Vincenzo 61
National Lampoon's Vacation 154, 313
Needham, Gary 26, 76, 318
neoliberalism 63–64, 129, 180–183, 187, 286–290, 292
Neon Genesis Evangelion 121–122, 124
Netflix 20, 21, 182–184, 204, 235, 369, 375
New Wave Hookers 39
Ng, Jenna 255, 275–284
Nguyen, James 45–46
Nicholson, Jack 280, 330, 337, 444, 448, 473
Night of the Lepus 20, 158

Night of the Living Dead 12, 38, 52–53, 56–57, 203–204, 207, 310–311
Nightmare on Elm Street 224, 226, 396
Ninn, Michael 39
Nolan, Christopher 329, 338–339, 348
Nosferatu, eine Symphonie des Grauens 472
Nosferatu: Phantom der Nacht (Nosferatu, Vampyr) 472–474
nostalgia 12, 21, 33, 57, 80, 133, 138–140, 149, 152–159, 162, 199, 204–205, 218–220, 224, 230, 233–234, 236, 266, 270, 291, 316–317, 338–343, 367, 389, 445, 480
Nowhere to Hide 112

Obayashi, Nobuhiko 36, 38, 115–116
occultism 61, 140, 161–169
Okada, Toshio 124–127
Oldboy 112
O'Meara, Jennifer 380, 381, 411–421
Once Upon a Time in Mexico 94
Opening of Misty Beethoven 19, 38
Orange Is the New Black 20, 21
Orientalism 3, 17, 85–86, 98, 111–112, 114, 118
Original Gangstas 135
Orridge, Genesis P. 166–168
Otaku 114, 122, 126–129, 233
Otomo, Katsuhiro 115, 121

Pacific Rim 93
Paint Your Wagon 302
Pan's Labyrinth 93
Paris Chic 38
Paris Trout 447
Park Chan-wook 37
Parks, Gordon 132–134, 309
Pasolini, Pier Paolo 20, 282, 469
patriarchy 3, 99, 440–441, 448
Pearson, Roberta 366–367, 393
Peary, Danny 41, 69, 358
Peary, Gerald 20, 403–407
Penn, Arthur 469
Penn, Sean 443
performance 31, 70–71, 73, 114, 122, 145, 147, 149, 167–168, 171, 177, 192–194, 209, 253–255, 262–263, 266, 269–270, 275–276, 287, 291, 295, 317–318, 320, 326, 330, 335–336, 355, 380, 386–388, 405, 408, 416, 426, 428, 431, 432–433, 440–441, 443, 446–449, 453–454, 463, 468–469, 471–473, 475, 478, 480–482; live performance 205–207, 248–249, 263, 269; performance art 167, 420, 431
Performance 310
Pett, Emma 140, 154, 180–189, 480
Phantom of the Opera 304
Phantom of Paradise 303–304
Philipps, Kendall R. 52, 55
Phillips, Todd 177, 337

Pillow Talk 301
Pinkett-Smith, Jada 266–267
Pink Flamingos 2, 27, 29, 36, 148, 172, 190, 192,
  203–204, 207, 296, 319–321, 367, 412, 432, 483
Pink Floyd 204, 301, 309, 206
Piranha 12, 55, 455–456
Pitt, Ingrid 30, 457
Plan 9 from Outer Space 29, 40, 43–44, 204, 310,
  326, 356, 367
Poe, Edgar Allan 12, 76, 116, 163, 354, 363,
  455, 471; *Masque of the Red Death* 38
Polanski, Roman 54, 164, 363
Poltergeist 55
pornography 17, 19–20, 37, 40, 50, 65, 106, 109,
  212, 144, 146, 171, 175, 182, 186, 216, 218–220,
  229, 270, 272, 290, 320, 387, 402, 406–408,
  415–416, 427
Portillo, Rafael 93
Potamkin, Harry Allan 69, 71
Powell, Anna 140, 161–169
Presley, Elvis 302, 442, 463
Price, Vincent 73, 248, 363
Primer 61
The Princess Bride 205, 207, 361
Priscilla, Queen of the Desert 204, 207
provocation 12, 14, 21, 42, 63, 108, 112, 134, 153,
  155, 165, 172, 175, 233, 241, 285, 341, 350, 363,
  389, 403, 407, 410, 416–418, 432
Psycho 52, 312–313
Pull My Daisy 25
Pulp Fiction 280, 309, 350
punk 63, 85, 118, 219, 262, 383, 406, 409,
  444–445; cyberpunk 17, 66, 115–116
Puppet Master (films) 225
Purple Rain 304
Pynchon, Thomas 359

Q: The Winged Serpent 158
Qarun's Treasure 99
Qasemi, Manuchehr 99
Qeysar 99
Quadrophenia 309
Queen of Sheba Meets the Atom Man 24–25, 28, 31
queer 30, 135–136, 143–144, 148, 196, 199, 220,
  272, 320, 440

Rabid 55
race 111, 115, 118, 135–136, 186, 258, 262,
  266, 290
Rathod, Kanjibhai 105
Read, Jacinda 139, 144, 267, 287
Re-Animator 225, 363
The Red Car Gang 90
Redneck Zombie 229
Red Shoe Diaries 26
Reefer Madness 21, 35, 203, 207
Reeves, Keanu 443

repertory theatre 2, 38, 153, 199, 215, 220, 235
Repo Man 61, 63–66, 309
Reservoir Dogs 309
Revenge of the Nerds 73
River's Edge 478, 480
Robot Monster 40
The Robot vs. the Aztec Mummy 93
Rock 'n' Roll High School 149, 97, 308
Rock 'n' Roll Nightmare 228
Rocky 138
Rocky Horror Picture Show 28, 29, 35, 59–60, 70, 74,
  95, 148, 153, 158, 190–191, 194, 199, 203–204,
  206–207, 209, 211–213, 233, 234, 248, 249, 254,
  269, 296, 297, 303, 305, 308, 316, 326, 350, 356,
  359, 367, 368
Rodriguez, Robert 36, 94, 220, 317, 347, 412
Roeg, Nicholas 295, 313
The Rolling Stones 165
Romero, George 12, 38, 53, 56–57, 60, 310–311
Ronan, Saorsie 457
The Room 29, 43, 45, 47, 70, 74, 85, 153, 172, 192,
  204, 209, 211, 248, 326, 350, 352, 367, 483
Room 237 326, 362
Rooney, Mickey
Rosemary's Baby 54, 164, 363
Rosenbaum, Jonathan 4, 28, 85, 140, 203,
  206–207, 209–210, 423, 426, 431
Rossellini, Isabella 387, 449
Roth, Eli 38, 118
Rothman, Stephanie 12, 20, 146, 403
Routt, William 42, 44, 446
Royal Space Force: The Wings of the Honneamise 124
Rubin, Barbara 26, 28, 30
Ruétalo, Victoria 18, 89–90, 93
Russian Doll 21

Le Samourai 114
Sandvoss, Cornel 254
Santa Sangre 424–425
Santo films 91, 93, 240, 424
Santos, Alessandra 18, 93
Sargeant, Jack 174, 410
Sarris 34, 161, 212, 379, 402
satanism 164–167, 363, 386, 409
Satan's Bed 406
Saw 184, 396
Scanners 53, 55, 455
Schaefer, Eric 7, 14–16, 90, 92, 316
Schneider, Romy 329
Schneider, Steven Jay 16, 93, 319
Schopenhauer, Arthur 297–298, 306
science fiction 2, 8, 17, 29–30, 40, 59–68, 89,
  92–94, 121, 124, 135, 171, 224, 244, 254–255,
  259–261, 268, 316, 322, 350
Sconce, Jeffrey 14, 16, 40–44, 47–48, 69, 72, 92–93,
  133, 145, 158, 183, 219, 225, 233, 237, 258, 272
Scorpio Rising 27–28, 164, 203

Scorsese, Martin 63, 219, 312
Scott, Ridley 57, 309, 361
Scott, Tony 447
Scream films 52, 310
The Secret History 360
self-reflexivity 13, 16, 21, 154, 167, 177, 282, 286, 319, 325, 380, 384, 386, 389, 431, 480
A Serbian Film 180, 185–186
Serenity 379, 392–399
Sestero, Greg 47
sexuality 12, 27–28, 30, 108, 111–112, 115–118, 132, 134–135, 143, 145–146, 148, 164, 194, 203, 255, 261, 268, 270, 272, 301, 303–304, 416, 431, 440, 448, 454; bisexuality 194; homosexuality 190, 193–196, 219, 301, 442, 449; hypersexuality 108, 132, 134; lesbian sexuality 194
Shaft 86, 131, 133–134, 309
Shah, Kishan 108, 109–110
Shaitani Aatma (*The Satanic Spirit*) 106–108
Shaitani Dracula 107–108
The Shape of Water 93
Sharknado 20
The Shawshank Redemption 208
Sheba Baby 135
Sheen, Martin 1
The Sheltering Sky 360
She's Gotta Have It 137
The Shining 54, 280, 362
Shivers 55, 364, 455–456
Showgirls 145
The Sign of Death 93
Silence of the Lambs 4, 51, 52, 455
Simon, King of the Witches 164
Sinatra, Frank 445, 449
Singh, Dara 106
Singh, Harinam 106
Singin' in the Rain 149, 297, 301, 308
Sirk, Douglas 411, 414, 470
The Sixth Sense 51, 52
The Slaughter 402, 407
Sledgehammer 223, 225, 230
Smith, Iain Robert 85, 183, 187, 200, 288
Smith, Jack 24, 26, 29–30, 203, 233–243
Smith, Justin 42, 187
Smith, Kevin 65, 260
Snakes on a Train 46
The Snowman 101
Snuff 227 402, 406–407
snuff movies 20, 175, 229
Soderbergh, Steven 255, 266–267
Something Weird Video 13, 91, 116, 289–290
Sontag, Susan 4, 34, 42–43, 46, 190–196, 300
Soska, Jen and Sylvia (Soska Sisters) 20
Soulstein, Seth 8, 69–75
The Sound of Music 205, 297, 302, 308, 313, 368
Southland Tales 61, 64–6

Spaghetti Western 17, 39, 77, 79, 99, 132, 310, 468, 470–471
Sparkle 132
Speed 446
Spider-Man 207, 396
Spielberg, Steven 54–56, 137
Spotify 239, 269
Staiger, Janet 4, 74, 159
Stargate 366, 367
A Star Is Born 4, 301, 437–438, 441–442
Star Trek (franchise and conventions) 121, 259, 261, 327, 340, 351, 366–369, 373, 375
Star Wars (films and franchise) 8, 61, 138, 204–205, 207, 209, 211, 296, 321–322, 339–340, 346–347, 368–369; *The Empire Strikes Back* 204, 291
Steele, Barbara 326, 432, 451–459
Stella Dallas 149
Stephen King's It 329
Steppenwolf 360
Sternagel, Jörg 326, 329–337
Stole, Mink 31, 320
Stone, Sharon 145
Stop Making Sense 309
Stray Cat Rock: Sex Hunter 115
Streets of Fire 308
Suárez, Juan 25–26, 29
Subba, Vibhusan 17, 86, 105–110
subculture 2, 29, 53–56, 81, 85, 94, 99, 115, 122–123, 126–128, 140, 144, 161, 164–165, 167, 171, 173–178, 180, 186–187, 199, 208, 210, 219–220, 225, 227, 233–236, 242, 247–248, 254, 258–259, 285–287, 295, 297, 330–334, 360, 362, 416, 433, 479, 481–482; subcultural capital 53–56, 164, 183, 187, 204–205, 210, 219, 234–236, 241, 247–248, 286, 290, 292; subcultural distinction 140, 183, 219, 234, 238–239; subcultural ideology 34, 81, 94, 105, 173–177, 235, 285–286; subculture and fandom 36, 175–176, 199, 258, 285, 287
Suicide Squad 329
Super Fly 131, 133–134
Super Mario Bros. 445
Supernatural 255, 367
Superstar: The Karen Carpenter Story 236, 483
surrealism 4, 17, 25, 86, 166, 249, 321, 370, 372, 383–384, 388–389, 422, 428, 473, 478–479
Surrealists 8, 25, 41, 72–73, 166
Suspiria 38, 173, 310
Sweet Sweetback's Badass Song 86

Tabarraee, Babak 86, 98–104
Tabrizi, Kamal 101
Takeda, Yasuhiro 123–124
Tales from the QuadeaD Zone 223
Tarantino, Quentin 37, 114–115, 118, 133, 135, 220–221, 312–313, 317, 405, 431, 443, 446
Tarō, Hirai (Edogawa Rampo) 116–117

taste 3–5, 12, 17, 19, 25, 33–34, 36–37, 40–43, 48, 51, 71–73, 80–81, 86, 101, 139–140, 143, 155, 171–172, 181, 183–184, 187, 190–193, 200, 204, 212, 215–216, 227, 245, 249, 256, 272, 286, 292, 316, 318–320, 322, 341, 367, 393, 402, 410, 416, 425–426, 428, 441, 448, 463; bad taste 33, 40, 50, 60, 133, 162, 192, 204, 319, 367, 402, 408, 419, 475
Taxi Driver 63, 319
Taylor, Aaron 431
Taylor, Elizabeth 31
Taylor, Greg 71–73
Taylor, J.R. 404–406, 409
television (TV): 3, 14, 20, 42, 54, 59, 62, 69, 91, 93, 112, 125, 139, 149, 154, 203, 209, 211, 218, 226, 239, 253, 255, 257, 259–261, 266, 276, 300, 307, 310, 312–313, 318, 327, 350, 356, 366–376, 379, 384, 387, 392–397, 425, 437, 442, 445, 456, 478, 480–481, 483
Telotte, J.P. 5, 7, 72, 157, 206, 212
Tenebrae 38, 78, 82–83, 310
Tetsuo 115–119
The Texas Chainsaw Massacre 4, 12, 29, 38, 52, 55, 74, 171, 211, 245
The Texas Vibrator Massacre 175
Thelma and Louise 125
They Live 35, 60
The Thing from Another World 307, 310
Thirst 37
The 36 Chambers of Shaolin 113
This Is Spinal Tap 73, 237
Thriller: A Cruel Picture 246
The Thrill of It All 301
Thomas, Rob 373–375
Thomas, Sarah 457, 478–487
Thor films 392
Thornton, Sarah 53, 144, 247, 286
Thrower, Stephen 82, 424
Tierney, Dolores 18–19, 85, 86, 89–97, 123, 429
Times Square 219
The Tingler 73–74, 248
To the Devil a Daughter 164
Tommy 309, 322, 365
Too Young to Die: Heath Ledger 329–332
Torso 78
torture porn 39, 84, 375
Touch of Evil 35–36, 404
Tourneur, Jacques 38, 164
transgression 2, 8, 28–29, 31, 32, 36, 40, 50–53, 56, 72–73, 85, 101, 110, 112, 115–116, 118–119, 121, 140, 143, 162, 170–179, 180, 185, 187, 204, 206, 241, 249, 255, 267, 272, 285, 287, 303, 306, 337, 358, 360, 367–368, 375–376, 393, 423, 431, 478; *see also* horror and transgression
trash (aesthetics) 13, 14, 23–24, 26, 30, 37, 41, 48, 73, 92–94, 105–106, 136, 172, 225, 228–229, 319–322, 358–359, 363, 415, 424

Troll 2 43, 172, 211
Troma 35, 228–229
Tron 340
True Romance 443, 447–448
Twilight 148, 255, 267–269, 272, 279, 359
The Twilight Zone 55, 313, 367, 418
Twin Peaks 327, 367, 369–373, 375, 383–390
Twin Peaks: Fire Walk With Me 371 372, 374
Twitter 356, 372, 411, 415, 418–420, 482
2001, A Space Odyssey 59, 61, 365, 368

Ulmer, Edgar 38
underground 2, 4, 7–8, 16, 18, 24–32, 36, 100–101, 112, 162, 165, 168, 175–176, 193, 203, 219, 315, 321, 358–359, 415–416, 429
Urueta, Chano 93

Valentine, Lucifer 175
Valentine's Day 153, 154, 158
Valley of the Dolls 190
Vampire Girl vs. Frankenstein Girl 119
El Vampiro 89, 94
El vampiro y el sexo 94
Vampyros Lesbos 36, 309
Vanilla Sky 280
Van Peebles, Melvin 86, 132–133, 135
Variety (film) 219
Veidt, Conrad 329
Velasco, Maria Elena (India Maria) 92, 93–94
Velvet Vampire 148
Verhoeven, Paul 18, 356, 362
Veronica Mars 369, 372–375
video 7, 9, 14, 15, 20, 30, 39, 60, 65, 80–81, 89, 91, 94, 112, 118, 122, 125–126, 129, 154, 157, 161–169, 173–176, 181–182, 199–200, 215, 218, 220, 223–230, 235–236, 246–247, 267, 278–281, 289–291, 295, 305, 310, 318, 339, 353–354, 386, 406, 408, 424, 447, 451, 478, 481; video cassette, videotape and VCR 60, 80, 100, 106, 125, 199–200, 215, 227–230; video rental stores 89, 91, 94, 106, 109, 126, 182, 215, 218, 223–230, 267
Videodrome 35, 61, 356, 455
video games 253–255, 276, 360, 446
Video Nasties 20, 81, 100, 175–176, 185, 469
Video Watchdog 22, 239, 458
The Village Voice 26, 27, 38, 203, 404, 426
vinyl 125, 156, 158, 230, 235–236, 317, 341
Viva! 36, 380, 411–416, 419
Vomit Gore films 175
Von Sternberg, Joseph 191, 193
Von Trier, Lars 37, 180, 184, 304
Voodoo 167

Walken, Christopher 318, 443, 448
Walker, Johnny 15, 200, 223–232
Wallace, Edgar 76, 470–471

Waller, Gregory 72–73, 204, 217, 320
Walsh, Raoul 25, 404
Warhol, Andy 25–31, 207, 443, 445, 479
Waters, John 18, 27, 31, 36, 73, 172, 190, 192, 207, 246, 255, 296, 304, 309–311, 319, 367, 405, 432
Waterworld 445
Watson, Thomas Joseph (Tom) 140, 170–179
We Can't Go Home Again 447
Weinstock, Jeffrey 60–61, 66, 356, 370, 380, 383–390
Weldon, Michael 15, 41, 91
Welles, Orson 35, 36, 404, 450
Wenders, Wim 443, 448
West Side Story 297, 302
Wet Rope Confession 245
What Have You Done to Solange? 78
What Is It? 478, 484
Wheatley, Ben 168, 364
Whedon, Joss 373, 379, 392–401
Whisperer in Darkness 364
White Nights 101
White Zombie 167, 310
The Wicker Man 164, 237
Wierzbicki, James 296, 307–314, 315
Wikipedia 236, 241, 358
Wild at Heart 387, 390–391, 478, 479, 483
Williams, Esther 297, 299–300, 302
Williams, Linda 5, 50, 146–147, 270, 431
Williams, Robin 71
Williamson, Fred 133, 135
Winnicott, D.W. 352, 355–356

Wiseau, Tommy 29, 44–45, 85, 172, 192, 248, 326, 329, 350
Wishman, Doris 20, 29, 36, 41, 146, 380, 403, 405
Wizard (distribution company) 226–228
The Wizard of Oz 155, 297, 300–301, 432, 435–436, 440–442
Woo, John 38, 112–114
Wood, Ed Jr. 18, 29, 36, 40, 42, 44, 47, 146, 172, 204, 310, 326, 356, 367
Wood, Robert P. 211–212, 269
Wood, Robin 4, 12
Woodstock 309
Wu Tang Clan 113, 114
Wynorski, Jim 37

The X-Files 367, 394

YouTube 91, 168, 173, 204, 233, 235, 237, 241, 276, 279, 281, 318, 419, 460, 478, 479, 481–482, 484
Young, Neil 443
Yuzna, Brian 60

Zedd, Nick 174
Zombie, Rob 310, 311
Zombie 225
Zombie Flesh Eaters 454
Zombie Nightmare 228
Zombie Strippers 35
Zubernis, Lynn 254–255, 257–265, 326, 352